CONTENTS

Chapter 1	Basic number	1
Chapter 2	Fractions	25
Chapter 3	Negative numbers	49
Chapter 4	More about number	67
Chapter 5	Perimeter and area	95
Chapter 6	Statistical representation	119
Chapter 7	Basic algebra	143
Chapter 8	Further number skills	167
Chapter 9	Ratios, fractions, speed and proportion	195
Chapter 10	Symmetry	213
Chapter 11	Averages	225
Chapter 12	Percentages	257
Chapter 13	Equations and inequalities	275
Chapter 14	Graphs	299
Chapter 15	Angles	327
Chapter 16	Circles	355
Chapter 17	Scale and drawing	373
Chapter 18	Probability	397
Chapter 19	Transformations	427
Chapter 20	Constructions	453
Chapter 21	Units	473
Chapter 22	Pie charts, scatter diagrams and surveys	483
Chapter 23	Pattern	505
Chapter 24	Surface area and volume of 3-D shapes	523
Chapter 25	Quadratic graphs	539
Chapter 26	Pythagoras' theorem	549
	Coursework guidance	561
	Answers	563
	Index	599

Welcome to Collins GCSE Maths, the easiest way to learn and succeed in Mathematics. This textbook uses a stimulating approach that really appeals to students. Here are some of the key features of the textbook, to explain why.

Each chapter of the textbook begins with an **Overview**. The Overview lists the Sections you will encounter in the chapter, the key ideas you will learn, and shows how these ideas relate to, and build upon, each other. The Overview also highlights what you should already know, and if you're not sure, there is a short Quick Check activity to test yourself and recap.

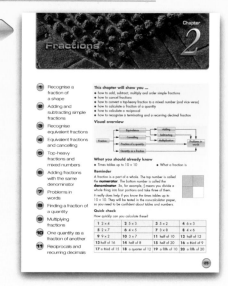

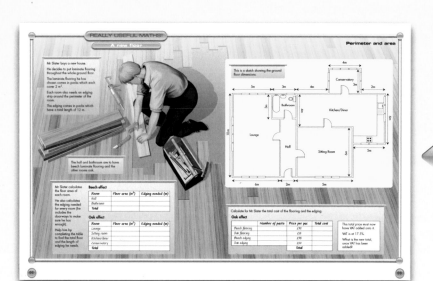

Maths can be useful to us every day of our lives, so look out for these **Really Useful Maths!** pages. These double page spreads use big, bright illustrations to depict real-life situations, and present a short series of real-world problems for you to practice your latest mathematical skills on.

Each **Section** begins first by explaining what mathematical ideas you are aiming to learn, and then lists the key words you will meet and use. The ideas are clearly explained, and this is followed by several examples showing how they can be applied to real problems. Then it's your turn to work through the exercises and improve your skills. Notice the different coloured panels along the outside of the exercise pages. These show the equivalent exam grade of the questions you are working on, so you can always tell how well you are doing.

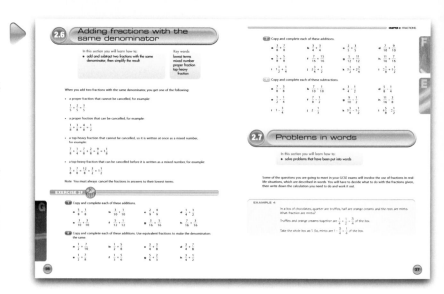

Collins

GCSE Maths
2 tier-foundation
for Edexcel A

BRIAN SPEED

KEITH GORDON

KEVIN EVANS

This high quality material is endorsed by Edexcel and has been through a rigorous quality assurance programme to ensure it is a suitable companion to the specification for both learners and teachers. This does not mean that the contents will be used verbatim when setting examinations nor is it to be read as being the official specification – a copy of which is available at www.edexcel.org.uk

This book provides indicators of the equivalent grade level of maths questions throughout. The publishers wish to make clear that these grade indicators have been provided by Collins Education, and are not the responsibility of Edexcel Ltd. Whilst every effort has been made to assure their accuracy, they should be regarded as indicators, and are not binding or definitive.

William Collins' dream of knowledge for all began with the publication of his first book in 1819. A self-educated mill worker, he not only enriched millions of lives, but also founded a flourishing publishing house. Today, staying true to this spirit, Collins books are packed with inspiration, innovation and a practical expertise. They place you at the centre of a world of possibility and give you exactly what you need to explore it.

Collins. Do more.

Published by Collins
An imprint of HarperCollins*Publishers*
77–85 Fulham Palace Road
Hammersmith
London
W6 8JB

Browse the complete Collins catalogue at
www.collinseducation.com

© HarperCollins*Publishers* Limited 2006

10 9 8 7 6
ISBN-13: 978-0-00-721560-7
ISBN-10: 0-00-721560-6

British Library Cataloguing in Publication Data. A Catalogue record for this publication is available from the British Library

Commissioned by Marie Taylor, Vicky Butt and Michael Cotter

Project managed by Penny Fowler

Edited by Joan Miller and Peta Abbott

Additional proof reader: Ruth Burns

Indexer: Dr Laurence Errington

Internal design by JPD

Cover design by JPD

Cover illustration by Andy Parker, JPD

Page make-up by Gray Publishing

Page make-up of Really Useful Maths! spreads by EMC Design

Illustrations by Gray Publishing, EMC Design, David Russel, Lazlo Veres, Lisa Alderson, Roger Wade Walker, Bob Lea, Peter Cornwell, Martin Sanders and Peters and Zabranksy

Production by Natasha Buckland

Printed and bound by Printing Express, Hong Kong

Acknowledgements

With special thanks to Lynn and Greg Byrd

The Publishers gratefully acknowledge the following for permission to reproduce copyright material. Whilst every effort has been made to trace the copyright holders, in cases where this has been unsuccessful or if any have inadvertently been overlooked, the Publishers will be pleased to make the necessary arrangements at the first opportunity.

Edexcel material reproduced with permission of Edexcel Limited. Edexcel Ltd accepts no responsibility whatsoever for the accuracy or method of working in the answers given.

Grade bar photos © 2006 JupiterImages Corporation and Photodisc Collection / Getty Images

© 2006 JupiterImages Corporation, p1, p22 Main, p23 Middle and BR, p49, p67, p95, p143, p167, p195, p213, p257, p275, p299, p327, p355, p427, p453, p473, p483, p523, p549

© Bernd Klumpp / Istock, p22 TL

© Karen Town / Istock, p22 TR

© David Wall / Alamy, p22 BL

© Neale Haynes/Buzz Pictures, p23 TL

© Christian Kretz / Istock, p22 TR

© PCL / Alamy, p119

© Images Etc Ltd / Alamy, p225

© Dave Roberts / Istock, p373

© Michal Galazka / Istock, p505

© Agence Images / Alamy, p539

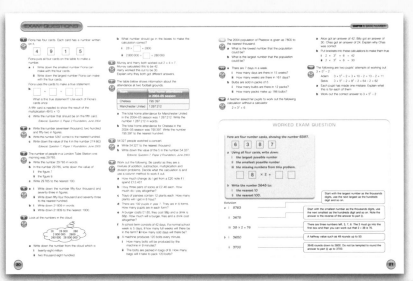

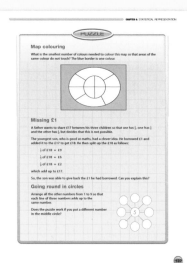

Every chapter in this textbook contains lots of **Exam Questions**. These provide ideal preparation for your examinations. Each exam question section also concludes with a fully worked example. Compare this with your own work, and pay special attention to the examiner's comments, which will ensure you understand how to score maximum marks.

Throughout the textbook you will find **Puzzles** and **Activities** – highlighted in the green panels – designed to challenge your thinking and improve your understanding.

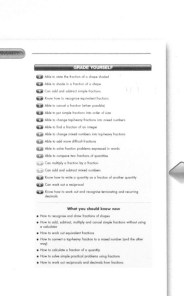

Review the **Grade Yourself** pages at the very end of the chapter. This will show what exam grade you are currently working at. Doublecheck **What you should now know** to confirm that you have the knowledge you need to progress.

Working through these sections in the right way should mean you achieve your very best in GCSE Maths. Remember though, if you get stuck, answers to all the questions are at the back of the book (except the exam question answers which your teacher has).

We do hope you enjoy using Collins GCSE Maths, and wish you every good luck in your studies!

Brian Speed, Keith Gordon, Kevin Evans

ICONS

 You may use your calculator for this question

 You should not use your calculator for this question

 Indicates a Using and Applying Mathematics question

 Indicates a Proof question

Basic number

1 Adding with grids

2 Times table check

3 Order of operations and BODMAS

4 Place value and ordering numbers

5 Rounding

6 Adding and subtracting numbers with up to four digits

7 Multiplying and dividing by single-digit numbers

This chapter will show you ...

● how to use basic number skills without a calculator

Visual overview

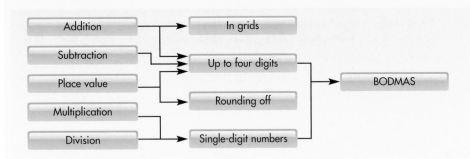

What you should already know

● Times tables up to 10×10

● Addition and subtraction of numbers less than 20

● Simple multiplication and division

● How to multiply numbers by 10 and 100

Quick check

How quickly can you complete these?

1 4×6	**2** 3×7	**3** 5×8	**4** 9×2
5 6×7	**6** $13 + 14$	**7** $15 + 15$	**8** $18 - 12$
9 $19 - 7$	**10** $11 - 6$	**11** $50 \div 5$	**12** $48 \div 6$
13 $35 \div 7$	**14** $42 \div 6$	**15** $36 \div 9$	**16** 8×10
17 9×100	**18** 3×10	**19** 14×100	**20** 17×10

1.1 Adding with grids

In this section you will learn how to:
- add and subtract single-digit numbers in a grid
- use row and column totals to find missing numbers in a grid

Key words

add
column
grid
row

ACTIVITY

Adding with grids

You need a set of cards marked 0 to 9.

0 1 2 3 4 5 6 7 8 9

Shuffle the cards and lay them out in a 3 by 3 **grid**. You will have one card left over.

3	5	0
7	6	4
8	2	9

Copy your grid onto a piece of paper. Then **add** up each **row** and each **column** and write down their totals. Finally, find the grand total and write it in the box at the bottom right.

3	5	0	8
7	6	4	17
8	2	9	19
18	13	13	44

Look out for things that help. For example:

- in the first column, $3 + 7$ make 10 and $10 + 8 = 18$

- in the last column, $9 + 4 = 9 + 1 + 3 = 10 + 3 = 13$

Reshuffle the cards, lay them out again and copy the new grid. Copy the new grid again on a fresh sheet of paper, leaving out some of the numbers.

4	5	8
0	2	6
9	1	7

4	5	8	17
0	2	6	8
9	1	7	17
13	8	21	42

4	☐	8	17
☐	2	☐	8
9	☐	7	☐
☐	8	21	42

Pass this last grid to a friend to work out the missing numbers. You can make it quite hard because you are using only the numbers from 0 to 9. Remember: once a number has been used, it *cannot* be used again in that grid.

Example Find the numbers missing from this grid.

☐	☐	9	17
☐	2	☐	11
8	☐	☐	☐
19	3	17	☐

Clues The two numbers missing from the second column must add up to 1, so they must be 0 and 1. The two numbers missing from the first column add to 11, so they could be 7 and 4 or 6 and 5. Now, 6 or 5 won't work with 0 or 1 to give 17 across the top row. That means it has to be:

7	1	9	17
4	2	□	11
8	0	□	□
19	3	17	□

giving

7	1	9	17
4	2	5	11
8	0	3	11
19	3	17	39

as the answer.

You can use your cards to try out your ideas.

EXERCISE 1A

1 Find the row and column totals for each of these grids.

a
1	3	7	□
9	2	8	□
6	5	4	□
□	□	□	□

b
0	6	7	□
8	1	4	□
9	5	3	□
□	□	□	□

c
0	8	7	□
1	6	2	□
9	3	4	□
□	□	□	□

d
2	4	6	□
3	5	7	□
8	9	1	□
□	□	□	□

e
5	9	3	□
6	1	8	□
2	7	4	□
□	□	□	□

f
0	8	3	□
7	2	4	□
1	6	5	□
□	□	□	□

g
9	4	8	□
7	0	5	□
1	6	3	□
□	□	□	□

h
0	8	6	□
7	1	4	□
5	9	2	□
□	□	□	□

i
1	8	7	□
6	2	5	□
0	9	3	□
□	□	□	□

2 Find the numbers missing from each of these grids. Remember: the numbers missing from each grid must be chosen from 0 to 9 without any repeats.

a
1	7	□	16
□	3	6	9
5	□	2	11
6	14	16	36

b
1	□	3	6
□	5	4	15
7	8	□	24
14	15	16	35

c
9	3	□	18
4	□	5	9
□	2	8	11
14	5	19	38

d
□	□	□	16
2	□	4	13
8	5	0	13
19	13	10	42

e
2	□	6	17
□	1	□	□
5	□	8	13
11	□	17	38

f
1	□	□	16
□	2	4	12
□	9	3	□
12	□	15	□

g
0	2	□	3
9	□	□	□
□	4	5	17
17	□	13	42

h
□	□	3	4
□	7	4	□
9	6	□	20
18	□	12	□

i
□	□	4	10
□	2	□	□
8	□	□	15
15	□	□	36

Times table check

In this section you will:

- recall and use your knowledge of times tables

ACTIVITY

Special table facts

You need a sheet of squared paper.

Start by writing in the easy tables. These are the 1 ×, 2 ×, 5 ×, 10 × and 9 × tables.

Now draw up a 10 by 10 tables square before you go any further. (Time yourself doing this and see if you can get faster.)

Once you have filled it in, shade in all the easy tables. You should be left with something like the square on the right.

×	1	2	3	4	5	6	7	8	9	10
1										
2										
3			9	12		18	21	24		
4			12	16		24	28	32		
5										
6			18	24		36	42	48		
7			21	28		42	49	56		
8			24	32		48	56	64		
9										
10										

Now cross out **one** of each pair that have the same answer, such as 3 × 4 and 4 × 3. This leaves you with:

×	1	2	3	4	5	6	7	8	9	10
1										
2										
3			9							
4			12	16						
5										
6			18	24		36				
7			21	28		42	49			
8			24	32		48	56	64		
9										
10										

Now there are just 15 table facts. Do learn them.

The rest are easy tables, so you should know all of them. But keep practising!

EXERCISE 1B

1 Write down the answer to each of the following without looking at the multiplication square.

a 4 × 5	**b** 7 × 3	**c** 6 × 4	**d** 3 × 5	**e** 8 × 2
f 3 × 4	**g** 5 × 2	**h** 6 × 7	**i** 3 × 8	**j** 9 × 2
k 5 × 6	**l** 4 × 7	**m** 3 × 6	**n** 8 × 7	**o** 5 × 5
p 5 × 9	**q** 3 × 9	**r** 6 × 5	**s** 7 × 7	**t** 4 × 6
u 6 × 6	**v** 7 × 5	**w** 4 × 8	**x** 4 × 9	**y** 6 × 8

2 Write down the answer to each of the following without looking at the multiplication square.

a 10 ÷ 2	**b** 28 ÷ 7	**c** 36 ÷ 6	**d** 30 ÷ 5	**e** 15 ÷ 3
f 20 ÷ 5	**g** 21 ÷ 3	**h** 24 ÷ 4	**i** 16 ÷ 8	**j** 12 ÷ 4
k 42 ÷ 6	**l** 24 ÷ 3	**m** 18 ÷ 2	**n** 25 ÷ 5	**o** 48 ÷ 6
p 36 ÷ 4	**q** 32 ÷ 8	**r** 35 ÷ 5	**s** 49 ÷ 7	**t** 27 ÷ 3
u 45 ÷ 9	**v** 16 ÷ 4	**w** 40 ÷ 8	**x** 63 ÷ 9	**y** 54 ÷ 9

3 Write down the answer to each of the following. Look carefully at the signs, because they are a mixture of ×, +, − and ÷ .

a 5 + 7	**b** 20 − 5	**c** 3 × 7	**d** 5 + 8	**e** 24 ÷ 3
f 15 − 8	**g** 6 + 8	**h** 27 ÷ 9	**i** 6 × 5	**j** 36 ÷ 6
k 7 × 5	**l** 15 ÷ 3	**m** 24 − 8	**n** 28 ÷ 4	**o** 7 + 9
p 9 + 6	**q** 36 − 9	**r** 30 ÷ 5	**s** 8 + 7	**t** 4 × 6
u 8 × 5	**v** 42 ÷ 7	**w** 8 + 9	**x** 9 × 8	**y** 54 − 8

4 Write down the answer to each of the following.

a 3 × 10	**b** 5 × 10	**c** 8 × 10	**d** 10 × 10	**e** 12 × 10
f 18 × 10	**g** 24 × 10	**h** 4 × 100	**i** 7 × 100	**j** 9 × 100
k 10 × 100	**l** 14 × 100	**m** 24 × 100	**n** 72 × 100	**o** 100 × 100
p 20 ÷ 10	**q** 70 ÷ 10	**r** 90 ÷ 10	**s** 170 ÷ 10	**t** 300 ÷ 10
u 300 ÷ 100	**v** 800 ÷ 100	**w** 1200 ÷ 100	**x** 2900 ÷ 100	**y** 5000 ÷ 100

In this section you will learn how to:

• work out the answers to a problem with a number of different signs

Key words

brackets
operation
sequence

Suppose you have to work out the answer to 4 + 5 × 2. You may say the answer is 18, but the correct answer is 14.

There is an order of **operations** which you *must* follow when working out calculations like this. The × is always done *before* the +.

In 4 + 5 × 2 this gives 4 + 10 = 14.

Now suppose you have to work out the answer to (3 + 2) × (9 − 5). The correct answer is 20.

You have probably realised that the parts in the **brackets** have to be done *first*, giving 5 × 4 = 20.

So, how do you work out a problem such as 9 ÷ 3 + 4 × 2?

To answer questions like this, you *must* follow the BODMAS rule. This tells you the **sequence** in which you *must* do the operations.

B Brackets
O Order (powers)
D Division
M Multiplication
A Addition
S Subtraction

For example, to work out 9 ÷ 3 + 4 × 2:

First divide:	9 ÷ 3 = 3	giving	3 + 4 × 2
Then multiply:	4 × 2 = 8	giving	3 + 8
Then add:	3 + 8 = 11		

And to work out $60 - 5 \times 3^2 + (4 \times 2)$:

First, work out the brackets:	(4 × 2) = 8	giving	$60 - 5 \times 3^2 + 8$
Then the order (power):	$3^2 = 9$	giving	60 − 5 × 9 + 8
Then multiply:	5 × 9 = 45	giving	60 − 45 + 8
Then add:	60 + 8 = 68	giving	68 − 45
Finally, subtract:	68 − 45 = 23		

ACTIVITY

Dice with BODMAS

You need a sheet of squared paper and three dice.

Draw a 5 by 5 grid and write the numbers from 1 to 25 in the spaces.

The numbers can be in *any order*.

14	13	18	7	24
15	1	16	17	6
23	8	2	12	5
3	22	4	10	19
25	21	9	20	11

Now throw three dice. Record the score on each one.

Use these numbers to make up a number problem.

You must use all three numbers, and you must not put them together to make a number like 136. For example, with 1, 3 and 6 you could make:

$$1 + 3 + 6 = 10 \qquad 3 \times 6 + 1 = 19 \qquad (1 + 3) \times 6 = 24$$

$$6 \div 3 + 1 = 3 \qquad 6 + 3 - 1 = 8 \qquad 6 \div (3 \times 1) = 2$$

and so on. Remember to use **BODMAS**.

You have to make only one problem with each set of numbers.

When you have made a problem, cross the answer off on the grid and throw the dice again. Make up a problem with the next three numbers and cross that answer off the grid. Throw the dice again and so on.

The first person to make a line of five numbers across, down or diagonally is the winner.

You must write down each problem and its answer so that they can be checked.

Just put a line through each number on the grid, as you use it. Do not cross it out so that it cannot be read, otherwise your problem and its answer cannot be checked.

This might be a typical game.

14	13	18	7	24
15	1	16	17	6
23	8	2	12	5
3	22	4	10	19
25	21	9	20	11

First set (1, 3, 6) $6 \times 3 \times 1 = 18$

Second set (2, 4, 4) $4 \times 4 - 2 = 14$

Third set (3, 5, 1) $(3 - 1) \times 5 = 10$

Fourth set (3, 3, 4) $(3 + 3) \times 4 = 24$

Fifth set (1, 2, 6) $6 \times 2 - 1 = 11$

Sixth set (5, 4, 6) $(6 + 4) \div 5 = 2$

Seventh set (4, 4, 2) $2 - (4 \div 4) = 1$

EXERCISE 1C

1 Work out each of these.

a $2 \times 3 + 5 =$ b $6 \div 3 + 4 =$ c $5 + 7 - 2 =$

d $4 \times 6 \div 2 =$ e $2 \times 8 - 5 =$ f $3 \times 4 + 1 =$

g $3 \times 4 - 1 =$ h $3 \times 4 \div 1 =$ i $12 \div 2 + 6 =$

j $12 \div 6 + 2 =$ k $3 + 5 \times 2 =$ l $12 - 3 \times 3 =$

2 Work out each of the following. Remember: first work out the bracket.

a $2 \times (3 + 5) =$ b $6 \div (2 + 1) =$ c $(5 + 7) - 2 =$

d $5 + (7 - 2) =$ e $3 \times (4 \div 2) =$ f $3 \times (4 + 2) =$

g $2 \times (8 - 5) =$ h $3 \times (4 + 1) =$ i $3 \times (4 - 1) =$

j $3 \times (4 \div 1) =$ k $12 \div (2 + 2) =$ l $(12 \div 2) + 2 =$

3 Copy each of these and put a loop round the part that you do first. Then work out the answer. The first one has been done for you.

a $\boxed{(3 \times 3)} - 2 = 7$ b $3 + 2 \times 4 =$ c $9 \div 3 - 2 =$

d $9 - 4 \div 2 =$ e $5 \times 2 + 3 =$ f $5 + 2 \times 3 =$

g $10 \div 5 - 2 =$ h $10 - 4 \div 2 =$ i $4 \times 6 - 7 =$

j $7 + 4 \times 6 =$ k $6 \div 3 + 7 =$ l $7 + 6 \div 2 =$

4 Work out each of these.

a $6 \times 6 + 2 =$ b $6 \times (6 + 2) =$ c $6 \div 6 + 2 =$

d $12 \div (4 + 2) =$ e $12 \div 4 + 2 =$ f $2 \times (3 + 4) =$

g $2 \times 3 + 4 =$ h $2 \times (4 - 3) =$ i $2 \times 4 - 3 =$

j $17 + 5 - 3 =$ k $17 - 5 + 3 =$ l $17 - 5 \times 3 =$

m $3 \times 5 + 5 =$ n $6 \times 2 + 7 =$ o $6 \times (2 + 7) =$

p $12 \div 3 + 3 =$ q $12 \div (3 + 3) =$ r $14 - 7 \times 1 =$

s $(14 - 7) \times 1 =$ t $2 + 6 \times 6 =$ u $(2 + 5) \times 6 =$

v $12 - 6 \div 3 =$ w $(12 - 6) \div 3 =$ x $15 - (5 \times 1) =$

y $(15 - 5) \times 1 =$ z $8 \times 9 \div 3 =$

5 Copy each of these and then put in brackets where necessary to make each answer true.

a $3 \times 4 + 1 = 15$ b $6 \div 2 + 1 = 4$ c $6 \div 2 + 1 = 2$

d $4 + 4 \div 4 = 5$ e $4 + 4 \div 4 = 2$ f $16 - 4 \div 3 = 4$

g $3 \times 4 + 1 = 13$ h $16 - 6 \div 3 = 14$ i $20 - 10 \div 2 = 5$

j $20 - 10 \div 2 = 15$ k $3 \times 5 + 5 = 30$ l $6 \times 4 + 2 = 36$

m $15 - 5 \times 2 = 20$ n $4 \times 7 - 2 = 20$ o $12 \div 3 + 3 = 2$

p $12 \div 3 + 3 = 7$ q $24 \div 8 - 2 = 1$ r $24 \div 8 - 2 = 4$

6 Three dice are thrown. They give scores of 3, 1 and 4.

A class makes the following questions with the numbers.
Work them out.

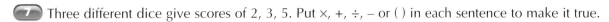

a 3 + 4 + 1 =   **b** 3 + 4 − 1 =   **c** 4 + 3 − 1 =

d 4 × 3 + 1 =   **e** 4 × 3 − 1 =   **f** (4 − 1) × 3 =

g 4 × 3 × 1 =   **h** (3 − 1) × 4 =   **i** (4 + 1) × 3 =

j 4 × (3 + 1) =   **k** 1 × (4 − 3) =   **l** 4 + 1 × 3 =

7 Three different dice give scores of 2, 3, 5. Put ×, +, ÷, − or ( ) in each sentence to make it true.

a 2   3   5 = 11   **b** 2   3   5 = 16   **c** 2   3   5 = 17

d 5   3   2 = 4   **e** 5   3   2 = 13   **f** 5   3   2 = 30

1.4 Place value and ordering numbers

In this section you will learn how to:
- identify the value of any digit in a number

Key words
digit
place value

The ordinary counting system uses **place value**, which means that the value of a **digit** depends upon its place in the number.

In the number 5348

the 5 stands for 5 thousands or 5000

the 3 stands for 3 hundreds or 300

the 4 stands for 4 tens or 40

the 8 stands for 8 units or 8

And in the number 4 073 520

the 4 stands for 4 millions or 4 000 000

the 73 stands for 73 thousands or 73 000

the 5 stands for 5 hundreds or 500

the 2 stands for 2 tens or 20

You write and say this number as:

four million, seventy-three thousand, five hundred and twenty

Note the use of narrow spaces between groups of three digits, starting from the right. All whole and mixed numbers with five or more digits are spaced in this way.

EXAMPLE 1

Put these numbers in order with the smallest first.

7031   3071   3701   7103   7130   1730

Look at the thousands column first and then each of the other columns in turn.
The correct order is:

1730   3071   3701   7031   7103   7130

EXERCISE 1D

1 Write the value of each underlined digit.

a 3<u>4</u>1   b 47<u>5</u>   c <u>1</u>86   d 2<u>9</u>8   e <u>8</u>3

f 83<u>9</u>   g 23<u>8</u>0   h 1<u>5</u>07   i 653<u>0</u>   j <u>2</u>5 436

k 29 <u>0</u>54   l 18 25<u>4</u>   m 4<u>3</u>08   n 52 9<u>9</u>4   o <u>8</u>3 205

2 Copy each of these sentences, writing the numbers in words.

a The last Olympic games in Greece had only 43 events and 200 competitors.

b The last Olympic games in Britain had 136 events and 4099 competitors.

c The last Olympic games in the USA had 271 events and 10 744 competitors.

3 Write each of the following numbers in words.

a 5 600 000   b 4 075 200   c 3 007 950   d 2 000 782

4 Write each of the following numbers in numerals or digits.

a Eight million, two hundred thousand and fifty-eight

b Nine million, four hundred and six thousand, one hundred and seven

c One million, five hundred and two

d Two million, seventy-six thousand and forty

5 Write these numbers in order, putting the *smallest* first.

a 21,   48,   23,   9,   15,   56,   85,   54

b 310,   86,   219,   25,   501,   62,   400,   151

c 357,   740,   2053,   888,   4366,   97,   368

6 Write these numbers in order, putting the *largest* first.

a 52,   23,   95,   34,   73,   7,   25,   89

b 65,   2,   174,   401,   80,   700,   18,   117

c 762,   2034,   395,   6227,   89,   3928,   59,   480

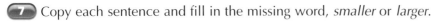

7 Copy each sentence and fill in the missing word, *smaller* or *larger*.

a 7 is ...... than 5

b 34 is ...... than 29

c 89 is ...... than 98

d 97 is ...... than 79

e 308 is ...... than 299

f 561 is ...... than 605

g 870 is ...... than 807

h 4275 is ...... than 4527

i 782 is ...... than 827

8 **a** Write as many three-digit numbers as you can using the digits 3, 6 and 8. (Only use each digit once in each number).

b Which of your numbers is the smallest?

c Which of your numbers is the largest?

9 Using each of the digits 0, 4 and 8 only once in each number, write as many different three-digit numbers as you can. (Do not start any number with 0.) Write your numbers down in order, smallest first.

10 Write down in order of size, smallest first, all the two-digit numbers that can be made using 3, 5 and 8. (Each digit can be repeated.)

1.5 Rounding

In this section you will learn how to:
● round a number

Key words
approximation
rounded down
rounded up

You use rounded information all the time. Look at these examples. All of these statements use rounded information. Each actual figure is either above or below the **approximation** shown here. But if the rounding is done correctly, you can find out what the maximum and the minimum figures really are. For example, if you know that the number of matches in the packet is rounded to the nearest 10,

Cook the pie for 30 minutes

THE DAILY PL...
23 000 PEOPLE RAN THE MARATHON

The Georgian HOTEL

AVERAGE CONTENTS 30 MATCHES

I drive for 40 minutes to get to school.

● the smallest figure to be **rounded up** to 30 is 25, and

● the largest figure to be **rounded down** to 30 is 34 (because 35 would be rounded up to 40).

So there could actually be from 25 to 34 matches in the packet.

What about the number of runners in the marathon? If you know that the number 23 000 is rounded to the nearest 1000,

- The smallest figure to be rounded up to 23 000 is 22 500.

- The largest figure to be rounded down to 23 000 is 23 499.

So there could actually be from 22 500 to 23 499 people in the marathon.

EXERCISE 1E

1 Round each of these numbers to the nearest 10.

a 24	**b** 57	**c** 78	**d** 54	**e** 96
f 21	**g** 88	**h** 66	**i** 14	**j** 26
k 29	**l** 51	**m** 77	**n** 49	**o** 94
p 35	**q** 65	**r** 15	**s** 102	**t** 107

2 Round each of these numbers to the nearest 100.

a 240	**b** 570	**c** 780	**d** 504	**e** 967
f 112	**g** 645	**h** 358	**i** 998	**j** 1050
k 299	**l** 511	**m** 777	**n** 512	**o** 940
p 350	**q** 650	**r** 750	**s** 1020	**t** 1070

3 On the shelf of a sweetshop there are three jars like the ones below.

Jar 1   Jar 2   Jar 3

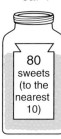
80 sweets (to the nearest 10)

120 sweets (to the nearest 10)

190 sweets (to the nearest 10)

Look at each of the numbers below and write down which jar it could be describing. (For example, 76 sweets could be in jar 1.)

a 78 sweets	**b** 119 sweets	**c** 84 sweets	**d** 75 sweets
e 186 sweets	**f** 122 sweets	**g** 194 sweets	**h** 115 sweets
i 81 sweets	**j** 79 sweets	**k** 192 sweets	**l** 124 sweets

m Which of these numbers of sweets *could not* be in jar 1: 74, 84, 81, 76?

n Which of these numbers of sweets *could not* be in jar 2: 124, 126, 120, 115?

o Which of these numbers of sweets *could not* be in jar 3: 194, 184, 191, 189?

4 Round each of these numbers to the nearest 1000.

a 2400	**b** 5700	**c** 7806	**d** 5040	**e** 9670
f 1120	**g** 6450	**h** 3499	**i** 9098	**j** 1500
k 2990	**l** 5110	**m** 7777	**n** 5020	**o** 9400
p 3500	**q** 6500	**r** 7500	**s** 1020	**t** 1770

5 Round each of these numbers to the nearest 10.

a 234	**b** 567	**c** 718	**d** 524	**e** 906
f 231	**g** 878	**h** 626	**i** 114	**j** 296
k 279	**l** 541	**m** 767	**n** 501	**o** 942
p 375	**q** 625	**r** 345	**s** 1012	**t** 1074

6 Which of these sentences could be true and which must be false?

Welcome to Elsecar	**Welcome to Hoyland**	**Welcome to Jump**
Population 800 (to the nearest 100)	**Population 1200** (to the nearest 100)	**Population 600** (to the nearest 100)

a There are 789 people living in Elsecar.

b There are 1278 people living in Hoyland.

c There are 550 people living in Jump.

d There are 843 people living in Elsecar.

e There are 1205 people living in Hoyland.

f There are 650 people living in Jump.

7 These were the numbers of spectators in the crowds at nine Premier Division games on a weekend in May 2005.

Aston Villa v Man City	39 645
Blackburn v Fulham	18 991
Chelsea v Charlton	42 065
C. Palace v Southampton	26 066
Everton v Newcastle	40 438
Man.Utd v West Brom	67 827
Middlesbrough v Tottenham	34 766
Norwich v Birmingham	25 477
Portsmouth v Bolton	20 188

a Which match had the largest crowd?

b Which had the smallest crowd?

c Round all the numbers to the nearest 1000.

d Round all the numbers to the nearest 100.

8 Give these cooking times to the nearest 5 minutes.

a 34 min	**b** 57 min	**c** 14 min	**d** 51 min	**e** 8 min
f 13 min	**g** 44 min	**h** 32.5 min	**i** 3 min	**j** 50 s

In this section you will learn how to:

- add and subtract numbers with more than one digit

Key words

addition
column
digit
subtract

Addition

There are three things to remember when you are adding two whole numbers.

- The answer will always be larger than the bigger number.

- Always add the units **column** first.

- When the total of the **digits** in a column is more than 9, you have to carry a digit into the next column on the left, as shown in Example 2. It is important to write down the carried digit, otherwise you may forget to include it in the **addition**.

EXAMPLE 2

Add: **a** 167 + 25 **b** 2296 + 1173

$$
\begin{array}{r}
\textbf{a} \quad 167 \\
+ \quad 25 \\
\hline
192 \\
\hline
{\scriptstyle 1}
\end{array}
\qquad
\begin{array}{r}
\textbf{b} \quad 2296 \\
+ \quad 1173 \\
\hline
3469 \\
\hline
{\scriptstyle 1}
\end{array}
$$

Subtraction

These are four things to remember when you are subtracting two whole numbers.

- The bigger number must always be written down first.

- The answer will always be smaller than the bigger number.

- Always **subtract** the units column first.

- When you have to take a bigger digit from a smaller digit in a column, you must first remove 10 from the next column on the left and put it with the smaller digit, as shown in Example 3.

EXAMPLE 3

Subtract: **a** 874 − 215 **b** 300 − 163

$$
\begin{array}{r}
\textbf{a} \quad 8{}^{6}7{}^{1}4 \\
- \quad 215 \\
\hline
659
\end{array}
\qquad
\begin{array}{r}
\textbf{b} \quad {}^{2}3{}^{9}\cancel{0}{}^{1}0 \\
- \quad 163 \\
\hline
137
\end{array}
$$

EXERCISE 1F

1 Copy and work out each of these additions.

a 365	**b** 95	**c** 4872	**d** 317
+ 348	+ 56	+ 1509	416
			+ 235

e 287
+ 335

f 483
+ 832

g 4676
+ 3584

h 438
147
+ 233

i 175
+ 276

j 562
93
+ 197

2 Copy and complete each of these additions.

a 128 + 518   **b** 563 + 85 + 178   **c** 3086 + 58 + 674

d 347 + 408   **e** 85 + 1852 + 659   **f** 759 + 43 + 89

g 257 + 93   **h** 605 + 26 + 2135   **i** 56 + 8407 + 395

j 89 + 752   **k** 6143 + 557 + 131   **l** 2593 + 45 + 4378

m 719 + 284   **n** 545 + 3838 + 67   **o** 5213 + 658 + 4073

3 Copy and complete each of these subtractions.

a 637
– 187

b 908
– 345

c 954
– 472

d 572
– 158

e 732
– 447

f 673
– 187

g 602
– 358

h 638
– 354

i 650
– 317

j 580
– 364

k 6254
– 3362

l 8043
– 3626

m 8432
– 4665

n 8034
– 3947

o 5375
– 3547

4 Copy and complete each of these subtractions.

a 354 – 226   **b** 285 – 256   **c** 663 – 329

d 506 – 328   **e** 654 – 377   **f** 733 – 448

g 592 – 257   **h** 753 – 354   **i** 6705 – 2673

j 8021 – 3256   **k** 7002 – 3207   **l** 8700 – 3263

5 Copy each of these additions and fill in the missing digits.

a   5 3
+ 2 ☐
─────
     ☐ 9

b   ☐ 7
+ 3 ☐
─────
     8 4

c   4 5
+ ☐ ☐
─────
     9 3

d   4 ☐ 7
+ ☐ 5 ☐
───────
     9 3 6

e
```
  □ 1 8
+ 2 5 □
  8 □ 7
```

f
```
  5 4 □
+ □ □ 6
  8 2 2
```

g
```
  4 6 9
+ □ □ □
  7 3 5
```

h
```
  □ □ □
+ 3 4 8
  8 0 7
```

i
```
  □ 4 □
+ 3 3 7
  7 □ 5
```

j
```
  3 5 7 8
+ □ □ □ □
  8 0 7 6
```

6 Copy each of these subtractions and fill in the missing digits.

a
```
  7 4
- 2 □
  □ 1
```

b
```
  □ 7
- 3 □
  5 4
```

c
```
  8 5
- □ □
  2 7
```

d
```
  6 7 □
- □ □ 3
  1 3 5
```

e
```
  □ 1 4
- 2 5 □
  3 □ 7
```

f
```
  5 4 □
- □ □ 6
  3 2 5
```

g
```
  4 6 2
- □ □ □
  1 8 5
```

h
```
  □ □ □
- 2 4 7
  3 0 9
```

i
```
  □ 4 □
- 5 5 8
  2 □ 5
```

j
```
  8 0 7 6
- □ □ □ □
  6 1 8 7
```

1.7 Multiplying and dividing by single-digit numbers

In this section you will learn how to:
- multiply and divide by a single-digit number

Key words
division
multiplication

Multiplication

There are two things to remember when you are multiplying two whole numbers.

- The bigger number must always be written down first.
- The answer will always be larger than the bigger number.

EXAMPLE 4

Multiply 231 by 4.
```
    2 1 3
×     4
─────────
    8 5 2
      1
```

Note that the first multiplication, 3×4, gives 12. So, you need to carry a digit into the next column on the left, as in the case of addition.

Division

There are two things to remember when you are dividing one whole number by another whole number:

- The answer will always be smaller than the bigger number.

- Division starts at the *left-hand side*.

EXAMPLE 5

Divide 417 by 3.

$417 \div 3$ is set out as:

$$
\begin{array}{r}
1\ 3\ 9 \\
3\,\overline{\smash{)}\,4^{1}1^{2}7}
\end{array}
$$

This is how the division was done:

- First, divide 3 into 4 to get 1 and remainder 1. Note where to put the 1 and the remainder 1.

- Then, divide 3 into 11 to get 3 and remainder 2. Note where to put the 3 and the remainder 2.

- Finally, divide 3 into 27 to get 9 with no remainder, giving the answer 139.

EXERCISE 1G

1 Copy and work out each of the following multiplications.

	a	14	b	13	c	17	d	19	e	18
		$\times\ 4$		$\times\ 5$		$\times\ 3$		$\times\ 2$		$\times\ 6$

	f	23	g	34	h	42	i	53	j	85
		$\times\ 5$		$\times\ 6$		$\times\ 7$		$\times\ 4$		$\times\ 5$

	k	50	l	200	m	320	n	340	o	253
		$\times\ 3$		$\times\ 4$		$\times\ 3$		$\times\ 4$		$\times\ 6$

2 Calculate each of the following multiplications by setting the work out in columns.

a 42×7 b 74×5 c 48×6

d 208×4 e 309×7 f 630×4

g 548×3 h 643×5 i 8×375

j 6×442 k 7×528 l 235×8

m 6043×9 n 5×4387 o 9×5432

3 Calculate each of the following divisions.

a   438 ÷ 2   b   634 ÷ 2   c   945 ÷ 3

d   636 ÷ 6   e   297 ÷ 3   f   847 ÷ 7

g   756 ÷ 3   h   846 ÷ 6   i   576 ÷ 4

j   344 ÷ 4   k   441 ÷ 7   l   5818 ÷ 2

m   3744 ÷ 9   n   2008 ÷ 8   o   7704 ÷ 6

4 By doing a suitable multiplication, answer each of these questions.

a   How many days are there in 17 weeks?

b   How many hours are there in 4 days?

c   Eggs are packed in boxes of 6. How many eggs are there in 24 boxes?

d   Joe bought 5 boxes of matches. Each box contained 42 matches. How many matches did Joe buy altogether?

e   A box of Tulip Sweets holds 35 sweets. How many sweets are there in 6 boxes?

5 By doing a suitable division, answer each of these questions.

a   How many weeks are there in 91 days?

b   How long will it take me to save £111, if I save £3 a week?

c   A rope, 215 metres long, is cut into 5 equal pieces. How long is each piece?

d   Granny has a bottle of 144 tablets. How many days will they last if she takes 4 each day?

e   I share a box of 360 sweets between 8 children. How many sweets will each child get?

Letter sets

Find the next letters in these sequences.

a O, T, T, F, F, ...   **b** T, F, S, E, T, ...

Valued letters

In the three additions below, each letter stands for a single numeral. But a letter may not necessarily stand for the same numeral when it is used in more than one sum.

a		**b**		**c**	
	O N E		T W O		F O U R
+	O N E	+	T W O	+	F I V E
	T W O		F O U R		N I N E

Write down each addition in numbers.

Four fours

Write number sentences to give answers from 1 to 10, using only four 4s and any number of the operations +, −, × and ÷ . For example:

$1 = (4 + 4) \div (4 + 4)$ $2 = (4 \times 4) \div (4 + 4)$

Heinz 57

Pick any number in the grid on the right. Circle the number and cross out all the other numbers in the row and column containing the number you have chosen. Now circle another number that is not crossed out and cross out all the other numbers in the row and column containing this number. Repeat until you have five numbers circled. Add these numbers together. What do you get? Now do it again but start with a different number.

19	8	11	25	7
12	1	4	18	0
16	5	8	22	4
21	10	13	27	9
14	3	6	20	2

Magic squares

This is a magic square. Add the numbers in any row, column or diagonal. The answer is *always* 15.

8	1	6
3	5	7
4	9	2

Now try to complete this magic square using every number from 1 to 16.

1		14	
	6		9
8		11	
	3		16

1 Fiona has four cards. Each card has a number written on it.

| 4 | 9 | 1 | 5 |

Fiona puts all four cards on the table to make a number.

a i Write down the smallest number Fiona can make with the four cards.

ii Write down the largest number Fiona can make with the four cards.

Fiona uses the cards to make a true statement.

b ☐ + ☐ = ☐ ☐

What is this true statement? Use each of Fiona's cards *once*.

A fifth card is needed to show the result of the multiplication 4915 × 10

c Write the number that should be on the fifth card.

Edexcel, Question 3, Paper 2 Foundation, June 2004

2 a Write the number seventeen thousand, two hundred and fifty-two in figures.

b Write the number 5367 correct to the nearest hundred.

c Write down the value of the 4 in the number 274 863

Edexcel, Question 1, Paper 1 Foundation, June 2005

3 The number of people in a London Tube Station one morning was 29 765.

a Write the number 29 765 in words.

b In the number 29 765, write down the value of

i the figure 7

ii the figure 9.

c Write 29 765 to the nearest 100.

4 a i Write down the number fifty-four thousand and seventy-three in figures.

ii Write down fifty-four thousand and seventy-three to the nearest hundred.

b i Write down 21 809 in words.

ii Write down 21 809 to the nearest 1000.

5 Look at the numbers in the cloud.

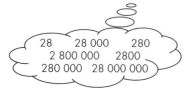

28   28 000   280
2 800 000   2800
280 000   28 000 000

a Write down the number from the cloud which is

i twenty eight million

ii two thousand eight hundred.

b What number should go in the boxes to make the calculation correct?

i 28 × ☐ = 2800

ii 2 800 000 ÷ ☐ = 280 000

6 Murray and Harry both worked out 2 + 4 × 7.
Murray calculated this to be 42.
Harry worked this out to be 30.
Explain why they both got different answers.

7 The table below shows information about the attendance at two football grounds.

Team	Total home attendance in 2004–05 season
Chelsea	795 397
Manchester United	1 287 212

a The total home attendance for Manchester United in the 2004–05 season was 1 287 212. Write the number 1 287 212 in words.

b The total home attendance for Chelsea in the 2004–05 season was 795 397. Write the number 795 397 to the nearest hundred.

8 54 327 people watched a concert.

a Write 54 327 to the nearest thousand.

b Write down the value of the 5 in the number 54 327.

Edexcel, Question 7, Paper 2 Foundation, June 2003

9 Work out the following. Be careful as they are a mixture of addition, subtraction, multiplication and division problems. Decide what the calculation is and use a column method to work it out.

a How much change do I get from a £20 note if I spend £13.45?

b I buy three pairs of socks at £2.46 each. How much do I pay altogether?

c Trays of pansies contain 12 plants each. How many plants will I get in 8 trays?

d There are 192 pupils in year 7. They are in 6 forms. How many pupils are in each form?

e A burger costs £1.65, fries cost 98p and a drink is 68p. How much will a burger, fries and a drink cost altogether?

f A school term consists of 42 days. If a normal school week is 5 days, **i** how many full weeks will there be in the term? **ii** How many odd days will there be?

g A machine produces 120 bolts every minute.

i How many bolts will be produced by the machine in 9 minutes?

ii The bolts are packed in bags of 8. How many bags will it take to pack 120 bolts?

10 The 2004 population of Plaistow is given as 7800 to the nearest thousand.

   a What is the lowest number that the population could be?

   b What is the largest number that the population could be?

11 **a** There are 7 days in a week.

   i How many days are there in 15 weeks?

   ii How many weeks are there in 161 days?

   b Bulbs are sold in packs of 6.

   i How many bulbs are there in 12 packs?

   ii How many packs make up 186 bulbs?

12 A teacher asked her pupils to work out the following calculation without a calculator

   $2 \times 3^2 + 6$

   a Alice got an answer of 42. Billy got an answer of 30. Chas got an answer of 24. Explain why Chas was correct

   b Put brackets into these calculations to make them true

   i $2 \times 3^2 + 6 = 42$

   ii $2 \times 3^2 + 6 = 30$

13 The following are two pupils' attempts at working out $3 + 5^2 - 2$

   Adam $3 + 5^2 - 2 = 3 + 10 - 2 = 13 - 2 = 11$

   Bekki $3 + 5^2 - 2 = 8^2 - 2 = 64 - 2 = 62$

   a Each pupil has made one mistake. Explain what this is for each of them

   b Work out the correct answer to $3 + 5^2 - 2$

WORKED EXAM QUESTION

Here are four number cards, showing the number 6387.

| 6 | 3 | 8 | 7 |

a Using all four cards, write down:

   i the largest possible number

   ii the smallest possible number

   iii the missing numbers from this problem.

   ☐ **8** × 2 = ☐ ☐

b Write the number 3648 to:

   i the nearest 10

   ii the nearest 100.

Solution

a i 8763 — Start with the largest number as the thousands digits, use the next largest as the hundreds digit and so on.

ii 3678 — Start with the smallest number as the thousands digits, use the next smallest as the hundreds digit and so on. Note the answer is the reverse of the answer to part (i).

iii 38 × 2 = 76 — There are three numbers left, 3, 7, 6. The 3 must go into the first box and then you can work out that 2 × 38 is 76.

b i 3650 — A halfway value such as 48 rounds up to 50.

ii 3700 — 3648 rounds down to 3600. Do not be tempted to round the answer to part (i) up to 3700.

Mr and Mrs Davies, their daughter, Alice (aged 15), and their son, Joe (aged 13), decide to take an activity holiday. The family want to stay in a cottage in Wales.

The activities on offer are shown below.

Mr Davies works out the total cost of their holiday, which includes the cost of the activities, the rental for the holiday cottage (in the high season) and the cost of the petrol they will use to travel to the cottage, for trips while they are there, and to get home again.

Paragliding:
adults £99

Quad bikes:
adults £21,
children (6–15) £12.50

Horse riding:
1½ hour valley ride £28,
1½ hour beach ride £32

Windsurfing:
half day £59,
full day £79

Water-jet boat:
adults £20,
children (under 14) £10

The table shows which activities they all chose. Copy it and complete the "Totals" row. Use it to work out the total cost of the activities.

	Horse riding	Water-jet boats	Conventional boats	Kayaking	Coast jumping	Windsurfing
Mr Davies	✗	✓	✓	½ day	✗	✗
Mrs Davies	1½ hour beach ride	✓	✓	✗	✓	✗
Alice Davies	1½ hour beach ride	✓	✓	½ day	✗	½ day
Joe Davies	✗	✓	✓	✗	✓	½ day
Totals						

Coast jumping:
adults £40,
children (under 16) £25

Holiday cottage:
low season: £300
mid season: £400
high season: £550

Kayaking:
half day £29,
full day £49

Diving:
adults £38

Conventional boat:
adults £10,
children (under 14) £6

Diving	Quad bikes	Paragliding
✗	✓	✓
✓	✗	✗
✗	✓	✗
✗	✓	✗
		£99

Cost of holiday (£)	
Activities	
Cottage	
Petrol	
Total:	

It is 250 miles from their home to their holiday cottage. They drive an extra 100 miles while they are on holiday. Their car travels, on average, 50 miles to the gallon. Petrol costs £1 per litre.

1 gallon = 4.5 litres

GRADE YOURSELF

G Able to add columns and rows in grids

G Know the times tables up to 10×10

G Can use BODMAS to find the correct order of operations

G Can identify the value of digits in different places

G Able to round to the nearest 10 and 100

G Can add and subtract numbers with up to four digits

G Can multiply numbers by a single-digit number

F Able to answer problems involving multiplication or division by a single-digit number

What you should know now

- How to use BODMAS

- How to put numbers in order

- How to round to the nearest ten, hundred, thousand

- How to solve simple problems, using the four operations of arithmetic: addition, subtraction, multiplication and division

This book provides indicators of the equivalent grade level of maths questions throughout. The publishers wish to make clear that these grade indicators have been provided by Collins Education, and are not the responsibility of Edexcel Ltd. Whilst every effort has been made to assure their accuracy, they should be regarded as indicators, and are not binding or definitive.

Fractions

1 Recognise a fraction of a shape

2 Adding and subtracting simple fractions

3 Recognise equivalent fractions

4 Equivalent fractions and cancelling

5 Top-heavy fractions and mixed numbers

6 Adding fractions with the same denominator

7 Problems in words

8 Finding a fraction of a quantity

9 Multiplying fractions

10 One quantity as a fraction of another

11 Reciprocals and recurring decimals

This chapter will show you ...

● how to add, subtract, multiply and order simple fractions
● how to cancel fractions
● how to convert a top-heavy fraction to a mixed number (and vice versa)
● how to calculate a fraction of a quantity
● how to calculate a reciprocal
● how to recognise a terminating and a recurring decimal fraction

Visual overview

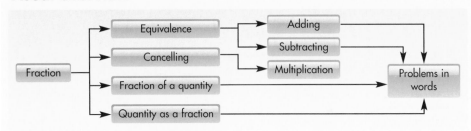

What you should already know

● Times tables up to 10×10 ● What a fraction is

Reminder

A fraction is a part of a whole. The top number is called the **numerator**. The bottom number is called the **denominator**. So, for example, $\frac{3}{4}$ means you divide a whole thing into four portions and take three of them.

It really does help if you know the times tables up to 10×10. They will be tested in the non-calculator paper, so you need to be confident about tables and numbers.

Quick check

How quickly can you calculate these?

1 2×4	**2** 5×3	**3** 5×2	**4** 6×3
5 2×7	**6** 4×5	**7** 3×8	**8** 4×6
9 9×2	**10** 3×7	**11** half of 10	**12** half of 12
13 half of 16	**14** half of 8	**15** half of 20	**16** a third of 9
17 a third of 15	**18** a quarter of 12	**19** a fifth of 10	**20** a fifth of 20

In this section you will learn how to:

- recognise what fraction of a shape has been shaded
- shade a given simple fraction of a shape

1 What fraction is shaded in each of these diagrams?

a   b   c   d

e   f   g   h

i   j   k   l

m   n   o   p

2 Draw diagrams as in question **1** to show these fractions.

a $\dfrac{3}{4}$ b $\dfrac{2}{3}$ c $\dfrac{1}{5}$ d $\dfrac{5}{8}$

e $\dfrac{1}{6}$ f $\dfrac{8}{9}$ g $\dfrac{1}{9}$ h $\dfrac{1}{10}$

i $\dfrac{4}{5}$ j $\dfrac{2}{7}$ k $\dfrac{3}{8}$ l $\dfrac{5}{6}$

In this section you will learn how to:
- add and subtract two fractions with the same denominator

Key words
denominator
numerator

Fractions that have the same **denominator** (bottom number) can easily be added or subtracted.
For example:

$$\frac{3}{10} + \frac{4}{10} = \frac{7}{10}$$

$$\frac{7}{8} - \frac{2}{8} = \frac{5}{8}$$

Just add or subtract the **numerators** (top numbers). The bottom number stays the same.

EXERCISE 2B

1 Calculate each of the following.

a $\frac{1}{4} + \frac{2}{4}$ b $\frac{1}{8} + \frac{3}{8}$ c $\frac{2}{5} + \frac{1}{5}$ d $\frac{3}{10} + \frac{5}{10}$

e $\frac{1}{3} + \frac{1}{3}$ f $\frac{2}{7} + \frac{3}{7}$ g $\frac{2}{9} + \frac{5}{9}$ h $\frac{1}{6} + \frac{4}{6}$

i $\frac{3}{5} + \frac{1}{5}$ j $\frac{5}{8} + \frac{2}{8}$ k $\frac{2}{10} + \frac{3}{10}$ l $\frac{4}{7} + \frac{1}{7}$

m $\frac{3}{5} + \frac{1}{5}$ n $\frac{2}{6} + \frac{3}{6}$ o $\frac{4}{9} + \frac{1}{9}$ p $\frac{2}{11} + \frac{5}{11}$

2 Calculate each of the following.

a $\frac{3}{4} - \frac{1}{4}$ b $\frac{4}{5} - \frac{1}{5}$ c $\frac{7}{8} - \frac{4}{8}$ d $\frac{8}{10} - \frac{5}{10}$

e $\frac{2}{3} - \frac{1}{3}$ f $\frac{5}{6} - \frac{1}{6}$ g $\frac{5}{7} - \frac{2}{7}$ h $\frac{7}{9} - \frac{2}{9}$

i $\frac{3}{5} - \frac{2}{5}$ j $\frac{4}{7} - \frac{1}{7}$ k $\frac{8}{9} - \frac{5}{9}$ l $\frac{9}{10} - \frac{3}{10}$

m $\frac{4}{6} - \frac{1}{6}$ n $\frac{5}{8} - \frac{3}{8}$ o $\frac{7}{11} - \frac{5}{11}$ p $\frac{7}{10} - \frac{3}{10}$

a Draw a diagram to show $\dfrac{2}{4}$

b Show on your diagram that $\dfrac{2}{4} = \dfrac{1}{2}$

c Use the above information to write down the answers to these.

    i $\dfrac{1}{4} + \dfrac{1}{2}$ **ii** $\dfrac{3}{4} - \dfrac{1}{2}$

 a Draw a diagram to show $\dfrac{5}{10}$

b Show on your diagram that $\dfrac{5}{10} = \dfrac{1}{2}$

c Use the above information to write down the answers to these.

    i $\dfrac{1}{2} + \dfrac{1}{10}$ **ii** $\dfrac{1}{2} + \dfrac{3}{10}$ **iii** $\dfrac{1}{2} + \dfrac{2}{10}$

2.3 Recognise equivalent fractions

In this section you will learn how to:
- recognise equivalent fractions

Key word
equivalent

ACTIVITY

Making eighths

You need lots of squared paper and a pair of scissors.

Draw three rectangles, each 4 cm by 2 cm, on squared paper.

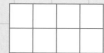 Each small square is called an *eighth* or $\frac{1}{8}$.

Cut one of the rectangles into halves, another into quarters and the third into eighths.

You can see that the strip equal to one half takes up 4 squares, so:

$$\dfrac{1}{2} = \dfrac{4}{8}$$

These are called **equivalent** fractions.

1 Use the strips to write down the following fractions as eighths.

  a $\dfrac{1}{4}$ **b** $\dfrac{3}{4}$

2 Use the strips to work out the following problems. Leave your answers as eighths.

  a $\dfrac{1}{4} + \dfrac{3}{8}$ **b** $\dfrac{3}{4} + \dfrac{1}{8}$ **c** $\dfrac{3}{8} + \dfrac{1}{2}$ **d** $\dfrac{1}{4} + \dfrac{1}{2}$

  e $\dfrac{1}{8} + \dfrac{1}{8}$ **f** $\dfrac{1}{8} + \dfrac{1}{4}$ **g** $\dfrac{3}{8} + \dfrac{3}{4}$ **h** $\dfrac{3}{4} + \dfrac{1}{2}$

Making twenty-fourths

You need lots of squared paper and a pair of scissors.

Draw four rectangles, each 6 cm by 4 cm, on squared paper.

Each small square is called a *twenty-fourth* or $\frac{1}{24}$. Cut one of the rectangles into quarters, another into sixths, another into thirds and the remaining one into eighths.

You can see that the strip equal to a quarter takes up 6 squares, so:

$$\frac{1}{4} = \frac{6}{24}$$

This is another example of equivalent fractions.

This idea is used to add fractions together. For example:

$$\frac{1}{4} + \frac{1}{6}$$

can be changed into:

$$\frac{6}{24} + \frac{4}{24} = \frac{10}{24}$$

EXERCISE 2C

1 Use the strips to write down each of these fractions as twenty-fourths.

a $\dfrac{1}{6}$ b $\dfrac{1}{3}$ c $\dfrac{1}{8}$ d $\dfrac{2}{3}$ e $\dfrac{5}{6}$

f $\dfrac{3}{4}$ g $\dfrac{3}{8}$ h $\dfrac{5}{8}$ i $\dfrac{7}{8}$ j $\dfrac{1}{2}$

2 Use the strips to write down the answer to each of the following problems. Each answer will be in twenty-fourths.

a $\dfrac{1}{3} + \dfrac{1}{8}$ b $\dfrac{1}{8} + \dfrac{1}{4}$ c $\dfrac{1}{6} + \dfrac{1}{8}$ d $\dfrac{2}{3} + \dfrac{1}{8}$ e $\dfrac{5}{8} + \dfrac{1}{3}$

f $\dfrac{1}{8} + \dfrac{5}{6}$ g $\dfrac{1}{2} + \dfrac{3}{8}$ h $\dfrac{1}{6} + \dfrac{3}{4}$ i $\dfrac{5}{8} + \dfrac{1}{6}$ j $\dfrac{1}{3} + \dfrac{5}{8}$

3 Draw three rectangles, each 5 cm by 4 cm. Cut one into quarters, another into fifths and the last into tenths.

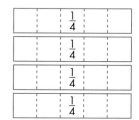 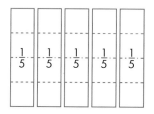 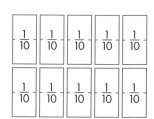

Use the strips to find the equivalent fraction in twentieths to each of the following.

a $\dfrac{1}{4}$ b $\dfrac{1}{5}$ c $\dfrac{3}{4}$ d $\dfrac{4}{5}$ e $\dfrac{1}{10}$

f $\dfrac{1}{2}$ g $\dfrac{3}{5}$ h $\dfrac{2}{5}$ i $\dfrac{7}{10}$ j $\dfrac{3}{10}$

4 Use the strips to write down the answer to each of the following.

a $\dfrac{1}{4} + \dfrac{1}{5}$ b $\dfrac{3}{5} + \dfrac{1}{10}$ c $\dfrac{3}{10} + \dfrac{1}{4}$ d $\dfrac{3}{4} + \dfrac{1}{5}$ e $\dfrac{7}{10} + \dfrac{1}{4}$

Equivalent fractions and cancelling

In this section you will learn how to:
- create equivalent fractions
- cancel fractions, where possible

Key words
denominator
lowest terms
numerator

Equivalent fractions are two or more fractions that represent the same part of a whole.

EXAMPLE 1

Complete these statements.

a $\dfrac{3}{4} \xrightarrow[\times 4]{\times 4} = \dfrac{\square}{16}$

b $\dfrac{2}{5} = \dfrac{\square}{15}$

a Multiplying the **numerator** by 4 gives 12. This means $\frac{12}{16}$ is an equivalent fraction to $\frac{3}{4}$.

b To change the **denominator** from 5 to 15, you multiply by 3. Do the same thing to the numerator, which gives $2 \times 3 = 6$. So, $\frac{2}{5} = \frac{6}{15}$.

The basic fraction, $\frac{3}{4}$ in Example 1, is in its **lowest terms**. This means that there is no number that is a factor of both the numerator and the denominator.

EXAMPLE 2

Cancel these fractions to their lowest terms.

a $\dfrac{15}{35}$

b $\dfrac{24}{54}$

a Here is one reason why you need to know the times tables. What is the biggest number that has both 15 and 35 in its times table? You should know that this is the five times table. So, divide both top and bottom numbers by 5.

$$\frac{15}{35} = \frac{15 \div 5}{35 \div 5} = \frac{3}{7}$$

You can say that you have 'cancelled by fives'.

b The biggest number that has both 24 and 54 in its times table is 6. So, divide both the numerator and denominator by 6.

$$\frac{24}{54} = \frac{24 \div 6}{54 \div 6} = \frac{4}{9}$$

Here, you have 'cancelled by sixes'.

EXAMPLE 3

Put the following fractions in order with the smallest first.

$$\frac{5}{6}, \frac{2}{3}, \frac{3}{4}$$

First write each fraction with the same denominator by using equivalent fractions.

$$\frac{5}{6} = \frac{10}{12}$$

$$\frac{2}{3} = \frac{4}{6} = \frac{6}{9} = \frac{8}{12}$$

$$\frac{3}{4} = \frac{6}{8} = \frac{9}{12}$$

This shows that $\frac{5}{6} = \frac{10}{12}$, $\frac{2}{3} = \frac{8}{12}$ and $\frac{3}{4} = \frac{9}{12}$.

In order, the fractions are:

$$\frac{2}{3}, \frac{3}{4}, \frac{5}{6}$$

EXERCISE 2D

1 Copy and complete each of these statements.

a $\dfrac{2}{5} \longrightarrow \dfrac{\times 4}{\times 4} = \dfrac{\square}{20}$

b $\dfrac{1}{4} \longrightarrow \dfrac{\times 3}{\times 3} = \dfrac{\square}{12}$

c $\dfrac{3}{8} \longrightarrow \dfrac{\times 5}{\times 5} = \dfrac{\square}{40}$

d $\dfrac{4}{5} \longrightarrow \dfrac{\times 3}{\times 3} = \dfrac{\square}{15}$

e $\dfrac{5}{6} \longrightarrow \dfrac{\times 3}{\times 3} = \dfrac{\square}{18}$

f $\dfrac{3}{7} \longrightarrow \dfrac{\times 4}{\times 4} = \dfrac{\square}{28}$

g $\dfrac{3}{10} \longrightarrow \dfrac{\times \square}{\times 2} = \dfrac{\square}{20}$

h $\dfrac{1}{3} \longrightarrow \dfrac{\times \square}{\times \square} = \dfrac{\square}{9}$

i $\dfrac{3}{5} \longrightarrow \dfrac{\times \square}{\times \square} = \dfrac{\square}{20}$

j $\dfrac{2}{3} \longrightarrow \dfrac{\times \square}{\times \square} = \dfrac{\square}{18}$

k $\dfrac{3}{4} \longrightarrow \dfrac{\times \square}{\times \square} = \dfrac{\square}{12}$

l $\dfrac{5}{8} \longrightarrow \dfrac{\times \square}{\times \square} = \dfrac{\square}{40}$

m $\dfrac{7}{10} \longrightarrow \dfrac{\times \square}{\times \square} = \dfrac{\square}{20}$

n $\dfrac{1}{6} \longrightarrow \dfrac{\times \square}{\times \square} = \dfrac{4}{\square}$

o $\dfrac{3}{8} \longrightarrow \dfrac{\times \square}{\times \square} = \dfrac{15}{\square}$

2 Copy and complete each of these statements.

a $\dfrac{1}{2} = \dfrac{2}{\square} = \dfrac{3}{\square} = \dfrac{\square}{8} = \dfrac{\square}{10} = \dfrac{6}{\square}$

b $\dfrac{1}{3} = \dfrac{2}{\square} = \dfrac{3}{\square} = \dfrac{\square}{12} = \dfrac{\square}{15} = \dfrac{6}{\square}$

c $\dfrac{3}{4} = \dfrac{6}{\square} = \dfrac{9}{\square} = \dfrac{\square}{16} = \dfrac{\square}{20} = \dfrac{18}{\square}$

d $\dfrac{2}{5} = \dfrac{4}{\square} = \dfrac{6}{\square} = \dfrac{\square}{20} = \dfrac{\square}{25} = \dfrac{12}{\square}$

e $\dfrac{3}{7} = \dfrac{6}{\square} = \dfrac{9}{\square} = \dfrac{\square}{28} = \dfrac{\square}{35} = \dfrac{18}{\square}$

3 Copy and complete each of these statements.

a $\dfrac{10}{15} = \dfrac{10 \div 5}{15 \div 5} = \dfrac{\square}{\square}$

b $\dfrac{12}{15} = \dfrac{12 \div 3}{15 \div 3} = \dfrac{\square}{\square}$

c $\dfrac{20}{28} = \dfrac{20 \div 4}{28 \div 4} = \dfrac{\square}{\square}$

d $\dfrac{12}{18} = \dfrac{12 \div \square}{\square \div \square} = \dfrac{\square}{\square}$

e $\dfrac{15}{25} = \dfrac{15 \div 5}{\square \div \square} = \dfrac{\square}{\square}$

f $\dfrac{21}{30} = \dfrac{21 \div \square}{\square \div \square} = \dfrac{\square}{\square}$

4 Cancel each of these fractions.

a $\dfrac{4}{6}$ b $\dfrac{5}{15}$ c $\dfrac{12}{18}$ d $\dfrac{6}{8}$ e $\dfrac{3}{9}$

f $\dfrac{5}{10}$ g $\dfrac{14}{16}$ h $\dfrac{28}{35}$ i $\dfrac{10}{20}$ j $\dfrac{4}{16}$

k $\dfrac{12}{15}$ l $\dfrac{15}{21}$ m $\dfrac{25}{35}$ n $\dfrac{14}{21}$ o $\dfrac{8}{20}$

p $\dfrac{10}{25}$ q $\dfrac{7}{21}$ r $\dfrac{42}{60}$ s $\dfrac{50}{200}$ t $\dfrac{18}{12}$

u $\dfrac{6}{9}$ v $\dfrac{18}{27}$ w $\dfrac{36}{48}$ x $\dfrac{21}{14}$ y $\dfrac{42}{12}$

5 Put the following fractions in order, with the smallest first.

a $\dfrac{1}{2}, \dfrac{5}{6}, \dfrac{2}{3}$ b $\dfrac{3}{4}, \dfrac{1}{2}, \dfrac{5}{8}$ c $\dfrac{7}{10}, \dfrac{2}{5}, \dfrac{1}{2}$ d $\dfrac{2}{3}, \dfrac{3}{4}, \dfrac{7}{12}$

e $\dfrac{1}{6}, \dfrac{1}{3}, \dfrac{1}{4}$ f $\dfrac{9}{10}, \dfrac{3}{4}, \dfrac{4}{5}$ g $\dfrac{4}{5}, \dfrac{7}{10}, \dfrac{5}{6}$ h $\dfrac{1}{3}, \dfrac{2}{5}, \dfrac{3}{10}$

> **HINTS AND TIPS**
>
> Make all denominators the same, e.g. $\dfrac{1}{2}, \dfrac{5}{6}, \dfrac{2}{3}$ is $\dfrac{3}{6}, \dfrac{5}{6}, \dfrac{4}{6}$.

2.5 Top-heavy fractions and mixed numbers

In this section you will learn how to:
- change top-heavy fractions into mixed numbers
- change a mixed number into a top-heavy fraction

Key word
mixed number
proper fraction
top-heavy

A fraction such as $\frac{9}{5}$ is called **top-heavy** because the numerator (top number) is bigger than the denominator (bottom number). You may also see a top-heavy fraction called an *improper* fraction.

A fraction that is not top-heavy, such as $\frac{4}{5}$, is sometimes called a **proper fraction**. The numerator of a proper fraction is smaller than its denominator.

Converting top-heavy fractions

You need a calculator with a fraction key, which will look like this. **a b/c**

Your calculator probably shows fractions like this. $2\lrcorner3$ or $2\ulcorner3$

This means $\frac{2}{3}$ or two-thirds.

Key the top-heavy fraction $\frac{9}{5}$ into your calculator. **9** **a b/c** **5**

The display will look like this. $9\lrcorner5$

Now press the equals key **=**. The display will change to: $1\lrcorner4\lrcorner5$

This is the **mixed number** $1\frac{4}{5}$.

(It is called a mixed number because it is a mixture of a whole number and a proper fraction.)

Write down the result: $\dfrac{9}{5} = 1\dfrac{4}{5}$

Key the top-heavy fraction $\frac{8}{4}$ into your calculator. **8** **a b/c** **4**

The display will look like this. $8\lrcorner4$

Now press the equals key **=**. The display will change to: 2

This represents the whole number 2. Whole numbers are special fractions with a denominator of 1. So, 2 is the fraction $\frac{2}{1}$.

Write down the result: $\dfrac{8}{4} = \dfrac{2}{1}$

- Now key at least ten top-heavy fractions and convert them to mixed numbers. Keep the numbers sensible. For example, don't use 37 or 17.

- Write down your results.

- Look at your results. Can you see a way of converting a top-heavy fraction to a mixed number without using a calculator?

- Test your idea. Then use your calculator to check it.

Converting mixed numbers

Key the mixed number $2\frac{3}{4}$ into your calculator. **2** **a b/c** **3** **a b/c** **4**

The display will look like this. $2\lrcorner3\lrcorner4$

Now press the shift (or **INV**) key and then press the fraction key **a b/c**

The display will change to: $11\lrcorner4$

This represents the top-heavy fraction $\frac{11}{4}$.

Write down the result. $2\frac{3}{4} = \frac{11}{4}$

- Now key at least ten more mixed numbers and convert them to top-heavy fractions. Keep your numbers sensible. For example, don't use $8\frac{16}{19}$ or $17\frac{11}{32}$.

- Write down your results.

- Look at your results. Can you see a way of converting a mixed number to a top-heavy fraction without using a calculator?

- Test your idea. Then use your calculator to check it.

EXERCISE 2E

Change each of these top-heavy fractions into a mixed number.

1 $\frac{7}{3}$	**2** $\frac{8}{3}$	**3** $\frac{9}{4}$	**4** $\frac{10}{7}$	**5** $\frac{12}{5}$	**6** $\frac{7}{5}$
7 $\frac{13}{5}$	**8** $\frac{15}{4}$	**9** $\frac{10}{3}$	**10** $\frac{15}{7}$	**11** $\frac{17}{6}$	**12** $\frac{18}{5}$
13 $\frac{19}{4}$	**14** $\frac{22}{7}$	**15** $\frac{14}{11}$	**16** $\frac{12}{11}$	**17** $\frac{28}{5}$	**18** $\frac{19}{7}$
19 $\frac{40}{7}$	**20** $\frac{42}{5}$	**21** $\frac{21}{10}$	**22** $\frac{5}{2}$	**23** $\frac{5}{3}$	**24** $\frac{25}{8}$
25 $\frac{23}{10}$	**26** $\frac{23}{11}$	**27** $\frac{38}{5}$	**28** $\frac{38}{7}$	**29** $\frac{40}{8}$	**30** $\frac{12}{6}$

Change each of these mixed numbers into a top-heavy fraction.

31 $3\frac{1}{3}$	**32** $5\frac{5}{6}$	**33** $1\frac{4}{5}$	**34** $5\frac{2}{7}$	**35** $4\frac{1}{10}$	**36** $5\frac{2}{3}$
37 $2\frac{1}{2}$	**38** $3\frac{1}{4}$	**39** $7\frac{1}{6}$	**40** $3\frac{5}{8}$	**41** $6\frac{1}{3}$	**42** $9\frac{8}{9}$
43 $11\frac{4}{5}$	**44** $3\frac{1}{5}$	**45** $4\frac{3}{8}$	**46** $3\frac{1}{9}$	**47** $5\frac{1}{5}$	**48** $2\frac{3}{4}$
49 $4\frac{2}{7}$	**50** $8\frac{1}{6}$	**51** $2\frac{8}{9}$	**52** $6\frac{1}{6}$	**53** $12\frac{1}{5}$	**54** $1\frac{5}{8}$
55 $7\frac{1}{10}$	**56** $8\frac{1}{9}$	**57** $7\frac{5}{8}$	**58** $10\frac{1}{2}$	**59** $1\frac{1}{16}$	**60** $4\frac{3}{4}$

Adding fractions with the same denominator

In this section you will learn how to:

- add and subtract two fractions with the same denominator, then simplify the result

Key words

lowest terms
mixed number
proper fraction
top-heavy
   fraction

When you add two fractions with the same denominator, you get one of the following:

- a **proper fraction** that cannot be cancelled, for example:

$$\frac{1}{5} + \frac{2}{5} = \frac{3}{5}$$

- a proper fraction that can be cancelled, for example:

$$\frac{1}{8} + \frac{3}{8} = \frac{4}{8} = \frac{1}{2}$$

- a **top-heavy fraction** that cannot be cancelled, so it is written at once as a **mixed number**, for example:

$$\frac{7}{8} + \frac{1}{4} = \frac{7}{8} + \frac{2}{8} = \frac{9}{8} = 1\frac{1}{8}$$

- a top-heavy fraction that can be cancelled before it is written as a mixed number, for example:

$$\frac{5}{8} + \frac{7}{8} = \frac{12}{8} = \frac{3}{2} = 1\frac{1}{2}$$

Note You must *always* cancel the fractions in answers to their **lowest terms**.

EXERCISE 2F

1 Copy and complete each of these additions.

  a $\dfrac{5}{8} + \dfrac{1}{8}$ **b** $\dfrac{3}{10} + \dfrac{1}{10}$ **c** $\dfrac{2}{9} + \dfrac{4}{9}$ **d** $\dfrac{1}{4} + \dfrac{1}{2}$

  e $\dfrac{3}{10} + \dfrac{3}{10}$ **f** $\dfrac{5}{12} + \dfrac{1}{12}$ **g** $\dfrac{3}{16} + \dfrac{5}{16}$ **h** $\dfrac{7}{16} + \dfrac{3}{16}$

2 Copy and complete each of these additions. Use equivalent fractions to make the denominators the same.

  a $\dfrac{1}{2} + \dfrac{7}{10}$ **b** $\dfrac{1}{2} + \dfrac{5}{8}$ **c** $\dfrac{3}{4} + \dfrac{3}{8}$ **d** $\dfrac{3}{4} + \dfrac{7}{8}$

  e $\dfrac{1}{2} + \dfrac{7}{8}$ **f** $\dfrac{1}{3} + \dfrac{5}{6}$ **g** $\dfrac{5}{6} + \dfrac{2}{3}$ **h** $\dfrac{3}{4} + \dfrac{1}{2}$

G

3 Copy and complete each of these additions.

a $\dfrac{3}{8} + \dfrac{7}{8}$ **b** $\dfrac{3}{4} + \dfrac{3}{4}$ **c** $\dfrac{2}{5} + \dfrac{3}{5}$ **d** $\dfrac{7}{10} + \dfrac{9}{10}$

e $\dfrac{5}{8} + \dfrac{5}{8}$ **f** $\dfrac{7}{16} + \dfrac{15}{16}$ **g** $\dfrac{5}{12} + \dfrac{11}{12}$ **h** $\dfrac{11}{16} + \dfrac{7}{16}$

i $1\dfrac{1}{2} + \dfrac{1}{4}$ **j** $2\dfrac{3}{4} + \dfrac{1}{2}$ **k** $3\dfrac{1}{2} + 2\dfrac{3}{4}$ **l** $2\dfrac{1}{8} + 1\dfrac{1}{2}$

4 Copy and complete each of these subtractions.

a $\dfrac{7}{8} - \dfrac{3}{8}$ **b** $\dfrac{7}{10} - \dfrac{1}{10}$ **c** $\dfrac{3}{4} - \dfrac{1}{2}$ **d** $\dfrac{5}{8} - \dfrac{1}{4}$

e $\dfrac{1}{2} - \dfrac{1}{4}$ **f** $\dfrac{7}{8} - \dfrac{1}{2}$ **g** $\dfrac{9}{10} - \dfrac{1}{2}$ **h** $\dfrac{11}{16} - \dfrac{3}{8}$

i $1 - \dfrac{3}{4}$ **j** $2 - \dfrac{1}{3}$ **k** $3\dfrac{3}{4} - 1\dfrac{1}{2}$ **l** $4\dfrac{5}{8} - 2\dfrac{1}{2}$

2.7 Problems in words

In this section you will learn how to:
- solve problems that have been put into words

Some of the questions you are going to meet in your GCSE exams will involve the use of fractions in real-life situations, which are described in words. You will have to decide what to do with the fractions given, then write down the calculation you need to do and work it out.

EXAMPLE 4

In a box of chocolates, quarter are truffles, half are orange creams and the rest are mints. What fraction are mints?

Truffles and orange creams together are $\dfrac{1}{4} + \dfrac{1}{2} = \dfrac{3}{4}$ of the box.

Take the whole box as 1. So, mints are $1 - \dfrac{3}{4} = \dfrac{1}{4}$ of the box.

EXERCISE 2G

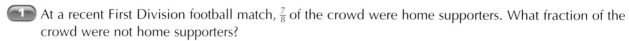

1. At a recent First Division football match, $\frac{7}{8}$ of the crowd were home supporters. What fraction of the crowd were not home supporters?

2. After Emma had taken a slice of cake, $\frac{3}{4}$ of the cake was left. Ayesha then had $\frac{1}{2}$ of what was left.

   a What fraction of the cake did Emma eat?

   b What fraction of the cake did Ayesha have?

   c Who had more cake?

3. Three friends share two pizzas. Each pizza is cut into six equal slices. What fraction of a pizza did each friend get?

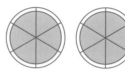

4. In a box of old CDs from a jumble sale, $\frac{1}{4}$ of them were rock music, $\frac{3}{8}$ of them were pop music and the rest were classical. What fraction of the CDs were classical?

5. In a car park, $\frac{1}{5}$ of the cars were British makes. Half of the rest were Japanese makes. What fraction of the cars were Japanese makes?

6. A fruit drink consists of $\frac{1}{2}$ orange juice, $\frac{1}{8}$ lemon juice and the rest is pineapple juice. What fraction of the drink is pineapple juice?

7. In a hockey team, $\frac{2}{11}$ of the team are French, $\frac{2}{11}$ are Italian, $\frac{3}{11}$ are Scottish and the rest are English. What fraction of the team is English?

8. In a packet of biscuits, $\frac{1}{6}$ are digestives, $\frac{2}{3}$ are bourbons and the rest are jammy dodgers. What fraction are jammy dodgers?

9. Jide pays $\frac{1}{4}$ of his wages in tax and $\frac{1}{8}$ of his wages in National Insurance. What fraction of his wages does he take home?

2.8 Finding a fraction of a quantity

In this section you will learn how to:
- find a fraction of a given quantity

To do this, you simply multiply the quantity by the fraction.

EXAMPLE 5

Find $\frac{3}{4}$ of £196.

First, find $\frac{1}{4}$ by dividing by 4. Then find $\frac{3}{4}$ by multiplying your answer by 3:

$196 \div 4 = 49$ then $49 \times 3 = 147$

The answer is £147.

Of course, you can use your calculator to do this problem by either:

- pressing the sequence: **1 9 6 ÷ 4 × 3 =**
- or using the **a b/c** key: **3 a b/c 4 × 1 9 6 =**

EXERCISE 2H

1 Calculate each of these.

  a $\frac{3}{5} \times 30$ **b** $\frac{2}{7} \times 35$ **c** $\frac{3}{8} \times 48$ **d** $\frac{7}{10} \times 40$

  e $\frac{5}{6} \times 18$ **f** $24 \times \frac{3}{4}$ **g** $60 \times \frac{4}{5}$ **h** $72 \times \frac{5}{8}$

2 Calculate each of these quantities.

  a $\frac{3}{4}$ of £2400   **b** $\frac{2}{5}$ of 320 grams   **c** $\frac{5}{8}$ of 256 kilograms

  d $\frac{2}{3}$ of £174   **e** $\frac{5}{6}$ of 78 litres   **f** $\frac{3}{4}$ of 120 minutes

  g $\frac{4}{5}$ of 365 days   **h** $\frac{7}{8}$ of 24 hours   **i** $\frac{3}{4}$ of 1 day

  j $\frac{5}{9}$ of 4266 miles

3 In each case, find out which is the larger number.

  a $\frac{2}{5}$ of 60 or $\frac{5}{8}$ of 40   **b** $\frac{3}{4}$ of 280 or $\frac{7}{10}$ of 290

  c $\frac{2}{3}$ of 78 or $\frac{4}{5}$ of 70   **d** $\frac{5}{6}$ of 72 or $\frac{11}{12}$ of 60

  e $\frac{4}{9}$ of 126 or $\frac{3}{5}$ of 95   **f** $\frac{3}{4}$ of 340 or $\frac{2}{3}$ of 381

4 A director was entitled to $\frac{2}{15}$ of his firm's profits. The firm made a profit of £45 600 in one year. What was the director's share of this profit?

5 A woman left $\frac{3}{8}$ of her estate to her favourite charity. What amount is this if her estate totalled £84 000?

6 There were 36 800 people at Hillsborough to see Sheffield Wednesday play Manchester United. Of this crowd, $\frac{3}{8}$ were female. How many male spectators were at the ground?

7 Two-thirds of a person's weight is water. Paul weighed 78 kg. How much of his body weight was water?

8 **a** Information from the first census in Singapore suggests that then $\frac{2}{25}$ of the population were Indian. The total population was 10 700. How many people were Indian?

   b By 1990 the population of Singapore had grown to 3 002 800. Only $\frac{1}{16}$ of this population were Indian. How many Indians were living in Singapore in 1990?

9 Mark normally earns £500 a week. One week he is given a bonus of $\frac{1}{10}$ of his wage.

   a Find $\frac{1}{10}$ of £500.

   b How much does he earn altogether for this week?

10 The contents of a standard box of cereals weigh 720 g. A new larger box holds $\frac{1}{4}$ more than the standard box.

   a Find $\frac{1}{4}$ of 720 g.

   b How much do the contents of the new box of cereals weigh?

11 The price of a new TV costing £360 is reduced by $\frac{1}{3}$ in a sale.

   a Find $\frac{1}{3}$ of £360.

   b How much does the TV cost in the sale?

12 The price of a car in a showroom is given as £8000. Find the price of the car if a discount of $\frac{1}{5}$ of the price is allowed.

2.9 Multiplying fractions

In this section you will learn how to:
- multiply a fraction by a fraction

What is $\frac{1}{2}$ of $\frac{1}{4}$?

The diagram shows the answer is $\frac{1}{8}$.

In mathematics, you always write $\frac{1}{2}$ of $\frac{1}{4}$ as $\frac{1}{2} \times \frac{1}{4}$

So you know that $\frac{1}{2} \times \frac{1}{4} = \frac{1}{8}$

To multiply fractions, you multiply the numerators together and you multiply the denominators together.

EXAMPLE 6

Work out $\frac{1}{4}$ of $\frac{2}{5}$.

$$\frac{1}{4} \times \frac{2}{5} = \frac{1 \times 2}{4 \times 5} = \frac{2}{20} = \frac{1}{10}$$

EXERCISE 2I

Work out each of these multiplications.

1. $\frac{1}{2} \times \frac{1}{3}$

2. $\frac{1}{4} \times \frac{1}{5}$

3. $\frac{1}{3} \times \frac{2}{3}$

4. $\frac{1}{4} \times \frac{2}{3}$

5. $\frac{1}{3} \times \frac{3}{4}$

6. $\frac{2}{3} \times \frac{3}{5}$

7. $\frac{3}{4} \times \frac{2}{3}$

8. $\frac{5}{6} \times \frac{3}{5}$

9. $\frac{2}{7} \times \frac{3}{4}$

10. $\frac{5}{6} \times \frac{7}{8}$

11. $\frac{4}{5} \times \frac{2}{3}$

12. $\frac{3}{4} \times \frac{7}{8}$

2.10 **One quantity as a fraction of another**

In this section you will learn how to:
● express one quantity as a fraction of another

You may often need to give one amount as a fraction of another amount.

EXAMPLE 7

Write £5 as a fraction of £20.

As a fraction this is written $\frac{5}{20}$. This cancels to $\frac{1}{4}$.

EXERCISE 2J

1 In each of the following, write the first quantity as a fraction of the second.

    a 2 cm, 6 cm   **b** 4 kg, 20 kg

    c £8, £20   **d** 5 hours, 24 hours

    e 12 days, 30 days   **f** 50p, £3

    g 4 days, 2 weeks   **h** 40 minutes, 2 hours

2 In a form of 30 pupils, 18 are boys. What fraction of the form consists of boys?

3 During March, it rained on 12 days. For what fraction of the month did it rain?

4 Reka wins £120 in a competition and puts £50 into her bank account. What fraction of her winnings does she keep to spend?

2.11 Reciprocals and rational numbers

In this section you will learn how to:
- recognise rational numbers, reciprocals, terminating decimals and recurring decimals
- convert terminal decimals to fractions
- convert fractions to recurring decimals
- find reciprocals of numbers or fractions

Key words
rational number
reciprocal
recurring decimal
terminating decimal

Rational decimal numbers

A fraction, also known as a **rational number**, can be expressed as a decimal that is either a **terminating decimal** or a **recurring decimal**.

A terminating decimal contains a finite number of digits (decimal places). For example, changing $\frac{3}{16}$ into a decimal gives 0.1875 exactly.

A recurring decimal contains a digit or a block of digits that repeats. For example, changing $\frac{5}{9}$ into a decimal gives 0.5555…, while changing $\frac{14}{27}$ into a decimal gives 0.518 518 5… with the recurring block 518

You can indicate recurring digits by placing a dot over the first and last digits in the recurring block; for example, 0.5555… becomes $0.\dot{5}$, 0.518 518 5… becomes $0.\dot{5}1\dot{8}$ and 0.583 33 becomes $0.58\dot{3}$

Converting terminal decimals into fractions

To convert a terminating decimal to a fraction, take the decimal number as the numerator. Then the denominator is 10, 100 or 1000, depending on the number of decimal places. Because a terminating decimal has a specific number of decimal places, you can use place value to work out exactly where the numerator and the denominator end. For example:

- $0.7 = \dfrac{7}{10}$

- $0.045 = \dfrac{45}{1000} = \dfrac{9}{200}$

- $2.34 = \dfrac{234}{100} = \dfrac{117}{50} = 2\dfrac{17}{50}$

- $0.625 = \dfrac{625}{1000} = \dfrac{5}{8}$

Converting fractions into recurring decimals

A fraction that does not convert to a terminating decimal will give a recurring decimal. You may already know that $\frac{1}{3} = 0.333\ldots = 0.\dot{3}$ This means that the 3s go on for ever and the decimal never ends.

To convert the fraction, you can usually use a calculator to divide the numerator by the denominator. Note that calculators round off the last digit so it may not always be a true recurring decimal in the display. Use a calculator to check the following recurring decimals.

$\dfrac{2}{11} = 0.181\,818\ldots = 0.\dot{1}\dot{8}$

$\dfrac{4}{15} = 0.2666\ldots = 0.2\dot{6}$

$\dfrac{8}{13} = 0.615\,384\,615\,384\,6\ldots = 0.\dot{6}15\,38\dot{4}$

Finding reciprocals of numbers or fractions

You can find the **reciprocal** of a number by dividing that number into 1. So the reciprocal of 2 is $1 \div 2 = \frac{1}{2}$ or 0.5

Reciprocals of fractions are quite easy to find as you just have to turn the fraction upside down. For example, the reciprocal of $\frac{2}{3}$ is $\frac{3}{2}$

1 Write each of these fractions as a decimal. Give them as terminating decimals or recurring decimals, as appropriate.

a $\dfrac{1}{2}$ b $\dfrac{1}{3}$ c $\dfrac{1}{4}$ d $\dfrac{1}{5}$ e $\dfrac{1}{6}$

f $\dfrac{1}{7}$ g $\dfrac{1}{8}$ h $\dfrac{1}{9}$ i $\dfrac{1}{10}$ j $\dfrac{1}{13}$

2 There are several patterns to be found in recurring decimals. For example:

$$\frac{1}{7} = 0.142\,857\,142\,857\,142\,857\,142\,857\ldots$$

$$\frac{2}{7} = 0.285\,714\,285\,714\,285\,714\,285\,714\ldots$$

$$\frac{3}{7} = 0.428\,571\,428\,571\,428\,571\,428\,571\ldots$$

and so on.

a Write down the decimals for each of the following to 24 decimal places.

i $\dfrac{4}{7}$ ii $\dfrac{5}{7}$ iii $\dfrac{6}{7}$

b What do you notice?

3 Work out the ninths, $\dfrac{1}{9}, \dfrac{2}{9}, \dfrac{3}{9}$, and so on up to $\dfrac{8}{9}$, as recurring decimals.

Describe any patterns that you notice.

4 Work out the elevenths, $\dfrac{1}{11}, \dfrac{2}{11}, \dfrac{3}{11}$, and so on up to $\dfrac{10}{11}$, as recurring decimals.

Describe any patterns that you notice.

5 Write each of these fractions as a decimal. Use your results to write the list in order of size, smallest first.

$\dfrac{4}{9}$ $\dfrac{5}{11}$ $\dfrac{3}{7}$ $\dfrac{9}{22}$ $\dfrac{16}{37}$ $\dfrac{6}{13}$

6 Write the following list of fractions in order of size, smallest first.

$\dfrac{19}{60}$ $\dfrac{7}{24}$ $\dfrac{3}{10}$ $\dfrac{2}{5}$ $\dfrac{5}{12}$

7 Convert each of these terminating decimals to a fraction.

a 0.125   b 0.34   c 0.725   d 0.3125

e 0.89   f 0.05   g 2.35   h 0.218 75

8 Use a calculator to work out the reciprocal of each of the following.

a 12   b 16   c 20   d 25   e 50

9 Write down the reciprocal of each of the following fractions.

a $\dfrac{3}{4}$ b $\dfrac{5}{6}$ c $\dfrac{2}{5}$

d $\dfrac{7}{10}$ e $\dfrac{11}{20}$ f $\dfrac{4}{15}$

10 Write the fractions and their reciprocals in question **9** as decimals. Write them as terminating decimals or recurring decimals, as appropriate.

Is it always true that a fraction that gives a terminating decimal has a reciprocal that gives a recurring decimal?

11 Multiply each of the fractions in question **9** by its reciprocal. What result do you get every time?

1 **a** What fraction of the shape below is shaded?

Give your answer as a fraction in its simplest form.

b Copy out and shade $\frac{3}{4}$ of the shape below.

2 Put the following fractions into order, smallest first.

$$\frac{3}{4} \quad \frac{1}{2} \quad \frac{2}{5} \quad \frac{1}{3}$$

3 Work out.

$$\frac{7}{10} - \frac{2}{5}$$

4 Work out $\frac{3}{5}$ of 185.

Edexcel, Question 4a, Paper 8B Foundation, January 2003

5 Alison travels by car to her meetings. Alison's company pays her 32p for each mile she travels.

One day Alison writes down the distance readings from her car.

    Start of the day: 2430 miles

    End of the day: 2658 miles

a Work out how much the company pays Alison for her day's travel.

The next day Alison travelled a total of 145 miles.

She travelled $\frac{2}{5}$ of this distance in the morning.

b How many miles did she travel during the rest of the day?

Edexcel, Question 9, Paper 2 Foundation, June 2005

6 Calculate the following, giving your answers as fractions in their simplest forms.

a $\frac{3}{8} + \frac{1}{8}$

b $\frac{9}{10} - \frac{1}{2}$

7 A fruit punch was made using $\frac{1}{2}$ lemonade, $\frac{1}{5}$ orange juice with the rest lemon juice. What fraction of the drink is lemon juice?

8 The land area of a farm is 385 acres. One-fifth of the land is used to grow barley. How many acres is this?

9 **a** Work out

     i $\frac{3}{5}$ of 175

     ii $\frac{3}{4} \times \frac{2}{3}$

b What fraction is 13 weeks out of a year of 52 weeks?

c What is $1 - \frac{2}{5}$?

10 Two-fifths of the price of a book goes to the bookshop. A book cost £12. How much goes to the bookshop?

11 When a cross is carved from a piece of wood, $\frac{4}{5}$ of the wood is cut away. The original block weighs 215 grams. What weight of wood is cut off?

12 Find $\frac{3}{5}$ of 45 kg.

13 Here are two fractions $\frac{3}{5}$ and $\frac{2}{3}$.

Explain which is the larger fraction.

You may copy and use the grids to help with your explanation.

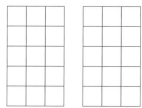

Edexcel, Question 19, Paper 1 Foundation, June 2003

14 **a** Work out $30 \times \frac{2}{3}$

b Work out the value of $\frac{14}{15} \times \frac{3}{4}$

Give your answer as a fraction in its simplest form.

15 Change the following fractions to decimals.

a $\frac{1}{5}$

b $\frac{1}{3}$

16 Packets of Wheetix used to contain 550 grams of cereal. New packets contain one-fifth more. How much does a new packet contain?

17 Change the following fractions to decimals.

a $\frac{1}{7}$

b $\frac{5}{13}$

WORKED EXAM QUESTION

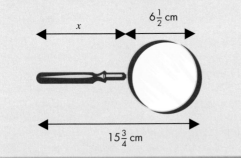

This is a drawing of a magnifying glass.
Calculate the length marked x.

$6\frac{1}{2}$ cm

x

$15\frac{3}{4}$ cm

Solution

$15\frac{3}{4} - 6\frac{1}{2}$ First identify the problem as a subtraction.

$= 15 - 6 + \frac{3}{4} - \frac{1}{2}$ Split the problem into whole numbers and fractions.

$= 9 + \frac{1}{4}$ Work out each part.

$= 9\frac{1}{4}$ Final answer

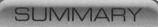

GRADE YOURSELF

- **G** Able to state the fraction of a shape shaded
- **G** Able to shade in a fraction of a shape
- **G** Can add and subtract simple fractions
- **G** Know how to recognise equivalent fractions
- **G** Able to cancel a fraction (when possible)
- **G** Able to put simple fractions into order of size
- **G** Able to change top-heavy fractions into mixed numbers
- **G** Able to find a fraction of an integer
- **F** Able to change mixed numbers into top-heavy fractions
- **F** Able to add more difficult fractions
- **F** Able to solve fraction problems expressed in words
- **F** Able to compare two fractions of quantities
- **E** Can multiply a fraction by a fraction
- **E** Can add and subtract mixed numbers
- **D** Know how to write a quantity as a fraction of another quantity
- **C** Can work out a reciprocal
- **C** Know how to work out and recognise terminating and recurring decimals

What you should know now

- How to recognise and draw fractions of shapes
- How to add, subtract, multiply and cancel simple fractions without using a calculator
- How to work out equivalent fractions
- How to convert a top-heavy fraction to a mixed number (and the other way)
- How to calculate a fraction of a quantity
- How to solve simple practical problems using fractions
- How to work out reciprocals and decimals from fractions

This book provides indicators of the equivalent grade level of maths questions throughout. The publishers wish to make clear that these grade indicators have been provided by Collins Education, and are not the responsibility of Edexcel Ltd. Whilst every effort has been made to assure their accuracy, they should be regarded as indicators, and are not binding or definitive.

Negative numbers

1 Introduction to negative numbers

2 Everyday use of negative numbers

3 The number line

4 Arithmetic with negative numbers

This chapter will show you ...
- how negative numbers are used in real life
- what is meant by a negative number
- how to use inequalities with negative numbers
- how to do arithmetic with negative numbers

Visual overview

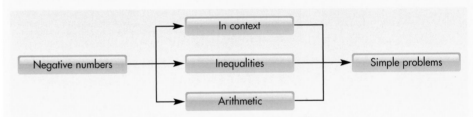

What you should already know
- What a negative number means
- How to put numbers in order

Quick check
Put the numbers in the following lists into order, smallest first.

1	8, 2, 5, 9, 1, 0, 4
2	14, 19, 11, 10, 17
3	51, 92, 24, 0, 32
4	87, 136, 12, 288, 56
5	5, 87, $\frac{1}{2}$, 100, 0, 50

In this section you will learn how:

● negative numbers can represent depths

Key word

negative number

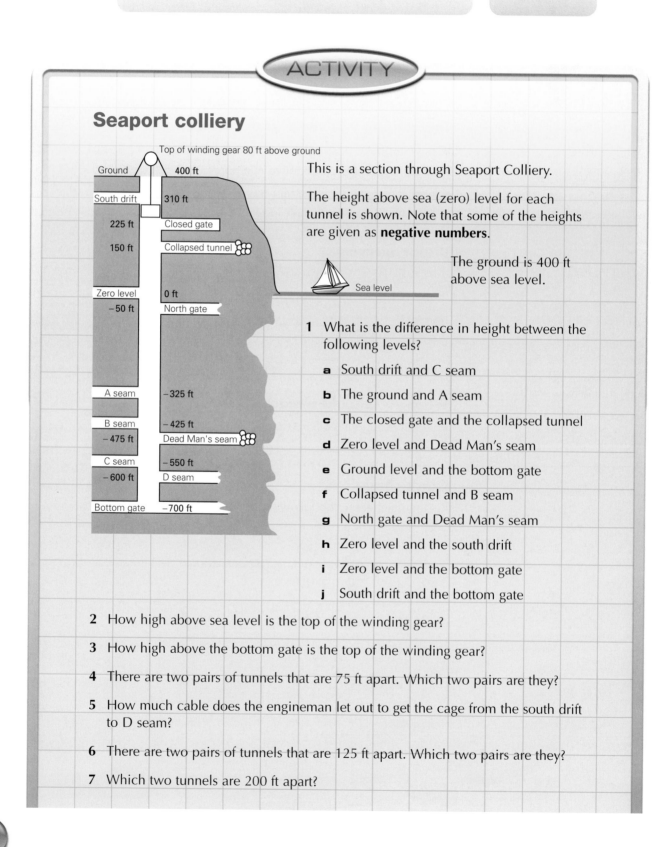

Seaport colliery

Top of winding gear 80 ft above ground

Ground	400 ft
South drift	310 ft
225 ft	Closed gate
150 ft	Collapsed tunnel
Zero level	0 ft
–50 ft	North gate
A seam	–325 ft
B seam	–425 ft
–475 ft	Dead Man's seam
C seam	–550 ft
–600 ft	D seam
Bottom gate	–700 ft

Sea level

This is a section through Seaport Colliery.

The height above sea (zero) level for each tunnel is shown. Note that some of the heights are given as **negative numbers**.

The ground is 400 ft above sea level.

1 What is the difference in height between the following levels?

   a South drift and C seam

   b The ground and A seam

   c The closed gate and the collapsed tunnel

   d Zero level and Dead Man's seam

   e Ground level and the bottom gate

   f Collapsed tunnel and B seam

   g North gate and Dead Man's seam

   h Zero level and the south drift

   i Zero level and the bottom gate

   j South drift and the bottom gate

2 How high above sea level is the top of the winding gear?

3 How high above the bottom gate is the top of the winding gear?

4 There are two pairs of tunnels that are 75 ft apart. Which two pairs are they?

5 How much cable does the engineman let out to get the cage from the south drift to D seam?

6 There are two pairs of tunnels that are 125 ft apart. Which two pairs are they?

7 Which two tunnels are 200 ft apart?

Caves and mountains

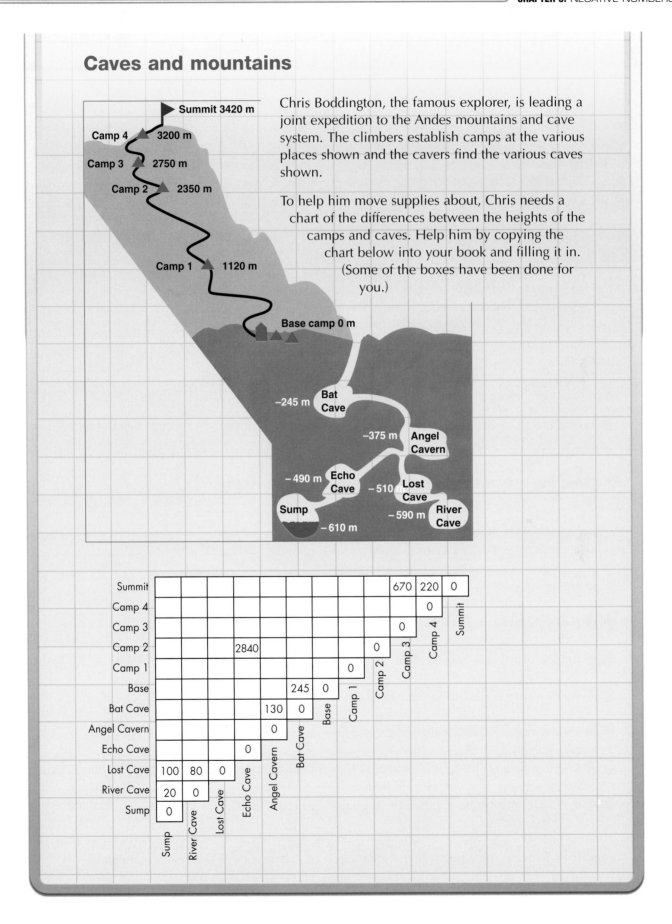

Chris Boddington, the famous explorer, is leading a joint expedition to the Andes mountains and cave system. The climbers establish camps at the various places shown and the cavers find the various caves shown.

To help him move supplies about, Chris needs a chart of the differences between the heights of the camps and caves. Help him by copying the chart below into your book and filling it in. (Some of the boxes have been done for you.)

Diagram labels:
- Summit 3420 m
- Camp 4 — 3200 m
- Camp 3 — 2750 m
- Camp 2 — 2350 m
- Camp 1 — 1120 m
- Base camp 0 m
- Bat Cave −245 m
- Angel Cavern −375 m
- Echo Cave −490 m
- Lost Cave −510 m
- Sump −610 m
- River Cave −590 m

	Sump	River Cave	Lost Cave	Echo Cave	Angel Cavern	Bat Cave	Base	Camp 1	Camp 2	Camp 3	Camp 4	Summit
Summit										670	220	0
Camp 4											0	
Camp 3										0		
Camp 2				2840					0			
Camp 1								0				
Base						245	0					
Bat Cave					130	0						
Angel Cavern					0							
Echo Cave				0								
Lost Cave	100	80	0									
River Cave	20	0										
Sump	0											

Everyday use of negative numbers

In this section you will learn about:

- using positive and negative numbers in everyday life

Key words
after
before
below
loss
negative
    number
profit

You meet **negative numbers** often in winter when the temperature falls **below** freezing (0 °C). Negative numbers are less than 0.

You also meet negative numbers on graphs, and you may already have plotted coordinates with negative numbers.

There are many other situations where negative numbers are used. Here are three examples.

- When +15 m means 15 metres above sea level, then –15 m means 15 metres **below** sea level.

- When +2 h means 2 hours **after** midday, then –2 h means 2 hours **before** midday.

- When +£60 means a **profit** of £60, then –£60 means a **loss** of £60.

EXERCISE 3A

Copy and complete each of the following.

1. If +£5 means a profit of five pounds, then …… means a loss of five pounds.

2. If +£9 means a profit of £9, then a loss of £9 is …… .

3. If –£4 means a loss of four pounds, then +£4 means a …… of four pounds.

4. If +200 m means 200 metres above sea level, then …… means 200 metres below sea level.

5. If +50 m means fifty metres above sea level, then fifty metres below sea level is written …… .

6. If –100 m means one hundred metres below sea level, then +100 m means one hundred metres …… sea level.

7. If +3 h means three hours after midday, then …… means three hours before midday.

8. If +5 h means 5 hours after midday, then …… means 5 hours before midday.

9. If –6 h means six hours before midday, then +6 h means six hours …… midday.

10 If +2 °C means two degrees above freezing point, then …… means two degrees below freezing point.

11 If +8 °C means 8 °C above freezing point, then …… means 8 °C below freezing point.

12 If –5 °C means five degrees below freezing point, then +5 °C means five degrees …… freezing point.

13 If +70 km means 70 kilometres north of the equator, then …… means 70 kilometres south of the equator.

14 If +200 km means 200 kilometres north of the equator, then 200 kilometres south of the equator is written …… .

15 If –50 km means fifty kilometres south of the equator, then +50 km means fifty kilometres …… of the equator.

16 If 10 minutes before midnight is represented by –10 minutes, then five minutes after midnight is represented by …… .

17 If a car moving forwards at 10 mph is represented by +10 mph, then a car moving backwards at 5 mph is represented by …… .

18 In an office building, the third floor above ground level is represented by +3. So, the second floor below ground level is represented by …… .

3.3 The number line

In this section you will learn how to:
- use a number line to represent negative numbers
- use inequalities with negative numbers

Key words
greater than
inequality
less than
more than
negative
number line
positive

Look at the **number line**.

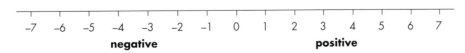

Notice that the **negative** numbers are to the left of 0, and the **positive** numbers are to the right of 0.

Numbers to the right of any number on the number line are always bigger than that number.

Numbers to the left of any number on the number line are always smaller than that number.

So, for example, you can see from a number line that:

2 is *smaller* than 5 because 2 is to the *left* of 5.

You can write this as 2 < 5.

−3 is *smaller* than 2 because −3 is to the *left* of 2.

You can write this as −3 < 2.

7 is *bigger* than 3 because 7 is to the *right* of 3.

You can write this as 7 > 3.

−1 is *bigger* than −4 because −1 is to the *right* of −4.

You can write this as −1 > −4.

Reminder   The **inequality** signs:

< means 'is **less than**'

> means 'is **greater than**' or 'is **more than**'

EXERCISE 3B

1 Copy and complete each of the following by putting a suitable number in the box.

a ☐ is smaller than 3   b ☐ is smaller than 1   c ☐ is smaller than −3

d ☐ is smaller than −7   e −5 is smaller than ☐   f −1 is smaller than ☐

g 3 is smaller than ☐   h −2 is smaller than ☐   i ☐ is smaller than 0

j −4 is smaller than ☐   k ☐ is smaller than −8   l −7 is smaller than ☐

2 Copy and complete each of the following by putting a suitable number in the box.

a ☐ is bigger than −3   b ☐ is bigger than 1   c ☐ is bigger than −2

d ☐ is bigger than −1   e −1 is bigger than ☐   f −8 is bigger than ☐

g 1 is bigger than ☐   h −5 is bigger than ☐   i ☐ is bigger than −5

j 2 is bigger than ☐   k ☐ is bigger than −4   l −2 is bigger than ☐

3 Copy each of these and put the correct phrase in each space.

a −1 3   b 3 2   c −4 ...... −1

d −5 ...... −4   e 1 ...... −6   f −3 0

g −2 ...... −1   h 2 ...... −3   i 5 ...... −6

j 3 4   k −7 ...... −5   l −2 ...... −4

4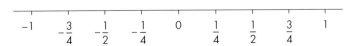

Copy each of these and put the correct phrase in each space.

a $\dfrac{1}{4}$ ...... $\dfrac{3}{4}$

b $-\dfrac{1}{2}$ 0

c $-\dfrac{3}{4}$ ...... $\dfrac{3}{4}$

d $\dfrac{1}{4}$ ...... $-\dfrac{1}{2}$

e -1 ...... $\dfrac{3}{4}$

f $\dfrac{1}{2}$ 1

5 In each case below, copy the statement and put the correct symbol, either < or >, in the box.

a $3 \ \square \ 5$

b $-2 \ \square \ -5$

c $-4 \ \square \ 3$

d $5 \ \square \ 9$

e $-3 \ \square \ 2$

f $4 \ \square \ -3$

g $-1 \ \square \ 0$

h $6 \ \square \ -4$

i $2 \ \square \ -3$

j $0 \ \square \ -2$

k $-5 \ \square \ -4$

l $1 \ \square \ 3$

m $-6 \ \square \ -7$

n $2 \ \square \ -3$

o $-1 \ \square \ 1$

p $4 \ \square \ 0$

6 Copy these number lines and fill in the missing numbers.

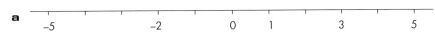

a $-5 \quad\quad -2 \quad 0 \quad 1 \quad\quad 3 \quad\quad 5$

b $-20 \quad\quad -10 \quad 0 \quad 5 \quad\quad 15$

c $-8 \quad\quad -4 \quad 0 \quad 2 \quad\quad 6$

d $-30 \quad\quad -10 \quad 0 \quad 10 \quad 20$

e $-9 \quad -6 \quad 0 \quad 3 \quad 6 \quad\quad 12$

f $-8 \quad 0 \quad\quad 8 \quad\quad 16$

g $-2 \quad\quad -1 \quad 0 \quad\quad 1 \quad\quad 2$

h $-100 \quad\quad -40 \quad 0 \quad 20 \quad\quad 60$

i $-100 \quad 0 \quad 50 \quad\quad\quad 200$

In this section you will learn how to:

- add and subtract positive and negative numbers to both positive and negative numbers

Key words

add

subtract

Adding and subtracting positive numbers

These two operations can be illustrated on a thermometer scale.

- **Adding** a positive number moves the marker *up* the thermometer scale. For example,

−2 + 6 = 4

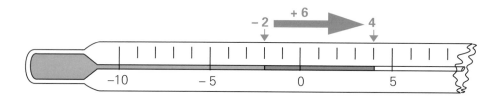

- **Subtracting** a positive number moves the marker *down* the thermometer scale. For example,

3 − 5 = −2

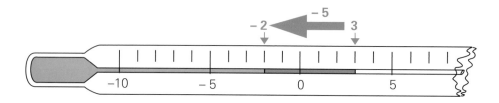

EXAMPLE 1

The temperature at midnight was 2 °C but then it fell by 5 degrees. What was the new temperature?

To put it simply, the problem is 2 − 5, which is equal to −3. So, the new temperature is −3°C.

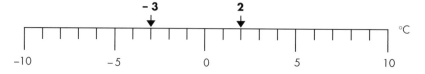

EXAMPLE 2

The temperature drops five degrees from −4 °C. What does it drop to?

To put it simply, the problem is −4 − 5, which is equal to −9. So, the new temperature is −9 °C.

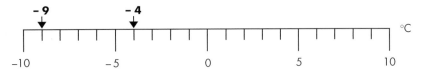

EXERCISE 3C

1 Use a thermometer scale to find the answer to each of the following.

a 2 °C − 4 °C =	**b** 4 °C − 7 °C =	**c** 3 °C − 5 °C =	**d** 1 °C − 4 °C =
e 6 °C − 8 °C =	**f** 5 °C − 8 °C =	**g** −2 + 5 =	**h** −1 + 4 =
i −4 + 3 =	**j** −6 + 5 =	**k** −3 + 5 =	**l** −5 + 2 =
m −1 − 3 =	**n** −2 − 4 =	**o** −5 − 1 =	**p** 3 − 4 =
q 2 − 7 =	**r** 1 − 5 =	**s** −3 + 7 =	**t** 5 − 6 =
u −2 − 3 =	**v** 2 − 6 =	**w** −8 + 3 =	**x** 4 − 9 =

2 Answer each of the following *without* the help of a thermometer scale.

a 5 − 9 =	**b** 3 − 7 =	**c** −2 − 8 =	**d** −5 + 7 =
e −1 + 9 =	**f** 4 − 9 =	**g** −10 + 12 =	**h** −15 + 20 =
i 23 − 30 =	**j** 30 − 42 =	**k** −12 + 25 =	**l** −30 + 55 =
m −10 − 22 =	**n** −13 − 17 =	**o** 45 − 50 =	**p** 17 − 25 =
q 18 − 30 =	**r** −25 + 35 =	**s** −23 − 13 =	**t** 31 − 45 =
u −24 + 65 =	**v** −19 + 31 =	**w** 25 − 65 =	**x** 199 − 300 =

3 Work out each of the following.

a 8 + 3 − 5 =	**b** −2 + 3 − 6 =	**c** −1 + 3 + 4 =
d −2 − 3 + 4 =	**e** −1 + 1 − 2 =	**f** −4 + 5 − 7 =
g −3 + 4 − 7 =	**h** 1 + 3 − 6 =	**i** 8 − 7 + 2 =
j −5 − 7 + 12 =	**k** −4 + 5 − 8 =	**l** −4 + 6 − 8 =
m 103 − 102 + 7 =	**n** −1 + 4 − 2 =	**o** −6 + 9 − 12 =
p −3 − 3 − 3 =	**q** −3 + 4 − 6 =	**r** −102 + 45 − 23 =
s 8 − 10 − 5 =	**t** 9 − 12 + 2 =	**u** 99 − 100 − 46 =

Adding and subtracting negative numbers

To *subtract a negative number ...*

... treat the − − as a +

For example: $4 - (-2) = 4 + 2 = 6$

To *add a negative number ...*

... treat the + − as a −

For example: $3 + (-5) = 3 - 5 = -2$

Using your calculator

Calculations involving negative numbers can be done on a calculator by using the [±] [(] [)] keys or the [(−)] key.

EXAMPLE 3

Work out $-3 + 7$.

Press [3] [±] [+] [7] [=]

The answer should be 4.

EXAMPLE 4

Work out $-6 - (-2)$.

Press [(−)] [6] [−] [(−)] [2] [=]

The answer should be −4.

EXERCISE 3D

1 Answer each of the following. Check your answers on a calculator.

a $2 - (-4) =$	**b** $4 - (-3) =$	**c** $3 - (-5) =$	**d** $5 - (-1) =$
e $6 - (-2) =$	**f** $8 - (-2) =$	**g** $-1 - (-3) =$	**h** $-4 - (-1) =$
i $-2 - (-3) =$	**j** $-5 - (-7) =$	**k** $-3 - (-2) =$	**l** $-8 - (-1) =$
m $4 + (-2) =$	**n** $2 + (-5) =$	**o** $3 + (-2) =$	**p** $1 + (-6) =$
q $5 + (-2) =$	**r** $4 + (-8) =$	**s** $-2 + (-1) =$	**t** $-6 + (-2) =$
u $-7 + (-3) =$	**v** $-2 + (-7) =$	**w** $-1 + (-3) =$	**x** $-7 + (-2) =$

2 Write down the answer to each of the following, then check your answers on a calculator.

a $-3 - 5 =$ **b** $-2 - 8 =$ **c** $-5 - 6 =$ **d** $6 - 9 =$

e $5 - 3 =$ **f** $3 - 8 =$ **g** $-4 + 5 =$ **h** $-3 + 7 =$

i $-2 + 9 =$ **j** $-6 + -2 =$ **k** $-1 + -4 =$ **l** $-8 + -3 =$

m $5 - -6 =$ **n** $3 - -3 =$ **o** $6 - -2 =$ **p** $3 - -5 =$

q $-5 - -3 =$ **r** $-2 - -1 =$ **s** $-4 - 5 =$ **t** $2 - 7 =$

u $-3 + 8 =$ **v** $-4 + - 5 =$ **w** $1 - -7 =$ **x** $-5 - -5 =$

3 The temperature at midnight was 4 °C. Find the temperature if it *fell* by:

a 1 degree **b** 4 degrees **c** 7 degrees **d** 9 degrees **e** 15 degrees

4 What is the *difference* between the following temperatures?

a 4 °C and –6 °C **b** –2 °C and –9 °C **c** –3 °C and 6 °C

5 Rewrite the following list, putting the numbers in order of size, lowest first.

1   –5   3   –6   –9   8   –1   2

6 Write down the answers to each of the following, then check your answers on a calculator.

a $2 - 5 =$ **b** $7 - 11 =$ **c** $4 - 6 =$ **d** $8 - 15 =$

e $9 - 23 =$ **f** $-2 - 4 =$ **g** $-5 - 7 =$ **h** $-1 - 9 =$

i $-4 + 8 =$ **j** $-9 + 5 =$ **k** $9 - -5 =$ **l** $8 - -3 =$

m $-8 - -4 =$ **n** $-3 - -2 =$ **o** $-7 + -3 =$ **p** $-9 + 4 =$

q $-6 + 3 =$ **r** $-1 + 6 =$ **s** $-9 - -5 =$ **t** $9 - 17 =$

7 Find what you have to *add to* 5 to get:

a 7 **b** 2 **c** 0 **d** –2 **e** –5 **f** –15

8 Find what you have to *subtract from* 4 to get:

a 2 **b** 0 **c** 5 **d** 9 **e** 15 **f** –4

9 Find what you have to *add to* –5 to get:

a 8 **b** –3 **c** 0 **d** –1 **e** 6 **f** –7

10 Find what you have to *subtract from* –3 to get:

a 7 **b** 2 **c** –1 **d** –7 **e** –10 **f** 1

11 Write down *ten* different addition sums that give the answer 1.

12 Write down *ten* different subtraction calculations that give the answer 1. There must be *one negative number* in each calculation.

13 Use a calculator to work out each of these.

a $-7 + - 3 - -5 =$ **b** $6 + 7 - 7 =$ **c** $-3 + -4 - -7 =$

d $-1 - 3 - -6 =$ **e** $8 - -7 + -2 =$ **f** $-5 - 7 - -12 =$

g $-4 + 5 - 7 =$ **h** $-4 + -6 - -8 =$ **i** $103 - -102 - -7 =$

j $-1 + 4 - -2 =$ **k** $6 - -9 - 12 =$ **l** $-3 - -3 - -3 =$

m $-45 + -56 - -34 =$ **n** $-3 + 4 - -6 =$ **o** $102 + -45 - 32 =$

14 Give the outputs of each of these function machines.

a $-4, -3, -2, -1, 0$ → $+ 3$ → ?, ?, ?, ?, ?

b $-4, -3, -2, -1, 0$ → $- 2$ → ?, ?, ?, ?, ?

c $-4, -3, -2, -1, 0$ → $+ 1$ → ?, ?, ?, ?, ?

d $-4, -3, -2, -1, 0$ → $- 4$ → ?, ?, ?, ?, ?

e $-4, -3, -2, -1, 0$ → $- 5$ → ?, ?, ?, ?, ?

f $-4, -3, -2, -1, 0$ → $+ 7$ → ?, ?, ?, ?, ?

g $-10, -9, -8, -7, -6$ → $- 2$ → ?, ?, ?, ?, ?

h $-10, -9, -8, -7, -6$ → $- 6$ → ?, ?, ?, ?, ?

i $-5, -4, -3, -2, -1, 0$ → $+ 3$ → ?, ?, ?, ?, ?, ? → $- 2$ → ?, ?, ?, ?, ?, ?

j $-5, -4, -3, -2, -1, 0$ → $- 7$ → ?, ?, ?, ?, ?, ? → $- 2$ → ?, ?, ?, ?, ?, ?

k $-5, -4, -3, -2, -1, 0$ → $+ 3$ → ?, ?, ?, ?, ?, ? → $+ 2$ → ?, ?, ?, ?, ?, ?

l $-3, -2, -1, 0, 1, 2, 3$ → $- 5$ → ?, ?, ?, ?, ?, ? → $+ 3$ → ?, ?, ?, ?, ?, ?

m $-3, -2, -1, 0, 1, 2, 3$ → $- 7$ → ?, ?, ?, ?, ?, ?, ? → $+ 9$ → ?, ?, ?, ?, ?, ?, ?

n $-3, -2, -1, 0, 1, 2, 3$ → $+ 6$ → ?, ?, ?, ?, ?, ?, ? → $- 8$ → ?, ?, ?, ?, ?, ?, ?

15 What numbers are missing from the boxes to make the number sentences true?

a $2 + -6 = \square$ **b** $4 + \square = 7$ **c** $-4 + \square = 0$ **d** $5 + \square = -1$

e $3 + 4 = \square$ **f** $\square - -5 = 7$ **g** $\square - 5 = 2$ **h** $6 + \square = 0$

i $\square - -5 = -2$ **j** $2 + -2 = \square$ **k** $\square - 2 = -2$ **l** $-2 + -4 = \square$

m $2 + 3 + \square = -2$ **n** $-2 + -3 + -4 = \square$ **o** $\square - 5 = -1$ **p** $\square - 8 = -8$

q $-4 + 2 + \square = 3$ **r** $-5 + 5 = \square$ **s** $7 - -3 = \square$ **t** $\square - -5 = 0$

u $3 - \square = 0$ **v** $-3 - \square = 0$ **w** $-6 + -3 = \square$ **x** $\square - 3 - -2 = -1$

y $\square - 1 = -4$ **z** $7 - \square = 10$

16 You have the following cards.

a Which card should you choose to make the answer to the following sum as large as possible? What is the answer?

$+6$ $+$ $\blacksquare$ $=$ ......

b Which card should you choose to make the answer to part **a** as small as possible? What is the answer?

c Which card should you choose to make the answer to the following subtraction as large as possible? What is the answer?

$+6$ $-$ $\blacksquare$ $=$ ......

d Which card should you choose to make the answer to part **c** as small as possible? What is the answer?

17 You have the following cards.

a Which cards should you choose to make the answer to the following calculation as large as possible? What is the answer?

$+5$ $+$ $\blacksquare$ $-$ $\blacksquare$ $=$ ......

b Which cards should you choose to make the answer to part **a** as small as possible? What is the answer?

c Which cards should you choose to make the answer to the following number sentence zero? Give all possible answers.

 $+$ $\blacksquare$ $= 0$

Negative magic squares

Make your own magic square with negative numbers. You need nine small square cards and two pens or pencils of different colours.

This is perhaps the best known magic square.

8	3	4
1	5	9
6	7	2

But magic squares can be made from many different sets of numbers, as shown by this second square.

8	13	6
7	9	11
12	5	10

This square is now used to show you how to make a magic square with negative numbers. But the method works with any magic square. So, if you can find one of your own, use it!

- Arrange the nine cards in a square and write on them the numbers of the magic square. Picture **a** below.

- Rearrange the cards in order, lowest number first, to form another square. Picture **b** below.

- Keeping the cards in order, turn them over so that the blank side of each card is face up. Picture **c** below.

a

8	13	6
7	9	11
12	5	10

b

5	6	7
8	9	10
11	12	13

c

- Now use a different coloured pen to avoid confusion.

- Choose any number (say 4) for the top left-hand corner of the square. Picture **d** below.

- Choose another number (say 3) and subtract it from each number in the first row to get the next number. Picture **e** below.

- Now choose a third number (say 2) and subtract it from each number in the top row to make the second row, and then again from each number in the second row. Picture **f** below.

d

4		

e

4	1	–2

f

4	1	–2
2	–1	–4
0	–3	–6

- Turn the cards over. Picture **g**.

- Rearrange the cards into the original magic square. Picture **h**.

- Turn them over again. Picture **i**.

g

5	6	7
8	9	10
11	12	13

h

8	13	6
7	9	11
12	5	10

i

2	–6	1
–2	–1	0
–3	4	–4

You should have a **magic square of negative numbers**.

Try it on any square. It works even with squares bigger than 3 × 3. Try it on this 4 × 4 square.

2	13	9	14
16	7	11	4
15	8	12	3
5	10	6	17

EXERCISE 3E

Copy and complete each of these magic squares. In each case, write down the 'magic number'.

1

–1		
–5	–4	–3
		–7

2

	–4	3
		–2
	4	–1

3

–6	–5	–4
		–10

4

2		
–4		
–7	6	–8

5

		–9
–3	–6	–9

6

		–1
	–7	
–13		–12

7

–4		
–8		–6
–9		

8

2	1	–3
	0	

9

–2		
	–5	
–7		–8

10

–8			–14
–8	–9		
		–4	–5
1	–10	–12	–5

11

–7		2	–16
	–8		
–11	–3	0	–2
		–13	–1

 1 The temperature in a school yard was measured at 9am each morning for one week.

Day	Monday	Tuesday	Wednesday	Thursday	Friday
9am temperature	−1	−3	−2	1	2

a Which day was the coldest at 9am?

b Which day was the warmest at 9am?

2 The table shows the temperature in each of 6 cities on 1st January 2003.

 a Write down the name of the city which had the *lowest* temperature.

b Work out the difference in temperature between Copenhagen and Cairo.

On 2nd January 2003, the temperature in Moscow had increased by 4 °C.

c Work out the new temperature in Moscow.

City	Temperature
Cairo	15 °C
Copenhagen	−1 °C
Helsinki	−9 °C
Manchester	3 °C
Moscow	−14 °C
Sydney	20 °C

Edexcel, Question 4, Paper 8A Foundation, March 2003

 3 Write out and complete the following to make a correct statement.

a $3 - \boxed{} = -5$ **b** $\boxed{} + 4 = -5$ **c** $1 - \boxed{} = 8$

4 The table shows the temperature on the surface of each of five planets.

a Work out the difference in temperature between Mars and Jupiter.

b Work out the difference in temperature between Venus and Mars.

c Which planet has a temperature 30 °C higher than the temperature on Saturn?

The temperature on Pluto is 20 °C lower than the temperature on Uranus.

d Work out the temperature on Pluto.

Planet	Temperature
Venus	480 °C
Mars	−60 °C
Jupiter	−150 °C
Saturn	−180 °C
Uranus	−210 °C

Edexcel, Question 8, Paper 2 Foundation, June 2005

5 Write these numbers in order of size. Start with the smallest number.

i 75, 56, 37, 9, 59 **ii** 5, −6, −10, 2, −4 **iii** $\frac{1}{2}, \frac{2}{3}, \frac{2}{5}, \frac{3}{4}$

Edexcel, Question 9, Paper 1 Foundation, June 2003

 6 The temperatures of the first few days of January were recorded as

1 °C, −1 °C, 0 °C and −2 °C

 a Write down the four temperatures, in order, with the lowest first.

b What is the difference between the coldest and the warmest of these four days?

 7 You have the following cards.

$\boxed{+3}$ $\boxed{+8}$ $\boxed{-4}$ $\boxed{-7}$

 a i What card should you choose to make the answer to the following sum as large as possible?

$\boxed{+1} + \boxed{} = \ldots\ldots$

ii What is the answer to the sum in **i**?

iii What card would you have chosen to make the sum as small as possible?

b i What card should you choose to make the answer to the following subtraction as large as possible?

$\boxed{+1} \; - \; \boxed{} \; = \; \ldots\ldots$

ii What is the answer to the subtraction sum in **i**?

iii What card would you have chosen to make the subtraction as small as possible?

8 Nitrogen gas makes up most of the air we breathe.

Nitrogen freezes under –210 °C and is a gas above –196 °C. In between it is liquid.

Write down a possible temperature where nitrogen is

i a liquid

ii a gas

iii frozen.

9 The most common rocket fuel is liquid hydrogen and liquid oxygen. These two gases are kept in storage, as a liquid, at the following temperatures:

Liquid hydrogen   –253 °C

Liquid oxygen   –183 °C

a i Which of the two gases is kept at the coldest temperature?

ii What is the difference between the two storage temperatures?

b Scientists are experimenting with liquid methane as its liquid storage temperature is only –162 °C. How much warmer is the stored liquid methane than the

i stored liquid oxygen?

ii stored liquid hydrogen?

WORKED EXAM QUESTION

The number $2\frac{1}{2}$ is halfway between 1 and 4.

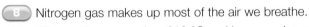

What number is halfway between:

a –8 and –1   b $\frac{1}{4}$ and $1\frac{1}{4}$?

Solution

a The number halfway between –8 and –1 is $-4\frac{1}{2}$.

The hint in the question is to sketch the numbers on a number line.

Just by counting from each end you can find the middle value.

b The number halfway between $\frac{1}{4}$ and $1\frac{1}{4}$ is $\frac{3}{4}$.

Sketch the number line and mark on the quarters.

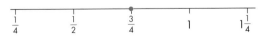

Count from each end to identify the middle value.

GRADE YOURSELF

G Use negative numbers in context

G Use negative numbers with inequalities

F Add positive and negative numbers to positive and negative numbers

F Subtract positive and negative numbers from positive and negative numbers

E Solve problems involving simple negative numbers

What you should know now

- How to order positive and negative numbers
- How to add and subtract positive and negative numbers
- How to use negative numbers in practical situations
- How to use a calculator when working with negative numbers

This book provides indicators of the equivalent grade level of maths questions throughout. The publishers wish to make clear that these grade indicators have been provided by Collins Education, and are not the responsibility of Edexcel Ltd. Whilst every effort has been made to assure their accuracy, they should be regarded as indicators, and are not binding or definitive.

More about number

Chapter 4

1 Multiples of whole numbers

2 Factors of whole numbers

3 Prime numbers

4 Square numbers

5 Square roots

6 Powers

7 Multiplying and dividing by powers of 10

8 Prime factors

9 Rules for multiplying and dividing powers

This chapter will show you ...

- the meaning of multiples
- the meaning of factors
- the meaning of prime numbers
- how to work out squares, square roots and powers
- how to break a number down into its prime factors
- how to work out the lowest common multiple of two numbers
- how to work out the highest common factor of two numbers

Visual overview

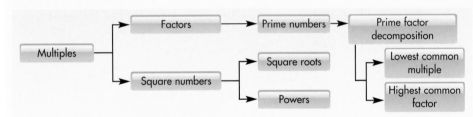

What you should already know

- Times tables up to 10×10

Quick check

Write down the answers to the following.

1	**a** 2×3	**b** 4×3	**c** 5×3
	d 6×3	**e** 7×3	**f** 8×3
2	**a** 2×4	**b** 4×4	**c** 5×4
	d 6×4	**e** 7×4	**f** 8×4
3	**a** 2×5	**b** 9×5	**c** 5×5
	d 6×5	**e** 7×5	**f** 8×5
4	**a** 2×6	**b** 9×6	**c** 8×8
	d 6×6	**e** 7×9	**f** 8×6
5	**a** 2×7	**b** 9×7	**c** 8×9
	d 6×7	**e** 7×7	**f** 8×7

Multiples of whole numbers

In this section you will learn how to:
- find multiples of whole numbers
- recognise multiples of numbers

Key words
multiple
times table

When you multiply any whole number by another whole number, the answer is called a **multiple** of either of those numbers.

For example, $5 \times 7 = 35$, which means that 35 is a multiple of 5 and it is also a multiple of 7. Here are some other multiples of 5 and 7:

multiples of 5 are   5   10   15   20   25   30   35   …

multiples of 7 are   7   14   21   28   35   42   …

Multiples are also called **times tables**.

Recognising multiples

You can recognise the multiples of 2, 3, 5 and 9 in the following ways.

- Multiples of 2 always end in an even number or 0. For example:

   12   34   96   1938   370

- Multiples of 3 are always made up of digits that add up to a multiple of 3. For example:

   15   because $1 + 5 = 6$ which is $2 \times \mathbf{3}$

   72   because $7 + 2 = 9$ which is $3 \times \mathbf{3}$

   201   because $2 + 0 + 1 = 3$ which is $1 \times \mathbf{3}$

- Multiples of 5 always end in 5 or 0. For example:

   35   60   155   300

- Multiples of 9 are always made up of digits that add up to a multiple of 9. For example:

   63   because $6 + 3 = 9$ which is $1 \times \mathbf{9}$

   738   because $7 + 3 + 8 = 18$ which is $2 \times \mathbf{9}$

You can find out whether numbers are multiples of 4, 6, 7 and 8 by using your calculator. For example, to find out whether 341 is a multiple of 7, you have to see whether 341 gives a whole number when it is divided by 7. You therefore key

The answer is 48.714 286, which is a decimal number, not a whole number. So, 341 is *not* a multiple of 7.

EXERCISE 4A

 1 Write out the first five multiples of:

    a 3   **b** 7   **c** 9   **d** 11   **e** 16

    Remember: the first multiple is the number itself.

 2 From the numbers below, write down those that are:

    a multiples of 2   **b** multiples of 3

    c multiples of 5   **d** multiples of 9

111	254	255	108	73
68	162	711	615	98
37	812	102	75	270

>
> **HINTS AND TIPS**
>
> Remember the rules on page 68

 3 Use your calculator to see which of the numbers below are:

    a multiples of 4   **b** multiples of 7

    c multiples of 6

72	135	102	161	197
132	78	91	216	514
312	168	75	144	294

> **HINTS AND TIPS**
>
> There is no point testing odd numbers for multiplies of even numbers such as 4 and 6

 4 Find the biggest number smaller than 100 that is:

    a a multiple of 2   **b** a multiple of 3   **c** a multiple of 4

    d a multiple of 5   **e** a multiple of 7   **f** a multiple of 6

5 Find the smallest number that is bigger than 1000 that is:

    a a multiple of 6   **b** a multiple of 8   **c** a multiple of 9

Grid locked

You need eight copies of this 10 × 10 grid.

1	2	3	4	5	6	7	8	9	10
11	12	13	14	15	16	17	18	19	20
21	22	23	24	25	26	27	28	29	30
31	32	33	34	35	36	37	38	39	40
41	42	43	44	45	46	47	48	49	50
51	52	53	54	55	56	57	58	59	60
61	62	63	64	65	66	67	68	69	70
71	72	73	74	75	76	77	78	79	80
81	82	83	84	85	86	87	88	89	90
91	92	93	94	95	96	97	98	99	100

Take one of the grids and shade in all the multiples of 2. You should find that they make a neat pattern.

Do the same thing for the multiples of 3, 4, … up to 9, using a fresh 10 × 10 grid for each number.

Next, draw a grid which is 9 squares wide and write the numbers from 1 to 100 in the grid, like this:

1	2	3	4	5	6	7	8	9
10	11	12	13	14	15	16	17	18
1…	…	21	…	…3	2…		…	27

Make seven more copies of this grid. Then shade in the multiples of 2, 3, … up to 9, using a fresh grid for each number.

Write out the numbers from 1 to 100 on grids of different widths and shade in the multiples of 2, 3, … up to 9, as before.

Describe the patterns that you get.

In this section you will learn how to:
- identify the factors of a number

Key word

factor

A **factor** of a whole number is any whole number that divides into it exactly. So:

the factors of 20 are   1   2   4   5   10   20

the factors of 12 are   1   2   3   4   6   12

This is where it helps to know your times tables!

Factor facts

Remember these facts:

- 1 is always a factor and so is the number itself.

- When you have found one factor, there is always another factor that goes with it – unless the factor is multiplied by itself to give the number. For example, look at the number 20:

  $1 \times 20 = 20$ so 1 and 20 are both factors of 20

  $2 \times 10 = 20$ so 2 and 10 are both factors of 20

  $4 \times 5 = 20$ so 4 and 5 are both factors of 20

You may need to use your calculator to find the factors of large numbers.

EXAMPLE 1

Find the factors of 32.

Look for the pairs of numbers that make 32 when multiplied together. These are:

$1 \times 32 = 32$ $2 \times 16 = 32$ $4 \times 8 = 32$

So, the factors of 32 are 1, 2, 4, 8, 16, 32.

EXAMPLE 2

Find the factors of 36.

Look for the pairs of numbers that make 36 when multiplied together. These are:

$1 \times 36 = 36$ $2 \times 18 = 36$ $3 \times 12 = 36$ $4 \times 9 = 36$ $6 \times 6 = 36$

6 is a repeated factor which is counted only once.

So, the factors of 36 are 1, 2, 3, 4, 6, 9, 12, 18, 36.

EXERCISE 4B

1 What are the factors of each of these numbers?

a	10	**b**	28
c	18	**d**	17
e	25	**f**	40
g	30	**h**	45
i	24	**j**	16

2 Use your calculator to find the factors of each of these numbers.

a	120	**b**	150
c	144	**d**	180
e	169	**f**	108
g	196	**h**	153
i	198	**j**	199

> **HINTS AND TIPS**
>
> Remember that once you find one factor this will give you another, unless it is a repeated factor such as 5×5.

3 What is the biggest factor that is less than 100 for each of these numbers?

a	110	**b**	201
c	145	**d**	117
e	130	**f**	240
g	160	**h**	210
i	162	**j**	250

4 Find the largest common factor for each of the following pairs of numbers. (Do not include 1.)

a	2 and 4	**b**	6 and 10
c	9 and 12	**d**	15 and 25
e	9 and 15	**f**	12 and 21
g	14 and 21	**h**	25 and 30
i	30 and 50	**j**	55 and 77

> **HINTS AND TIPS**
>
> Look for the largest number that has both numbers in its times table.

Prime numbers

In this section you will learn how to:

- identify prime numbers

Key word

prime
 number

What are the factors of 2, 3, 5, 7, 11 and 13?

Notice that each of these numbers has only two factors: itself and 1. They are all examples of **prime numbers**.

So, a prime number is a whole number that has only two factors: itself and 1.

Note: 1 is *not* a prime number, since it has only one factor – itself.

The prime numbers up to 50 are:

2, 3, 5, 7, 11, 13, 17, 19, 23, 29, 31, 37, 41, 43, 47

It will be useful to recognise all these as prime numbers.

ACTIVITY

Prime search

You need a 10 × 10 grid.

Cross out 1.

Leave 2 and cross out the rest of the multiples of 2.

Leave 3 and cross out the rest of the multiples of 3. Some of them will already have been crossed out.

Leave 5 and cross out the rest of the multiples of 5. Some of them will already have been crossed out.

Leave 7 and cross out the rest of the multiples of 7. All but three of them will already have been crossed out.

1	2	3	4	5	6	7	8	9	10
11	12	13	14	15	16	17	18	19	20
21	22	23	24	25	26	27	28	29	30
31	32	33	34	35	36	37	38	39	40
41	42	43	44	45	46	47	48	49	50
51	52	53	54	55	56	57	58	59	60
61	62	63	64	65	66	67	68	69	70
71	72	73	74	75	76	77	78	79	80
81	82	83	84	85	86	87	88	89	90
91	92	93	94	95	96	97	98	99	100

The numbers left are prime numbers.

The activity is known as the Sieve of Eratosthenes. (Eratosthenes, a Greek scholar, lived from about 275 BC to 194 BC.)

In this section you will learn how to:
- identify square numbers
- use a calculator to find the square of a number

What is the next number in this sequence?

    1, 4, 9, 16, 25, …

Writing each number in terms of its factors gives:

    $1 \times 1, 2 \times 2, 3 \times 3, 4 \times 4, 5 \times 5, …$

These factors can be represented by **square** patterns of dots:

From these patterns, you can see that the next pair of factors must be $6 \times 6 = 36$, therefore 36 is the next number in the sequence.

Because they form square patterns, the numbers 1, 4, 9, 16, 25, 36, … are called **square numbers**.

When you multiply any number by itself, the answer is called the *square of the number* or *the number squared*. This is because the answer is a square number. For example:

    the square of 5 (or 5 squared) is $5 \times 5 = 25$

    the square of 6 (or 6 squared) is $6 \times 6 = 36$

There is a short way to write the square of any number. For example:

    5 squared (5×5) can be written as 5^2

    13 squared (13×13) can be written as 13^2

So, the sequence of square numbers, 1, 4, 9, 16, 25, 36, …, can be written as:

    $1^2, \quad 2^2, \quad 3^2, \quad 4^2, \quad 5^2, \quad 6^2, \quad …$

You are expected to know the square numbers up to 15×15 (= 225) for the GCSE exam.

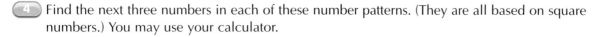

EXERCISE 4C

 1 The square number pattern starts:

   1   4   9   16   25   …

Copy and continue the pattern above until you have written down the first 20 square numbers. You may use your calculator for this.

 2 Work out the answer to each of these number sentences.

   $1 + 3 =$

   $1 + 3 + 5 =$

   $1 + 3 + 5 + 7 =$

Look carefully at the pattern of the three number sentences. Then write down the next three number sentences in the pattern and work them out.

 3 Draw one counter.

Now add more counters to your picture to make the next square number.

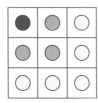

a How many extra counters did you add?

Now add more counters to your picture to make the next square number.

b How many extra counters did you add?

c Without drawing, how many more counters will you need to make the next square number?

d Describe the pattern of counters you are adding.

4 Find the next three numbers in each of these number patterns. (They are all based on square numbers.) You may use your calculator.

	1	4	9	16	25	36	49	64	81
a	2	5	10	17	26	37	…	…	…
b	2	8	18	32	50	72	…	…	…
c	3	6	11	18	27	38	…	…	…
d	0	3	8	15	24	35	…	…	…
e	101	104	109	116	125	136	…	…	…

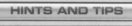

HINTS AND TIPS

Look for the connection with the square numbers on the top line.

5 Write down the answer to each of the following. You will need to use your calculator. Look for the x^2 key.

a 23^2 **b** 57^2 **c** 77^2 **d** 123^2 **e** 152^2

f 3.2^2 **g** 9.5^2 **h** 23.8^2 **i** $(-4)^2$ **j** $(-12)^2$

6 a Work out each of the following. You may use your calculator.

$$3^2 + 4^2 \quad \text{and} \quad 5^2$$
$$5^2 + 12^2 \quad \text{and} \quad 13^2$$
$$7^2 + 24^2 \quad \text{and} \quad 25^2$$
$$9^2 + 40^2 \quad \text{and} \quad 41^2$$
$$11^2 + 60^2 \quad \text{and} \quad 61^2$$

b Describe what you notice about your answers to part **a**.

EXERCISE 4D

The following exercise will give you some practice on multiplies, factors, square numbers and prime numbers.

1 Write out the first five multiples of:

a 6   **b** 13   **c** 8   **d** 20   **e** 18

Remember: the first multiple is the number itself.

2 Write out the first three numbers that are multiples of both of the numbers shown.

a 3 and 4   **b** 4 and 5   **c** 3 and 5   **d** 6 and 9   **e** 5 and 7

3 What are the factors of these numbers?

a 12   **b** 20   **c** 9   **d** 32   **e** 24

f 38   **g** 13   **h** 42   **i** 45   **j** 36

4 In question **3**, part **g**, there were only two factors. Why?

5 In question **3**, every number had an even number of factors except parts **c** and **j**. What sort of numbers are 9 and 36?

6 Write down the prime numbers up to 20.

7 Write down the square numbers up to 100.

8 If hot-dog sausages are sold in packs of 10 and hot-dog buns are sold in packs of 8, how many of each must you buy to have complete hot dogs with no extra sausages or buns?

9 Rover barks every 8 seconds and Spot barks every 12 seconds. If they both bark together, how many seconds will it be before they both bark together again?

10 A bell chimes every 6 seconds. Another bell chimes every 5 seconds. If they both chime together, how many seconds will it be before they both chime together again?

11 Fred runs round a running track in 4 minutes. Debbie runs round in 3 minutes. If they both start together on the line at the end of the finishing straight, when will they both be on the same line together again? How many laps will Debbie have run? How many laps will Fred have run?

12 From this box, choose one number that fits each of these descriptions.

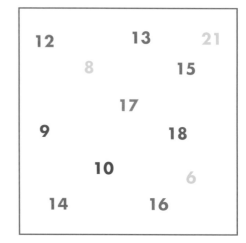

12   13   21
8   15
17
9   18
10   6
14   16

 a a multiple of 3 and a multiple of 4

 b a square number and an odd number

 c a factor of 24 and a factor of 18

 d a prime number and a factor of 39

 e an odd factor of 30 and a multiple of 3

 f a number with 4 factors and a multiple of 2 and 7

 g a number with 5 factors exactly

 h a multiple of 5 and a factor of 20

 i an even number and a factor of 36 and a multiple of 9

 j a prime number that is one more than a square number

 k written in order, the four factors of this number make a number pattern in which each number is twice the one before

 l an odd number that is a multiple of 7.

13 Copy these number sentences and write out the *next four* sentences in the pattern.

   1 = 1

   1 + 3 = 4

   1 + 3 + 5 = 9

   1 + 3 + 5 + 7 = 16

14 The following numbers are described as triangular numbers:

   1, 3, 6, 10, 15

 a Investigate why they are called triangular numbers.

 b Write down the next five triangular numbers.

4.5 # Square roots

In this section you will learn how to:
- find a square root of a square number
- use a calculator to find the square roots of any number

Key word

square root

The **square root** of a given number is a number that, when multiplied by itself, produces the given number.

For example, the square root of 9 is 3, since $3 \times 3 = 9$.

Numbers also have a negative square root, since -3×-3 also equals 9.

A square root is represented by the symbol $\sqrt{\ }$. For example, $\sqrt{16} = 4$.

EXERCISE 4E

1 Write down the positive square root of each of these numbers.

a 4	**b** 25	**c** 49	**d** 1	**e** 81
f 100	**g** 64	**h** 9	**i** 36	**j** 16
k 121	**l** 144	**m** 400	**n** 900	**o** 169

2 Write down both possible values of each of these square roots.

a $\sqrt{25}$	**b** $\sqrt{36}$	**c** $\sqrt{100}$	**d** $\sqrt{49}$	**e** $\sqrt{64}$
f $\sqrt{16}$	**g** $\sqrt{9}$	**h** $\sqrt{81}$	**i** $\sqrt{1}$	**j** $\sqrt{144}$

3 Write down the value of each of these. You need only give positive square roots. You will need to use your calculator for some of them. Look for the $\boxed{\sqrt{x}}$ key.

a 9^2	**b** $\sqrt{1600}$	**c** 10^2	**d** $\sqrt{196}$	**e** 6^2
f $\sqrt{225}$	**g** 7^2	**h** $\sqrt{144}$	**i** 5^2	**j** $\sqrt{441}$
k 11^2	**l** $\sqrt{256}$	**m** 8^2	**n** $\sqrt{289}$	**o** 21^2

4 Write down the positive value of each of the following. You will need to use your calculator.

a $\sqrt{576}$	**b** $\sqrt{961}$	**c** $\sqrt{2025}$	**d** $\sqrt{1600}$	**e** $\sqrt{4489}$
f $\sqrt{10\,201}$	**g** $\sqrt{12.96}$	**h** $\sqrt{42.25}$	**i** $\sqrt{193.21}$	**j** $\sqrt{492.84}$

Powers

In this section you will learn how to:

- use powers

Powers are a convenient way of writing repetitive multiplications. (Powers are also called **indices** – singular, index.)

The power that you will use most often is 2, which has the special name **square**. The only other power with a special name is 3, which is called **cube**.

You are expected to know the cubes of numbers, $1^3 = 1$, $2^3 = 8$, $3^3 = 27$, $4^3 = 64$, $5^3 = 125$ and $10^3 = 1000$, for the GCSE exam.

EXAMPLE 3

a What is the value of:

   i 7 squared   **ii** 5 cubed?

b Write each of these numbers out in full.

   i 4^6 **ii** 6^4 **iii** 7^3 **iv** 12^2

c Write the following numbers in index form.

   i $3 \times 3 \times 3 \times 3 \times 3 \times 3 \times 3 \times 3$

   ii $13 \times 13 \times 13 \times 13 \times 13$

   iii $7 \times 7 \times 7 \times 7$

   iv $5 \times 5 \times 5 \times 5 \times 5 \times 5 \times 5$

a The value of 7 squared is $7^2 = 7 \times 7 = 49$

   The value of 5 cubed is $5^3 = 5 \times 5 \times 5 = 125$

b **i** $4^6 = 4 \times 4 \times 4 \times 4 \times 4 \times 4$

   ii $6^4 = 6 \times 6 \times 6 \times 6$

   iii $7^3 = 7 \times 7 \times 7$

   iv $12^2 = 12 \times 12$

c **i** $3 \times 3 \times 3 \times 3 \times 3 \times 3 \times 3 \times 3 = 3^8$

   ii $13 \times 13 \times 13 \times 13 \times 13 = 13^5$

   iii $7 \times 7 \times 7 \times 7 = 7^4$

   iv $5 \times 5 \times 5 \times 5 \times 5 \times 5 \times 5 = 5^7$

Working out powers on your calculator

How would you work out the value of 5^7 on a calculator?

You could key it in as $5 \times 5 \times 5 \times 5 \times 5 \times 5 \times 5 =$. But as you key it in, you may miss a number or press a wrong key. If your calculator has one, you could use the power key, **x^y** or **y^x**.

$$5^7 = \boxed{5} \ \boxed{x^y} \ \boxed{7} \ \boxed{=} \ 78\,125$$

Make sure you know where to find the power key on your calculator. It may be an INV or SHIFT function.

Try using your calculator to work out 3^4, 7^8, 23^4 and 72^3.

Check that you get 81, 5 764 801, 279 841 and 373 248.

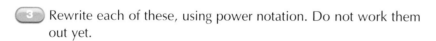

EXERCISE 4F

1 Use your calculator to work out the value of each of the following.

a 3^3 b 5^3 c 6^3 d 12^3 e 2^4

f 4^4 g 5^4 h 2^5 i 3^7 j 2^{10}

2 Work out the values of the following powers of 10.

a 10^2 b 10^3 c 10^4 d 10^5 e 10^6

f Describe what you notice about your answers.

g Now write down the value of each of these.

i 10^8 ii 10^{10} iii 10^{15}

> **HINTS AND TIPS**
>
> When working out a power, make sure you multiply the number by itself and not by the power. A very common error is to write, for example, $2^3 = 6$ instead of $2^3 = 2 \times 2 \times 2 = 8$.

3 Rewrite each of these, using power notation. Do not work them out yet.

a $2 \times 2 \times 2 \times 2$ b $3 \times 3 \times 3 \times 3 \times 3$

c 7×7 d $5 \times 5 \times 5$

e $10 \times 10 \times 10 \times 10 \times 10 \times 10 \times 10$ f $6 \times 6 \times 6 \times 6$

g $4 \times 4 \times 4 \times 4$ h $1 \times 1 \times 1 \times 1 \times 1 \times 1 \times 1$

i $0.5 \times 0.5 \times 0.5 \times 0.5$ j $100 \times 100 \times 100$

4 Write these power terms out in full. Do not work them out yet.

a 3^4 b 9^3 c 6^2 d 10^5 e 2^{10}

f 8^6 g 0.1^3 h 2.5^2 i 0.7^3 j 1000^2

5 Using the power key on your calculator (or another method), work out the values of the power terms in question **3**.

6 Using the power key on your calculator (or another method), work out the values of the power terms in question **4**.

7 Write the answer to question **3**, part **j** as a power of 10.

8 Write the answer to question **4**, part **j** as a power of 10.

> **HINTS AND TIPS**
>
> Use the answer you found for question **2f** to help you.

9 Copy this pattern of powers of 2 and continue it for another five terms.

2^2 2^3 2^4 ... ...

4 8 16 ... ...

10 Copy the pattern of powers of 10 and fill in the previous five and the next five terms.

... ... 10^2 10^3 ... ...

... ... 100 1000 ... ...

4.7 Multiplying and dividing by powers of 10

In this section you will learn how to:
- multiply and divide by powers of 10

The last question in the above exercise uses powers of 10, which you have already seen are special.

When you write a million in figures, how many zeros does it have? What is a million as a power of 10? This table shows some of the pattern of the powers of 10.

Number	0.001	0.01	0.1	1	10	100	1000	10 000	100 000
Powers	10^{-3}	10^{-2}	10^{-1}	10^0	10^1	10^2	10^3	10^4	10^5

What pattern is there in the top row?

What pattern is there in the powers in the bottom row?

The easiest number to multiply by is zero, because any number multiplied by zero is zero.

The next easiest number to multiply by is 1, because any number multiplied by 1 stays the same.

After that it is a matter of opinion, but it is generally accepted that multiplying by 10 is simple. Try these on your calculator.

a 7×10

b 7.34×10

c 43×10

d 0.678×10

e 0.007×10

f 34.5×10

Can you see the rule for multiplying by 10? You may have learnt that when you multiply a number by 10, you add a zero to the number. This is only true when you start with a whole number. It is not true for a decimal. The rule is:

● Every time you multiply a number by 10, move the digits in the number one place to the left.

Check to make sure that this happened in examples **a** to **f** above.

It is almost as easy to multiply by 100. Try these on your calculator.

a 7×100

b 7.34×100

c 43×100

d 0.678×100

e 0.007×100

f 34.5×100

This time you should find that the digits move two places to the left.

You can write 100, 1000, 10 000 as powers of 10. For example:

$$100 = 10 \times 10 = 10^2$$

$$1000 = 10 \times 10 \times 10 = 10^3$$

$$10\,000 = 10 \times 10 \times 10 \times 10 = 10^4$$

You should know the connection between the number of zeros and the power of 10. Try these on your calculator. Look for the connection between the calculation and the answer.

a 12.3×10

b 3.45×1000

c 3.45×10^3

d $0.075 \times 10\,000$

e 2.045×10^2

f 6.78×1000

g 25.67×10^4

h 34.21×100

i $0.032\,4 \times 10^4$

Can you find a similar connection for division by multiples of 10? Try these on your calculator. Look for the connection between the calculation and the answer.

a $12.3 \div 10$

b $3.45 \div 1000$

c $3.45 \div 10^3$

d $0.075 \div 100$

e $2.045 \div 10^2$

f $6.78 \div 1000$

g $25.67 \div 10^4$

h $34.21 \div 100$

i $0.032\,4 \div 10^4$

You can use this principle to multiply multiples of 10 – 100 and so on. You use this method in estimation. You should have the skill to do this mentally so that you can check that your answers to calculations are about right. (Approximation of calculations is covered on page 190.)

Use a calculator to work out these multiplications.

a $200 \times 300 =$

b $100 \times 40 =$

c $2000 \times 3000 =$

d $200 \times 50 =$

e $200 \times 5000 =$

f $300 \times 40 =$

Can you see a way of doing them without using a calculator or pencil and paper? Dividing is almost as simple. Use a calculator to do these divisions.

a $400 \div 20 =$

b $200 \div 50 =$

c $1000 \div 200 =$

d $300 \div 30 =$

e $250 \div 50 =$

f $30\,000 \div 600 =$

Once again, there is an easy way of doing these 'in your head'. Look at these examples.

$300 \times 4000 = 1\,200\,000$ $5000 \div 200 = 25$ $200 \times 50 = 10\,000$

$60 \times 5000 = 300\,000$ $400 \div 20 = 20$ $30\,000 \div 600 = 500$

In 200×3000, for example, you multiply the non-zero digits ($2 \times 3 = 6$) and then write the total number of zeros in both numbers at the end, to give $600\,000$.

$$200 \times 3000 = 2 \times 100 \times 3 \times 1000 = 6 \times 100\,000 = 600\,000$$

For division, you divide the non-zero digits and then cancel the zeros. For example:

$$400\,000 \div 80 = \frac{400\,000}{80} = \frac{{}^{5}\cancel{400\,000}}{{}_{1}\cancel{80}} = 5000$$

Standard form on a calculator

Sometimes calculators display small and large numbers in this format

$$\boxed{1.7^{-03}} \qquad \boxed{5.3^{12}}$$

This is known as standard form and means 1.7×10^{-3} and 5.3×10^{12}.

This means the first display represents $1.7 \times 10^{-3} = 0.0017$ and the second display represents $5.3 \times 10^{12} = 5\,300\,000\,000\,000$.

EXAMPLE 4

On a calculator, calculate $3.7 \times 10^5 \times 2.8 \times 10^7$, giving your answer as the normal number represented by the display.

Using a scientific calculator, key in

The calculator shows a display similar to

$$\boxed{1.036^{13}}$$

Which as a normal number is $10\,360\,000\,000\,000$

EXERCISE 4G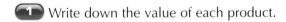

1 Write down the value of each product.

     a 3.1×10 **b** 3.1×100 **c** 3.1×1000 **d** $3.1 \times 10\,000$

2 Write down the value of each product.

     a 6.5×10 **b** 6.5×10^2 **c** 6.5×10^3 **d** 6.5×10^4

3 In questions **1** and **2** there is a connection between the multipliers. What is the connection? (It isn't that the first number is the same.)

D

4 This list of answers came from a set of questions very similar to those in questions **1** and **2**. Write down what the questions must have been, using numbers written out in full and powers of 10. (There is a slight catch!)

    a 73   **b** 730   **c** 7300   **d** 730 000

5 Write down the value of each of the following.

    a $3.1 \div 10$ **b** $3.1 \div 100$ **c** $3.1 \div 1000$ **d** $3.1 \div 10\,000$

6 Write down the value of each of the following.

    a $6.5 \div 10$ **b** $6.5 \div 10^2$ **c** $6.5 \div 10^3$ **d** $6.5 \div 10^4$

7 In questions **5** and **6** there is a connection between the divisors. What is it?

8 This list of answers came from a set of questions very similar to those in questions **5** and **6**. Write down what the questions must have been, using numbers written out in full and powers of 10. (There is a slight catch!)

    a 0.73   **b** 0.073   **c** 0.0073   **d** 0.000 073

9 Without using a calculator, write down the answers to these.

    a 2.5×100 **b** 3.45×10 **c** 4.67×1000

    d 34.6×10 **e** 20.789×10 **f** 56.78×1000

    g 0.897×10^5 **h** 0.865×1000 **i** 100.5×10^2

    j 0.999×10^6 **k** 234.56×10^2 **l** 98.7654×10^3

10 Without using a calculator, write down the answers to these.

    a $2.5 \div 100$ **b** $3.45 \div 10$

    c $4.67 \div 1000$ **d** $34.6 \div 10$

    e $20.789 \div 100$ **f** $56.78 \div 1000$

    g $2.46 \div 10^2$ **h** $0.865 \div 1000$ **i** $100.5 \div 10^2$

    j $0.999 \div 10^6$ **k** $203.67 \div 10^1$ **l** $76.43 \div 10$

> **HINTS AND TIPS**
>
> Even though you are really moving digits left or right, you may think of it as if the decimal point moves right or left.

11 Without using a calculator, write down the answers to these.

    a 200×300 **b** 30×4000 **c** 50×200

    d 100×2000 **e** 20×1400 **f** 30×30

    g $(20)^2$ **h** $(20)^3$ **i** $(400)^2$

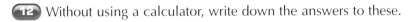

12 Without using a calculator, write down the answers to these.

a 3000 ÷ 150   b 400 ÷ 200   c 5000 ÷ 5000

d 4000 ÷ 250   e 300 ÷ 2   f 6000 ÷ 500

g 30 000 ÷ 2000 h 2000 × 40 ÷ 2000   i 200 × 20 ÷ 800

j 200 × 6000 ÷ 30 000   k 20 × 80 × 600 ÷ 3000

13 i Write down what each of these calculator display means in the form $a \times 10n$.
   ii Work out the value of each display as an ordinary number.

a $\boxed{2.3^{07}}$ b $\boxed{3.4^{-02}}$ c $\boxed{6.3^{10}}$

d $\boxed{1.6^{-03}}$ e $\boxed{5.5^{-04}}$ f $\boxed{1.2^{14}}$

14 Using a scientific calculator, evaluate each of the following.

Write down the ordinary number represented by the calculator display.

a $6.8 \times 10^4 \times 7.5 \times 10^5$ b $9.6 \times 10^5 \times 8.5 \times 10^6$

c $6.4 \times 10^{12} \div 1.2 \times 10$ d $2.2^5 \times 10^{15} \div 1.5 \times 10^9$

4.8 Prime factors

In this section you will learn how to:
- identify prime factors
- identify the lowest common multiple (LCM) of two numbers
- identify the highest common factor (HCF) of two numbers

Key words
prime factor
prime factor tree
lowest common multiple
highest common factor

Start with a number, such as 110, and find two numbers that, when multiplied together, give that number, for example, 2 × 55. Are they both prime? No, 55 isn't. So take 55 and repeat the operation, to get 5 × 11. Are these both prime? Yes. So:

110 = 2 × 5 × 11

The **prime factors** of 110 are 2, 5 and 11.

This method is not very logical and you need to know your times tables well to use it. There are, however, two methods that you can use to make sure you do not miss any of the prime factors.

EXAMPLE 5

Find the prime factors of 24.

Divide 24 by any prime number that goes into it. (2 is an obvious choice.)

Now divide the answer (12) by a prime number. As 12 is even, again 2 is the obvious choice.

Repeat this process until you finally have a prime number as the answer.

So, written as a product of its prime factors, $24 = 2 \times 2 \times 2 \times 3$.

A quicker and neater way to write this answer is to use index notation, expressing the answer in powers. (Powers are dealt with on pages 79–81.)

In index notation, as a product of its prime factors, $24 = 2^3 \times 3$.

$$\begin{array}{c|c} 2 & 24 \\ \hline 2 & 12 \\ \hline 3 & 6 \\ \hline & 2 \end{array}$$

EXAMPLE 6

Find the prime factors of 96.

As a product of prime factors, 96 is $2 \times 2 \times 2 \times 2 \times 2 \times 3 = 2^5 \times 3$.

$$\begin{array}{c|c} 2 & 96 \\ \hline 2 & 48 \\ \hline 2 & 24 \\ \hline 2 & 12 \\ \hline 2 & 6 \\ \hline & 3 \end{array}$$

The method shown below is called a **prime factor tree**.

You start by splitting the number into a product of two factors. Then you split these factors, and carry on splitting, until you reach prime numbers.

EXAMPLE 7

Find the prime factors of 76.

Stop splitting the factors here because 2, 2 and 19 are all prime numbers.

So, as a product of prime factors, 76 is $2 \times 2 \times 19 = 2^2 \times 19$.

EXAMPLE 8

Find the prime factors of 420.

You can work it upside down, to make an upright tree.

So, as a product of prime factors:

$420 = 2 \times 5 \times 2 \times 3 \times 7 = 2^2 \times 3 \times 5 \times 7$

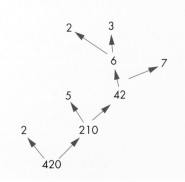

EXERCISE 4H

1 Copy and complete these prime factor trees.

a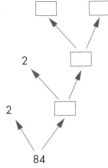

$84 = 2 \times 2 \ldots \times \ldots$

b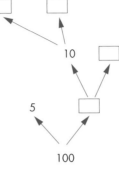

$100 = 5 \times 2 \ldots \times \ldots$

c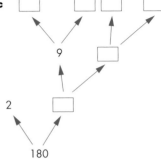

$180 = 2 \times \ldots \times \ldots \times \ldots \times \ldots$

d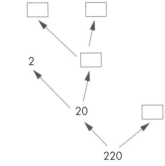

$220 = 2 \times \ldots \times \ldots \times \ldots$

e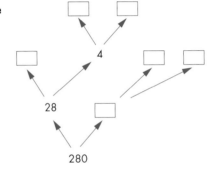

$280 = \ldots \times \ldots \times \ldots \times \ldots \times \ldots$

f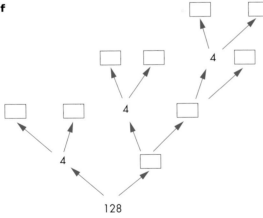

$128 = \ldots \times \ldots \times \ldots \times \ldots \times \ldots \times \ldots \times \ldots$

g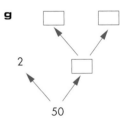

$50 = \ldots \times \ldots \times \ldots$

h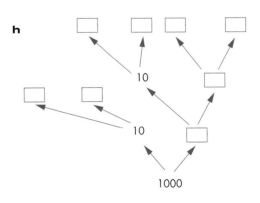

$1000 = \ldots \times \ldots \times \ldots \times \ldots \times \ldots \times \ldots$

i

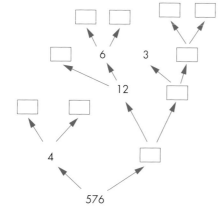

$$576 = \ldots \times \ldots \times \ldots \times \ldots \times \ldots \times \ldots \times \ldots \times \ldots \times \ldots$$

j

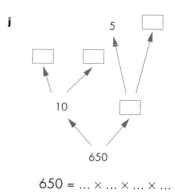

$$650 = \ldots \times \ldots \times \ldots \times \ldots$$

2 Using index notation, for example:

$$100 = 2 \times 2 \times 5 \times 5 = 2^2 \times 5^2$$

and $\qquad 540 = 2 \times 2 \times 3 \times 3 \times 3 \times 5 = 2^2 \times 3^3 \times 5$

rewrite your answers to question **1**, parts **a** to **j**.

3 Write the numbers from 1 to 50 as products of their prime factors. Use index notation. For example:

$$1 = 1 \qquad 2 = 2 \qquad 3 = 3 \qquad 4 = 2^2 \qquad 5 = 5 \qquad 6 = 2 \times 3 \qquad \ldots$$

> **HINTS AND TIPS**
>
> Use your previous answers to help you. For example, $9 = 3^2$ so as $18 = 2 \times 9$, $18 = 2 \times 3^2$.

4 **a** What is special about the numbers 2, 4, 8, 16, 32, …?

  b What are the next two terms in this series?

  c What are the next three terms in the series 3, 9, 27, …?

  d Continue the series 4, 16, 64, …, for three more terms.

  e Rewrite all the series in parts **a**, **b**, **c** and **d** in index notation. For example, the first series is:

$$2^2, 2^3, 2^4, 2^5, 2^6, 2^7, \ldots$$

Lowest common multiple

The **lowest common multiple** (or *least common multiple*, usually called the LCM) of two numbers is the smallest number that appears in the times tables of both numbers.

For example, the LCM of 3 and 5 is 15, the LCM of 2 and 7 is 14 and the LCM of 6 and 9 is 18.

There are two ways of working out the LCM.

EXAMPLE 9

Find the LCM of 18 and 24.

Write out the 18 times table: 18, 36, 54, (72), 90, 108, …

Write out the 24 times table: 24, 48, (72), 96, 120, …

Numbers that appear in both tables are *common multiples*. You can see that 72 is the smallest (lowest) number that appears in both tables, so it is the lowest common multiple.

EXAMPLE 10

Find the LCM of 42 and 63.

Write 42 in prime factor form: $42 = 2 \times 3 \times 7$

Write 63 in prime factor form: $63 = 3^2 \times 7$

Write down the smallest number, in prime factor form, that includes all the prime factors of both 42 and 63.

$2 \times 3^2 \times 7$ (This includes $2 \times 3 \times 7$ and $3^2 \times 7$.)

Then work it out:

$2 \times 3^2 \times 7 = 2 \times 9 \times 7 = 18 \times 7 = 126$

Highest common factor

The **highest common factor** (usually called the HCF) of two numbers is the biggest number that divides exactly into both of them.

For example, the HCF of 24 and 18 is 6, the HCF of 45 and 36 is 9 and the HCF of 15 and 22 is 1.

There are two ways of working out the HCF.

EXAMPLE 11

Find the HCF of 28 and 16.

Write out the factors of 28:   {1, 2, (4), 7, 14, 28}

Write out the factors of 16:   {1, 2, (4), 8, 16}

Numbers that appear in both sets of factors are *common factors*. You can see that 4 is the biggest (highest) number that appears in both lists, so it is the highest common factor.

EXAMPLE 12

Find the HCF of 48 and 120.

Write 48 in prime factor form: $48 = 2^4 \times 3$

Write 120 in prime factor form: $120 = 2^3 \times 3 \times 5$

Write down, in prime factor form, the biggest number that is in the prime factors of 48 and 120.

$2^3 \times 3$ (This is in both $2^4 \times 3$ and $2^3 \times 3 \times 5$.)

Then work it out.

$2^3 \times 3 = 8 \times 3 = 24$

EXERCISE 4I

1. Find the LCM of the numbers in each pair.

   a 4 and 5   **b** 7 and 8   **c** 2 and 3   **d** 4 and 7

   e 2 and 5   **f** 3 and 5   **g** 3 and 8   **h** 5 and 6

2. What connection is there between the LCMs and the pairs of numbers in question **1**?

3. Find the LCM of the numbers in each pair.

   a 4 and 8   **b** 6 and 9   **c** 4 and 6   **d** 10 and 15

4. Does the connection you found in question **2** still work for the numbers in question **3**? If not, can you explain why not?

5. Find the LCM of these pairs of numbers.

   a 24 and 56   **b** 21 and 35   **c** 12 and 28   **d** 28 and 42

   e 12 and 32   **f** 18 and 27   **g** 15 and 25   **h** 16 and 36

6. Find the HCF of these pairs of numbers.

   a 24 and 56   **b** 21 and 35   **c** 12 and 28   **d** 28 and 42

   e 12 and 32   **f** 18 and 27   **g** 15 and 25   **h** 16 and 36

   i 42 and 27   **j** 48 and 64   **k** 25 and 35   **l** 36 and 54

7. In prime factor form $1250 = 2 \times 5^4$ and $525 = 3 \times 5^2 \times 7$.

   a Which of these are common multiples of 1250 and 525?

   i $2 \times 3 \times 5^3 \times 7$ **ii** $2^3 \times 3 \times 5^4 \times 7^2$ **iii** $2 \times 3 \times 5^4 \times 7$ **iv** $2 \times 3 \times 5 \times 7$

   b Which of these are common factors of 1250 and 525?

   i 2×3 **ii** 2×5 **iii** 5^2 **iv** $2 \times 3 \times 5 \times 7$

Rules for multiplying and dividing powers

In this section you will learn how to:
- use rules for multiplying and dividing powers

When you multiply numbers that are written as powers of the same variable or number, something unexpected happens. For example:

$$a^2 \times a^3 = (a \times a) \times (a \times a \times a) = a^5$$

$$3^3 \times 3^5 = (3 \times 3 \times 3) \times (3 \times 3 \times 3 \times 3 \times 3) = 3^8$$

Can you see the rule? You can find these products just by *adding* the powers. For example:

$$a^3 \times a^4 = a^{3+4} = a^7 \qquad 2^3 \times 2^4 \times 2^5 = 2^{12}$$

A similar rule applies when you divide powers of the same variable or number. For example:

$$a^5 \div a^2 = (a \times a \times a \times a \times a) \div (a \times a) = a \times a \times a = a^3$$

$$7^6 \div 7 = (7 \times 7 \times 7 \times 7 \times 7 \times 7) \div (7) = 7 \times 7 \times 7 \times 7 \times 7 = 7^5$$

Can you see the rule? You can do these divisions just by *subtracting* the powers. For example:

$$a^4 \div a^3 = a^{4-3} = a^1 = a \qquad b^7 \div b^4 = b^3$$

EXERCISE 4J

1 Write these as single powers of 5.

a $5^2 \times 5^2$	**b** $5^4 \times 5^6$	**c** $5^2 \times 5^3$	**d** 5×5^2	**e** $5^6 \times 5^9$
f 5×5^8	**g** $5^2 \times 5^4$	**h** $5^6 \times 5^3$	**i** $5^2 \times 5^6$	

2 Write these as single powers of 6.

a $6^5 \div 6^2$	**b** $6^7 \div 6^2$	**c** $6^3 \div 6^2$	**d** $6^4 \div 6^4$	**e** $6^5 \div 6^4$
f $6^5 \div 6^2$	**g** $6^4 \div 6^2$	**h** $6^4 \div 6^3$	**i** $6^5 \div 6^3$	

3 Simplify these (write them as single powers of x).

a $x^2 \times x^6$	**b** $x^5 \times x^4$	**c** $x^6 \times x^2$	**d** $x^3 \times x^2$	**e** $x^6 \times x^6$
f $x^5 \times x^8$	**g** $x^7 \times x^4$	**h** $x^2 \times x^8$	**i** $x^{12} \times x^4$	

4 Simplify these (write them as single powers of x).

a $x^7 \div x^3$	**b** $x^8 \div x^3$	**c** $x^4 \div x$	**d** $x^6 \div x^3$	**e** $x^{10} \div x^4$
f $x^6 \div x$	**g** $x^8 \div x^6$	**h** $x^8 \div x^2$	**i** $x^{12} \div x^3$	

1 **a** Write down the largest multiple of 3 smaller than 100.

b Write down the smallest multiple of 6 larger than 100.

2 Look at the numbers in this cloud.

4 8 15 16 21 25
32 36 45 49 50 54
64 66 75 80 81 90

Write down all the square numbers that are inside the cloud.

3 **a** Write down the largest factor of 360, smaller than 100.

b Write down the smallest factor of 315 larger than 100.

4 Using only the numbers in the cloud, write down

8 12 27
4 6
16 5 3

i all the multiples of 6,

ii all the square numbers,

iii all the factors of 12,

iv all the cube numbers.

Edexcel, Question 11, Paper 1 Foundation, June 2003

5 **a** Copy and complete the missing numbers in the following pattern:

Last digit

$4^1 = 4 = 4$ → $\boxed{4}$

$4^2 = 4 \times 4 = 16$ → $\boxed{6}$

$4^3 = 4 \times 4 \times 4 = 64$ → $\boxed{}$

$4^4 = 4 \times 4 \times 4 \times 4 = 256$ → $\boxed{}$

$4^5 = \boxed{} = \boxed{}$ → $\boxed{}$

b What will the last digit of 4^{17} be?

6 **a** Write down the first five multiples of 6.

b Write down the factors of 12.

c Write down a square number between 20 and 30.

d Write down two prime numbers between 20 and 30.

7 Here are six number cards.

$\boxed{4}$ $\boxed{5}$ $\boxed{8}$ $\boxed{9}$ $\boxed{10}$ $\boxed{11}$

a Which of the numbers are multiples of 4?

b Which of the numbers are factors of 10?

c Which of the numbers are prime numbers?

d Which numbers are square numbers?

e Which number is a cube number?

f Use the numbers to complete the magic square below so that every row, every column and both diagonals add up to 21.

		6
3	7	

8 **a** Find the value of 3.7^2

The table shows some numbers.

51	52	53	54	55	56	57	58	59

Two of the numbers are prime numbers.

b Which two numbers are these?

9 Write down the value of

a 2^3

b $\sqrt{64}$

10 John set up two computer virus checkers on his computer on January 1st.

Checker A would check every 8 days.

Checker B would check every 10 days.

After how many days will both checkers be checking on the same day again?

11 Mary set up her Christmas Tree with two sets of twinkling lights.

Set A would twinkle every 3 seconds.

Set B would twinkle every 4 seconds.

How many times in a minute will both sets be twinkling at the same time?

12 Write down the answers to

a 4000×20

b $4000 \div 20$

c $\dfrac{120\,000}{200 \times 300}$

Write as a power of 5

 a $5^4 \times 5^2$

b $5^9 \div 5^6$

Edexcel, Question 15a, Paper 3 Intermediate, June 2005

 a Write down 44 as the product of its prime numbers.

 b Find the lowest common multiple (LCM) of 44 and 66.

 Find the Highest Common Factor of 108 and 252.

WORKED EXAM QUESTION

a Write 36 as a product of prime factors.

b Find the lowest common multiple (LCM) of 36 and 45.

c Find the highest common factor (HCF) of 45 and 60.

Solution

a $2^2 \times 3^2$

> Split 36 into products until there are only prime numbers. $36 = 4 \times 9 = 2 \times 2 \times 9 = 2 \times 2 \times 3 \times 3$
> Write the answer in index form.

b 36, 72, 108, 144, (180), ...

45, 90, 135, (180), ...

So the LCM of 36 and 45 is 180.

> Write out the multiples of 36 and 45 until there is a common multiple then pick out the smallest (lowest), value in both (common) lists (multiples).

c Factors of 45 = {3, 5, 9, (15), 45}

Factors of 60 = {1, 2, 3, 4, 5, 6, 10, 12, (15), 20, 30, 60}

So the HCF of 45 and 60 is 15.

> Write out the factors of 48 and 60, then pick out the largest (highest) value in both (common) lists (factors).

GRADE YOURSELF

G Able to recognise multiples of the first ten whole numbers

G Able to find factors of numbers less than 100

G Able to recognise the square numbers up to 100

F Able to write down the square of any number up to $15 \times 15 = 225$

F Able to write down the cubes of 1, 2, 3, 4, 5 and 10

F Know how to find the square root of any number using a calculator

E Can calculate simple powers of whole numbers

E Able to recognise two-digit prime numbers

D Can multiply and divide by powers of 10

D Can multiply together numbers that are multiples of 10

C Can work out the prime factor form of numbers

C Can work out the LCM and HCF of two numbers

C Can simplify multiplications and divisions of powers

What you should know now

- What multiples are
- How to find the factors of any whole number
- What a prime number is
- What square numbers are
- What square roots are
- How to find powers of numbers
- How to write numbers in prime factor form
- How to find the LCM and HCF of any pair of numbers

This book provides indicators of the equivalent grade level of maths questions throughout. The publishers wish to make clear that these grade indicators have been provided by Collins Education, and are not the responsibility of Edexcel Ltd. Whilst every effort has been made to assure their accuracy, they should be regarded as indicators, and are not binding or definitive.

Perimeter and area

Chapter 5

1 Perimeter

2 Area of an irregular shape

3 Area of a rectangle

4 Area of a compound shape

5 Area of a triangle

6 Area of a parallelogram

7 Area of a trapezium

8 Dimensional analysis

This chapter will show you ...

● how to work out the perimeters and the areas of some common 2-D shapes

● the types of problem you will be able to solve with knowledge of area

● how to recognise compound formulae for length, area and volume

Visual overview

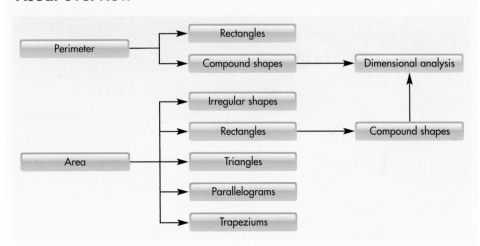

What you should already know

● The common units of length are millimetre (mm), centimetre (cm), metre (m) and kilometre (km).

● Area is the amount of space inside a shape. The common units of area are the square millimetre (mm^2), the square centimetre (cm^2), the square metre (m^2) and the square kilometre (km^2).

Quick check

This rectangle has sides of length 8 cm and 2 cm.

a What is the total length of all four sides?

b How many centimetre squares are there in the rectangle?

8 cm

2 cm

Perimeter

In this section you will learn how to:

- find the perimeter of a rectangle and compound shapes

Key words

compound shape
perimeter
rectangle

The **perimeter** of a rectangle is the sum of the lengths of all its sides.

ACTIVITY

Round about

On a piece of 1-cm squared paper draw this **rectangle**.

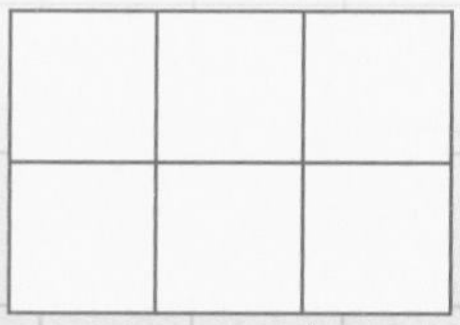

Measure its perimeter. You should get:

3 cm + 2 cm + 3 cm + 2 cm = 10 cm

Draw a different rectangle that also has a perimeter of 10 cm.

See how many different rectangles you can draw that each have a perimeter of 10 cm.

There are only three different rectangles that each have a perimeter of 12 cm and whole numbers of centimetres for their length and breadth. Can you draw all three?

Can you draw a rectangle that has a perimeter of 7 cm?

If not, why not? If you can, what is so strange about it?

Try drawing a rectangle that has a perimeter of 13 cm.

EXAMPLE 1

Find the perimeter of this rectangle.

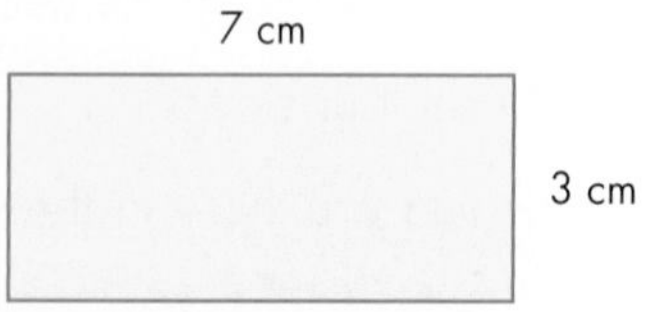

7 cm

3 cm

Perimeter = 7 + 3 + 7 + 3 = 20 cm

A **compound shape** is any 2-D shape that is made up of other simple shapes such as rectangles and triangles.

EXAMPLE 2

Find the perimeter of this compound shape.

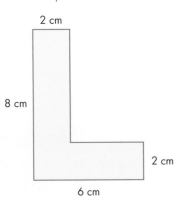

2 cm

8 cm

2 cm

6 cm

The lengths of the two missing sides are 6 cm and 4 cm.

So, the perimeter = 2 + 6 + 4 + 2 + 6 + 8 = 28 cm

EXERCISE 5A

Calculate the perimeter of each of the following shapes. Draw them first on squared paper if it helps you.

1
4 cm
1 cm

2
2 cm
2 cm

3
4 cm
3 cm

4
3 cm
3 cm

5
6 cm
2 cm

6
2 cm
1 cm

7
3 cm
2 cm
1 cm
1 cm

8
4 cm
2 cm
1 cm
1 cm
1 cm

9
4 cm
1 cm
2 cm
3 cm

10
2 cm
1 cm
3 cm
1 cm
1 cm
4 cm

11
2 cm
1 cm
1 cm
3 cm
1 cm

12
1 cm
1 cm
1 cm
1 cm

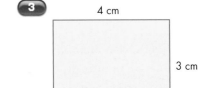
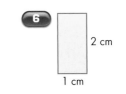
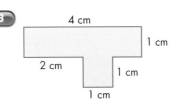

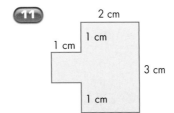
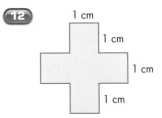
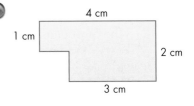

5.2 Area of an irregular shape

In this section you will learn how to:

- estimate the area of an irregular 2-D shape by counting squares

Key words
area
estimate

ACTIVITY

A different area

Take a piece of 1-cm squared paper. Draw on it a rectangle of 2 cm by 6 cm.

Check that it has a perimeter of 16 cm.

Count the number of squares inside the rectangle. This should come to 12.

This means that the **area** of this shape is 12 square centimetres.

Draw a different rectangle that has an area of 12 square centimetres but a perimeter that is smaller than 16 cm.

Draw another different rectangle that also has an area of 12 square centimetres, but a perimeter that is larger than 16 cm.

Using whole squares only, how many rectangles can you draw that have *different* perimeters but the *same* area of 16 square centimetres?

To find the area of an irregular shape, you can put a square grid over the shape and **estimate** the number of complete squares that are covered.

The most efficient way to do this is:

- First, count all the whole squares.
- Second, put together parts of squares to make whole and almost whole squares.
- Finally, add together the two results.

EXAMPLE 3

Below is a map of a lake. Each square represents 1 km². Estimate the area of the lake.

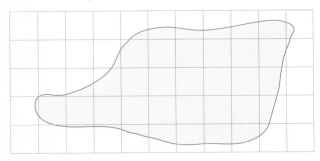

First, count all the whole squares. You should count 16.

Next, put together the parts of squares around the edge of the lake.

This should make up about ten squares.

Finally, add together the 16 and the 10 to get an area of 26 km².

Note: This is only an *estimate*. Someone else may get a slightly different answer. However, provided the answer is close to 26, it is acceptable.

EXERCISE 5B

1 These shapes were drawn on centimetre-squared paper. By counting squares, estimate the area of each of them, giving your answers in square centimetres.

a
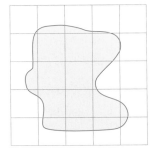

b
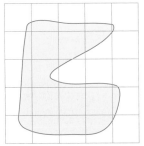

c
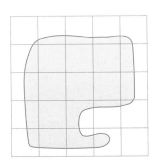

d
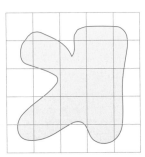

2 On a piece of 1-cm squared paper, draw round each of your hands to find its area. Do both hands have the same area?

3 Draw some shapes of your own on squared paper. First, guess the area of each shape. Then count up the squares and see how close your estimate was.

5.3 Area of a rectangle

In this section you will learn how to:
- find the area of a rectangle
- use the formula for the area of a rectangle

Key words

area
length
width

Look at these rectangles and their areas.

 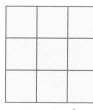 

Area 6 cm²   Area 9 cm²   Area 15 cm²

Notice that the area of each rectangle is given by its length multiplied by its width.

So, the formula to find the area of a rectangle is:

area = length × width

As an algebraic formula, this is written as:

$A = lw$

EXAMPLE 4

Calculate the area of this rectangle.

Area of rectangle = length × width
= 11 cm × 4 cm
= 44 cm²

11 cm

4 cm

EXERCISE 5C

Calculate the area and the perimeter for each of the rectangles 1 to 8.

1   7 cm
5 cm

2   11 cm
3 cm

3   15 cm
3 cm

4   10 cm
7 cm

5   8 cm
7 cm

6   5 cm
2 cm

F

7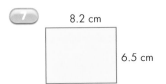
8.2 cm

6.5 cm

8
11.8 cm

7.2 cm

9 Copy and complete the table on the right for rectangles **a** to **h**.

	Length	Width	Perimeter	Area
a	7 cm	3 cm		
b	5 cm	4 cm		
c	4 cm		12 cm	
d	5 cm		16 cm	
e	6 mm			18 mm^2
f	7 mm			28 mm^2
g		2 m	14 m	
h		5 m		35 m^2

10 A rectangular field is 150 m long and 45 m wide.

  a What length of fencing is needed to go all the way round the field?

  b What is the area of the field?

11 A rugby pitch is 160 m long and 70 m wide.

  a Before a game, the players have to run all the way round the pitch twice to help them loosen up. What is the distance that they have to run?

  b The groundsman waters the pitch at the rate of 100 m^2 per minute. How long will it take him to water the whole pitch?

12 How much will it cost to buy enough carpet for a rectangular room 12 m by 5 m, if the carpet costs £13.99 per square metre?

13 What is the perimeter of a square with an area of 100 cm^2?

UAM

14 a The two squares on the right have the same area. Calculate the areas of square A and square B. Copy and complete: 1 cm^2 = ... mm^2

  b Change the following into square millimetres.

    i 3 cm^2 **ii** 5 cm^2 **iii** 6.3 cm^2

1 cm   10 mm

A 1 cm   **B** 10 mm

15 a The two squares on the right have the same area. Calculate the areas of square A and square B. Copy and complete: 1 m^2 = ... cm^2

  b Change the following into square centimetres.

    i 2 m^2 **ii** 4 m^2 **iii** 5.6 m^2

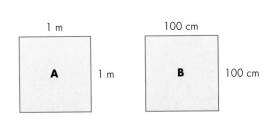
1 m   100 cm

A 1 m   **B** 100 cm

Area of a compound shape

In this section you will learn how to:

- find the area of a compound shape by splitting it into rectangles

Key words

area

compound shape

Some 2-D shapes are made up of two or more rectangles or triangles.

These **compound shapes** can be split into simpler shapes, which makes it easy to calculate the **areas** of these shapes.

EXAMPLE 5

Find the area of the shape on the right.

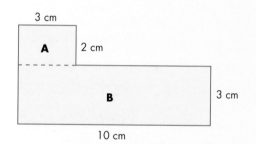

First, split the shape into two rectangles, A and B.

Then, calculate the area of each one.

area of A = 2 × 3 = 6 cm^2

area of B = 10 × 3 = 30 cm^2

The area of the shape is given by:

area of A + area of B = 6 + 30 = 36 cm^2

EXERCISE 5D

Calculate the area of each of the compound shapes below as follows.

- First, split it into rectangles.

- Then, calculate the area of each rectangle.

- Finally, add together the areas of the rectangles.

 1

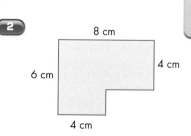 **2**

D

D

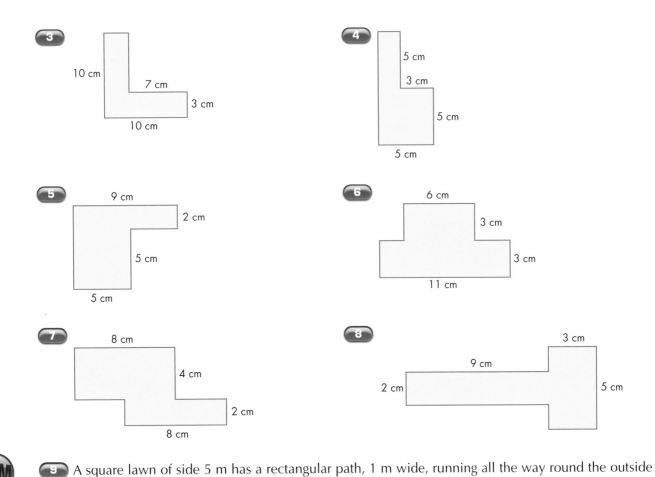

3
10 cm
7 cm
3 cm
10 cm

4
5 cm
3 cm
5 cm
5 cm

5
9 cm
2 cm
5 cm
5 cm

6
6 cm
3 cm
3 cm
11 cm

7
8 cm
4 cm
2 cm
8 cm

8
3 cm
9 cm
2 cm
5 cm

UAM **9** A square lawn of side 5 m has a rectangular path, 1 m wide, running all the way round the outside of it. What is the area of the path?

5.5 Area of a triangle

In this section you will learn how to:
- find the area of a triangle
- use the formula for the area of a triangle

Key words
area
base
height
perpendicular
  height
triangle

Area of a right-angled triangle

It is easy to see that the **area** of a right-angled **triangle** is half the area of the rectangle with the same **base** and **height**. Hence:

area = $\frac{1}{2} \times$ base $\times$ height

As an algebraic formula, this is written as:

$A = \frac{1}{2} bh$

Length
Width
Height
Base

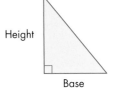

EXAMPLE 6

Find the area of this right-angled triangle.

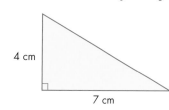

4 cm

7 cm

$$\text{Area} = \tfrac{1}{2} \times 7 \text{ cm} \times 4 \text{ cm}$$
$$= \tfrac{1}{2} \times 28 \text{ cm}^2$$
$$= 14 \text{ cm}^2$$

EXERCISE 5E

1 Write down the area and the perimeter of each triangle.

a

4 cm   5 cm

3 cm

b

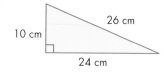

26 cm

10 cm

24 cm

c

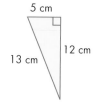

5 cm

13 cm   12 cm

2 Find the area of the shaded triangle RST.

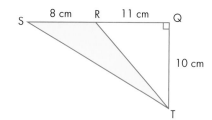

S   8 cm   R   11 cm   Q

10 cm

T

HINTS AND TIPS

Find the area of triangle QST and subtract the area of triangle QRT.

3 A tree is in the middle of a garden.
Around the tree there is a square region where nothing will be planted. The dimensions of the garden are shown in the diagram.

How much area can be planted?

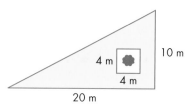

4 m   10 m

4 m

20 m

4 Find the area of the shaded part of each triangle.

a

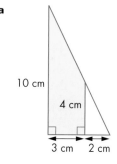

10 cm

4 cm

3 cm   2 cm

b

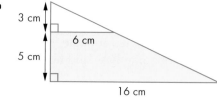

3 cm

6 cm

5 cm

16 cm

c

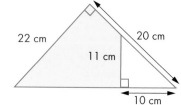

22 cm   20 cm

11 cm

10 cm

Area of any triangle

A rectangle can be drawn around any triangle with dimensions base × vertical height.

This triangle can be split into two smaller rectangles of which each is halved to show part of the larger triangle as shown.

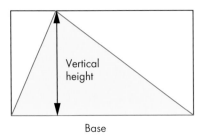

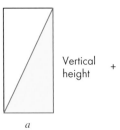

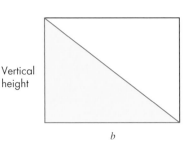

Area of triangle $= \frac{1}{2} \times a \times$ vertical height $\quad + \quad \frac{1}{2} \times b \times$ vertical height
$= \frac{1}{2} \times (a + b) \times$ vertical height

In algebraic form, this is written as $\quad A = \frac{1}{2}bh$

EXAMPLE 7

Calculate the area of this triangle.

$\begin{aligned} \text{Area} \ &= \tfrac{1}{2} \times 9 \text{ cm} \times 4 \text{ cm} \\ &= \tfrac{1}{2} \times 36 \text{ cm}^2 \\ &= 18 \text{ cm}^2 \end{aligned}$

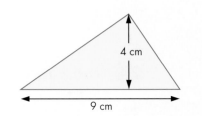

EXAMPLE 8

Calculate the area of the shape shown below.

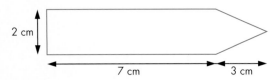

This is a compound shape that can be split into a rectangle (R) and a triangle (T).

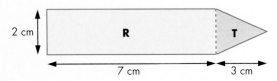

$\begin{aligned} \text{Area of the shape} \ &= \text{ area of R} + \text{area of T} \\ &= 7 \times 2 + \tfrac{1}{2} \times 2 \times 3 \\ &= 14 + 3 \\ &= 17 \text{ cm}^2 \end{aligned}$

EXERCISE 5F

1 Calculate the area of each of these triangles.

a
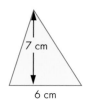
7 cm
6 cm

b
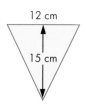
3 cm
8 cm

c
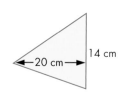
7 cm
4 cm

d
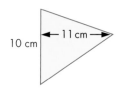
10 cm
11 cm

e
12 cm
15 cm

f
20 cm
14 cm

2 Copy and complete the following table for triangles **a** to **f**.

	Base	Perpendicular height	Area
a	8 cm	7 cm	
b		9 cm	36 cm^2
c		5 cm	10 cm^2
d	4 cm		6 cm^2
e	6 cm		21 cm^2
f	8 cm	11 cm	

3 Find the area of each of these shapes.

a
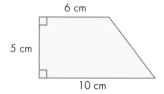
6 cm
5 cm
10 cm

b
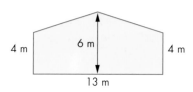
4 m
6 m
4 m
13 m

HINTS AND TIPS

Refer to Example 8 on how to find the area of a compound shape.

c
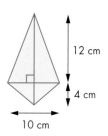
12 cm
4 cm
10 cm

4 Find the area of each shaded shape.

a
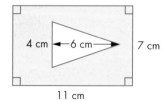
4 cm
6 cm
7 cm
11 cm

b
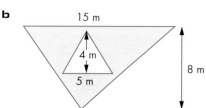
15 m
4 m
5 m
8 m

HINTS AND TIPS

Find the area of the outer shape and subtract the area of the inner shape.

5 Write down the dimensions of two different-sized triangles that have the same area of 50 cm^2.

Area of a parallelogram

In this section you will learn how to:
- find the area of a parallelogram
- use the formula for the area of a parallelogram

Key words

parallelogram
area
base
height
vertices

A **parallelogram** can be changed into a rectangle by moving a triangle.

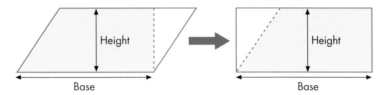

This shows that the **area** of the parallelogram is the area of a rectangle with the same **base** and **height**. The formula is:

area of a parallelogram = base × height

As an algebraic formula, this is written as:

$A = bh$

EXAMPLE 9

Find the area of this parallelogram.

Area = 8 cm × 6 cm
     = 48 cm²

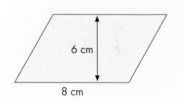

ACTIVITY

Pick's theorem

This quadrilateral has an area of $16\frac{1}{2}$ square units.

The perimeter of the quadrilateral passes through nine dots. Thirteen dots are contained within the perimeter of the quadrilateral.

Draw some quadrilaterals of different shapes and sizes on dotty paper. Make sure the **vertices** are all on dots on the paper. Investigate the connection between the area and the total number of dots inside and the total number of dots on the perimeter of the shape.

Then, from your findings, write down Pick's theorem.

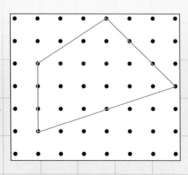

Calculate the area of each parallelogram below.

1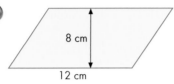

8 cm

12 cm

2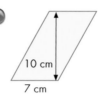

10 cm

7 cm

3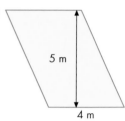

5 m

4 m

4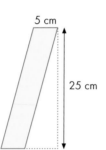

5 cm

25 cm

5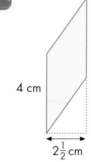

4 cm

$2\frac{1}{2}$ cm

6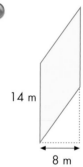

14 m

8 m

5.7 Area of a trapezium

In this section you will learn how to:
- find the area of a trapezium
- use the formula for the area of a trapezium

Key words
area
height
trapezium

The **area** of a **trapezium** is calculated by finding the average of the lengths of its parallel sides and multiplying this by the perpendicular **height** between them.

The area of a trapezium is given by this formula:

$$A = \tfrac{1}{2}(a + b)h$$

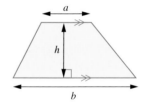

EXAMPLE 10

Find the area of the trapezium ABCD.

Area $= \tfrac{1}{2}(4 + 7) \times 3$

$= \tfrac{1}{2} \times 11 \times 3$

$= 16.5 \text{ cm}^2$

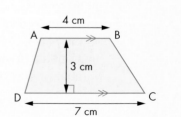

EXERCISE 5H

1 Copy and complete the following table for each trapezium.

	Parallel side 1	Parallel side 2	Perpendicular height	Area
a	8 cm	4 cm	5 cm	
b	10 cm	12 cm	7 cm	
c	7 cm	5 cm	4 cm	
d	5 cm	9 cm	6 cm	
e	3 cm	13 cm	5 cm	
f	4 cm	10 cm		42 cm^2
g	7 cm	8 cm		22.5 cm^2

2 Calculate the perimeter and the area of each trapezium.

a
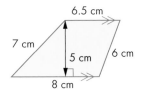
6.5 cm
7 cm
5 cm
6 cm
8 cm

b
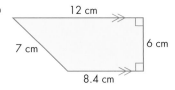
12 cm
7 cm
6 cm
8.4 cm

c
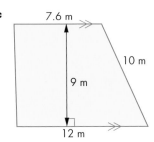
7.6 m
10 m
9 m
12 m

HINTS AND TIPS

Make sure you use the right value for the height. GCSE exam questions sometimes include the slant side length, which is not used for the area.

3 A trapezium has an area of 25 cm^2. Its vertical height is 5 cm. Write down five different possible pairs of lengths for the two parallel sides.

4 Which of the following shapes has the largest area?

a
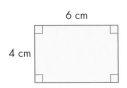
6 cm
4 cm

b
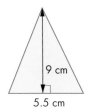
9 cm
5.5 cm

c
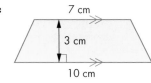
7 cm
3 cm
10 cm

5 Which of the following shapes has the smallest area?

a
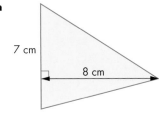
7 cm
8 cm

b
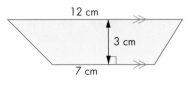
12 cm
3 cm
7 cm

c
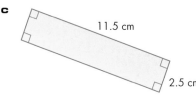
11.5 cm
2.5 cm

In this section you will learn how to:
- recognise whether a formula represents a length, an area or a volume

Key words
area
dimension
length
volume

Dimensions of length

When we have an unknown **length** or distance in a problem, we represent it by a single letter, followed by the unit in which it is measured. For example, t centimetres, x miles and y kilometres

---

EXAMPLE 11

Find a formula the perimeters of these shapes.

a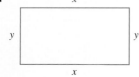

b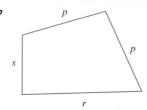

Shape **a** is a rectangle. Its perimeter is given by the formula

$P = x + y + x + y = 2x + 2y$

Shape **b** is irregular quadrilateral. Its perimeter is given by the formula

$P = p + p + r + s = 2p + r + s$

In the example, each letter is a length and has the **dimension** or measure of length, i.e. centimetre, metre, kilometre, etc. The numbers or coefficients written before the letters are *not* lengths and therefore have *no* dimensions. So, for example, $2x$, $5y$ or $\frac{1}{2}p$ have the same dimension as x, y or p respectively.

When just lengths are involved in a formula, the formula is said to have one dimension or 1-D, which is sometimes represented by the symbol [L].

EXERCISE 5I

D

Find a formula for the perimeter of each of these shapes. Each letter represents a length.

1

2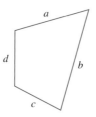

3

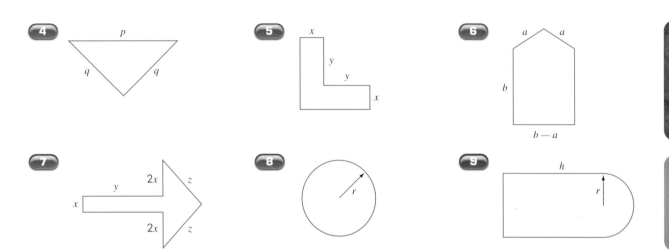

Dimensions of area

EXAMPLE 12

Look at these four examples of formulae for calculating area.

$A = lb$ gives the area of a rectangle
$A = x^2$ gives the area of a square
$A = 2ab + 2ac + 2bc$ gives the surface area of a cuboid
$A = \pi r^2$ gives the area of a circle

These formulae have one thing in common. They all consist of terms that are the product of two lengths. You can recognise this by counting the number of letters in each term of the formula. The first formula has two (l and b). The second has two (x and x). The third has three terms, each of two letters (a and b, a and c, b and c). The fourth also has only two letters (r and r) because π is a number (3.14159…) which has no dimension.

We can recognise formulae for **area** because they only have terms that consist of two letters – that is, two lengths multiplied together. Numbers are not defined as lengths, since they have no dimensions. These formulae therefore have two dimensions or 2-D, which is sometimes represented by the symbol [L^2].

This confirms the units in which area is usually measured. For example, square metres (m × m or m^2) and square centimetres (cm × cm or cm^2)

EXERCISE 5J

Find a formula for the area of each of these shapes. Each letter represents a length.

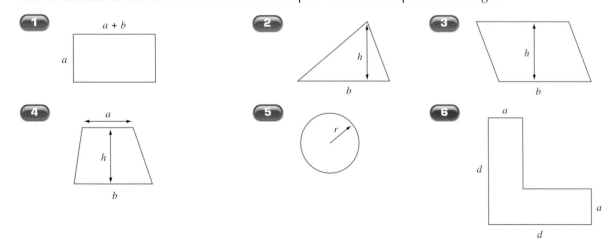

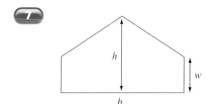

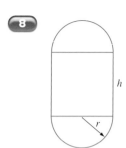

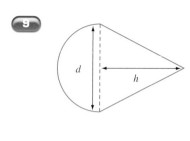

Dimensions of volume

EXAMPLE 13

Look at these three examples of formulae for calculating volume.

$V = lbh$ gives the volume of a cuboid

$V = x^3$ gives the volume of a cube

$V = \pi r^2 h + \pi r^3$ gives the volume of a cylinder with hemispherical ends

Again, these formulae have one thing in common. They all consist of terms that are the product of three lengths. You can recognise this by counting the number of letters in each term of the formula. The first formula has three (l, b and h). The second has three (x, x and x). The third has two terms, each of three letters (r, r and h; r, r and r). Remember, π has no dimension.

We can recognise formulae for **volume** because they only have terms that consist of three letters – that is, three lengths multiplied together. They therefore have three dimensions or 3-D, which is sometimes represented by the symbol $[L^3]$. Once more, numbers are not defined as lengths, since they have no dimensions.

This confirms the units in which volume is usually measured. For example,

cubic metres (m × m × m or m³)

cubic centimetres (cm × cm × cm or cm³)

EXERCISE 5K

Find a formula for the volume of each of these shapes. Each letter represents a length.

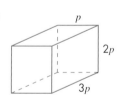

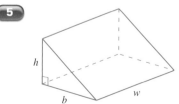

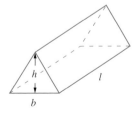

Recognising formulae

Scientists use dimensional analysis to check if complicated formulae are consistent. We are only concerned with length, areas or volume. It is possible to recognise if a formula is a length, area or volume by looking at the number of variables in each term.

Each term in a formula must have the correct number of dimensions. It is not possible to have a formula with a mixture of terms, some of which have, for example, one dimension and some two dimensions. When terms are found to be mixed, the formula is said to be *inconsistent* and is not possible.

We are only concerned with lengths, areas and volumes, so it is easy for us to test for consistency.

EXAMPLE 14

One of the these formulae represents a length (L), one represents an area (A), and one represents a volume (V). Which is which?

a $\pi r^2 + ab$ **b** $\dfrac{(ab^2 + a^2b)}{2}$ **c** $\pi(R + r)$

a This is an area because the first term has two letters (r and r) multiplied by a dimensionless number (π), and the second term also has two letters (a and b). $[L^2] + [L^2] = [L^2]$.

b This is a volume because each term is 3-D. $[L^3] + [L^3] = [L^3]$ is consistent.

c This is a length. There are two terms which are both single letters. So $[L] + [L] = [L]$.

EXERCISE 5L

1 Each of these expressions represents a length, an area or a volume. Indicate by writing L, A or V which it is. Each letter represents a length.

a x^2 **b** $2y$ **c** πa **d** πab

e xyz **f** $3x^3$ **g** x^2y **h** $2xy$

i $4y$ **j** $3ab^2$ **k** $4xz$ **l** $5z$

m abc **n** $ab + bc$ **o** $abc + d^3$ **p** $2ab + 3bc$

q $a^2b + ab^2$ **r** $a^2 + b^2$ **s** πa^2 **t** $\dfrac{abc}{d}$

u $\dfrac{(ab + bc)}{d}$ **v** $\dfrac{ab}{2}$ **w** $(a + b)^2$ **x** $4a^2 + 2ab$

y $3abc + 2abd + 4bcd + 2acd$ **z** $4\pi r^3 + \pi r^2 h$

2 One of these formulae is a length (L), 5 of them are areas (A), 4 of them are volumes (V) and the remaining 6 are mixtures which are impossible formulae (I). Indicate which are which by writing L, A, V or I.

a $a + b$ **b** $a^2 + b$ **c** $a^2 + b^2$ **d** $ab + c$

e $ab + c^2$ **f** $a^3 + bc$ **g** $a^3 + abc$ **h** $a^2 + abc$

i $3a^2 + bc$ **j** $4a^3b + 2ab^2$ **k** $3abc + 2x^2y$ **l** $3a(ab + bc)$

m $4a^2 + 3ab$ **n** $\pi a^2(a + b)$ **o** $\pi a^2 + 2r^2$ **p** $\pi r^2 h + \pi rh$

1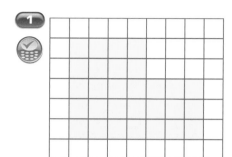

A shaded shape is shown on the grid of centimetre squares.

a Find the area of the shaded shape.

b Find the perimeter of the shaded shape.

Edexcel, Question 5, Paper 11B Foundation, January 2003

2 Here is a rectangle.

a Find the perimeter of the rectangle. State the units of your answer.

b Find the area of the rectangle. State the units of your answer.

3 A parallelogram is drawn on a centimetre square grid.

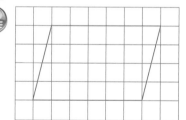

Calculate the area of the parallelogram.

4

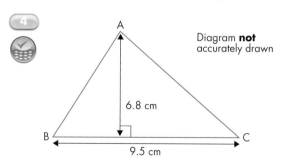

Diagram **not** accurately drawn

Work out the area of triangle ABC.

Edexcel, Question 7, Paper 11B Foundation, March 2004

5 This diagram shows a wall with a door in it.

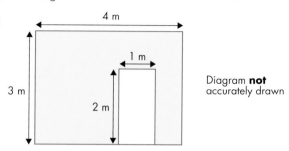

Diagram **not** accurately drawn

Work out the shaded area.

Edexcel, Question 23a, Paper 1 Foundation, June 2005

6 The diagram shows a trapezium ABCD.

AB = 8 cm, AD = 7 cm, DC = 12 cm

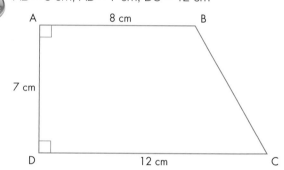

Find the area of the trapezium ABCD. Remember to state the units of your answer.

7 In this question, the letters x, y and z represent lengths. State whether each expression could represent a length, an area or a volume.

a xyz **b** $\pi(x + y + z)$

8 In this question, the letters x, y and z represent lengths. State whether each expression could represent a length, an area or a volume.

a $\pi x^2 y$ **b** $x + y + z$ **c** $x^2 + y^2$

WORKED EXAM QUESTIONS

1   A tile is shown below.

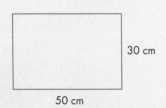

30 cm

50 cm

Find the area of the tile. Give your answer in square metres.

Solution

Area of tile = 50 × 30 = 1500 cm^2

10 000 cm^2 = 1 m^2

So: area = 1500 ÷ 10 000 = 0.15 m^2

2   The diagram shows a Tangram.

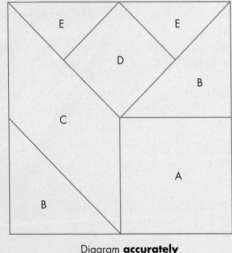

E   E

D

B

C

A

B

Diagram **accurately** drawn

The Tangram is a large square that is made up from

one square A,

two triangles B,

one parallelogram C,

another square D and

two small triangles E.

The total area of the Tangram is 64 cm^2.

Find the area of

a   square A,

b   triangle B,

c   parallelogram C.

Edexcel, Question 4, Paper 3 Intermediate, November 2004

Solution

a   Area of square A = 64 ÷ 4 = 16 cm^2 ——— Square A is $\frac{1}{4}$ of the large square

b   Area of triangle B = 16 ÷ 2 = 8 cm^2 ——— Triangle B is $\frac{1}{2}$ square A

c   Area of parallelogram C = 2 × 8 = 16 cm^2 ——— Parallelogram C is made from two triangles B

Mr Slater buys a new house.

He decides to put laminate flooring throughout the whole ground floor.

The laminate flooring he has chosen comes in packs which each cover 2 m².

Each room also needs an edging strip around the perimeter of the room.

The edging comes in packs which have a total length of 12 m.

The hall and bathroom are to have beech laminate flooring and the other rooms oak.

Mr Slater calculates the floor area of each room.

He also calculates the edging needed for every room (he includes the doorways to make sure he has enough).

Help him by completing the table to find the total floor area and the length of edging he needs.

Beech effect

Room	Floor area (m²)	Edging needed (m)
Hall		
Bathroom		
Total		

Oak effect

Room	Floor area (m²)	Edging needed (m)
Lounge		
Sitting room		
Kitchen/diner		
Conservatory		
Total		

This is a sketch showing the ground floor dimensions.

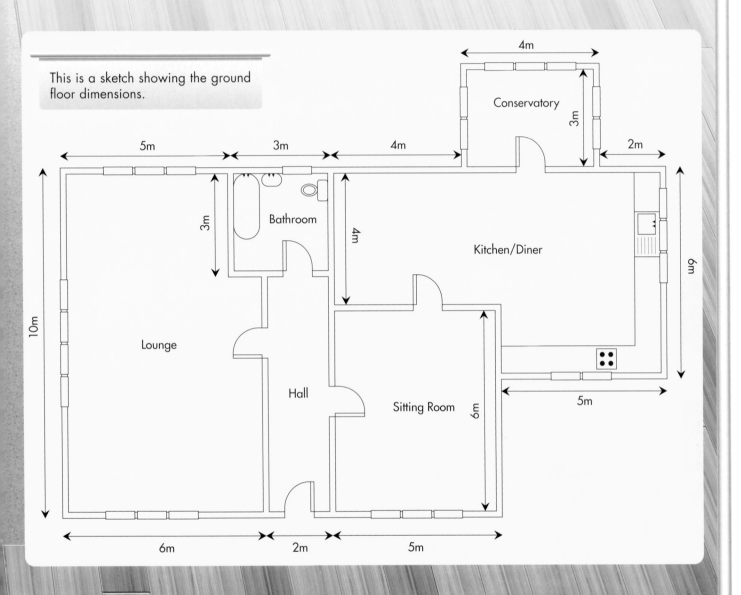

Calculate for Mr Slater the total cost of the flooring and the edging.

Oak effect

	Number of packs	Price per pack	Total cost
Beech flooring		£32	
Beech edging		£18	
Oak flooring		£38	
Oak edging		£22	
		Total	

This total price must now have VAT added onto it.

VAT is at 17.5%.

What is the new total, once VAT has been added?

GRADE YOURSELF

G Can find the perimeter of a 2-D shape

G Can find the area of a 2-D shape by counting squares

F Can find the area of a rectangle using the formula $A = lw$

E Can find the area of a triangle using the formula $A = \frac{1}{2}bh$

D Can find the area of a parallelogram using the formula $A = bh$

D Can find the area of a trapezium using the formula $A = \frac{1}{2}(a + b)h$

D Can find the area of a compound shape

D Able to work out a formula for the perimeter, area or volume of simple shapes

C Able to work out a formula for the perimeter, area or volume of complex shapes

C Able to work out whether an expression or formula is dimensionally consistent and whether it represents a length, an area or a volume

What you should know now

- How to find the perimeter and area of 2-D shapes by counting squares
- How to find the area of a rectangle
- How to find the area of a triangle
- How to find the area of a parallelogram and a trapezium
- How to find the area of a compound shape

Statistical representation

1 Frequency diagrams

2 Statistical diagrams

3 Bar charts

4 Line graphs

5 Stem-and-leaf diagrams

This chapter will show you ...

- how to collect and organise data, and how to represent data on various types of diagram
- how to draw diagrams for data, including line graphs for time series and frequency diagrams
- how to draw diagrams for discrete data, including stem-and-leaf diagrams

Visual overview

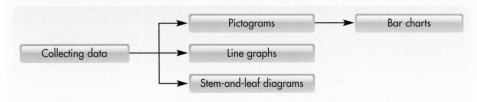

What you should already know

- How to use a tally for recording data
- How to read information from charts and tables

Quick check

Zoe works in a dress shop. She recorded the sizes of all the dresses sold during a week. The table shows the results.

Day	Size of dresses sold									
Monday	12	8	10	8	14	8	12	8	8	
Tuesday	10	10	8	12	14	16	8	12	14	16
Wednesday	16	8	12	10						
Thursday	12	8	8	10	12	14	16	12	8	
Friday	10	10	8	10	12	14	14	12	10	8
Saturday	10	8	8	12	10	12	8	10		

a Use a tallying method to make a table showing how many dresses of each size were sold in the week.

b Which dress size had the most sales?

Frequency diagrams

In this section you will learn how to:
- collect and represent discrete and grouped data using tally charts and frequency tables

Key words
class
class interval
data collection sheet
experiment
frequency
frequency table
grouped data
grouped frequency table
observation
sample
tally chart

Statistics is concerned with the collection and organisation of data, the representation of data on diagrams and the interpretation of data.

When you are collecting data for simple surveys, it is usual to use a **data collection sheet**, also called a **tally chart**. For example, data collection sheets are used to gather information on how people travel to work, how students spend their free time and the amount of time people spend watching TV.

It is easy to record the data by using tally marks, as shown in Example 1. Counting up the tally marks in each row of the chart gives the **frequency** of each category. By listing the frequencies in a column on the right-hand side of the chart, you can make a **frequency table** (see Example 1). Frequency tables are an important part of making statistical calculations, as you will see in Chapter 11.

Three methods are used to collect data.

- **Taking a sample**   For example, to find out which 'soaps' students watch, you would need to take a sample from the whole school population by asking at random an equal number of boys and girls from each year group. In this case, a good sample size would be 50.

- **Observation**   For example, to find how many vehicles a day use a certain road, you would need to count and record the number of vehicles passing a point at different times of the day.

- **Experiment**   For example, to find out how often a six occurs when you throw a dice, you would need to throw the dice 50 times or more and record each score.

EXAMPLE 1

Sandra wanted to find out about the ways in which students travelled to school. She carried out a survey. Her frequency table looked like this:

Method of travel	Tally	Frequency
Walk	ⅢⅢ ⅢⅢ ⅢⅢ ⅢⅢ ⅢⅢ |||	28
Car	ⅢⅢ ⅢⅢ ||	12
Bus	ⅢⅢ ⅢⅢ ⅢⅢ ⅢⅢ |||	23
Bicycle	ⅢⅢ	5
Taxi	||	2

By adding together all the frequencies, you can see that 70 students took part in the survey. The frequencies also show you that more students travelled to school on foot than by any other method of transport.

EXAMPLE 2

Andrew wanted to find out the most likely outcome when two coins are tossed. He carried out an experiment by tossing two coins 50 times. His frequency table looked like this.

Number of heads	Tally	Frequency
0	ЖЖ ЖЖ II	12
1	ЖЖ ЖЖ ЖЖ ЖЖ ЖЖ II	27
2	ЖЖ ЖЖ I	11

From Andrew's table, you can see that a single head appeared the highest number of times.

Grouped data

Many surveys produce a lot of data that covers a wide range of values. In these cases, it is sensible to put the data into groups before attempting to compile a frequency table. These groups of data are called **classes** or **class intervals**.

Once the data has been grouped into classes, a **grouped frequency table** can be completed. The method is shown in Example 3.

EXAMPLE 3

These marks are for 36 students in a Year 10 mathematics examination.

31	49	52	79	40	29	66	71	73	19	51	47
81	67	40	52	20	84	65	73	60	54	60	59
25	89	21	91	84	77	18	37	55	41	72	38

a Construct a frequency table, using classes of 1–20, 21–40 and so on.

b What was the most common mark interval?

a Draw the grid of the table shown below and put in the headings.

Next, list the classes, in order, in the column headed 'Marks'.

Using tally marks, indicate each student's score against the class to which it belongs. For example, 81, 84, 89 and 91 belong to the class 81–100, giving five tally marks, as shown below.

Finally, count the tally marks for each class and enter the result in the column headed 'Frequency'. The table is now complete.

Marks	Tally	Frequency
1–20	III	3
21–40	ЖЖ III	8
41–60	ЖЖ ЖЖ I	11
61–80	ЖЖ IIII	9
81–100	ЖЖ	5

b From the grouped frequency table, you can see that the highest number of students obtained a mark in the 41–60 interval.

EXERCISE 6A

1 Philip kept a record of the number of goals scored by Burnley Rangers in the last 20 matches. These are his results:

0 1 1 0 2 0 1 3 2 1

0 1 0 3 2 1 0 2 1 1

a Draw a frequency table for his data.

b Which score had the highest frequency?

c How many goals were scored in total for the 20 matches?

2 Monica was doing a geography project on the weather. As part of her work, she kept a record of the daily midday temperatures in June.

Daily temperatures for June (°C)

15 18 19 21 23 22
20 23 22 24 24 25
26 26 20 19 19 20
18 18 19 17 16 15
16 16 17 18 20 22

a Copy and complete the grouped frequency table for her data.

Temperature (°C)	Tally	Frequency
14–16		
17–19		
20–22		
23–25		
26–28		

b In which interval do the most temperatures lie?

c Describe what the weather was probably like throughout the month.

3 For the following surveys, decide whether the data should be collected by:

    i sampling

    ii observation

    iii experiment.

> **HINTS AND TIPS**
>
> Look back to page 120 where each method of collecting data is discussed.

    a The number of people using a new superstore.

    b How people will vote in a forthcoming election.

    c The number of times a person scores double top in a game of darts.

    d Where people go for their summer holidays.

    e The frequency of a bus service on a particular route.

    f The number of times a drawing pin lands point up when dropped.

4 In a game of Hextuple, Mitesh used a six-sided dice. He decided to keep a record of his scores to see whether the dice was fair. His scores were:

    2 4 2 6 1 5 4 3 3 2 3 6 2 1 3

    5 4 3 4 2 1 6 5 1 6 4 1 2 3 4

    a Draw a frequency table for his data.

    b How many throws did Mitesh have during the game?

    c Do you think the dice was a fair one? Explain why.

5 The data shows the heights, in centimetres, of a sample of 32 Year 10 students.

    172   158   160   175   180   167   159   180

    167   166   178   184   179   156   165   166

    184   175   170   165   164   172   154   186

    167   172   170   181   157   165   152   164

    a Draw a grouped frequency table for the data, using class intervals 151–155, 156–160, …

    b In which interval do the most heights lie?

    c Does this agree with a survey of the students in your class?

6 Conduct some surveys of your own choice and draw frequency tables for your data.

Double dice

This is an activity for two or more players. Each player needs two six-sided dice.

Each player throws their two dice together 100 times. For each throw, add together the two scores to get a total score.

What is the lowest total score anyone can get? What is the highest total score?

Everyone keeps a record of their 100 throws in a frequency table.

Compare your frequency table with someone else's and comment on what you notice. For example: Which scores appear the most often? What about 'doubles'?

How might this information be useful in games that use two dice?

Repeat the activity in one or more of the following ways.

- For each throw, multiply the score on one dice by the score on the other.

- Use two four-sided dice (tetrahedral dice), adding or multiplying the scores.

- Use two different-sided dice, adding or multiplying the scores.

- Use three or more dice, adding and/or multiplying the scores.

6.2 Statistical diagrams

In this section you will learn how to:
- show collected data as pictograms

Key words
key
pictograms
symbol

Data collected from a survey can be presented in pictorial or diagrammatic form to help people to understand it more quickly. You see plenty of examples of this in newspapers and magazines and on TV, where every type of visual aid is used to communicate statistical information.

Pictograms

A **pictogram** is a frequency table in which frequency is represented by a repeated **symbol**. The symbol itself usually represents a number of items, as Example 5 shows. However, sometimes it is more sensible to let a symbol represent just a single unit, as in Example 4. The **key** tells you how many items are represented by a symbol.

EXAMPLE 4

The pictogram shows the number of telephone calls made by Mandy during a week.

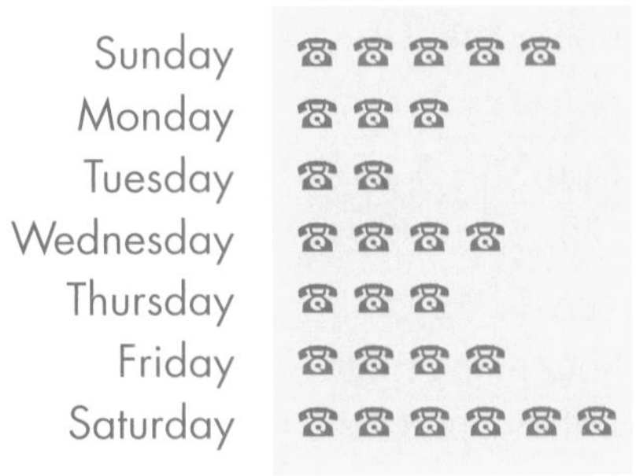

Sunday   ☎ ☎ ☎ ☎ ☎
Monday   ☎ ☎ ☎
Tuesday   ☎ ☎
Wednesday   ☎ ☎ ☎ ☎
Thursday   ☎ ☎ ☎
Friday   ☎ ☎ ☎ ☎
Saturday   ☎ ☎ ☎ ☎ ☎ ☎

Key ☎ represents 1 call

How many calls did Mandy make in the week?

From the pictogram, you can see that Mandy made a total of 27 telephone calls.

Although pictograms can have great visual impact (particularly as used in advertising) and are easy to understand, they have a serious drawback. Apart from a half, fractions of a symbol cannot usually be drawn accurately and so frequencies are often represented only approximately by symbols.

Example 5 highlights this difficulty.

EXAMPLE 5

The pictogram shows the number of Year 10 students who were late for school during a week.

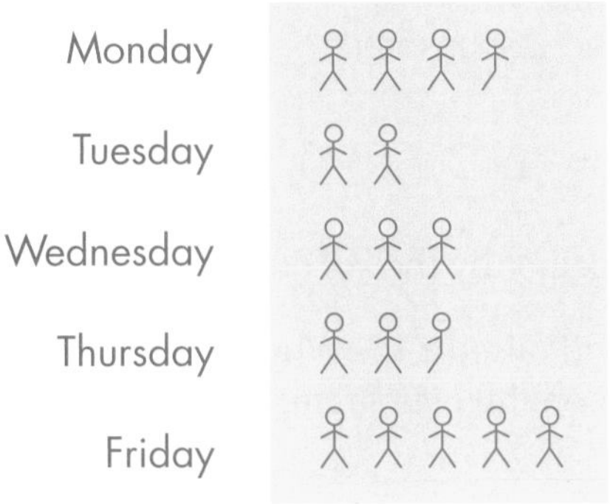

Key 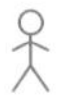 represents 5 pupils

How many pupils were late on:

a Monday

b Thursday?

Precisely how many students were late on Monday and Thursday respectively?

If you assume that each 'limb' of the symbol represents one student and its 'body' also represents one student, then the answers are:

a 19 students were late on Monday.

b 13 on Thursday.

EXERCISE 6B

1 The frequency table shows the numbers of cars parked in a supermarket's car park at various times of the day. Draw a pictogram to illustrate the data. Use a key of 1 symbol = 5 cars.

Time	9 am	11 am	1 pm	3 pm	5 pm
Frequency	40	50	70	65	45

2 Mr Weeks, a milkman, kept a record of how many pints of milk he delivered to ten flats on a particular morning. Draw a pictogram for the data. Use a key of 1 symbol = 1 pint.

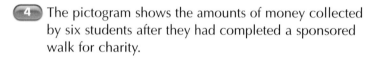

Flat 1	Flat 2	Flat 3	Flat 4	Flat 5	Flat 6	Flat 7	Flat 8	Flat 9	Flat 10
2	3	1	2	4	3	2	1	5	1

3 The pictogram, taken from a Suntours brochure, shows the average daily hours of sunshine for five months in Tenerife.

a Write down the average daily hours of sunshine for each month.

b Which month had the most sunshine?

c Give a reason why pictograms are useful in holiday brochures.

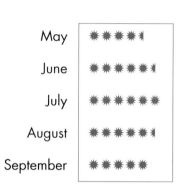

Key ✳ represents 2 hours

4 The pictogram shows the amounts of money collected by six students after they had completed a sponsored walk for charity.

a Who raised the most money?

b How much money was raised altogether by the six pupils?

c Robert also took part in the walk and raised £32. Why would it be difficult to include him on the pictogram?

Anthony £ £ £ £ £
Ben £ £ £ £ £ £
Emma £ £ £ £ £
Leanne £ £ £ £
Reena £ £ £ £ £ £
Simon £ £ £ £ £ £ £

Key £ represents £5

5 Draw pictograms of your own to show the following data.

a The number of hours for which you watched TV every evening last week.

b The magazines that students in your class read.

c The favourite colours of students in your class.

In this section you will learn how to:

- draw bar charts to represent statistical data

Key words

axis
bar chart
class interval
dual bar
    chart

A **bar chart** consists of a series of bars or blocks of the *same* width, drawn either vertically or horizontally from an **axis**.

The heights or lengths of the bars always represent *frequencies*.

Sometimes, the bars are separated by narrow gaps of equal width, which makes the chart easier to read.

EXAMPLE 6

The grouped frequency table below shows the marks of 24 students in a test. Draw a bar chart for the data.

Marks	1–10	11–20	21–30	31–40	41–50
Frequency	2	3	5	8	6

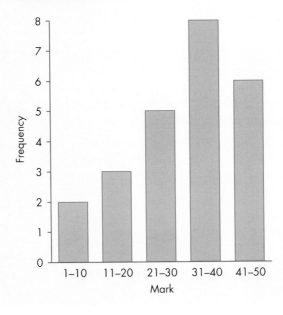

Note:

- Both axes are labelled.

- The **class intervals** are written under the middle of each bar.

- Bars are separated by equal spaces.

By using a **dual bar chart**, it is easy to compare two sets of related data, as Example 7 shows.

EXAMPLE 7

This dual bar chart shows the average daily maximum temperatures for England and Turkey over a five-month period.

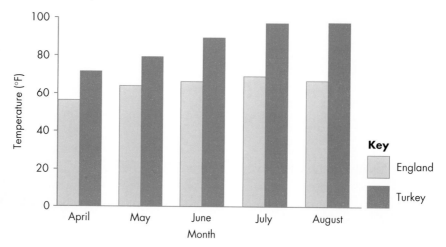

In which month was the difference between temperatures in England and Turkey the greatest?

The largest difference can be seen in August.

Note: You must always include a key to identify the two different sets of data.

EXERCISE 6C

1 For her survey on fitness, Maureen asked a sample of people, as they left a sports centre, which activity they had taken part in. She then drew a bar chart to show her data.

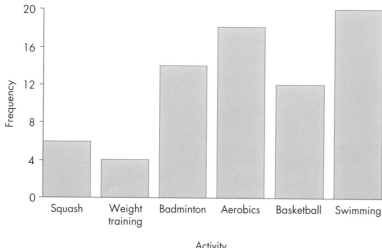

a Which was the most popular activity?

b How many people took part in Maureen's survey?

c Give a probable reason why fewer people took part in weight training than in any other activity.

d Is a sports centre a good place in which to do a survey on fitness? Explain why.

2 The frequency table below shows the levels achieved by 100 Year 9 students in their KS3 mathematics tests.

Level	3	4	5	6	7	8
Frequency	12	22	24	25	15	2

a Draw a suitable bar chart to illustrate the data.

b What fraction of the students achieved Level 6 or Level 7?

c State an advantage of drawing a bar chart rather than a pictogram for this data.

3 This table shows the number of points Richard and Derek were each awarded in eight rounds of a general knowledge quiz.

Round	1	2	3	4	5	6	7	8
Richard	7	8	7	6	8	6	9	4
Derek	6	7	6	9	6	8	5	6

a Draw a dual bar chart to illustrate the data.

b Comment on how well each of them did in the quiz.

4 Kay did a survey on the time it took students in her form to get to school on a particular morning. She wrote down their times to the nearest minute.

15   23   36   45   8   20   34   15   27   49

10   60   5   48   30   18   21   2   12   56

49   33   17   44   50   35   46   24   11   34

a Draw a grouped frequency table for Kay's data, using class intervals 1–10, 11–20, …

b Draw a bar chart to illustrate the data.

c Comment on how far from school the students live.

F

5 This table shows the number of accidents at a dangerous crossroads over a six-year period.

Year	2000	2001	2002	2003	2004	2005
No. of accidents	6	8	7	9	6	4

a Draw a pictogram for the data.

b Draw a bar chart for the data.

c Which diagram would you use if you were going to write to your local council to suggest that traffic lights should be installed at the crossroads? Explain why.

6 Conduct a survey to find the colours of cars that pass your school or your home.

a Draw pictograms and bar charts to illustrate your data.

b Compare your results with someone else's in your class and comment on anything you find about the colours of cars in your area.

7 Choose two daily newspapers (for example, the *Sun* and *The Times*) and take a fairly long article from each paper. Count the number of words in the first 50 sentences of each article.

a For each article, draw a grouped frequency table for the number of words in each of the first 50 sentences.

b Draw a dual bar chart for your data.

c Comment on your results.

6.4 Line graphs

In this section you will learn how to:
- draw a line graph to show trends in data

Key words
line graphs
trends

Line graphs are usually used in statistics to show how data changes over a period of time. One such use is to indicate **trends**, for example, whether the Earth's temperature is increasing as the concentration of carbon dioxide builds up in the atmosphere, or whether a firm's profit margin is falling year on year.

Line graphs are best drawn on graph paper.

EXAMPLE 8

This line graph shows the outside temperature at a weather station, taken at hourly intervals. Estimate the temperature at 3:30 pm.

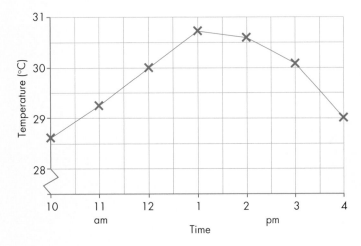

At 3.30 the temperature is approximately 29.5 °C.

Note: The temperature axis starts at 28 °C rather than 0 °C. This allows the use of a scale which makes it easy to plot the points and then to read the graph. The points are joined with lines so that the intermediate temperatures can be estimated for other times of the day.

EXAMPLE 9

This line graph shows the profit made each year by a company over a six-year period. Between which years did the company have the greatest increase in profits?

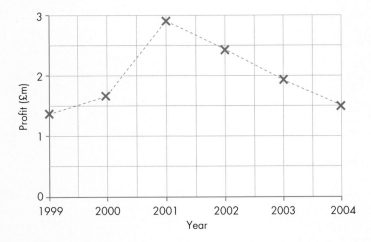

The greatest increase in profits was between 2000 and 2001.

For this graph, the values between the plotted points have no meaning because the profit of the company would have been calculated at the end of every year. In cases like this, the lines are often dashed. Although the trend appears to be that profits have fallen after 2001, it would not be sensible to predict what would happen after 2004.

EXERCISE 6D

1   This line graph shows the value of Spevadon shares on seven consecutive trading days.

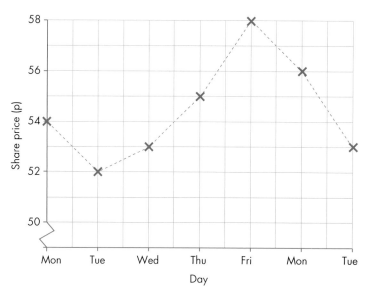

a   On which day did the share price have its lowest value and what was that value?

b   By how much did the share price rise from Wednesday to Thursday?

c   Which day had the greatest rise in the share price from the previous day?

d   Mr Hardy sold 500 shares on Friday. How much profit did he make if he originally bought the shares at 40p each?

2   The table shows the population of a town, rounded to the nearest thousand, after each census.

Year	1941	1951	1961	1971	1981	1991	2001
Population (1000s)	12	14	15	18	21	25	23

a   Draw a line graph for the data.

b   From your graph estimate the population in 1966.

c   Between which two consecutive censuses did the population increase the most?

d   Can you predict the population for 2011? Give a reason for your answer.

The table shows the estimated number of tourists worldwide.

Year	1965	1970	1975	1980	1985	1990	1995	2000
No. of tourists (millions)	60	100	150	220	280	290	320	340

a Draw a line graph for the data.

b From your graph estimate the number of tourists in 1977.

c Between which two consecutive years did world tourism increase the most?

d Explain the trend in world tourism. What reasons can you give to explain this trend?

4 The table shows the maximum and minimum daily temperatures for London over a week.

Day	Sunday	Monday	Tuesday	Wednesday	Thursday	Friday	Saturday
Maximum (°C)	12	14	16	15	16	14	10
Minimum (°C)	4	5	7	8	7	4	3

a Draw line graphs on the *same* axes to show the maximum and minimum temperatures.

b Find the smallest and greatest differences between the maximum and minimum temperatures.

Diagrams from the press

This is an activity for a group of two or more people. You will need a large selection of recent newspapers and magazines.

In a group, look through the newspapers and magazines.

Cut out any statistical diagrams and stick them on large sheets of coloured paper.

Underneath each diagram, explain what the diagram shows and how useful the diagram is in showing that information.

If any of the diagrams appears to be misleading, explain why.

You now have a lot of up-to-date statistics to display in your classroom.

Stem-and-leaf diagrams

In this section you will learn how to:

- draw and read information from an ordered stem-and-leaf diagram

Key words
discrete data
ordered data
raw data
unordered data

Raw data

If you were recording the ages of the first 20 people who line up at a bus stop in the morning, the **raw data** might look like this.

23, 13, 34, 44, 26, 12, 41, 31, 20, 18, 19, 31, 48, 32, 45, 14, 12, 27, 31, 19

This data is **unordered** and is difficult to read and analyse. When the data is **ordered**, it will look like this.

12, 12, 13, 14, 18, 19, 19, 20, 23, 26, 27, 31, 31, 31, 32, 34, 41, 44, 45, 48

This is easier to read and analyse.

Another method for displaying **discrete data** is a stem-and-leaf diagram. The tens digits will be the 'stem' and the units digits will be the 'leaves'.

Key 1 | 2 represents 12

1	2	2	3	4	8	9	9
2	0	3	6	7			
3	1	1	1	2	4		
4	1	4	5	8			

This is called an ordered stem-and-leaf diagram and gives a better idea of how the data is distributed.

A stem-and-leaf diagram should always have a key.

EXAMPLE 10

Put the following data into an ordered stem-and-leaf diagram.

45, 62, 58, 58, 61, 49, 61, 47, 52, 58, 48, 56, 65, 46, 54

a What is the largest value?

b What is the most common value?

c What is the difference between the largest and smallest values?

First decide on the stem and the leaf.

In this case, the tens digit will be the stem and the units digit will be the leaf.

Key 4 | 5 represents 45

4	5	6	7	8	9	
5	2	4	6	8	8	8
6	1	1	2	5		

a The largest value is 65.

b The most common value is 58 which occurs three times.

c The difference between the largest and the smallest is 65 − 45 = 20.

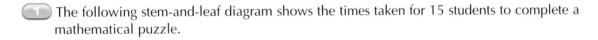

EXERCISE 6E

1 The following stem-and-leaf diagram shows the times taken for 15 students to complete a mathematical puzzle.

Key 1 | 7 represents 17 seconds

1	7	8	8	9		
2	2	2	2	5	6	9
3	3	4	5	5	8	

a What is the shortest time to complete the puzzle?

b What is the most common time to complete the puzzle?

c What is the difference between the longest time and the shortest time to complete the puzzle?

2 This stem-and-leaf diagram shows the marks for the boys and girls in form 7E in a maths test.

Key Boys: 2 | 4 means 42 marks

Girls: 3 | 5 means 35 marks

HINTS AND TIPS

Read the boys' marks from right to left.

Boys						Girls					
6	4	2	3	3	3	5	7	9			
9	9	6	2	4	4	2	2	3	8	8	8
7	6	6	6	5	5	1	1	5			

a What was the highest mark for the boys?

b What was the highest mark for the girls?

c What was the most common mark for the boys?

d What was the most common mark for the girls?

e Overall, who did better in the test, the boys or the girls? Give a reason for your answer.

3 The heights of 15 sunflowers were measured.

43 cm, 39 cm, 41 cm, 29 cm, 36 cm,

34 cm, 43 cm, 48 cm, 38 cm, 35 cm,

41 cm, 38 cm, 43 cm, 28 cm, 48 cm

a Show the results in an ordered stem-and-leaf diagram, using this key:

Key 4 | 3 represents 43 cm

b What was the largest height measured?

c What was the most common height measured?

d What is the difference between the largest and smallest heights measured?

4 A student records the number of text messages she receives each day for two weeks.

12, 18, 21, 9, 17, 23, 8, 2, 20, 13, 17, 22, 9, 9

a Show the results in an ordered stem-and-leaf diagram, using this key:

Key 1 | 2 represents 12 messages

b What was the largest number of text messages received in a day?

c What is the most common number of text messages received in a day?

Map colouring

What is the smallest number of colours needed to colour this map so that areas of the same colour do not touch? The blue border is one colour.

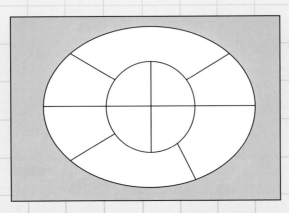

Missing £1

A father wants to share £17 between his three children so that one has $\frac{1}{2}$, one has $\frac{1}{3}$ and the other has $\frac{1}{9}$, but decides that this is not possible.

The youngest son, who is good at maths, had a clever idea. He borrowed £1 and added it to the £17 to get £18. He then split up the £18 as follows:

$\frac{1}{2}$ of £18 = £9

$\frac{1}{3}$ of £18 = £6

$\frac{1}{9}$ of £18 = £2

which add up to £17.

So, the son was able to give back the £1 he had borrowed. Can you explain this?

Going round in circles

Arrange all the other numbers from 1 to 9 so that each line of three numbers adds up to the same number.

Does the puzzle work if you put a different number in the middle circle?

1 The pictogram shows the number of packets of crisps sold by a shop on each of Monday, Tuesday and Wednesday.

Monday	☺ ☺ ☺ ☺ ☺ ☺ ☾
Tuesday	☺ ☺ ☺ ☺ ☺
Wednesday	☺ ☺
Thursday	
Friday	

Key ☺ = 4 packets

a Write down the number of packets sold on Tuesday.

16 packets were sold on Thursday.

6 packets were sold on Friday.

b Using this information copy and complete the pictogram.

Edexcel, Question 1, Paper 11A Foundation, January 2003

2 The pictogram below shows the number of football matches attended by four members of a family in one season.

 represents four matches

Name		Number of matches
Joy	⚽ ⚽ ⚽	
Joe	⚽ ◖	
John		20
James		28

a How many matches did Joy attend?

b Copy and complete the pictogram.

3 The bar chart shows the number of DVDs Beth, Terry and Abbas watched in one week.

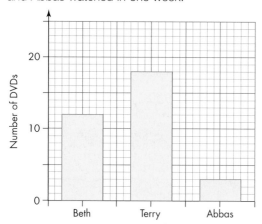

a How many DVDs did Beth watch?

b How many DVDs did Beth, Terry and Abbas watch altogether?

c How many more DVDs did Terry watch than Abbas?

4 The bar chart shows the number of packets of different flavoured crisps sold at a canteen one morning.

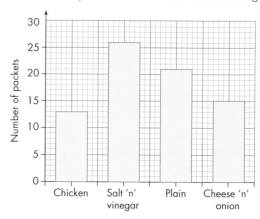

a How many packets of chicken-flavoured crisps were sold?

b Which was the most popular flavour?

c How many more packets of plain crisps than packets of cheese 'n' onion were sold?

d How many packets of crisps were sold altogether?

5 Martin asked his friends to choose, from a list, which Star Trek series they like best.

Their replies were:

Deep Space 9	Enterprise	Deep Space 9
Voyager	Deep Space 9	Voyager
Deep Space 9	Next Generation	Deep Space 9
Next Generation	Enterprise	Next Generation
Enterprise	Next Generation	Deep Space 9

a Copy and complete the tally and the frequency columns in the table below.

Star Trek series	Tally	Frequency
Deep Space 9		
Voyager		
Enterprise		
Next Generation		

b Draw a pictogram to show these results.

Use the symbol 𝗔 to represent two replies.

6 The table shows the average height in centimetres of boys and girls in a village school for six years.

a i The difference between the heights of the two sexes is calculated. Complete the last row to show these differences.

	2000	2001	2002	2003	2004	2005
Boys	112.7	112.2	113.1	113.5	113.0	113.5
Girls	111.4	111.0	111.2	111.5	111.8	112.1
Difference	1.3			2.0		1.4

ii Compare the heights of the boys with the heights of the girls. What do you notice?

b A bar chart to show the heights of the boys and girls is drawn.

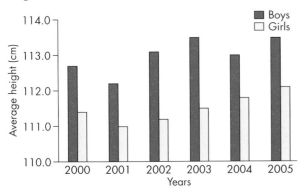

Explain why the bar chart is misleading.

7 A shop has a sale. The bar chart shows some information about the sale.

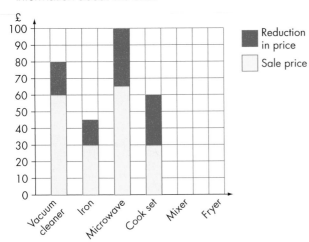

The normal price of a vacuum cleaner is £80.
The sale price of a vacuum cleaner is £60.

a Write the sale price of a vacuum clearner as a fraction of its normal price. Give your answer in its simplest form.

b Find the reduction in the price of the iron.

c Which two items have the same sale price?

Edexcel, Question 9, Paper 2 Foundation, June 2004

8 A coach company asks some of its passengers if their service has improved. Here are the results.

Reply	Percentage
Improved	35%
Same	24%
Not as good	29%
Don't know	12%

Copy and complete the bar chart to show these results.

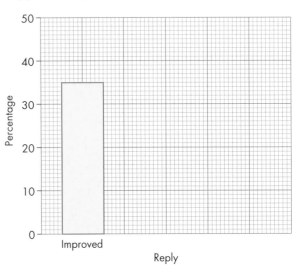

9 The diagram shows the number of babies born in hospital or at home on one weekend in five towns.

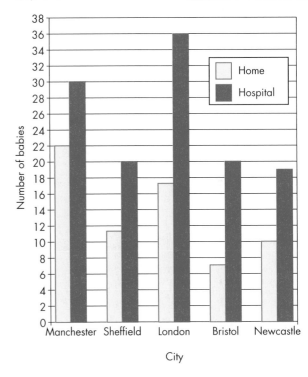

a Which two cities had the same number of babies born in hospital?

b Work out the difference between the number of babies born at home and in hospital for:

i Manchester

ii Newcastle

c Lisa says the number of babies born in hospital is double those born at home.

Give an example to show that Lisa is wrong.

Give a reason for your choice.

10 Anil counted the number of letters in each of 30 sentences in a newspaper. Anil showed his results in a stem and leaf diagram.

Key 4 | 1 stands for 41 letters

```
0 | 8  8  9
1 | 1  2  3  4  4  8  9
2 | 0  3  5  5  7  7  8
3 | 2  2  3  3  6  6  8  8
4 | 1  2  3  3  5
```

a Write down the number of sentences with 36 letters.

b Work out the range.

c Work out the median.

Edexcel, Question 7, Paper 4 Foundation, November 2004

11 The graph shows the average annual water rates in a town.

a By how much did the average annual water rates increase from 2003 to 2005?

b Between which two years was there the largest annual increase in water rates?

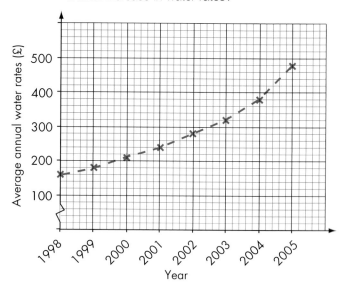

12 The height of a sunflower is measured at the end of each week.

The graph shows the height of the sunflower. At the end of week 5 the height of the sunflower was 100 cm.

a At the end of week 6 the height of the sunflower was 106 cm. At the end of week 10 the height of the sunflower was 118 cm.

   i Copy the graph and plot these points on the graph.

   ii Complete the graph with straight lines.

b Use your graph to estimate the height of the sunflower in centimetres at the end of week 9.

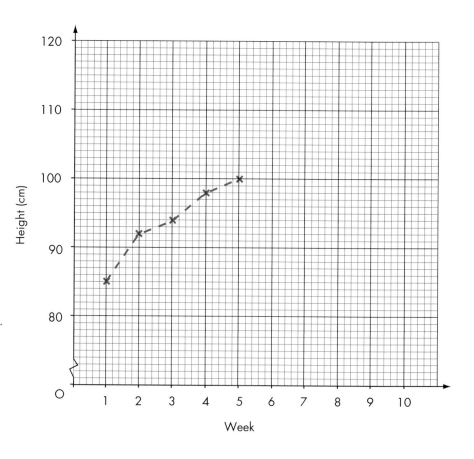

WORKED EXAM QUESTION

The number of cars stolen in 20 cities in one weekend is recorded.

8 20 1 10 6 22 4 3 17 3

13 14 9 16 23 17 10 19 22 19

Draw a stem-and-leaf diagram to represent these data and complete the key.

Key 1 | represents ....

0 ....

1 ....

2 ....

Solution

Key 1 | 5 represents 15 ———————

> You can see from the basic diagram that the stem is the tens digits and the leaves are the units digits. Complete the key, using any value.

0	1	3	3	4	6	8	9
1	0	0	3	4	6	7	7	9	9
2	0	2	2	3

> Now complete the stem-and-leaf diagram keeping the data in order.

GRADE YOURSELF

G Able to draw and read information from bar charts, dual bar charts and pictograms

F Able to work out the total frequency from a frequency table and compare data in bar charts

E Able to read information from a stem-and-leaf diagram

D Able to draw an ordered stem-and-leaf diagram

What you should know now

- How to draw frequency tables for grouped and ungrouped data
- How to draw and interpret pictograms, bar charts and line graphs
- How to read information from statistical diagrams, including stem-and-leaf diagrams

Basic algebra

1 The language of algebra

2 Simplifying expressions

3 Expanding brackets

4 Factorisation

5 Quadratic expansion

6 Substitution

This chapter will show you ...

- how to use letters to represent numbers
- how to form simple algebraic expressions
- how to simplify such expressions by collecting like terms
- how to factorise expressions
- how to express simple rules in algebraic form
- how to substitute numbers into expressions and formulae
- how to expand the product of two linear brackets

Visual overview

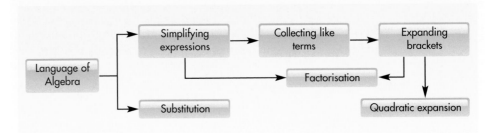

What you should already know

- The **BODMAS** rule, which gives the order in which you must do the operations of arithmetic when they occur together

Quick check

1 Write the answer to each expression.

  a $(5 - 1) \times 2$

  b $5 - (1 \times 2)$

2 Work out $(7 - 5) \times (5 + 4 - 2)$.

3 a Put brackets in the calculation to make the answer 40.

    $2 + 3 + 5 \times 4$

  b Put brackets in the calculation to make the answer 34.

    $2 + 3 + 5 \times 4$

The language of algebra

In this section you will learn how to:

- use letters, numbers and mathematical symbols to write algebraic expressions and formulae

Key words

expression
formula
symbol

Algebra is based on the idea that if something works with numbers, it will work with letters. The main difference is that when you work only with numbers, the answer is also a number. When you work with letters, you get an **expression** as the answer.

Algebra follows the same rules as arithmetic, and uses the same **symbols** ($+$, $-$, $\times$ and $\div$). Below are seven important algebraic rules.

- Write '4 more than x' as $4 + x$ or $x + 4$.

- Write '6 less than p' or 'p minus 6' as $p - 6$.

- Write '4 times y' as $4 \times y$ or $y \times 4$ or $4y$. The last one of these is the neatest way to write it.

- Write 'b divided by 2' as $b \div 2$ or $\dfrac{b}{2}$.

- When a number and a letter or a letter and a letter appear together, there is a hidden multiplication sign between them. So, $7x$ means $7 \times x$ and ab means $a \times b$.

- Always write '$1 \times x$' as x.

- Write 't times t' as $t \times t$ or t^2.

EXAMPLE 1

What is the area of each of these rectangles?

a 4 cm by 6 cm **b** 4 cm by w cm **c** l cm by w cm

You have already met the rule for working out the area of a rectangle:

area = length $\times$ width

So, the area of rectangle **a** is $4 \times 6 = 24$ cm^2

The area of rectangle **b** is $4 \times w = 4w$ cm^2

The area of rectangle **c** is $l \times w = lw$ cm^2

Now, if A represents the area of rectangle **c**:

$A = lw$

This is an example of a rule expressed algebraically.

EXAMPLE 2

What is the perimeter of each of these rectangles?

a 6 cm by 4 cm   **b** 4 cm by w cm   **c** l cm by w cm

The rule for working out the perimeter of a rectangle is:

perimeter = twice the longer side + twice the shorter side

So, the perimeter of rectangle **a** is $2 \times 6 + 2 \times 4 = 20$ cm

The perimeter of rectangle **b** is $2 \times 4 + 2 \times w = 8 + 2w$ cm

The perimeter of rectangle **c** is $2 \times l + 2 \times w = 2l + 2w$ cm

Now, let P represent the perimeter of rectangle **c**, so:

$$P = 2l + 2w$$

which is another example of a rule expressed algebraically.

Expressions such as $A = lw$ and $P = 2l + 2w$ are called **formulae** (the plural of formula).

As the two examples above show, a formula states the connection between two or more quantities, each of which is represented by a different letter.

In a formula, the letters are replaced by numbers when a calculation has to be made. This is called *substitution* and is explained on page 159.

EXERCISE 7A

1 Write down the algebraic expression for:

a 2 more than x **b** 6 less than x

c k more than x **d** x minus t

e x added to 3   **f** d added to m

g y taken away from b **h** p added to t added to w

i 8 multiplied by x **j** h multiplied by j

k x divided by 4   **l** 2 divided by x

m y divided by t **n** w multiplied by t

o a multiplied by a **p** g multiplied by itself

2 Here are four squares.

  i   **ii**   **iii**   **iv**

a Work out the area and perimeter of each square.

b Copy and complete these rules.

  i The perimeter, P, of a square of side s centimetres is $P = \ldots\ldots$

  ii The area, A, of a square of side s centimetres is $A = \ldots\ldots$

3 Asha, Bernice and Charu are three sisters. Bernice is *x* years old. Asha is three years older than Bernice. Charu is four years younger than Bernice.

    a How old is Asha?

    b How old is Charu?

4 An approximation method of converting from degrees Celsius to degrees Fahrenheit is given by this rule:

    Multiply by 2 and add 30.

Using *C* to stand for degrees Celsius and *F* to stand for degrees Fahrenheit, complete this formula.

    F = ...

5 Cows have four legs. Which of these formulae connects the number of legs (*L*) and the number of cows (*C*)?

    a $C = 4L$ **b** $L = C + 4$ **c** $L = 4C$ **d** $L + C = 4$

6 There are 3 feet in a yard. The rule $F = 3Y$ connects the number of feet (*F*) and the number of yards (*Y*). Write down rules, using the letters shown, to connect:

    a the number of centimetres (*C*) in metres (*M*)

    b the number of inches (*N*) in feet (*F*)

    c the number of wheels (*W*) on cars (*C*)

    d the number of heads (*H*) on people (*P*).

> **HINTS AND TIPS**
>
> Check your formula with a numerical example. In 4 yards there are 12 feet, so, if $F = 3Y$ is correct, then $12 = 3 \times 4$, which is true.

7 **a** Anne has three bags of marbles. Each bag contains *n* marbles. How many marbles does she have altogether?

    b Beryl gives her another three marbles. How many marbles does Anne have now?

    c Anne puts one of her new marbles in each bag. How many marbles are there now in each bag?

    d Anne takes two marbles out of each bag. How many marbles are there now in each bag?

8 Simon has *n* cubes.

    • Rob has twice as many cubes as Simon.

    • Tom has two more than Simon.

    • Vic has three fewer than Simon.

    • Wes has three more than Rob.

How many cubes does each person have?

> **HINTS AND TIPS**
>
> Remember that you do not have to write down a multiplication sign between numbers and letters, or letters and letters.

9 **a** John has been drawing squares and writing down the area and the perimeter of each of them. He has drawn three squares. Finish his work by writing down the missing areas and perimeters.

$P = 4n$
$A = n^2$

$P = ...$
$A = 4n^2$

$P = 12n$
$A = ...$

b Write down the area and the perimeter of this partly covered square.

$6n$

10 **a** I go shopping with £10 and spend £6. How much do I have left?

b I go shopping with £10 and spend £x. How much do I have left?

c I go shopping with £y and spend £x. How much do I have left?

d I go shopping with £$3x$ and spend £x. How much do I have left?

11 Give the total cost of:

a 5 pens at 15p each

b x pens at 15p each

c 4 pens at Ap each

d y pens at Ap each.

12 A boy went shopping with £A. He spent £B. How much has he got left?

13 Five ties cost £A. What is the cost of one tie?

14 My dad is 72 and I am T years old. How old shall we each be in x years' time?

15 I am twice as old as my son. I am T years old.

a How old is my son?

b How old will my son be in four years' time?

c How old was I x years ago?

16 What is the total perimeter of each of these figures?

a

$2x$

Square

b

$4m$

Equilateral triangle

c

$3t$

Regular hexagon

17 Write down the number of marbles each pupil ends up with.

Pupil	Action	Marbles
Andrea	Start with three bags each containing n marbles and give away one marble from each bag	
Bert	Start with three bags each containing n marbles and give away one marble from one bag	
Colin	Start with three bags each containing n marbles and give away two marbles from each bag	
Davina	Start with three bags each containing n marbles and give away n marbles from each bag	
Emma	Start with three bags each containing n marbles and give away n marbles from one bag	
Florinda	Start with three bags each containing n marbles and give away m marbles from each bag	

7.2 Simplifying expressions

In this section you will learn how to:

- simplify algebraic expressions by multiplying terms
- simplify algebraic expressions by collecting like terms

Key words

like terms
simplify

Simplifying an algebraic expression means making it neater and, usually, shorter by combining its terms where possible.

Multiplying expressions

When you multiply algebraic expressions, first you combine the numbers, then the letters.

EXAMPLE 3

Simplify:

a $2 \times t$ **b** $m \times t$ **c** $2t \times 5$ **d** $3y \times 2m$

The convention is to write the number first then the letters, but if there is no number just put the letters in alphabetical order.

a $2 \times t = 2t$ **b** $m \times t = mt$ **c** $2t \times 5 = 10t$ **d** $3y \times 2m = 6my$

In an examination you will not be penalised for writing $2ba$ instead of $2ab$, but you will be penalised if you write $ab2$ as this can be confused with powers, so *always* write the number first.

EXAMPLE 4

Simplify:

a $t \times t$ **b** $3t \times 2t$ **c** $3t^2 \times 4t$ **d** $2t^3 \times 4t^2$

Combine the same letters together using powers. The indices are added together.

a $t \times t = t^2$ (Remember: $t = t^1$) **b** $3t \times 2t = 6t^2$

c $3t^2 \times 4t = 12t^3$ **d** $2t^3 \times 4t^2 = 8t^5$

EXERCISE 7B

Simplify the following expressions:

1 $2 \times 3t$	**2** $3 \times 4y$	**3** $5y \times 3$
4 $2w \times 4$	**5** $3t \times t$	**6** $5b \times b$
7 $2w \times w$	**8** $5y \times 3y$	**9** $4p \times 2p$
10 $3t \times 2t$	**11** $4m \times 3m$	**12** $5t \times 3t$

HINTS AND TIPS

Remember to multiply numbers and add indices.

13 $m \times 2t$	**14** $3y \times w$	**15** $5t \times q$	**16** $n \times 6m$
17 $3t \times 2q$	**18** $4f \times 3g$	**19** $5h \times 2k$	**20** $3p \times 7r$
21 $y^2 \times y$	**22** $t \times t^2$	**23** $3m \times m^2$	**24** $4t^2 \times t$
25 $3n \times 2n^2$	**26** $4r^2 \times 5r$	**27** $t^2 \times t^2$	**28** $h^3 \times h^2$
29 $3n^2 \times 4n^3$	**30** $5t^3 \times 2t^4$	**31** $3a^4 \times 2a^3$	**32** $k^5 \times 4k^2$
33 $-t^2 \times -t$	**34** $-2y \times -3y$	**35** $-4d^2 \times -3d$	**36** $-3p^4 \times -5p^2$
37 $3mp \times p$	**38** $2ty \times 3t$	**39** $3mn \times 2m$	**40** $4mp \times 2mp$

Collecting like terms

Collecting **like terms** generally involves two steps.

- Collect like terms into groups.

- Then combine the like terms in each group.

Like terms are those that are multiples of the same letter or of the same combination of letters. For example, a, $3a$, $9a$, $\frac{1}{4}a$ and $-5a$ are all like terms.

So are $2xy$, $7xy$ and $-5xy$, and so are $6x^2$, x^2 and $-3x^2$.

Only like terms can be added or subtracted to simplify an expression. For example,

$a + 3a + 9a - 5a$ simplifies to $8a$

$2xy + 7xy - 5xy$ simplifies to $4xy$

and

$6x^2 + x^2 - 3x^2$ simplifies to $4x^2$

But an expression such as $4p + 8t + 5x - 9$ cannot be made simpler, because $4p$, $8t$, $5x$ and -9 are *unlike terms*, which *cannot* be combined.

EXAMPLE 5

Simplify $7x^2 + 3y - 6z + 2x^2 + 3z - y + w + 9$

Write out the expression: $7x^2 + 3y - 6z + 2x^2 + 3z - y + w + 9$

Then collect like terms: $\boxed{7x^2 + 2x^2}\ \boxed{+3y - y}\ \boxed{-6z + 3z}\ \boxed{+ w}\ \boxed{+ 9}$

Then combine them: $9x^2 \quad + \quad 2y \quad - \quad 3z \quad + w \ + 9$

So, the expression in its simplest form is:

$9x^2 + 2y - 3z + w + 9$

EXERCISE 7C

1 Joseph is given £t, John has £3 more than Joseph, Joy has £$2t$.

  a How much more money has Joy than Joseph?

  b How much do the three of them have altogether?

2 Write down an expression for the perimeter of each of these shapes.

  a

  b

  c
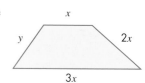

3 Write each of these expressions in a shorter form.

  a $a + a + a + a + a$ **b** $c + c + c + c + c + c$

  c $4e + 5e$ **d** $f + 2f + 3f$

  e $g + g + g + g - g$ **f** $3i + 2i - i$

  g $5j + j - 2j$ **h** $9q - 3q - 3q$

  i $3r - 3r$ **j** $2w + 4w - 7w$

  k $5x^2 + 6x^2 - 7x^2 + 2x^2$ **l** $8y^2 + 5y^2 - 7y^2 - y^2$ **m** $2z^2 - 2z^2 + 3z^2 - 3z^2$

> **HINTS AND TIPS**
>
> The term a has a coefficient of 1.
> i.e. $a = 1a$, but you do not need to write the 1.

4 Simplify each of the following expressions.

a $3x + 4x$ **b** $4y + 2y$

c $5t - 2t$ **d** $t - 4t$

e $-2x - 3x$ **f** $-k - 4k$

g $m^2 + 2m^2 - m^2$ **h** $2y^2 + 3y^2 - 5y^2$

i $-f^2 + 4f^2 - 2f^2$

> **HINTS AND TIPS**
>
> Remember that only **like** terms can be added or subtracted.
> If all the terms cancel out, just write 0 rather than $0x^2$ for example.

5 Simplify each of the following expressions.

a $5x + 8 + 2x - 3$ **b** $7 - 2x - 1 + 7x$

c $4p + 2t + p - 2t$ **d** $8 + x + 4x - 2$

e $3 + 2t + p - t + 2 + 4p$ **f** $5w - 2k - 2w - 3k + 5w$

g $a + b + c + d - a - b - d$ **h** $9k - y - 5y - k + 10$

6 Write each of these in a shorter form. (Be careful – two of them will not simplify.)

a $c + d + d + d + c$ **b** $2d + 2e + 3d$

c $f + 3g + 4h$ **d** $3i + 2k - i + k$

e $4k + 5p - 2k + 4p$ **f** $3k + 2m + 5p$

g $4m - 5n + 3m - 2n$ **h** $n + 3p - 6p + 5n$

i $5u - 4v + u + v$ **j** $2v - 5w + 5w$

k $2w + 4y - 7y$ **l** $5x^2 + 6x^2 - 7y + 2y$

m $8y^2 + 5z - 7z - 9y^2$ **n** $2z^2 - 2x^2 + 3x^2 - 3z^2$

7 Find the perimeter of each of these shapes, giving it in its simplest form.

a

b

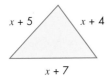

c

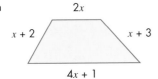

Expanding brackets

In this section you will learn how to:
- expand brackets such as $2(x - 3)$
- expand and simplify brackets

Key words

expand
expand and
   simplify
multiply out
simplify

Expanding

In mathematics, the term '**expand**' usually means '**multiply out**'. For example, expressions such as $3(y + 2)$ and $4y^2(2y + 3)$ can be expanded by multiplying them out.

Remember that there is an invisible multiplication sign between the outside number and the opening bracket. So $3(y + 2)$ is really $3 \times (y + 2)$, and $4y^2(2y + 3)$ is really $4y^2 \times (2y + 3)$.

You expand by multiplying *everything inside* the brackets by what is outside the brackets.

EXAMPLE 6

Expand $3(y + 2)$.

$3(y + 2) = 3 \times (y + 2) = 3 \times y + 3 \times 2 = 3y + 6$

EXAMPLE 7

Expand $4y^2(2y + 3)$.

$4y^2(2y + 3) = 4y^2 \times (2y + 3) = 4y^2 \times 2y + 4y^2 \times 3 = 8y^3 + 12y^2$

Look at these next examples of expansion, which show clearly how each term inside the brackets has been multiplied by the term outside the brackets.

$2(m + 3) = 2m + 6$

$3(2t + 5) = 6t + 15$

$m(p + 7) = mp + 7m$

$x(x - 6) = x^2 - 6x$

$4t(t + 2) = 4t^2 + 8t$

$y(y^2 - 4x) = y^3 - 4xy$

$3x^2(4x + 5) = 12x^3 + 15x^2$

$-3(2 + 3x) = -6 - 9x$

$-2x(3 - 4x) = -6x + 8x^2$

$3t(2 + 5t - p) = 6t + 15t^2 - 3pt$

Expand these expressions.

1 $2(3 + m)$ **2** $5(2 + l)$ **3** $3(4 - y)$ **4** $4(5 + 2k)$

5 $3(2 - 4f)$ **6** $2(5 - 3w)$ **7** $3(g + h)$ **8** $5(2k + 3m)$

9 $4(3d - 2n)$ **10** $t(t + 3)$ **11** $m(m + 5)$ **12** $k(k - 3)$

13 $g(3g + 2)$ **14** $y(5y - 1)$ **15** $p(5 - 3p)$ **16** $3m(m + 4)$

17 $4t(t - 1)$ **18** $2k(4 - k)$ **19** $4g(2g + 5)$ **20** $5h(3h - 2)$

21 $3t(5 - 4t)$ **22** $3d(2d + 4e)$ **23** $2y(3y + 4k)$ **24** $5m(3m - 2p)$

25 $y(y^2 + 5)$ **26** $h(h^3 + 7)$ **27** $k(k^2 - 5)$ **28** $3t(t^2 + 4)$

29 $4h(h^3 - 1)$ **30** $5g(g^3 - 2)$ **31** $4m(3m^2 + m)$ **32** $5k(2k^3 + k^2)$

33 $3d(5d^2 - d^3)$ **34** $3w(2w^2 + t)$ **35** $5a(3a^2 - 2b)$ **36** $3p(4p^3 - 5m)$

37 $m^2(5 + 4m)$ **38** $t^3(t + 2t)$ **39** $g^2(5t - 4g^2)$ **40** $3t^2(5t + m)$

41 $4h^2(3h + 2g)$ **42** $2m^2(4m + m^2)$

Expand and simplify

This usually means that you need to expand more than one set of brackets and **simplify** the resulting expressions.

You will often be asked to **expand and simplify** expressions.

EXAMPLE 8

Expand and simplify $3(4 + m) + 2(5 + 2m)$.

$$3(4 + m) + 2(5 + 2m) = 12 + 3m + 10 + 4m = 22 + 7m$$

EXAMPLE 9

Expand and simplify $3t(5t + 4) - 2t(3t - 5)$.

$$3t(5t + 4) - 2t(3t - 5) = 15t^2 + 12t - 6t^2 + 10t = 9t^2 + 22t$$

EXAMPLE 10

Expand and simplify $4a(2b - 3f) - 3b(a + 2f)$.

$$4a(2b - 3f) - 3b(a + 2f) = 8ab - 12af - 3ab - 6bf = 5ab - 12af - 6bf$$

EXERCISE 7E

1 Simplify these expressions.

a $4t + 3t$ **b** $5m + 4m$ **c** $2y + y$ **d** $3d + 2d + 4d$

e $5e - 2e$ **f** $7g - 5g$ **g** $4p - p$ **h** $3t - t$

i $2t^2 + 3t^2$ **j** $6y^2 - 2y^2$ **k** $3ab + 2ab$ **l** $7a^2d - 4a^2d$

2 Expand and simplify these expressions.

a $3(4 + t) + 2(5 + t)$ **b** $5(3 + 2k) + 3(2 + 3k)$

c $4(1 + 3m) + 2(3 + 2m)$ **d** $2(5 + 4y) + 3(2 + 3y)$

e $4(3 + 2f) + 2(5 - 3f)$ **f** $5(1 + 3g) + 3(3 - 4g)$

g $3(2 + 5t) + 4(1 - t)$ **h** $4(3 + 3w) + 2(5 - 4w)$

> **HINTS AND TIPS**
>
> Expand the expression before trying to collect like terms. If you try to expand and collect at the same time you will probably make a mistake.

3 Expand and simplify these expressions.

a $4(3 + 2h) - 2(5 + 3h)$ **b** $5(3g + 4) - 3(2g + 5)$

c $3(4y + 5) - 2(3y + 2)$ **d** $3(5t + 2) - 2(4t + 5)$

e $5(5k + 2) - 2(4k - 3)$ **f** $4(4e + 3) - 2(5e - 4)$

g $3(5m - 2) - 2(4m - 5)$ **h** $2(6t - 1) - 3(3t - 4)$

4 Expand and simplify these expressions.

a $m(4 + p) + p(3 + m)$ **b** $k(3 + 2h) + h(4 + 3k)$

c $t(2 + 3n) + n(3 + 4t)$ **d** $p(2q + 3) + q(4p + 7)$

e $3h(2 + 3j) + 2j(2h + 3)$ **f** $2y(3t + 4) + 3t(2 + 5y)$

g $4r(3 + 4p) + 3p(8 - r)$ **h** $5k(3m + 4) - 2m(3 - 2k)$

> **HINTS AND TIPS**
>
> Be careful with minus signs. They are causes of the most common errors students make in examinations. Remember $-2 \times -4 = 8$ but $-2 \times 5 = -10$. You will learn more about multiplying and dividing with negative numbers in Chapter 8.

5 Expand and simplify these expressions.

a $t(3t + 4) + 3t(3 + 2t)$ **b** $2y(3 + 4y) + y(5y - 1)$

c $4w(2w + 3) + 3w(2 - w)$ **d** $5p(3p + 4) - 2p(3 - 4p)$

e $3m(2m - 1) + 2m(5 - m)$ **f** $6d(4 - 2d) + d(3d - 2)$

g $4e(3e - 5) - 2e(e - 7)$ **h** $3k(2k + p) - 2k(3p - 4k)$

6 Expand and simplify these expressions.

a $4a(2b + 3c) + 3b(3a + 2c)$ **b** $3y(4w + 2t) + 2w(3y - 4t)$

c $2g(3h - k) + 5h(2g - 2k)$ **d** $3h(2t - p) + 4t(h - 3p)$

e $a(3b - 2c) - 2b(a - 3c)$ **f** $4p(3q - 2w) - 2w(p - q)$

g $5m(2n - 3p) - 2n(3p - 2m)$ **h** $2r(3r + r^2) - 3r^2(4 - 2r)$

Factorisation

In this section you will learn how to:
- 'reverse' the process of expanding brackets by taking out a common factor from each term in an expression

Key words
factor
factorisation

Factorisation is the opposite of expansion. It puts an expression back into the brackets it may have come from.

To factorise an expression, look for the common **factors** in every term of the expression. Follow through the examples below to see how this works.

EXAMPLE 11

Factorise each expression. **a** $6t + 9m$ **b** $6my + 4py$
     c $8kp + 4k - 12km$ **d** $8kp + 4kt - 12km$

a The common factor is 3, so $6t + 9m = 3(2t + 3m)$

b The common factor is 2y, so $6my + 4py = 2y(3m + 2p)$

c The common factor is 4k, so $8kp + 4k - 12km = 4k(2p + 1 - 3m)$

d The common factor is 4k, so $8kp + 4kt - 12km = 4k(2p + t - 3m)$

Notice that if you multiply out each answer you will get the expressions you started with.

This diagram may help you to see the difference and the connection between expansion and factorisation.

Note: When the whole term is the common factor, as in part **c**, then you are left with 1, not 0, inside the brackets.

Expanding

$3(2t + 3m) = 6t + 9m$

Factorising

EXERCISE 7F

Factorise the following expressions.

1 $6m + 12t$ **2** $9t + 3p$ **3** $8m + 12k$

4 $4r + 8t$ **5** $mn + 3m$ **6** $5g^2 + 3g$

7 $4w - 6t$ **8** $8p - 6k$ **9** $16h - 10k$

10 $2mp + 2mk$ **11** $4bc + 2bk$ **12** $6ab + 4ac$

13 $3y^2 + 2y$ **14** $4t^2 - 3t$ **15** $4d^2 - 2d$ **16** $3m^2 - 3mp$

> **HINTS AND TIPS**
>
> First look for a common factor of the numbers and then look for common factors of the letters.

D

17 $6p^2 + 9pt$

18 $8pt + 6mp$

19 $8ab - 4bc$

20 $12a^2 - 8ab$

21 $9mt - 6pt$

22 $16at^2 + 12at$

23 $5b^2c - 10bc$

24 $8abc + 6bed$

25 $4a^2 + 6a + 8$

26 $6ab + 9bc + 3bd$

27 $5t^2 + 4t + at$

28 $6mt^2 - 3mt + 9m^2t$

29 $8ab^2 + 2ab - 4a^2b$

30 $10pt^2 + 15pt + 5p^2t$

Factorise the following expressions where possible. List those that cannot be factorised.

31 $7m - 6t$

32 $5m + 2mp$

33 $t^2 - 7t$

34 $8pt + 5ab$

35 $4m^2 - 6mp$

36 $a^2 + b$

37 $4a^2 - 5ab$

38 $3ab + 4cd$

39 $5ab - 3b^2c$

7.5 Quadratic expansion

In this section you will learn how to:

- expand the product of two linear expressions to obtain a quadratic expression

Key words
quadratic expansion
quadratic expression

A **quadratic expression** is one in which the highest power of any of its terms is 2. For example:

$$y^2 \qquad 3t^2 + 5t \qquad 5m^2 + 3m + 8$$

are quadratic expressions.

An expression such as $(3y + 2)(4y - 5)$ can be expanded to give a quadratic expression. Multiplying out pairs of brackets in this way is usually called **quadratic expansion**.

The rule for expanding expressions such as $(t + 5)(3t - 4)$ is similar to that for expanding single brackets: multiply everything in one pair of brackets by everything in the other pair of brackets.

Follow through the four examples below to see how brackets can be expanded. Notice how to split up the terms in the first pair of brackets and make each of these terms multiply everything in the second pair of brackets. Then simplify the outcome.

EXAMPLE 12

Expand $(x + 3)(x + 4)$.

$$
\begin{aligned}
(x + 3)(x + 4) &= x(x + 4) + 3(x + 4) \\
&= x^2 + 4x + 3x + 12 \\
&= x^2 + 7x + 12
\end{aligned}
$$

EXAMPLE 13

Expand $(t + 5)(t - 2)$.

$$
\begin{aligned}
(t + 5)(t - 2) &= t(t - 2) + 5(t - 2) \\
&= t^2 - 2t + 5t - 10 \\
&= t^2 + 3t - 10
\end{aligned}
$$

EXAMPLE 14

Expand $(m - 3)(m + 1)$.

$$
\begin{aligned}
(m - 3)(m + 1) &= m(m + 1) - 3(m + 1) \\
&= m^2 + m - 3m - 3 \\
&= m^2 - 2m - 3
\end{aligned}
$$

EXAMPLE 15

Expand $(k - 3)^2$.

$$
\begin{aligned}
(k - 3)^2 &= (k - 3)(k - 3) = k(k - 3) - 3(k - 3) \\
&= k^2 - 3k - 3k + 9 \\
&= k^2 - 6k + 9
\end{aligned}
$$

Warning: Be careful with the signs! This is the main reason that marks are lost in examination questions involving the expansion of brackets.

HINTS AND TIPS

You can also use FOIL. FOIL stands for First, Outer, Inner and Last terms.

$(t + 5)(t - 2)$

F gives t^2
O gives $-2t$
I gives $5t$
L gives -10

$= t^2 - 2t + 5t - 10$
$= t^2 + 3t - 10$

HINTS AND TIPS

You can also use the box method.

	k	-3
k	k^2	$-3k$
-3	$-3k$	$+9$

$= (k - 3)(k - 3)$
$= k^2 - 3k - 3k + 9$
$= k^2 - 6k + 9$

EXERCISE 7G

Expand the following expressions.

1 $(x + 3)(x + 2)$ **2** $(t + 4)(t + 3)$ **3** $(w + 1)(w + 3)$ **4** $(m + 5)(m + 1)$

5 $(k + 3)(k + 5)$ **6** $(a + 4)(a + 1)$ **7** $(x + 4)(x - 2)$ **8** $(t + 5)(t - 3)$

9 $(w + 3)(w - 1)$ **10** $(f + 2)(f - 3)$ **11** $(g + 1)(g - 4)$ **12** $(y + 4)(y - 3)$

13 $(x - 3)(x + 4)$ **14** $(p - 2)(p + 1)$ **15** $(k - 4)(k + 2)$

16 $(y - 2)(y + 5)$ **17** $(a - 1)(a + 3)$ **18** $(t - 3)(t + 4)$

19 $(x - 4)(x - 1)$ **20** $(r - 3)(r - 2)$ **21** $(m - 3)(m - 1)$

22 $(g - 4)(g - 2)$ **23** $(h - 5)(h - 3)$ **24** $(n - 1)^2$

25 $(x + 5)^2$ **26** $(t + 6)^2$ **27** $(3 - b)(5 + b)$

28 $(5 - y)(1 - y)$ **29** $(p - 4)^2$ **30** $(k - 2)^2$

HINTS AND TIPS

If you need to work out the square of an expression in brackets, always write down the brackets twice.
For example,
$(n - 1)^2 = (n - 1)(n - 1)$.

C

The expansions of the expressions below follow a pattern. Work out the first few and try to spot the pattern that will allow you immediately to write down the answers to the rest.

31 $(x + 3)(x - 3)$ **32** $(t + 5)(t - 5)$ **33** $(m + 4)(m - 4)$ **34** $(t + 2)(t - 2)$

35 $(y + 8)(y - 8)$ **36** $(p + 1)(p - 1)$ **37** $(5 + x)(5 - x)$ **38** $(7 + g)(7 - g)$

39 $(x - 6)(x + 6)$

7.6 Substitution

In this section you will learn how to:

- substitute numbers for letters in formulae and evaluate the resulting numerical expression
- use a calculator to evaluate numerical expressions

Key words

brackets
calculator
formula
substitution

One of the most important features of algebra is the use of expressions and **formulae**, and the **substitution** of real numbers into them.

The value of an expression, such as $3x + 2$, changes when different values of x are substituted into it. For example, the expression $3x + 2$ has the value:

5 when $x = 1$ 14 when $x = 4$

and so on. A formula expresses the value of one variable as the others in the formula change. For example, the formula for the area, A, of a triangle of base b and height h is:

$$A = \frac{b \times h}{2}$$

When $b = 4$ and $h = 8$:

$$A = \frac{4 \times 8}{2} = 16$$

EXAMPLE 16

The formula for the area of a trapezium is:

$$A = \frac{(a + b)h}{2}$$

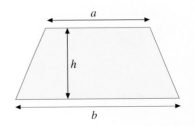

Find the area of the trapezium when $a = 5$, $b = 9$ and $h = 3$.

$$A = \frac{(5 + 9) \times 3}{2} = \frac{14 \times 3}{2} = 21$$

Always substitute the numbers for the letters before trying to work out the value of the expression. You are less likely to make a mistake this way. It is also useful to write **brackets** around each number, especially with negative numbers.

EXERCISE 7H

1 Find the value of $3x + 2$ when:

    a $x = 2$ **b** $x = 5$ **c** $x = 10$

2 Find the value of $4k - 1$ when:

    a $k = 1$ **b** $k = 3$ **c** $k = 11$

3 Find the value of $5 + 2t$ when:

    a $t = 2$ **b** $t = 5$ **c** $t = 12$

4 Evaluate $15 - 2f$ when: **a** $f = 3$ **b** $f = 5$ **c** $f = 8$

5 Evaluate $5m + 3$ when: **a** $m = 2$ **b** $m = 6$ **c** $m = 15$

6 Evaluate $3d - 2$ when: **a** $d = 4$ **b** $d = 5$ **c** $d = 20$

7 Find the value of $\dfrac{8 \times 4h}{5}$ when:

    a $h = 5$ **b** $h = 10$ **c** $h = 25$

8 Find the value of $\dfrac{25 - 3p}{2}$ when:

    a $p = 4$ **b** $p = 8$ **c** $p = 10$

9 Evaluate $\dfrac{x}{3}$ when: **a** $x = 6$ **b** $x = 24$ **c** $x = -30$

HINTS AND TIPS

It helps to put the numbers in brackets.
$3(2) + 2 = 6 + 2 = 8$
$3(5) + 2 = 15 + 2 = 17$
etc ...

10 Evaluate $\dfrac{A}{4}$ when: **a** $A = 12$ **b** $A = 10$ **c** $A = -20$

11 Find the value of $\dfrac{12}{y}$ when: **a** $y = 2$ **b** $y = 4$ **c** $y = 6$

12 Find the value of $\dfrac{24}{x}$ when: **a** $x = 2$ **b** $x = 3$ **c** $x = 16$

Using your calculator

Now try working out a solution on your calculator, making up values for w and d. Remember to put in the brackets as required.

Look at this expression.

$$t = 5\left(\frac{w + 2d}{4}\right)$$

To find t when, for example, $w = 6$ and $d = 3$, key into your calculator:

You should get the answer 15.

Sometimes you need to work out the bottom part (denominator) of a fraction, such as:

$$k = \frac{8}{b - d}$$

You will need to use brackets to do this.

For example, to evaluate k when $b = 7$ and $d = 3$, key into your calculator:

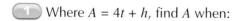

You should get the answer 2.

Notice that the expression does *not* include brackets, but you need to use them on your calculator.

EXERCISE 7I

1 Where $A = 4t + h$, find A when:

    a $t = 2$ and $h = 3$ **b** $t = 3$ and $h = 5$ **c** $t = 1$ and $h = 9$

2 Where $P = 5w - 4y$, find P when:

    a $w = 3$ and $y = 2$ **b** $w = 6$ and $y = 4$ **c** $w = 2$ and $y = 3$

3 Where $A = b^2 + c$, find A when:

    a $b = 2$ and $c = 3$ **b** $b = 5$ and $c = 7$ **c** $b = 1$ and $c = -4$

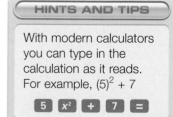

HINTS AND TIPS

With modern calculators you can type in the calculation as it reads. For example, $(5)^2 + 7$

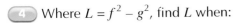

4 Where $L = f^2 - g^2$, find L when:

   a $f = 6$ and $g = 3$ **b** $f = 3$ and $g = 2$ **c** $f = 5$ and $g = 5$

5 Where $T = P - n^2$, find T when:

   a $P = 100$ and $n = 5$ **b** $P = 17$ and $n = 3$ **c** $P = 10$ and $n = 4$

6 Where $A = 180(n - 2)$, find A when:

   a $n = 7$ **b** $n = 3$ **c** $n = 2$

7 Where $t = 10 - \sqrt{P}$, find t when:

   a $P = 25$ **b** $P = 4$ **c** $P = 81$

8 Where $W = v + \dfrac{m}{5}$, find W when:

   a $v = 3$ and $m = 7$ **b** $v = 2$ and $m = 3$ **c** $v = -3$ and $m = 8$

ACTIVITY

In algebra, an *Identity* is an expression which is true for all values of the variable used.

For example:

$$x^2 - 4 \equiv (x - 2)(x + 2)$$

the three horizontal lines indicate an *Identity*.

Whatever value of x is put into the left-hand expression, makes the same value if placed into the right-hand expression.

e.g. $x = 3 : x^2 - 4 = 9 - 4 = 5$ $(x - 2)(x + 2) = 1 \times 5 = 5$

         $x = 7 : x^2 - 4 = 49 - 4 = 45$ $(x - 2)(x + 2) = 5 \times 9 = 45$

Note: Substitution alone will not prove an identity, only show it may be true. Algebra will be the means of sure proof. However a substitution can be used to show an identity is not true if an example can be found showing it not to be.

Find, by substitution or otherwise, which of the following pairs of expressions are identities, may be identities or are not identities.

Those that you feel are (or may be) write them out using the $\equiv$ sign.

a $6n$, $\dfrac{12n^2}{2n}$

b $n^3 - 1$, $(n + 1)(n^2 - 1)$

c $x + 1$, $\dfrac{x^2 - 1}{x - 1}$

d $x^2 - 6$, $(x + 3)(x - 3)$

e $(x - 2)^2 + 1$, $x^2 - 4n + 5$

1 Here is a two-step number machine.

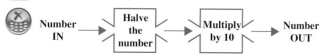

Number IN → Halve the number → Multiply by 10 → Number OUT

a Use the number machine to complete this table.

Number IN	Number OUT
6	30
18	
	170
27	

b The number machine can be simplifed. The two steps can be made into one step. What will this step be?

Number IN → ⬜ → Number OUT

c The number IN is n. Write an expression for the Number OUT.

Number IN	Number OUT
n	

2 Simplify each expression.

a $t + 4t - 2t$ **b** $4p \times 3q$

c $8x - 12x$

3 The table shows some expressions.

$2(y + y)$	$2y + y$	$2y \times 2y$	$2y + 2y$	$2 + 2y$

Two of the expressions *always* have the same value as $4y$.

Which two are these?

4 An approximate rule for converting degrees Fahrenheit into degrees Celsius is:

$$C = \frac{F - 30}{2}$$

Use this rule to convert 18 °F into degrees Celsius.

5 **a** At a café, a cup of tea costs 55p. Write down an expression for the cost, in pence, of x cups of tea.

b **i** The cafe sells twice as many cups of coffee as it does cups of tea. Write down an expression for the number of cups of coffee sold when x cups of tea are sold.

ii Each cup of coffee costs 80p. Write down an expression for the cost, in pence, of the cups of coffee sold.

6 **a** Simplify: $5a + 2b - a + 5b$

b Expand: $5(p + 2q - 3r)$

7 Using the formula $v = 4u - 3t$, calculate the value of v when $u = 12.1$ and $t = 7.2$.

8 **a** Simplify: $2x + 4y - x + 4y$

b Find the value of $3p + 5q$ when $p = 2$ and $q = -1$.

c Find the value of $u^2 + v^2$ when $u = 4$ and $v = -3$.

9 **a** Matt buys 10 boxes of apple juice at 24 pence each.

i Calculate the total cost.

ii He pays with a £10 note. How much change will he receive?

b Aisha buys c oranges at 20 pence each.

i Write down an expression for the total cost in terms of c.

ii She now buys d apples at 15 pence each. Write down an expression for the total cost of the apples and oranges.

10 Graham is y years old.

Harriet is 5 years older than Graham.

a Write down an expression for Harriet's age.

b Jane is half as old as Harriet. Write down an expression for Jane's age.

11 **a** Find the value of t^3 when $t = 5$.

b Find the value of $3t + 4m$ when $t = -1$ and $m = 3$.

c There are p seats in one single-decker bus and q seats in one double-decker bus. An outing uses four single-decker and six double-decker buses.

Write down an expression in terms of p and q for the number of seats available on the outing.

12 Using $m = 17.6$, $t = 42.3$, $r = 0.2$, work out the value of:

a $m + \dfrac{t}{r}$ **b** $\dfrac{m + t}{r}$

13 $d = 3e + 2h^2$

Calculate the value of d when $e = 3.7$ and $h = 2$.

14 **a** Expand and simplify this expression.

$2(x + 3) + 5(x + 2)$

b Expand and simplify this expression.

$(4x + y) - (2x - y)$

15 **a** Simplify

    i $3a + 4b - 2a - b$

    ii $5x^2 + 2x - 3x^2 - x$

b Expand the brackets

    i $4(2x - 3)$

    ii $p(q - p^2)$

c Expand and simplify $5(3p + 2) - 2(5p - 3)$

    Edexcel, Question 5, Paper 3 Intermediate, November 2004

16 **a** Simplify this expression. $3x + 4y + 6x - 3y - 5x$

b Factorise this expression. $6c + 9$

c Factorise this expression. $z^2 + 6z$

17 **a** **i** Multiply out and simplify this expression.

    $3(x - 3) + 2(x + 2)$

    ii Multiply out and simplify this expression.

    $(n - 1)^2$

b Factorise completely the following expressions.

    i $6a^2 + a$

    ii $6x^2y^3 - 4xy^2$

18 **a** Factorise $p^2 + 6p$

b Expand and simplify $(x + 7)(x - 4)$

    Edexcel, Question 11, Paper 3 Intermediate, June 2005

19 **a** Expand and simplify this expression.

    $3(x - 1) + 2(3x - 5)$

b Expand and simplify this expression.

    $(x - 3)(x - 2)$

WORKED EXAM QUESTION

a Factorise completely: $6m^2 - 12mp$

b Simplify: $(2mt^2) \times (5tm^3)$

Solution

a $6m^2 - 12mp = 6m \times m - 6m \times 2p$ — Look for a common factor of 6 and 12, e.g. 6. Look for a common factor of m^2 and mp, e.g. m.

$= 6m(m - 2p)$ — Split up the terms, using the common factors.

— Write as a factorised expression.

b $(2mt^2) \times (5tm^3) = 2 \times 5 \times t^2 \times t \times m \times m^3$ — Rearrange the expression to put numbers together and letters together.

$= 10t^3m^4$ — Work out each part, remembering to add the indices.

A group of friends are planning a five-day walking holiday. The profile of their daily walks is shown below.

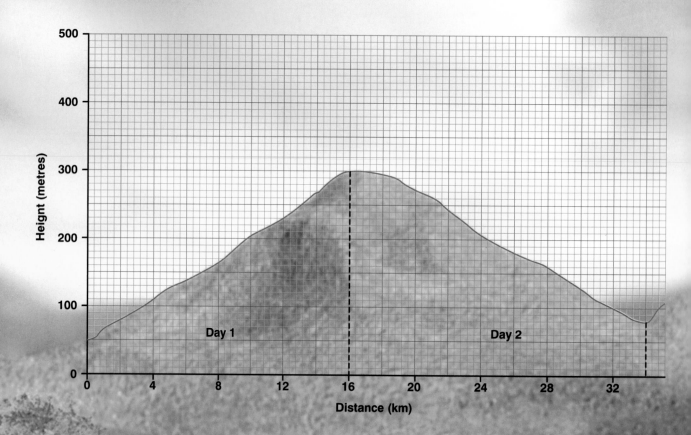

For every day, they work out the horizontal distance they will walk, in kilometres, and the height they climb, in metres. They calculate the length of time that each day's walk will take them, using the formula below.

$$T = 15D + \frac{H}{10}$$

where: T = time, in minutes
         D = distance, in kilometres
         H = height climbed, in metres

This formula assumes an average walking speed of 4km/h and an extra minute for each 10 metres climbed.

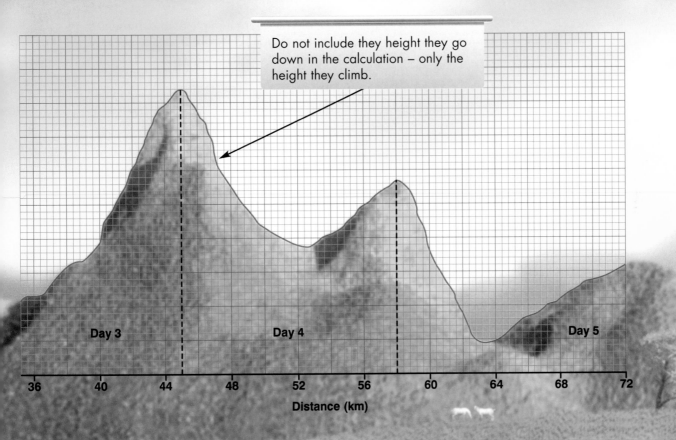

Do not include they height they go down in the calculation – only the height they climb.

Day 3

Day 4

Day 5

| 36 | 40 | 44 | 48 | 52 | 56 | 60 | 64 | 68 | 72 |

Distance (km)

Help them to complete the table so that they can work out how much time each day's walk will take, and the time at which they expect to finish.

Day	Distance (km)	Height climbed (m)	Time (minutes)	Time (hours and minutes)	Start time	Time allowed for breaks	Finish time
1					10.00 am	2 hours	
2	18	0	270	4 h 30 min	10.00 am	$1\frac{1}{2}$ hours	4.00 pm
3					9.30 am	$2\frac{1}{2}$ hours	
4					10.30 am	$2\frac{1}{2}$ hours	
5					10.30 am	$2\frac{1}{2}$ hours	

GRADE YOURSELF

G Able to use a formula expressed in words

F Can substitute numbers into expressions and use letters to write a simple algebraic expression

E Able to simplify expressions by collecting like terms

D Know how to use letters to write more complicated expressions, expand expressions with brackets and factorise simple expressions

C Can expand and simplify expressions with brackets, factorise expressions involving letters and numbers, and expand pairs of linear brackets to give quadratic expressions

What you should know now

- How to simplify a variety of algebraic expressions by multiplying, collecting like terms and expanding brackets
- How to factorise expressions by removing common factors
- How to substitute into expressions, using positive or negative whole numbers and decimals

Further number skills

1 Long multiplication

2 Long division

3 Solving real-life problems

4 Arithmetic with decimal numbers

5 Arithmetic with fractions

6 Multiplying and dividing with negative numbers

7 Approximation of calculations

This chapter will show you ...

- a reminder of the ways you can multiply a three-digit number by a two-digit number
- a reminder of long division
- how to calculate with decimal numbers
- how to interchange decimals and fractions
- further fraction calculations
- how to multiply and divide negative numbers
- how to use decimal places and significant figures to make approximations
- sensible rounding methods

Visual overview

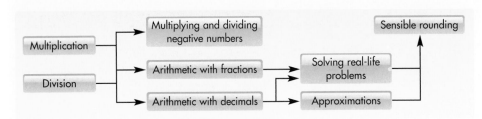

What you should already know

- Times tables up to 10×10
- How to cancel fractions

Quick check

1 Write down the first five multiples of 6.

2 Write down the first five multiples of 8.

3 Write down a number that is both a multiple of 3 and a multiple of 5.

4 Write down the smallest number that is a multiple of 4 and a multiple of 5.

5 Write down the smallest number that is a multiple of 4 and a multiple of 6.

6 Cancel the following fractions.

    a $\dfrac{8}{10}$ **b** $\dfrac{5}{20}$ **c** $\dfrac{4}{16}$ **d** $\dfrac{32}{100}$ **e** $\dfrac{36}{100}$ **f** $\dfrac{16}{24}$ **g** $\dfrac{16}{50}$

Long multiplication

In this section you will learn how to:

- multiply a three-digit number (e.g. 358) by a two-digit number (e.g. 74) using
  - the partition method
  - the traditional method
  - the box method

Key words

carry mark
column
partition

When you are asked to do long multiplication on the GCSE non-calculator paper, you will be expected to use an appropriate method. The three most common are:

(1) the **partition** method, see Example 1 below

(2) the traditional method, see Example 2 below

(3) the box method, see Example 3 below.

EXAMPLE 1

Work out 358 × 74 by the partition method.

Set out a grid as shown.

- Put the larger number along the top and the smaller number down the right-hand side.

- Multiply each possible pair in the grid, putting the numbers into each half as shown.

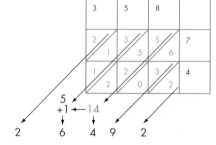

- Add up the numbers in each diagonal. If a total is larger than nine (in this example there is a total of **14**), split the number and put the 1 in the next **column** on the left ready to be added in that diagonal.

- When you have completed the totalling, the number you are left with is the answer to the multiplication.

So, 358 × 74 = 26 492

EXAMPLE 2

Work out 357 × 24 without using a calculator.

There are several different ways to do long multiplication, but the following is perhaps the method that is most commonly used.

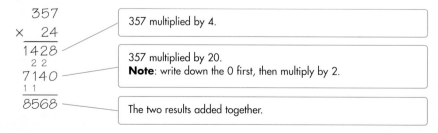

So 357 × 24 = 8568

Note the use of **carry marks** to help with the calculation. Always try to keep carry marks much smaller than the other numbers, so that you don't confuse them with the main calculation.

EXAMPLE 3

Work out 243×68.

Split the two numbers into hundreds, tens and units and write them in a grid like the one below. Multiply all the pairs of numbers.

×	200	40	3
60	12 000	2400	180
8	1600	320	24

Add the separate answers to find the total.

```
  12 000
   2 400
     180
   1 600
     320
      24
  ──────
  16 524
     1 1
```

So, $243 \times 68 = 16\,524$

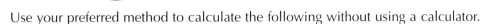

EXERCISE 8A

Use your preferred method to calculate the following without using a calculator.

1 357×34 **2** 724×63 **3** 714×42 **4** 898×23

5 958×54 **6** 676×37 **7** 239×81 **8** 437×29

9 539×37 **10** 477×55 **11** 371×85 **12** 843×93

13 507×34 **14** 810×54 **15** 905×73 **16** 1435×72

17 2504×56 **18** 4037×23 **19** 8009×65 **20** 2070×38

8.2 Long division

In this section you will learn how to:
- divide, without a calculator, a three- or four-digit number by a two-digit number, e.g. $840 \div 24$

Key words
long
division
remainder

There are several different ways of doing **long division**. It is acceptable to use any of them, provided it gives the correct answer and you can show all your working clearly. Two methods are shown in this book. Example 4 shows the *Italian method*. It is the most commonly used way of doing long division.

Example 5 shows a method of repeated subtraction, which is sometimes called the *chunking method*.

Sometimes, as here, you will not need a whole times table, and so you could jot down only those parts of the table that you will need. But, don't forget, you are going to have to work *without* a calculator, so you do need all the help you can get.

You may do a long division without writing down all the numbers. It will look like this:

$$24 \overline{\smash{)}8\ 4^{12}0}\ \ ^{3\ \ 5}$$

Notice how the **remainder** from 84 is placed in front of the 0 to make it 120.

EXAMPLE 4

Work out $840 \div 24$.

It is a good idea to jot down the appropriate times table before you start the long division. In this case, it will be the 24 times table.

1	2	3	4	5	6	7	8	9
24	48	72	96	120	144	168	192	216

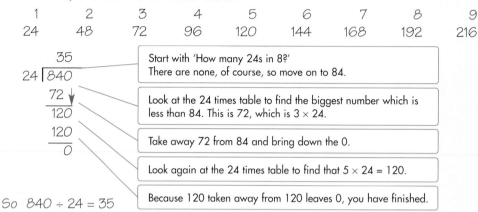

Start with 'How many 24s in 8?'
There are none, of course, so move on to 84.

Look at the 24 times table to find the biggest number which is less than 84. This is 72, which is 3×24.

Take away 72 from 84 and bring down the 0.

Look again at the 24 times table to find that $5 \times 24 = 120$.

Because 120 taken away from 120 leaves 0, you have finished.

So $840 \div 24 = 35$

EXAMPLE 5

Work out $1655 \div 35$.

Jot down some of the multiples of 35 that may be useful.

$1 \times 35 = 35 \qquad 2 \times 35 = 70 \qquad 5 \times 35 = 175 \qquad 10 \times 35 = 350 \qquad 20 \times 35 = 700$

```
  1655
-  700    20 × 35   ⟷   From 1655, subtract a large multiple of 35, such as 20 × 35 = 700.
   955
-  700    20 × 35   ⟷   From 955, subtract a large multiple of 35, such as 20 × 35 = 700.
   255
-  175     5 × 35   ⟷   From 255, subtract a multiple of 35, such as 5 × 35 = 175.
    80
-   70     2 × 35   ⟷   From 80, subtract a multiple of 35, such as 2 × 35 = 70.
    10     47
```

Once the remainder of 10 has been found, you cannot subtract any more multiples of 35. Add up the multiples to see how many times 35 has been subtracted.

So, $1655 \div 35 = 47$, remainder 10

EXERCISE 8B

Solve the following by long division.

1. $525 \div 21$ 2. $480 \div 32$ 3. $925 \div 25$ 4. $645 \div 15$

5. $621 \div 23$ 6. $576 \div 12$ 7. $1643 \div 31$ 8. $728 \div 14$

9. $832 \div 26$ 10. $2394 \div 42$ 11. $829 \div 22$ 12. $780 \div 31$

13. $895 \div 26$ 14. $873 \div 16$ 15. $875 \div 24$ 16. $225 \div 13$

17. $759 \div 33$ 18. $1478 \div 24$ 19. $756 \div 18$ 20. $1163 \div 43$

8.3 Solving real-life problems

In this section you will learn how to:
- identify which arithmetical process you need to solve some real-life problems

In your GCSE examination, you will not always be given simple, straightforward problems like those in Exercises 8A and 8B but *real* problems that you have to *read carefully*, *think about* and then *sort out* without using a calculator.

EXAMPLE 6

Naseema is organising a coach trip for 640 people. Each coach will carry 46 people. How many coaches are needed?

You need to divide the number of people (640) by the number of people in a coach (46).

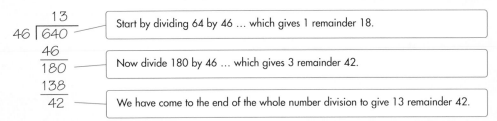

```
      13
46 | 640
     46
     180
     138
      42
```

Start by dividing 64 by 46 ... which gives 1 remainder 18.

Now divide 180 by 46 ... which gives 3 remainder 42.

We have come to the end of the whole number division to give 13 remainder 42.

This tells Naseema that 14 coaches are needed to take all 640 passengers.
(There will be 46 − 42 = 4 spare seats)

EXERCISE 8C

1. There are 48 cans of soup in a crate. A supermarket had a delivery of 125 crates of soup. How many cans of soup were there in this delivery?

2. Greystones Primary School has 12 classes, each of which has 26 pupils. How many pupils are there at Greystones Primary School?

3. 3600 supporters of Barnsley Football Club want to go to an away game by coach. Each coach can hold 53 passengers. How many coaches will they need altogether?

4. How many stamps costing 26p each can I buy for £10?

5. Suhail walks to school each day, there and back. The distance to school is 450 metres. How far will he walk in a school term consisting of 64 days?

6. On one page of a newspaper there are seven columns. In each column there are 172 lines, and in each line there are 50 letters. How many letters are there on the page?

7. A tank of water was emptied into casks. Each cask held 81 litres. 71 casks were filled and there were 68 litres left over. How much water was there in the tank to start with?

8. Joy was going to do a sponsored walk to raise money for the Macmillan Nurses. She managed to get 18 people to sponsor her, each for 35p per kilometre. She walked a total of 48 kilometres. How much sponsor money should she expect to collect?

F

9 Kirsty collects small models of animals. Each one costs 45p. Her pocket money is £15 a month. How many model animals could Kirsty buy with one month's pocket money?

10 Amina wanted to save up to see a concert. The cost of a ticket was £25. She was paid 75p per hour to mind her little sister. For how many hours would Amina have to mind her sister to be able to afford the ticket?

11 The magazine *Teen Dance* comes out every month. The annual (yearly) subscription for the magazine is £21. How much does each magazine cost per month?

12 Paula buys a music centre for her club at a cost of 95p a week for 144 weeks. How much will she actually pay for this music centre?

8.4 Arithmetic with decimal numbers

In this section you will learn how to:
- identify the information that a decimal number shows
- round a decimal number
- identify decimal places
- add and subtract two decimal numbers
- multiply and divide a decimal number by a whole number less than 10
- multiply a decimal number by a two-digit number
- multiply a decimal number by another decimal number

Key words

decimal fraction
decimal place
decimal point
digit

The number system is extended by using decimal numbers to represent fractions.

The **decimal point** separates the **decimal fraction** from the whole-number part.

For example, the number 25.374 means:

Tens	Units		Tenths	Hundredths	Thousandths
10	1		$\frac{1}{10}$	$\frac{1}{100}$	$\frac{1}{1000}$
2	**5**	**.**	**3**	**7**	**4**

You already use decimal notation to express amounts of money. For example:

£32.67   means $3 \times £10$
$2 \times £1$
$6 \times £0.10$ (10 pence)
$7 \times £0.01$ (1 penny)

Decimal places

When a number is written in decimal form, the **digits** to the right of the decimal point are called **decimal places**. For example:

79.4 is written 'with one decimal place'

6.83 is written 'with two decimal places'

0.526 is written 'with three decimal places'.

To round a decimal number to a particular number of decimal places, take these steps:

- Count along the decimal places from the decimal point and look at the first digit to be removed.

- When the value of this digit is less than 5, just remove the unwanted places.

- When the value of this digit is 5 or more, add 1 onto the digit in the last decimal place then remove the unwanted places.

Here are some examples.

5.852 rounds to 5.85 to two decimal places

7.156 rounds to 7.16 to two decimal places

0.274 rounds to 0.3 to one decimal place

15.3518 rounds to 15.4 to one decimal place

EXERCISE 8D

1 Round each of the following numbers to one decimal place.

a 4.83	**b** 3.79	**c** 2.16	**d** 8.25
e 3.673	**f** 46.935	**g** 23.883	**h** 9.549
i 11.08	**j** 33.509	**k** 7.054	**l** 46.807
m 0.057	**n** 0.109	**o** 0.599	**p** 64.99
q 213.86	**r** 76.07	**s** 455.177	**t** 50.999

> **HINTS AND TIPS**
>
> Just look at the value of the digit in the second decimal place.

2 Round each of the following numbers to two decimal places.

a 5.783	**b** 2.358	**c** 0.977	**d** 33.085
e 6.007	**f** 23.5652	**g** 91.7895	**h** 7.995
i 2.3076	**j** 23.9158	**k** 5.9999	**l** 1.0075
m 3.5137	**n** 96.508	**o** 0.009	**p** 0.065
q 7.8091	**r** 569.897	**s** 300.004	**t** 0.0099

3 Round each of the following to the number of decimal places (dp) indicated.

a 4.568 (1 dp)	**b** 0.0832 (2 dp)	**c** 45.715 93 (3 dp)
d 94.8531 (2 dp)	**e** 602.099 (1 dp)	**f** 671.7629 (2 dp)
g 7.1124 (1 dp)	**h** 6.903 54 (3 dp)	**i** 13.7809 (2 dp)
j 0.075 11 (1 dp)	**k** 4.001 84 (3 dp)	**l** 59.983 (1 dp)
m 11.9854 (2 dp)	**n** 899.995 85 (3 dp)	**o** 0.0699 (1 dp)
p 0.009 87 (2 dp)	**q** 6.0708 (1 dp)	**r** 78.3925 (3 dp)
s 199.9999 (2 dp)	**t** 5.0907 (1 dp)	

4 Round each of the following to the nearest whole number.

a 8.7	**b** 9.2	**c** 2.7	**d** 6.5
e 3.28	**f** 7.82	**g** 3.19	**h** 7.55
i 6.172	**j** 3.961	**k** 7.388	**l** 1.514
m 46.78	**n** 23.19	**o** 96.45	**p** 32.77
q 153.9	**r** 342.5	**s** 704.19	**t** 909.5

Adding and subtracting with decimals

When you are working with decimals, you must *always* set out your work properly.

Make sure that the decimal points are in line underneath the first point and each digit is in its correct place or column.

Then you can add or subtract just as you have done before. The decimal point of the answer will be placed directly underneath the other decimal points.

EXAMPLE 7

Work out 4.72 + 13.53

$$\begin{array}{r} 4.72 \\ + 13.53 \\ \hline 18.25 \\ \hline 1 \end{array}$$

So, 4.72 + 13.53 = 18.25

Notice how to deal with 7 + 5 = 12, the 1 carrying forward into the next column.

EXAMPLE 8

Work out 7.3 − 1.5

$$\begin{array}{r} {}^{6}7.{}^{1}3 \\ - \ 1.5 \\ \hline 5.8 \end{array}$$

So, 7.3 − 1.5 = 5.8

Notice how to deal with the fact that you cannot take 5 from 3. You have to take one of the units from 7, replace the 7 with a 6 and make the 3 into 13.

Hidden decimal point

Whole numbers are usually written without decimal points. Sometimes you *do* need to show the decimal point in a whole number (see Example 9), in which case it is placed at the right-hand side of the number, followed by a zero.

EXAMPLE 9

Work out 4.2 + 8 + 12.9

```
    4.2
    8.0
+ 12.9
  25.1
  ‾‾‾
  1 1
```

So 4.2 + 8 + 12.9 = 25.1

EXERCISE 8E

1 Work out each of these.

a 47.3 + 2.5   b 16.7 + 4.6   c 43.5 + 4.8

d 28.5 + 4.8   e 1.26 + 4.73   f 2.25 + 5.83

g 83.5 + 6.7   h 8.3 + 12.9   i 3.65 + 8.5

j 7.38 + 5.7   k 7.3 + 5.96   l 6.5 + 17.86

2 Work out each of these.

a 3.8 − 2.4   b 4.3 − 2.5   c 7.6 − 2.8

d 8.7 − 4.9   e 8.25 − 4.5   f 19.7 − 13.8

g 9.4 − 5.7   h 8.62 − 4.85   i 8 − 4.3

j 9 − 7.6   k 15 − 3.2   l 24 − 8.7

> **HINTS AND TIPS**
>
> When the numbers to be added or subtracted do not have the same number of decimal places, put in extra zeros, for example:
>
> ```
>   3.65       8.25
> + 8.50     − 4.50
> ```

3 Evaluate each of the following. (Take care – they are a mixture.)

a 23.8 + 6.9   b 8.3 − 1.7   c 9 − 5.2

d 12.9 + 3.8   e 17.4 − 5.6   f 23.4 + 6.8

g 35 + 8.3   h 9.54 − 2.81   i 34.8 + 3.15

j 8.1 − 3.4   k 12.5 − 8.7   l 198.5 + 12

Multiplying and dividing decimals by single-digit numbers

You can carry out these operations in exactly the same way as with whole numbers, as long as you remember to put each digit in its correct column.

Again, the decimal point is kept in line underneath or above the first point.

EXAMPLE 10

Work out 4.5×3

$$\begin{array}{r} 4.5 \\ \times \quad 3 \\ \hline 13.5 \\ 1 \end{array}$$

So, $4.5 \times 3 = 13.5$

EXAMPLE 11

Work out $8.25 \div 5$

$$5\overline{)8.^32^25} \quad \begin{array}{r} 1.65 \end{array}$$

So, $8.25 \div 5 = 1.65$

EXAMPLE 12

Work out $5.7 \div 2$

$$2\overline{)5.^17^10} \quad \begin{array}{r} 2.85 \end{array}$$

So, $5.7 \div 2 = 2.85$

> **HINTS AND TIPS**
>
> We add a 0 after the 5.7 in order to continue dividing.
> We do not use remainders with decimal places.

EXERCISE 8F

1 Evaluate each of these.

a 2.4×3	**b** 3.8×2	**c** 4.7×4	**d** 5.3×7
e 6.5×5	**f** 3.6×8	**g** 2.5×4	**h** 9.2×6
i 12.3×5	**j** 24.4×7	**k** 13.6×6	**l** 19.3×5

2 Evaluate each of these.

a 2.34×4	**b** 3.45×3	**c** 5.17×5	**d** 4.26×3
e 0.26×7	**f** 0.82×4	**g** 0.56×5	**h** 0.92×6
i 6.03×7	**j** 7.02×8	**k** 2.55×3	**l** 8.16×6

3 Evaluate each of these.

a 3.6 ÷ 2	**b** 5.6 ÷ 4	**c** 4.2 ÷ 3	**d** 8.4 ÷ 7
e 4.26 ÷ 2	**f** 3.45 ÷ 5	**g** 8.37 ÷ 3	**h** 9.68 ÷ 8
i 7.56 ÷ 4	**j** 5.43 ÷ 3	**k** 1.32 ÷ 4	**l** 7.6 ÷ 4

4 Evaluate each of these.

a 3.5 ÷ 2	**b** 6.4 ÷ 5	**c** 7.4 ÷ 4	**d** 7.3 ÷ 2
e 8.3 ÷ 5	**f** 5.8 ÷ 4	**g** 7.1 ÷ 5	**h** 9.2 ÷ 8
i 6.7 ÷ 2	**j** 4.9 ÷ 5	**k** 9.2 ÷ 4	**l** 7.3 ÷ 5

> **HINTS AND TIPS**
>
> Remember to keep the decimal points in line.

5 Evaluate each of these.

a 7.56 ÷ 4	**b** 4.53 ÷ 3	**c** 1.32 ÷ 5	**d** 8.53 ÷ 2
e 2.448 ÷ 2	**f** 1.274 ÷ 7	**g** 0.837 ÷ 9	**h** 16.336 ÷ 8
i 9.54 ÷ 5	**j** 14 ÷ 5	**k** 17 ÷ 4	**l** 37 ÷ 2

6 Soup is sold in packs of five for £3.25 and packs of eight for £5. Which is the cheaper way of buying soup?

7 Mike took his wife and four children to a theme park. The tickets were £13.25 for each adult and £5.85 for each child. How much did all the tickets cost Mike?

8 Mary was laying a path through her garden. She bought nine paving stones, each 1.35 m long. She wanted the path to run straight down the garden, which is 10 m long. Has Mary bought too many paving stones? Show all your working.

Long multiplication with decimals

As before, you must put each digit in its correct column and keep the decimal point in line.

EXAMPLE 13

Evaluate 4.27 × 34

```
       4.27
  ×      34
     17.08
      1 2
   128.10
      2
   145.18
      1
```

So, 4.27 × 34 = 145.18

EXERCISE 8G

1 Evaluate each of these.

a 3.72×24 b 5.63×53 c 1.27×52 d 4.54×37

e 67.2×35 f 12.4×26 g 62.1×18 h 81.3×55

i 5.67×82 j 0.73×35 k 23.8×44 l 99.5×19

2 Find the total cost of each of the following purchases.

a Eighteen ties at £12.45 each

b Twenty-five shirts at £8.95 each

c Thirteen pairs of tights at £2.30 a pair

> **HINTS AND TIPS**
>
> When the answer is an amount of money, in pounds, you must write it with two places of decimals. Writing £224.1 may lose you a mark. It should be £224.10.

3 A party of 24 scouts and their leader went into a zoo. The cost of a ticket for each scout was £2.15, and the cost of a ticket for the leader was £2.60. What was the total cost of entering the zoo?

4 A market gardener bought 35 trays of seedlings. Each tray cost £3.45. What was the total cost of the trays of seedlings?

Multiplying two decimal numbers together

Follow these steps to multiply one decimal number by another decimal number.

- First, complete the whole calculation as if the decimal points were not there.

- Then, count the total number of decimal places in the two decimal numbers. This gives the number of decimal places in the answer.

EXAMPLE 14

Evaluate 3.42 × 2.7

Ignoring the decimal points gives the following calculation:

$$
\begin{array}{r}
342 \\
\times\ \ 27 \\
\hline
2394 \\
{\scriptstyle 2\ 1} \\
6840 \\
\hline
9234 \\
{\scriptstyle 1\ 1}
\end{array}
$$

Now, 3.42 has two decimal places (.42) and 2.7 has one decimal place (.7). So, the total number of decimal places in the answer is three.

So 3.42 × 2.7 = 9.234

EXERCISE 8H

1 Evaluate each of these.

   a 2.4×0.2 **b** 7.3×0.4 **c** 5.6×0.2 **d** 0.3×0.4

   e 0.14×0.2 **f** 0.3×0.3 **g** 0.24×0.8 **h** 5.82×0.52

   i 5.8×1.23 **j** 5.6×9.1 **k** 0.875×3.5 **l** 9.12×5.1

2 For each of the following:

   i estimate the answer by first rounding each number to the nearest whole number

   ii calculate the exact answer, and then calculate the difference between this and your answers to part **i**.

   a 4.8×7.3 **b** 2.4×7.6 **c** 15.3×3.9 **d** 20.1×8.6

   e 4.35×2.8 **f** 8.13×3.2 **g** 7.82×5.2 **h** 19.8×7.1

8.5 Arithmetic with fractions

In this section you will learn how to:

- change a decimal number to a fraction
- change a fraction to a decimal
- add and subtract fractions with different denominators
- multiply a mixed number by a fraction
- divide one fraction by another fraction

Key words

decimal
denominator
fraction
mixed
   number
numerator

Changing a decimal into a fraction

A **decimal** can be changed into a **fraction** by using the place-value table on page 172.

EXAMPLE 15

Express 0.32 as a fraction.

$$0.32 = \frac{32}{100}$$

This cancels to $\frac{8}{25}$

So $0.32 = \frac{8}{25}$

Changing a fraction into a decimal

You can change a fraction into a decimal by dividing the **numerator** by the **denominator**. Example 16 shows how this can be done without a calculator.

EXAMPLE 16

Express $\frac{3}{8}$ as a decimal.

$\frac{3}{8}$ means $3 \div 8$. This is done as a division calculation:

$$8 \overline{\smash{\big)}\, 3.^30^60^40} \quad \begin{array}{c} 0.375 \end{array}$$

So $\frac{3}{8} = 0.375$

Notice that extra zeros have been put at the end to be able to complete the division.

EXERCISE 8I

1 Change each of these decimals to fractions, cancelling where possible.

    a 0.7   **b** 0.4   **c** 0.5   **d** 0.03   **e** 0.06

    f 0.13   **g** 0.25   **h** 0.38   **i** 0.55   **j** 0.64

2 Change each of these fractions to decimals. Where necessary, give your answer correct to three decimal places.

    a $\frac{1}{2}$ **b** $\frac{3}{4}$ **c** $\frac{3}{5}$ **d** $\frac{9}{10}$ **e** $\frac{1}{3}$

    f $\frac{5}{8}$ **g** $\frac{2}{3}$ **h** $\frac{7}{20}$ **i** $\frac{7}{11}$ **j** $\frac{4}{9}$

3 Put each of the following sets of numbers in order, with the smallest first.

    a 0.6, 0.3, $\frac{1}{2}$ **b** $\frac{2}{5}$, 0.8, 0.3

    c 0.35, $\frac{1}{4}$, 0.15   **d** $\frac{7}{10}$, 0.72, 0.71

    e 0.8, $\frac{3}{4}$, 0.7   **f** 0.08, 0.1, $\frac{1}{20}$

    g 0.55, $\frac{1}{2}$, 0.4   **h** $1\frac{1}{4}$, 1.2, 1.23

> **HINTS AND TIPS**
>
> Convert the fractions to decimals first.

Addition and subtraction of fractions

Fractions can only be added or subtracted after you have changed them to equivalent fractions with the same denominator.

For example:

i $\dfrac{2}{3} + \dfrac{1}{5}$

Note you can change both fractions to equivalent fractions with a denominator of 15.

This then becomes:

$$\dfrac{2 \times 5}{3 \times 5} + \dfrac{1 \times 3}{5 \times 3} = \dfrac{10}{15} + \dfrac{3}{15} = \dfrac{13}{15}$$

ii $2\dfrac{3}{4} - 1\dfrac{5}{6}$

Split the calculation into $\left(2 + \dfrac{3}{4}\right) - \left(1 + \dfrac{5}{6}\right)$.

This then becomes:

$$2 - 1 + \dfrac{3}{4} - \dfrac{5}{6}$$

Note you can change both fractions to equivalent fractions with a denominator of 12.

$$= 1 + \dfrac{9}{12} - \dfrac{10}{12} = 1 - \dfrac{1}{12}$$

$$= \dfrac{11}{12}$$

EXERCISE 8J

1 Evaluate the following.

a $\dfrac{1}{3} + \dfrac{1}{5}$ **b** $\dfrac{1}{3} + \dfrac{1}{4}$ **c** $\dfrac{1}{5} + \dfrac{1}{10}$

d $\dfrac{2}{3} + \dfrac{1}{4}$ **e** $\dfrac{3}{4} + \dfrac{1}{8}$ **f** $\dfrac{1}{3} + \dfrac{1}{6}$

g $\dfrac{1}{2} - \dfrac{1}{3}$ **h** $\dfrac{1}{4} - \dfrac{1}{5}$ **i** $\dfrac{1}{5} - \dfrac{1}{10}$

j $\dfrac{7}{8} - \dfrac{3}{4}$ **k** $\dfrac{5}{6} - \dfrac{3}{4}$ **l** $\dfrac{5}{6} - \dfrac{1}{2}$

m $\dfrac{5}{12} - \dfrac{1}{4}$ **n** $\dfrac{1}{3} + \dfrac{4}{9}$ **o** $\dfrac{1}{4} + \dfrac{3}{8}$

p $\dfrac{7}{8} - \dfrac{1}{2}$ **q** $\dfrac{3}{5} - \dfrac{8}{15}$ **r** $\dfrac{11}{12} + \dfrac{5}{8}$

s $\dfrac{7}{16} + \dfrac{3}{10}$ **t** $\dfrac{4}{9} - \dfrac{2}{21}$ **u** $\dfrac{5}{6} - \dfrac{4}{27}$

D

2 Evaluate the following.

a $2\frac{1}{7} + 1\frac{3}{14}$

b $6\frac{3}{10} + 1\frac{4}{5} + 2\frac{1}{2}$

c $3\frac{1}{2} - 1\frac{1}{3}$

d $1\frac{7}{18} + 2\frac{3}{10}$

e $3\frac{2}{6} + 1\frac{9}{20}$

f $1\frac{1}{8} - \frac{5}{9}$

g $1\frac{3}{16} - \frac{7}{12}$

h $\frac{5}{6} + \frac{7}{16} + \frac{5}{8}$

i $\frac{7}{10} + \frac{3}{8} + \frac{5}{6}$

j $1\frac{1}{3} + \frac{7}{10} - \frac{4}{15}$

k $\frac{5}{14} + 1\frac{3}{7} - \frac{5}{12}$

3 In a class of children, three-quarters are Chinese, one-fifth are Malay and the rest are Indian. What fraction of the class are Indian?

4 In a class election, half of the people voted for Aminah, one-third voted for Janet and the rest voted for Peter. What fraction of the class voted for Peter?

5 A group of people travelled from Hope to Castletown. One-twentieth of them decided to walk, one-twelfth went by car and all the rest went by bus. What fraction went by bus?

6 A one-litre flask filled with milk is used to fill two glasses, one of capacity half a litre and the other of capacity one-sixth of a litre. What fraction of a litre will remain in the flask?

7 Katie spent three-eighths of her income on rent, and two-fifths of what was left on food. What fraction of her income was left after buying her food?

Multiplication of fractions

Remember:

• To multiply two fractions, multiply the numerators (top numbers) and multiply the denominators (bottom numbers) and cancel if possible.

• When multiplying a **mixed number**, change the mixed number to a top-heavy fraction before you start multiplying.

EXAMPLE 17

Work out $1\frac{3}{4} \times \frac{2}{5}$.

Change the mixed number to a top-heavy fraction.

$1\frac{3}{4}$ to $\frac{7}{4}$

The problem is now:

$\frac{7}{4} \times \frac{2}{5}$

So, $\frac{7}{4} \times \frac{2}{5} = \frac{14}{20}$ which cancels to $\frac{7}{10}$.

EXAMPLE 18

A boy had 930 stamps in his collection. $\frac{2}{15}$ of them were British stamps. How many British stamps did he have?

The problem is:

$$\frac{2}{15} \times 930$$

First, calculate $\frac{1}{15}$ of 930.

$$\frac{1}{15} \times 930 = 930 \div 15 = 62$$

So, $\frac{2}{15}$ of $930 = 2 \times 62 = 124$

He has 124 British stamps.

EXERCISE 8K

1. Evaluate the following, leaving each answer in its simplest form.

a $\dfrac{1}{2} \times \dfrac{1}{3}$ b $\dfrac{1}{4} \times \dfrac{2}{5}$ c $\dfrac{3}{4} \times \dfrac{1}{2}$ d $\dfrac{3}{7} \times \dfrac{1}{2}$

e $\dfrac{2}{3} \times \dfrac{4}{5}$ f $\dfrac{1}{3} \times \dfrac{3}{5}$ g $\dfrac{1}{3} \times \dfrac{6}{7}$ h $\dfrac{3}{4} \times \dfrac{2}{5}$

i $\dfrac{5}{16} \times \dfrac{3}{10}$ j $\dfrac{2}{3} \times \dfrac{3}{4}$ k $\dfrac{1}{2} \times \dfrac{4}{5}$ l $\dfrac{9}{10} \times \dfrac{5}{12}$

m $\dfrac{14}{15} \times \dfrac{3}{8}$ n $\dfrac{8}{9} \times \dfrac{6}{15}$ o $\dfrac{6}{7} \times \dfrac{21}{30}$ p $\dfrac{9}{14} \times \dfrac{35}{36}$

2. I walked two-thirds of the way along Pungol Road which is four and a half kilometres long. How far have I walked?

3. One-quarter of Alan's stamp collection was given to him by his sister. Unfortunately two-thirds of these were torn. What fraction of his collection was given to him by his sister and were not torn?

4. Bilal eats one-quarter of a cake, and then half of what is left. How much cake is left uneaten?

5. A merchant buys 28 crates, each containing three-quarters of a tonne of waste metal. What is the total weight of this order?

6. Because of illness, on one day $\frac{2}{5}$ of a school was absent. If the school had 650 pupils on the register, how many were absent that day?

7. To increase sales, a shop reduced the price of a car stereo radio by $\frac{2}{5}$. If the original price was £85, what was the new price?

8. Two-fifths of a class were boys. If the class contained 30 children, how many were girls?

9 Evaluate the following, giving each answer as a mixed number where possible.

a $1\frac{1}{4} \times \frac{1}{3}$ **b** $1\frac{2}{3} \times 1\frac{1}{4}$ **c** $2\frac{1}{2} \times 2\frac{1}{2}$ **d** $1\frac{3}{4} \times 1\frac{2}{3}$

e $3\frac{1}{4} \times 1\frac{1}{5}$ **f** $1\frac{1}{4} \times 2\frac{2}{3}$ **g** $2\frac{1}{2} \times 5$ **h** $7\frac{1}{2} \times 4$

10 Which is larger, $\frac{3}{4}$ of $2\frac{1}{2}$ or $\frac{2}{5}$ of $6\frac{1}{2}$?

11 After James spent $\frac{2}{5}$ of his pocket money on magazines, and $\frac{1}{4}$ of his pocket money at a football match, he had £1.75 left. How much pocket money did he have in the beginning?

12 Which is the biggest: half of 96, one-third of 141, two-fifths of 120, or three-quarters of 68?

13 At a burger-eating competition, Lionel ate 34 burgers in 20 minutes while Ahmed ate 26 burgers in 20 minutes. How long after the start of the competition would they have consumed a total of 21 burgers between them?

14 If £5.20 is two-thirds of three-quarters of a sum of money, what is the sum?

15 Emily lost $\frac{3}{4}$ of her money in the market, but then found $\frac{3}{5}$ of what she had lost. She now had £21 altogether. How much did she start with?

Dividing fractions

Look at the problem $3 \div \frac{3}{4}$. This is like asking, 'How many $\frac{3}{4}$s are there in 3?'

Look at the diagram.

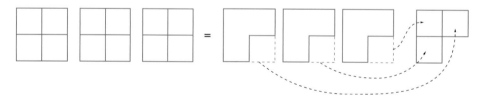

Each of the three whole shapes is divided into quarters. How many 3s go into the total number of quarters?

Can you see that you could fit the four shapes on the right-hand side of the = sign into the three shapes on the left-hand side?

i.e. $3 \div \frac{3}{4} = 4$

or $3 \div \frac{3}{4} = 3 \times \frac{4}{3} = \frac{3 \times 4}{3} = \frac{12}{3} = 4$

So, to divide by a fraction, you turn the fraction upside down (finding its reciprocal), and then multiply.

EXERCISE 8L

1 Evaluate the following, giving your answer as a mixed number where possible.

   a $\dfrac{1}{4} \div \dfrac{1}{3}$ **b** $\dfrac{2}{5} \div \dfrac{2}{7}$ **c** $\dfrac{4}{5} \div \dfrac{3}{4}$ **d** $\dfrac{3}{7} \div \dfrac{2}{5}$

   e $5 \div 1\dfrac{1}{4}$ **f** $6 \div 1\dfrac{1}{2}$ **g** $7\dfrac{1}{2} \div 1\dfrac{1}{2}$ **h** $3 \div 1\dfrac{3}{4}$

   i $1\dfrac{5}{12} \div 3\dfrac{3}{16}$ **j** $3\dfrac{3}{5} \div 2\dfrac{1}{4}$

2 A grain merchant has only thirteen and a half tonnes in stock. He has several customers who are all ordering three-quarters of a tonne. How many customers can he supply?

3 For a party, Zahar made twelve and a half litres of lemonade. His glasses could each hold $\frac{5}{16}$ of a litre. How many of the glasses could he fill from the twelve and a half litres of lemonade?

4 How many strips of ribbon, each three and a half centimetres long, can I cut from a roll of ribbon that is fifty-two and a half centimetres long?

5 Joe's stride is three-quarters of a metre long. How many strides does he take to walk the length of a bus twelve metres long?

6 Evaluate the following, giving your answers as a mixed number where possible.

   a $2\dfrac{2}{9} \times 2\dfrac{1}{10} \times \dfrac{16}{35}$ **b** $3\dfrac{1}{5} \times 2\dfrac{1}{2} \times 4\dfrac{3}{4}$

   c $1\dfrac{1}{4} \times 1\dfrac{2}{7} \times 1\dfrac{1}{6}$ **d** $\dfrac{18}{25} \times \dfrac{15}{16} \div 2\dfrac{2}{5}$

   e $\left(\dfrac{2}{5} \times \dfrac{2}{5}\right) \times \left(\dfrac{5}{6} \times \dfrac{5}{6}\right) \times \left(\dfrac{3}{4} \times \dfrac{3}{4}\right)$ **f** $\left(\dfrac{4}{5} \times \dfrac{4}{5}\right) \div \left(1\dfrac{1}{4} \times 1\dfrac{1}{4}\right)$

8.6 # Multiplying and dividing with negative numbers

In this section you will learn how to:
- multiply and divide with negative numbers

The rules for multiplying and dividing with negative numbers are very easy.

- When the signs of the numbers are the *same*, the answer is *positive*.

- When the signs of the numbers are *different*, the answer is *negative*.

Here are some examples.

   $2 \times 4 = 8$ $12 \div -3 = -4$ $-2 \times -3 = 6$ $-12 \div -3 = 4$

EXERCISE 8M

1 Write down the answers to the following.

a −3 × 5	**b** −2 × 7	**c** −4 × 6	**d** −2 × −3	**e** −7 × −2
f −12 ÷ −6	**g** −16 ÷ 8	**h** 24 ÷ −3	**i** 16 ÷ −4	**j** −6 ÷ −2
k 4 × −6	**l** 5 × −2	**m** 6 × −3	**n** −2 × −8	**o** −9 × −4
p 24 ÷ −6	**q** 12 ÷ −1	**r** −36 ÷ 9	**s** −14 ÷ −2	**t** 100 ÷ 4
u −2 × −9	**v** 32 ÷ −4	**w** 5 × −9	**x** −21 ÷ −7	**y** −5 × 8

2 Write down the answers to the following.

a −3 + −6	**b** −2 × −8	**c** 2 + −5	**d** 8 × −4	**e** −36 ÷ −2
f −3 × −6	**g** −3 − −9	**h** 48 ÷ −12	**i** −5 × −4	**j** 7 − −9
k −40 ÷ −5	**l** −40 + −8	**m** 4 − −9	**n** 5 − 18	**o** 72 ÷ −9
p −7 − −7	**q** 8 − −8	**r** 6 × −7	**s** −6 ÷ −1	**t** −5 ÷ −5
u −9 − 5	**v** 4 − −2	**w** 4 ÷ −1	**x** −7 ÷ −1	**y** −4 × 0

3 What number do you multiply by −3 to get the following?

a 6	**b** −90	**c** −45	**d** 81	**e** 21

4 What number do you divide −36 by to get the following?

a −9	**b** 4	**c** 12	**d** −6	**e** 9

5 Evaluate the following.

a −6 + (4 − 7)	**b** −3 − (−9 − −3)	**c** 8 + (2 − 9)

6 Evaluate the following.

a 4 × (−8 ÷ −2)	**b** −8 − (3 × −2)	**c** −1 × (8 − −4)

7 What do you get if you divide −48 by the following?

a −2	**b** −8	**c** 12	**d** 24

8 Write down six different multiplications that give the answer −12.

9 Write down six different divisions that give the answer −4.

10 Find the answers to the following.

a −3 × −7	**b** 3 + −7	**c** −4 ÷ −2	**d** −7 − 9	**e** −12 ÷ −6
f −12 − −7	**g** 5 × −7	**h** −8 + −9	**i** −4 + −8	**j** −3 + 9
k −5 × −9	**l** −16 ÷ 8	**m** −8 − −8	**n** 6 ÷ −6	**o** −4 + −3
p −9 × 4	**q** −36 ÷ −4	**r** −4 × −8	**s** −1 − −1	**t** 2 − 67

Approximation of calculations

In this section you will learn how to:
- identify significant figures
- round to one significant figure
- approximate the result before multiplying two numbers together
- approximate the result before dividing two numbers
- round a calculation, at the end of a problem, to give what is considered to be a sensible answer

Key words

approximate
round
significant
    figure

Rounding to significant figures

You will often use **significant figures** when you want to **approximate** a number with quite a few digits in it.

The following table illustrates some numbers written correct to one, two and three significant figures (sf).

One sf	8	50	200	90 000	0.000 07	0.003	0.4
Two sf	67	4.8	0.76	45 000	730	0.006 7	0.40
Three sf	312	65.9	40.3	0.0761	7.05	0.003 01	0.400

In the GCSE exam you only have to **round** numbers correct to one significant figure.

The steps taken to round a number to one significant figure are very similar to those used for decimal places.

- From the left, find the second digit. If the original number is less than 1, start counting from the first non-zero digit.

- When the value of the second digit is less than 5, leave the first digit as it is.

- When the value of the second digit is equal to or greater than 5, add 1 to the first digit.

- Put in enough zeros at the end to keep the number the right size.

For example, the following tables show some numbers rounded to one significant figure.

Number	Rounded to 1 sf
78	80
32	30
0.69	0.7
1.89	2
998	1000
0.432	0.4

Number	Rounded to 1 sf
45 281	50 000
568	600
8054	8000
7.837	8
99.8	100
0.078	0.08

EXERCISE 8N

D

 Round each of the following numbers to 1 significant figure.

a	46 313	**b**	57 123	**c**	30 569	**d**	94 558	**e**	85 299
f	54.26	**g**	85.18	**h**	27.09	**i**	96.432	**j**	167.77
k	0.5388	**l**	0.2823	**m**	0.005 84	**n**	0.047 85	**o**	0.000 876
p	9.9	**q**	89.5	**r**	90.78	**s**	199	**t**	999.99

2 Write down the smallest and the greatest numbers of sweets that can be found in each of these jars.

a    **b**    **c**

3 Write down the smallest and the greatest numbers of people that might live in these towns.

Elsecar   population 800 (to 1 significant figure)

Hoyland   population 1000 (to 1 significant figure)

Barnsley   population 200 000 (to 1 significant figure)

4 Round each of the following numbers to 1 significant figure.

a	56 147	**b**	26 813	**c**	79 611	**d**	30 578	**e**	14 009
f	5876	**g**	1065	**h**	847	**i**	109	**j**	638.7
k	1.689	**l**	4.0854	**m**	2.658	**n**	8.0089	**o**	41.564
p	0.8006	**q**	0.458	**r**	0.0658	**s**	0.9996	**t**	0.009 82

Approximation of calculations

How would you approximate the value of a calculation? What would you actually do when you try to approximate an answer to a problem?

For example, what is the approximate answer to 35.1 × 6.58?

To find the approximate answer, you simply round each number to 1 significant figure, then complete the calculation. So in this case, the approximation is:

$$35.1 \times 6.58 \approx 40 \times 7 = 280$$

Sometimes, especially when dividing, it is more sensible to round to 2 sf instead of 1 sf. For example:

$$57.3 \div 6.87$$

Since 6.87 rounds to 7, round 57.3 to 56 because 7 divides exactly into 56. Hence:

$$57.3 \div 6.87 \approx 56 \div 7 = 8$$

A quick approximation is always a great help in any calculation since it often stops you giving a silly answer.

EXERCISE 8P

1 Find approximate answers to the following.

a 5435×7.31 **b** 5280×3.211 **c** $63.24 \times 3.514 \times 4.2$

d 3508×2.79 **e** $72.1 \times 3.225 \times 5.23$ **f** $470 \times 7.85 \times 0.99$

g $354 \div 79.8$ **h** $36.8 \div 1.876$ **i** $5974 \div 5.29$

Check your answers on a calculator to see how close you were.

2 Find the approximate monthly pay of the following people whose annual salaries are given.

a Paul £35 200 **b** Michael £25 600 **c** Jennifer £18 125 **d** Ross £8420

3 Find the approximate annual pay of the following people who earn:

a Kevin £270 a week **b** Malcolm £1528 a month **c** David £347 a week

4 A litre of paint will cover an area of about 8.7 m². Approximately how many litre cans will I need to buy to paint a room with a total surface area of 73 m²?

5 A farmer bought 2713 kg of seed at a cost of £7.34 per kg. Find the approximate total cost of this seed.

6 By rounding, find an approximate answer to each of the following.

a $\dfrac{573 + 783}{107}$ **b** $\dfrac{783 - 572}{24}$ **c** $\dfrac{354 + 656}{997 - 656}$ **d** $\dfrac{1124 - 661}{355 + 570}$

e $\dfrac{28.3 \times 19.5}{97.4}$ **f** $\dfrac{78.3 \times 22.6}{3.69}$ **g** $\dfrac{3.52 \times 7.95}{15.9}$ **h** $\dfrac{11.78 \times 77.8}{39.4}$

7 It took me 6 hours and 40 minutes to drive from Sheffield to Bude, a distance of 295 miles. My car uses petrol at the rate of about 32 miles per gallon. The petrol cost £3.51 per gallon.

a Approximately how many miles did I travel each hour?

b Approximately how many gallons of petrol did I use in going from Sheffield to Bude?

c What was the approximate cost of all the petrol I used in the journey to Bude and back again?

8 Kirsty arranges for magazines to be put into envelopes. She sorts out 178 magazines between 10.00 am and 1.00 pm. Approximately how many magazines will she be able to sort in a week in which she works for 17 hours?

9 An athlete's training routine is to run 3.75 km every day. Approximately how far does he run in:

a a week **b** a month **c** a year?

10 A box full of magazines weighs 8 kg. One magazine weighs about 15 g. Approximately how many magazines are there in the box?

189

11 An apple weighs about 280 grams.

    a What is the approximate weight of a bag containing a dozen apples?

    b Approximately how many apples will there be in a sack weighing 50 kg?

12 One marble weighs 8 grams to the nearest gram.

    a What is **i** the greatest **ii** the least possible weight of 100 marbles identical to this one?

    b I buy 1 kg of these identical marbles, what is **i** the greatest **ii** the least number of marbles I might have bought?

Sensible rounding

In your GCSE examination you will be required to round off answers to problems to a suitable degree of accuracy without being told specifically what that is.

Generally, you can use common sense. For example, you would not give the length of a pencil as 14.574 cm; you would round off to something like 14.6 cm. If you were asked how many tins you need to buy to do a particular job, then you would give a whole-number answer and not a decimal fraction such as 5.91 tins.

It is hard to make rules about this, as there is much disagreement even among the 'experts' as to how you ought to do it. But, generally, when you are in any doubt as to how many significant figures to use for the final answer to a problem, round to the same accuracy as the numbers used in the original data.

Remember too, that measurements given to the nearest whole unit may be inaccurate by up to one half in either direction.

EXERCISE 8Q

1 Round each of the following figures to a suitable degree of accuracy.

    a I am 1.7359 metres tall.

    b It took me 5 minutes 44.83 seconds to mend the television.

    c My kitten weighs 237.97 grams.

    d The correct temperature at which to drink Earl Grey tea is 82.739 °C.

    e There were 34 827 people at the Test Match yesterday.

    f The distance from Wath to Sheffield is 15.528 miles.

    g My telephone number is 284 519.

    h The area of the floor is 13.673 m^2.

2 Rewrite the following article, rounding all the numbers to a suitable degree of accuracy if necessary.

It was a hot day, the temperature was 81.699 °F and still rising. I had now walked 5.3289 km in just over 113.98 minutes. But I didn't care since I knew that the 43 275 people watching the race were cheering me on. I won by clipping 6.2 seconds off the record time. This was the 67th time the race had taken place since records first began in 1788. Well, next year I will only have 15 practice walks beforehand as I strive to beat the record by at least another 4.9 seconds.

1 a Copy and complete the shopping bill for Dean.

4 kg potatoes	at £0.85 per kg	
3 kg apples	at £1.45 per kg	
2 bottles of orange	at £1.15 each	
	Total	

b The shop assistant gives Dean 10p off for every £2 he spends. How much is Dean given off his bill?

c Dean buys six balloons at 45p each. He pays with a £10 note. How much change should he receive?

2 450 people go on a Football trip. Each coach will seat 54 people.

a How many coaches are needed?

b How many seats will be empty?

3 Every day, a quarter of a million babies are born in the world.

a Write a quarter of a million using figures.

b Work out the number of babies born in 28 days. Give your answer in millions.

Edexcel, Question 14, Paper 2 Foundation, June 2003

4 a Write $\frac{5}{8}$ as a decimal.

b Write 0.6 as a fraction. Give your answer in its lowest terms.

5 Nick takes 26 boxes out of his van. The weight of each box is 32.9 kg.

Work out the *total* weight of the 26 boxes.

Edexcel, Question 3, Paper 3 Intermediate, June 2004

6 Estimate the value of each expression:

a 15.7×29.2 **b** 143.1×17.8

7 a Work out $13 \times 17 - 11 \times 17$.

b Find an approximate value of $\frac{51 \times 250}{82}$.

You *must* show all your working.

8 John says 'For all prime numbers, n, the value of $n^2 + 3$ is always an even number'. Give an example to show that John is *not* correct.

9 Three pupils use calculators to work out $\frac{32.7 + 14.3}{1.28 - 0.49}$

Arnie gets 43.4, Bert gets 36.2 and Chuck gets 59.5. Use approximations to show which one of them is correct.

10 Work out $3\frac{2}{5} - 1\frac{2}{3}$

11 Use approximations to estimate the value of

$$\sqrt{\frac{323\,407}{0.48}}$$

12 Each term of a sequence is formed by multiplying the previous term by −2 and then subtracting 1. The first three terms are

2, −5, 9 …

a Write down the next two terms of the sequence

b A later term in the sequence is 119. What was the previous term?

WORKED EXAM QUESTION

In a survey the number of visitors to a Theme Park was recorded daily. Altogether 20 million visitors went to the Theme Park. Each day there were approximately 400 000 visitors.
Based on this information, for how many days did the survey last?

Read the question to decide what you have to do.
You need to find the number of days: total times visited ÷ number of visits a day

Solution

$20\,000\,000 \div 400\,000 = \dfrac{20\,000\,000}{400\,000}$

Show the calculation, you get a mark for this.

You can cancel the five zeros on the top and the bottom.

$= \dfrac{200}{4} = 50$ days

Check the final answer is sensible. Here, it is.

A health and fitness club has six new members.

The manager measures their heights and weights and uses the height–weight chart to identify the category into which each of them falls.

Help him to complete the table.

Person	Weight category
Dave	
Pete	
Andy	OK
Sue	
Sally	
Lynn	

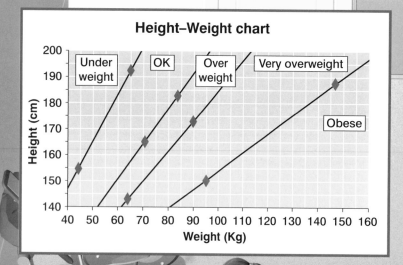

Height–Weight chart

Under weight | OK | Over weight | Very overweight | Obese

Height (cm) — Weight (Kg)

Lynn
height 162 cm
weight 60 kg

150 g toast (bread)
20 g butter
250 ml orange juice

Cross trainer 9 cal/min

Sue
height 168 cm
weight 82 kg

50 g bacon
200 g sausages
50 g egg
tea with 40 ml
semi-skimmed milk

Walking 6 cal/min

Andy
height 180 cm
weight 75 kg

100 g apple
100 g banana
150 g yoghurt
200 ml apple juice

Running 8 cal/min

Further number skills

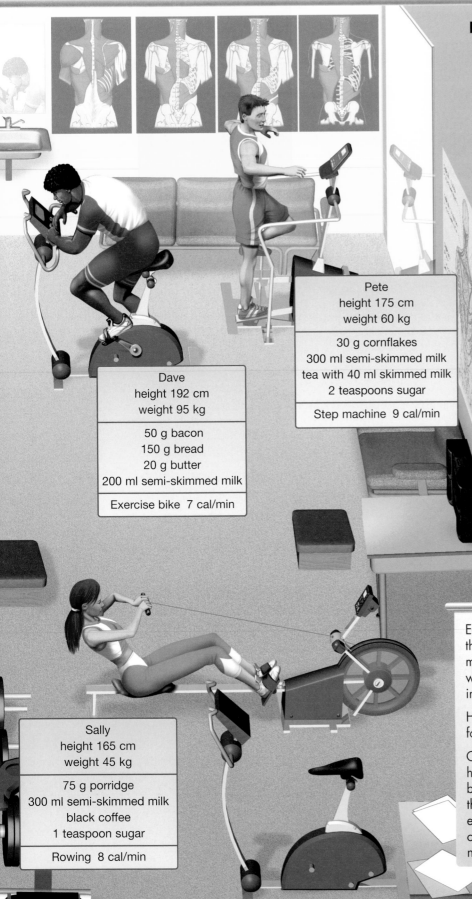

Calories per 100 g of food	
apple	46
bacon	440
banana	76
bread	246
butter	740
cornflakes	370
eggs	148
porridge	368
sausages	186
yoghurt	62
apple juice (100 ml)	41
orange juice (100 ml)	36
semi-skimmed milk (100 ml)	48
skimmed milk (100 ml)	34
sugar (1 teaspoonful)	20
tea or coffee (black)	0

Pete
height 175 cm
weight 60 kg

30 g cornflakes
300 ml semi-skimmed milk
tea with 40 ml skimmed milk
2 teaspoons sugar

Step machine 9 cal/min

Dave
height 192 cm
weight 95 kg

50 g bacon
150 g bread
20 g butter
200 ml semi-skimmed milk

Exercise bike 7 cal/min

Person	Calories in breakfast	Minutes exercising
Dave		
Pete		
Andy		
Sue		
Sally	440	55
Lynn		

Sally
height 165 cm
weight 45 kg

75 g porridge
300 ml semi-skimmed milk
black coffee
1 teaspoon sugar

Rowing 8 cal/min

Each new member writes down what they usually have for breakfast. The manager uses the calorie table to work out how many calories there are in each breakfast.

He also selects an exercise machine for each of them to use.

Copy and complete the table to show how many calories there are in each breakfast and how many minutes on the exercise machine it would take each member to burn off these calories. Round each time up to the nearest minute.

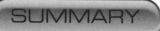

GRADE YOURSELF

F Multiply a three-digit number by a two-digit number without using a calculator

F Divide a three- or four-digit number by a two-digit number

F Solve real problems involving multiplication and division

F Round decimal numbers to a specific number of places

E Evaluate calculations involving decimal numbers

E Change decimals to fractions

E Change fractions to decimals

D Estimate the approximate value of a calculation before calculating

D Order a list containing decimals and fractions

D Round numbers to one significant figure

C Multiply and divide by negative numbers

C Round answers to a suitable degree of accuracy

C Multiply and divide fractions

What you should know now

- How to do long multiplication
- How to do long division
- How to perform calculations with decimal numbers
- How to round to a specific number of decimal places
- How to round to a specific number of significant figures
- How to add fractions with different denominators
- How to multiply and divide fractions
- How to multiply and divide with negative numbers
- How to interchange decimals and fractions
- How to make estimates by suitable rounding

Ratios, fractions, speed and proportion

1 Ratio

2 Speed, time and distance

3 Direct proportion problems

4 Best buys

This chapter will show you ...

- what a ratio is
- how to divide an amount according to a given ratio
- how to solve problems involving direct proportion
- how to compare prices of products
- how to calculate speed

Visual overview

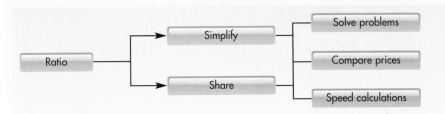

What you should already know

- Times tables up to 10×10
- How to cancel fractions
- How to find a fraction of a quantity
- How to multiply and divide, with and without a calculator

Quick check

1 Cancel the following fractions.

    a $\dfrac{6}{10}$ **b** $\dfrac{4}{20}$ **c** $\dfrac{4}{12}$ **d** $\dfrac{32}{50}$ **e** $\dfrac{36}{90}$ **f** $\dfrac{18}{24}$ **g** $\dfrac{16}{48}$

2 Find the following quantities.

    a $\dfrac{2}{5}$ of £30   **b** $\dfrac{3}{4}$ of £88   **c** $\dfrac{7}{10}$ of 250 litres   **d** $\dfrac{5}{8}$ of 24 kg

    e $\dfrac{2}{3}$ of 60 m   **f** $\dfrac{5}{6}$ of £42   **g** $\dfrac{9}{20}$ of 300 g   **h** $\dfrac{3}{10}$ of 3.5 litres

In this section you will learn how to:
- simplify a ratio
- express a ratio as a fraction
- divide amounts according to ratios
- complete calculations from a given ratio and partial information

Key words

cancel

common
unit

ratio

simplest
form

A **ratio** is a way of comparing the sizes of two or more quantities.

A ratio can be expressed in a number of ways. For example, if Joy is five years old and James is 20 years old, the ratio of their ages is:

Joy's age : James's age

which is: 5 : 20

which simplifies to: 1 : 4 (dividing both sides by 5)

A ratio is usually given in one of these three ways.

Joy's age : James's age or 5 : 20 or 1 : 4

Joy's age to James's age or 5 to 20 or 1 to 4

$$\frac{\text{Joy's age}}{\text{James's age}} \quad \text{or} \quad \frac{5}{20} \quad \text{or} \quad \frac{1}{4}$$

Common units

When working with a ratio involving different units, *always change them to a* **common unit**. A ratio can be simplified only when the units of each quantity are the *same*, because the ratio itself has no units. Once the units are the same, the ratio can be simplified or **cancelled**.

For example, the ratio 125 g to 2 kg must be changed to 125 g to 2000 g, so that you can simplify it.

125 : 2000

Divide both sides by 25: 5 : 80   The ratio 125 : 2000 can be cancelled to 1 : 16.

Divide both sides by 5: 1 : 16

Ratios as fractions

A ratio in its **simplest form** can be expressed as portions by changing the whole numbers in the ratio into fractions with the same denominator (bottom number).

For example, in a garden that is divided into lawn and shrubs in the ratio 3 : 2, you should see that:

the lawn covers $\frac{3}{5}$ of the garden

and the shrubs cover $\frac{2}{5}$ of the garden.

The common denominator (bottom number) 5 is the *sum of the numbers in the ratio.*

EXERCISE 9A

1 Express each of the following ratios in its simplest form.

a 6 : 18   **b** 15 : 20   **c** 16 : 24   **d** 24 : 36

e 20 to 50   **f** 12 to 30   **g** 25 to 40   **h** 125 to 30

i 15 : 10   **j** 32 : 12   **k** 28 to 12   **l** 100 to 40

m 0.5 to 3   **n** 1.5 to 4   **o** 2.5 to 1.5   **p** 3.2 to 4

2 Express each of the following ratios of quantities in its simplest form. (Remember always to express both parts in a common unit before you simplify.)

a £5 to £15   **b** £24 to £16

c 125 g to 300 g   **d** 40 minutes : 5 minutes

e 34 kg to 30 kg   **f** £2.50 to 70p

g 3 kg to 750 g   **h** 50 minutes to 1 hour

i 1 hour to 1 day   **j** 12 cm to 2.5 mm

k 1.25 kg : 500 g   **l** 75p : £3.50

m 4 weeks : 14 days   **n** 600 m: 2 km

o 465 mm : 3 m   **p** 15 hours : 1 day

3 A length of wood is cut into two pieces in the ratio 3 : 7. What fraction of the original length is the longer piece?

4 Jack and Thomas find a bag of marbles that they share between them in the ratio of their ages. Jack is 10 years old and Thomas is 15. What fraction of the marbles did Jack get?

5 Dave and Sue share a pizza in the ratio 2 : 3. They eat it all.

a What fraction of the pizza did Dave eat?   **b** What fraction of the pizza did Sue eat?

6 A camp site allocates space to caravans and tents in the ratio 7 : 3. What fraction of the total space is given to:

a the caravans   **b** the tents?

7 Two sisters, Amy and Katie, share a packet of sweets in the ratio of their ages. Amy is 15 and Katie is 10. What fraction of the sweets does each sister get?

8 The recipe for a fruit punch is 1.25 litres of fruit crush to 6.75 litres of lemonade. What fraction of the punch is each ingredient?

9 One morning a farmer notices that her hens, Gertrude, Gladys and Henrietta, have laid eggs in the ratio 2 : 3 : 4.

    a What fraction of the eggs did Gertrude lay?

    b What fraction of the eggs did Gladys lay?

    c How many more eggs did Henrietta lay than Gertrude?

10 In a safari park at feeding time, the elephants, the lions and the chimpanzees are given food in the ratio 10 to 7 to 3. What fraction of the total food is given to:

    a the elephants   **b** the lions   **c** the chimpanzees?

11 Three brothers, James, John and Joseph, share a huge block of chocolate in the ratio of their ages. James is 20, John is 12 and Joseph is 8. What fraction of the bar of chocolate does each brother get?

12 The recipe for a pudding is 125 g of sugar, 150 g of flour, 100 g of margarine and 175 g of fruit. What fraction of the pudding is each ingredient?

Dividing amounts according to ratios

To divide an amount into portions according to a given ratio, you first change the whole numbers in the ratio into fractions with the same common denominator. Then you multiply the amount by each fraction.

EXAMPLE 1

Divide £40 between Peter and Hitan in the ratio 2 : 3

Changing the ratio to fractions gives:

$$\text{Peter's share} = \frac{2}{(2+3)} = \frac{2}{5}$$

$$\text{Hitan's share} = \frac{3}{(2+3)} = \frac{3}{5}$$

So Peter receives £40 × $\frac{2}{5}$ = £16 and Hitan receives £40 × $\frac{3}{5}$ = £24.

EXERCISE 9B

1 Divide the following amounts according to the given ratios.

    a 400 g in the ratio 2 : 3   **b** 280 kg in the ratio 2 : 5

    c 500 in the ratio 3 : 7   **d** 1 km in the ratio 19 : 1

    e 5 hours in the ratio 7 : 5   **f** £100 in the ratio 2 : 3 : 5

    g £240 in the ratio 3 : 5 : 12   **h** 600 g in the ratio 1 : 5 : 6

    i £5 in the ratio 7 : 10 : 8   **j** 200 kg in the ratio 15 : 9 : 1

 2 The ratio of female to male members of Lakeside Gardening Club is 5 : 3. The total number of members of the group is 256.

    a How many members are female?   **b** What percentage of members are male?

 3 A supermarket aims to stock branded goods and their own goods in the ratio 2 : 5. They stock 350 kg of breakfast cereal.

    a What percentage of the cereal stock is branded?

    b How much of the cereal stock is their own?

 4 The Illinois Department of Health reported that, for the years 1981 to 1992 when they tested a total of 357 horses for rabies, the ratio of horses with rabies to those without was 1 : 16.

    a How many of these horses had rabies?

    b What percentage of the horses did not have rabies?

 5 Being overweight increases the chances of an adult suffering from heart disease. A way to test whether an adult has an increased risk is shown below:

    For women, increased risk when $W/H > 0.8$

    For men, increased risk when $W/H > 1.0$

W = waist measurement
H = hip measurement

    a Find whether the following people have an increased risk of heart disease.

       Miss Mott: waist 26 inches, hips 35 inches

       Mrs Wright: waist 32 inches, hips 37 inches

       Mr Brennan: waist 32 inches, hips 34 inches

       Ms Smith: waist 31 inches, hips 40 inches

       Mr Kaye: waist 34 inches, hips 33 inches

    b Give three examples of waist and hip measurements that would suggest no risk of heart disease for a man, but would suggest a risk for a woman.

 6 Rewrite the following scales as ratios as simply as possible.

    a 1 cm to 4 km   **b** 4 cm to 5 km   **c** 2 cm to 5 km

    d 4 cm to 1 km   **e** 5 cm to 1 km   **f** 2.5 cm to 1 km

    g 8 cm to 5 km   **h** 10 cm to 1 km   **i** 5 cm to 3 km

 7 A map has a scale of 1 cm to 10 km.

    a Rewrite the scale as a ratio in its simplest form.

    b What is the actual length of a lake that is 4.7 cm long on the map?

    c How long will a road be on the map if its actual length is 8 km?

HINTS AND TIPS

1 km = 1000 m
     = 100 000 cm

8 A map has a scale of 2 cm to 5 km.

a Rewrite the scale as a ratio in its simplest form.

b How long is a path that measures 0.8 cm on the map?

c How long should a 12 km road be on the map?

9 The scale of a map is 5 cm to 1 km.

a Rewrite the scale as a ratio in its simplest form.

b How long is a wall that is shown as 2.7 cm on the map?

c The distance between two points is 8 km; how far will this be on the map?

10 You can simplify a ratio by changing it into the form 1 : *n*. For example, 5 : 7 can be rewritten as

$$\frac{5}{5} : \frac{7}{5} = 1 : 1.4$$

Rewrite each of the following ratios in the form 1 : *n*.

a 5 : 8

b 4 : 13

c 8 : 9

d 25 : 36

e 5 : 27

f 12 : 18

g 5 hours : 1 day

h 4 hours : 1 week

i £4 : £5

Calculating according to a ratio when only part of the information is known

---

EXAMPLE 2

Two business partners, Lubna and Adama, divided their total profit in the ratio 3 : 5. Lubna received £2100. How much did Adama get?

Lubna's £2100 was $\frac{3}{8}$ of the total profit. (Check that you know why.)

$\frac{1}{8}$ of the total profit = £2100 ÷ 3 = £700

So Adama's share, which was $\frac{5}{8}$, amounted to £700 × 5 = £3500.

EXERCISE 9C

1 Derek, aged 15, and Ricki, aged 10, shared all the conkers they found in the woods in the same ratio as their ages. Derek had 48 conkers.

a Simplify the ratio of their ages.

b How many conkers did Ricki have?

c How many conkers did they find altogether?

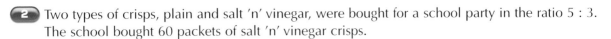

2 Two types of crisps, plain and salt 'n' vinegar, were bought for a school party in the ratio 5 : 3. The school bought 60 packets of salt 'n' vinegar crisps.

a How many packets of plain crisps did they buy?

b How many packets of crisps altogether did they buy?

3 Robin is making a drink from orange juice and lemon juice in the ratio 9 : 1. If Robin has only 3.6 litres of orange juice, how much lemon juice does he need to make the drink?

4 When I picked my strawberries, I found some had been spoilt by snails. The rest were good. These were in the ratio 3 : 17. Eighteen of my strawberries had been spoilt by snails. How many good strawberries did I find?

5 A blend of tea is made by mixing Lapsang with Assam in the ratio 3 : 5. I have a lot of Assam tea but only 600 g of Lapsang. How much Assam do I need to make the blend using all the Lapsang?

6 The ratio of male to female spectators at ice hockey games is 4 : 5. At the Steelers' last match, 4500 men watched the match. What was the total attendance at the game?

7 'Proper tea' is made by putting milk and tea together in the ratio 2 : 9. How much 'proper tea' can be made if you have 1 litre of milk?

8 A teacher always arranged the content of each of his lessons to Y10 as 'teaching' and 'practising learnt skills' in the ratio 2 : 3.

a If a lesson lasted 35 minutes, how much teaching would he do?

b If he decided to teach for 30 minutes, how long would the lesson be?

9 A 'good' children's book is supposed to have pictures and text in the ratio 17 : 8. In a book I have just looked at, the pictures occupy 23 pages. Approximately how many pages of text should this book have to be deemed a 'good' children's book?

10 Three business partners, Kevin, John and Margaret, put money into a venture in the ratio 3 : 4 : 5. They shared any profits in the same ratio. Last year, Margaret made £3400 out of the profits. How much did Kevin and John make last year?

11 The soft drinks Coke, Orange and Vimto were bought for the school disco in the ratio 10 : 5 : 3. The school bought 80 cans of Orange.

a How much Coke did they buy? **b** How much Vimto did they buy?

12 Iqra is making a drink from lemonade, orange and ginger in the ratio 40 : 9 : 1. If Iqra has only 4.5 litres of orange, how much of the other two ingredients does she need to make the drink?

13 When I harvested my apples I found some had been eaten by wasps, some were rotten and some were good. These were in the ratio 6 : 5 : 25. Eighteen of my apples had been eaten by wasps.

a What fraction of my apples were rotten? **b** How many good apples did I get?

Speed, time and distance

In this section you will learn how to:

- recognise the relationship between speed, distance and time
- calculate average speed from distance and time
- calculate distance travelled from the speed and the time taken
- calculate the time taken on a journey from the speed and the distance

Key word

average

The relationship between speed, time and distance can be expressed in three ways:

$$\text{speed} = \frac{\text{distance}}{\text{time}} \qquad \text{distance} = \text{speed} \times \text{time} \qquad \text{time} = \frac{\text{distance}}{\text{speed}}$$

In problems relating to speed, you usually mean **average** speed, as it would be unusual to maintain one exact speed for the whole of a journey.

This diagram will help you remember the relationships between distance (D), time (T) and speed (S).

$$D = S \times T \qquad S = \frac{D}{T} \qquad T = \frac{D}{S}$$

EXAMPLE 3

Paula drove a distance of 270 miles in 5 hours. What was her average speed?

$$\text{Paula's average speed} = \frac{\text{distance she drove}}{\text{time she took}} = \frac{270}{5} = 54 \text{ miles/h}$$

EXAMPLE 4

Sarah drove from Sheffield to Peebles in $3\frac{1}{2}$ hours at an average speed of 60 miles/h. How far is it from Sheffield to Peebles?

Since:

$$\text{distance} = \text{speed} \times \text{time}$$

the distance from Sheffield to Peebles is given by:

$$60 \times 3.5 = 210 \text{ miles}$$

Note: You need to change the time to a decimal number and use 3.5 (*not* 3.30).

EXAMPLE 5

Sean is going to drive from Newcastle upon Tyne to Nottingham, a distance of 190 miles. He estimates that he will drive at an average speed of 50 miles/h. How long will it take him?

$$\text{Sean's time} = \frac{\text{distance he covers}}{\text{his average speed}} = \frac{190}{50} = 3.8 \text{ hours}$$

Change the 0.8 hour to minutes by multiplying by 60, to give 48 minutes.

So, the time for Sean's journey will be 3 hours 48 minutes. A sensible rounding would give 4 hours.

Remember: When you calculate a time and get a decimal answer, as in Example 5, *do not mistake* the decimal part for minutes. You must either:

- leave the time as a decimal number and give the unit as hours, or

- change the decimal part to minutes by multiplying it by 60 (1 hour = 60 minutes) and give the answer in hours and minutes.

EXERCISE 9D

1 A cyclist travels a distance of 90 miles in 5 hours. What was her average speed?

> **HINTS AND TIPS**
>
> Remember to convert time to a decimal if you are using a calculator, for example, 8 hours 30 minutes is 8.5 hours.

2 How far along a motorway would you travel if you drove at 70 mph for 4 hours?

3 I drive to Bude in Cornwall from Sheffield in about 6 hours. The distance from Sheffield to Bude is 315 miles. What is my average speed?

4 The distance from Leeds to London is 210 miles. The train travels at an average speed of 90 mph. If I catch the 9.30 am train in London, at what time should I expect to arrive in Leeds?

5 How long will an athlete take to run 2000 metres at an average speed of 4 metres per second?

6 Copy and complete the following table.

	Distance travelled	Time taken	Average speed
a	150 miles	2 hours	
b	260 miles		40 mph
c		5 hours	35 mph
d		3 hours	80 km/h
e	544 km	8 hours 30 minutes	
f		3 hours 15 minutes	100 km/h
g	215 km		50 km/h

D

7 A train travels at 50 km/h for 2 hours, then slows down to do the last 30 minutes of its journey at 40 km/h.

   a What is the total distance of this journey?

   b What is the average speed of the train over the whole journey?

8 Jade runs and walks the 3 miles from home to work each day. She runs the first 2 miles at a speed of 8 mph, then walks the next mile at a steady 4 mph.

   a How long does it take Jade to get to work?   **b** What is her average speed?

9 Eliot drove from Sheffield to Inverness, a distance of 410 miles, in 7 hours 45 minutes.

   a Change the time 7 hours 45 minutes to a decimal.

   b What was the average speed of the journey? Round your answer to 1 decimal place.

10 Colin drives home from his son's house in 2 hours 15 minutes. He says that he drives at an average speed of 44 mph.

   a Change the 2 hours 15 minutes to a decimal.

   b How far is it from Colin's home to his son's house?

11 The distance between Paris and Le Mans is 200 km. The express train between Paris and Le Mans travels at an average speed of 160 km/h.

   a Calculate the time taken for the journey from Paris to Le Mans, giving your answer as a decimal number of hours.

   b Change your answer to part **a** to hours and minutes.

C

12 The distance between Sheffield and Land's End is 420 miles.

   a What is the average speed of a journey from Sheffield to Land's End that takes 8 hours 45 minutes?

   b If Sam covered the distance at an average speed of 63 mph, how long would it take him?

13 Change the following speeds to metres per second.

   a 36 km/h   **b** 12 km/h   **c** 60 km/h

   d 150 km/h   **e** 75 km/h

> **HINTS AND TIPS**
>
> Remember that there are 3600 seconds in an hour and 1000 metres in a kilometre.

14 Change the following speeds to kilometres per hour.

   a 25 m/s   **b** 12 m/s   **c** 4 m/s

   d 30 m/s   **e** 0.5 m/s

15 A train travels at an average speed of 18 m/s.

   a Express its average speed in km/h.

   b Find the approximate time the train would take to travel 500 m.

   c The train set off at 7.30 on a 40 km journey. At approximately what time will it reach its destination?

> **HINTS AND TIPS**
>
> To convert a decimal fraction of an hour to minutes, just multiply by 60.

16 A cyclist is travelling at an average speed of 24 km/h.

    a What is this speed in metres per second?

    b What distance does he travel in 2 hours 45 minutes?

    c How long does it take him to travel 2 km?

    d How far does he travel in 20 seconds?

9.3 Direct proportion problems

In this section you will learn how to:
- recognise and solve problems using direct proportion

Key words
direct
   proportion
unit cost
unitary method

Suppose you buy 12 items which each cost the *same*. The total amount you spend is 12 times the cost of one item.

That is, the total cost is said to be in **direct proportion** to the number of items bought. The cost of a single item (the **unit cost**) is the constant factor that links the two quantities.

Direct proportion is concerned not only with costs. Any two related quantities can be in direct proportion to each other.

The best way to solve all problems involving direct proportion is to start by finding the single unit value. This method is called the **unitary method**, because it involves referring to a single unit value. Work through Examples 6 and 7 to see how it is done.

Remember: Before solving a direct proportion problem, think about it carefully to make sure that you know how to find the required single unit value.

EXAMPLE 6

If eight pens cost £2.64, what is the cost of five pens?

First, find the cost of one pen. This is £2.64 ÷ 8 = £0.33

So, the cost of five pens is £0.33 × 5 = £1.65

EXAMPLE 7

Eight loaves of bread will make packed lunches for 18 people. How many packed lunches can be made from 20 loaves?

First, find how many lunches *one* loaf will make.

One loaf will make 18 ÷ 8 = 2.25 lunches.

So, 20 loaves will make 2.25 × 20 = 45 lunches.

EXERCISE 9E

1 If 30 matches weigh 45 g, what would 40 matches weigh?

2 Five bars of chocolate cost £2.90. Find the cost of nine bars.

3 Eight men can chop down 18 trees in a day. How many trees can 20 men chop down in a day?

4 Find the cost of 48 eggs when 15 eggs can be bought for £2.10.

5 Seventy maths textbooks cost £875.

    a How much will 25 maths textbooks cost?

    b How many maths textbooks can you buy for £100?

> **HINTS AND TIPS**
>
> Remember to work out the value of one unit each time. Always check that answers are sensible.

6 A lorry uses 80 litres of diesel fuel on a trip of 280 miles.

    a How much diesel would the same lorry use on a trip of 196 miles?

    b How far would the lorry get on a full tank of 100 litres of diesel?

7 During the winter, I find that 200 kg of coal keeps my open fire burning for 12 weeks.

    a If I want an open fire all through the winter (18 weeks), how much coal will I need to buy?

    b Last year I bought 150 kg of coal. For how many weeks did I have an open fire?

8 It takes a photocopier 16 seconds to produce 12 copies. How long will it take to produce 30 copies?

9 A recipe for 12 biscuits uses:

    200 g margarine

    400 g sugar

    500 g flour

    300 g ground rice

    a What quantities are needed for:

        i 6 biscuits   **ii** 9 biscuits   **iii** 15 biscuits?

    b What is the maximum number of biscuits I could make if I had just 1 kg of each ingredient?

Best buys

In this section you will learn how to:
- find the cost per unit weight
- find the weight per unit cost
- use the above to find which product is the cheaper

Key words
best buy
value for money

When you wander around a supermarket and see all the different prices for the many different-sized packets, it is rarely obvious which are the '**best buys**'. However, with a calculator you can easily compare **value for money** by finding either:

the cost per unit weight **or** the weight per unit cost

To find:

- *cost per unit weight*, divide *cost by weight*

- *weight per unit cost*, divide *weight by cost*.

The next two examples show you how to do this.

EXAMPLE 8

A 300 g tin of cocoa costs £1.20. Find the cost per unit weight and the weight per unit cost.

First change £1.20 to 120p. Then divide, using a calculator, to get:

Cost per unit weight $120 \div 300 = 0.4$p per gram

Weight per unit cost $300 \div 120 = 2.5$ g per penny

EXAMPLE 9

A supermarket sells two different-sized packets of Whito soap powder. The medium size contains 800 g and costs £1.60 and the large size contains 2.5 kg and costs £4.75. Which is the better buy?

Find the weight per unit cost for both packets.

Medium: $800 \div 160 = 5$ g per penny

Large: $2500 \div 475 = 5.26$ g per penny

From these it is clear that there is more weight per penny with the large size, which means that the large size is the better buy.

EXERCISE 9F

D

1 Compare the following pairs of products and state which is the better buy. Explain why.

a Coffee: a medium jar which contains 140 g for £1.10 or a large jar which contains 300 g for £2.18

b Beans: a 125 g tin at 16p or a 600 g tin at 59p

c Flour: a 3 kg bag at 75p or a 5 kg bag at £1.20

d Toothpaste: a large tube containing 110 ml for £1.79 or a medium tube containing 75 ml for £1.15

e Frosties: a large box which contains 750 g for £1.64 or a medium box which contains 500 g for £1.10

f Rice Crispies: a medium box which contains 440 g for £1.64 or a large box which contains 600 g for £2.13

g Hair shampoo: a bottle containing 400 ml for £1.15 or a bottle containing 550 ml for £1.60

2 Julie wants to respray her car with yellow paint. In the local automart, she sees the following tins:

Small tin   350 ml at a cost of £1.79
Medium tin   500 ml at a cost of £2.40
Large tin   1.5 litres at a cost of £6.70

a What is the cost per litre of paint in the small tin?

b Which tin is offered at the lowest price per litre?

3 Tisco's sells bottled water in three sizes.

a Work out the cost per litre of the 'handy' size.

b Which bottle is the best value for money?

Handy size 40 cl   Family size 2 l   Giant size 5 l
£0.38   £0.98   £2.50

4 Two drivers are comparing the petrol consumption of their cars.

Ahmed says, 'I get 320 miles on a tank of 45 litres.'

Bashir says, 'I get 230 miles on a tank of 32 litres.'

Whose car is the more economical?

5 Mary and Jane are arguing about which of them is better at mathematics.

Mary scored 49 out of 80 on a test.

Jane scored 60 out of 100 on a test of the same standard.

Who is better at mathematics?

6 Paula and Kelly are comparing their running times.

Paula completed a 10-mile run in 65 minutes.

Kelly completed a 10-kilometre run in 40 minutes.

Given that 8 kilometres are equal to 5 miles, which girl has the greater average speed?

1 Breakfast cereal is sold in two sizes of packet.

The small packet holds 500 grams and costs £2.10.

The large packet holds 875 grams and costs £3.85.

Which packet is better value for money? You *must* show all your working.

2 **a** Brian travels 234 miles by train. His journey takes $2\frac{1}{2}$ hours.

What is the average speed of the train?

b Val drives 234 miles at an average speed of 45 mph.

How long does her journey take?

3 A country walk is 15 miles long. A leaflet states that this walk can be done in 4 hours.

a Calculate the average speed required to complete the walk in the time stated.

b A walker completes the route in 4 hours. She averages 5 miles an hour for the first hour.

Calculate her average speed for the remainder of the journey.

4 The only pets a pet shop sells are hamsters and fish. The ratio of the number of hamsters to the number of fish is 12 : 28

a What fraction of these pets are hamsters? Give your fraction in its simplest form.

The only fish the pet shop sells are goldfish and tropical fish.

The ratio of goldfish to tropical fish is 1 : 4.

The shop has 280 fish.

b Work out the number of goldfish the shop has.

Edexcel, Question 2, Paper 12A Intermediate, March 2005

5 The length of a coach is 15 metres. Jonathan makes a model of the coach. He uses a scale of 1 : 24

Work out the length, in centimetres, of the model coach.

Edexcel, Question 2, Paper 4 Intermediate, June 2005

6 Mr Bandle wins £18 000. He divides the £18 000 between his three children, Charlotte, James and Louise, in the ratio 4 : 5 : 6, respectively.

How much does Charlotte receive?

7 **a** The most popular picture frames are those for which the ratio of width to length is 5 : 8.

Which frames are in the ratio 5 : 8?

b There are 52 cards in a normal pack of cards. For a game, Dad shares the pack between Jack and Kenny in the ratio of 6 : 7.

How many cards does each player receive?

8 There are 40 chocolates in a box. 12 chocolates are plain chocolates. The remaining chocolates are milk chocolates.

a Work out the ratio of the number of plain chocolates to the number of milk chocolates in the box. Give your ratio in its simplest form.

Some plain chocolates are added to the box so that the ratio of the number of plain chocolates to the number of milk chocolates is 1 : 2

b Work out how many plain chocolates are added to the box.

Edexcel, Question 3, Paper 12B Intermediate, January 2005

9 In a school the ratio of teachers to pupils is 5 : 92. There are 644 pupils. How many teachers are there?

WORKED EXAM QUESTION

Cream is sold in small pots and large pots.

The ratio of the weight of a small pot to the weight of a large pot is 5 : 14. The weight of a small pot is 110 g.

What is the weight of a large pot?

> Read the question.
> Let W be the weight of the large pot.
> The ratio of the weights of the pots is $110 : W$, which is equal to 5 : 14.

Solution

$$W = \frac{14 \times 110}{5}$$

> Set up the equation $\frac{W}{110} = \frac{14}{5}$.
> You get 1 mark for this.

$$= \frac{14 \times 22}{1} = 308 \text{ g}$$

> Perform the final calculation (after maybe cancelling the fraction).
> Check the final answer is sensible.

Party time!

Alison and Bob have invited four friends to a dinner party.

They choose a menu but they have to change all the recipes to serve six people.

Copy their notebook pages and fill in the correct amounts.

Menu

* * * * *

Marinated mushrooms

* * * * *

Leek and macaroni bake
Mixed salad

* * * * *

Crème caramel

Marinated mushrooms (serves 2)
225 g mushrooms
15 ml wine vinegar
45 ml olive oil

Marinated mushrooms
(serves 6)
mushrooms _____ g
wine vinegar _____ ml
olive oil _____ ml

Leek and macaroni bake (serves 4)
130 g macaroni
50 g butter
270 g leeks
30 g flour
600 ml milk
180 g cheese
20 g breadcrumbs

Leek and macaroni bake
(serves 6)
macaroni _____ g
butter _____ g
leeks _____ g
flour _____ g
milk _____ ml
cheese _____ g
breadcrumbs _____ g

Crème caramel (serves 8)
240 g sugar
8 eggs
1.2 litres milk

Crème caramel (serves 6)
sugar _____ g
eggs _____
milk _____ litres

Bob arranges the seating plan for the table.

He sits everyone in order, male, female, male, female, and so on.

The plan shows where he places Alison and himself.

How many different ways are there to seat Claire, Derek, Elizabeth and Frank?

Bob
Alison

Bob estimates how many bottles of wine they will need.

A wine glass holds 150 ml. A bottle of wine holds 75 cl.

If each person at the party drinks two glasses of wine, apart from Frank who is driving, how many bottles will they need?

GRADE YOURSELF

E Simplify a ratio

D Calculate average speeds from data

D Calculate distance from speed and time

D Calculate time from speed and distance

D Compare prices of products to find the 'best buy'

C Solve problems, using ratio in appropriate situations

What you should know now

- How to divide any amount according to a given ratio
- The relationships between speed, time and distance
- How to solve problems involving direct proportion
- How to compare the prices of products

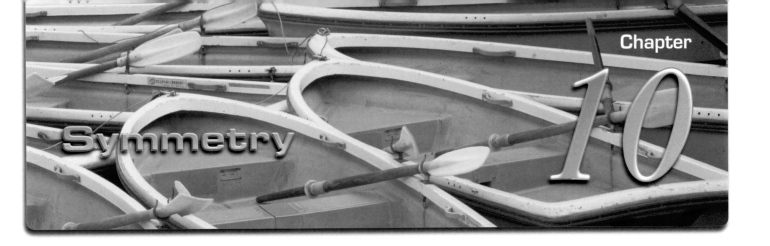

Chapter 10

Symmetry

1 Lines of symmetry

2 Rotational symmetry

3 Planes of symmetry

This chapter will show you ...

- how to draw the lines of symmetry on a 2-D shape
- how to find the order of rotational symmetry for a 2-D shape
- how to find the planes of symmetry for a 3-D shape

Visual overview

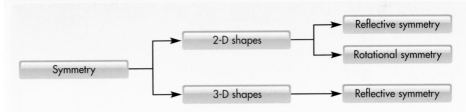

What you should already know

- The names of these 2-D shapes: isosceles triangle, equilateral triangle, right-angled triangle, square, rectangle, parallelogram, rhombus, trapezium and kite
- The names of these 3-D shapes: cone, cube, cuboid, cylinder, prism, sphere

Quick check

Name these 3-D shapes.

a 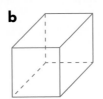   **b**   **c** 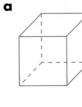   **d**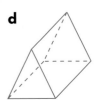

e   **f**   **g**

Mirror writing

You need a plane mirror and some plain or squared paper.

You probably know that certain styles of some upright capital letters have one or more lines of symmetry. For example, the upright A given below has one line of symmetry (shown here as a dashed line).

Draw a large A on your paper and put the mirror along the line of symmetry.

What do you notice when you look in the mirror?

Upright capital letters such as A, O and M have a vertical line of symmetry. Can you find any others?

Other upright capital letters (E, for example) have a horizontal line of symmetry. Can you find any others?

Now try to form words that have a vertical or a horizontal line of symmetry.

Here are two examples:

Make a display of all the different words you have found.

In this section you will learn how to:
- draw the lines of symmetry on a 2-D shape
- recognise shapes with reflective symmetry

Key words
line of symmetry
mirror line
symmetry

Many 2-D shapes have one or more lines of **symmetry**.

A **line of symmetry** is a line that can be drawn through a shape so that what can be seen on one side of the line is the mirror image of what is on the other side. This is why a line of symmetry is sometimes called a **mirror line**.

It is also the line along which a shape can be folded exactly onto itself.

Finding lines of symmetry

In an examination, you cannot use a mirror to find lines of symmetry but it is just as easy to use tracing paper, which is always available in any mathematics examination.

For example, to find the lines of symmetry for a rectangle, follow these steps.

1   Trace the rectangle.

2   Draw a line on the tracing paper where you think there is a line of symmetry.

3   Fold the tracing paper along this line. If the parts match, you have found a line of symmetry. If they do not match, try a line in another position.

4   Next, find out whether this is also a line of symmetry. You will find that it is.

5   Now see whether this is a line of symmetry. You will find that it is *not* a line of symmetry.

6   Your completed diagram should look like this. It shows that a rectangle has *two* lines of symmetry.

EXAMPLE 1

Find the number of lines of symmetry for this cross.

First, follow steps 1 to 4, which give the vertical and horizontal lines of symmetry.

Then, search for any other lines of symmetry in the same way.

There are two more, as the diagram shows.

So, this cross has a total of four lines of symmetry.

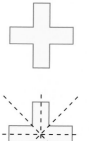

EXERCISE 10A

1 Copy these shapes and draw on the lines of symmetry for each one. If it will help you, use tracing paper or a mirror to check your results.

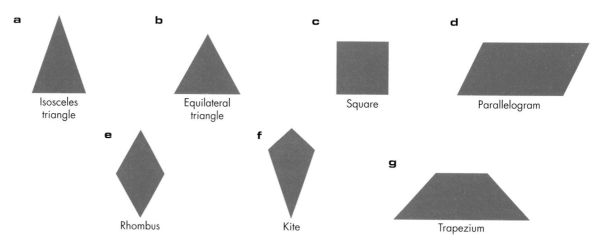

a Isosceles triangle

b Equilateral triangle

c Square

d Parallelogram

e Rhombus

f Kite

g Trapezium

2 **a** Find the number of lines of symmetry for each of these regular polygons.

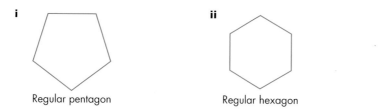

i Regular pentagon

ii Regular hexagon

iii Regular octagon

b How many lines of symmetry do you think a regular decagon has? (A decagon is a ten-sided polygon.)

3 Copy these star shapes and draw in all the lines of symmetry for each one.

a

b

c

4 Copy these patterns and draw in all the lines of symmetry for each one.

a

b

c

d

e

f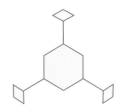

5 Write down the number of lines of symmetry for each of these flags.

Austria   Canada   Iceland   Switzerland   Greece

6 **a** These road signs all have lines of symmetry. Copy them and draw on the lines of symmetry for each one.

b Draw sketches of other common signs that also have lines of symmetry. State the number of lines of symmetry in each case.

7 The animal and plant kingdoms are full of symmetry. Four examples are given below. Sketch them and state the number of lines of symmetry for each one. Can you find other examples? Find suitable pictures, copy them and state the number of lines of symmetry each one has.

a

b

c

d

8 **a** Draw a circle with a radius of 3 cm.

b Draw on any lines of symmetry. What do you notice?

c How many lines of symmetry does a circle have?

217

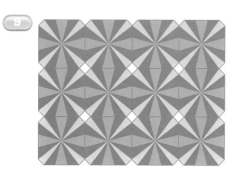

This decorative pattern is made by repeating shapes that have lines of symmetry. By using squared or isometric paper, try to make a similar pattern of your own.

10.2 Rotational symmetry

In this section you will learn how to:
- find the order of rotational symmetry for a 2-D shape
- recognise shapes with rotational symmetry

Key words
order of rotational symmetry
rotational symmetry

A 2-D shape has **rotational symmetry** if it can be rotated about a point to look exactly the same in a new position.

The **order of rotational symmetry** is the number of different positions in which the shape looks the same when it is rotated about the point.

The easiest way to find the order of rotational symmetry for any shape is to trace it and count the number of times that the shape stays the same as you turn the tracing paper through one complete turn.

EXAMPLE 2

Find the order of rotational symmetry for this shape.

First, hold the tracing paper on top of the shape and trace the shape. Then rotate the tracing paper and count the number of times the tracing matches the original shape in one complete turn.

You will find three different positions.

So, the order of rotational symmetry for the shape is 3.

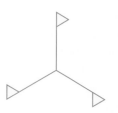

EXERCISE 10B

1 Copy these shapes and write below each one the order of rotational symmetry. If it will help you, use tracing paper.

a
Square

b
Rectangle

c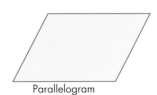
Parallelogram

d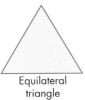
Equilateral triangle

e
Regular hexagon

2 Find the order of rotational symmetry for each of these shapes.

a   **b**   **c**   **d**   **e**

3 The following are Greek capital letters. Write down the order of rotational symmetry for each one.

a Φ **b** H **c** Z **d** Θ **e** Ξ

4 Copy these shapes on tracing paper and find the order of rotational symmetry for each one.

a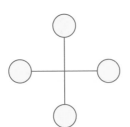

b

c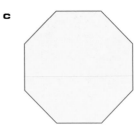

d

e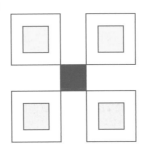

f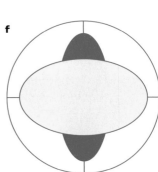

5 The upright capital letter A fits exactly onto itself only *once*. So, its order of rotational symmetry is 1. This means that it has *no* rotational symmetry. Write down all the upright capital letters of the alphabet that have rotational symmetry of order 1.

6 Find the order of rotational symmetry for a circle.

7 Obtain a pack of playing cards or a set of dominoes. Which cards or dominoes have rotational symmetry? Can you find any patterns? Write down everything you discover about the symmetry of the cards or dominoes.

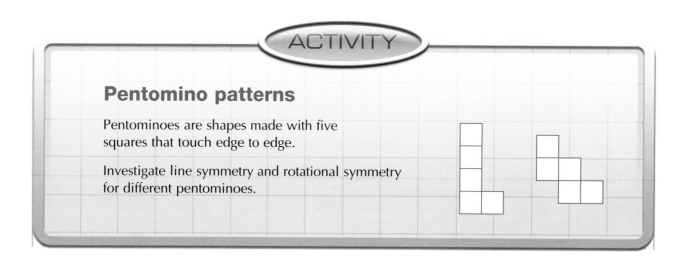

ACTIVITY

Pentomino patterns

Pentominoes are shapes made with five squares that touch edge to edge.

Investigate line symmetry and rotational symmetry for different pentominoes.

10.3 Planes of symmetry

In this section you will learn how to:
- find the number of planes of symmetry for a 3-D shape
- recognise shapes with planes of symmetry

Key words
plane of
  symmetry

Because of their 'depth', 3-D shapes have **planes of symmetry**, instead of the lines of symmetry found in 2-D shapes.

A plane of symmetry divides a 3-D shape into two identical parts or halves.

That is, one half of the shape is the reflection of the other half in the plane of symmetry.

EXAMPLE 3

How many planes of symmetry does this cuboid have?

A cuboid has three planes of symmetry because it can be sliced into halves in three different ways.

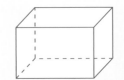

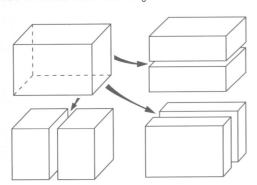

EXERCISE 10C

1 Find the number of planes of symmetry in each of these 3-D shapes.

a

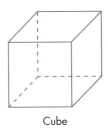

Cube

b

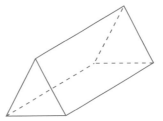

Triangular prism

c

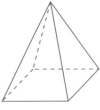

Square-based pyramid

2 This 3-D shape has five planes of symmetry.
Draw diagrams to show where they are.

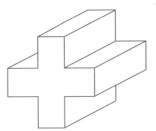

3 a The diagram shows half of a 3-D shape. Draw the complete shape so that the shaded part forms a plane of symmetry. What name do we give to this 3-D shape?

   b Draw similar diagrams to show a plane of symmetry for a cylinder and for a cone.

4 How many planes of symmetry does each of the following have?

   a brick   **b** shovel   **c** chair

   d spoon   **e** milk bottle   **f** kettle

1 The diagram shows a pentagon. It has one line of symmetry.

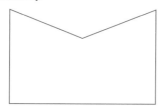

Copy the diagram and draw the line of symmetry.

  2 a Copy this rectangle and draw the lines of symmetry on it.

b What is the order of rotational symmetry of a rectangle?

  3 Here is a list of 8 numbers.

11   16   18   36
68   69   82   88

From these numbers, write down a number which has

a exactly *one* line of symmetry,

b 2 lines of symmetry *and* rotational symmetry of order 2,

c rotational symmetry of order 2 but *no* lines of symmetry.

Edexcel, Question 5d, Paper 1 Foundation, June 2005

  4 A pattern is to be drawn. It will have rotational symmetry of order 4. The pattern has been started.

Copy the diagram and shade *six* more squares to complete the pattern.

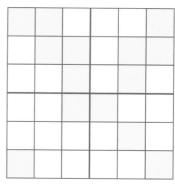

Edexcel, Question 6, Paper 8A Foundation, January 2003

  5

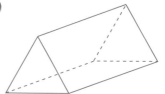

The diagram shows a triangular prism. The cross-section of the prism is an equilateral triangle.

Copy the diagram and draw in one plane of symmetry for the triangular prism.

Edexcel, Question 19a, Paper 2 Foundation, June 2005

  6 The diagram shows a square-based pyramid.

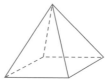

How many planes of symmetry does the pyramid have?

WORKED EXAM QUESTIONS

B A T H S

1 Which of the letters above has
   a line symmetry
   b rotational symmetry of order 2?

Solution

a  These letters have line symmetry as shown

b **H S**

2 A pattern has rotational symmetry of order 4 and no line symmetry. Part of the pattern is shown below. Complete the pattern.

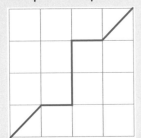

Solution

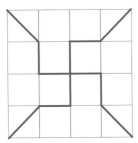

Trace the part of the pattern and rotate it about the centre of the grid three times through 90° to form the pattern.

SUMMARY

G Able to draw lines of symmetry on basic 2-D shapes

F Able to find the order of rotational symmetry for basic 2-D shapes

E Able to draw lines of symmetry on more complex 2-D shapes

E Able to find the order of rotational symmetry for more complex 2-D shapes

D Able to identify the number of planes of symmetry for 3-D shapes

What you should know now

- How to recognise lines of symmetry and draw them on 2-D shapes
- How to recognise whether a 2-D shape has rotational symmetry and find its order of rotational symmetry
- How to find the number of planes of symmetry for a 3-D shape

Averages

1 The mode

2 The median

3 The mean

4 The range

5 Which average to use

6 Frequency tables

7 Grouped data

8 Frequency polygons

This chapter will show you ...

- how to calculate the mode, median, mean and range of small sets of discrete data
- how to calculate the mode, median, mean and range from frequency tables of discrete data
- how to decide which is the best average for different types of data
- how to use and recognise the modal class and calculate an estimate of the mean from frequency tables of grouped data
- how to draw frequency polygons

Visual overview

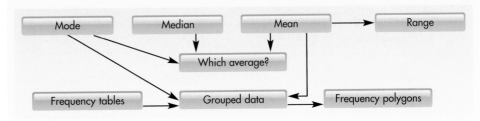

What you should already know

- How to collect and organise data
- How to draw frequency tables
- How to extract information from tables and diagrams

Quick check

The marks for 15 students in a maths test are:

2, 3, 4, 5, 5, 6, 6, 6, 7, 7, 7, 7, 7, 8, 10

a What is the most common mark?

b What is the middle value in the list?

c Find the difference between the highest mark and the lowest mark.

d Find the total of all 15 marks.

Average is a term often used when describing or comparing sets of data, for example, the average rainfall in Britain, the average score of a batsman, an average weekly wage or the average mark in an examination.

In each of the above examples, you are representing the whole set of many values by just a single, 'typical' value, which is called the average.

The idea of an average is extremely useful, because it enables you to compare one set of data with another set by comparing just two values – their averages.

There are several ways of expressing an average, but the most commonly used averages are the **mode**, the **median** and the **mean**.

11.1 The mode

In this section you will learn how to:
- find the mode from lists of data and from frequency tables

Key words
frequency
modal class
modal value
mode

The **mode** is the value that occurs the most in a set of data. That is, it is the value with the highest **frequency**.

The mode is a useful average because it is very easy to find and it can be applied to non-numerical data (qualitative data). For example, you could find the modal style of skirts sold in a particular month.

EXAMPLE 1

Suhail scored the following number of goals in 12 school football matches:

1 2 1 0 1 0 0 1 2 1 0 2

What is the mode of his scores?

The number which occurs most often in this list is 1. So, the mode is 1.

You can also say that the modal score or **modal value** is 1.

EXAMPLE 2

Barbara asked her friends how many books they had each taken out of the school library during the previous month. Their responses were:

2 1 3 4 6 4 1 3 0 2 6 0

Find the mode.

Here, there is no mode, because no number occurs more than the others.

EXERCISE 11A

1 Find the mode for each set of data.

a 3, 4, 7, 3, 2, 4, 5, 3, 4, 6, 8, 4, 2, 7

b 47, 49, 45, 50, 47, 48, 51, 48, 51, 48, 52, 48

c –1, 1, 0, –1, 2, –2, –2, –1, 0, 1, –1, 1, 0, –1, 2, –1, 2

d $\frac{1}{2}$, $\frac{1}{4}$, 1, $\frac{1}{2}$, $\frac{3}{4}$, $\frac{1}{4}$, 0, 1, $\frac{3}{4}$, $\frac{1}{4}$, 1, $\frac{1}{4}$, $\frac{3}{4}$, $\frac{1}{4}$, $\frac{1}{2}$

e 100, 10, 1000, 10, 100, 1000, 10, 1000, 100, 1000, 100, 10

f 1.23, 3.21, 2.31, 3.21, 1.23, 3.12, 2.31, 1.32, 3.21, 2.31, 3.21

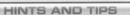

> **HINTS AND TIPS**
>
> It helps to put the data in order or group all the same things together.

2 Find the modal category for each set of data.

a red, green, red, amber, green, red, amber, green, red, amber

b rain, sun, cloud, sun, rain, fog, snow, rain, fog, sun, snow, sun

c α, γ, α, β, γ, α, α, γ, β, α, β, γ, β, β, α, β, γ, β

d ❄, ☆, ★, ★, ☆, ❄, ★, ✰, ★, ✰, ✦, ❄, ✪, ✰, ★, ✦, ✰

3 Joan did a survey to find the shoe sizes of pupils in her class. The bar chart illustrates her data.

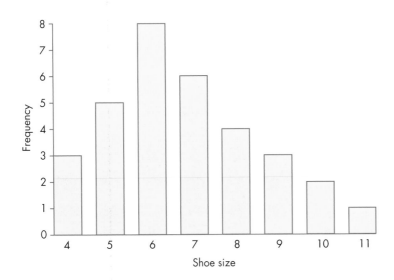

a How many pupils are in Joan's class?

b What is the modal shoe size?

c Can you tell from the bar chart which are the boys or which are the girls in her class?

 d Joan then decided to draw a bar chart to show the shoe sizes of the boys and the girls separately. Do you think that the mode for the boys and the mode for the girls will be the same as the mode for the whole class? Explain your answer.

4 The frequency table shows the marks that Form 10MP obtained in a spelling test.

Mark	3	4	5	6	7	8	9	10
Frequency	1	2	6	5	5	4	3	4

a Write down the mode for their marks.

b Do you think this is a typical mark for the form? Explain your answer.

5 The grouped frequency table shows the number of e-mails each household in Corporation Street received during one week.

No. of e-mails	0–4	5–9	10–14	15–19	20–24	25–29	30–34	35–39
Frequency	9	12	14	11	10	8	4	2

a Draw a bar chart to illustrate the data.

b How many households are there in Corporation Street?

c How many households received 20 or more e-mails?

d How many households did not receive any e-mails during the week? Explain your answer.

e Write down the modal class for the data in the table.

> **HINTS AND TIPS**
>
> You cannot find the mode of the data in a grouped frequency table. So, instead, you need to find the **modal class**, which is the class interval with the highest frequency.

6 Explain why the mode is often referred to as the 'shopkeeper's average'.

7 This table shows the colours of eyes for the pupils in form 7P.

	Blue	Brown	Green
Boys	4	8	1
Girls	8	5	2

a How many pupils are in form 7P?

b What is the modal eye colour for:

   i boys   ii girls   iii the whole form?

c After two pupils join the form the modal eye colour for the whole form is blue. Which of the following statements is true?

- Both pupils had green eyes.
- Both pupils had brown eyes.
- Both pupils had blue eyes.
- You cannot tell what their eye colours were.

The median

In this section you will learn how to:
- find the median from a list of data, a table of data and a stem-and-leaf diagram

Key words
median
middle
value

The **median** is the **middle value** of a list of values when they are put in *order* of size, from lowest to highest.

The advantage of using the median as an average is that half the data-values are below the median value and half are above it. Therefore, the average is only slightly affected by the presence of any particularly high or low values that are not typical of the data as a whole.

EXAMPLE 3

Find the median for the following list of numbers:

2, 3, 5, 6, 1, 2, 3, 4, 5, 4, 6

Putting the list in numerical order gives:

1, 2, 2, 3, 3, **4**, 4, 5, 5, 6, 6

There are 11 numbers in the list, so the middle of the list is the 6th number.
Therefore, the median is 4.

EXAMPLE 4

Find the median of the data shown in the frequency table.

Value	2	3	4	5	6	7
Frequency	2	4	6	7	8	3

First, add up the frequencies to find out how many pieces of data there are.

The total is 30 so the median value will be between the 15th and 16th values.

Now, add up the frequencies to give a running total, to find out where the 15th and 16th values are.

Value	2	3	4	5	6	7
Frequency	2	4	6	7	8	3
Total frequency	2	6	12	19	27	30

There are 12 data-values up to the value 4 and 19 up to the value 5.

Both the 15th and 16th values are 5, so the median is 5.

To find the median in a list of n values, written in order, use the rule:

$$\text{median} = \frac{n+1}{2}\text{th value}$$

For a set of data that has a lot of values, it is sometimes more convenient and quicker to draw a stem-and-leaf diagram. Example 5 shows you how to do this.

EXAMPLE 5

The ages of 20 people attending a conference were as follows:

28, 34, 46, 23, 28, 34, 52, 61, 45, 34, 39, 50, 26, 44, 60, 53, 31, 25, 37, 48

Find the modal age and median age of the group.

Taking the tens to be the 'stem' and the units to be the 'leaves', draw the stem-and-leaf diagram as shown below.

```
2 | 3  5  6  8  8
3 | 1  4  4  4  7  9
4 | 4  5  6  8
5 | 0  2  3
6 | 0  1
```
Key 2 | 3 represents 23 people

The most common value is 34, so the mode is 34.

There is an even number of values in this list, so the middle of the list is between the two central values, which are the 10th and 11th values. To find the central values count *up* 10 from the lowest value, 23, 25, 26, 28, 28, 31 … or *down* 10 from the highest value 61, 60, 53, 52, 50, 48 …

Therefore, the median is exactly midway between 37 and 39.

Hence, the median is 38.

EXERCISE 11B

1 Find the median for each set of data.

a 7, 6, 2, 3, 1, 9, 5, 4, 8

b 26, 34, 45, 28, 27, 38, 40, 24, 27, 33, 32, 41, 38

c 4, 12, 7, 6, 10, 5, 11, 8, 14, 3, 2, 9

d 12, 16, 12, 32, 28, 24, 20, 28, 24, 32, 36, 16

e 10, 6, 0, 5, 7, 13, 11, 14, 6, 13, 15, 1, 4, 15

f −1, −8, 5, −3, 0, 1, −2, 4, 0, 2, −4, −3, 2

g 5.5, 5.05, 5.15, 5.2, 5.3, 5.35, 5.08, 5.9, 5.25

> **HINTS AND TIPS**
>
> Remember to put the data in order before finding the median.

> **HINTS AND TIPS**
>
> If there is an even number of pieces of data, the median will be halfway between the two middle values.

2 A group of 15 sixth-formers had lunch in the school's cafeteria. Given below are the amounts that they spent.

£2.30, £2.20, £2, £2.50, £2.20, £3.50, £2.20, £2.25, £2.20, £2.30, £2.40, £2.20, £2.30, £2, £2.35

a Find the mode for the data.

b Find the median for the data.

c Which is the better average to use? Explain your answer.

3 **a** Find the median of 7, 4, 3, 8, 2, 6, 5, 2, 9, 8, 3.

b Without putting them in numerical order, write down the median for each of these sets.

i 17, 14, 13, 18, 12, 16, 15, 12, 19, 18, 13

ii 217, 214, 213, 218, 212, 216, 215, 212, 219, 218, 213

iii 12, 9, 8, 13, 7, 11, 10, 7, 14, 13, 8

iv 14, 8, 6, 16, 4, 12, 10, 4, 18, 16, 6

> **HINTS AND TIPS**
>
> Look for a connection between the original data and the new data. For example, in **i**, the numbers are each 10 more than those in part **a**.

4 Given below are the age, height and weight of each of the seven players in a netball team.

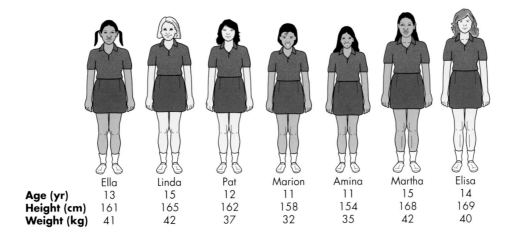

	Ella	Linda	Pat	Marion	Amina	Martha	Elisa
Age (yr)	13	15	12	11	11	15	14
Height (cm)	161	165	162	158	154	168	169
Weight (kg)	41	42	37	32	35	42	40

a Find the median age of the team. Which player has the median age?

b Find the median height of the team. Which player has the median height?

c Find the median weight of the team. Which player has the median weight?

d Who would you choose as the average player in the team? Give a reason for your answer.

5 The table shows the number of sandwiches sold in a corner shop over 25 days.

Sandwiches sold	10	11	12	13	14	15	16
Frequency	2	3	6	4	3	4	3

a What is the modal number of sandwiches sold?

b What is the median number of sandwiches sold?

6 The bar chart shows the marks that Mrs Woodhead gave her students for their first mathematics coursework task.

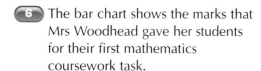

a How many students are there in Mrs Woodhead's class?

b What is the modal mark?

c Copy and complete this frequency table.

Mark	12	13	14	15	16	17	18
Frequency	1	3					

d What is the median mark?

7 **a** Write down a list of nine numbers that has a median of 12.

b Write down a list of ten numbers that has a median of 12.

c Write down a list of nine numbers that has a median of 12 and a mode of 8.

d Write down a list of ten numbers that has a median of 12 and a mode of 8.

8 The following stem-and-leaf diagram shows the times taken for 15 students to complete a mathematical puzzle.

```
1 | 7   8   8   9
2 | 2   2   2   5   6   9
3 | 3   4   5   5   8
```
Key 1 | 7 represents 17 seconds

a What is the modal time taken to complete the puzzle?

b What is the median time taken to complete the puzzle?

9 The stem-and-leaf diagram shows the marks for 13 boys and 12 girls in form 7E in a science test.

Key 2 | 3 represents 32 marks for boys
3 | 5 represents 35 marks for girls

```
            Boys  |  | Girls
        6   4   2 | 3 | 5   7   9
    9   9   6   2 | 4 | 2   2   3   8   8   8
7   6   6   6   5   3 | 5 | 1   1   5
```

> **HINTS AND TIPS**
>
> Read the boys' marks from right to left.

a What was the modal mark for the boys?

b What was the modal mark for the girls?

c What was the median mark for the boys?

d What was the median mark for the girls?

> **HINTS AND TIPS**
>
> To find the middle value of two numbers, add them together and divide the result by 2. For example, for 43 and 48, 43 + 48 = 91, 91 ÷ 2 = 45.5.

e Who did better in the test, the boys or the girls? Give a reason for your answer.

10 A list contains seven even numbers. The largest number is 24. The smallest number is half the largest. The mode is 14 and the median is 16. Two of the numbers add up to 42. What are the seven numbers?

11 The marks of 25 students in an English examination were as follows:

55, 63, 24, 47, 60, 45, 50, 89, 39, 47, 38, 42, 69, 73, 38, 47, 53, 64, 58, 71, 41, 48, 68, 64, 75

Draw a stem-and-leaf diagram to find the median.

11.3 The mean

In this section you will learn how to:	Key words
• calculate the mean of a set of data	average
	mean

The **mean** of a set of data is the sum of all the values in the set divided by the total number of values in the set. That is:

$$\text{mean} = \frac{\text{sum of all values}}{\text{total number of values}}$$

This is what most people mean when they use the term '**average**'.

The advantage of using the mean as an average is that it takes into account all the values in the set of data.

EXAMPLE 6

Find the mean of 4, 8, 7, 5, 9, 4, 8, 3.

Sum of all the values = 4 + 8 + 7 + 5 + 9 + 4 + 8 + 3 = 48

Total number of values = 8

Therefore, mean = $\frac{48}{8}$ = 6

EXAMPLE 7

The ages of 11 players in a football squad are:

21, 23, 20, 27, 25, 24, 25, 30, 21, 22, 28

What is the mean age of the squad?

Sum of all the ages = 266

Total number in squad = 11

Therefore, mean age = $\dfrac{266}{11}$ = 24.1818... = 24.2 (1 decimal place)

When the answer is not exact, it is usual to round the mean to 1 decimal place.

Using a calculator

If your calculator has a statistical mode, the mean of a set of numbers can be found by simply entering the numbers and then pressing the $\bar{x}$ key. On some calculators, the statistical mode is represented by SD.

Try this example. Find the mean of 2, 3, 7, 8 and 10.

First put your calculator into statistical mode. Then press the following keys:

2 DATA 3 DATA 7 DATA 8 DATA 1 0 DATA $\bar{x}$

You should find that the mean is given by $\bar{x}$ = 6.

You can also find the number of data-values by pressing the n key.

EXERCISE 11C

1 Find, without the help of a calculator, the mean for each set of data.

   a 7, 8, 3, 6, 7, 3, 8, 5, 4, 9

   b 47, 3, 23, 19, 30, 22

   c 42, 53, 47, 41, 37, 55, 40, 39, 44, 52

   d 1.53, 1.51, 1.64, 1.55, 1.48, 1.62, 1.58, 1.65

   e 1, 2, 0, 2, 5, 3, 1, 0, 1, 2, 3, 4

2 Calculate the mean for each set of data, giving your answer correct to 1 decimal place. You may use your calculator.

   a 34, 56, 89, 34, 37, 56, 72, 60, 35, 66, 67

   b 235, 256, 345, 267, 398, 456, 376, 307, 282

   c 50, 70, 60, 50, 40, 80, 70, 60, 80, 40, 50, 40, 70

   d 43.2, 56.5, 40.5, 37.9, 44.8, 49.7, 38.1, 41.6, 51.4

   e 2, 3, 1, 0, 2, 5, 4, 3, 2, 0, 1, 3, 4, 5, 0, 3, 1, 2

3 The table shows the marks that ten students obtained in mathematics, English and science in their Year 10 examinations.

Student	Abigail	Brian	Chloe	David	Eric	Frances	Graham	Howard	Ingrid	Jane
Maths	45	56	47	77	82	39	78	32	92	62
English	54	55	59	69	66	49	60	56	88	44
Science	62	58	48	41	80	56	72	40	81	52

  a Calculate the mean mark for mathematics.

  b Calculate the mean mark for English.

  c Calculate the mean mark for science.

  d Which student obtained marks closest to the mean in all three subjects?

  e How many students were above the average mark in all three subjects?

4 Heather kept a record of the amount of time she spent on her homework over 10 days:

$\frac{1}{2}$ h, 20 min, 35 min, $\frac{1}{4}$ h, 1 h, $\frac{1}{2}$ h, $1\frac{1}{2}$ h, 40 min, $\frac{3}{4}$ h, 55 min

Calculate the mean time, in minutes, that Heather spent on her homework.

> **HINTS AND TIPS**
>
> Convert all times to minutes, for example, $\frac{1}{4}$h = 15 minutes.

5 The weekly wages of ten people working in an office are:

£350   £200   £180   £200   £350   £200   £240   £480   £300   £280

  a Find the modal wage.

  b Find the median wage.

  c Calculate the mean wage.

> **HINTS AND TIPS**
>
> Remember that the mean can be distorted by extreme values.

  d Which of the three averages best represents the office staff's wages? Give a reason for your answer.

6 The ages of five people in a group of walkers are 38, 28, 30, 42 and 37.

  a Calculate the mean age of the group.

  b Steve, who is 41, joins the group. Calculate the new mean age of the group.

7 **a** Calculate the mean of 3, 7, 5, 8, 4, 6, 7, 8, 9 and 3.

  b Calculate the mean of 13, 17, 15, 18, 14, 16, 17, 18, 19 and 13. What do you notice?

  c Write down, without calculating, the mean for each of the following sets of data.

> **HINTS AND TIPS**
>
> Look for a connection between the original data and the new data. For example in **i** the numbers are 50 more.

    i 53, 57, 55, 58, 54, 56, 57, 58, 59, 53

    ii 103, 107, 105, 108, 104, 106, 107, 108, 109, 103

    iii 4, 8, 6, 9, 5, 7, 8, 9, 10, 4

8 The mean age of a group of eight walkers is 42. Joanne joins the group and the mean age changes to 40. How old is Joanne?

The range

In this section you will learn how to:

● find the range of a set of data and compare different sets of data using the mean and the range

Key words
consistency
range
spread

The **range** for a set of data is the highest value of the set minus the lowest value.

The range is *not* an average. It shows the **spread** of the data. It is, therefore, used when comparing two or more sets of similar data. You can also use it to comment on the **consistency** of two or more sets of data.

EXAMPLE 8

Rachel's marks in ten mental arithmetic tests were 4, 4, 7, 6, 6, 5, 7, 6, 9 and 6.

Therefore, her mean mark is $60 \div 10 = 6$ and the range is $9 - 4 = 5$.

Adil's marks in the same tests were 6, 7, 6, 8, 5, 6, 5, 6, 5 and 6.

Therefore, his mean mark is $60 \div 10 = 6$ and the range is $8 - 5 = 3$.

Although the means are the same, Adil has a smaller range. This shows that Adil's results are more consistent.

EXERCISE 11D

1 Find the range for each set of data.

a 3, 8, 7, 4, 5, 9, 10, 6, 7, 4

b 62, 59, 81, 56, 70, 66, 82, 78, 62, 75

c 1, 0, 4, 5, 3, 2, 5, 4, 2, 1, 0, 1, 4, 4

d 3.5, 4.2, 5.5, 3.7, 3.2, 4.8, 5.6, 3.9, 5.5, 3.8

e 2, –1, 0, 3, –1, –2, 1, –4, 2, 3, 0, 2, –2, 0, –3

2 The table shows the maximum and minimum temperatures at midday for five cities in England during a week in August.

	Birmingham	Leeds	London	Newcastle	Sheffield
Maximum temperature (°C)	28	25	26	27	24
Minimum temperature (°C)	23	22	24	20	21

a Write down the range of the temperatures for each city.

b What do the ranges tell you about the weather for England during the week?

3 Over a three-week period, the school tuck shop took the following amounts.

	Monday	Tuesday	Wednesday	Thursday	Friday
Week 1	£32	£29	£36	£30	£28
Week 2	£34	£33	£25	£28	£20
Week 3	£35	£34	£31	£33	£32

a Calculate the mean amount taken each week.

b Find the range for each week.

c What can you say about the total amounts taken for each of the three weeks?

4 In a ladies' golf tournament, the club chairperson had to choose either Sheila or Fay to play in the first round. In the previous eight rounds, their scores were as follows:

Sheila's scores: 75, 92, 80, 73, 72, 88, 86, 90

Fay's scores: 80, 87, 85, 76, 85, 79, 84, 88

a Calculate the mean score for each golfer.

b Find the range for each golfer.

c Which golfer would you choose to play in the tournament? Explain why.

HINTS AND TIPS

The best person to choose may not be the one with the biggest mean but could be the most consistent player.

5 Dan has a choice of two buses to get to school: Number 50 or Number 63. Over a month, he kept a record of the number of minutes each bus was late when it set off from his home bus stop.

No. 50: 4, 2, 0, 6, 4, 8, 8, 6, 3, 9

No. 63: 3, 4, 0, 10, 3, 5, 13, 1, 0, 1

a For each bus, calculate the mean number of minutes late.

b Find the range for each bus.

c Which bus would you advise Dan to catch? Give a reason for your answer.

Your time is up

You are going to find out how good you are at estimating 1 minute.

You need a stopwatch and a calculator.

This is a group activity. One person in the group acts as a timekeeper, says 'Start' and starts the stopwatch.

When someone thinks 1 minute has passed, they say 'Stop', and the timekeeper writes down the actual time, in seconds, that has passed. The timekeeper should try to record everyone's estimate.

Repeat the activity, with every member of the group taking a turn as the timekeeper.

Collate all the times and, from the data, find the mean (to the nearest second) and the range.

- How close is the mean to 1 minute?

- Why is the range useful?

- What strategies did people use to estimate 1 minute?

Repeat the activity for estimating different times, for example, 30 seconds or 2 minutes.

Write a brief report on what you find out about people's ability to estimate time.

11.5 Which average to use

In this section you will learn how to:

- understand the advantages and disadvantages of each type of average and decide which one to use in different situations

Key words

appropriate
extreme values
representative

An average must be truly **representative** of a set of data. So, when you have to find an average, it is crucial to choose the **appropriate** type of average for this particular set of data.

If you use the wrong average, your results will be distorted and give misleading information.

This table, which compares the advantages and disadvantages of each type of average, will help you to make the correct decision.

	Mode	Median	Mean

Advantages	Very easy to find
	Not affected by
	   extreme values
	Can be used for
	   non-numerical data
		Easy to find for
		   ungrouped data
		Not affected by extreme
		   values
			Easy to find
			Uses all the values
			The total for a given
			   number of values can
			   be calculated from it

Disadvantages	Does not use all the values
	May not exist
		Does not use all the
		   values
		Often not understood
			Extreme values can
			   distort it
			Has to be calculated

Use for	Non-numerical data
	Finding the most
	   likely value
		Data with extreme
		   values
			Data with values that
			   are spread in a
			   balanced way

EXERCISE 11E

1 The ages of the members of a hockey team were:

   29   26   21   24   26   28   35   23   29   28   29

a What is:

   i the modal age?   **ii** the median age?   **iii** the mean age?

b What is the range of the ages?

2 **a** For each set of data, find the mode, the median and the mean.

   i 6, 10, 3, 4, 3, 6, 2, 9, 3, 4

   ii 6, 8, 6, 10, 6, 9, 6, 10, 6, 8

   iii 7, 4, 5, 3, 28, 8, 2, 4, 10, 9

b For each set of data, decide which average is the best one to use and give a reason.

3 A newsagent sold the following number of copies of *The Evening Star* on 12 consecutive evenings during a promotion exercise organised by the newspaper's publisher:

   65   73   75   86   90   112   92   87   77   73   68   62

a Find the mode, the median and the mean for the sales.

b The newsagent had to report the average sale to the publisher after the promotion. Which of the three averages would you advise the newsagent to use? Explain why.

4 The mean age of a group of ten young people was 15.

   a What do all their ages add up to?

   b What will be their mean age in five years' time?

5 **a** Find the median of each list below.

i 2, 4, 6, 7, 9

ii 12, 14, 16, 17, 19

iii 22, 24, 26, 27, 29

iv 52, 54, 56, 57, 59

v 92, 94, 96, 97, 99

b What do you notice about the lists and your answers?

c Use your answer above to help find the medians of the following lists.

i 132, 134, 136, 137, 139

ii 577, 576, 572, 574, 579

iii 431, 438, 439, 432, 435

iv 855, 859, 856, 851, 857

d Find the mean of each of the sets of numbers in part **a**.

6 Decide which average you would use for each of the following. Give a reason for your answer.

a The average mark in an examination

b The average pocket money for a group of 16-year-old students

c The average shoe size for all the girls in Year 10

d The average height for all the artistes on tour with a circus

e The average hair colour for pupils in your school

f The average weight of all newborn babies in a hospital's maternity ward

7 A pack of matches consisted of 12 boxes. The contents of each box were counted as:

34   31   29   35   33   30   31   28   29   35   32   31

On the box it stated 'Average contents 32 matches'. Is this correct?

8 A firm showed the annual salaries for its employees as:

Chairman	£43 000
Managing director	£37 000
Floor manager	£25 000
Skilled worker 1	£24 000
Skilled worker 2	£24 000
Machinist	£18 000
Computer engineer	£18 000
Secretary	£18 000
Office junior	£7 000

a What is:

   i the modal salary?   **ii** the median salary?   **iii** the mean salary?

b The management suggested a pay rise of 6% for all employees. The shopfloor workers suggested a pay rise of £1500 for all employees.

   i One of the suggestions would cause problems for the firm. Which one is that and why?

   ii What difference would each suggestion make to the modal, median and mean salaries?

9 Mr Brennan, a caring maths teacher, told each pupil their test mark and only gave the test statistics to the whole class. He gave the class the modal mark, the median mark and the mean mark.

   a Which average would tell a pupil whether they were in the top half or the bottom half of the class?

   b Which average tells the pupils nothing really?

   c Which average allows a pupil to gauge how well they have done compared with everyone else?

10 A list of nine numbers has a mean of 7.6. What number must be added to the list to give a new mean of 8?

11 A dance group of 17 teenagers had a mean weight of 44.5 kg. To enter a competition there needed to be 18 teenagers with an average weight of 44.4 kg or less. What is the maximum weight that the eighteenth person must be?

11.6 Frequency tables

In this section you will:
- revise finding the mode and median from a frequency table
- learn how to calculate the mean from a frequency table

Key words
frequency table

When a lot of information has been gathered, it is often convenient to put it together in a **frequency table**. From this table you can then find the values of the three averages and the range.

EXAMPLE 9

A survey was done on the number of people in each car leaving the Meadowhall Shopping Centre, in Sheffield. The results are summarised in the table below.

Number of people in each car	1	2	3	4	5	6
Frequency	45	198	121	76	52	13

For the number of people in a car, calculate the following.

a the mode   **b** the median   **c** the mean

a The modal number of people in a car is easy to spot. It is the number with the largest frequency, that is 198. Hence, the modal number of people in a car is 2.

b The median number of people in a car is found by working out where the middle of the set of numbers is located. First, add up frequencies to get the total number of cars surveyed, which comes to 505. Next, calculate the middle position:

$$(505 + 1) \div 2 = 253$$

Now add the frequencies across the table to find which group contains the 253rd item. The 243rd item is the end of the group with 2 in a car. Therefore, the 253rd item must be in the group with 3 in a car. Hence, the median number of people in a car is 3.

c To calculate the mean number of people in a car, multiply the number of people in the car by the frequency. This is best done in an extra column. Add these to find the total number of people and divide by the total frequency (the number of cars surveyed).

Number in car	Frequency	Number in these cars
1	45	$1 \times 45 = 45$
2	198	$2 \times 198 = 396$
3	121	$3 \times 121 = 363$
4	76	$4 \times 76 = 304$
5	52	$5 \times 52 = 260$
6	13	$6 \times 13 = 78$
Totals	505	1446

Hence, the mean number of people in a car is $1446 \div 505 = 2.9$ (to 1 decimal place).

Using your calculator

The previous example can also be done by using the statistical mode which is available on some calculators. However, not all calculators are the same, so you will have to either read your instruction manual or experiment with the statistical keys on your calculator.

You may find one labelled:

DATA or **M+** or **Σ+** or **$\bar{x}$** , where $\bar{x}$ is printed in blue.

Try the following key strokes:

EXERCISE 11F

1 Find **i** the mode, **ii** the median and **iii** the mean from each frequency tables below.

a A survey of the shoe sizes of all the Y10 boys in a school gave these results.

Shoe size	4	5	6	7	8	9	10
Number of pupils	12	30	34	35	23	8	3

b A survey of the number of eggs laid by hens over a period of one week gave these results.

Number of eggs	0	1	2	3	4	5	6
Frequency	6	8	15	35	48	37	12

c This is a record of the number of babies born each week over one year in a small maternity unit.

Number of babies	0	1	2	3	4	5	6	7	8	9	10	11	12	13	14
Frequency	1	1	1	2	2	2	3	5	9	8	6	4	5	2	1

d A school did a survey on how many times in a week pupils arrived late at school. These are the findings.

Number of times late	0	1	2	3	4	5
Frequency	481	34	23	15	3	4

2 A survey of the number of children in each family of a school's intake gave these results.

Number of children	1	2	3	4	5
Frequency	214	328	97	26	3

a Assuming each child at the school is shown in the data, how many children are at the school?

b Calculate the mean number of children in a family.

c How many families have this mean number of children?

d How many families would consider themselves average from this survey?

3 A dentist kept records of how many teeth he extracted from his patients.

In 1980 he extracted 598 teeth from 271 patients.

In 1990 he extracted 332 teeth from 196 patients.

In 2000 he extracted 374 teeth from 288 patients.

a Calculate the average number of teeth taken from each patient in each year.

b Explain why you think the average number of teeth extracted falls each year.

4 One hundred cases of apples delivered to a supermarket were inspected and the numbers of bad apples were recorded.

Bad apples	0	1	2	3	4	5	6	7	8	9
Frequency	52	29	9	3	2	1	3	0	0	1

What is:

a the modal number of bad apples per case?

b the mean number of bad apples per case?

5 Two dice are thrown together 60 times. The sum of the scores is shown below.

Score	2	3	4	5	6	7	8	9	10	11	12
Frequency	1	2	6	9	12	15	6	5	2	1	1

Find **a** the modal score, **b** the median score and **c** the mean score.

6 During a one-month period, the number of days off by 100 workers in a factory were noted as follows.

Number of days off	0	1	2	3	4
Number of workers	35	42	16	4	3

Calculate the following.

a the modal number of days off

b the median number of days off

c the mean number of days off

7 Two friends often played golf together. They recorded their scores for each hole over the last five games to compare who was more consistent and who was the better player. Their results were summarised in the following table.

No. of shots to hole ball	1	2	3	4	5	6	7	8	9
Roger	0	0	0	14	37	27	12	0	0
Brian	5	12	15	18	14	8	8	8	2

a What is the modal score for each player?

b What is the range of scores for each player?

c What is the median score for each player?

d What is the mean score for each player?

e Which player is the more consistent and why?

f Who would you say is the better player and why?

Grouped data

In this section you will learn how to:
- identify the modal class
- calculate an estimate of the mean from a grouped table

Key words

grouped data
estimated mean
modal class

Sometimes the information you are given is grouped in some way (called **grouped data**), as in Example 10, which shows the range of weekly pocket money given to Y10 students in a particular class.

Normally, grouped tables use continuous data, which is data that can have any value within a range of values, for example, height, weight, time, area and capacity. In these situations, the **mean** can only be **estimated** as you do not have all the information.

Discrete data is data that consists of separate numbers, for example, goals scored, marks in a test, number of children and shoe sizes.

In both cases, when using a grouped table to estimate the mean, first find the midpoint of the interval by adding the two end values and then dividing by two.

EXAMPLE 10

Pocket money, p (£)	$0 < p \leqslant 1$	$1 < p \leqslant 2$	$2 < p \leqslant 3$	$3 < p \leqslant 4$	$4 < p \leqslant 5$
No. of students	2	5	5	9	15

a Write down the **modal class**. **b** Calculate an estimate of the mean weekly pocket money.

a The modal class is easy to pick out, since it is simply the one with the largest frequency. Here the modal class is £4 to £5.

b To estimate the mean, assume that each person in each class has the 'midpoint' amount, then build up the following table.

To find the midpoint value, the two end values are added together and then divided by two.

Pocket money, p (£)	Frequency (f)	Midpoint (m)	$f \times m$
$0 < p \leqslant 1$	2	0.50	1.00
$1 < p \leqslant 2$	5	1.50	7.50
$2 < p \leqslant 3$	5	2.50	12.50
$3 < p \leqslant 4$	9	3.50	31.50
$4 < p \leqslant 5$	15	4.50	67.50
Totals	36		120

The estimated mean will be £120 ÷ 36 = £3.33 (rounded to the nearest penny).

Note the notation for the classes:

$0 < p \leqslant 1$ means any amount above 0p up to and including £1.

$1 < p \leqslant 2$ means any amount above £1 up to and including £2, and so on.

If you had written 0.01 – 1.00, 1.01 – 2.00 and so on for the groups, then the midpoints would have been 0.505, 1.505 and so on. This would not have had a significant effect on the final answer as it is only an estimate.

1 For each table of values given below, find:

i the modal group

ii an estimate for the mean.

a

x	$0 < x \leqslant 10$	$10 < x \leqslant 20$	$20 < x \leqslant 30$	$30 < x \leqslant 40$	$40 < x \leqslant 50$
Frequency	4	6	11	17	9

b

y	$0 < y \leqslant 100$	$100 < y \leqslant 200$	$200 < y \leqslant 300$	$300 < y \leqslant 400$	$400 < y \leqslant 500$	$500 < x \leqslant 600$
Frequency	95	56	32	21	9	3

c

z	$0 < z \leqslant 5$	$5 < z \leqslant 10$	$10 < z \leqslant 15$	$15 < z \leqslant 20$
Frequency	16	27	19	13

> **HINTS AND TIPS**
>
> When you copy the tables, drawn them vertically as in Example 10.

d

Weeks	1–3	4–6	7–9	10–12	13–15
Frequency	5	8	14	10	7

2 Jason brought 100 pebbles back from the beach and weighed them all, recording each weight to the nearest gram. His results are summarised in the table below.

Weight, w (g)	$40 < w \leqslant 60$	$60 < w \leqslant 80$	$80 < w \leqslant 100$	$100 < w \leqslant 120$	$120 < w \leqslant 140$	$140 < w \leqslant 160$
Frequency	5	9	22	27	26	11

Find the following.

a the modal weight of the pebbles

b an estimate of the total weight of all the pebbles

c an estimate of the mean weight of the pebbles

3 A gardener measured the heights of all his daffodils to the nearest centimetre and summarised his results as follows.

Height (cm)	10–14	15–18	19–22	23–26	27–40
Frequency	21	57	65	52	12

a How many daffodils did the gardener have?

b What is the modal height of the daffodils?

c What is the estimated mean height of the daffodils?

4 A survey was made to see how quickly the AA attended calls that were not on a motorway. The following table summarises the results.

Time (min)	1–15	16–30	31–45	46–60	61–75	76–90	91–105
Frequency	2	23	48	31	27	18	11

a How many calls were used in the survey?

b Estimate the mean time taken per call.

c Which average would the AA use for the average call-out time?

d What percentage of calls do the AA get to within the hour?

5 One hundred light bulbs were tested by their manufacturer to see whether the average life-span of the manufacturer's bulbs was over 200 hours. The following table summarises the results.

Life span, h (hours)	$150 < h \leqslant 175$	$175 < h \leqslant 200$	$200 < h \leqslant 225$	$225 < h \leqslant 250$	$250 < h \leqslant 275$
Frequency	24	45	18	10	3

a What is the modal length of time a bulb lasts?

b What percentage of bulbs last longer than 200 hours?

c Estimate the mean life-span of the light bulbs.

d Do you think the test shows that the average life-span is over 200 hours? Fully explain your answer.

6 Three supermarkets each claimed to have the lowest average price increase over the year. The following table summarises their price increases.

Price increase (p)	1–5	6–10	11–15	16–20	21–25	26–30	31–35
Soundbuy	4	10	14	23	19	8	2
Springfields	5	11	12	19	25	9	6
Setco	3	8	15	31	21	7	3

Using their average price increases, make a comparison of the supermarkets and write a report on which supermarket, in your opinion, has the lowest price increases over the year. Do not forget to justify your answers.

7 The table shows the distances run, over a month, by an athlete who is training for a marathon.

Distance, d (miles)	$0 < d \leqslant 5$	$5 < d \leqslant 10$	$10 < d \leqslant 15$	$15 < d \leqslant 20$	$20 < d \leqslant 25$
Frequency	3	8	13	5	2

a A marathon is 26.2 miles. It is recommended that an athlete's daily average mileage should be at least a third of the distance of the race for which they are training. Is this athlete doing enough training?

b The athlete records the times of some runs and calculates that her average pace for all runs is $6\frac{1}{2}$ minutes to a mile. Explain why she is wrong to expect a finishing time for the marathon of $26.2 \times 6\frac{1}{2}$ minutes ≈ 170 minutes.

c The runner claims that the difference in length between her shortest and longest run is 21 miles. Could this be correct? Explain your answer.

Frequency polygons

In this section you will learn how to:

- draw frequency polygons for discrete and continuous data

Key words

frequency
    polygon
discrete data
continuous
    data

To help people understand it, statistical information is often presented in pictorial or diagrammatic form, which includes the pie chart, the line graph, the bar chart and stem-and-leaf diagrams. These were covered in Chapter 6. Another method of showing data is by **frequency polygons**.

Frequency polygons can be used to represent both ungrouped data and grouped data, as shown in Example 11 and Example 12 respectively and are appropriate for both **discrete data** and **continuous data**.

Frequency polygons show the shapes of distributions and can be used to compare distributions.

EXAMPLE 11

No. of children	0	1	2	3	4	5
Frequency	12	23	36	28	16	11

This is the frequency polygon for the ungrouped data in the table.

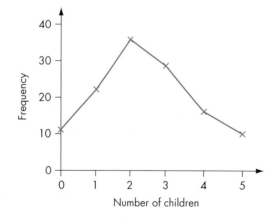

Note:

- The coordinates are plotted from each ordered pair in the table.

- The polygon is completed by joining up the plotted points with straight lines.

EXAMPLE 12

Weight, w (kg)	0 < w ≤ 5	5 < w ≤ 10	10 < w ≤ 15	15 < w ≤ 20	20 < w ≤ 25	25 < w ≤ 30
Frequency	4	13	25	32	17	9

This is the frequency polygon for the grouped data in the table.

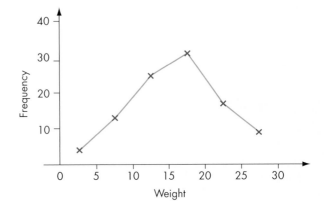

Note:

- The midpoint of each group is used, just as it was in estimating the mean.

- The ordered pairs of midpoints with frequency are plotted, namely:

  (2.5, 4), (7.5, 13), (12.5, 25), (17.5, 32), (22.5, 17), (27.5, 9)

- The polygon should be left like this. Any lines you draw before and after this have no meaning.

EXERCISE 11H

1. The following table shows how many students were absent from one particular class throughout the year.

Students absent	1	2	3	4	5
Frequency	48	32	12	3	1

   a Draw a frequency polygon to illustrate the data.

   b Estimate the mean number of absences each lesson.

2. The table below shows the number of goals scored by a hockey team in one season.

Goals	1	2	3	4	5
Frequency	3	9	7	5	2

   a Draw the frequency polygon for this data.

   b Estimate the mean number of goals scored per game this season.

3 After a spelling test, all the results were collated for girls and boys as below.

Number correct	1–4	5–8	9–12	13–16	17–20
Boys	3	7	21	26	15
Girls	4	8	17	23	20

a Draw frequency polygons to illustrate the differences between the boys' scores and the girls' scores.

b Estimate the mean score for boys and girls separately, and comment on the results.

4 A doctor was concerned at the length of time her patients had to wait to see her when they came to the morning surgery. The survey she did gave her the following results.

Time, m (min)	$0 < m \leqslant 10$	$10 < m \leqslant 20$	$20 < m \leqslant 30$	$30 < m \leqslant 40$	$40 < m \leqslant 50$	$50 < m \leqslant 60$
Monday	5	8	17	9	7	4
Tuesday	9	8	16	3	2	1
Wednesday	7	6	18	2	1	1

a Using the same pair of axes, draw a frequency polygon for each day.

b What is the average amount of time spent waiting each day?

c Why might the average time for each day be different?

5 The frequency polygon shows the amounts of money spent in a corner shop by the first 40 customers one morning.

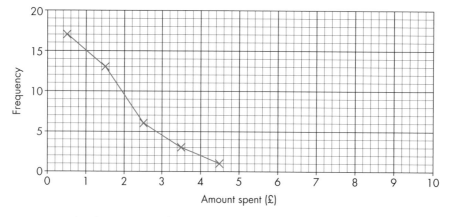

Amount spent (£)

a i Use the frequency polygon to complete the table for the amounts spent by the first 40 customers.

Amount spent, m (£)	$0 < m \leqslant 1$	$1 < m \leqslant 2$	$2 < m \leqslant 3$	$3 < m \leqslant 4$	$4 < m \leqslant 5$
Frequency					

ii Work out the mean amount of money spent by these 40 customers.

b Mid-morning another 40 customers visit the shop and the shopkeeper records the amounts they spend. The table below shows the data.

Amount spent, m (£)	$0 < m \leqslant 2$	$2 < m \leqslant 4$	$4 < m \leqslant 6$	$6 < m \leqslant 8$	$8 < m \leqslant 10$
Frequency	3	5	18	10	4

i Copy the graph above and draw the frequency polygon to show this data.

ii Calculate the mean amount spent by the 40 mid-morning customers.

c Comment on the differences between the frequency polygons and the average amounts spent by the different groups of customers.

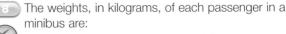

1 The table shows how many children there were in the family of each member of a class.

Number of children	Frequency
1	6
2	10
3	4
4	3
5	1

a How many children were in the class?

b What is the modal number of children per family?

c What is the median number of children per family?

d What is the mean number of children per family?

2 Find: **a** the mode **b** the median of:

6, 6, 6, 8, 9, 10, 11, 12, 13

3 Here are the test marks of 6 girls and 4 boys.

Girls: 5 3 10 2 7 3

Boys: 2 5 9 3

a Write down the mode of the 10 marks.

b Work out the median mark of the boys.

c Work out the range of the girls' marks.

d Work out the mean mark of all 10 students.

Edexcel, Question 4, Paper 8B Foundation, January 2004

4 Find the mean of 5, 7, 8, 9, 10, 10, 11, 12, 13 and 35.

5 Use your calculator to work out the value of

$$\frac{5.4 \times 8.1}{12.3 - 5.9}$$

Write down all the figures on your calculator display.

Edexcel, Question 2, Paper 12B Intermediate, March 2005

6 a Work out:

i the mean ii the range

of 61, 63, 61, 86, 78, 75, 80, 68, 84 and 84.

b Fred wants to plant a conifer hedge. At the local garden centre he looks at 10 plants from two different varieties of conifer.

All the plants have been growing for six months.

The Sprucy Pine plants have a mean height of 74 cm and a range of 25 cm.

The Evergreen plants have a mean height of 52 cm and a range of 5 cm.

i Give one reason why Fred might decide to plant a hedge of Sprucy Pine trees.

ii Give one reason why Fred might decide to plant a hedge of Evergreen trees.

7 The stem-and leaf-diagram shows the number of packages 15 drivers delivered.

Key 3 | 5 means 35 packages

```
3 | 5 7
4 | 1 3 8 8
5 | 0 2 5 6 7 9
6 | 6 9
7 | 2
```

a What is the range of the packets delivered?

b What is the median of the packets delivered?

c What is the mode of the packets delivered?

8 The weights, in kilograms, of each passenger in a minibus are:

86, 76, 84, 84, 81, 85, 80, 86, 33

a Calculate:

i their median weight

ii the range of their weights

iii their mean weight.

b Which of the two averages, mean or median, better describes the data above? Give a reason for your answer.

9 A company puts this advert in the local paper.

NCS Engineers
Mechanic needed
Average wage over £500 per week

The following people work for the company.

Job	Wage per week (£)
Apprentice	210
Cleaner	210
Foreman	360
Manager	850
Mechanic	255
Parts Manager	650
Sales Manager	680

a What is the mode of these wages?

b What is the median wage?

c Calculate the mean wage.

d Explain why the advert is misleading.

10 The numbers of people in 50 cars are recorded.

Number of people	Frequency
1	24
2	13
3	8
4	4
5	1

Calculate the mean number of people per car.

11 The table shows the distances travelled to work by 40 office workers.

Distance travelled, d (km)	Frequency
$0 < d \leqslant 2$	10
$2 < d \leqslant 4$	16
$4 < d \leqslant 6$	8
$6 < d \leqslant 8$	5
$8 < d \leqslant 10$	1

Calculate an estimate of the mean distance travelled to work by these office workers.

12 Tom and Barbara grew tomatoes. They compared their tomatoes by selecting 100 of each one weekend. The table shows the mean weight of Tom's tomatoes.

Weight, w (grams)	Tom's Tomatoes
$50 \leqslant w < 100$	21
$100 \leqslant w < 150$	28
$150 \leqslant w < 200$	26
$200 \leqslant w < 250$	14
$250 \leqslant w < 300$	9
$300 \leqslant w < 350$	2

a Which class interval contains the median weight for Tom's Tomatoes?

b The frequency polygon for Barbara's Tomatoes is drawn on the following grid. Copy it on to graph paper. On the same grid draw the frequency polygon for Tom's Tomatoes.

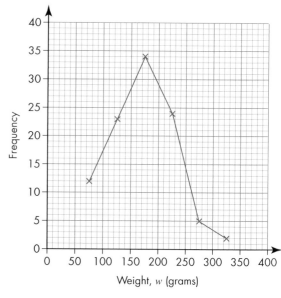

c Use the frequency polygons to write down one comparison between Tom and Barbara's Tomatoes.

13 The mean weight of five rowers is 49.2 kg.

a Find the total weight of the rowers.

b The mean weight of the five rowers and the reserve is 50.5 kg.
Calculate the weight of the reserve.

14 The table shows information about the number of hours that 120 children used a computer last week.

Number of hours (h)	Frequency
$0 < h \leqslant 2$	10
$2 < h \leqslant 4$	15
$4 < h \leqslant 6$	30
$6 < h \leqslant 8$	35
$8 < h \leqslant 10$	25
$10 < h \leqslant 12$	5

Work out an estimate for the mean number of hours that the children used a computer. Give your answer correct to 2 decimal places.

Edexcel, Question 10, Paper 17 Intermediate, June 2005

WORKED EXAM QUESTIONS

1 A teacher asks all his class: 'How many children are there in your family?' Their replies are given below.

Number of children in a family	Number of replies
1	7
2	12
3	5
4	2
5	0

a How many children are in the class?
b What is the modal number of children in a family?
c What is the median number in a family?
d What is the mean number in a family?

Solution

1 a $7 + 12 + 5 + 2 + 0 = 26$
  The total number of children is 26.
b The modal number of children is 2.
c The median number of children is 2.
d The mean number of children $= 54 ÷ 26 = 2.1$

> Add up the frequencies.

> The largest frequency is 12 so the modal number is 2.

> The median will be between the 13th and 14th values. Adding up the frequencies gives 7, 19, 24, 26, 26. So the required value is in the second row.

> Add an extra column to the table and multiply the number of children by the number of replies. This gives 7, 24, 15, 8, 0.
> Add these to get 54.
> Divide 54 by 26.

2 A teacher shows her class 25 objects on a tray. She leaves it in view for one minute.
She then covers the objects and asks the class to write down the names of as many objects as they can remember.
The results are shown in the table.
What is the mean number of objects recalled by the class?

Number of objects recalled, x	Frequency, f
$0 < x \leqslant 5$	2
$5 < x \leqslant 10$	5
$10 < x \leqslant 15$	13
$15 < x \leqslant 20$	8
$20 < x \leqslant 25$	2
	30

Solution

2

Number of objects recalled, x	Frequency, f	Midpoint, m	$m \times f$
$0 < x \leqslant 5$	2	2.5	5
$5 < x \leqslant 10$	5	7.5	37.5
$10 < x \leqslant 15$	13	12.5	162.5
$15 < x \leqslant 20$	8	17.5	140
$20 < x \leqslant 25$	2	22.5	45
	30		390

> First add a column for the midpoints. This is the two end values added and divided by 2.

> Next, add a column for midpoint multiplied by frequency.

> Next, work out the totals for the frequency and the $m \times f$ columns.

Mean $= 390 ÷ 30$
     $= 13$

> Finally, divide the total of the $m \times f$ column by the total frequency.

Mr Davies is a dairy farmer. Every month he records how many thousands of litres of milk are produced by his cows.

For his business plan he compares the amount of milk produced in 2004 with the amount in 2005.

Monthly milk production (thousands of litres)		
Month	2004	2005
Jan	51	62
Feb	53	65
Mar	55	62
Apr	56	67
May	64	72
Jun	72	83
Jul	70	81
Aug	75	86
Sep	64	75
Oct	64	73
Nov	62	70
Dec	58	68

Copy and comple the table below.

Monthly milk production (thousands of litres)		
	2004	2005
mean		
median		
mode		
range		

Copy this bar chart into your book and complete it for Mr Davies' milk production in 2005.

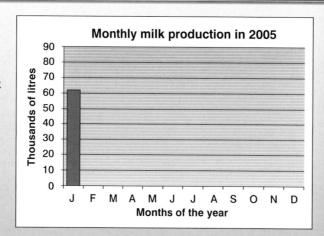

254

For his business plan Mr Davies compares the amount of milk he produces in 2005 with the graphs showing the hours of sunshine and amount of rain that year.

Compare your milk production bar chart with the rainfall bar chart.

What do you notice?

Compare your milk production bar chart with the hours of sunshine bar chart.

What do you notice?

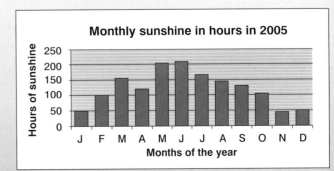

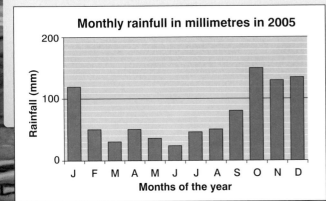

GRADE YOURSELF

G Able to find the mode and median of a list of data

F Able to find the range of a set of data and find the mean of a small set of data

E Able to find the mean and range from a stem-and-leaf diagram

D Able to find the mean from a frequency table of discrete data and draw a frequency polygon for discrete data

D Able to find the median from a stem-and-leaf diagram

C Able to find an estimate of the mean from a grouped table of continuous data and draw a frequency polygon for continuous data

What you should know now

- How to find the range, mode, median and mean of sets of discrete data
- Which average to use in different situations
- How to find the modal class and an estimated mean for continuous data
- How to draw frequency polygons for discrete and continuous data

Percentages

1 Equivalent percentages, fractions and decimals

2 Calculating a percentage of a quantity

3 Calculating a percentage increase or decrease

4 Expressing one quantity as a percentage of another

This chapter will show you ...

- what is meant by percentage
- how to do calculations involving percentages
- how to use your calculator to work out percentages by using a multiplier
- how to work out percentage increases and decreases

Visual overview

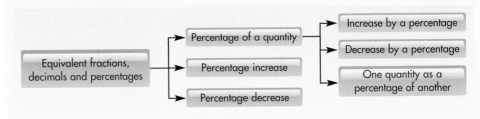

What you should already know

- How to cancel fractions
- How to calculate with fractions
- How to multiply decimals by 100 (move the digits two places to the left)
- How to divide decimals by 100 (move the digits two places to the right)

Quick check

1 Cancel these fractions.

    a $\dfrac{12}{32}$ **b** $\dfrac{20}{45}$ **c** $\dfrac{28}{48}$ **d** $\dfrac{36}{60}$

2 Work out these amounts.

    a $\dfrac{2}{3}$ of 27   **b** $\dfrac{5}{8}$ of 32   **c** $\dfrac{1}{4} \times 76$ **d** $\dfrac{3}{5} \times 45$

3 Work out these amounts.

    a 12×100 **b** $34 \div 100$ **c** 0.23×100 **d** $4.7 \div 100$

In this section you will learn how to:

- convert percentages to fractions and decimals and vice versa

Key words

decimal
decimal equivalents
fraction
percentage

Per cent means 'out of 100'. So, any **percentage** can be expressed as a **fraction** with denominator 100. For example:

$$32\% = \frac{32}{100} \text{ which can be cancelled to } \frac{8}{25}$$

Also, any percentage can be expressed as a **decimal** by dividing by 100. This means moving the digits two places to the right. For example:

$$65\% = 65 \div 100 = 0.65$$

Any decimal can be expressed as a percentage simply by multiplying by 100.

Any fraction can be expressed as a percentage either by making the denominator into 100 or dividing the numerator by the denominator and multiplying by 100.

Knowing the percentage and **decimal equivalents** of the common fractions is extremely useful. So, do try to learn them.

$$\frac{1}{2} = 0.5 = 50\% \qquad \frac{1}{4} = 0.25 = 25\% \qquad \frac{3}{4} = 0.75 = 75\% \qquad \frac{1}{8} = 0.125 = 12.5\%$$

$$\frac{1}{10} = 0.1 = 10\% \qquad \frac{1}{5} = 0.2 = 20\% \qquad \frac{1}{3} = 0.33 = 33\frac{1}{3}\% \qquad \frac{2}{3} = 0.67 = 67\%$$

The following table shows how to convert from one to the other.

Convert from percentage to:	
Decimal	**Fraction**
Divide the percentage by 100, for example, 52% = 52 ÷ 100 = 0.52	Make the percentage into a fraction with a denominator of 100 and cancel down if possible, for example, $52\% = \frac{52}{100} = \frac{13}{25}$

Convert from decimal to:	
Percentage	**Fraction**
Multiply the decimal by 100, for example, 0.65 = 0.65 × 100 = 65%	If the decimal has 1 decimal place put it over the denominator 10, if it has 2 decimal places put it over the denominator 100, etc. Then cancel down if possible, for example, $0.65 = \frac{65}{100} = \frac{13}{20}$

Convert from fraction to:	
Percentage	**Decimal**
If the denominator is a factor of 100 multiply numerator and denominator to make the denominator 100, then the numerator is the percentage, for example, $\frac{3}{20} = \frac{15}{100} = 15\%$, or convert to a decimal and change the decimal to a percentage, for example, $\frac{7}{8} = 7 \div 8 = 0.875 = 87.5\%$	Divide the numerator by the denominator, for example, $\frac{9}{40} = 9 \div 40 = 0.225$

100% means the *whole* of something. So, if you want to, you can express *part* of the whole as a percentage.

EXAMPLE 1

Change the following to decimals.　**a** 78%　**b** 35%　**c** $\frac{3}{25}$　**d** $\frac{7}{40}$

a $78 \div 100 = 0.78$　　　　**b** $35 \div 100 = 0.35$

c $3 \div 25 = 0.12$　　　　　**d** $7 \div 40 = 0.175$

EXAMPLE 2

Change the following to percentages.　**a** 0.85　**b** 0.125　**c** $\frac{7}{20}$　**d** $\frac{3}{8}$

a $0.85 \times 100 = 85\%$　　　　**b** $0.125 \times 100 = 12.5\%$

c $\frac{7}{20} = \frac{35}{100} = 35\%$　　　　**d** $\frac{3}{8} = 3 \div 8 = 0.375 = 37.5\%$

EXAMPLE 3

Change the following to fractions.　**a** 0.45　**b** 0.4　**c** 32%　**d** 15%

a $0.45 = \frac{45}{100} = \frac{9}{20}$　　　　**b** $0.4 = \frac{4}{10} = \frac{2}{5}$

c $32\% = \frac{32}{100} = \frac{8}{25}$　　　　**d** $15\% = \frac{15}{100} = \frac{3}{20}$

EXAMPLE 4

Put the following set of fractions into order, putting the smallest on the left hand side.

$25\%, \frac{1}{10}, 0.2, 0.195$

Change each fraction into a decimal for easier comparison

$25\% = 0.25, \frac{1}{10} = 0.1, 0.2, 0.195$

Re-order as: 0.1, 0.195, 0.2, 0.25

smallest

> **HINTS AND TIPS**
>
> It will help to think of
> 0.1　as　0.100
> and　0.2　as　0.20

EXERCISE 12A

1 Write each percentage as a fraction in its lowest terms.

    a 8%   **b** 50%   **c** 25%

    d 35%   **e** 90%   **f** 75%

2 Write each percentage as a decimal.

    a 27%   **b** 85%   **c** 13%

    d 6%   **e** 80%   **f** 32%

3 Write each decimal as a fraction in its lowest terms.

    a 0.12   **b** 0.4   **c** 0.45

    d 0.68   **e** 0.25   **f** 0.625

4 Write each decimal as a percentage.

    a 0.29   **b** 0.55   **c** 0.03

    d 0.16   **e** 0.6   **f** 1.25

5 Write each fraction as a percentage.

    a $\frac{7}{25}$ **b** $\frac{3}{10}$ **c** $\frac{19}{20}$

    d $\frac{17}{50}$ **e** $\frac{11}{40}$ **f** $\frac{7}{8}$

6 Write each fraction as a decimal.

    a $\frac{9}{15}$ **b** $\frac{3}{40}$ **c** $\frac{19}{25}$

    d $\frac{5}{16}$ **e** $\frac{1}{20}$ **f** $\frac{1}{8}$

7 Of the 300 members of a social club 50% are men. How many members are women?

8 Gillian came home and told her dad that she got 100% of her spellings correct. She told her mum that there were 25 spellings to learn. How many spellings did Gillian get wrong?

9 Every year a school library likes to replace 1% of its books. One year the library had 2000 books. How many did it replace?

10 a If 23% of pupils go home for lunch, what percentage do not go home for lunch?

    b If 61% of the population takes part in the National Lottery, what percentage do not take part?

    c If 37% of members of a gym are males, what percentage of the members are females?

11 I calculated that 28% of my time is spent sleeping and 45% is spent working. How much time is left to spend doing something else?

12 In one country, 24.7% of the population is below the age of 16 and 13.8% of the population is aged over 65. How much of the population is aged from 16 to 65 inclusive?

13 Approximately what percentage of each bottle is filled with water?

a   b   c

14 Helen made a cake for James. The amount of cake left each day is shown in the diagram.

a What percentage is left each day?

b What percentage has been eaten each day?

Monday   Tuesday   Wednesday   Thursday   Friday

15 Change each of these fractions into a percentage.

a $\frac{1}{5}$ b $\frac{1}{4}$ c $\frac{3}{4}$ d $\frac{9}{20}$ e $\frac{7}{50}$

f $\frac{1}{2}$ g $\frac{3}{5}$ h $\frac{7}{40}$ i $\frac{11}{20}$ j $\frac{13}{10}$

16 Change each of these fractions into a percentage. Give your answers to one decimal place.

a $\frac{1}{3}$ b $\frac{1}{6}$ c $\frac{2}{3}$ d $\frac{5}{6}$ e $\frac{2}{7}$

f $\frac{47}{60}$ g $\frac{31}{45}$ h $\frac{8}{9}$ i $\frac{73}{90}$ j $\frac{23}{110}$

17 Change each of these decimals into a percentage.

a 0.07   b 0.8   c 0.66   d 0.25   e 0.545

f 0.82   g 0.3   h 0.891   i 1.2   j 2.78

18 Chris scored 24 marks out of a possible 40 in a maths test.

a Write this score as a fraction.

b Write this score as a decimal.

c Write this score as a percentage.

19 Convert each of the following test scores into a percentage. Give each answer to the nearest whole number.

Subject	Result	Percentage
Mathematics	38 out of 60	
English	29 out of 35	
Science	27 out of 70	
History	56 out of 90	
Technology	58 out of 75	

20 The air you breathe consists of about $\frac{4}{5}$ nitrogen and $\frac{1}{5}$ oxygen. What percentage of the air is **a** nitrogen **b** oxygen?

21 There were two students missing from my class of 30. What percentage of my class were away?

22 In one season, Robbie Keane had 110 shots at goal. He scored with 28 of these shots. What percentage of his shots resulted in goals?

23 Copy and complete the table.

Percentage	Decimal	Fraction
34%		
	0.85	
		$\frac{3}{40}$

24 Put the following sets of fractions into order, the smallest being on the left.

a 0.8, 0.35, 0.3, 0.75

b 0.15, $\frac{1}{2}$, 10%, $\frac{1}{5}$

c 30%, $\frac{1}{4}$, 0.275, 26%

d $\frac{3}{4}$, 0.32, 3%, $\frac{3}{8}$

e 0.6, 45%, $\frac{1}{2}$, 0.55

f 9%, $\frac{1}{8}$, 0.111, $\frac{1}{10}$

g 28%, 0.23, $\frac{1}{4}$, 0.275

h 0.8, 8%, $\frac{1}{8}$, 0.88

i 0.3, 35%, $\frac{1}{3}$, 0.325

j $\frac{1}{5}$, 50%, $\frac{3}{5}$, 0.35

In this section you will learn how to:
- calculate a percentage of a quantity

Key word
multiplier

To calculate a percentage of a quantity, you multiply the quantity by the percentage. The percentage may be expressed as either a fraction or a decimal. When finding percentages without a calculator, base the calculation on 10% (or 1%) as these are easy to calculate.

EXAMPLE 5

Calculate: **a** 10% **b** 15% of 54 kg.

a 10% is $\frac{1}{10}$ so divide 54 by 10. 54 ÷ 10 = 5.4 kg

b 15% is 10% + 5% = 5.4 + 2.7 = 8.1 kg

EXAMPLE 6

Calculate 12% of £80.

10% of £80 is £8 and 1% of £80 is £0.80

12% = 10% + 1% + 1% = £8 + £0.80 + £0.80 = £9.60

Using a percentage multiplier

You have already seen that percentages and decimals are equivalent so it is easier, particularly when using a calculator, to express a percentage as a decimal and use this to do the calculation.

For example, 13% is a multiplier of 0.13, 20% is a multiplier of 0.2 (or 0.20) and so on.

EXAMPLE 7

Calculate 45% of 16 cm.

45% = 0.45, so 45% of 160 = 0.45 × 160 = 72 cm

 EXERCISE 12B

1 What multiplier is equivalent to a percentage of:

 a 88% **b** 30% **c** 25% **d** 8% **e** 115%?

2 What percentage is equivalent to a multiplier of:

 a 0.78 **b** 0.4 **c** 0.75 **d** 0.05 **e** 1.1?

E

3 Calculate the following.

a 15% of £300

b 6% of £105

c 23% of 560 kg

d 45% of 2.5 kg

e 12% of 9 hours

f 21% of 180 cm

g 4% of £3

h 35% of 8.4 m

i 95% of £8

j 11% of 308 minutes

k 20% of 680 kg

l 45% of £360

4 In a school 15% of the pupils bring sandwiches with them. If there are 640 pupils in the school, how many bring sandwiches?

5 An estate agent charges 2% commission on every house he sells. How much commission will he earn on a house that he sells for £60 250?

6 A department store had 250 employees. During one week of a flu epidemic, 14% of the store's employees were absent.

a What percentage of the employees went into work?

b How many of the employees went into work?

7 It is thought that about 20% of fans at a rugby match are women. For a match at Twickenham there were 42 600 fans. How many of these do you think would be women?

8 At St Pancras Railway Station, in one week 350 trains arrived. Of these trains, 5% arrived early and 13% arrived late. How many arrived on time?

9 For the FA Cup Final that was held at Wembley, each year the 75 000 tickets were split up as follows.

Each of the teams playing received 30% of the tickets.

The referees' association received 1% of the tickets.

The other 90 teams received 10% of the tickets among them.

The FA associates received 20% of the tickets among them.

The rest were for the special celebrities.

How many tickets went to each set of people?

> **HINTS AND TIPS**
>
> Always read the question carefully. **Each** team received 30% of the tickets.

10 A school estimates that during a parents' evening it will see the parents of 60% of all the students. Year 10 consists of 190 students. How many of them expected to be represented by their parents?

11 A school had 850 pupils and the attendance record in the week before Christmas was:

Monday 96%   Tuesday 98%   Wednesday 100%   Thursday 94%   Friday 88%

How many pupils were present each day?

12 Soft solder consists of 60% lead, 35% tin and 5% bismuth (by weight). How much of each metal is there in 250 grams of solder?

13 Calculate the following.

    a 12.5% of £26   **b** 6.5% of 34 kg   **c** 26.8% of £2100

    d 7.75% of £84   **e** 16.2% of 265 m   **f** 0.8% of £3000

14 Air consists of 80% nitrogen and 20% oxygen (by volume). A man's lungs have a capacity of 600 cm^3. How much of each gas will he have in his lungs when he has just taken a deep breath?

15 A factory estimates that 1.5% of all the garments it produces will have a fault in them. One week the factory produces 850 garments. How many are likely to have a fault?

16 An insurance firm sells house insurance and the annual premiums are usually set at 0.3% of the value of the house. What will be the annual premium for a house valued at £90 000?

12.3 Calculating a percentage increase or decrease

In this section you will learn how to:
- calculate percentage increases and decreases

Key word
multiplier

Increase

There are two methods for increasing by a percentage.

Method 1
Find the increase and add it to the original amount.

EXAMPLE 8

Increase £6 by 5%.

Find 5% of £6: $(5 \div 100) \times 6 = £0.30$

Add the £0.30 to the original amount: £6 + £0.30 = £6.30

Method 2
Use a **multiplier**. An increase of 6% is equivalent to the original 100% *plus* the extra 6%. This is a total of 106% and is equivalent to the multiplier 1.06.

EXAMPLE 9

Increase £6.80 by 5%.

A 5% increase is a multiplier of 1.05.

So £6.80 increased by 5% is 6.80 × 1.05 = £7.14

EXERCISE 12C

1 What multiplier is equivalent to a percentage increase of:

    a 10%   **b** 3%   **c** 20%   **d** 7%   **e** 12%?

2 Increase each of the following by the given percentage. (Use any method you like.)

    a £60 by 4%   **b** 12 kg by 8%   **c** 450 g by 5%   **d** 545 m by 10%

    e £34 by 12%   **f** £75 by 20%   **g** 340 kg by 15%   **h** 670 cm by 23%

    i 130 g by 95%   **j** £82 by 75%   **k** 640 m by 15%   **l** £28 by 8%

3 Kevin, who was on a salary of £27 500, was given a pay rise of 7%. What was his new salary?

4 In 2000 the population of Melchester was 1 565 000. By 2005 it had increased by 8%. What was the population of Melchester in 2005?

5 A small firm made the same pay increase of 5% for all its employees.

    a Calculate the new pay of each employee listed below. Each of their salaries before the increase is given.

        Bob, caretaker, £16 500   Jean, supervisor, £19 500
        Anne, tea lady, £17 300   Brian, manager, £25 300

    b Is the actual pay increase the same for each worker?

6 A bank pays 7% interest on the money that each saver keeps in the bank for a year. Allison keeps £385 in this bank for a year. How much will she have in the bank after the year?

7 In 1980 the number of cars on the roads of Sheffield was about 102 000. Since then it has increased by 90%. Approximately how many cars are there on the roads of Sheffield now?

8 An advertisement for a breakfast cereal states that a special offer packet contains 15% more cereal for the same price as a normal 500 g packet. How much breakfast cereal is there in a special offer packet?

9 A headteacher was proud to point out that, since he had arrived at the school, the number of students had increased by 35%. How many students are now in the school, if there were 680 when the headteacher started at the school?

10 At a school disco there are always about 20% more girls than boys. If there were 50 boys at a recent disco, how many girls were there?

11 The Government adds a tax called VAT to the price of most goods in shops. At the moment, it is 17.5% on all electrical equipment.

Calculate the price of the following electrical equipment after VAT of 17.5% has been added.

Equipment	Pre-VAT price
TV set	£245
Microwave oven	£72
CD player	£115
Personal stereo	£29.50

Decrease

There are two methods for decreasing by a percentage.

Method 1
Find the decrease and take it away from the original amount.

EXAMPLE 10

Decrease £8 by 4%.

Find 4% of £8: (4 ÷ 100) × 8 = £0.32

Take the £0.32 away from the original amount: £8 − £0.32 = £7.68

Method 2
Use a multiplier. A 7% decrease is 7% less than the original 100% so it represents 100 − 7 = 93% of the original. This is a multiplier of 0.93.

EXAMPLE 11

Decrease £8.60 by 5%.

A decrease of 5% is a multiplier of 0.95.

So £8.60 decreased by 5% is 8.60 × 0.95 = £8.17

EXERCISE 12D

1 What multiplier is equivalent to a percentage decrease of:

    a 8%   **b** 15%   **c** 25%   **d** 9%   **e** 12%?

2 Decrease each of the following by the given percentage. (Use any method you like.)

    a £10 by 6%   **b** 25 kg by 8%   **c** 236 g by 10%

    d 350 m by 3%   **e** £5 by 2%   **f** 45 m by 12%

    g 860 m by 15%   **h** 96 g by 13%   **i** 480 cm by 25%

    j 180 minutes by 35%   **k** 86 kg by 5%   **l** £65 by 42%

3 A car valued at £6500 last year is now worth 15% less. What is its value now?

4 A new P-plan diet guarantees that you will lose 12% of your weight in the first month. How much should the following people weigh after one month on the diet?

    a Gillian, who started at 60 kg

    b Peter, who started at 75 kg

    c Margaret, who started at 52 kg

D

5 A motor insurance firm offers no-claims discounts off the given premium, as follows.

1 year no claim	15% discount
2 years no claim	25% discount
3 years no claim	45% discount
4 years no claim	60% discount

Mr Speed and his family are all offered motor insurance from this firm:

Mr Speed, who has four years' no-claim discount, is quoted a premium of £440.

Mrs Speed, who has one year's no-claim discount, is quoted a premium of £350.

James, who has three years' no-claim discount, is quoted a premium of £620.

John, who has two years' no-claim discount, is quoted a premium of £750.

Calculate the actual amount each member of the family has to pay for the motor insurance.

6 A large factory employed 640 people. It had to streamline its workforce and lose 30% of the workers. How big is the workforce now?

7 On the last day of the Christmas term, a school expects to have an absence rate of 6%. If the school population is 750 pupils, how many pupils will the school expect to see on the last day of the Christmas term?

8 A particular charity called *Young Ones* said that since the start of the National Lottery they have had a decrease of 45% in the amount of money raised by scratch cards. If before the Lottery the charity had an annual income of £34 500 from their scratch cards, how much do they collect now?

9 Most speedometers in cars have an error of about 5% from the true reading. When my speedometer says I am driving at 70 mph:

a what is the lowest speed I could be doing

b what is the highest speed I could be doing?

10 You are a member of a club that allows you to claim a 12% discount off any marked price in shops. What will you pay in total for the following goods?

Sweatshirt	£19
Track suit	£26

11 I read an advertisement in my local newspaper last week that stated: "By lagging your roof and hot water system you will use 18% less fuel." Since I was using an average of 640 units of gas a year, I thought I would lag my roof and my hot water system. How much gas would I expect to use now?

12 Shops add VAT to the basic price of goods to find the selling price that customers will be asked to pay. In a sale, a shop reduces the selling price by a certain percentage to set the sale price. Calculate the sale price of each of these items.

Item	Basic price	VAT rate	Sale discount	Sale price
TV	£220	17.5%	14%	
DVD player	£180	17.5%	20%	

C

12.4 Expressing one quantity as a percentage of another

In this section you will learn how to:
- express one quantity as a percentage of another

You can express one quantity as a percentage of another by setting up the first quantity as a fraction of the second, making sure that the *units of each are the same*. Then, you convert that fraction to a percentage by simply multiplying it by 100.

EXAMPLE 12

Express £6 as a percentage of £40.

Set up the fraction and multiply it by 100. This gives:

$(6 \div 40) \times 100 = 15\%$

EXAMPLE 13

Express 75 cm as a percentage of 2.5 m.

First, change 2.5 m to 250 cm to work in a common unit.

Hence, the problem becomes 75 cm as a percentage of 250 cm.

Set up the fraction and multiply it by 100. This gives:

$(75 \div 250) \times 100 = 30\%$

You can use this method to calculate percentage gain or loss in a financial transaction.

EXAMPLE 14

Jabeer buys a car for £1500 and sells it for £1800. What is Jabeer's percentage gain?

Jabeer's gain is £300, so his percentage gain is:

$\dfrac{300}{1500} \times 100 = 20\%$

Notice how the percentage gain is found as: $\dfrac{\text{difference}}{\text{original}} \times 100$

Using a multiplier

Find the multiplier by dividing the increase by the original quantity, then change the resulting decimal to a percentage.

EXAMPLE 15

Express 5 as a percentage of 40.

$5 \div 40 = 0.125$

$0.125 = 12.5\%$

EXERCISE 12E

1 Express each of the following as a percentage. Give suitably rounded figures where necessary.

   a £5 of £20   **b** £4 of £6.60   **c** 241 kg of 520 kg

   d 3 hours of 1 day   **e** 25 minutes of 1 hour   **f** 12 m of 20 m

   g 125 g of 600 g   **h** 12 minutes of 2 hours   **i** 1 week of a year

   j 1 month of 1 year   **k** 25 cm of 55 cm   **l** 105 g of 1 kg

2 Liam went to school with his pocket money of £2.50. He spent 80p at the tuck shop. What percentage of his pocket money had he spent?

3 In Greece, there are 3 654 000 acres of agricultural land. Olives are grown on 237 000 acres of this land. What percentage of the agricultural land is used for olives?

4 During the wet year of 1981, it rained in Manchester on 123 days of the year. What percentage of days were wet?

5 Find, correct to one decimal place, the percentage profit on the following.

Item	Retail price (selling price)	Wholesale price (price the shop paid)
a CD player	£89.50	£60
b TV set	£345.50	£210
c Computer	£829.50	£750

6 Before Anton started to diet, he weighed 95 kg. He now weighs 78 kg. What percentage of his original weight has he lost?

7 In 2004 the Melchester County Council raised £14 870 000 in council tax. In 2005 it raised £15 597 000 in council tax. What was the percentage increase?

8 When Blackburn Rovers won the championship in 1995, they lost only four of their 42 league games. What percentage of games did they *not* lose?

9 In the year 1900 Britain's imports were as follows.

British Commonwealth	£109 530 000
USA	£138 790 000
France	£53 620 000
Other countries	£221 140 000

   a What percentage of the total imports came from each source? Give your answers to 1 decimal place.

   b Add up your answer to part **a**. What do you notice? Explain your answer.

EXERCISE 12F Ⓧ

This exercise includes a mixture of percentage questions, which you should answer without using a calculator.

1 Copy and complete this table.

	Fraction	Decimal	Percentage
a	$\frac{3}{5}$		
b		0.7	
c			55%

2 Work out these amounts.

   a 15% of £68

   b 12% of 400 kg

   c 30% of £4.20

3 What percentage is:

   a 28 out of 50

   b 17 out of 25

   c 75 out of 200?

4 What is the result if:

   a 240 is increased by 15%

   b 3600 is decreased by 11%?

5 **a** A paperboy's weekly wage went up from £10 to £12. What was the percentage increase in his wages?

   b The number of houses he has to deliver to increases from 60 to 78. What is the percentage increase in the number of houses he delivers to?

   c The newsagent then increased his new wage of £12 by 10%. What are the boy's wages now?

6 The on-the-road price of a new car was £8000.

   a In the first year it depreciated in value by 20%. What was the value of the car at the end of the first year?

   b In the second year it depreciated by a further 15%. What was the value of the car at the end of the second year?

7 The members of a slimming club had a mean weight of 80 kg before they started dieting. After a month they calculated that they had lost an average of 12% in weight.

   a What was the average weight after the month?

   b One of the members realised she had misread the scale and she was 10 kg heavier than she thought. Which of these statements is true?

     i The mean weight loss will have decreased by more than 12%.

     ii The mean weight loss will have stayed at 12%.

     iii The mean weight loss will have decreased by less than 12%.

     iv There is not enough information to answer the question.

1 **a** Write $\frac{1}{4}$ as a percentage.

b Write 0.23 as a percentage.

c Write 42% as a fraction. Give your answer in its simplest form.

Edexcel, Question 3, Paper 11A Foundation, January 2004

2 **a** This diagram is made from equilateral triangles.

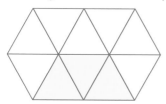

i What percentage of the diagram is shaded?

ii What percentage of the diagram is not shaded?

b Another diagram has 70% shaded. What fraction of the diagram is shaded?
Simplify your answer.

c Another diagram has $\frac{3}{5}$ shaded.
Write $\frac{3}{5}$ as a decimal.

3 **a** **i** Write $\frac{7}{16}$ as a decimal.

ii Write 27% as a decimal.

b Write these values in order of size, smallest first.

0.7 $\frac{6}{10}$ 65%   0.095

4 Mr and Mrs Jones are buying a tumble dryer that normally costs £250. They save 12% in a sale.

a What is 12% of £250?

b How much do they pay for the tumble dryer?

5 Cat facts
- 40% of people named cats as their favourite pet.
- 98% of women said they would rather go out with someone who liked cats.
- About $7\frac{1}{2}$ million families have a cat.
- $\frac{1}{4}$ of cat owners keep a cat because cats are easy to look after.

a Write 40% as a fraction.
Give your fraction in its simplest form.

b Write 98% as a decimal.

c Write $7\frac{1}{2}$ million in figures.

d Write $\frac{1}{4}$ as a percentage.

e What percentage of people did *not* name cats as their favourite pet?

Edexcel, Question 7, Paper 1 Foundation, June 2005

6 Which is the larger amount?

40% of £30 $\frac{3}{5}$ of £25

7 Mrs Senior earns £320 per week. She is awarded a pay rise of 4%.

How much does she earn each week after the pay rise?

8 Five girls swim a 50 metre race. Their times are shown in the table.

Name	Time (seconds)
Amy	12.8
Joy	14.6
Sophie	13.5
Lydia	13.9
Charlotte	15.8

a Write down the median time.

b The five girls swim another 50 metre race. They all reduce their times by 8%.

i Who won the race?

ii Who improved her time by the greatest amount of time?

9 Mr Shaw's bill for new tyres is £120 plus VAT. VAT is charged at $17\frac{1}{2}$%.

What is his total bill?

10 Two shops sell DVDs.

HTV Vision	CUS Video
DVDs £9.60 each	DVD SALE
Buy 2 DVDs and get a third one FREE	30% OFF normal price of £9.60 each

Lewis wants to buy three DVDs from one of the above shops. Which shop offers the better value?
You must show all your working.

11 Supermarkets often make 'Buy one, get one free' offers. What percentage saving is this?

10%, 50%, 100% or 200%

12 There are 75 penguins at a zoo. There are 15 baby penguins.

What percentage of the penguins are babies?

13 Alistair sells books. He sells each book for £7.60 plus VAT at $17\frac{1}{2}\%$.

He sells 1650 books.

Work out how much money Alistair receives.

Edexcel, Question 26, Paper 2 Foundation, June 2005

 14 ABCD is a rectangle with length 35 cm and width 15 cm.

The length of the rectangle is increased by 10%.
The width of the rectangle is increased by 20%.
Find the percentage increase in the area of the rectangle.

 15 In a sale the price of a dress, originally marked as £80, was reduced by 30%.

  a What was the sale price of the dress?

  b On a special promotion day the shop offered 20% off sale prices.

    i What was the reduced price of the dress after 20% was taken off the sale price?

    ii What percentage was this price of the original £80?

 16 A TV originally cost £300.

In a sale, its price was reduced by 20%, then this sale price was reduced by a further 10%.

Show why this is not a 30% reduction of the original price.

WORKED EXAM QUESTION

The land area of a farm is 385 acres.

a Two-fifths of the land is used to grow barley. How many acres is this?

b Fifteen per cent of the land is not used. How many acres is this?

c On the farm, 96 acres is pasture. What percentage of the total land is pasture? Give your answer to the nearest 1%.

Solution

a 154 acres

> The calculation is $\frac{2}{5} \times 385$.
> Divide 385 by 5, 385 ÷ 5 = 77
> Multiply 77 by 2, 2 × 77 = 154

b 57.75 acres

> First work out 10%, 10% of 385 = 38.5
> Now work out 5%, 5% of 385 = 19.25
> Add to get 15%.
> Alternatively use a multiplier, 0.15 × 385

c 25%

> The fraction is $\frac{96}{385}$.
> Divide the numerator by the denominator and multiply by 100.
> This gives 24.935, which is 25% to the nearest per cent.

GRADE YOURSELF

G Able to find equivalent fractions, decimals and percentages

F Able to find simple percentages of a quantity

E Able to find any percentages of a quantity

D Able to find a new quantity after an increase or decrease by a percentage and find one quantity as a percentage of another

C Able to find a percentage increase

What you should know now

- How to find equivalent percentages, decimals and fractions
- How to calculate percentages, percentage increases and decreases
- How to calculate one quantity as a percentage of another

Equations and inequalities

1 Solving simple linear equations

2 Solving equations with brackets

3 Equations with the letter on both sides

4 Setting up equations

5 Trial and improvement

6 Rearranging formulae

7 Solving linear inequalities

This chapter will show you ...

- how to solve linear equations with the variable on one side only
- how to solve linear equations with the variable on both sides
- how to solve equations using trial and improvement
- how to rearrange simple formulae
- how to solve simple linear inequalities

Visual overview

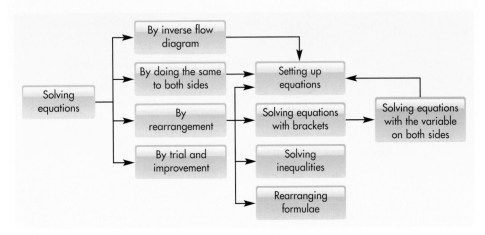

What you should already know

- The basic language of algebra
- How to expand brackets and collect like terms
- That addition and subtraction are opposite (inverse) operations
- That multiplication and division are opposite (inverse) operations

Quick check

1 a Simplify $5x + 3x - 2x$.　　**b** Expand $4(3x - 1)$.

　c Expand and simplify $2(3x - 1) + 3(4x + 3)$.

2 What number can go in the box to make the calculation true?

　a $13 + \square = 9$　　　**b** $4 \times \square = 10$

In this section you will learn how to:

- solve a variety of simple linear equations, such as $3x - 1 = 11$, where the variable only appears on one side
- use inverse operations and inverse flow charts
- solve equations by doing the same on both sides
- deal with negative numbers
- solve equations by rearrangement

Key words

do the same to both sides
equation
inverse flow diagram
inverse operations
rearrangement
solution
variable

A teacher gave these instructions to her class.

What algebraic expression represents the teacher's statement? (See Chapter 7.)

- Think of a number.
- Double it.
- Add 3.

This is what two of her students said.

Can you work out Kim's answer and the number that Freda started with?

Kim's answer will be $2 \times 5 + 3 = 13$.

Freda's answer can be set up as an **equation**.

An equation is formed when an expression is put equal to a number or another expression. You are expected to deal with equations that have only one **variable** or letter.

My final answer was 10.

I chose the number 5.

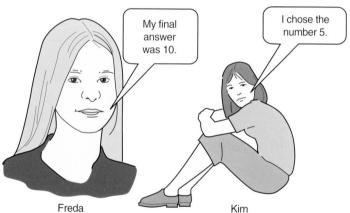

Freda   Kim

The **solution** to an equation is the value of the variable that makes the equation true. For example, the equation for Freda's answer is

$$2x + 3 = 10$$

where x represents Freda's number.

The value of x that makes this true is $x = 3\frac{1}{2}$.

To solve an equation, you have to 'undo' it. That is, you have to reverse the processes that set up the equation in the first place.

Freda did two things. First she multiplied by 2 and then she added 3. The reverse process is first to subtract 3 and then to divide by 2. So, to solve:

$$2x + 3 = 10$$

Subtract 3

$$2x + 3 - 3 = 10 - 3$$

$$2x = 7$$

Divide by 2

$$\frac{2x}{2} = \frac{7}{2}$$

$$x = 3\frac{1}{2}$$

The problem is knowing how an equation is set up in the first place, so that you can undo it in the right order.

There are four ways to solve equations: **inverse operations, inverse flow diagrams**, **'doing the same to both sides'** and **rearrangement**. They are all essentially the same. You will have to decide which method you prefer, although you should know how to use all three.

There is one rule about equations that you should *always* follow.

Check that your answer works in the original equation.

For example, to check the answer to Freda's equation, put $x = 3\frac{1}{2}$ into Freda's equation. This gives:

$$2 \times 3\frac{1}{2} + 3 = 7 + 3 = 10$$

which is correct.

Inverse operations

One way to solve equations is to use **inverse operations**. The opposite or inverse operation to addition is subtraction (and vice versa) and the opposite or inverse operation to multiplication is division (and vice versa).

That means you can 'undo' the four basic operations by using the inverse operation.

EXAMPLE 1

Solve these equations.

a $w + 7 = 9$ **b** $x - 8 = 10$ **c** $2y = 8$ **d** $\dfrac{z}{5} = 3$

a The opposite operation to $+ 7$ is $- 7$, so the solution is $9 - 7 = 2$.

   Check: $2 + 7 = 9$

b The opposite operation to $- 8$ is $+ 8$, so the solution is $10 + 8 = 18$.

   Check: $18 - 8 = 10$

c $2y$ means $2 \times y$. The opposite operation to $\times 2$ is $\div 2$, so the solution is $8 \div 2 = 4$.

   Check: $2 \times 4 = 8$

d $\dfrac{z}{5}$ means $z \div 5$. The opposite operation to $\div 5$ is $\times 5$, so the solution is $3 \times 5 = 15$.

   Check: $15 \div 5 = 3$

EXERCISE 13A

Solve the following equations by applying the inverse on the operation on the left-hand side to the right-hand side.

1 $x + 6 = 10$ **2** $w - 5 = 9$

3 $y + 3 = 8$ **4** $p - 9 = 1$

5 $2x = 10$ **6** $3x = 18$

7 $\dfrac{z}{3} = 8$ **8** $4x = 10$

9 $\dfrac{q}{4} = 1$ **10** $x + 9 = 10$

11 $r - 7 = 21$ **12** $\dfrac{s}{6} = 2$

> **HINTS AND TIPS**
>
> Remember to perform the inverse operation on the number on the right-hand side.

Inverse flow diagrams

Another way to solve simple linear equations is to use inverse flow diagrams.

This flow diagram represents the instructions that their teacher gave to Kim and Freda.

$\longrightarrow \boxed{\times 2} \longrightarrow \boxed{+ 3} \longrightarrow$

The **inverse flow diagram** looks like this.

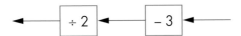

Running Freda's answer through this gives:

$$3\tfrac{1}{2} \xleftarrow{} \boxed{\div 2} \xleftarrow{7} \boxed{-3} \xleftarrow{10}$$

So, Freda started with $3\tfrac{1}{2}$ to get an answer of 10.

EXAMPLE 2

Use an inverse flow diagram to solve the following equation.

$3x - 4 = 11$

Flow diagram:

$$\xrightarrow{} \boxed{\times 3} \xrightarrow{} \boxed{-4} \xrightarrow{}$$

Inverse flow diagram:

$$\xleftarrow{} \boxed{\div 3} \xleftarrow{} \boxed{+4} \xleftarrow{}$$

Put through the value on the right-hand side of the equals sign.

$$\xleftarrow{5} \boxed{\div 3} \xleftarrow{15} \boxed{+4} \xleftarrow{11}$$

So, the answer is $x = 5$.

Checking the answer gives:

$3 \times 5 - 4 = 11$

which is correct.

EXERCISE 13B

Use inverse flow diagrams to solve each of the following equations. Remember to check that each answer works for its original equation.

1 $3x + 5 = 11$

2 $3x - 13 = 26$

3 $3x - 7 = 32$

4 $4y - 19 = 5$

5 $3a + 8 = 11$

6 $2x + 8 = 14$

7 $2y + 6 = 18$

8 $8x + 4 = 12$

> **HINTS AND TIPS**
>
> Remember the rules of BODMAS. So $3x + 5$ means do $x \times 3$ first then $+5$ in the flow diagram. Then do the opposite (inverse) operations in the inverse flow diagram.

9 $2x - 10 = 8$

10 $\dfrac{x}{5} + 2 = 3$

11 $\dfrac{t}{3} - 4 = 2$

12 $\dfrac{y}{4} + 1 = 7$

13 $\dfrac{k}{2} - 6 = 3$

14 $\dfrac{h}{8} - 4 = 1$

15 $\dfrac{w}{6} + 1 = 4$

16 $\dfrac{x}{4} + 5 = 7$

17 $\dfrac{y}{2} - 3 = 5$

18 $\dfrac{f}{5} + 2 = 8$

Doing the same to both sides

You need to know how to solve equations by performing the same operation on both sides of the equals sign.

Mary had two bags of marbles, each of which contained the same number of marbles, and five spare marbles.

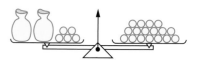

She put them on scales and balanced them with 17 single marbles.

How many marbles were there in each bag?

If x is the number of marbles in each bag, then the equation representing Mary's balanced scales is:

$2x + 5 = 17$

Take five marbles from each pan:

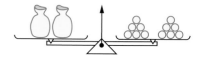

$2x + 5 - 5 = 17 - 5$
$2x = 12$

Now halve the number of marbles on each pan.

That is, divide both sides by 2:

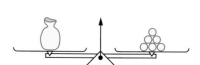

$\dfrac{2x}{2} = \dfrac{12}{2}$

$x = 6$

Checking the answer gives $2 \times 6 + 5 = 17$, which is correct.

EXAMPLE 3

Solve each of these equations by 'doing the same to both sides'.

a $3x - 5 = 16$

b $\dfrac{x}{2} + 2 = 10$

Add 5 to both sides.

Subtract 2 from both sides.

$3x - 5 + 5 = 16 + 5$

$\dfrac{x}{2} + 2 - 2 = 10 - 2$

$3x = 21$

$\dfrac{x}{2} = 8$

Divide both sides by 3.

Multiply both sides by 2.

$\dfrac{3x}{3} = \dfrac{21}{3}$

$\dfrac{x}{2} \times 2 = 8 \times 2$

$x = 7$

$x = 16$

Checking the answer gives:

Checking the answer gives:

$3 \times 7 - 5 = 16$

$16 \div 2 + 2 = 10$

which is correct.

which is correct.

Dealing with negative numbers

The solution to an equation may be a negative number. You need to know that when a negative number is multiplied or divided by a positive number, then the answer is also a negative number. For example:

$-3 \times 4 = -12$ and $-10 \div 5 = -2$

Check these on your calculator.

EXERCISE 13C

Solve each of the following equations by 'doing the same to both sides'. Remember to check that each answer works for its original equation.

1 $x + 4 = 60$

2 $3y - 2 = 4$

3 $3x - 7 = 11$

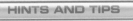

HINTS AND TIPS

Be careful with negative numbers.

4 $5y + 3 = 18$

5 $7 + 3t = 19$

6 $5 + 4f = 15$

7 $3 + 6k = 24$

8 $4x + 7 = 17$

9 $5m - 3 = 17$

10 $\dfrac{w}{3} - 5 = 2$

11 $\dfrac{x}{8} + 3 = 12$

12 $\dfrac{m}{7} - 3 = 5$

13 $\dfrac{x}{5} + 3 = 3$

14 $\dfrac{h}{7} + 2 = 1$

15 $\dfrac{w}{3} + 10 = 4$

16 $\dfrac{x}{3} - 5 = 7$

17 $\dfrac{y}{2} - 13 = 5$

18 $\dfrac{f}{6} - 2 = 8$

E

ACTIVITY

Balancing with unknowns

Suppose you want to solve an equation such as:

$2x + 3 = x + 4$

You can imagine it as a balancing problem with marbles.

2 bags + 3 marbles = 1 bag + 4 marbles

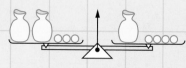

Take one bag from each side.

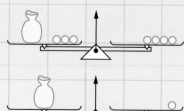

Take three marbles from each side.

There must be one marble in the bag.

This means that $x = 1$.

Checking the answer gives $2 \times \mathbf{1} + 3 = \mathbf{1} + 4$, which is correct.

Set up each of the following problems as a 'balancing picture' and solve it by 'doing the same to both sides'. Remember to check that each answer works. The first two problems include the pictures to start you off.

1 $2x + 6 = 3x + 1$  **2** $4x + 2 = x + 8$

3 $5x + 1 = 3x + 11$ **4** $x + 9 = 2x + 7$ (Some of the
5 $3x + 8 = 2x + 10$ **6** $5x + 7 = 3x + 21$ marbles could
7 $2x + 12 = 5x + 6$ **8** $3x + 6 = x + 9$ be broken in
                                                           half!)

9 Explain why there is no answer to this problem:

$x + 3 = x + 4$

10 One of the bags of marbles on the left-hand pan has had three marbles taken out.

Try to draw the pictures to solve this problem:

$4x - 3 = 2x + 5$

Rearrangement

Solving equations by rearrangement is the most efficient method and the one used throughout the rest of this chapter. The terms of the equation are rearranged until the variable is on its own – usually on the left-hand side of the equals sign.

EXAMPLE 4

Solve $4x + 3 = 23$.

Move the 3 to give: $\qquad\qquad\qquad 4x = 23 - 3 = 20$

Now divide both sides by 4 to give: $\qquad x = \dfrac{20}{4} = 5$

So, the solution is $x = 5$.

EXAMPLE 5

Solve $\dfrac{y - 4}{5} = 3$.

Move the 5 to give: $\qquad\qquad y - 4 = 3 \times 5 = 15$

Now move the 4 to give: $\qquad\quad y = 15 + 4 = 19$

So, the solution is $y = 19$.

EXERCISE 13D

Solve each of the following equations. Remember to check that each answer works for its original equation.

1 $2x + 4 = 6$

2 $2t + 7 = 13$

3 $3x + 10 = 16$

4 $4y + 15 = 23$

5 $2x - 8 = 10$

6 $4t - 3 = 17$

7 $5x - 6 = 24$

8 $7 - x = 3$

9 $12 - 3y = 6$

10 $2k + 8 = 4$

11 $\dfrac{x}{3} + 7 = 15$

12 $\dfrac{t}{5} + 3 = 5$

13 $\dfrac{w}{3} - 5 = 2$

14 $\dfrac{x}{8} + 3 = 12$

15 $\dfrac{m}{7} - 3 = 5$

16 $\dfrac{k + 1}{2} = 3$

17 $\dfrac{h - 4}{8} = 3$

18 $\dfrac{w + 1}{6} = 1$

19 $\dfrac{x + 5}{4} = 10$

20 $\dfrac{y - 3}{6} = 5$

21 $\dfrac{f + 2}{5} = 5$

> **HINTS AND TIPS**
>
> When a variable changes sides of the equals sign, it also changes signs, that is, plus becomes minus and vice versa, multiply becomes divide and vice versa. This is sometimes called 'Change sides, change signs'.

Solving equations with brackets

In this section you will learn how to:

- solve equations that include brackets

When an equation contains brackets, you must first multiply out the brackets and then solve the equation by using one of the previous methods.

EXAMPLE 6

Solve $5(x + 3) = 25$.

First multiply out the brackets: $5x + 15 = 25$

Rearrange. $\quad 5x = 25 - 15 = 10$

Divide by 5. $\quad \dfrac{5x}{5} = \dfrac{10}{5}$

$\qquad\qquad\quad x = 2$

EXAMPLE 7

Solve $3(2x - 7) = 15$.

Multiply out the brackets: $6x - 21 = 15$

Add 21 to both sides. $\quad 6x = 36$

Divide both sides by 6. $\quad x = 6$

EXERCISE 13E

Solve each of the following equations. Some of the answers may be decimals or negative numbers. Remember to check that each answer works for its original equation. Use your calculator if necessary.

1 $2(x + 5) = 16$

2 $5(x - 3) = 20$

3 $3(t + 1) = 18$

4 $4(2x + 5) = 44$

5 $2(3y - 5) = 14$

6 $5(4x + 3) = 135$

7 $4(3t - 2) = 88$

8 $6(2t + 5) = 42$

9 $2(3x + 1) = 11$

10 $4(5y - 2) = 42$

11 $6(3k + 5) = 39$

12 $5(2x + 3) = 27$

13 $5(2x - 1) = -45$

14 $7(3y + 5) = -7$

HINTS AND TIPS

Once the brackets have been expanded the equations are the same sort as those you have already been dealing with. Remember to multiply everything inside the brackets with what is outside.

D

Equations with the letter on both sides

In this section you will learn how to:

- solve equations where the variable appears on both sides of the equation

When a letter appears on both sides of an equation, it is best to use the 'do the same to both sides' method of solution and collect all the terms containing the letter on the left-hand side of the equation. If there are more of the letter on the right-hand side, it is easier to turn the equation round. When an equation contains brackets, they must be multiplied out first.

EXAMPLE 8

Solve $5x + 4 = 3x + 10$.

There are more xs on the left-hand side, so leave the equation as it is.

Subtract $3x$ from both sides.	$2x + 4 = 10$
Subtract 4 from both sides.	$2x = 6$
Divide both sides by 2.	$x = 3$

EXAMPLE 9

Solve $2x + 3 = 6x - 5$.

There are more xs on the right-hand side, so turn the equation round.

$$6x - 5 = 2x + 3$$

Subtract $2x$ from both sides.	$4x - 5 = 3$
Add 5 to both sides.	$4x = 8$
Divide both sides by 4.	$x = 2$

EXAMPLE 10

Solve $3(2x + 5) + x = 2(2 - x) + 2$.

| Multiply out both brackets. | $6x + 15 + x = 4 - 2x + 2$ |
| Simplify both sides. | $7x + 15 = 6 - 2x$ |

There are more xs on the left-hand side, so leave the equation as it is.

Add $2x$ to both sides.	$9x + 15 = 6$
Subtract 15 from both sides.	$9x = -9$
Divide both sides by 9.	$x = -1$

EXERCISE 13F

Solve each of the following equations.

1 $2x + 3 = x + 5$

2 $5y + 4 = 3y + 6$

3 $4a - 3 = 3a + 4$

4 $5t + 3 = 2t + 15$

5 $7p - 5 = 3p + 3$

6 $6k + 5 = 2k + 1$

7 $2t - 7 = 4t - 3$

8 $2p - 1 = 9 - 3p$

9 $2(d + 3) = d + 12$

10 $5(x - 2) = 3(x + 4)$

11 $3(2y + 3) = 5(2y + 1)$

12 $3(h - 6) = 2(5 - 2h)$

13 $4(3b - 1) + 6 = 5(2b + 4)$

14 $2(5c + 2) - 2c = 3(2c + 3) + 7$

> **HINTS AND TIPS**
>
> Remember the rule 'Change sides, change signs'. Show all your working on this type of question. Rearrange before you simplify. If you try to rearrange and simplify at the same time, you will probably get it wrong.

13.4 Setting up equations

In this section you will learn how to:

- set up equations from given information and then use the methods already seen to solve them

Equations are used to represent situations, so that you can solve real-life problems.

EXAMPLE 11

A milkman sets off from the dairy with eight crates of milk each containing b bottles. He delivers 92 bottles to a large factory and finds that he has exactly 100 bottles left on his milk float. How many bottles were in each crate?

The equation is:

$8b - 92 = 100$

$8b = 192$ (Add 92 to both sides.)

$b = 24$ (Divide both sides by 8.)

EXAMPLE 12

The rectangle shown has a perimeter of 40 cm.

Find the value of x.

The perimeter of the rectangle is:

$3x + 1 + x + 3 + 3x + 1 + x + 3 = 40$

This simplifies to $8x + 8 = 40$.

Subtract 8. $8x = 32$

Divide by 8. $x = 4$

$3x + 1$

$x + 3$

EXERCISE 13G

Set up an equation to represent each situation described below. Then solve the equation. Remember to check each answer.

1 A man buys a daily paper from Monday to Saturday for *d* pence. On Sunday he buys his paper for £1. His weekly paper bill is £4.30.
What is the price of his daily paper?

2 The diagram shows a rectangle.

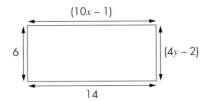

a What is the value of *x*?

b What is the value of *y*?

> **HINTS AND TIPS**
>
> Use the letter *x* for the variable unless you are given a letter to use. Once the equation is set up solve it by the methods above.

3 In this rectangle, the length is 3 cm more than the width. The perimeter is 12 cm.

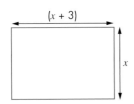

a What is the value of *x*?

b What is the area of the rectangle?

4 Mary has two bags, each of which contains the same number of sweets. She eats four sweets. She then finds that she has 30 sweets left. How many sweets were there in each bag to start with?

5 A boy is *Y* years old. His father is 25 years older than he is. The sum of their ages is 31. How old is the boy?

6 Another boy is *X* years old. His sister is twice as old as he is. The sum of their ages is 27. How old is the boy?

7 The diagram shows a square.
Find *x* if the perimeter is 44 cm.

$(4x - 1)$

8 Max thought of a number. He then multiplied his number by 3. He added 4 to the answer. He then doubled that answer to get a final value of 38. What number did he start with?

9 The angles of a triangle are $2x$, $x + 5°$ and $x + 35°$.

a Write down an equation to show this.

b Solve your equation to find the value of *x*.

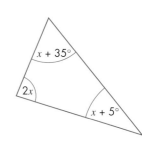

Trial and improvement

In this section you will learn how to:

- use the method of trial and improvement to estimate the answer to equations that do not have exact solutions

Key words

comment
decimal place
guess
trial and improvement

Certain equations cannot be solved exactly. However, a close enough solution to such an equation can be found by the **trial-and-improvement** method. (Sometimes wrongly called the trial-and-error method.)

The idea is to keep trying different values in the equation to take it closer and closer to the 'true' solution. This step-by-step process is continued until a value is found that gives a solution that is close enough to the accuracy required.

The trial-and-improvement method is the way in which computers are programmed to solve equations.

EXAMPLE 13

Solve the equation $x^3 + x = 105$, giving the solution correct to one **decimal place**.

Step 1 You must find the two consecutive whole numbers between which x lies. You do this by intelligent guessing.

Try $x = 5$: $125 + 5 = 130$ Too high – next trial needs to be much smaller.

Try $x = 4$: $64 + 4 = 68$ Too low.

So you now know that the solution lies between $x = 4$ and $x = 5$.

Step 2 You must find the two consecutive one-decimal-place numbers between which x lies. Try 4.5, which is halfway between 4 and 5.

This gives $91.125 + 4.5 = 95.625$ Too small.

Now attempt to improve this by trying 4.6.

This gives $97.336 + 4.6 = 101.936$ Still too small.

Try 4.7 which gives 108.523.   This is too high, so the solution is between 4.6 and 4.7.

It looks as though 4.7 is closer but there is a very important final step.

Step 3 Now try the value that is halfway between the two one-decimal-place values. In this case 4.65.

This gives 105.194 625.

This means that 4.6 is nearer the actual solution than 4.7 is, so never assume that the one-decimal-place number that gives the closest value to the solution is the answer.

The diagram on the right shows why this is.

The approximate answer is $x = 4.6$ to 1 decimal place.

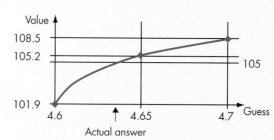

The best way to answer this type of question is to set up a table to show working. There will be three columns: **guess** (the trial); the equation to be solved; and a **comment** whether the value of the equation is too high or too low.

Guess	$x^3 + x$	Comment
4	68	Too low
5	130	Too high
4.5	95.625	Too low
4.6	101.936	Too low
4.7	108.523	Too high
4.65	105.194 625	Too high

EXERCISE 13H

1 Find the two consecutive *whole numbers* between which the solution to each of the following equations lies.

    a $x^2 + x = 24$ **b** $x^3 + 2x = 80$ **c** $x^3 - x = 20$

2 Copy and complete the table by using trial and improvement to find an approximate solution to:

    $x^3 + 2x = 50$

Guess	$x^3 + 2x$	Comment
3	33	Too low
4	72	Too high

    Give your answer correct to 1 decimal place.

3 Copy and complete the table by using trial and improvement to find an approximate solution to:

    $x^3 - 3x = 40$

Guess	$x^3 - 3x$	Comment
4	52	Too high

    Give your answer correct to 1 decimal place.

4 Use trial and improvement to find an approximate solution to:

    $2x^3 + x = 35$

    Give your answer correct to 1 decimal place.

    You are given that the solution lies between 2 and 3.

> **HINTS AND TIPS**
>
> Set up a table to show your working. This makes it easier for you to show method and the examiner to mark.

5 Use trial and improvement to find an exact solution to:

    $4x^2 + 2x = 12$

    Do not use a calculator.

6 Find a solution to each of the following equations, correct to 1 decimal place.

    a $2x^3 + 3x = 35$ **b** $3x^3 - 4x = 52$ **c** $2x^3 + 5x = 79$

7 A rectangle has an area of 100 cm². Its length is 5 cm longer than its width.

   a Show that, if x is the width, then $x^2 + 5x = 100$.

   b Find, correct to 1 decimal place, the dimensions of the rectangle.

8 Use trial and improvement to find a solution to the equation $x^2 + x = 40$.

13.6 Rearranging formulae

In this section you will learn how to:

- rearrange formulae, using the same methods as for solving equations

Key words

expression
rearrange
subject
transpose
variable

The **subject** of a formula is the **variable** (letter) in the formula that stands on its own, usually on the left-hand side of the 'equals' sign. For example, x is the subject of each of the following.

$$x = 5t + 4 \qquad x = 4(2y - 7) \qquad x = \frac{1}{t}$$

If you need to change the existing subject to a different variable, you have to **rearrange** (**transpose**) the formula to get that variable on the left-hand side.

You do this by using the same rule as that for solving equations, that is, move the terms concerned from one side of the 'equals' sign to the other.

The main difference is that when you solve an equation each step gives a numerical value. When you rearrange a formula each step gives an algebraic **expression**.

EXAMPLE 14

Make m the subject of $T = m - 3$.

Move the 3 away from the m. $T + 3 = m$

Reverse the formula. $m = T + 3$

EXAMPLE 15

From the formula $P = 4t$, express t in terms of P.

(This is another common way of asking you to make t the subject.)

Divide both sides by 4. $\dfrac{P}{4} = \dfrac{4t}{4}$

Reverse the formula. $t = \dfrac{P}{4}$

EXAMPLE 16

From the formula $C = 2m + 3$, make m the subject.

Move the 3 away from the $2m$.　　$C - 3 = 2m$

Divide both sides by 2.　　$\dfrac{C - 3}{2} = \dfrac{2m}{2}$

Reverse the formula.　　$m = \dfrac{C - 3}{2}$

EXERCISE 13I

1 $T = 3k$　　Make k the subject.

2 $P = m + 7$　　Make m the subject.

3 $X = y - 1$　　Express y in terms of X.

4 $Q = \dfrac{p}{3}$　　Express p in terms of Q.

5 $p = m + t$　　**a** Make m the subject.

　　　　　　　　b Make t the subject.

6 $t = 2k + 7$　　Express k in terms of t.

7 $g = \dfrac{m}{v}$　　Make m the subject.

8 $t = m^2$　　Make m the subject.

9 $C = 2\pi r$　　Make r the subject.

10 $A = bh$　　Make b the subject.

11 $P = 2l + 2w$　　Make l the subject.

12 $m = p^2 + 2$　　Make p the subject.

> **HINTS AND TIPS**
>
> Remember about inverse operations and the rule 'Change sides, change signs'.

13.7 Solving linear inequalities

In this section you will learn how to:

• solve a simple linear inequality

Key words

integer
linear inequality
number line

Inequalities behave similarly to equations, which you have already met. In the case of **linear inequalities**, you can use the same rules to solve them as you use for linear equations. There are four inequality signs, < which means 'less than', > which means 'greater than', ⩽ which means 'less than or equal to' and ⩾ which means 'greater than or equal to'.

EXAMPLE 17

Solve $2x + 3 < 14$.

This is rewritten as:

$2x < 14 - 3$

that is $2x < 11$.

Divide both sides by 2. $\qquad \dfrac{2x}{2} < \dfrac{11}{2}$

$\Rightarrow \quad x < 5.5$

This means that x can take any value below 5.5 but it *cannot* take the value 5.5.

Note: The inequality sign given in the problem is the sign to give in the answer.

EXAMPLE 18

Solve $\dfrac{x}{2} + 4 \geqslant 13$.

Solve just like an equation but leave the inequality sign in place of the equals sign.

Subtract 4 from both sides. $\qquad \dfrac{x}{2} \geqslant 9$

Multiply both sides by 2. $\qquad x \geqslant 18$

This means that x can take any value above 18 and including 18.

EXERCISE 13J

1 Solve the following linear inequalities.

a $\quad x + 4 < 7$

b $\quad t - 3 > 5$

c $\quad p + 2 \geqslant 12$

d $\quad 2x - 3 < 7$

e $\quad 4y + 5 \leqslant 17$

f $\quad 3t - 4 > 11$

g $\quad \dfrac{x}{2} + 4 < 7$

h $\quad \dfrac{y}{5} + 3 \leqslant 6$

i $\quad \dfrac{t}{3} - 2 \geqslant 4$

j $\quad 3(x - 2) < 15$

k $\quad 5(2x + 1) \leqslant 35$

l $\quad 2(4t - 3) \geqslant 34$

2 Write down the largest value of x that satisfies each of the following.

a $\quad x - 3 \leqslant 5$, where x is a positive **integer**.

b $\quad x + 2 < 9$, where x is a positive, even integer.

c $\quad 3x - 11 < 40$, where x is a square number.

d $\quad 5x - 8 \leqslant 15$, where x is a positive, odd number.

e $\quad 2x + 1 < 19$, where x is a positive, prime number.

3 Write down the smallest value of x that satisfies each of the following.

a $x - 2 \geqslant 9$, where x is a positive integer.

b $x - 2 > 13$, where x is a positive, even integer.

c $2x - 11 \geqslant 19$, where x is a square number.

d $3x + 7 \geqslant 15$, where x is a positive, odd number.

e $4x - 1 > 23$, where x is a positive, prime number.

The number line

The solution to a linear inequality can be shown on the **number line** by using the following conventions.

Below are five examples.

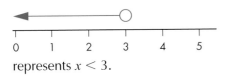

represents $x < 3$.

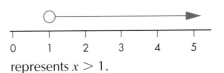

represents $x > 1$.

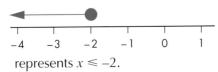

represents $x \leqslant -2$.

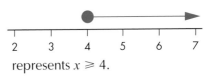

represents $x \geqslant 4$.

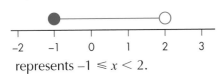

represents $-1 \leqslant x < 2$.

EXAMPLE 19

a Write down the inequality shown by this diagram.

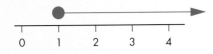

b i Solve the inequality $2x + 3 < 11$.   **ii** Mark the solution to **b** on a number line.

c Write down the integers that satisfy both the inequality in **a** and the inequality in **b**.

a The inequality shown is $x \geqslant 1$.

b i $2x + 3 < 11 \Rightarrow 2x < 8 \Rightarrow x < 4$

ii

c The integers that satisfy both inequalities are 1, 2 and 3.

1 Write down the inequality that is represented by each diagram below.

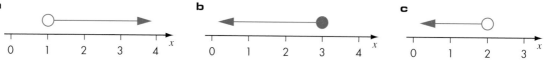

a

b

c

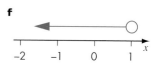

d

e

f

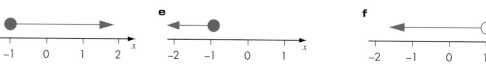

g

h

i

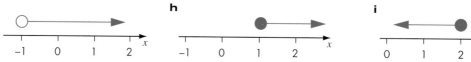

j

k

l

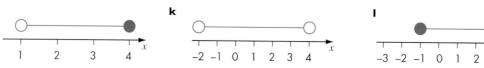

2 Draw diagrams to illustrate the following.

a $x \leqslant 3$ b $x > -2$ c $x \geqslant 0$ d $x < 5$

e $x \geqslant -1$ f $2 < x \leqslant 5$ g $-1 \leqslant x \leqslant 3$ h $-3 < x < 4$

i $-4 \leqslant x \leqslant 4$ j $3 \leqslant x < 7$

3 Solve the following inequalities and illustrate their solutions on number lines.

a $x + 4 \geqslant 8$ b $x + 5 < 3$ c $x - 1 \leqslant 2$ d $x - 4 > -1$

e $2x > 8$ f $3x \leqslant 15$ g $4x < 10$ h $2x \geqslant 9$

i $\dfrac{x}{2} \leqslant 5$ j $\dfrac{x}{4} > 3$ k $\dfrac{3x}{4} \geqslant 9$ l $\dfrac{2x}{5} < 10$

4 Solve the following equations and illustrate the solutions to **a**, **b**, **c** and **d** on number lines.

a $2x + 3 \leqslant 7$ b $4x - 2 \geqslant 12$ c $3x - 1 > 14$ d $2x + 5 < 3$

e $2x - 5 < 3$ f $5x + 1 \geqslant 11$ g $3x + 7 > 4$ h $2x - 3 \geqslant 4$

i $\dfrac{x}{3} + 1 > 6$ j $\dfrac{x}{4} - 3 \leqslant 3$ k $\dfrac{x}{2} + 3 < 9$ l $\dfrac{x}{7} - 1 \geqslant 9$

5 Solve the following equations and illustrate the solutions to **a**, **b**, **c** and **d** on number lines.

a $2(4x + 3) < 18$ b $\dfrac{x}{2} + 3 \leqslant 2$ c $\dfrac{x}{5} - 2 > 8$ d $\dfrac{x}{3} + 5 \geqslant 3$

e $3(x + 4) > 9$ f $2(x - 1) \leqslant 7$ g $5(x + 3) \geqslant 10$ h $2(x - 7) < 2$

i $\dfrac{x + 2}{3} > 4$ j $\dfrac{x - 5}{4} \leqslant 1$ k $\dfrac{x + 1}{5} \geqslant 2$ l $\dfrac{x - 1}{4} < 3$

1 Solve these equations.

a $4x = 20$

b $y + 5 = 14$

c $8t - 3 = 13$

d $4(m - 5) = 16$

2 Solve these equations.

a $5x - 1 = 9$

b $3 + x = 9$

c $4x + 3 = 2x + 13$

3 Solve these equations.

a $5x + 3 = 38$

b $4(x - 3) = 16$

c $\dfrac{x + 5}{3} = 9$

4

a What answer did Zara get?

b What was the number Jason thought of?

5 An orange costs z pence. A lemon costs 4 pence more than an orange.

a Write down an expression, in terms of z, for the cost of one lemon.

b Write down an expression, in terms of z, for the total cost of three oranges and one lemon.

c The total cost of three oranges and one lemon is 60 pence.

Form an equation in terms of z and solve it to find the cost of one orange.

6 **a** Solve these equations.

   i $2x = 9$

   ii $3x - 8 = 13$

   iii $6x + 9 = x + 24$

b Simplify these expressions.

   i $5q + 6q + 2q$

   ii $5n + 4p + 2n - p$

7 The length of a rectangle is twice its width.

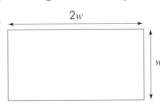

The area of the rectangle is 128 cm^2.

Show that the length of the rectangle is 16 cm.

8 In the table below, the letters a, b, c and d represent different numbers. The total of each row is given at the side of the table.

a	a	a	a	20
a	b	b	a	24
c	c	c	d	11
d	d	b	c	14

Find the values of a, b, c and d.

9 **a** Write down an expression for the cost, in pence, of x buns at 30p each and four tarts at 40p each.
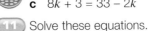
b The total cost of x buns and four tarts is £3.10. Find the number of buns sold.

10 Solve these equations.

a $5x - 4 = 11$ **b** $3(m + 7) = 27$

c $8k + 3 = 33 - 2k$

11 Solve these equations.

a $5x + 4 = 9$

b $9p + 7 = 6p + 16$

c $\dfrac{11 - t}{4} = 7$

12 Solve these equations.
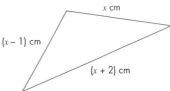
a $4x + 3 = 13$

b $12x + 1 = 4x + 5$

13 The lengths of the sides of a triangle are x cm, $(x + 2)$ cm and $(x - 1)$ cm.

x cm

$(x - 1)$ cm

$(x + 2)$ cm

a Write an expression, in terms of x, for the perimeter of this triangle. Give your answer in its simplest form.

b The perimeter is 22 cm.
Write down an equation in x and use it to find the value of x.

14 The width of a rectangle is x centimetres. The length of the rectangle is $(x + 4)$ centimetres.

x + 4

x

a Find an expression, in terms of x, for the perimeter of the rectangle. Give your expression in its simplest form.

The perimeter of the rectangle is 54 centimetres.

b Work out the length of the rectangle.

Edexcel, Question 5, Paper 17 Intermediate, June 2005

15 Solve the equation $5x + 6 = 6 - x$.

16 ABC is a triangle with angles, given in degrees, of x, $x + 40°$ and $x + 80°$.

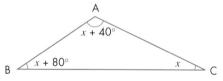

A

x + 40°

x + 80°

B   x   C

a Write down an expression, in terms of x, for the sum of the angles in the triangle.

b Calculate the value of x.

17 **a** Solve $20y - 16 = 18y - 9$

b Solve $\dfrac{40 - x}{3} = 4 + x$

Edexcel, Question 13, Paper 4 Intermediate, June 2004

18 You are given that $y = 12 + 3x$.

a When $x = -4$, work out the value of y.

b When $y = 0$, work out the value of x.

c Make x the subject of the formula.

19 Make x the subject of the formula:

$5x + 7 = 6y$

Simplify your answer as much as possible.

20 Make m the subject of the formula:

$p = \dfrac{m + 1}{4}$

21 Parveen is using trial and improvement to find a solution to the equation:

$x^2 + 9x = 40$

The table shows her first two tries.

x	$x^2 + 9x = 40$	Comment
3	36	Too low
4	52	Too high

Continue the table to find a solution to the equation. Give your answer correct to one decimal place.

22 ABC is a triangle with sides, given in centimetres, of x, $2x + 1$ and $3x - 3$.

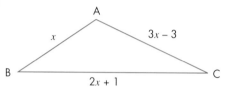

A

x   3x – 3

B   2x + 1   C

The perimeter of the triangle is 22 cm. Find the value of x.

23 **a** Rearrange the formula:

$T = 5p$

to make p the subject.

b Rearrange the formula:

$V = 5t^2$

to make t the subject.

24 Solve the equation:

$3(x + 4) = 8 - 2x$

25 **a** Solve $5 - 3x = 2(x + 1)$

b $-3 \leqslant y < 3$

y is an integer. Write down all the possible values of y.

Edexcel, Question 10, Paper 16 Intermediate, June 2005

WORKED EXAM QUESTIONS

1 The angles of a quadrilateral are 83°, x°, $4x$° and 97°.

   a Write down an equation in x.

   b Use your equation to find the largest angle in the quadrilateral.

Solution

1 a $5x + 180 = 360$

   b 144°

> You should know that the angles in a quadrilateral add up to 360°. This means that:
> $x + 4x + 83 + 97 = 360$
> This would get the marks for part (a) but you will need to simplify this equation. You should always try to simplify expressions whenever you can.

> Solving the equation gives:
> subtracting 180 $5x = 360 - 180 = 180$
> dividing by 5 $x = 36$
> Do not stop at this point as the question asks for the largest angle. This is the angle $4x$°, which is $4 \times 36 = 144°$.

2 Mark is x years old.
   Nell is eight years older than Mark.
   Oliver is twice as old as Nell.

   a Write down expressions in x for the ages of Nell and Oliver.
   b Show that the total of their ages is given by the expression $4(x + 6)$.
   c Given that their total age is 44, find Mark's age.

Solution

2 a Nell: $x + 8$
      Oliver: $2(x + 8)$

   b $x + x + 8 + 2(x + 8)$
      $= 2x + 8 + 2x + 16$
      $= 4x + 24$
      $= 4(x + 6)$

   c $4(x + 6) = 44$
      $4x + 24 = 44$
      $4x = 20$
      $x = 5$
      Mark is five years old.

> '8 years older' means an addition, so Nell's age is $x + 8$.
>
> 'Twice as' means multiply. Use brackets around Nell's age, as $2x + 8$ is wrong.

> Write down the total of all the ages.
>
> Expand the brackets and collect terms.
>
> Either expand $4(x + 6)$ or factorise $4x + 24$.

> Set up the equation and expand the brackets.
>
> Subtract 24, then divide by 4.

GRADE YOURSELF

F Able to solve equations such as $4x = 12$ and $x - 8 = 3$

E Able to solve equations such as $3x + 2 = 7$ or $\dfrac{x}{3} - 7 = 1$

D Able to solve equations such as $\dfrac{x - 2}{3} = 6$ or $3x + 7 = x - 6$

D Able to set up simple equations from given information

C Able to solve equations such as $3(x - 4) = 5x + 8$

C Able to solve inequalities such as $3x + 2 < 5$

C Able to solve equations by trial and improvement

C Able to rearrange simple formulae

What you should know now

- How to solve a variety of linear equations using rearrangement or 'doing the same thing to both sides'
- How to solve equations using trial and improvement
- How to rearrange simple formulae
- How to solve simple inequalities

This book provides indicators of the equivalent grade level of maths questions throughout. The publishers wish to make clear that these grade indicators have been provided by Collins Education, and are not the responsibility of Edexcel Ltd. Whilst every effort has been made to assure their accuracy, they should be regarded as indicators, and are not binding or definitive.

Graphs

1 Conversion graphs

2 Travel graphs

3 Flow diagrams and graphs

4 Linear graphs

This chapter will show you ...

- how to read information from a conversion graph
- how to read information from a travel graph
- how to draw a straight-line graph from its equation

Visual overview

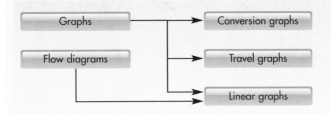

What you should already know

- How to plot coordinates in the first quadrant
- How speed, distance and time are related (from Chapter 9)
- How to substitute numbers into a formula (from Chapter 7)

Quick check

Write down the coordinates of the following points.

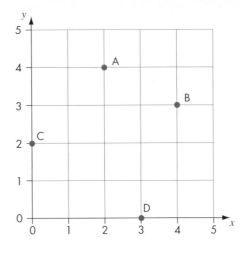

In this section you will learn how to:

- convert from one unit to another unit by using a graph

Key word

conversion graph

Look at Examples 1 and 2, and make sure that you can follow through the conversions.

EXAMPLE 1

This is a **conversion graph** between litres and gallons.

a How many litres are there in 5 gallons?

b How many gallons are there in 15 litres?

From the graph you can see that:

a 5 gallons are approximately equivalent to 23 litres.

b 15 litres are approximately equivalent to $3\frac{1}{4}$ gallons.

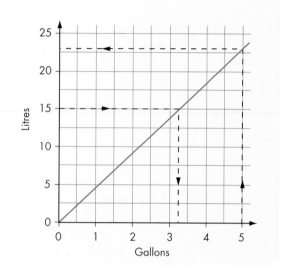

EXAMPLE 2

This is a graph of the charges made for units of electricity used in the home.

a How much will a customer who uses 500 units of electricity be charged?

b How many units of electricity will a customer who is charged £20 have used?

From the graph you can see that:

a A customer who uses 500 units of electricity will be charged £45.

b A customer who is charged £20 will have used about 150 units.

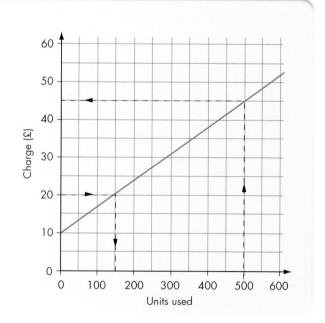

You need to be able to read these types of graph by finding a value on one axis and following it through to the other axis.

EXERCISE 14A

1 This is a conversion graph between kilograms (kg) and pounds (lb).

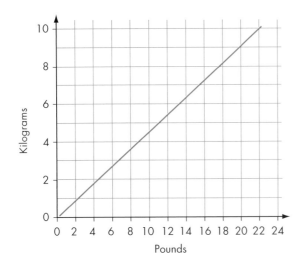

a Use the graph to make an approximate conversion of:

   i 18 lb to kilograms

   ii 5 lb to kilograms

   iii 4 kg to pounds

   iv 10 kg to pounds.

b Approximately how many pounds are equivalent to 1 kg?

2 This is a conversion graph between inches (in) and centimetres (cm).

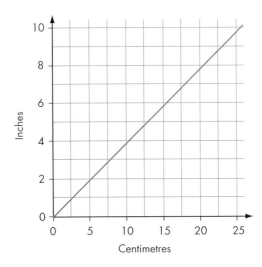

a Use the graph to make an approximate conversion of:

   i 4 inches to centimetres

   ii 9 inches to centimetres

   iii 5 cm to inches

   iv 22 cm to inches.

b Approximately how many centimetres are equivalent to 1 inch?

3 This graph was produced to show the approximate equivalence of the British pound (£) to the Singapore dollar ($).

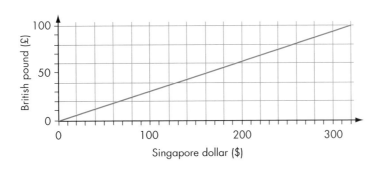

a Use the graph to make an approximate conversion of:

   i £100 to Singapore dollars

   ii £30 to Singapore dollars

   iii $150 to British pounds

   iv $250 to British pounds.

b Approximately how many Singapore dollars are equivalent to £1?

4 A hire firm hired out industrial blow heaters. They used the following graph to approximate what the charges would be.

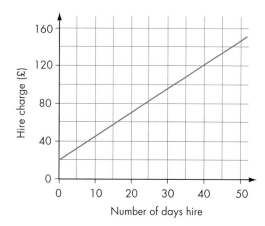

a Use the graph to find the approximate charge for hiring a heater for:

   i 40 days

   ii 25 days.

b Use the graph to find out how many days' hire you would get for a cost of:

   i £100

   ii £140.

5 A conference centre had the following chart on the office wall so that the staff could see the approximate cost of a conference, based on the number of people attending it.

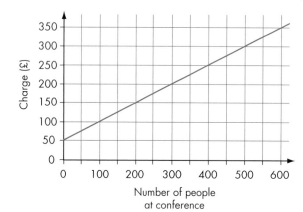

a Use the graph to find the approximate charge for:

   i 100 people

   ii 550 people.

b Use the graph to estimate how many people can attend a conference at the centre for a cost of:

   i £300

   ii £175.

6 At a small shop, the manager marked all goods at the pre-VAT prices and the sales assistant had to use the following chart to convert these marked prices to selling prices.

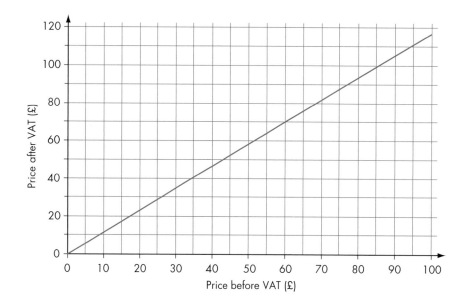

a Use the chart to find the selling price of goods marked:

   i £60

   ii £25.

b What was the marked price if you bought something for:

   i £100

   ii £45?

7 When Leon travelled abroad in his car, he always took this conversion graph. It helped him to convert between miles and kilometres.

  a Use the graph to make an approximate conversion of:

    i 25 miles to kilometres

    ii 10 miles to kilometres

    iii 40 kilometres to miles

    iv 15 kilometres to miles.

  b Approximately how many kilometres are equivalent to 5 miles?

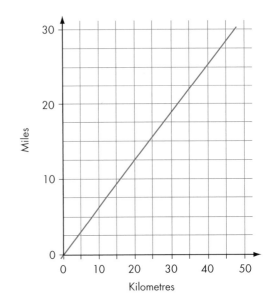

8 Granny McAllister still finds it hard to think in degrees Celsius. So she always uses the following conversion graph to help her to understand the weather forecast.

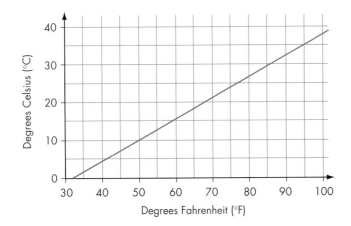

  a Use the graph to make an approximate conversion of:

    i 35 °C to Fahrenheit

    ii 20 °C to Fahrenheit

    iii 50 °F to Celsius

    iv 90 °F to Celsius.

  b Water freezes at 0 °C. What temperature is this in Fahrenheit?

9 Tea is sold at a school fete between 1.00 pm and 2.30 pm. The numbers of cups of tea that had been sold were noted at half-hour intervals.

Time	1.00	1.30	2.00	2.30	3.00	3.30
No. of cups of tea sold	0	24	48	72	96	120

  a Draw a graph to illustrate this information. Use a scale from 1 to 4 hours on the horizontal time axis, and from 1 to 120 on the vertical axis for numbers of cups of tea sold.

  b Use your graph to estimate when the 60th cup of tea was sold.

10 I lost my fuel bill, but while talking to my friends I found out that:

Bill who had used 850 units was charged £57.50
Wendy who had used 320 units was charged £31
Rhanni who had used 540 units was charged £42.

  a Plot the given information and draw a straight-line graph. Use a scale from 0 to 900 on the horizontal units axis, and from £0 to £60 on the vertical cost axis.

  b Use your graph to find what I will be charged for 700 units.

Travel graphs

In this section you will learn how to:
- read information from a travel graph
- find an average speed from a travel graph

Key words

average
  speed
distance–time
  graph
travel graph

As the name suggests, a **travel graph** gives information about how someone or something has travelled over a given time period. It is also called a **distance–time graph**.

A travel graph is read in a similar way to the conversion graphs you have just done. But you can also find the **average speed** from a distance–time graph by using the formula:

$$\text{average speed} = \frac{\text{total distance travelled}}{\text{total time taken}}$$

EXAMPLE 3

The distance–time graph below represents a car journey from Barnsley to Nottingham, a distance of 50 km, and back again.

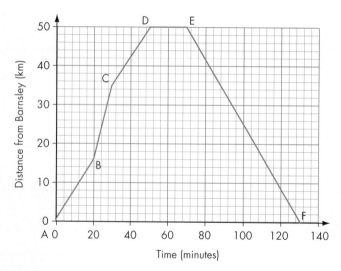

a What can you say about points B, C and D?

b What can you say about the journey from D to F?

c Work out the average speed for each of the five stages of the journey.

From the graph:

a B: After 20 minutes the car was 16 km away from Barnsley.

C: After 30 minutes the car was 35 km away from Barnsley.

D: After 50 minutes the car was 50 km away from Barnsley, so at Nottingham.

b D–F: The car stayed at Nottingham for 20 minutes, and then took 60 minutes for the return journey.

c The average speeds over the five stages of the journey are worked out as follows.

A to B represents 16 km in 20 minutes.

Multiplying both numbers by 3 gives 48 km in 60 minutes, which is 48 km/h.

B to C represents 19 km in 10 minutes.

Multiplying both numbers by 6 gives 114 km in 60 minutes, which is 114 km/h.

C to D represents 15 km in 20 minutes.

Multiplying both numbers by 3 gives 45 km in 60 minutes, which is 45 km/h.

D to E represents a stop: no further distance travelled.

E to F represents the return journey of 50 km in 60 minutes, which is 50 km/h.

So, the return journey was at an average speed of 50 km/h.

You always work out the distance travelled in 1 hour to get the speed in kilometres per hour (km/h) or miles per hour (mph or miles/h).

EXERCISE 14B

1 Paul was travelling in his car to a meeting. He set off from home at 7.00 am and stopped on the way for a break. This distance–time graph illustrates his journey.

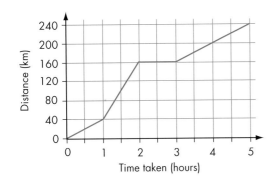

> **HINTS AND TIPS**
>
> Read the question carefully. Paul set off at 7 o'clock in the morning and the graph shows the time after this.

a At what time did he:

i stop for his break

ii set off after his break

iii get to his meeting place?

b At what average speed was he travelling:

i over the first hour

ii over the second hour

iii for the last part of his journey?

2 James was travelling to Cornwall on his holidays. This distance–time graph illustrates his journey.

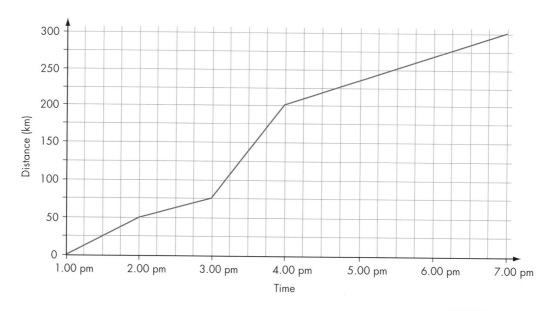

a His greatest speed was on the motorway.

   i   How far did he travel along the motorway?

   ii What was his average speed on the motorway?

b i   When did he travel most slowly?

   ii What was his lowest average speed?

HINTS AND TIPS

Remember that the graph is made up of straight lines, as it shows average speed for each section of the journey. In reality, speed is rarely constant – except sometimes on motorways.

3 A small bus set off from Leeds to pick up Mike and his family. It then went on to pick up Mike's parents and grandparents. It then travelled further, dropping them all off at a hotel. The bus then went on a further 10 km to pick up another party and took them back to Leeds. This distance–time graph illustrates the journey.

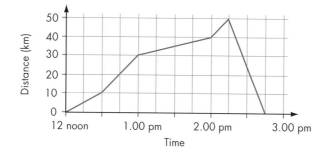

a How far from Leeds did Mike's parents and grandparents live?

b How far from Leeds is the hotel at which they all stayed?

c What was the average speed of the bus on its way back to Leeds?

4 Azam and Jafar were having a race. The distance–time graph below illustrates the distances covered.

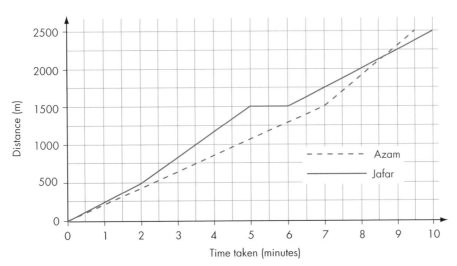

a Jafar stopped during the race. Why might this have happened?

b i When Jafar was running at his fastest, he ran from 500 metres to 1500 metres in 3 minutes. What was his speed in metres per minute?

ii How many seconds are there in three minutes?

iii What is Jafar's speed in metres per second?

c i At about what time into the race did Azam overtake Jafar?

ii By how many seconds did Azam beat Jafar?

5 Three friends, Patrick, Araf and Sean, ran a 1000 metres race. The race is illustrated on the distance–time graph below.

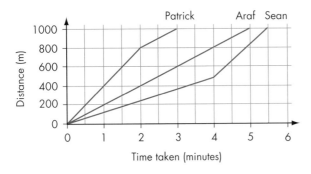

The school newspaper gave the following report of Patrick's race:

'Patrick took an early lead, running the first 800 metres in 2 minutes. He then slowed down a lot and ran the last 200 metres in 1 minute, to finish first in a total time of 3 minutes.'

a Describe the races of Araf and Sean in a similar way.

b i What is the average speed of Patrick in kilometres per hour?

ii What is the average speed of Araf in kilometres per hour?

iii What is the average speed of Sean in kilometres per hour?

6 Three school friends all set off from school at the same time, 3.45 pm. They all lived 12 km away from the school. The distance–time graph below illustrates their journeys.

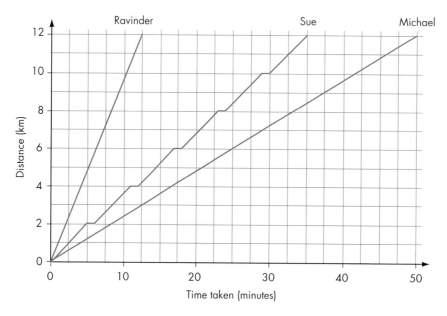

One of them went by bus, one cycled and one was taken by car.

a i Explain how you know that Sue used the bus.

ii Who went by car?

b At what time did each friend get home?

c i When the bus was moving, it covered 2 kilometres in 5 minutes. What is this speed in kilometres per hour?

ii Overall, the bus covered 12 kilometres in 35 minutes. What is this speed in kilometres per hour?

iii How many stops did the bus make before Sue got home?

14.3 Flow diagrams and graphs

In this section you will learn how to:
- find the equations of horizontal and vertical lines
- use flow diagrams to draw graphs

Key words

equation of
a line
flow diagram
function
input value
negative
coordinates
output value
x-value
y-value

Plotting negative coordinates

So far, all the points you have read or plotted on graphs have been coordinates in the first quadrant. The grid below shows you how to read and plot coordinates in all four quadrants and how to find the equations of vertical and horizontal lines. This involves using **negative coordinates**.

The coordinates of a point are given in the form (x, y), where x is the number along the x-axis and y is the number up the y-axis.

The coordinates of the four points on the grid are:

   A(2, 3)   B(–1, 2)   C(–3, –4)   D(1, –3)

The x-coordinate of all the points on line X are 3. So you can say the **equation of line** X is $x = 3$.

The y-coordinate of all the points on line Y are –2. So you can say the equation of line Y is $y = –2$.

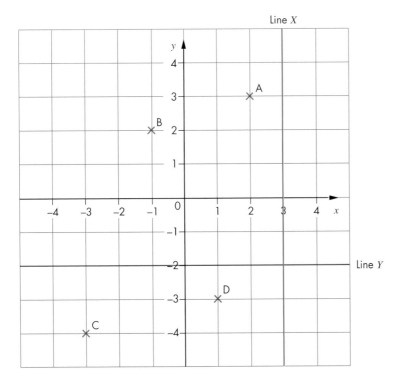

Note: The equation of the x-axis is $y = 0$ and the equation of the y-axis is $x = 0$.

Flow diagrams

One way of drawing a graph is to obtain a set of coordinates from an equation by means of a **flow diagram**. These coordinates are then plotted and the graph is drawn.

In its simplest form, a flow diagram consists of a single box, which may be thought of as containing a mathematical operation, called a **function**. A set of numbers fed into one side of the box is changed by the operation into another set, which comes out from the opposite side of the box. For example, the box shown below represents the operation of multiplying by 3.

Input   Output
0, 1, 2, 3, 4 $\boxed{\times 3}$ 0, 3, 6, 9, 12

The numbers that are fed into the box are called **input values** and the numbers that come out are called **output values**.

The input and output values can be arranged in a table.

x	0	1	2	3	4
y	0	3	6	9	12

The input values are called ***x*-values** and the output values are called ***y*-values**. These form a set of coordinates that can be *plotted on a graph*. In this case, the coordinates are (0, 0), (1, 3), (2, 6), (3, 9) and (4, 12).

Most functions consist of more than one operation, so the flow diagrams consist of more than one box. In such cases, you need to match the *first* input values to the *last* output values. The values produced in the middle operations are just working numbers and can be missed out.

0, 1, 2, 3, 4 → × 2 → 0, 2, 4, 6, 8 → + 3 → 3, 5, 7, 9, 11

So, for the two-box flow diagram the table looks like this.

x	0	1	2	3	4
y	3	5	7	9	11

This gives the coordinates (0, 3), (1, 5), (2, 7), (3, 9) and (4, 11).

The two flow diagrams above represent respectively the equation $y = 3x$ and the equation $y = 2x + 3$, as shown below.

x → × 3 → 3*x*
$y = 3x$

x → × 2 → 2*x* → + 3 → 2*x* + 3
$y = 2x + 3$

It is now an easy step to plot the coordinates for each equation on a set of axes, to produce the graphs of $y = 3x$ and $y = 2x + 3$, as shown below.

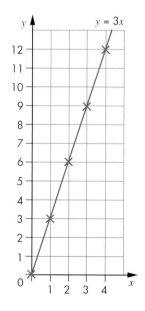

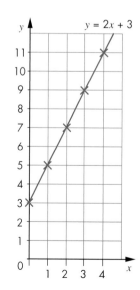

One of the practical problems in graph work is deciding the range of values for the axes. In examinations this is not usually a problem as the axes are drawn for you. Throughout this section, diagrams like the one on the right will show you the range for your axes for each question. These diagrams are not necessarily drawn to scale.

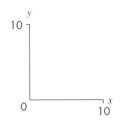

This particular diagram means draw the *x*-axis (horizontal axis) from 0 to 10 and the *y*-axis (vertical axis) from 0 to 10. You can use any type of graph or squared paper to draw your axes.

Note that the *scale* on each axis need *not always be the same*.

EXAMPLE 4

Use the flow diagram below to draw the graph of *y* = 4*x* − 1.

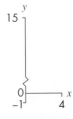

Now enter the values in a table.

x	0	1	2	3	4
y					

The table becomes:

x	0	1	2	3	4
y	−1	3	7	11	15

So, the coordinates are:

(0, −1), (1, 3), (2, 7), (3, 11), (4, 15)

Plot these points and join them up to obtain the graph shown on the right.

This is the graph of *y* = 4*x* − 1.

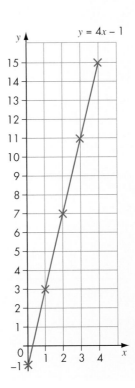

Always label your graphs. In an examination, you may need to draw more than one graph on the same axes. If you do not label your graphs you may lose marks.

EXERCISE 14C

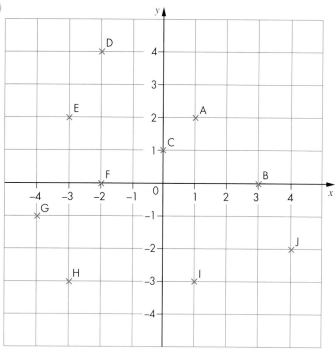

a Write down the coordinates of all the points A to J on the grid.

b Write down the coordinates of the midpoint of the line joining:

i A and B   ii H and I   iii D and J.

c Write down the equations of the lines labelled 1 to 4 on the grid.

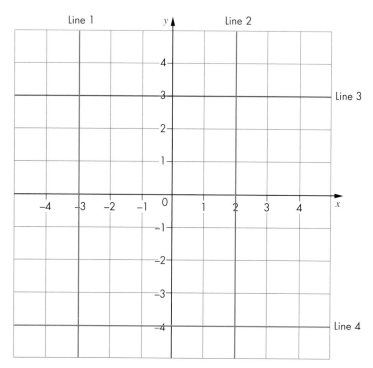

d Write down the equation of the line that is exactly halfway between:

i line 1 and line 2   ii line 3 and line 4.

2 Draw the graph of $y = x + 2$.

$$x \xrightarrow{\;0, 1, 2, 3, 4\;} \boxed{+ 2} \xrightarrow{\;?, ?, ?, ?, ?\;} y$$

x	0	1	2	3	4
y					

3 Draw the graph of $y = 2x - 2$.

$$x \xrightarrow{\;0, 1, 2, 3, 4\;} \boxed{\times 2} \xrightarrow{\;?, ?, ?, ?, ?\;} \boxed{- 2} \xrightarrow{\;?, ?, ?, ?, ?\;} y$$

x	0	1	2	3	4
y					

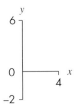

4 Draw the graph of $y = \dfrac{x}{3} + 1$.

$$x \xrightarrow{\;0, 3, 6, 9, 12\;} \boxed{\div 3} \xrightarrow{\;?, ?, ?, ?, ?\;} \boxed{+ 1} \xrightarrow{\;?, ?, ?, ?, ?\;} y$$

x	0	3	6	9	12
y					

5 Draw the graph of $y = \dfrac{x}{2} - 4$.

$$x \xrightarrow{\;0, 2, 4, 6, 8\;} \boxed{\div 2} \xrightarrow{\;?, ?, ?, ?, ?\;} \boxed{- 4} \xrightarrow{\;?, ?, ?, ?, ?\;} y$$

x	0	2	4	6	8
y					

6 **a** Draw the graphs of $y = x - 3$ and $y = 2x - 6$ on the same grid.

$$x \xrightarrow{\;0, 1, 2, 3, 4\;} \boxed{- 3} \xrightarrow{\;?, ?, ?, ?, ?\;} y$$

$$x \xrightarrow{\;0, 1, 2, 3, 4\;} \boxed{\times 2} \xrightarrow{\;?, ?, ?, ?, ?\;} \boxed{- 6} \xrightarrow{\;?, ?, ?, ?, ?\;} y$$

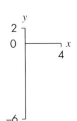

b At which point do the lines intersect?

a Draw the graphs of $y = 2x$ and $y = x + 6$ on the same grid.

$x \xrightarrow{\quad 0, 2, 4, 6, 8 \quad} \boxed{\times 2} \xrightarrow{\quad ?, ?, ?, ?, ?, ? \quad} y$

$x \xrightarrow{\quad 0, 2, 4, 6, 8 \quad} \boxed{+ 6} \xrightarrow{\quad ?, ?, ?, ?, ?, ? \quad} y$

b At which point do the lines intersect?

8 Draw the graph of $y = 5x - 1$. Choose your own inputs and axes.

14.4 Linear graphs

In this section you will learn how to:
- draw linear graphs without using flow diagrams
- find the gradient of a straight line
- use the gradient to draw a straight line
- use the gradient-intercept method to draw a linear graph

Key word
coefficient
constant term
gradient
gradient-intercept
linear graphs
slope

This chapter is concerned with drawing straight-line graphs. These graphs are usually referred to as **linear graphs**.

The minimum number of points needed to draw a linear graph is two but it is better to plot three or more because that gives at least one point to act as a check. There is no rule about how many points to plot but here are some tips for drawing graphs.

- Use a sharp pencil and mark each point with an accurate cross.

- Position your eyes directly over the graph. If you look from the side, you will not be able to line up your ruler accurately.

Drawing graphs by finding points

This method is a bit quicker and does not need flow diagrams. However, if you prefer flow diagrams, use them.

Follow through Example 5 to see how this method works.

EXAMPLE 5

Draw the graph of $y = 4x - 5$ for values of x from 0 to 5. This is usually written as $0 \leqslant x \leqslant 5$.

Choose three values for x: these should be the highest and lowest x-values and one in between.

Work out the y-values by substituting the x-values into the equation.

Keep a record of your calculations in a table, as shown below.

x	0	3	5
y			

When $x = 0$, $y = 4(0) - 5 = -5$
This gives the point $(0, -5)$.

When $x = 3$, $y = 4(3) - 5 = 7$
This gives the point $(3, 7)$.

When $x = 5$, $y = 4(5) - 5 = 15$
This gives the point $(5, 15)$.

Hence your table is:

x	0	3	5
y	-5	7	15

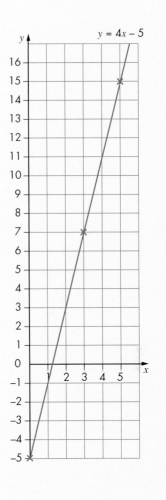

You now have to decide the extent (range) of the axes. You can find this out by looking at the coordinates that you have so far.

The smallest x-value is 0, the largest is 5.
The smallest y-value is -5, the largest is 15.

Now draw the axes, plot the points and complete the graph.

It is nearly always a good idea to choose 0 as one of the x-values. In an examination, the range for the x-values will usually be given and the axes will already be drawn.

EXERCISE 14D

Read through these hints before drawing the following linear graphs.

- Use the highest and lowest values of x given in the range.

- Do not pick x-values that are too close together, such as 1 and 2. Try to space them out so that you can draw a more accurate graph.

- Always label your graph with its equation. This is particularly important when you are drawing two graphs on the same set of axes.

- If you want to use a flow diagram, use one.

- Create a table of values. You will often have to complete these in your examinations.

D

1 Draw the graph of $y = 3x + 4$ for x-values from 0 to 5 ($0 \leq x \leq 5$).

2 Draw the graph of $y = 2x - 5$ for $0 \leq x \leq 5$.

3 Draw the graph of $y = \frac{x}{2} - 3$ for $0 \leq x \leq 10$.

4 Draw the graph of $y = 3x + 5$ for $-3 \leq x \leq 3$.

5 **a** On the same set of axes, draw the graphs of $y = 3x - 2$ and $y = 2x + 1$ for $0 \leq x \leq 5$.

   b At which point do the two lines intersect?

6 **a** On the same axes, draw the graphs of $y = \frac{x}{3} - 1$ and $y = \frac{x}{2} - 2$ for $0 \leq x \leq 12$.

   b At which point do the two lines intersect?

7 **a** On the same axes, draw the graphs of $y = 3x + 1$ and $y = 3x - 2$ for $0 \leq x \leq 4$.

   b Do the two lines intersect? If not, why not?

8 **a** Copy and complete the table to draw the graph of $x + y = 5$ for $0 \leq x \leq 5$.

x	0	1	2	3	4	5
y	5		3		1	

   b Now draw the graph of $x + y = 7$ for $0 \leq x \leq 7$.

Gradient

The **slope** of a line is called its **gradient**. The steeper the slope of the line, the larger the value of the gradient.

The gradient of the line shown here can be measured by drawing, as large as possible, a right-angled triangle which has part of the line as its hypotenuse (sloping side). The gradient is then given by:

$$\text{gradient} = \frac{\text{distance measured up}}{\text{distance measured along}}$$

$$= \frac{\text{difference on } y\text{-axis}}{\text{difference on } x\text{-axis}}$$

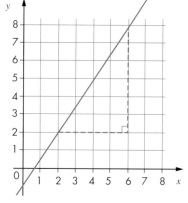

For example, to measure the steepness of the line in the first diagram, below, you first draw a right-angled triangle that has part of this line as its hypotenuse. It does not matter where you draw the triangle but it makes the calculations much easier if you choose a sensible place. This usually means using existing grid lines, so that you avoid fractional values. See the second and third diagrams below.

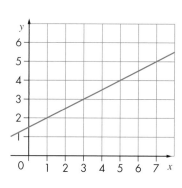

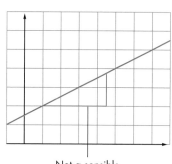

Not a sensible choice of triangle

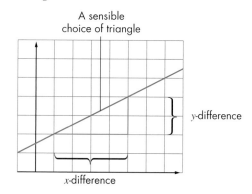

A sensible choice of triangle

y-difference

x-difference

After you have drawn the triangle, measure (or count) how many squares there are on the vertical side. This is the difference between the *y*-coordinates. In the case above, this is 2.

Then measure (or count) how many squares there are on the horizontal side. This is the difference between the *x*-coordinates. In the case above, this is 4.

To work out the gradient, you make the following calculation.

$$\text{gradient} = \frac{\text{difference of the } y\text{-coordinates}}{\text{difference of the } x\text{-coordinates}} = \frac{2}{4} = \frac{1}{2} \text{ or } 0.5$$

Note that the value of the gradient is not affected by where the triangle is drawn. As you are calculating the ratio of two sides of the triangle, the gradient will always be the same wherever you draw the triangle.

Remember: Take care when finding the differences between the coordinates of the two points. Choose one point as the first and the other as the second, and subtract in the *same order* each time to find the difference. When a line slopes *down from right to left* (/) the gradient is always positive, but when a line slopes *down from left to right* (\) the gradient is always negative, so you must make sure there is a minus sign in front of the fraction.

EXAMPLE 6

Find the gradient of each of these lines.

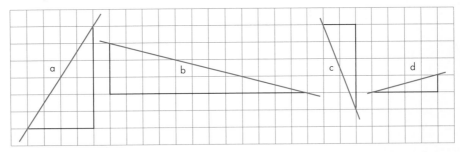

In each case, a sensible choice of triangle has already been made.

a *y*-difference = 6, *x*-difference = 4   Gradient = $6 \div 4 = \frac{3}{2} = 1.5$

b *y*-difference = 3, *x*-difference = 12   Line slopes down from left to right,

so gradient = $-(3 \div 12) = -\frac{1}{4} = -0.25$

c *y*-difference = 5, *x*-difference = 2   Line slopes down from left to right,

so gradient = $-(5 \div 2) = -\frac{5}{2} = -2.5$

d *y*-difference = 1, *x*-difference = 4   Gradient = $1 \div 4 = \frac{1}{4} = 0.25$

Drawing a line with a certain gradient

To draw a line with a certain gradient, you need to 'reverse' the process described above. Use the given gradient to draw the right-angled triangle first. For example, take a gradient of 2.

Start at a convenient point (A in the diagrams below). A gradient of 2 means for an *x*-step of 1 the *y*-step must be 2 (because 2 is the fraction $\frac{2}{1}$). So, move one square across and two squares up, and mark a dot.

Repeat this as many times as you like and draw the line. You can also move one square back and two squares down, which gives the same gradient, as the third diagram shows.

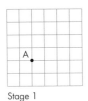

Stage 1   Stage 2

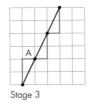

Stage 3

Remember: For a positive gradient you move across (left to right) and then *up*. For a negative gradient you move across (left to right) and then *down*.

EXAMPLE 7

Draw lines with these gradients. **a** $\frac{1}{3}$ **b** -3 **c** $-\frac{1}{4}$

a This is a fractional gradient which has a y-step of 1 and an x-step of 3. Move three squares across and one square up every time.

b This is a negative gradient, so for every one square across, move three squares down.

c This is also a negative gradient and it is a fraction. So for every four squares across, move one square down.

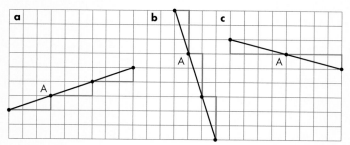

EXERCISE 14E

1 Find the gradient of each of these lines.

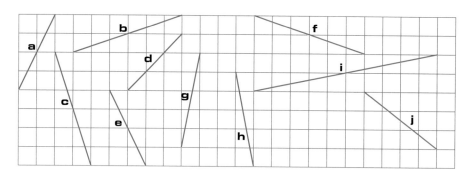

2 Find the gradient of each of these lines. What is special about these lines?

a 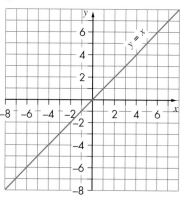   **b**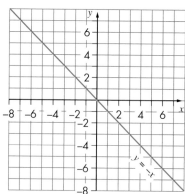

3 Draw lines with these gradients.

a 4   **b** $\frac{2}{3}$ **c** -2 **d** $-\frac{4}{5}$ **e** 6   **f** -6

Gradient-intercept method for drawing graphs

The ideas that you have already discovered in this section lead to another way of plotting lines, known as the **gradient-intercept** method.

EXAMPLE 8

Draw the graph of $y = 3x - 1$, using the gradient-intercept method.

- Because the **constant term** is -1, you know that the graph crosses or intercepts the y-axis at -1. Mark this point with a dot or a cross (**A** on diagram **i**).

- The number in front of x (called the **coefficient** of x) gives the relationship between y and x. Because the coefficient of x is 3, this tells you that the y-value is 3 times the x-value, so the gradient of the line is 3. For an x-step of one unit, there is a y-step of three. Starting at -1 on the y-axis, move one square across and three squares up and mark this point with a dot or a cross (**B** on diagram **i**).

Repeat this from every new point. You can also move one square back and three squares down. When enough points have been marked, join the dots (or crosses) to make the graph (diagram **ii**).

i

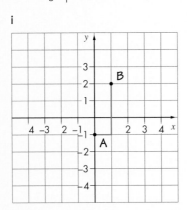

ii

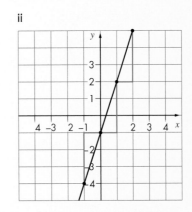

Note: If the points are not in a straight line, you have made a mistake.

You have found that a line with an equation in the form of $y = mx + c$

has a gradient of m

and cuts the y-axis at c

We can use this to help us find the equation of a line of best fit when looking at points plotted from an experiment.

For example:

In an experiment, the following results were obtained. Plot the points and find the equation of the line of best fit.

Distance x	1	2	3	4
Temperature y	5.1	6.9	8.8	11.1

Plot the points and join up the line of best fit.

The line cuts the y-axis at 3

The gradient (m) can be found to be 2

So the equation of the line is $y = 2x + 3$

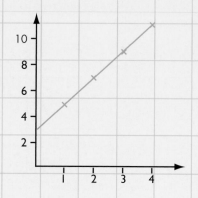

1 In another experiment, a ball was dropped from different heights onto a surface and the height of the bounce was measured. The results are given in the table.

Height dropped x cm	75	100	125	150	175	200
Bounce y cm	82	95	108	120	133	145

a Plot the points on a graph and draw the line of best fit.

b Find the equation of this line.

c What height was the surface that the ball bounced on?

d How high would the ball bounce if it was dropped from 300 cm?

2 Repeat the above experiment for different balls onto different surfaces and see if the equations you find help you to verify part **c** and also check the prediction for part **d**.

EXERCISE 14F

1 Use the gradient-intercept method to draw these lines. Use the same grid, taking x from -10 to 10 and y from -10 to 10. If the grid gets too full, draw another one.

a $y = 2x + 6$ **b** $y = 3x - 4$ **c** $y = \dfrac{1}{2}x + 5$

d $y = x + 7$ **e** $y = 4x - 3$ **f** $y = 2x - 7$

g $y = \dfrac{1}{4}x - 3$ **h** $y = \dfrac{2}{3}x + 4$ **i** $y = 6x - 5$

j $y = x + 8$ **k** $y = \dfrac{4}{5}x - 2$ **l** $y = 3x - 9$

For questions **2** to **4** use axes with ranges $-6 \leqslant x \leqslant 6$ and $-8 \leqslant y \leqslant 8$.

2 **a** Using the gradient–intercept method, draw the following lines on the same grid.

     i $y = 3x + 1$

     ii $y = 2x + 3$

   b Where do the lines cross?

3 **a** Using the gradient–intercept method, draw the following lines on the same grid.

     i $y = \dfrac{x}{3} + 3$

     ii $y = \dfrac{x}{4} + 2$

   b Where do the lines cross?

4 **a** Using the gradient–intercept method, draw the following lines on the same grid.

     i $y = x + 3$

     ii $y = 2x$

   b Where do the lines cross?

1 The conversion graph can be used for changing between miles and kilometres.

   a Use the graph to change 3 miles to kilometres.

   b Use the graph to change 11 kilometres to miles.

   Edexcel, Question 5, Paper 14 Foundation, June 2004

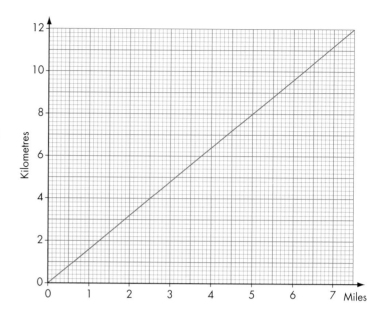

2 **a** Complete the table of values for $y = 2x - 3$.

x	−1	0	1	2	3
y	−5		−1		3

   b On a grid draw the graph of $y = 2x - 3$ for values of x from −1 to +3. Take the x-axis from −1 to +3 and the y-axis from −5 to 3.

   c Find the coordinates of the point where the line $y = 2x - 3$ crosses the line $y = -2$.

3 **a** Draw a set of axes on a grid and label the x-axis from −4 to +4 and the y-axis from −8 to +10. On this grid, draw and label the lines $y = -5$ and $y = 2x + 1$.

   b Write down the coordinates of the point where the lines $y = -5$ and $y = 2x + 1$ cross.

4 A man left home at 12 noon to go for a cycle ride. The travel graph represents part of the man's journey.

At 12.45 pm the man stopped for a rest.

   a For how many minutes did he rest?

   b Find his distance from home at 1.30 pm.

The man stopped for another rest at 2 pm. He rested for one hour.

Then he cycled home at a steady speed. It took him 2 hours.

   c Copy and complete the travel graph.

   Edexcel, Question 8, Paper 4 Intermediate, June 2005

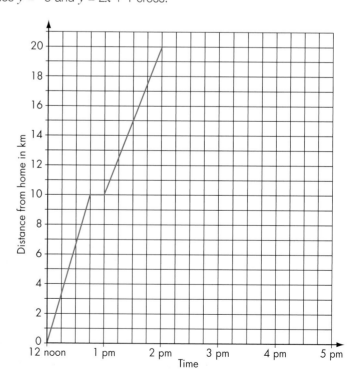

5 Here is part of a travel graph of Siân's journey from her house to the shops and back.

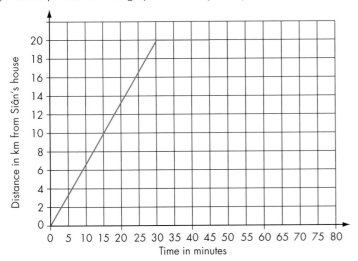

Distance in km from Siân's house

Time in minutes

a Work out Siân's speed for the first 30 minutes of her journey. Give your answer in km/h.

Siân spends 15 minutes at the shops. She then travels back to her house at 60 km/h.

b Copy and complete the travel graph.

Edexcel, Question 18, Paper 14 Foundation, June 2003

WORKED EXAM QUESTIONS

The distance–time graph shows the journey of a train between two stations. The stations are 12 miles apart.

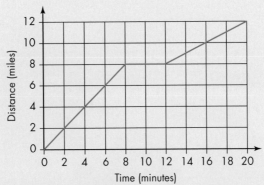

Distance (miles)

Time (minutes)

a During the journey the train stopped at a signal. For how long was the train stopped?

b What was the average speed of the train for the *whole* journey? Give your answer in miles per hour.

Solution

a The train stopped for 4 minutes (where the line is horizontal).

b The train travels 12 miles in 20 minutes. This is 36 miles in 60 minutes (multiply both numbers by 3).
So the average speed is 36 mph.

A trip to France

The Bright family plan to take a camping holiday in France. They book a campsite near Perpignan in the south of France.

This map shows the main roads. The distances between the towns are shown in red and approximate driving times are in black.

Boulogne
115 km **1h 20 min**
Arras
180 km **1¾ h**
170 km **1½ h**
Rouen
190 km **2h**
Reims
135 km **1h 20 min**
PARIS
130 km **1h 20 min**
300 km **2¾ h**
Orleans
310km **3h**
120 km **1h 10min**
Bourges
Dijon
190 km **1h 50min**
300 km **3h**
190 km **2h**
Clermont - Ferrand
175 km **2h**
Lyon
340 km **3¾ h**
200 km **1h 50 min**
Orange
Montpellier
100 km **1h**
155 km **1½ h**
Perpignan

Use the map to plan four different routes from the ferry port at Boulogne to Perpignan.

What are the total distances and driving times for each of your routes?

Which route is the quickest and shortest if they want to avoid Paris?

Find the average speed for each of your routes.

130 **110**

80 **90**

100 **50**

In France the speed limits are in kilometres per hour (km/h).

The speed limits are:

50 km/h   in towns
90 km/h   on open roads (80 km/h in wet weather)
110 km/h   on dual carriageways (100 km/h in wet
              weather)
130 km/h   on motorways (110 km/h in wet weather)

Mrs Bright notices on the car speedometer that 50 miles per hour (mph) is the same as 80 kilometres per hour (km/h).

Draw a conversion graph between km/h and mph and use it to help her complete this table.

km/h	mph
50	
80	50
90	
100	
110	
130	

In France, tyre pressures are measured in **bars**. In the UK tyre pressures are measured in **pounds per square inch** (lb/in^2).

Mr Bright uses the conversion graph to work out tyre pressures, in bars, for his car.

He knows the front tyres need 32 lb/in^2 and the back tyres need 34 lb/in^2.

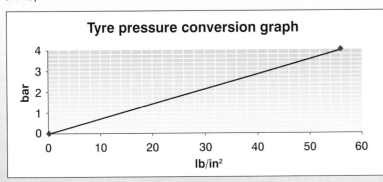

Tyre pressure conversion graph

Help him to decide what the pressures in his tyres should be.

Front tyres   _____ bars   Back tyres   _____ bars

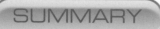

GRADE YOURSELF

F Able to read off values from a conversion graph

F Able to plot points in all four quadrants

E Able to read off distances and times from a travel graph

E Able to draw a linear graph given a table of values to complete

D Able to find an average speed from a travel graph

D Able to draw a linear graph without being given a table of values

What you should know now

- How to use conversion graphs
- How to use travel graphs to find distances, times and speeds
- How to draw a linear graph

This book provides indicators of the equivalent grade level of maths questions throughout. The publishers wish to make clear that these grade indicators have been provided by Collins Education, and are not the responsibility of Edexcel Ltd. Whilst every effort has been made to assure their accuracy, they should be regarded as indicators, and are not binding or definitive.

Angles

Chapter 15

1 Measuring and drawing angles

2 Angle facts

3 Angles in a triangle

4 Angles in a polygon

5 Regular polygons

6 Parallel lines

7 Special quadrilaterals

8 Bearings

This chapter will show you ...

- how to measure and draw angles
- how to find angles on a line and at a point
- how to find angles in a triangle and in any polygon
- how to calculate interior and exterior angles in polygons
- how to calculate angles in parallel lines
- how to use bearings

Visual overview

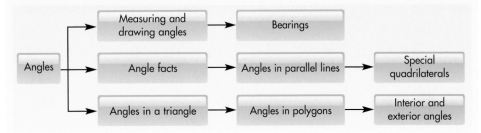

What you should already know

- How to use a protractor to find the size of any angle
- The meaning of the terms 'acute', 'obtuse', 'reflex', 'right' and how to use these terms to describe angles
- That a polygon is a 2-D shape with any number of straight sides
- That a diagonal is a line joining two vertices of a polygon
- The meaning of the terms 'parallel lines' and 'perpendicular lines'
- How to solve an equation (see Chapter 13)

Quick check

State whether these angles are acute, obtuse or reflex.

1 135°   **2** 68°   **3** 202°   **4** 98°   **5** 315°

In this section you will learn how to:

● measure and draw an angle of any size

Key words

acute angle
obtuse angle
protractor
reflex angle

When you are using a **protractor**, it is important that you:

● place the centre of the protractor *exactly* on the corner (vertex) of the angle

● lay the base-line of the protractor *exactly* along one side of the angle.

You must follow these two steps to obtain an accurate value for the angle you are measuring.

You should already have discovered how easy it is to measure **acute angles** and **obtuse angles**, using the common semicircular protractor.

EXAMPLE 1

Measure the angles ABC, DEF and GHI in the diagrams below.

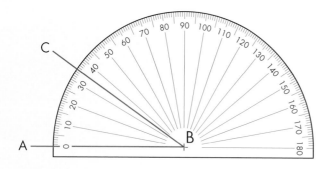
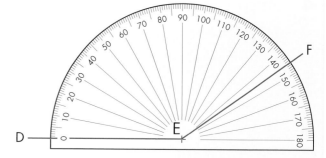

Acute angle ABC is 35° and obtuse angle DEF is 145°.

To measure **reflex angles**, such as angle GHI,
it is easier to use a circular protractor
if you have one.

Note the notation for angles.

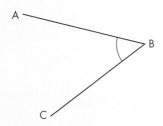

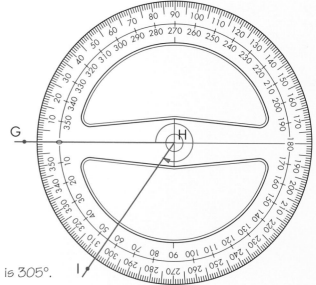

Angle ABC, or ∠ABC, means the
angle at B between the lines AB
and BC.

Reflex angle GHI is 305°.

EXERCISE 15A

1 Use a protractor to measure the size of each marked angle.

a

b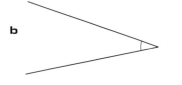

c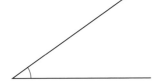

d

e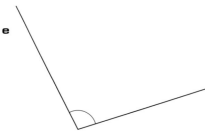

f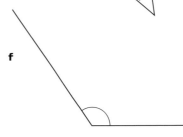

g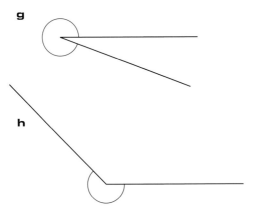

h

2 Use a protractor to draw angles of the following sizes.

    a 30°   **b** 60°

    c 90°   **d** 10°

    e 20°   **f** 45°

    g 75°

3 **a** **i** Draw any three acute angles.

   ii Estimate their sizes. Record your results.

   iii Measure the angles. Record your results.

   iv Work out the difference between your estimate and your measurement for each angle. Add all the differences together. This is your total error.

b Repeat parts **i** to **iv** of part **a** for three obtuse angles.

c Repeat parts **i** to **iv** of part **a** for three reflex angles.

d Which type of angle are you most accurate with, and which type are you least accurate with?

4 Sketch the following triangles. Do not make any measurements but try to get them as accurate as you can by estimating. Then use a ruler and a protractor to draw them accurately to see how accurate you were.

a

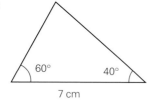

60°   40°
7 cm

b

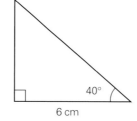

40°
6 cm

c

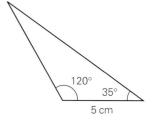

120°   35°
5 cm

15.2 Angle facts

In this section you will learn how to:

● calculate angles on a straight line and angles around a point

Key words
angles around a point
angles on a straight line

Angles on a line

The **angles on a straight line** add up to 180°.

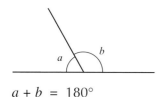

$a + b = 180°$

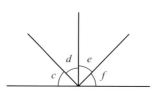

$c + d + e + f = 180°$

Draw an example for yourself (and measure a and b) to show that the statement is true.

Angles around a point

The sum of the **angles around a point** is 360°. For example:

$a + b + c + d + e = 360°$

Again, check this for yourself by drawing an example and measuring the angles.

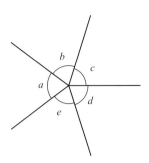

EXAMPLE 2

Find the size of angle x in the diagram.

Angles on a straight line add up to 180°.

$$x + 72° = 180°$$
$$\text{So, } x = 180° - 72°$$
$$x = 108°$$

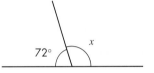

Sometimes equations can be used to solve angle problems.

EXAMPLE 3

Find the value of x in the diagram.

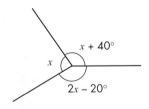

These angles are around a point, so they must add up to 360°.

$$\text{Therefore, } x + x + 40° + 2x - 20° = 360°$$
$$4x + 20° = 360°$$
$$4x = 340°$$
$$x = 85°$$

EXERCISE 15B

Calculate the size of the angle marked *x* in each of these examples.

1

132°   *x*

2
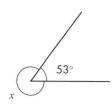
53°
x

3
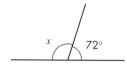
x   72°

4

x
38°

5
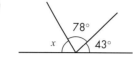
78°
x   43°

6
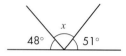
x
48°   51°

7
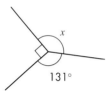
x
131°

8

129°
x

9

x   42°

10
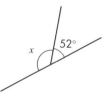
x   52°

11

313°
x

12
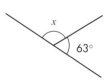
x
63°

13
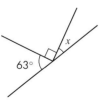
x
63°

14
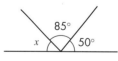
85°
x   50°

15
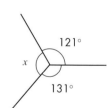
121°
x
131°

16

x   111°

17

x   45°

18
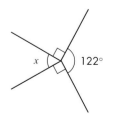
x   122°

19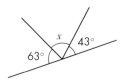

20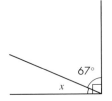

21

22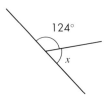

23 Calculate the value of *x* in each of these examples.

a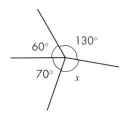

b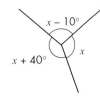

c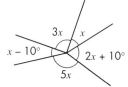

24 Calculate the value of *x* in each of these examples.

a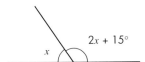

b

c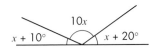

25 Calculate the value of *x* first and then calculate the value of *y* in each of these examples.

a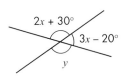

b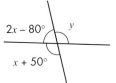

c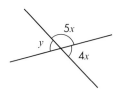

15.3 # Angles in a triangle

In this section you will learn how to:
- calculate the size of angles in a triangle

Key words
angles in a triangle
equilateral triangle
exterior angle
interior angle
isosceles triangle

ACTIVITY

Angles in a triangle

You need a protractor.

Draw a triangle. Label the corners
(vertices) A, B and C.

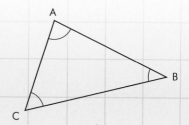

Use a ruler and make sure that the corners of your triangle form proper angles.

Like this.   Not like this...   ... or this.

Measure each angle, A, B and C.

Write them down and add them up:

Angle A = ...°

Angle B = ...°

Angle C = ...°

Total   =

Repeat this for five more triangles, including at least one with an obtuse angle.

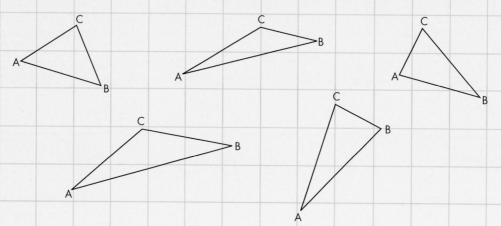

What conclusion can you draw about the sum of the angles in a triangle?

Remember

You will not be able to measure with total accuracy.

You should have discovered that the three **angles in a triangle** add up to 180°.

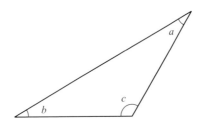

$a + b + c = 180°$

EXAMPLE 4

Calculate the size of angle a in the triangle below.

Angles in a triangle add up to 180°

Therefore, $a + 20° + 125° = 180°$

$a + 145° = 180°$

So $a = 35°$

Special triangles

Equilateral triangle

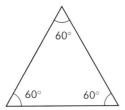

An **equilateral triangle** is a triangle with all its sides equal. Therefore, all three **interior angles** are 60°.

Isosceles triangle

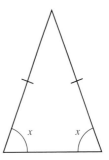

An **isosceles triangle** is a triangle with two equal sides and, therefore, with two equal interior angles (at the foot of the equal sides).

Notice how to mark the equal sides and equal angles.

1 Find the size of the angle marked with a letter in each of these triangles.

a

b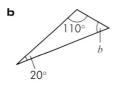

c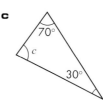

d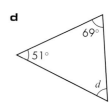

e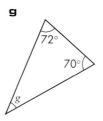

f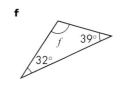

g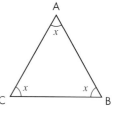

h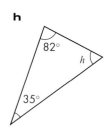

2 Do any of these sets of angles form the three angles of a triangle? Explain your answer.

a 35°, 75°, 80°

b 50°, 60°, 70°

c 55°, 55°, 60°

d 60°, 60°, 60°

e 35°, 35°, 110°

f 102°, 38°, 30°

3 Two interior angles of a triangle are given in each case. Find the third one indicated by a letter.

a 20°, 80°, *a*

b 52°, 61°, *b*

c 80°, 80°, *c*

d 25°, 112°, *d*

e 120°, 50°, *e*

f 122°, 57°, *f*

4 In the triangle on the right, all the interior angles are the same.

a What is the size of each angle?

b What is the name of a special triangle like this?

c What is special about the sides of this triangle?

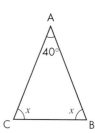

5 In the triangle on the right, two of the angles are the same.

a Work out the size of the lettered angles.

b What is the name of a special triangle like this?

c What is special about the sides AC and AB of this triangle?

6 In the triangle on the right, the angles at B and C are the same. Work out the size of the lettered angles.

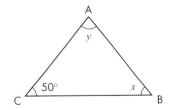

7 Find the size of the **exterior angle** marked with a letter in each of these diagrams.

a

b

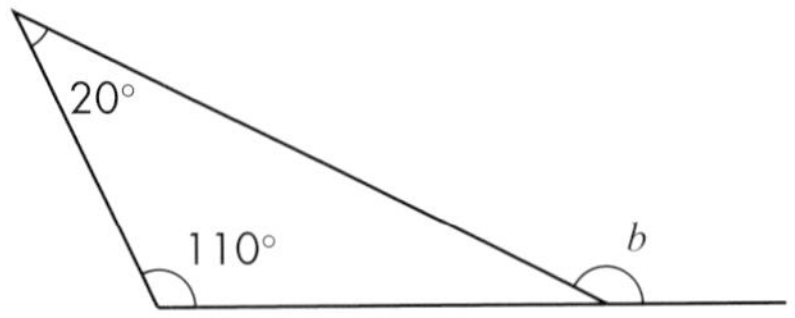

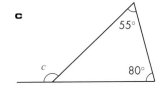

c

PROOF

8 By using algebra, show that $x = a + b$.

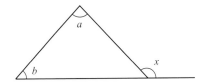

E

D

15.4 **Angles in a polygon**

In this section you will learn how to:

• calculate the sum of the interior angles in a polygon

Key words

decagon
heptagon
hexagon
interior angle
nonagon
octagon
pentagon
polygon
quadrilateral

Angle sums from triangles

Draw a **quadrilateral** (a four-sided shape).
Draw in a diagonal to make it into two triangles.

You should be able to copy and complete this statement:

> The sum of the angles in a quadrilateral is equal to the sum of
> the angles in ...... triangles, which is ...... × 180° = ...°.

Now draw a **pentagon** (a five-sided shape).

Draw in the diagonals to make it into three triangles.

You should be able to copy and complete this statement:

> The sum of the angles in a pentagon is equal to the
> sum of the angles in ...... triangles,
> which is ...... × 180° = ...°.

Next, draw a **hexagon** (a six-sided shape).

Draw in the diagonals to make it into four triangles.

You should be able to copy and complete this statement:

> The sum of the angles in a hexagon is equal to the sum of
> the angles in ...... triangles, which is ...... × 180° = ...°.

Now, complete the table below. Use the number pattern to carry on the angle sum
up to a **decagon** (ten-sided shape).

Shape	Sides	Triangles	Angle sum
triangle	3	1	180°
quadrilateral	4	2	
pentagon	5	3	
hexagon	6	4	
heptagon	7		
octagon	8		
nonagon	9		
decagon	10		

If you have spotted the number pattern, you should be able to copy and complete
this statement:

> The number of triangles in a 20-sided shape is ......, so the sum of the angles in a
> 20-sided shape is ...... × 180° = ...°.

So for an n-sided **polygon**, the sum of the **interior angles** is $180(n - 2)°$.

EXAMPLE 5

Calculate the size of angle a in the quadrilateral below.

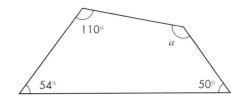

Angles in a quadrilateral add up to 360°.

Therefore, $a + 50° + 54° + 110° = 360°$

$$a + 214° = 360°$$

$$\text{So, } a = 146°$$

EXERCISE 15D

1 Find the size of the angle marked with a letter in each of these quadrilaterals.

a

95° 95°
80° a

b

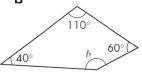

110° 60°
40° b

c

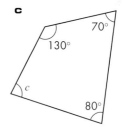

70°
130°
c
80°

d

69°
121°
d

e

78°
88°
117°
e

f

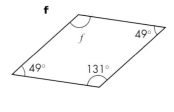

49°
f
49° 131°

g

72°
110°
g 86°

h

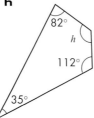

82°
h
112°
35°

HINTS AND TIPS

Remember, the sum of the interior angles of a quadrilateral is 360°.

2 Do any of these sets of angles form the four interior angles of a quadrilateral? Explain your answer.

a 135°, 75°, 60°, 80°

b 150°, 60°, 80°, 70°

c 85°, 85°, 120°, 60°

d 80°, 90°, 90°, 110°

e 95°, 95°, 60°, 110°

f 102°, 138°, 90°, 30°

3 Three interior angles of a quadrilateral are given. Find the fourth one indicated by a letter.

a 120°, 80°, 60°, *a*

b 102°, 101°, 90°, *b*

c 80°, 80°, 80°, *c*

d 125°, 112°, 83°, *d*

e 120°, 150°, 50°, *e*

f 122°, 157°, 80°, *f*

4 In the quadrilateral on the right, all the angles are the same.

a What is each angle?

b What is the name of a special quadrilateral like this?

c Is there another quadrilateral with all the angles the same? What is it called?

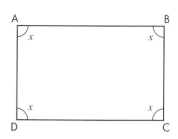

5 Work out the size of the angle marked with a letter in each of the polygons below. You may find the table you did on page 338 useful.

a

b
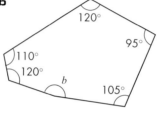

c
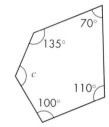

d
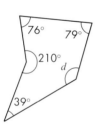

e
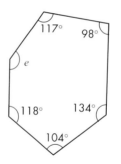

f
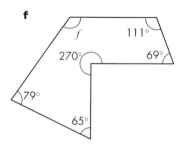

g

h
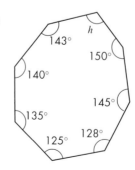

> **HINTS AND TIPS**
>
> Remember, the sum of the interior angles of an *n*-sided polygon is 180(*n* − 2)°.

15.5 Regular polygons

In this section you will learn how to:
- calculate the exterior angles and the interior angles of a regular polygon

Key words
exterior angle
interior angle
regular
   polygon

Regular polygons

To do this activity, you will need to have done the one on page 338.

You will also need a calculator.

Below are five **regular polygons**.

Square 4 sides   Pentagon 5 sides   Hexagon 6 sides   Octagon 8 sides   Decagon 10 sides

A polygon is regular if all its **interior angles** are equal and all its sides have the same length.

A square is a regular four-sided shape that has an angle sum of 360°.

So, each angle is 360° ÷ 4 = 90°.

A regular pentagon has an angle sum of 540°.

So, each angle is 540° ÷ 5 = 108°.

Copy and complete the table below.

Shape	Sides	Angle sum	Each angle
square	4	360°	90°
pentagon	5	540°	108°
hexagon	6	720°	
octagon	8		
nonagon	9		
decagon	10		

Interior and exterior angles

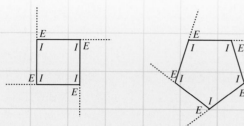 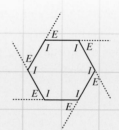

Look at these three regular polygons. At each vertex of each regular polygon, there is an interior angle, I, and an **exterior angle**, E. Notice that: $I + E = 180°$

Clearly, the exterior angles of a square are each 90°. So, the sum of the exterior angles of a square is $4 \times 90° = 360°$.

You can calculate the exterior angle of a regular pentagon as follows. From the table on the previous page, you know that the interior angle of a regular pentagon is 108°.

108° $\backslash$ E So, the exterior angle is $180° - 108° = 72°$.

Therefore, the sum of the exterior angles is $5 \times 72° = 360°$.

Now copy and complete the table below for regular polygons.

Regular polygon	No. of sides	Interior angle	Exterior angle	Sum of exterior angles
square	4	90°	90°	$4 \times 90° = 360°$
pentagon	5	108°	72°	$5 \times 72° =$
hexagon	6	120°		
octagon	8			
nonagon	9			
decagon	10			

From the table, you can see that the sum of the exterior angles is always 360°.

You can use this information to find the exterior angle and the interior angle for any regular polygon.

For an n-sided regular polygon, the exterior angle is given by $E = \dfrac{360°}{n}$

and the interior angle is given by $I = 180° - E$.

EXAMPLE 6

Calculate the size of the exterior and interior angle for a regular 12-sided polygon (a regular dodecagon).

$$E = \frac{360°}{12} = 30° \quad \text{and} \quad I = 180° - 30° = 150°$$

EXERCISE 15E

1 Each diagram shows one vertex of a regular polygon. For each polygon, answer the following.

 i   What is its exterior angle?

 ii How many sides does it have?

 iii What is the sum of its interior angles?

 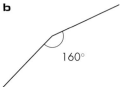 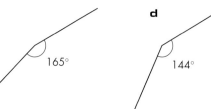

2 Each diagram shows one vertex of a regular polygon. For each polygon, answer the following.

 i   What is its interior angle?

 ii How many sides does it have?

 iii What is the sum of its interior angles?

   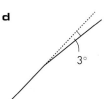

3 Each of these cannot be the interior angle of a regular polygon. Explain why.

4 Each of these cannot be the exterior angle of a regular polygon. Explain why.

 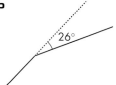  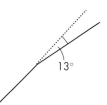

Draw a sketch of a regular octagon and join each vertex to the centre.

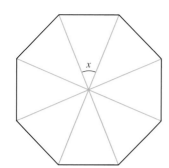

Calculate the value of the angle at the centre (marked x).

What connection does this have with the exterior angle?

Is this true for all regular polygons?

15.6 Parallel lines

In this section you will learn how to:
- find angles in parallel lines

Key words
allied angles
alternate angles
corresponding
 angles
vertically
 opposite angles

ACTIVITY

Angles in parallel lines

You need tracing paper or a protractor.

Draw two parallel lines about 5 cm apart and
a third line that crosses both of them.

The arrowheads indicate that the lines are parallel and
the line that crosses the parallel lines is called a *transversal*.

Notice that eight angles are formed. Label these a, b, c, d, e, f, g and h.

Measure or trace angle a. Find all the angles on the diagram that are the same size as
angle a.

Measure or trace angle b. Find all the angles on the diagram that are the same size as
angle b.

What is the sum of $a + b$?

Find all the pairs of angles on the diagram that add up to 180°.

Angles like these

are called **corresponding angles** (also known as F angles).

Corresponding angles are equal.

Angles like these

are called **alternate angles** (also known as Z angles).

Alternate angles are equal.

Angles like these

are called **vertically opposite angles** or **opposite angles** (also known as X angles).

Vertically opposite angles are equal.

Angles like these

are called **allied angles** or **co-interior angles** (also known as C angles).

Allied angles add to 180°.

Copy and complete these statements to make them true.

1 Angles h and ...... are corresponding angles.

2 Angles e and ...... are vertically opposite angles.

3 Angles d and ...... are alternate angles.

4 Angles e and ...... are allied angles.

5 Angles b and ...... are corresponding angles.

6 Angles b and ...... are vertically opposite angles.

7 Angles c and ...... are allied angles.

8 Angles c and ...... are alternate angles.

Note that in examinations you should use the correct terms for types of angles. Do *not* call them F, Z, X or C angles.

EXAMPLE 7

State the size of each of the lettered angles in the diagram.

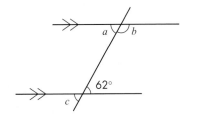

a = 62° (alternate angle)

b = 118° (allied angle or angles on a line)

c = 62° (vertically opposite angle)

EXERCISE 15F

1 State the sizes of the lettered angles in each diagram.

a
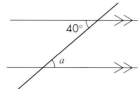

b
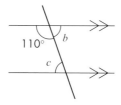

c
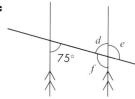

d
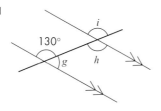

e
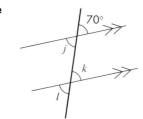

f
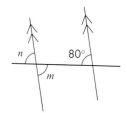

2 State the sizes of the lettered angles in each diagram.

a
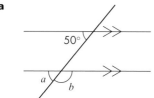

b
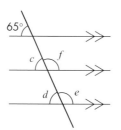

c
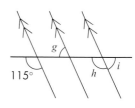

d
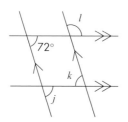

e
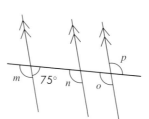

f
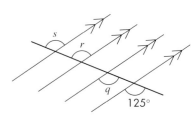

3 Two angles with a sum of 180° are called supplementary angles. Write down *all* the angles in the diagram that are supplementary to angle *a*.

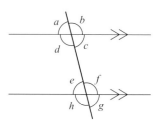

4 State the sizes of the lettered angles in these diagrams.

a
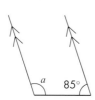

b
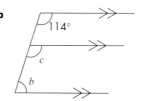

5 Calculate the values of *x* and *y* in these diagrams.

a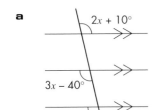

b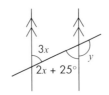

c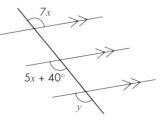

6 Calculate the values of *x* and *y* in these diagrams.

a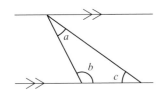

b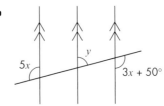

c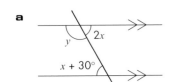

PROOF

7 Use the following diagram to prove that the three angles in a triangle add up to 180°.

PROOF

8 **a** Calculate the size of angle *p*.

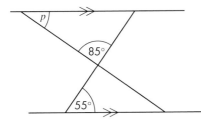

b Show that *p* + *q* + *r* = 180°.

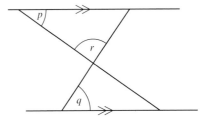

PROOF

9 **a** Use the diagram to illustrate that the angles in a triangle add up to 180°.

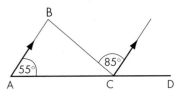

b Use a similar diagram to help you prove that the angles of any triangle add up to 180°.

HINTS AND TIPS

Use algebra and label your angles *a*, *b* and *c*.

In this section you will learn how to:
● use angle properties in quadrilaterals

Key words
kite
parallelogram
rhombus
trapezium

You should know the names of the following quadrilaterals, be familiar with their angle properties and know how to describe any angle using the three-letter notation.

Parallelogram

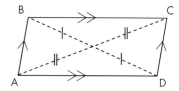

* A **parallelogram** has opposite sides parallel.
* Its opposite sides are equal.
* Its diagonals bisect each other.
* Its opposite angles are equal. That is:

    angle BAD = angle BCD
    angle ABC = angle ADC

Rhombus

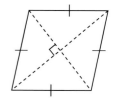

* A **rhombus** is a parallelogram with all its sides equal.
* Its diagonals bisect each other at right angles.
* Its diagonals also bisect the angles.

Kite

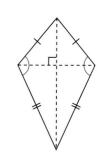

* A **kite** is a quadrilateral with two pairs of equal adjacent sides.
* Its longer diagonal bisects its shorter diagonal at right angles.
* The opposite angles between the sides of different lengths are equal.

Trapezium

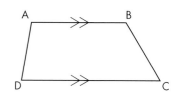

* A **trapezium** has two parallel sides.
* The sum of the interior angles at the ends of each non-parallel side is 180°. That is:

    angle BAD + angle ADC = 180°
    angle ABC + angle BCD = 180°

EXERCISE 15G

1 For each of the trapeziums, calculate the sizes of the lettered angles.

a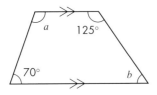

b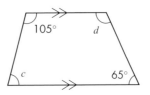

c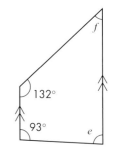

2 For each of these parallelograms, calculate the sizes of the lettered angles.

a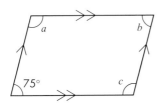

b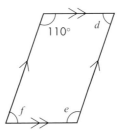

c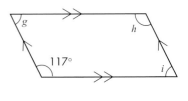

3 For each of these kites, calculate the sizes of the lettered angles.

a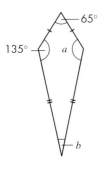

b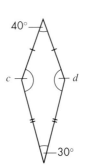

c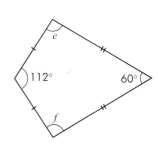

4 For each of these rhombuses, calculate the sizes of the lettered angles.

a

b

c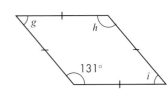

5 For each of these shapes, calculate the sizes of the lettered angles.

a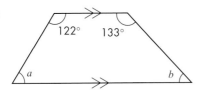

b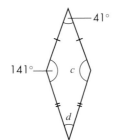

c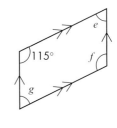

Bearings

In this section you will learn how to:
- use a bearing to specify a direction

Key words
bearing
three-figure
bearing

The **bearing** of a point B from a point A is the angle through which you turn *clockwise* as you change direction from *due north* to the direction of B.

For example, in this diagram the bearing of B from A is 60°.

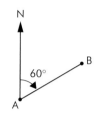

As a bearing can have any value from 0° to 360°, it is customary to give all bearings in three figures.
This is known as a **three-figure bearing**.
So, in the example on the previous page, the bearing becomes 060°, using three figures. Here are three more examples.

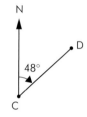

D is on a bearing of 048° from C

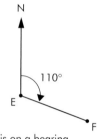

F is on a bearing of 110° from E

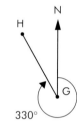

H is on a bearing of 330° from G

There are eight bearings with which you should be familiar. They are shown in the diagram.

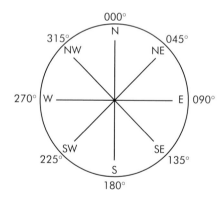

EXAMPLE 8

A, B and C are three towns.

Write down the bearing of B from A and the bearing of C from A.

The bearing of B from A is 070°.

The bearing of C from A is
360° − 115° = 245°.

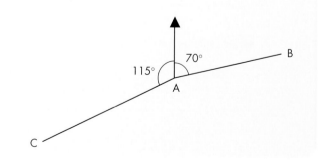

EXERCISE 15H

1 Draw sketches to illustrate the following situations.

   a Castleton is on a bearing of 170° from Hope.

   b Bude is on a bearing of 310° from Wadebridge.

2 A is due north from C. B is due east from A. B is on a bearing of 045° from C. Sketch the layout of the three points, A, B and C.

3 Captain Bird decided to sail his ship around the four sides of a square kilometre.

   a Assuming he started sailing due north, write down the further three bearings he would use in order to complete the square in a clockwise direction.

   b Assuming he started sailing on a bearing of 090°, write down the further three bearings he would use in order to complete the square in an anticlockwise direction.

4 The map shows a boat journey around an island, starting and finishing at S. On the map, 1 centimetre represents 10 kilometres. Measure the distance and bearing of each leg of the journey. Copy and complete the table below.

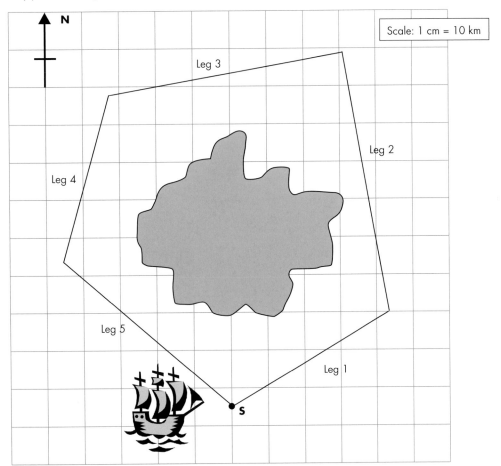

Leg	Actual distance	Bearing
1		
2		
3		
4		
5		

1 **a** The diagram shows three angles on a straight line AB.

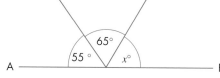

Work out the value of x.

b The diagram shows three angles meeting at point.

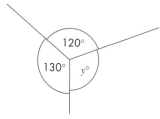

Work out the value of y.

2 This triangle has two equal sides.

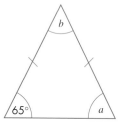

a What name is given to this type of triangle?
b Find the values of a and b.

3 ABCD is a quadrilateral.

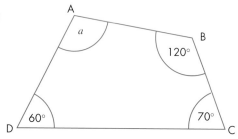

Work out the value of a.

4 The diagram shows a kite.

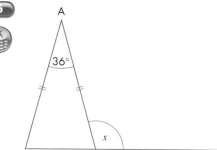

Calculate the size of the angle marked z.

5

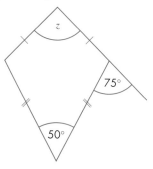

Triangle ABC is isosceles.
AB = AC.

Work out the size of angle x.

6

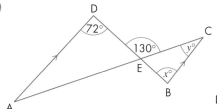

Diagram **not** accurately drawn

AC and BD are straight lines which cross at E.
AD is parallel to BC.

a i Find the size of the angle marked $x°$.
   ii Give a reason for your answer.
b i Find the size of the angle marked $y°$.
   ii Give a reason for your answer.

Edexcel, Question 5, Paper 9A Intermediate, March 2003

7 The lines AB and CD are parallel. Angle BAD = 35°.
Angle BCD = 40°.

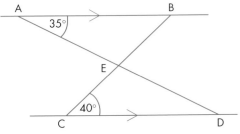

Show clearly why angle AEC is 75°.

8 The diagram shows a regular hexagon.

Explain clearly why the interior angles of the hexagon
add up to 720°.

9

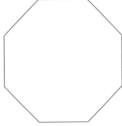

Diagram **not**
accurately drawn

a Work out the size of each interior angle of a regular
octagon.

The size of each exterior angle of a regular polygon
is 30°.

b Work out the number of sides of the polygon.

Edexcel, Question 5, Paper 9B Intermediate, January 2003

WORKED EXAM QUESTION

ABC is a triangle. D is a point on AB such that
BC = BD.

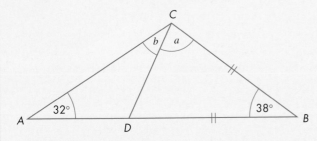

a Work out the value of *a*.

b Work out the value of *b*.

c Is it true that AD = DC? Give a reason for your answer.

Solution

a Triangle BCD is isosceles, so angle BDC is also *a*.

Angles in a triangle = 180°,

so $2a + 38° = 180°$

$2a = 142°$

So $a = 71°$

b Angle ADC = 180° − 71° = 109° (angles on a line)

$b + 32° + 109° = 180°$ (angles in a
triangle)

$b + 141° = 180°$

So $b = 39°$

c No, since triangle ACD is not an isosceles triangle.

GRADE YOURSELF

F Able to measure and draw angles

F Know the sum of the angles on a line is 180° and the sum of the angles at a point is 360°

E Able to use bearings

E Know the sum of the angles in a triangle is 180° and the sum of the angles in a quadrilateral is 360°

E Know how to find the exterior angle of a triangle and quadrilateral

D Know how to find angles in parallel lines

D Know all the properties of special quadrilaterals

D Know how to find interior and exterior angles in regular polygons

C Use interior angles and exterior angles to find the number of sides in a regular polygon

What you should know now

- How to measure and draw angles
- How to find angles on a line or at a point
- How to find angles in triangles, quadrilaterals and polygons
- How to find interior and exterior angles in polygons
- How to use bearings

Circles

Chapter

16

1 Drawing circles

2 The circumference of a circle

3 The area of a circle

4 Answers in terms of π

This chapter will show you ...

- how to draw circles
- how to calculate the circumference of a circle
- how to calculate the area of a circle
- how to write answers in terms of π

Visual overview

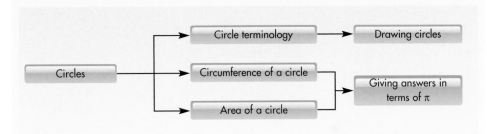

What you should already know

- How to use a pair of compasses to draw a circle
- The words 'radius', 'diameter' and 'semicircle'
- How to use a protractor to draw angles
- How to round numbers to a given number of decimal places
- How to find the square and square root of a number

Quick check

Write down the answer to each of the following, giving your answers to one decimal place.

1 5.21^2 **2** 8.78^2 **3** 15.5^2

4 $\sqrt{10}$ **5** $\sqrt{65}$ **6** $\sqrt{230}$

In this section you will learn how to:
- draw accurate circles
- draw diagrams made from circles

Key words

arc
centre
chord
circumference
diameter
radius
sector
segment
tangent

You need to know the following terms when dealing with circles.

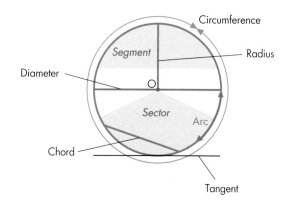

O	The **centre** of a circle.
Diameter	The 'width' of a circle. Any diameter passes through O.
Radius	The distance from O to the edge of a circle. The length of the diameter is twice the length of the radius.
Circumference	The perimeter of a circle.
Chord	A line joining two points on the circumference.
Tangent	A line that touches the circumference at one point only.
Arc	A part of the circumference of a circle.
Sector	A part of the area of a circle, lying between two radii and an arc.
Segment	A part of the area of a circle, lying between a chord and an arc.

When drawing a circle, you first need to set your compasses to a given radius.

EXAMPLE 1

Draw a circle with a radius of 3 cm.

Set your compasses to a radius of 3 cm, as shown in the diagram.

Draw a circle and mark the centre O.

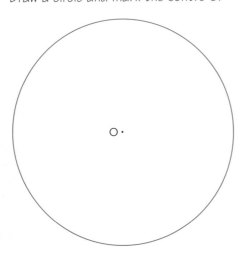

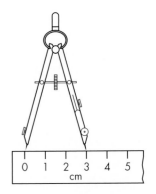

EXERCISE 16A

1 Measure the radius of each of the following circles, giving your answers in centimetres. Write down the diameter of each circle.

a

b

c

2 Draw circles with the following measurements.

a radius = 2 cm   **b** radius = 3.5 cm   **c** diameter = 8 cm   **d** diameter = 10.6 cm

3 Draw the following shapes accurately.

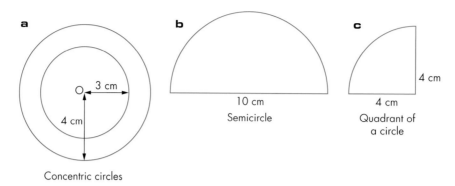

a

3 cm

4 cm

Concentric circles

b

10 cm

Semicircle

c

4 cm

4 cm

Quadrant of
a circle

4 Draw accurate copies of these diagrams.

a

8 cm

8 cm

b

4 cm

6 cm   2 cm

c

5 cm

5 cm

5 **a** Draw a circle of radius 4 cm.

b Keeping your compasses set to a radius of 4 cm, step round the circle making marks on the circumference that are 4 cm apart.

c Join the points with a pencil and ruler to make a polygon.

d What name is given to the polygon you have drawn?

6 **a** Draw a circle of radius 4 cm.

b Draw a tangent at any point on the circumference.

c Draw a radius to meet the tangent.

d Measure the angle between the tangent and the radius.

e Repeat the exercise for circles with different radii.

f Write down what you have found out about a radius touching a tangent at a point.

The circumference of a circle

In this section you will learn how to:
● calculate the circumference of a circle

ACTIVITY

Round and round

Find six cylindrical objects – bottles, cans, tubes, or piping will do. You also need about 2 metres of string.

Copy the following table so that you can fill it in as you do this activity.

Object number	Diameter	Circumference	Circumference / Diameter
1			
2			
3			
4			
5			
6			

Measure, as accurately as you can, the **diameter** of the first object. Write this measurement in your table.

Wrap the string around the object ten times, as shown in the diagram. Make sure you start and finish along the *same line*. Mark clearly the point on the string where the tenth wrap ends.

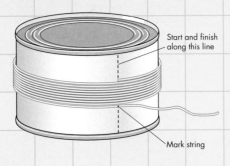

Start and finish along this line

Mark string

Then measure, as accurately as you can, the length of your ten wraps. This should be the distance from the start end of the string to the mark you made on it.

Next, divide this length of string by 10. You have now found the length of the **circumference** of the first object. Write this in the table.

Repeat this procedure for each of the remaining objects.

Finally, complete the last column in the table by using your calculator to divide the circumference by the diameter. In each case, round your answer to two decimal places.

If your measurements have been accurate, all the numbers you get should be about 3.14.

This is the well-known number that is represented by the Greek letter **π**. You can obtain a very accurate value for π by pressing the π key on your calculator. Try it and see how close your numbers are to it.

You calculate the circumference, c, of a circle by multiplying its diameter, d, by π, and then rounding your answer to one or two decimal places.

The value of π is found on all scientific calculators, with $\pi = 3.141\,592\,654$, but if it is not on your calculator, then take $\pi = 3.142$.

The circumference of a circle is given by the formula:

circumference = $\pi \times$ diameter   *or* $c = \pi d$

As the diameter is twice the **radius**, r, this formula can also be written as $c = 2\pi r$.

EXAMPLE 2

Calculate the circumference of the circle with a diameter of 4 cm.

Use the formula:

$$c = \pi d$$
$$= \pi \times 4$$
$$= 12.6 \text{ cm (rounded to 1 decimal place)}$$

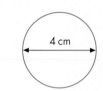

Remember The length of the radius of a circle is half the length of its diameter. So, when you are given a radius, in order to find a circumference you must first *double* the radius to get the diameter.

EXAMPLE 3

Calculate the diameter of a circle that has a circumference of 40 cm.

$$c = \pi \times d$$
$$40 = \pi \times d$$
$$d = \frac{40}{\pi} = 12.7 \text{ cm (rounded to 1 decimal place)}$$

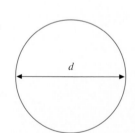

EXERCISE 16B

1 Calculate the circumference of each circle illustrated below. Give your answers to 1 decimal place.

a
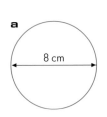
8 cm

b
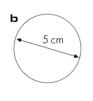
5 cm

c
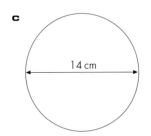
14 cm

d
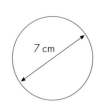
7 cm

e
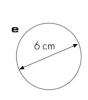
6 cm

f
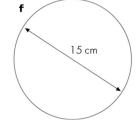
15 cm

g
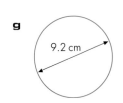
9.2 cm

h
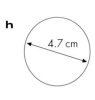
4.7 cm

2 Find the circumference of each of the following coins. Give your answers to 1 decimal place.

a 1p coin, diameter 2 cm

b 2p coin, diameter 2.6 cm

c 5p coin, diameter 1.7 cm

d 10p coin, diameter 2.4 cm

3 Calculate the circumference of each circle illustrated below. Give your answers to 1 decimal place.

a
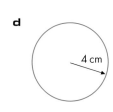
5 cm

b
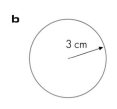
3 cm

c

1.5 cm

HINTS AND TIPS

Remember to double the radius to find the diameter, or use the formula $c = 2\pi r$.

d
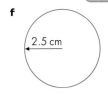
4 cm

e
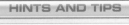
0.9 cm

f
2.5 cm

g
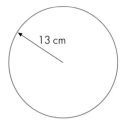
13 cm

h

6.3 cm

D

4 A bicycle wheel has a diameter of 32 cm. What is its circumference?

5 The diagram represents a race-track on a school playing field. The diameter of each circle is shown.

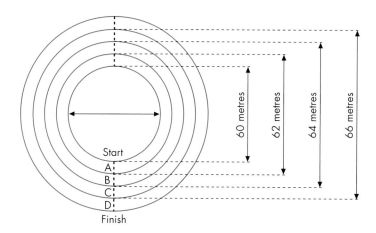

In a race with four runners, each runner starts and finishes on the same inner circle of their lane after completing one circuit.

a Calculate the distance run by each runner in their lane.

b How much further than A does D have to run?

6 A rope is wrapped eight times round a capstan (cylindrical post), the diameter of which is 35 cm. How long is the rope?

7 A hamster has a treadmill of diameter 12 cm.

a What is the circumference of the treadmill?

b How many centimetres has the hamster run when the wheel has made 100 complete revolutions.

c Change the answer to part **b** into metres.

d One night, the hamster runs and runs and runs. He turns the wheel 100 000 times. How many kilometres has he run?

C

8 A circle has a circumference of 314 cm. Calculate the diameter of the circle.

9 What is the diameter of a circle if its circumference is 76 cm? Give your answer to 1 decimal place.

10 What is the radius of a circle with a circumference of 100 cm? Give your answer to 1 decimal place.

11 Calculate the perimeters of the following shapes. Give your answers to 1 decimal place.

a

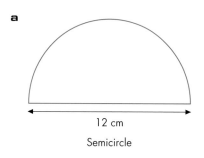

12 cm

Semicircle

b

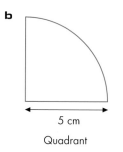

5 cm

Quadrant

12 Assume that the human waist is circular.

a What are the distances around the waists of the following people?

Sue: waist radius of 10 cm   Dave: waist radius of 12 cm

Julie: waist radius of 11 cm   Brian: waist radius of 13 cm

b Compare differences between pairs of waist circumferences. What connection do they have to π?

c What would be the difference in length between a rope stretched tightly round the Earth and another rope always held 1 m above it?

13 **a** Calculate the perimeter of each of shapes A and B.

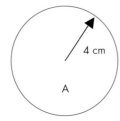
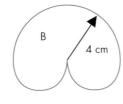
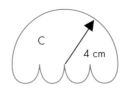

b Write down the perimeter of shape C.

16.3 The area of a circle

In this section you will learn how to:

- calculate the area of a circle

Key words

area
diameter
π
radius

The **area** of a circle is given by the formula:

$$\text{area} = \boldsymbol{\pi} \times \textbf{radius}^2 \quad or \quad A = \pi \times r \times r \quad or \quad A = \pi r^2$$

Remember This formula uses the radius of a circle. So, when you are given the **diameter** of a circle, you must *halve* it to get the radius.

EXAMPLE 4

Radius given

Calculate the area of a circle with a radius of 7 cm.

$$\begin{aligned}
\text{Area} &= \pi r^2 \\
&= \pi \times 7^2 \\
&= \pi \times 49 \\
&= 153.9 \text{ cm}^2 \text{ (rounded to 1 decimal place)}
\end{aligned}$$

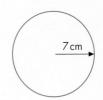

EXAMPLE 5

Diameter given

Calculate the area of a circle with a diameter of 12 cm.

First, halve the diameter to get the radius:

radius = 12 ÷ 2 = 6 cm

Then, find the area:

$$\text{area} = \pi r^2$$
$$= \pi \times 6^2$$
$$= \pi \times 36$$
$$= 113.1 \text{ cm}^2 \text{ (rounded to 1 decimal place)}$$

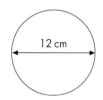
12 cm

EXERCISE 16C

1 Calculate the area of each circle illustrated below. Give your answers to 1 decimal place.

a
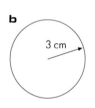
5 cm

b

3 cm

c

1.5 cm

d

4 cm

e

0.9 cm

f

2.5 cm

g
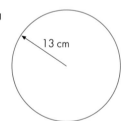
13 cm

h

6.3 cm

2 Find the area of one face of the following coins. Give your answers to 1 decimal place.

a 1p coin, radius 1 cm

b 2p coin, radius 1.3 cm

c 5p coin, radius 0.85 cm

d 10p coin, radius 1.2 cm

3 Calculate the area of each circle illustrated below.
Give your answers to 1 decimal place.

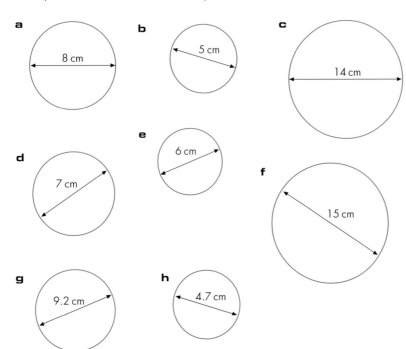

a 8 cm

b 5 cm

c 14 cm

d 7 cm

e 6 cm

f 15 cm

g 9.2 cm

h 4.7 cm

HINTS AND TIPS

Remember to halve the diameter to find the radius. The only formula for the area of a circle is $A = \pi r^2$.

4 Milk-bottle tops are stamped from rectangular strips as shown.

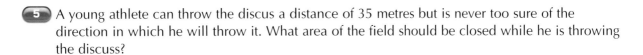

Each milk-bottle top is made from a circle of radius 1.7 cm.
Each rectangular strip measures 4 cm by 500 cm.

a What is the area of one milk-bottle top?

b How many milk-bottle tops can be stamped out of one strip 500 cm long when there is a 0.2 cm gap between adjacent tops?

c What is the area of the rectangular strip?

d What will be the total area of all the milk-bottle tops stamped out of the one strip?

e What waste is produced by one stamping?

5 A young athlete can throw the discus a distance of 35 metres but is never too sure of the direction in which he will throw it. What area of the field should be closed while he is throwing the discuss?

6 Calculate **i** the circumference and **ii** the area of each of these circles. Give your answers to 1 decimal place.

a 9 cm

b 22 cm

c 6.5 cm

d 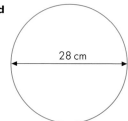 28 cm

7 A circle has a circumference of 60 cm.

   a Calculate the diameter of the circle to 1 decimal place.

   b What is the radius of the circle to 1 decimal place?

   c Calculate the area of the circle to 1 decimal place.

HINTS AND TIPS

Because π can be taken as 3.14 or 3.142, answers need not be exact. Examiners usually accept a range of answer.

8 Calculate the area of a circle with a circumference of 110 cm.

9 Calculate the area of the following shapes. Give your answers to 1 decimal place.

a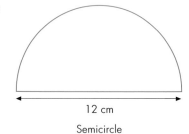
12 cm
Semicircle

b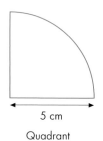
5 cm
Quadrant

10 Calculate the area of the shaded part of each of these diagrams.

a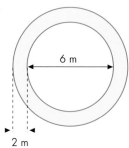
6 m
2 m

b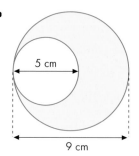
5 cm
9 cm

c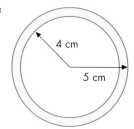
4 cm
5 cm

Answers in term of π

In this section you will learn how to:

- give answers for circle calculations in terms of π

Key words

area
circumference
diameter
π
radius

There are times when you do not want a numerical answer to a circle problem but need to evaluate the answer in terms of **π**. (The numerical answer could be evaluated later.)

EXAMPLE 6

What is the **circumference** and **area** of this circle?

Leave your answers in terms of π.

Circumference $= \pi d = \pi \times 14 = 14\pi$ cm

Area $= \pi r^2 = \pi \times 7^2 = \pi \times 49 = 49\pi$ cm^2

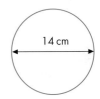

14 cm

If a question asks you to leave an answer in terms of π, it is most likely to be on the non-calculator paper and hence saves you the trouble of using your calculator.

However, if you did, and calculated the numerical answer, you could well lose a mark.

EXERCISE 16D

In this exercise, all answers should be given in terms of π.

1 A circle has diameter 10 cm.

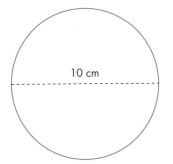

10 cm

State the circumference of the circle.

D

2 State the circumference of each of the following circles.

    a diameter 4 cm

    b radius 10 cm

    c diameter 15 cm

    d radius 2 cm

3 State the area of each of the following circles.

    a radius 4 cm

    b diameter 10 cm

    c radius 3 cm

    d diameter 18 cm

4 State the radius of the circle with a circumference of 50π cm.

5 State the radius of the circle with an area of 100π cm^2.

6 State the diameter of a circle with a circumference of 200 cm.

7 State the radius of a circle with an area of 25π cm^2.

8 Work out the area for each of the following shapes, giving your answers in terms of π.

a

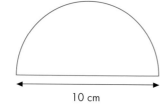

10 cm

b

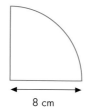

8 cm

c

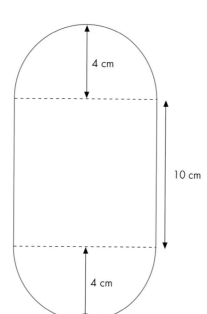

4 cm

10 cm

4 cm

d

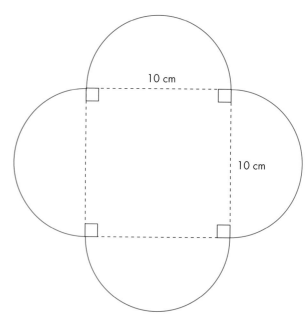

10 cm

10 cm

9 **a** Work out the area of a semicircle with radius 8 cm.

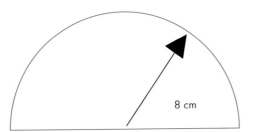

8 cm

b Work out the area of two semicircles with radii 4 cm.

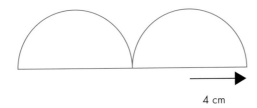

4 cm

c Work out the area of four semicircles with radii 2 cm.

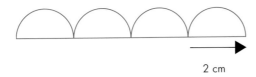

2 cm

d By looking at the pattern of areas of the answers to **a**, **b** and **c**, write down the area of eight semicircles with radii 1 cm.

1
  a Draw accurately a circle of radius 5 cm.
  b Write down the length of the diameter of the circle (in centimetres).
  c On your diagram draw a tangent to the circle.
  d On your diagram draw a chord of length 7 cm inside the circle.

2
Work out the circumference of the coin.
Give your answer correct to 1 decimal place.

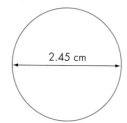

2.45 cm

Edexcel, Question 23b, Paper 2 Foundation, June 2005

3
The radius of a circle is 6.4 cm.
Work out the circumference of this circle.
Give your answer correct to 1 decimal place.

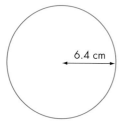

6.4 cm   Diagram **not** accurately drawn

Edexcel, Question 12, Paper 15 Foundation, June 2004

4
The radius of a circle is 4 m.
Work out the area of the circle.
Give your answer in terms of π.

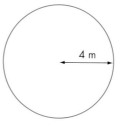

4 m   Diagram **not** accurately drawn

Edexcel, Question 4, Paper 12B Intermediate, January 2005

5
  a Calculate the area of a circle of radius 6 cm.
     Give your answer to 1 decimal place.
  b A semi-circular protractor has a diameter of 10 cm.

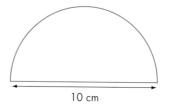

10 cm

Calculate its perimeter. Give your answer in terms of π.

WORKED EXAM QUESTION

A circular flowerbed has a radius of 2.7 m.
a Calculate the circumference of the flowerbed.
b Calculate the area of the flowerbed.

Solution
a $r = 2.7$, so $d = 5.4$ m
   $c = \pi d$
      $= \pi \times 5.4$
      $= 17.0$ m (1 decimal place)
b $A = \pi r^2$
      $= \pi \times 2.7^2$
      $= \pi \times 7.29$
      $= 22.9$ m^2 (1 decimal place)

GRADE YOURSELF

G Know the words 'radius', 'diameter', 'circumference', 'chord', 'tangent'

G Able to draw circles given the radius

F Able to draw shapes made up of circles

D Know the words 'sector' and 'segment'

D Able to calculate the circumference of a circle

D Able to calculate the area of a circle

C Able to find the perimeter and the area of shapes such as semicircles

What you should know now

- How to draw circles
- All the words associated with circles
- How to calculate the circumference of a circle
- How to calculate the area of a circle

Scale and drawing

1 Reading scales

2 Sensible estimates

3 Scale drawings

4 Nets

5 Using an isometric grid

This chapter will show you ...

- how to read scales and scale drawings and do accurate constructions
- how to draw and read isometric representations of 3-D shapes

Visual overview

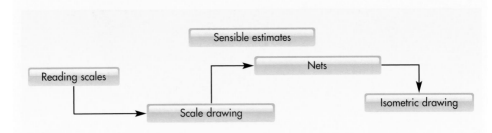

What you should already know

- The names of common 3-D shapes
- How to measure lengths of lines
- How to measure angles with a protractor

Quick check

Name the following 3-D shapes.

1

2

3

In this section you will learn how to:
- read and interpret scales

You will come across **scales** in a lot of different places.

For example, there are scales on thermometers, car speedometers and weighing scales. It is important that you can read scales accurately.

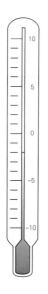

There are two things to do when reading a scale. First, make sure that you know what each **division** on the scale represents. Second, make sure you read the scale in the right direction, for example some scales read from right to left.

Also, make sure you note the **units**, if given, and include them in your answer.

EXAMPLE 1

Read the values from the following scales.

a
```
 0                 10
```

b
```
20      30      40
        kg
```

c
```
200            100
       mph
```

a The scale shows 7. This is a very straightforward scale. It reads from left to right and each division is worth 1 unit.

b The scale shows 34 kg. The scale reads from left to right and each division is worth 2 units.

c The scale shows 130 mph. The scale reads from right to left and each division is worth 10 units. You should know that mph stands for miles per hour. This is a unit of speed found on most British car speedometers.

EXERCISE 17A

1 Read the values from the following scales. Remember to state the units if they are shown.

a **i**    **ii**   **iii**

b **i**    **ii**   **iii**

c **i** 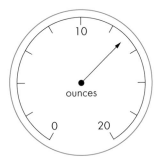   **ii**    **iii**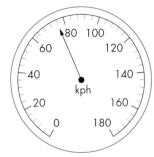

d **i** 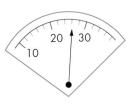   **ii** 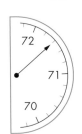   **iii**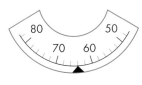

2 Copy (or trace) the following dials and mark on the values shown.

a

7 kg

b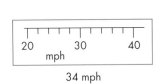

34 mph

c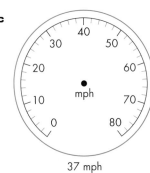

37 mph

d

470 kg

e

92 kph

f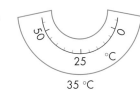

35 °C

3 Read the temperatures shown by each of these thermometers.

HINTS AND TIPS

Remember to check what each division is worth.

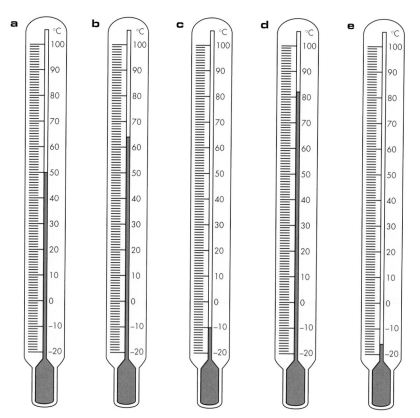

4 Read the values shown on these scales.

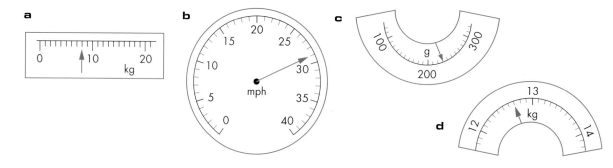

5 A pineapple was weighed.

A pineapple and an orange were weighed together.

a How much does the pineapple weigh? Give your answer in kilograms.

b How much does the orange weigh? Give your answer in grams.

Sensible estimates

In this section you will learn how to:

- make sensible estimates using standard measures

Key word

estimate

The average height of a man is 1.78 m. This is about 5 feet 10 inches. You should be able to **estimate** other heights or lengths if you use some basic information like this.

EXAMPLE 2

Look at the picture.

Estimate, in metres, the height of the lamppost and the length of the bus.

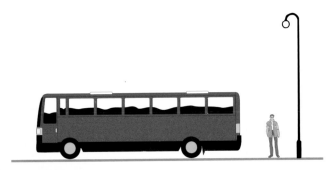

Assume the man is about 1.8 m tall. The lamppost is about three times as high as he is. (**Note:** One way to check this is to use tracing paper to mark off the length (or height) of the man and then measure the other lengths against this.) This makes the lamppost about 5.4 m tall. You can say 5 m. As it is an estimate, there is no need for an exact value.

The bus is about four times as long as the man so the bus is about 7.2 m long. You could say 7 m.

EXAMPLE 3

Look at the picture.

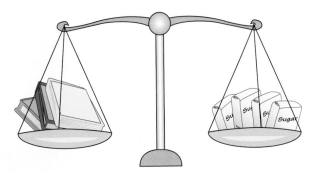

It shows three maths textbooks balanced by four bags of sugar. Estimate the mass of one textbook.

You should know that a bag of sugar weighs 1 kilogram, so the three maths books weigh 4000 grams. This means that each one weighs about 1333 grams or about 1.3 kg.

EXERCISE 17B

1 The car in the picture is 4 metres long. Use this to estimate the length of the bus, the train and the bicycle.

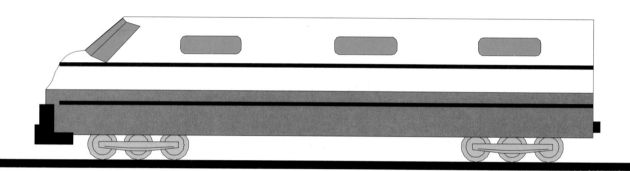

2 Estimate the height and length of the whale.

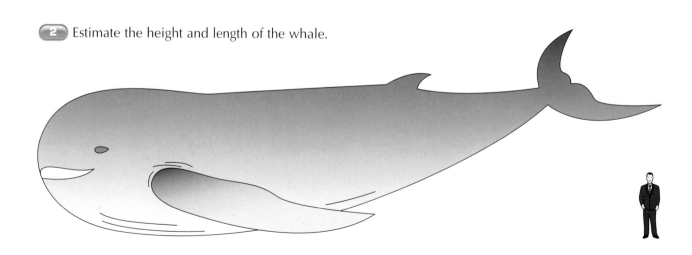

3 Estimate the weight of one apple.

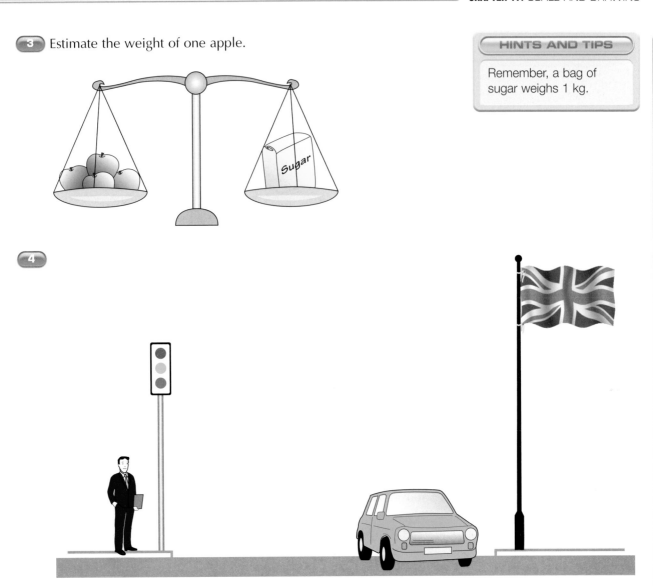

4

Estimate the following.

a the height of the traffic lights

b the width of the road

c the height of the flagpole

5

A charity collection balances pound coins against a bag of sugar. It take £105 to balance the bag of sugar. Estimate the weight of one pound coin.

Scale drawings

In this section you will learn how to:

● read scales and draw scale drawings

Key words

measurement
ratio
scale
    drawing
scale factor

A **scale drawing** is an accurate representation of a real object.

Scale drawings are usually smaller in size than the original objects. However, in certain cases, they have to be enlargements, typical examples of which are drawings of miniature electronic circuits and very small watch movements.

In a scale drawing:

● all the measurements must be in proportion to the corresponding measurements on the original object

● all the angles must be equal to the corresponding angles on the original object.

To obtain the measurements for a scale drawing, all the actual measurements are multiplied by a common **scale factor**, usually referred to as a scale. (See the section on enlargements in Chapter 19.)

Scales are often given as **ratios**, for example, 1 cm : 1 m.

When the units in a ratio are the *same*, they are normally not given. For example, a scale of 1 cm : 1000 cm is written as 1 : 1000.

Note When you are making a scale drawing, take care to express *all* **measurements** in the *same* unit.

EXAMPLE 4

The diagram shows the front of a kennel.
It is drawn to a scale of 1 : 30. Find:

a the actual width of the front

b the actual height of the doorway.

The scale of 1 : 30 means that a measurement of 1 cm on the diagram represents a measurement of 30 cm on the actual kennel.

a So, the actual width of the front is

4 cm × 30 = 120 cm

b The actual height of the doorway is

1.5 cm × 30 = 45 cm

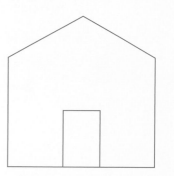

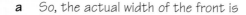

Map scales are usually expressed as ratios, such as 1 : 50 000 or 1 : 200 000.

The first ratio means that 1 cm on the map represents 50 000 cm or 500 m on the land. The second ratio means that 1 cm represents 200 000 cm or 2 km.

EXAMPLE 5

Find the actual distances between the following towns.

a Bran and Kelv　　　**b** Bran and Daid　　　**c** Daid and Malm

This map is drawn to a scale of 1 cm to 20 km.

The scale means that a distance of 1 cm on the map represents a distance of 20 km on the land.

So, the actual distances are:

a Bran and Kelv: 4 × 20 km = 80 km

b Bran and Daid: 3 × 20 km = 60 km

c Daid and Malm: 2.5 × 20 km = 50 km

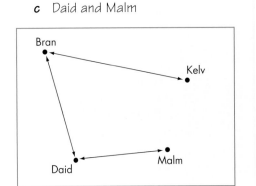

EXERCISE 17C

1 Look at this plan of a garden, drawn to a scale of 1 cm to 10 m.

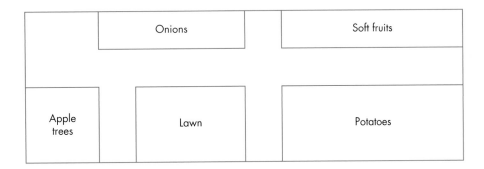

a State the actual dimensions of each plot of the garden.

b Calculate the actual area of each plot.

2 Below is a plan for a mouse mat. It is drawn to a scale of 1 to 6.

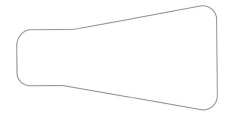

> **HINTS AND TIPS**
>
> Remember to check the scale.

a How long is the actual mouse mat?

b How wide is the narrowest part of the mouse mat?

3 Look at the map below, drawn to a scale of 1 : 200 000.

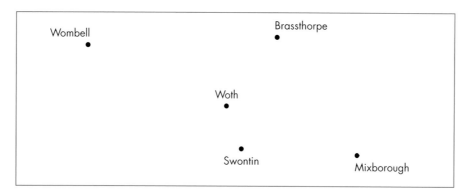

State the following actual distances to the nearest tenth of a kilometre.

a Wombell to Woth

b Woth to Brassthorpe

c Brassthorpe to Swontin

d Swontin to Mixborough

e Mixborough to Woth

f Woth to Swontin

4 This map is drawn to a scale of 1 cm to 40 km.

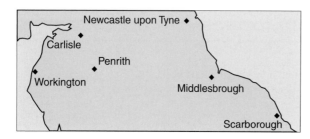

Give the approximate direct distances for each of the following.

a Penrith to:

   i Workington

   ii Scarborough

   iii Newcastle-upon-Tyne

   iv Carlisle

b Middlesbrough to:

   i Scarborough

   ii Workington

   iii Carlisle

   iv Penrith

5 This map is drawn to a scale of 1 cm to 20 kilometres.

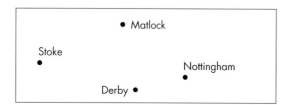

State the direct distance, to the nearest 5 kilometres, from Matlock to the following.

a Stoke   **b** Derby   **c** Nottingham

6 Below is a scale plan of the top of Derek's desk, where the scale is 1 : 10.

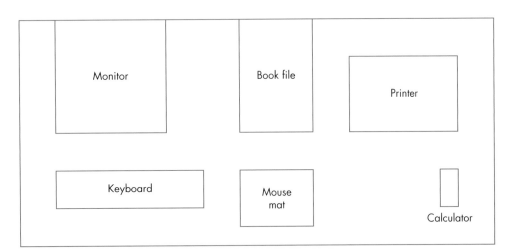

What are the actual dimensions of each of these articles?

a monitor   **b** keyboard   **c** mouse mat

d book file   **e** printer   **f** calculator

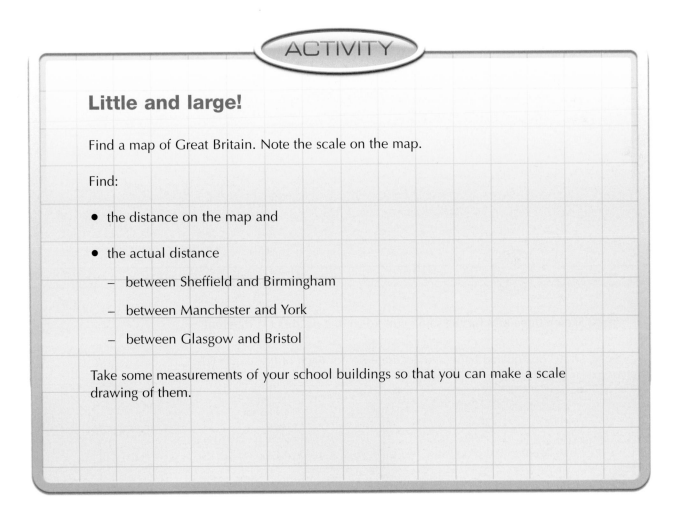

ACTIVITY

Little and large!

Find a map of Great Britain. Note the scale on the map.

Find:

- the distance on the map and

- the actual distance

  - between Sheffield and Birmingham

  - between Manchester and York

  - between Glasgow and Bristol

Take some measurements of your school buildings so that you can make a scale drawing of them.

17.4 Nets

In this section you will learn how to:
● draw and recognise shapes from their nets

Key words
net
3-D shape

Many of the **3-D shapes** that you come across can be made from **nets**.

A net is a flat shape that can be folded into a 3-D shape.

EXAMPLE 6

Sketch the net for each of these shapes.

a cube

b square-based pyramid

a This is a sketch of a net for a cube.

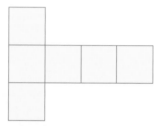

b This is a sketch of a net for a square-based pyramid.

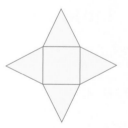

---

1 Sketch three nets for the same cuboid so that each net is different.

2 Draw, on squared paper, an accurate net for each of these cuboids.

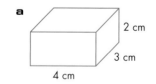
a 2 cm, 3 cm, 4 cm

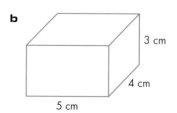
b 3 cm, 4 cm, 5 cm

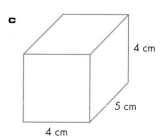
c 4 cm, 4 cm, 5 cm

3 Draw an accurate net for each of these pyramids. For each pyramid, the base is a rectangle and the sloping edges are all the same length.

a

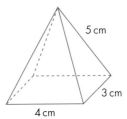

5 cm

3 cm

4 cm

b

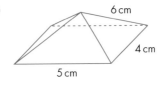

6 cm

4 cm

5 cm

4 The shape on the right is a triangular prism. Its ends are isosceles triangles and its other faces are rectangles. Draw an accurate net for this prism.

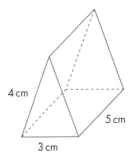

4 cm

5 cm

3 cm

5 The tetrahedron on the right is made up of four equilateral triangles, with all lengths being 4 cm. Draw an accurate net for this shape.

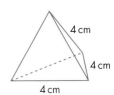

4 cm

4 cm

4 cm

6 Sketch the nets of these shapes.

a

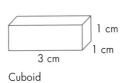

1 cm

1 cm

3 cm

Cuboid

b

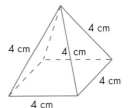

4 cm

4 cm

4 cm

4 cm

4 cm

Square-based pyramid

c

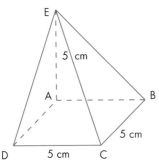

E

5 cm

A   B

5 cm

D   5 cm   C

Square-based pyramid, with point E directly above point A

d

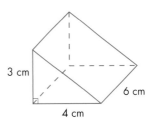

3 cm

6 cm

4 cm

Right-angled triangular prism

In this section you will learn how to:
● read from and draw on isometric grids
● interpret diagrams to find plans and elevations

Key words
elevation
isometric
  grid
plan

Isometric grids

The problem with drawing a 3-D shape is that you have to draw it on a flat (2-D) surface so that it looks like the original 3-D shape. The drawing is given the appearance of depth by slanting the view.

One easy way to draw a 3-D shape is to use an **isometric grid** (a grid of equilateral triangles).

Below are two drawings of the same cuboid, one on squared paper, the other on isometric paper. The cuboid measures $5 \times 4 \times 2$ units.

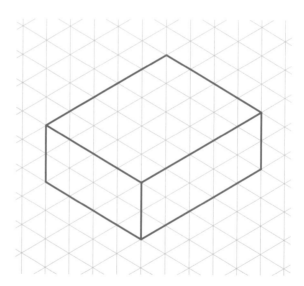

Note: The dimensions of the cuboid can be taken straight from the isometric drawing, whereas they cannot be taken from the drawing on squared paper.

You can use a triangular dot grid instead of an isometric grid but you *must* make sure that it is the correct way round – as shown here.

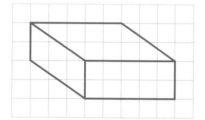

Plans and elevations

A **plan** is the view of a 3-D shape when it is seen from above.

An **elevation** is the view of a 3-D shape when it is seen from the front or from another side.

The 3-D shape below is drawn on an triangular dot grid.

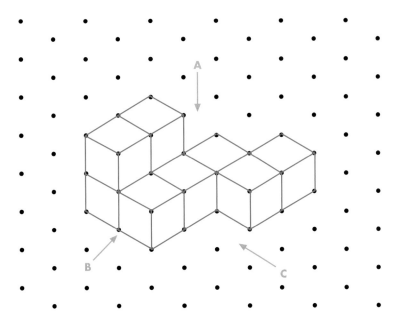

Its plan, front elevation and side elevation can be drawn on squared paper.

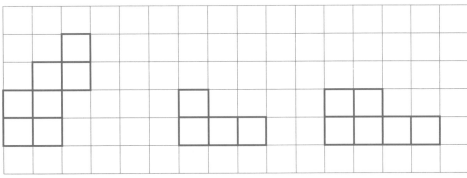

Plan from **A**   Front elevation from **B**   Side elevation from **C**

EXERCISE 17E

1 Draw each of these cuboids on an isometric grid.

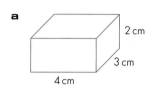

a

2 cm
3 cm
4 cm

b

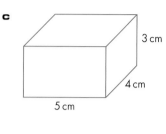

5 cm
4 cm
2 cm

c

3 cm
4 cm
5 cm

2 Draw each of these shapes on an isometric grid.

a

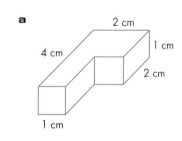

2 cm
4 cm
1 cm
2 cm
1 cm

b

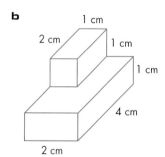

1 cm
2 cm
1 cm
1 cm
4 cm
2 cm

c

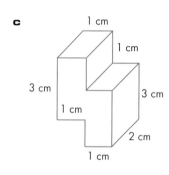

1 cm
1 cm
3 cm
3 cm
1 cm
2 cm
1 cm

3 Imagine that this shape falls and lands on the shaded side. Draw, on isometric paper, the position of the shape after it has landed.

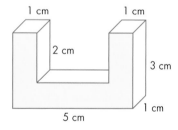

1 cm
1 cm
2 cm
3 cm
1 cm
5 cm

4 The firm TIL want their name made into a solid shape from 1 metre cubes of concrete. Draw, on isometric paper, a representation of these letters made from the blocks.

5 For each of the following 3-D shapes, draw the following.

i the plan

ii the front elevation

iii the side elevation

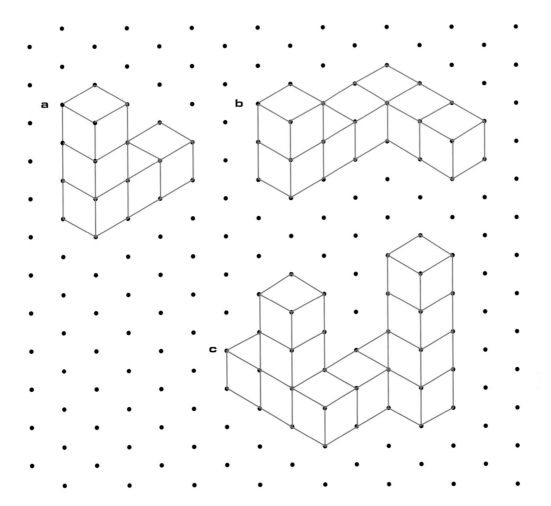

6 This drawing shows a solid made from centimetre cubes.

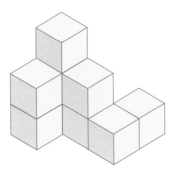

a How many centimetre cubes are there in the solid?

b Draw a plan view of the solid.

7 This drawing shows a plan view of a solid made from five cubes.

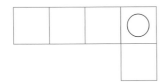

Draw the solid on an isometric grid.

Pentomino cubes

A pentomino is a shape made from five squares that touch edge to edge. These are two examples of pentominoes.

There are 13 different pentominoes. Draw as many of them as you can. Can you find them all?

Note that   and   are the same.

If two pentominoes can be turned round or turned over so that they both look the same, they are not different.

How many of the pentominoes can be folded to make an open-topped cube?

Hexomino cubes

A hexomino is a shape made from six squares that touch edge to edge. These are two examples of hexominoes.

Draw as many different hexominoes as you can.

Which of the hexominoes that you find are nets for a closed cube?

1 The diagram shows a line PQ and a point R.

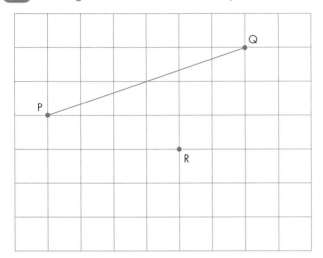

Copy the diagram onto squared paper.

a Measure the length of the line PQ, in centimetres.

b Draw the line parallel to PQ that passes through R.

2 The diagram shows a 1 litre measuring flask.
700 ml of milk are needed for a recipe.
Copy the scale. Draw an arrow to show where 700 ml is on the scale.

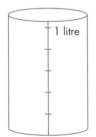

3

a The thermometer shows Peter's temperature in degrees Celsius. What is his temperature?

b

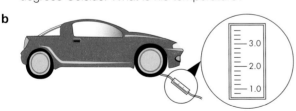

The tyre pressure for Peter's car is 2.7 units.

Copy the scale. Use an arrow to show 2.7 on your scale.

4 The diagram shows some kitchen scales.

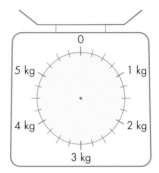

a Mrs Hall weighs a chicken on the scales.
The chicken weights $3\frac{1}{2}$ kilograms.
Copy the scale and draw an arrow on your diagram to show $3\frac{1}{2}$ kilograms.

b Mrs Kitchen weighs a pumpkin on the scales.
The pumpkin weighs $2\frac{3}{4}$ kg.
Draw an arrow on your diagram to show $2\frac{3}{4}$ kilograms.

5 Six nets are shown below.
List the nets that would not make a cube.

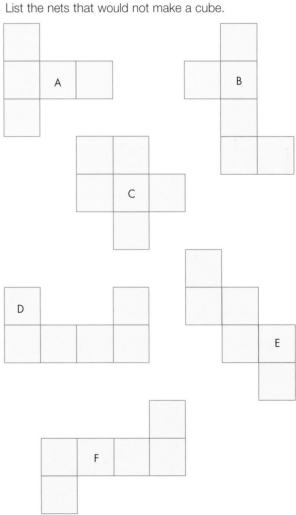

6 Here is a cuboid.

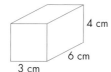

Diagram **not** accurately drawn

a Write down

i the number of edges of this cuboid,

ii the number of vertices of the cuboid.

b Draw an accurate net for the cuboid.

Edexcel, Question 10, Paper 14 Foundation, June 2003

7 a This is the petrol gauge on Patricia's car.

When full, the tank contains 32 litres.
Estimate the amount of petrol in the tank.

b Petrol costs 97p per litre.
Calculate the cost of 30 litres.

8 The diagram shows the position of Colwyn Bay and the position of Blackpool.

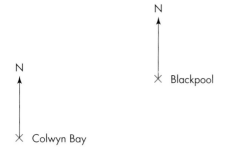

The bearing of a ship from Colwyn Bay is 032°.
The bearing of the ship from Blackpool is 290°.

Copy the diagram and accurately show the position of the ship.

Mark this position with a cross ✕. Label it S.

Edexcel, Question 3, Paper 9B Intermediate, January 2003

9 Here are the plan and front elevation of a prism.
The front elevation shows the cross section of the prism.

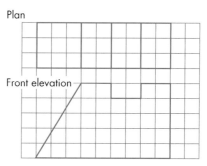

a Copy the grid below and draw a side elevation of the prism.

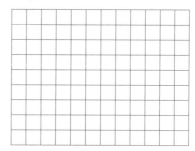

b Draw a 3-D sketch of the prism.

Edexcel, Question 6, Paper 16 Intermediate, June 2003

10 A triangular prism has dimensions as shown.

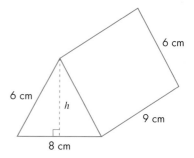

a *Sketch* a net of the prism.

b *Measure* the height *h* of the prism.

c Calculate the *total surface area* of the prism.

11 The diagram shows a solid shape made from five 1-centimetre cubes.

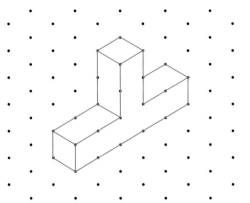

What is the surface area of the solid shape?

12 a Use isometric paper to copy and complete the drawing of a cuboid 4 cm by 2 cm by 3 cm.

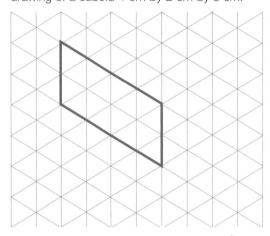

b Calculate the volume of the cuboid (in cm³).

WORKED EXAM QUESTION

Draw the net of a cuboid that is 2 cm by 3 cm by 6 cm.

Solution

Step 1: Start with the base. Draw a 3 cm by 6 cm rectangle.

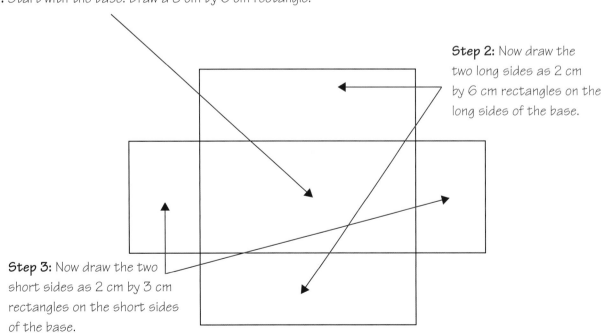

Step 2: Now draw the two long sides as 2 cm by 6 cm rectangles on the long sides of the base.

Step 3: Now draw the two short sides as 2 cm by 3 cm rectangles on the short sides of the base.

Villa Hinojos
Cost: €264 000
Floor space: 110 m^2
Rent per week: £500
Weeks rented per year: 24

Villa Cartref
Cost: €189 000
Floor space: 90 m^2
Rent per week: £300
Weeks rented per year: 20

Villa Rosa
Cost: €180 000
Floor space: 80 m^2
Rent per week: £350
Weeks rented per year: 25

Villa Amapola
Cost: €252 000
Floor space: 105 m^2
Rent per week: £400
Weeks rented per year: 25

Villa Blanca
Cost: €198 000
Floor space: 72 m^2
Rent per week: £350
Weeks rented per year: 30

Villa Azul
Cost: €237 000
Floor space: 100 m^2
Rent per week: £450
Weeks rented per year: 26

£1 = €1.50

Map scale 1 : 300 000

Mr Smith wants to buy a villa in Spain to use for holiday rent.

He compares the six villas shown on the map.

For each villa he uses the map to work out the distance by road from the airport and the distance by road to the coast, in kilometres.

He calculates the cost in euros for each square metre of floor space (€/m²).

He calculates the cost of each villa in pounds (£).

He also calculates the income he might get from each villa.

Help him by filling in the table.

Villa	Distance from airport (km)	Distance to coast (km)	Cost per square metre (€/m²)	Cost (£) of villa	Rental income per year (£)
Rosa	9.5				
Cartref		20			
Blanca			2750		
Azul				158 000	
Amapola					10 000
Hinojos					

GRADE YOURSELF

G Able to recognise the net of a simple shape, such as a cuboid, and to name basic 3-D shapes

F Can measure a line and draw the net of simple 3-D shapes

F Can read a variety of scales with different divisions

E Able to draw a simple shape, such as a cuboid, on an isometric grid

D Can recognise plans and elevations from isometric drawings

What you should know now

- How to read a variety of scales
- How to draw scale diagrams and construct accurate diagrams, using mathematical instruments
- How to interpret and draw 3-D representations on an isometric grid

Probability

1 Probability scale

2 Calculating probabilities

3 Probability that an outcome of an event will not happen

4 Addition rule for outcomes

5 Experimental probability

6 Combined events

7 Expectation

8 Two-way tables

This chapter will show you ...

- how to use the the language of probability
- how to work out the probability of outcomes of events, using either theoretical models or experimental models
- how to predict outcomes using theoretical models, and compare experimental and theoretical data

Visual overview

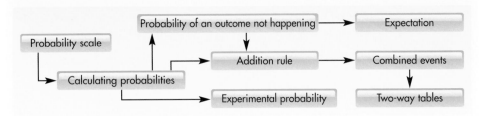

What you should already know

- How to add, subtract and cancel fractions
- That outcomes of events cannot always be predicted and that the laws of chance apply to everyday events
- How to list all the outcomes of an event in a systematic manner

Quick check

1 Cancel the following fractions.

a $\frac{6}{8}$ b $\frac{6}{36}$ c $\frac{3}{12}$

d $\frac{8}{10}$ e $\frac{6}{9}$ f $\frac{5}{20}$

2 Do the following fraction additions.

a $\frac{1}{8} + \frac{3}{8}$ b $\frac{5}{12} + \frac{3}{12}$ c $\frac{5}{36} + \frac{3}{36}$ d $\frac{2}{9} + \frac{1}{6}$ e $\frac{3}{5} + \frac{3}{20}$

3 Frank likes to wear brightly coloured hats and socks.

He has two hats, one is green and the other is yellow.
He has three pairs of socks which are red, purple and pink.

Write down all the six possible combinations of hats and socks Frank could wear.

For example, he could wear a green hat and red socks.

In this section you will learn how to:

- use the probability scale and the basic language of probability

Key words

certain
chance
event
impossible
likely
outcome
probability
probability
    scale
unlikely

Almost daily, you hear somebody talking about the probability of whether this or that will happen. Only usually they use words like '**chance**', 'likelihood' or 'risk' rather than 'probability'. For example:

"What is the likelihood of rain tomorrow?"
"What chance does she have of winning the 100 metres?"
"Is there a risk that his company will go bankrupt?"

You can give a value to the chance of any of these **outcomes** of **events** happening – and millions of others, as well. This value is called the **probability**.

It is true that some things are certain to happen and that some things cannot happen, that is, the chance of something happening can be anywhere between **impossible** and **certain**. This situation is represented on a sliding scale, called the **probability scale**, as shown below.

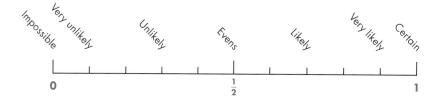

Note: All probabilities lie between **0** and **1**.

An outcome of an event that cannot happen (is impossible) has a probability of 0. For example, the probability that pigs will fly is 0.

An outcome of an event that is certain to happen has a probability of 1. For example, the probability that the sun will rise tomorrow is 1.

EXAMPLE 1

Put arrows on the probability scale to show roughly the probability of each of these outcomes of events.

    a You will get a head when throwing a coin.

    b You will get a six when throwing a dice.

    c You will have maths homework this week.

a This outcome is an even chance. (Commonly described as a fifty-fifty chance.)

b This outcome is fairly **unlikely**.

c This outcome is **likely**.

So, the arrows will be approximately in these positions on the probability scale.

 EXERCISE 18A

1 State whether each of the following outcomes is impossible, very unlikely, unlikely, evens, likely, very likely or certain.

    a Picking out a heart from a well-shuffled pack of cards.

    b January 1st 2012 will be on a Sunday.

    c Someone in your class is left-handed.

    d You will live to be 100.

    e A score of seven is obtained when throwing a dice.

    f You will watch some TV this evening.

    g A new-born baby will be a girl.

2 Draw a probability scale and put an arrow to show approximately the probability of each of the following outcomes of events happening.

    a The next car you see will have been made in Europe.

    b A person in your class will have been born in the twentieth century.

    c It will rain tomorrow.

    d In the next Olympic Games, someone will run the 1500 m race in 3 minutes.

    e During this week, you will have chips with a meal.

3 Give two events of your own where you think the probability of an outcome is as follows.

    a impossible   **b** very unlikely   **c** unlikely   **d** evens

    e likely   **f** very likely   **g** certain

Calculating probabilities

In this section you will learn how to:

● calculate the probability of outcomes of events

Key words
equally likely
event
outcome
probability
    fraction
random

In question **2** of Exercise 18A, you undoubtedly had difficulty in knowing exactly where to put some of the arrows on the probability scale. It would have been easier for you if each result of the **event** could have been given a value between 0 and 1 to represent the probability for that event.

For some events, this can be done by first finding all the possible results, or **outcomes**, for a particular event. For example, when you throw a coin there are two **equally likely** outcomes: heads or tails. If you want to calculate the probability of getting a head, there is only one outcome that is possible. So, you can say that there is a 1 in 2, or 1 out of 2, chance of getting a head. This is usually given as a **probability fraction**, namely $\frac{1}{2}$. So, you would write the event as:

P(head) $= \frac{1}{2}$

Probabilities can also be written as decimals or percentages, so that:

P(head) $= \frac{1}{2}$ or 0.5 or 50%

It is more usual to give probabilities as fractions in GCSE examinations but you will frequently come across probabilities given as percentages, for example, in the weather forecasts on TV.

The probability of an outcome is defined as:

$$P(\text{outcome}) = \frac{\text{number of ways the outcome can happen}}{\text{total number of possible outcomes}}$$

This definition always leads to a fraction, which should be cancelled to its simplest form.

Another probability term you will meet is at **random**. This means 'without looking' or 'not knowing what the outcome is in advance'.

EXAMPLE 2

A bag contains five red balls and three blue balls. A ball is taken out at random.

What is the probability that it is:

a red? **b** blue? **c** green?

Use the above formula to work out these probabilities.

a There are five red balls out of a total of eight, so P(red) $= \frac{5}{8}$

b There are three blue balls out of a total of eight, so P(blue) $= \frac{3}{8}$

c There are no green balls, so this event is impossible: P(green) $= 0$

EXAMPLE 3

The spinner shown here is spun and the score on the side on which it lands is recorded.

What is the probability that the score is:

a 2?   **b** odd?   **c** less than 5?

a There are two 2s out of six sides, so $P(2) = \frac{2}{6} = \frac{1}{3}$

b There are four odd numbers, so $P(\text{odd}) = \frac{4}{6} = \frac{2}{3}$

c All of the numbers are less than 5, so this is a certain event.

$P(\text{less than 5}) = 1$

EXAMPLE 4

Bernice is always early, just in time or late for work.

The probability that she is early is 0.1, the probability she is just on time is 0.5.

What is the probability that she is late?

As all the possibilities are covered, that is 'early', 'on time' and 'late', the total probability is 1. So:

$P(\text{early}) + P(\text{on time}) = 0.1 + 0.5 = 0.6$

So, the probability of Bernice being late is $1 - 0.6 = 0.4$.

EXERCISE 18B

1 What is the probability of each of the following outcomes?

a Throwing a 2 with a dice.

b Throwing a 6 with a dice.

c Tossing a coin and getting a tail.

d Drawing a queen from a pack of cards.

e Drawing a heart from a pack of cards.

f Drawing a black card from a pack of cards.

g Throwing a 2 or a 6 with a dice.

h Drawing a black queen from a pack of cards.

i Drawing an ace from a pack of cards.

j Throwing a 7 with a dice.

> **HINTS AND TIPS**
>
> If an event is impossible, just write the probability as 0, not as a fraction such as $\frac{0}{6}$. If it is certain, write the probability as 1, not as a fraction such as $\frac{6}{6}$.

> **HINTS AND TIPS**
>
> Remember to cancel the fractions if possible.

2 What is the probability of each of the following outcomes?

   a Throwing an even number with a dice.

   b Throwing a prime number with a dice.

   c Getting a heart or a club from a pack of cards.

   d Drawing the king of hearts from a pack of cards.

   e Drawing a picture card or an ace from a pack of cards.

   f Drawing the seven of diamonds from a pack of cards.

3 A bag contains only blue balls. If I take one out at random, what is the probability of each of these outcomes?

   a I get a black ball.   **b** I get a blue ball.

4 The numbers 1 to 10 inclusive are placed in a hat. Bob takes a number out of the bag without looking. What is the probability that he draws the following?

   a the number 7   **b** an even number   **c** a number greater than 6

   d a number less than 3   **e** a number between 3 and 8

5 A bag contains one blue ball, one pink ball and one black ball. Craig takes a ball from the bag without looking. What is the probability that he takes out the following?

   a the blue ball   **b** the pink ball

   c a ball that is not black

> **HINTS AND TIPS**
>
> A ball that is not black must be pink or blue.

6 A pencil case contains six red pens and five blue pens. Geoff takes out a pen without looking what it is. What is the probability that he takes out the following?

   a a red pen   **b** a blue pen   **c** a pen that is not blue

7 A bag contains 50 balls. Ten are green, 15 are red and the rest are white. Gemma takes a ball from the bag at random. What is the probability that she takes the following?

   a a green ball   **b** a white ball

   c a ball that is not white   **d** a ball that is green or white

8 A box contains seven bags of cheese and onion crisps, two bags of beef crisps and six bags of plain crisps. Iklil takes out a bag of crisps at random. What is the probability that he gets the following?

   a a bag of cheese and onion crisps   **b** a bag of beef crisps

   c a bag of crisps that are not cheese and onion   **d** a bag of prawn cracker crisps

   e a bag of crisps that is either plain or beef

9 In a Christmas raffle, 2500 tickets are sold. One family has 50 tickets. What is the probability that that family wins the first prize?

10 Ashley, Bianca, Charles, Debbie and Eliza are in the same class. Their teacher wants two pupils to do a special job.

a Write down all the possible combinations of two people, for example, Ashley and Bianca, Ashley and Charles. (There are ten combinations altogether).

b How many pairs give two boys?

c What is the probability of choosing two boys?

d How many pairs give a boy and a girl?

e What is the probability of choosing a boy and a girl?

f What is the probability of choosing two girls?

11 In a sale at the supermarket, there is a box of ten unlabelled tins. On the side it says: 4 tins of Creamed Rice and 6 tins of Chicken Soup. Mitesh buys this box. When he gets home he wants to have a lunch of chicken soup followed by creamed rice.

a What is the smallest number of tins he could open to get his lunch?

b What is the largest number of tins he could open to get his lunch?

c The first tin he opens is soup. What is the chance that the second tin he opens is

   i soup?   **ii** rice?

12 What is the probability of each of the following outcomes?

a Drawing a jack from a pack of cards.

b Drawing a 10 from a pack of cards.

c Drawing a red card from a pack of cards.

d Drawing a 10 or a jack from a pack of cards.

e Drawing a jack or a red card from a pack of cards.

f Drawing a red jack from a pack of cards.

13 A bag contains 25 coloured balls. Twelve are red, seven are blue and the rest are green. Martin takes a ball at random from the bag.

a Find the following.

   i P(he chooses a red)   **ii** P(he chooses a blue)   **iii** P(he chooses a green)

b Add together the three probabilities. What do you notice?

c Explain your answer to part **b**.

14 The weather tomorrow will be sunny, cloudy or raining.

If P(sunny) = 40%, P(cloudy) = 25%, what is P(raining)?

15 At morning break, Pauline has a choice of coffee, tea or hot chocolate.

If P(she chooses coffee) = 0.3 and P(she chooses hot chocolate) = 0.2, what is P(she chooses tea)?

Probability that an outcome of an event will not happen

In this section you will learn how to:

- calculate the probability of an outcome of an event not happening when you know the probability of the outcome happening

Key words

outcome

In some questions in Exercise 18B, you were asked for the probability of something not happening. For example, in question 5 you were asked for the probability of picking a ball that is *not* black. You could answer this because you knew how many balls were in the bag. However, sometimes you do not have this type of information.

The probability of throwing a six on a dice is $P(6) = \dfrac{1}{6}$.

There are five **outcomes** that are not sixes: {1, 2, 3, 4, 5}.

So, the probability of not throwing a six on a dice is:

$$P(\text{not a } 6) = \dfrac{5}{6}$$

Notice that:

$$P(6) = \dfrac{1}{6} \quad \text{and} \quad P(\text{not a } 6) = \dfrac{5}{6}$$

So:

$$P(6) + P(\text{not a } 6) = 1$$

If you know that $P(6) = \dfrac{1}{6}$, then $P(\text{not a } 6)$ is:

$$1 - \dfrac{1}{6} = \dfrac{5}{6}$$

So, if you know P(outcome happening), then:

$$P(\text{outcome not happening}) = 1 - P(\text{outcome happening})$$

EXAMPLE 5

What is the probability of not picking an ace from a pack of cards?

First, find the probability of picking an ace:

$$P(\text{picking an ace from a pack of cards}) = \tfrac{4}{52} = \tfrac{1}{13}$$

Therefore:

$$P(\text{not picking an ace from a pack of cards}) = 1 - \tfrac{1}{13} = \tfrac{12}{13}$$

EXERCISE 18C

1 a The probability of winning a prize in a raffle is $\frac{1}{20}$. What is the probability of not winning a prize in the raffle?

b The probability that snow will fall during the Christmas holidays is 45%. What is the probability that it will not snow?

c The probability that Paddy wins a game of chess is 0.7 and the probability that he draws the game is 0.1. What is the probability that he loses the game?

2 Millicent picks a card from a pack of well-shuffled playing cards.

Find the probability that she picks the following.

a i a picture card   **ii** a card that is not a picture

b i a club   **ii** not a club

c i an ace or a king   **ii** neither an ace nor a king

3 The following letters are put into a bag.

a Steve takes a letter at random.

i What is the probability he takes a letter A?

ii What is the probability he does not take a letter A?

b Richard picks an M and keeps it. Sue now takes a letter from those remaining.

i What is the probability she takes a letter A?

ii What is the probability she does not take a letter A?

18.4 Addition rule for outcomes

In this section you will learn how to:

● work out the probability of two outcomes such as P(outcome A) or P(outcome B)

Key words

mutually exclusive
outcome

You have used this rule already but it has not yet been formally defined.

When two **outcomes** of one event are **mutually exclusive**, you can work out the probability of either of them occurring by adding up the separate probabilities. Mutually exclusive outcomes are outcomes for which, when one occurs, it does not have any effect on the probability of other outcomes.

EXAMPLE 6

A bag contains twelve red balls, eight green balls, five blue balls and fifteen black balls. A ball is drawn at random. What is the probability that it is the following?

a red   **b** black   **c** red or black   **d** not green

a $P(\text{red}) = \frac{12}{40} = \frac{3}{10}$

b $P(\text{black}) = \frac{15}{40} = \frac{3}{8}$

c $P(\text{red or black}) = P(\text{red}) + P(\text{black}) = \frac{3}{10} + \frac{3}{8} = \frac{27}{40}$

d $P(\text{not green}) = \frac{32}{40} = \frac{4}{5}$

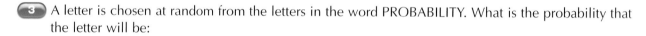

EXERCISE 18D

1 Iqbal throws an ordinary dice. What is the probability that he throws:

     a a 2?   **b** a 5?   **c** a 2 or a 5?

2 Jennifer draws a card from a pack of cards. What is the probability that she draws:

     a a heart?   **b** a club?   **c** a heart or a club?

3 A letter is chosen at random from the letters in the word PROBABILITY. What is the probability that the letter will be:

     a B?   **b** a vowel?   **c** B or a vowel?

4 A bag contains ten white balls, twelve black balls and eight red balls. A ball is drawn at random from the bag. What is the probability that it will be the following?

     a white   **b** black

     c black or white   **d** not red

     e not red or black

> **HINTS AND TIPS**
>
> You can only add fractions with the same denominator.

5 At the local School Fayre the tombola stall gives out a prize if you draw from the drum a numbered ticket that ends in 0 or 5. There are 300 tickets in the drum altogether and the probability of getting a winning ticket is 0.4.

     a What is the probability of getting a losing ticket?

     b How many winning tickets are there in the drum?

6 John needs his calculator for his mathematics lesson. It is always in his pocket, bag or locker. The probability it is in his pocket is 0.35 and the probability it is in his bag is 0.45. What is the probability that:

     a he will have the calculator for the lesson?

     b his calculator is in his locker?

Aneesa has twenty unlabelled CDs, twelve of which are rock, five are pop and three are classical. She picks a CD at random. What is the probability that it will be the following?

a rock or pop   **b** pop or classical   **c** not pop

8 The probability that it rains on Monday is 0.5. The probability that it rains on Tuesday is 0.5 and the probability that it rains on Wednesday is 0.5. Kelly argues that it is certain to rain on Monday, Tuesday or Wednesday because 0.5 + 0.5 + 0.5 = 1.5, which is bigger than 1 so it is a certain event. Explain why she is wrong.

C

18.5 Experimental probability

In this section you will learn how to:

- calculate experimental probabilities and relative frequencies from experiments
- recognise different methods for estimating probabilities

Key words

bias
equally likely
experimental data
experimental probability
historical data
relative frequency
trials

Heads or tails?

Toss a coin ten times and record the results like this:

H	T	H	H	T	T	H	T	H	H

Record how many heads you obtained.

Now repeat the above so that altogether you toss the coin 50 times. Record your results and count how many heads you obtained. Now toss the coin another 50 times and once again record your results and count the heads.

It helps if you work with a partner. First, your partner records while you toss the coin. Then you swap over and record, while your partner tosses the coin. Add the number of heads you obtained to the number your partner obtained.

Now find three more people to do the same activity and add together the number of heads that all five of you obtained.

Now find five more people and add their results to the previous total.

Combine as many results together as possible.

You should now be able to fill in a table like the one below. The first column is the number of times coins were tossed. The second column is the number of heads obtained. The third column is the number in the second column divided by the number in the first column.

The results below are from a group who did the same experiment.

Number of tosses	Number of heads	$\dfrac{\text{Number of heads}}{\text{Number of tosses}}$
10	6	0.6
50	24	0.48
100	47	0.47
200	92	0.46
500	237	0.474
1000	488	0.488
2000	960	0.48
5000	2482	0.4964

If you drew a graph of these results, plotting the first column against the last column, it would look like this.

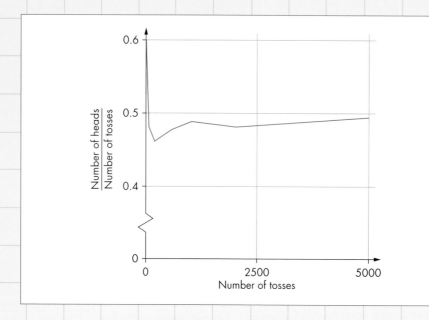

Your results should look very similar.

What happens to the value of $\dfrac{\text{number of heads}}{\text{number of tosses}}$ as the total number of tosses increases?

You should find that it gets closer and closer to 0.5.

The value of 'number of heads ÷ number of tosses' is called an **experimental probability**. As the number of **trials**, or experiments, increases, the value of the experimental probability gets closer to the true or theoretical probability.

Experimental probability is also known as the **relative frequency** of an outcome of an event. The relative frequency of an outcome is an estimate for the theoretical probability. It is given by:

$$\text{relative frequency of an outcome } = \frac{\text{frequency of the outcome}}{\text{total number of trials}}$$

EXAMPLE 7

The frequency table shows the speeds of 160 vehicles that pass a radar speed check on a dual carriageway.

Speed (mph)	20–29	30–39	40–49	50–59	60–69	70+
Frequency	14	23	28	35	52	8

a What is the experimental probability that a car is travelling faster than 70 mph?

b If 500 vehicles pass the speed check, estimate how many will be travelling faster than 70 mph.

a The experimental probability is the relative frequency, which is $\frac{8}{160} = \frac{1}{20}$.

b The number of vehicles travelling faster than 70 mph will be $\frac{1}{20}$ of 500.

That is:

$$500 \div 20 = 25$$

Finding probabilities

There are three ways in which the probability of an outcome of an event can be found.

- **First method** If you can work out the theoretical probability of an outcome – for example, drawing a king from a pack of cards – this is called using **equally likely** outcomes.

- **Second method** Some probabilities, such as people buying a certain brand of dog food, cannot be calculated using equally likely outcomes. To find the probabilities for such an event, you can perform an experiment such as you already have or conduct a survey. This is called collecting **experimental data**. The more data you collect, the better the estimate is.

- **Third method** The probabilities of some events, such as an earthquake occurring in Japan, cannot be found by either of the above methods. One of the things you can do is to look at data collected over a long period of time and make an estimate (sometimes called a 'best guess') at the chance of the event happening. This is called looking at **historical data**.

EXAMPLE 8

Which method (A, B or C) would you use to estimate the probabilities for the events **a** to **e**?

A: Use equally likely outcomes

B: Conduct a survey/collect data

C: Look at historical data

a Someone in your class will go abroad for a holiday this year.

b You will win the National Lottery.

c Your bus home will be late.

d It will snow on Christmas Day.

e You will pick a red seven from a pack of cards.

a You would have to ask all the members of your class what they intended to do for their holidays this year. You would therefore conduct a survey, Method B.

b The odds on winning are about 14 million to 1, so this is an equally likely outcome, Method A.

c If you catch the bus every day, you can collect data over several weeks. This would be Method C.

d If you check whether it snowed on Christmas Day for the last few years, you would be able to make a good estimate of the probability. This would be Method C.

e There are 2 red sevens out of 52 cards, so the probability of picking one can be calculated:

$$P(\text{red seven}) = \frac{2}{52} = \frac{1}{26}$$

This is Method A.

EXERCISE 18E

1 Which of these methods would you use to estimate or state the probabilities for each of the events **a** to **h**?

Method A: Use equally likely outcomes

Method B: Conduct a survey or experiment

Method C: Look at historical data

a How people will vote in the next election.

b A drawing pin dropped on a desk will land point up.

c A Premier League team will win the FA Cup.

d You will win a school raffle.

e The next car to drive down the road will be red.

f You will throw a 'double six' with two dice.

g Someone in your class likes classical music.

h A person picked at random from your school will be a vegetarian.

2 Naseer throws a dice and records the number of sixes that he gets after various numbers of throws. The table shows his results.

Number of throws	10	50	100	200	500	1000	2000
Number of sixes	2	4	10	21	74	163	329

  a Calculate the experimental probability of scoring a six at each stage that Naseer recorded his results.

  b How many ways can a dice land?

  c How many of these ways give a six?

  d What is the theoretical probability of throwing a six with a dice?

  e If Naseer threw the dice a total of 6000 times, how many sixes would you expect him to get?

3 Marie made a five-sided spinner, like the one shown in the diagram. She used it to play a board game with her friend Sarah. The girls thought that the spinner was not very fair as it seemed to land on some numbers more than others. They threw the spinner 200 times and recorded the results. The results are shown in the table.

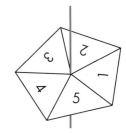

Side spinner lands on	1	2	3	4	5
Number of times	19	27	32	53	69

  a Work out the experimental probability of each number.

  b How many times would you expect each number to occur if the spinner is fair?

  c Do you think that the spinner is fair? Give a reason for your answer.

4 A sampling bottle contains 20 balls. The balls are either black or white. (A sampling bottle is a sealed bottle with a clear plastic tube at one end into which one of the balls can be tipped.) Kenny conducts an experiment to see how many black balls are in the bottle. He takes various numbers of samples and records how many of them showed a black ball. The results are shown in the table.

Number of samples	Number of black balls	Experimental probability
10	2	
100	25	
200	76	
500	210	
1000	385	
5000	1987	

  a Copy the table and complete it by calculating the experimental probability of getting a black ball at each stage.

  b Using this information, how many black balls do you think are in the bottle?

5 Use a set of number cards from 1 to 10 (or make your own set) and work with a partner. Take it in turns to choose a card and keep a record each time of what card you get. Shuffle the cards each time and repeat the experiment 60 times. Put your results in a copy of this table.

Score	1	2	3	4	5	6	7	8	9	10
Total										

a How many times would you expect to get each number?

b Do you think you and your partner conducted this experiment fairly?

c Explain your answer to part **b**.

6 A four-sided dice has faces numbered 1, 2, 3 and 4. The 'score' is the face on which it lands. Five pupils throw the dice to see if it is biased. They each throw it a different number of times. Their results are shown in the table.

Pupil	Total number of throws	Score			
		1	2	3	4
Alfred	20	7	6	3	4
Brian	50	19	16	8	7
Caryl	250	102	76	42	30
Deema	80	25	25	12	18
Emma	150	61	46	26	17

a Which pupil will have the most reliable set of results? Why?

b Add up all the score columns and work out the relative frequency of each score. Give your answers to 2 decimal places.

c Is the dice biased? Explain your answer.

7 If you were about to choose a card from a pack of yellow cards numbered from 1 to 10, what would be the chance of each of the events **a** to **i** occurring? Copy and complete each of these statements with a word or phrase chosen from 'impossible', 'not likely', '50–50 chance', 'quite likely', or 'certain'.

a The likelihood that the next card chosen will be a four is …

b The likelihood that the next card chosen will be pink is …

c The likelihood that the next card chosen will be a seven is …

d The likelihood that the next card chosen will be a number less than 11 is …

e The likelihood that the next card chosen will be a number bigger than 11 is …

f The likelihood that the next card chosen will be an even number is …

g The likelihood that the next card chosen will be a number more than 5 is …

h The likelihood that the next card chosen will be a multiple of 1 is …

i The likelihood that the next card chosen will be a prime number is …

Biased spinner

You need a piece of stiff card, a cocktail stick and some Blu-Tack.

You may find that it is easier to work in pairs.

Make a copy of this hexagon on the card and push the cocktail stick through its centre to make a six-sided spinner. The size of the hexagon does not really matter, but it does need to be *accurately* drawn.

Stick a small piece of Blu-Tack underneath one of the numbers. You now have a **biased** spinner.

Spin it 100 times and record your results in a frequency table.

Estimate the experimental probability of getting each number.

How can you tell that your spinner is biased?

Put Blu-Tack underneath a different number and see whether your partner can predict the number towards which the spinner is biased.

18.6 Combined events

In this section you will learn how to:
- work out the probabilities for two outcomes occurring at the same time

Key words
probability
space
diagram
sample space
diagram

There are many situations where two events occur together. Four examples are given below.

Throwing two dice

Imagine that two dice, one red and one blue, are thrown. The red dice can land with any one of six scores: 1, 2, 3, 4, 5 or 6. The blue dice can also land with any one of six scores. This gives a total of 36 possible combinations. These are shown in the left-hand diagram at the top of the next page, where each combination is given as (2, 3) and so on. The first number is the score on the blue dice and the second number is the score on the red dice.

The combination (2, 3) gives a total of 5. The total scores for all the combinations are shown in the diagram on the right-hand side. Diagrams that show all the outcomes of combined events are called **sample space diagrams** or **probability space diagrams**.

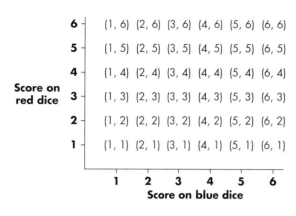

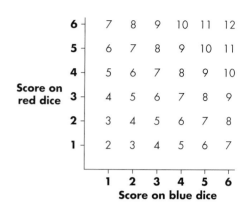

From the diagram on the right, you can see that there are two ways to get a score of 3. This gives a probability of scoring 3 as:

$$P(3) = \frac{2}{36} = \frac{1}{18}$$

From the diagram on the left, you can see that there are six ways to get a 'double'. This gives a probability of scoring a double as:

$$P(double) = \frac{6}{36} = \frac{1}{6}$$

Throwing coins

Throwing one coin
There are two equally likely outcomes, head or tail:

Throwing two coins together
There are four equally likely outcomes: (T)(T)
Hence:

$$P(2 \text{ heads}) = \frac{1}{4}$$

$$P(\text{head and tail}) = 2 \text{ ways out of } 4 = \frac{2}{4} = \frac{1}{2}$$

Dice and coins

Throwing a dice and a coin

Outcome on coin	H	(1, H)	(2, H)	(3, H)	(4, H)	(5, H)	(6, H)
	T	(1, T)	(2, T)	(3, T)	(4, T)	(5, T)	(6, T)
		1	2	3	4	5	6

Score on dice

Hence:

$$P \text{ (head and an even number)} = 3 \text{ ways out of } 12 = \frac{3}{12} = \frac{1}{4}$$

EXERCISE 18F

1 To answer these questions, use the diagram on page 414 for the total scores when two dice are thrown together.

   a What is the most likely score?

   b Which two scores are least likely?

   c Write down the probabilities of throwing all the scores from 2 to 12.

   d What is the probability of a score that is each of the following?

      i bigger than 10   **ii** between 3 and 7

      iii even   **iv** a square number

      v a prime number   **vi** a triangular number

2 Use the diagram on page 414 that shows the outcomes when two dice are thrown together as coordinates. What is the probability of each of the following?

   a the score is an even 'double'

   b at least one of the dice shows 2

   c the score on one dice is twice the score on the other dice

   d at least one of the dice shows a multiple of 3

3 Use the diagram on page 414 that shows the outcomes when two dice are thrown together as coordinates. What is the probability of each of the following?

   a both dice show a 6

   b at least one of the dice will show a six

   c exactly one dice shows a six

4 The diagram shows the score for the event 'the difference between the scores when two dice are thrown'. Copy and complete the diagram.

For the event described above, what is the probability of a difference of each of these numbers?

   a 1   **b** 0   **c** 4

   d 6   **e** an odd number

Score on second dice

	1	2	3	4	5	6
6	5	4			1	0
5	4	3				1
4	3					
3	2					
2	1					
1	0					

Score on first dice

5 When two coins are thrown together, what is the probability of each of these?

   a two heads   **b** a head and a tail

   c at least one tail   **d** no tails

Use the diagram of the outcomes when two coins are thrown together, on page 414.

6 Two five-sided spinners are spun together and the total score of the faces that they land on is worked out. Copy and complete the probability space diagram shown.

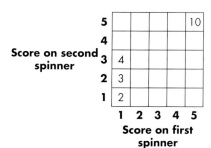

a What is the most likely score?

b When two five-sided spinners are spun together, what is the probability that:

i the total score is 5?

ii the total score is an even number?

iii the score is a 'double'?

iv the total score is less than 7?

18.7 Expectation

In this section you will learn how to:

* predict the likely number of successful events given the number of trials and the probability of any one outcome

Key words

expect

When you know the probability of an outcome of an event, you can predict how many times you would expect that outcome to happen in a certain number of trials.

Note that this is what you **expect**. It is not what is going to happen. If what you expected always happened, life would be very dull and boring, and the National Lottery would be a waste of time.

EXAMPLE 9

A bag contains twenty balls, nine of which are black, six white and five yellow. A ball is drawn at random from the bag, its colour is noted and then it is put back in the bag. This is repeated 500 times.

a How many times would you expect a black ball to be drawn?

b How many times would you expect a yellow ball to be drawn?

c How many times would you expect a black or a yellow ball to be drawn?

a P(black ball) = $\frac{9}{20}$

Expected number of black balls = $\frac{9}{20} \times 500 = 225$

b P(yellow ball) = $\frac{5}{20} = \frac{1}{4}$

Expected number of yellow balls = $\frac{1}{4} \times 500 = 125$

c Expected number of black or yellow balls = 225 + 125 = 350

EXERCISE 18G

1 **a** What is the probability of throwing a 6 with an ordinary dice?

b I throw an ordinary dice 150 times. How many times can I expect to get a score of 6?

2 **a** What is the probability of tossing a head with a coin?

b I toss a coin 2000 times. How many times can I expect to get a head?

3 **a** A card is taken at random from a pack of cards. What is the probability that it is:

  i a black card? **ii** a king? **iii** a heart? **iv** the king of hearts?

b I draw a card from a pack of cards and replace it. I do this 520 times. How many times would I expect to get:

  i a black card? **ii** a king? **iii** a heart? **iv** the king of hearts?

4 The ball in a roulette wheel can land in one of 37 spaces that are marked with numbers from 0 to 36 inclusive. I always bet on the same number, 13.

a What is the probability of the ball landing in 13?

b If I play all evening and there is a total of 185 spins of the wheel in that time, how many times could I expect to win?

5 In a bag there are 30 balls, 15 of which are red, five yellow, five green, and five blue. A ball is taken out at random and then replaced. This is done 300 times. How many times would I expect to get:

  a a red ball? **b** a yellow or blue ball? **c** a ball that is not blue? **d** a pink ball?

6 The experiment described in question **5** is carried out 1000 times. Approximately how many times would you expect to get:

  a a green ball? **b** a ball that is not blue?

7 A sampling bottle (as described in question **4** of Exercise 18E) contains red and white balls. It is known that the probability of getting a red ball is 0.3. If 1500 samples are taken, how many of them would you expect to give a white ball?

8 Josie said, "When I throw a dice, I expect to get a score of 3.5."

"Impossible," said Paul, "You can't score 3.5 with a dice".
'Do this and I'll prove it,' said Josie.

a An ordinary dice is thrown 60 times. Fill in the table for the expected number of times each score will occur.

Score						
Expected occurrences						

b Now work out the average score that is expected over 60 throws.

c There is an easy way to get an answer of 3.5 for the expected average score. Can you see what it is?

Two-way tables

In this section you will learn how to:

- read a two-way table and use them to do probability and other mathematics

A **two-way table** is a table that links together two variables. For example, the following table shows how many boys and girls are in a form and whether they are left- or right-handed.

	Boys	Girls
Left-handed	2	4
Right-handed	10	13

This table shows the colour and make of cars in the school car park.

	Red	Blue	White
Ford	2	4	1
Vauxhall	0	1	2
Toyota	3	3	4
Peugeot	2	0	3

As you can see, one variable is the rows of the table and the other variable is the columns of the table.

EXAMPLE 10

Use the first two-way table above to answer the following.

a How many left-handed boys are in the form?

b How many girls are in the form, in total?

c How many pupils are in the form altogether?

d How many pupils altogether are right-handed?

e If a pupil is selected at random from the form, what is the probability that the pupil is:

   i a left-handed boy?   **ii** right-handed?

a 2 boys.   Read this value from where the 'Boys' column and the 'Left-handed' row meet.

b 17 girls.   Add up the 'Girls' column.

c 29 pupils.   Add up all the numbers in the table.

d 23.   Add up the 'Right-handed' row.

e **i** P (left-handed boy) $= \frac{2}{29}$.   Use the answers to parts **a** and **c**.

    ii P (right-handed) $= \frac{23}{29}$.   Use the answer to parts **c** and **d**.

EXAMPLE 11

Use the second two-way table on the previous page to answer the following.

a How many cars were in the car park altogether?

b How many red cars were in the car park?

c What percentage of the cars in the car park were red?

d How many cars in the car park were white?

e What percentage of the white cars were Vauxhalls?

a 25. Add up all the numbers in the table.

b 7. Add up the 'Red' column.

c 28%. 7 out of 25 is the same as 28 out of 100.

d 10. Add up the 'White' column.

e 20%. 2 out of 10 is 20%.

EXERCISE 18H

1 The following table shows the top five clubs in the top division of the English Football League at the end of the season for the years 1965, 1975, 1985, 1995 and 2005.

		Year				
		1965	**1975**	**1985**	**1995**	**2005**
Position	**1st**	Man Utd	Derby	Everton	Blackburn	Chelsea
	2nd	Leeds	Liverpool	Liverpool	Man Utd	Arsenal
	3rd	Chelsea	Ipswich	Tottenham	Notts Forest	Man Utd
	4th	Everton	Everton	Man Utd	Liverpool	Everton
	5th	Notts Forest	Stoke	Southampton	Leeds	Liverpool

a Which team was in fourth place in 1975?

b Which three teams are in the top five for four of the five years?

c Which team finished three places lower between 1965 and 1995?

2 Here is a display of ten cards.

a Complete the two-way table.

		Shaded	Unshaded
Shape	**Circles**		
	Triangles		

b One of the cards is picked at random. What is the probability it shows either a shaded triangle or an unshaded circle?

3 The two-way table shows the number of doors and the number of windows in each room in a primary school.

		Number of doors		
		1	**2**	**3**
	1	5	4	2
Number of windows	**2**	4	5	4
	3	0	4	6
	4	1	3	2

a How many rooms are in the school altogether?

b How many rooms had two doors?

c What percentage of the rooms in the school had two doors?

d What percentage of the rooms that had one door also had two windows?

e How many rooms had the same number of windows as doors?

4 Three cards are lettered A, B and C. Three discs are numbered 4, 5 and 6.

One card and one disc are chosen at random.

If the card shows A, 1 is deducted from the score on the disc.
If the card shows B, the score on the disc stays the same.
If the card shows C, 1 is added to the score on the disc.

a Copy and complete the table to show all the possible scores.

		Number on disc		
		4	**5**	**6**
	A	3		
Letter on card	**B**	4		
	C	5		

b What is the probability of getting a score that is an even number?

c In a different game the probability of getting a total that is even is $\frac{2}{3}$.
What is the probability of getting a total that is an odd number?

5 The two-way table shows the age and sex of a sample of 50 pupils in a school.

		Age (years)					
		11	**12**	**13**	**14**	**15**	**16**
Sex	**Boys**	4	3	6	2	5	4
	Girls	2	5	3	6	4	6

a How many pupils are aged 13 years or less?

b What percentage of the pupils in the table are 16?

c A pupil from the table is selected at random. What is the probability that the pupil will be 14 years of age? Give your answer as a fraction in its lowest form.

d There are 1000 pupils in the school. Use the table to estimate how many boys are in the school altogether.

6 The two-way table shows the numbers of adults and the numbers of cars in 50 houses in one street.

		Number of adults			
		1	**2**	**3**	**4**
Number of cars	**0**	2	1	0	0
	1	3	13	3	1
	2	0	10	6	4
	3	0	1	4	2

a How many houses have exactly two adults and two cars?

b How many houses altogether have three cars?

c What percentage of the houses have three cars?

d What percentage of the houses with just one car have three adults living in the house?

7 Jane has two four-sided spinners. Spinner A has the numbers 1 to 4 on it and Spinner B has the numbers 5 to 8 on it.

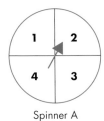

Spinner A

Spinner B

Both spinners are spun together.

The two-way table shows all the ways the two spinners can land.

Some of the total scores are filled in.

		Score on Spinner A			
		1	**2**	**3**	**4**
Score on Spinner B	**5**	6	7		
	6	7			
	7				
	8				

a Complete the table to show all the possible total scores.

b How many of the total scores are 9?

c When the two spinners are spun together, what is the probability that the total score will be:

   i 9?   **ii** 8?   **iii** a prime number?

8 The table shows information about the number of items in Flossy's music collection.

		Type of music		
		Pop	Folk	Classical
Format	Tape	16	5	2
	CD	51	9	13
	Mini disc	9	2	0

a How many pop tapes does Flossy have?

b How many items of folk music does Flossy have?

c How many CDs does Flossy have?

d If a CD is chosen at random from all the CDs, what is the probability that it will be a pop CD?

9 Zoe throws a fair coin and rolls a fair dice.

If the coin shows a head, she records the score on the dice.
If the coin shows tails, she doubles the number on the dice.

a Complete the two-way table to show Zoe's possible scores.

		Number on dice					
		1	2	3	4	5	6
Coin	Head	1	2				
	Tail	2	4				

b How many of the scores are square numbers?

c What is the probability of getting a score that is a square number?

10 A gardener plants some sunflower seeds in a greenhouse and some in the garden. After they have fully grown, he measures the diameter of the sunflower heads. The table shows his results.

		Greenhouse	Garden
Diameter	Mean diameter	16.8 cm	14.5 cm
	Range of diameter	3.2 cm	1.8 cm

a The gardener, who wants to enter competitions, says, "The sunflowers from the greenhouse are better."

Using the data in the table, give a reason to justify this statement.

b The gardener's wife, who does flower arranging, says, "The sunflowers from the garden are better."

Using the data in the table, give a reason to justify this statement.

1 Some bulbs were planted in October. The ticks in the table shows the months in which each type of bulb grows into flowers.

a In which months do tulips flower?

b Which type of bulb flowers in March?

c In which month do most types of bulb flower?

d Which type of bulb flowers in the same months as the iris?

Type of bulb	Month					
	Jan	Feb	March	April	May	June
Allium					✓	✓
Crocus	✓	✓				
Daffodil		✓	✓	✓		
Iris	✓	✓				
Tulip				✓	✓	

Ben puts one of each type of these bulbs in a bag. He takes a bulb from the bag without looking.

e i Write down the probability that he will take a crocus bulb.

   ii Copy the probability scale and mark with a cross (✗) the probability that he will take a bulb which flowers in February.

Edexcel, Question 6, Paper 1 Foundation, June 2005

2 A six-sided fair dice has either an odd number or an even number on each face. Bavna throws the dice 60 times and records the results in a table.

Number	Tally	Frequency
Odd		27
Even	⊪⊪ ⊪⊪ ⊪⊪ ⊪⊪ ⊪⊪ ⊪⊪ ‖‖	33

a Write down the tally for the frequency of 27.

b How many faces do you think have an even number marked on them?

c How many faces do you think have an odd number marked on them?

3 The probability that a paper girl delivers the wrong newspaper to a house is $\frac{1}{30}$.

a What is the probability that she delivers the correct newspaper to a house?

b One day she delivers newspapers to 90 houses. Estimate the number of houses that receive the *wrong* newspaper.

4 A quiz consists of twelve questions. Ann, Bill and Carol take part. The two-way table shows the results.

	Ann	Bill	Carol
Correct	5	6	5
Incorrect	4	5	0
Not attempted	3	1	7

A correct answer scores 4 points.
An incorrect answer scores −2 points.
A question not attempted scores 0 points.
Who scores the most points?

5 A farm sells two varieties of plum, 'Palmers' and 'Sturroks'. They are sold in boxes of 4 kilograms.

The table shows the mean weight and range of weights for the plums in each of two boxes.

	Mean weight	Range of weights
Plamers	68 g	18 g
Sturroks	39 g	29 g

a Ben buys a box of plums. He wants all the plums to be about the same weight. Which box should he buy? Give a reason for your answer.

b Martin buys a box of plums. He wants as many plums as possible in his box. Which box should he buy? Give a reason for your answer.

c In the box of Palmers plums the lightest plum weighs 61 g. What is the weight of the heaviest plum?

6 Anne and Peter have a choice of two bus routes to go to work. Data is collected for the journey times over one week. Here are the results.

	Mean (minutes)	Range (minutes)
Route X	15.7	18
Route Y	20.3	7

a Anne says, "It is better to use Route X."
Using the data given in the table, give a reason to justify her statement.

b Peter says, "It is better to use Route Y."
Using the data given in the table, give a reason to justify his statement.

7 **a** Alice has a spinner that has five equal sections. The numbers 1, 2 and 3 are written on the spinner.

Alice spins the spinner once. On what number is the spinner least likely to land?

b

There are three numbers.

There are two number 2s.

The chance of getting a 2 is $\frac{2}{3}$.

Alice thinks that the chance of getting a 2 is $\frac{2}{3}$. Explain why Alice is wrong.

8 The two-way table shows the number of computers and the number of TVs owned by each of 40 families.

Number of computers

		0	1	2
Number of TVs	1	2	16	4
	2	3	9	3
	3	1	3	2

a How many families have exactly one computer and one TV?

b How many families have more than one TV?

9 A bag contains some beads which are red or green or blue or yellow.

The table shows the number of beads of each colour.

Colour	Red	Green	Blue	Yellow
Number of beads	3	2	5	2

Samire takes a bead at random from the bag. Write down the probability that she takes a blue bead.

Edexcel, Question 1, Paper 12A Intermediate, March 2005

10 Here are two fair spinners. They have numbers on each section.

The spinners are spun. The two numbers are added together.

Spinner A   Spinner B

    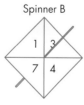

a Copy and complete the table to show all the possible total scores.

Spinner B

		1	3	4	7
Spinner A	1	2	4		
	4				
	5				
	8				

b What is the most likely score?

c What is the probability of getting a score of 5?

d What is the probability of getting a score of 11 or more?

e What is the probability of getting a score that is an odd number?

11 Fifty people take a maths exam. The table shows the results.

	Pass	Fail
Male	12	16
Female	9	13

a A person is chosen at random from the group. What is the probability that the person is male?

b A person is chosen at random from the group. What is the probability that the person passed the test?

12 A fair six-sided dice and a fair coin are thrown at the same time. This shows the outcome 1H or (1, head).

a Complete the list of all the possible outcomes.

b What is the probability of getting a head and an even number?

c What is the probability of getting a tail *or* an odd number *or* both?

13 Doris has a bag in which there are nine counters, all green. Alex has a bag in which there are 15 counters, all red. Jade has a bag in which there are some blue counters.

a What is the probability of picking a red counter from Doris's bag?

b Doris and Alex put all their counters into a box. What is the probability of choosing a green counter from the box?

c Jade now adds her blue counters to the box. The probability of choosing a blue counter from the box is now $\frac{1}{3}$. How many blue counters does Jade put in the box?

14 A spinner has a blue sector (B) and a white sector (W).

The arrow is spun 1000 times.

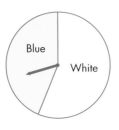

a The results for the first 20 spins are shown below.

B W W B W W B W W W
W B B B W B W B W W

Work out the relative frequency of a blue after 20 spins. Give your answer as a decimal.

b The table shows the relative frequency of a white after different numbers of spins.

Number of spins	Relative frequency of a white
50	0.61
100	0.59
150	0.57
200	0.56
500	0.55
1000	0.53

How many times was a white obtained after 500 spins?

15 Here is a 4-sided spinner.

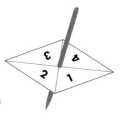

The sides of the spinner are labelled 1, 2, 3 and 4.

The spinner is biased.

The probability that the spinner will land on each of the numbers 2 and 3 is given in the table.

The probability that the spinner will land on 1 is equal to the probability that it will land on 4.

Number	1	2	3	4
Probability	x	0.3	0.2	x

a Work out the value of x.

Sarah is going to spin the spinner 200 times.

b Work out an estimate for the number of times it will land on 2.

Edexcel, Question 21, Paper 3 Intermediate, June 2005

WORKED EXAM QUESTION

Jing has a bag containing orange, black, purple, brown and yellow discs.

a Complete the table to show the probability of each colour being chosen at random.

b Which colour of disc is most likely to be chosen at random?

c Calculate the probability that a disc chosen at random is black or purple.

Colour of marble	Probability
Orange	0.25
Black	0.15
Purple	0.2
Brown	
Yellow	0.05

Solution

a 0.35

The probabilities in the table should add up to 1 so:
0.25 + 0.15 + 0.2 + 0.05 + ? = 1
0.65 + ? = 1
So the missing probability is 0.35.

b Brown disc

The brown disc is most likely as it has the largest probability of being chosen.

c 0.35

The word 'or' means you add probabilities of separate events.
P(black or purple) = P(black) + P(purple) = 0.15 + 0.2 = 0.35

GRADE YOURSELF

G Can understand basic terms such as 'certain', 'impossible', 'likely' and so on

F Can understand that the probability scale runs from 0 to 1 and are able to calculate the probability of outcomes of events

E Able to list all outcomes of two independent events such as tossing a coin and throwing a dice, and calculate probabilities from lists or tables

D Able to calculate the probability of an outcome of an event happening when the probability that the outcome does not happen is known and understand that the total probability of all possible outcomes is 1

D Able to predict the expected number of successes from a given number of trials if the probability of one success is known

C Able to calculate relative frequency from experimental evidence and compare this with the theoretical probability

What you should know now

- How to use the probability scale and estimate the likelihood of outcomes of events depending on their position on the scale

- How to calculate theoretical probabilities from different situations

- How to calculate relative frequency and understand that the reliability of experimental results depends on the number of experiments carried out

This book provides indicators of the equivalent grade level of maths questions throughout. The publishers wish to make clear that these grade indicators have been provided by Collins Education, and are not the responsibility of Edexcel Ltd. Whilst every effort has been made to assure their accuracy, they should be regarded as indicators, and are not binding or definitive.

Transformations

1 Congruent shapes

2 Tessellations

3 Translations

4 Reflections

5 Rotations

6 Enlargements

This chapter will show you ...

- how to recognise congruent shapes
- how 2-D shapes tessellate
- what is meant by a transformation
- how to translate 2-D shapes
- how to reflect 2-D shapes
- how to rotate 2-D shapes
- how to enlarge 2-D shapes

Visual overview

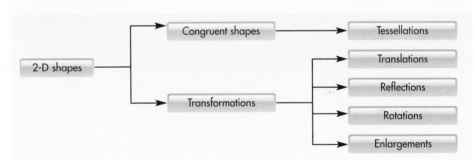

What you should already know

- How to find the lines of symmetry of a 2-D shape (Chapter 10)
- How to find the order of rotational symmetry of a 2-D shape (Chapter 10)
- How to find the equation of a line (Chapter 14)

Quick check

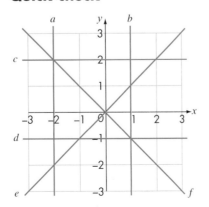

Write down the equations of the lines drawn on the grid.

19.1 Congruent shapes

In this section you will learn how to:
- recognise congruent shapes

Key word
congruent

Two-dimensional shapes which are exactly the *same* size and shape are said to be **congruent**. For example, although they are in different positions, the triangles below are congruent, because they are all exactly the same size and shape.

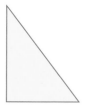  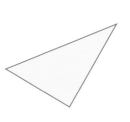 

Congruent shapes fit exactly on top of each other. So, one way to see whether shapes are congruent is to trace one of them and check that it exactly covers the other shapes. For some of the shapes, you may have to turn over your tracing.

EXAMPLE 1

Which of these shapes is not congruent to the others?

a 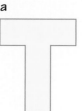 b c d

Trace shape **a** and check whether it fits exactly on top of the others.

You should find that shape **b** is not congruent to the others.

EXERCISE 19A

1. State whether the shapes in each pair, **a** to **f** are congruent or not.

a

b

c

d

e

f

G

2 Which figure in each group, **a** to **c**, is not congruent to the other two?

a i   ii    iii

b i 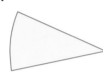   ii 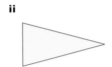   iii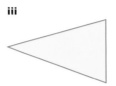

c i    ii    iii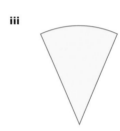

3 For each of the following sets of shapes, write down the numbers of the shapes that are congruent to each other.

a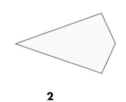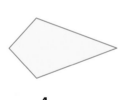

1   2   3   4

b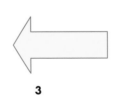

1   2   3   4

c

1   2   3   4

d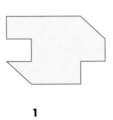

1   2   3   4

4 Draw a square PQRS. Draw in the diagonals PR and QS. Which triangles are congruent to each other?

5 Draw a rectangle EFGH. Draw in the diagonals EG and FH. Which triangles are congruent to each other?

6 Draw a parallelogram ABCD. Draw in the diagonals AC and BD. Which triangles are congruent to each other?

7 Draw an isosceles triangle ABC where AB = AC. Draw the line from A to the midpoint of BC. Which triangles are congruent to each other?

19.2 Tessellations

In this section you will learn how to:
● tessellate a 2-D shape

Key words
tessellate
tessellation

ACTIVITY

Tiling patterns

You need centimetre-squared paper and some card in several different colours.

Make a template for each of the following shapes on the centimetre-squared paper.

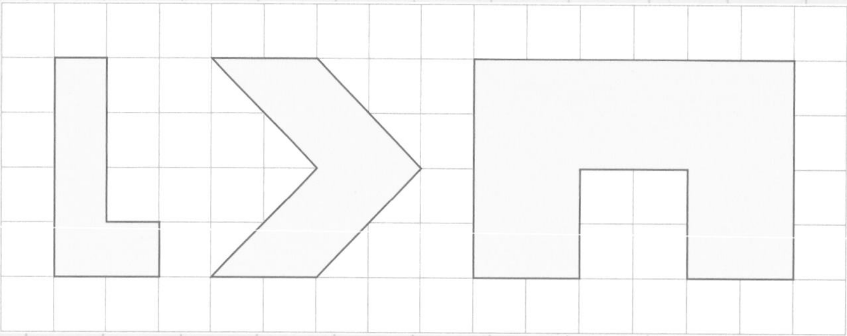

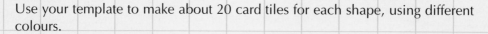

Use your template to make about 20 card tiles for each shape, using different colours.

For each shape, put all the tiles together to create a tiling pattern without any gaps.

What do you find?

From this activity you should have found that you could cover as much space as you wanted, using the *same* shape in a repeating pattern. You can say that the shape **tessellates**.

So, a **tessellation** is a regular pattern made with identical plane shapes, which fit together exactly, without overlapping and leaving no gaps.

EXAMPLE 2

Draw tessellations using each of these shapes.

a   b   c

These patterns show how each of the shapes tessellates.

a   b   c

   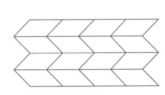

 **EXERCISE 19B**

1 On squared paper, show how each of these shapes tessellates.

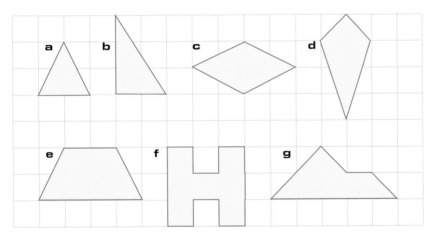

2 Invent some of your own tessellating patterns.

 3 'Every quadrilateral will form a tessellation'. Investigate this statement to see whether it is true.

 4 Explain why equilateral triangles, squares and regular hexagons tessellate.

E

D

In this section you will learn how to:

- translate a 2-D shape

Key words

image
object
transformation
translate
translation
vector

A **transformation** changes the position or the size of a 2-D shape in a particular way. You will deal with the four basic ways of using transformations to change a shape: **translation**, reflection, rotation and enlargement.

When a transformation is carried out, the shape's original position is called the **object** and its 'new' position is called the **image**. For translations, reflections and rotations, the object and image are congruent.

A translation is the movement of a shape from one position to another without reflecting it or rotating it. It is sometimes called a 'sliding' transformation, since the shape appears to slide from one position to another.

Every point in the shape moves in the same direction and through the same distance. The object shape **translates** to the image position.

EXAMPLE 3

Describe the following translations.

a triangle A to triangle B

b triangle A to triangle C

c triangle A to triangle D

a Triangle A has been transformed into triangle B by a translation of 5 squares right.

b Triangle A has been transformed into triangle C by a translation of 4 squares up.

c Triangle A has been transformed into triangle D by a translation of 3 squares right and 4 squares up.

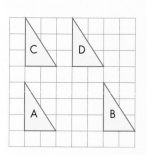

A translation can also be described by using a **vector**. (This is sometimes called a 'column vector'.)

A vector is written in the form $\begin{pmatrix} a \\ b \end{pmatrix}$, where a describes the horizontal movement and b describes the vertical movement.

EXAMPLE 4

Find the vectors for the following translations.

a A to B

b B to C

c C to D

d D to A

a The vector describing the translation from A to B is $\begin{pmatrix} 2 \\ 1 \end{pmatrix}$.

b The vector describing the translation from B to C is $\begin{pmatrix} 2 \\ 0 \end{pmatrix}$.

c The vector describing the translation from C to D is $\begin{pmatrix} -3 \\ 2 \end{pmatrix}$.

d The vector describing the translation from D to A is $\begin{pmatrix} -1 \\ -3 \end{pmatrix}$.

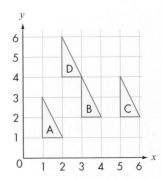

EXERCISE 19C

1 Copy each of these shapes onto squared paper and draw its image, using the given translation.

a

b

c

d

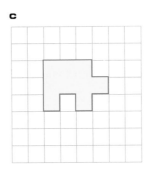

3 squares right   3 squares up   3 squares down   3 squares left

2 Copy each of these shapes onto squared paper and draw its image, using the given translation.

a

b

c

d

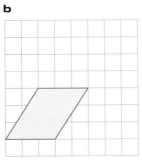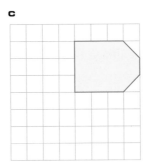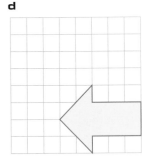

4 squares right and 3 squares down

3 squares right and 3 squares up

4 squares left and 3 squares down

1 square left and 4 squares up

3 Use vectors to describe these translations.

a i A to B   **ii** A to C   **iii** A to D   **iv** A to E   **v** A to F   **vi** A to G

b i B to A   **ii** B to C   **iii** B to D   **iv** B to E   **v** B to F   **vi** B to G

c i C to A   **ii** C to B   **iii** C to D   **iv** C to E   **v** C to F   **vi** C to G

d i D to E   **ii** E to B   **iii** F to C   **iv** G to D   **v** F to G   **vi** G to E

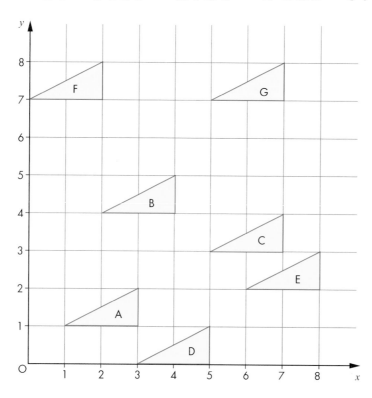

4 Draw a coordinate grid with $-1 \leqslant x \leqslant 6$ and $-4 \leqslant y \leqslant 6$.

a Draw the triangle with coordinates A(1, 1), B(2, 1) and C(1, 3).

b Draw the image of triangle ABC after a translation with vector $\begin{pmatrix} 2 \\ 3 \end{pmatrix}$. Label this P.

c Draw the image of triangle ABC after a translation with vector $\begin{pmatrix} -1 \\ 2 \end{pmatrix}$. Label this Q.

d Draw the image of triangle ABC after a translation with vector $\begin{pmatrix} 3 \\ -2 \end{pmatrix}$. Label this R.

e Draw the image of triangle ABC after a translation with vector $\begin{pmatrix} -2 \\ -4 \end{pmatrix}$. Label this S.

5 Using your diagram from question **4**, use vectors to describe the following translations.

a P to Q   **b** Q to R   **c** R to S   **d** S to P

e R to P   **f** S to Q   **g** R to Q   **h** P to S

6 Take a 10 × 10 grid and draw the triangle with coordinates A(0, 0), B(1, 0) and C(0, 1). How many different translations are there that use integer values only and will move the triangle ABC to somewhere in the grid? (Do not draw them all.)

Reflections

In this section you will learn how to:

- reflect a 2-D shape in a mirror line

Key words

image
mirror line
object
reflect
reflection

A **reflection** is a transformation of a 2-D shape so that it becomes the mirror **image** of itself.

Notice that each point on the image is the same perpendicular distance from the **mirror line** as the corresponding point on the **object**.

So, if you could 'fold' the whole diagram along the mirror line, every point on the object would coincide with its reflection.

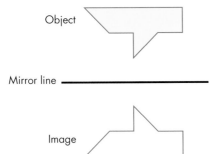

EXAMPLE 5

a **Reflect** the triangle ABC in the *x*-axis. Label the image P.

b Reflect the triangle ABC in the *y*-axis. Label the image Q.

a The mirror line is the *x*-axis. So, each vertex on triangle P will be the same distance from the *x*-axis as the corresponding vertex on the object.

b The mirror line is the *y*-axis. So, each vertex on triangle Q will be the same distance from the *y*-axis as the corresponding vertex on the object.

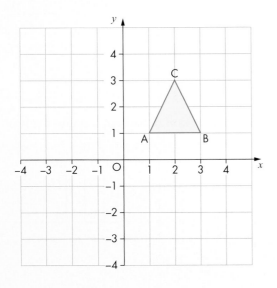

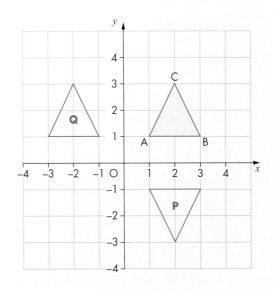

EXERCISE 19D

1 Copy each shape onto squared paper and draw its image after a reflection in the given mirror line.

a
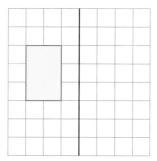

b
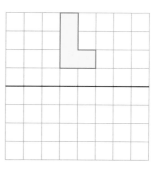

c
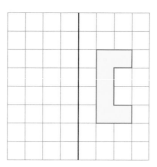

d
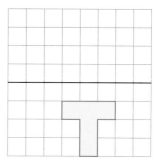

2 Copy these figures onto squared paper and then draw the reflection of each in the given mirror line.

a
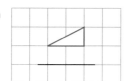

b

c
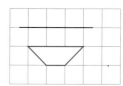

d
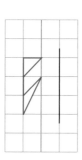

e
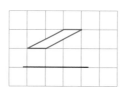

f
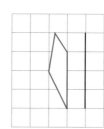

g
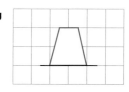

3 Copy these figures onto squared paper and then draw the reflection of each in the given mirror line.

a
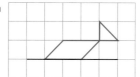

b
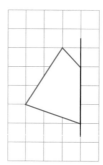

c
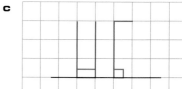

4 Copy this diagram onto squared paper.

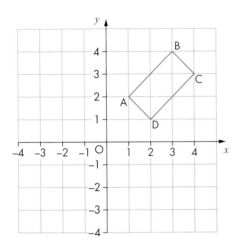

a Reflect the rectangle ABCD in the *x*-axis. Label the image R.

b Reflect the rectangle ABCD in the *y*-axis. Label the image S.

c What special name is given to figures that are exactly the same shape and size?

5 **a** Draw a coordinate grid with $-5 \leqslant x \leqslant 5$ and $-5 \leqslant y \leqslant 5$.

b Draw the triangle with coordinates A(1, 1), B(3, 1) and C(4, 5).

c Reflect triangle ABC in the *x*-axis. Label the image P.

d Reflect triangle P in the *y*-axis. Label the image Q.

e Reflect triangle Q in the *x*-axis. Label the image R.

f Describe the reflection that will transform triangle ABC onto triangle R.

6 Copy this diagram onto squared paper.

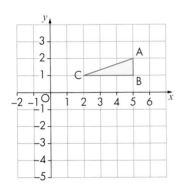

HINTS AND TIPS

Remember that *x*-lines are parallel to the *y*-axis and *y*-lines are parallel to the *x*-axis.

a Reflect triangle ABC in the line $x = 2$. Label the image X.

b Reflect triangle ABC in the line $y = -1$. Label the image Y.

D

 Draw these figures on squared paper and then draw the reflection of each in the given mirror line.

a 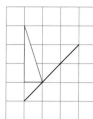 **b** 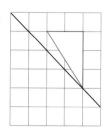 **c**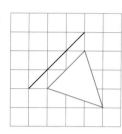

8 Draw these figures on squared paper and then draw the reflection of each in the given mirror line.

a 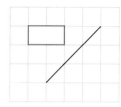 **b** 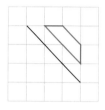 **c**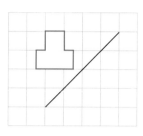

C

9 **a** Draw a pair of axes and the lines $y = x$ and $y = -x$, as shown below.

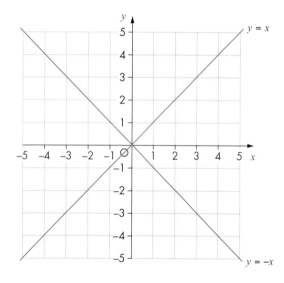

b Draw the triangle with coordinates A(2, 1), B(5, 1) and C(5, 3).

c Draw the reflection of triangle ABC in the x-axis and label the image P.

d Draw the reflection of triangle P in the line $y = -x$ and label the image Q.

e Draw the reflection of triangle Q in the y-axis and label the image R.

f Draw the reflection of triangle R in the line $y = x$ and label the image S.

g Draw the reflection of triangle S in the x-axis and label the image T.

h Draw the reflection of triangle T in the line $y = -x$ and label the image U.

i Draw the reflection of triangle U in the y-axis and label the image W.

j What single reflection will move triangle W to triangle ABC?

10 a Repeat the steps of question **9** but start with any shape you like.

b Is your answer to part **j** the same as before?

c Would your answer to part **j** always be the same no matter what shape you started with?

19.5 Rotations

In this section you will learn how to:
● rotate a 2-D shape about a point

Key words
angle of rotation
anticlockwise
centre of rotation
clockwise
image
object
rotate
rotation

A **rotation** transforms a 2-D shape to a new position by turning it about a fixed point called the **centre of rotation**.

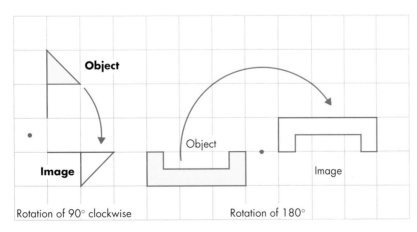

Rotation of 90° clockwise   Rotation of 180°

Note:

- The turn is called the **angle of rotation** and the direction is expressed as **clockwise** or **anticlockwise**.

- The position of the centre of rotation is always specified.

- The angles of rotation that occur in GCSE examinations are a $\frac{1}{4}$ turn or 90°, a $\frac{1}{2}$ turn or 180° and a $\frac{3}{4}$ turn or 270°.

- The rotations 180° clockwise and 180° anticlockwise are the same.

EXAMPLE 6

Draw the **image** of this shape after it has been rotated through 90° clockwise about the point X.

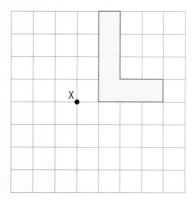

Using tracing paper is always the easiest way of tackling rotations.

First trace the **object** shape and fix the centre of rotation with a pencil point. Then **rotate** the tracing paper through 90° clockwise.

The tracing now shows the position of the image.

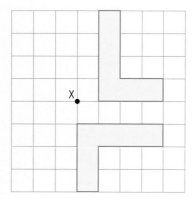

EXERCISE 19E

1 Copy each of these diagrams onto squared paper. Draw each image, using the given rotation about the centre of rotation, X.

a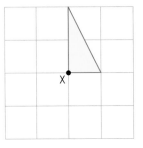

$\frac{1}{2}$ turn

b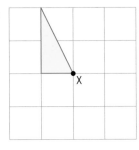

$\frac{1}{4}$ turn clockwise

c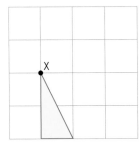

$\frac{1}{4}$ turn anticlockwise

d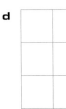

$\frac{3}{4}$ turn clockwise

2 Copy each of these diagrams onto squared paper. Draw each image, using the given rotation about the centre of rotation, X.

a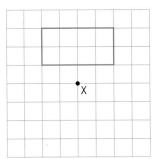

$\frac{1}{2}$ turn

b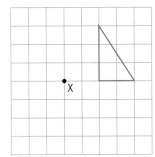

$\frac{1}{4}$ turn clockwise

c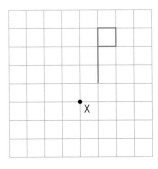

$\frac{1}{4}$ turn anticlockwise

d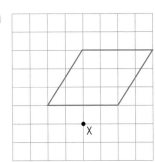

$\frac{3}{4}$ turn clockwise

D

3 Copy this diagram onto squared paper.

a Rotate the shape through 90° clockwise about the origin O. Label the image P.

b Rotate the shape through 180° clockwise about the origin O. Label the image Q.

c Rotate the shape through 270° clockwise about the origin O. Label the image R.

d What rotation takes R back to the original shape?

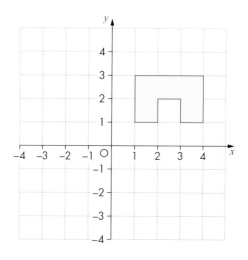

4 Copy this diagram onto squared paper.

a Write down the coordinates of the triangle ABC.

b Rotate the triangle ABC through 90° clockwise about the origin O. Label the image S.
Write down the coordinates of triangle S.

c Rotate the triangle ABC through 180° clockwise about the origin O. Label the image T.
Write down the coordinates of triangle T.

d Rotate the triangle ABC through 270° clockwise about the origin O. Label the image U.
Write down the coordinates of triangle U.

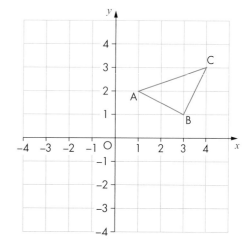

e What do you notice about the coordinates of the four triangles?

5 On squared paper, copy these shapes and their centres of rotation.

a

b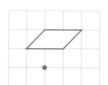

c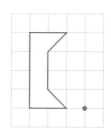

d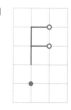

a Rotate each shape about its centre of rotation as follows.

i first by 90° anticlockwise

ii then by a further 180°

b Describe, in each case, the transformation that would take the original shape to the final image.

6 Copy this diagram onto squared paper.

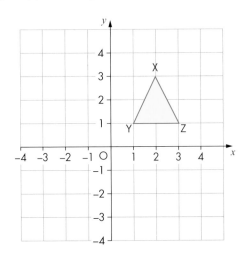

a Rotate triangle XYZ through 90° anticlockwise about the point (1, –2). Label the image P.

b Reflect triangle P in the *x*-axis. Label this triangle Q.

c Describe the transformation that maps triangle Q onto triangle XYZ.

7 **a** Draw a pair of axes where both the *x*- and *y*-values are from –5 to 5.

b Draw the triangle with vertices A(2, 1), B(3, 1) and C(3, 5).

c Reflect triangle ABC in the *x*-axis, then reflect the image in the *y*-axis. Label the final position A'B'C'.

d Describe the transformation that maps triangle ABC onto triangle A'B'C'.

e Will this always happen no matter what shape you start with?

f Will this still happen if you reflect in the *y*-axis first, then reflect in the *x*-axis?

19.6 Enlargements

In this section you will learn how to:
● enlarge a 2-D shape by a scale factor

Key words
centre of enlargement
enlarge
enlargement
image
object
scale factor

An **enlargement** is a transformation that changes the size of a 2-D shape to give a similar **image**. It always has a **centre of enlargement** and a **scale factor**.

The length of each side of the enlarged shape will be:

length of each side of the **object** × scale factor

The distance of each image point on the enlargement from the centre of enlargement will be:

distance of original point from centre of enlargement × scale factor

EXAMPLE 7

Enlarge the object triangle ABC by a scale factor 3 about O to give the image triangle A'B'C'.

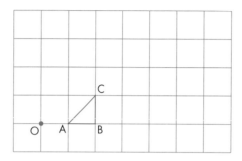

The image triangle A'B'C' is shown below.

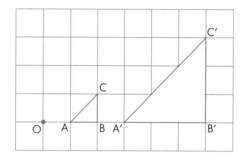

Note

- The length of each side on the enlarged triangle A'B'C' is three times the corresponding length of each side on the original triangle, so that the sides are in the ratio 1 : 3.

- The distance of any point on the enlarged triangle from the centre of enlargement is three times the corresponding distance from the original triangle.

There are two distinct ways to **enlarge** a shape: the ray method and the coordinate method.

Ray method

This is the *only* way to construct an enlargement when the diagram is not on a grid. The following example shows how to enlarge a triangle ABC by scale factor 3 about a centre of enlargement O by the ray method.

Coordinate method

Triangle A'B'C' is an enlargement of triangle ABC by scale factor 2, with the origin, O, as the centre of enlargement.

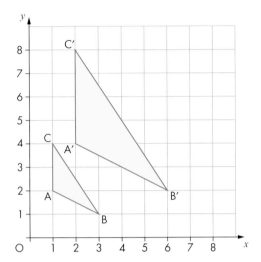

The coordinates of A are (1, 2) and the coordinates of A' are (2, 4). Notice that the coordinates of A' are the coordinates of A multiplied by 2, which is the scale factor of enlargement.

Check that the same happens for the other vertices.

This is a useful method for enlarging shapes on a coordinate grid, when the origin, O, is the centre of enlargement.

EXAMPLE 9

Enlarge the square by scale factor 3, using the origin as the centre of enlargement.

The coordinates of the original square are (1, 1), (2, 1), (2, 2) and (1, 2).

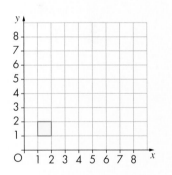

The enlarged square will have these coordinates multiplied by 3.

The coordinates are, therefore, (3, 3), (6, 3), (6, 6) and (3, 6), as shown on the diagram.

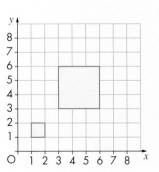

Note: This only works for enlargements centred on the origin. It is not always the case that the origin is the centre of enlargement. Always read the question carefully.

EXAMPLE 10

Counting squares

Enlarge triangle ABC by a scale factor 2, with the point P(O, 1) as the centre of enlargement.

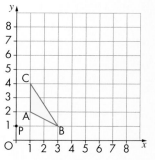

The point A is one square right and one square up from P. As the scale factor is 2, mark A'
two squares right and two squares up from P (2 × 1 = 2).

The point B is three squares right from P, so mark B' six squares right from P (2 × 3 = 6).

The point C is one square right and three squares up from P, so mark C' two squares right and six squares up from P (2 × 1 = 2, 2 × 3 = 6).

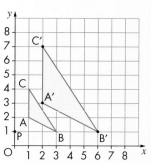

EXERCISE 19F

D

1 Copy each of these figures with its centre of enlargement. Then enlarge it by the given scale factor, using the ray method.

a

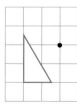

Scale factor 2

b

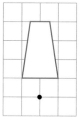

Scale factor 3

c

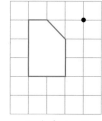

Scale factor 2

d

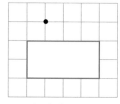

Scale factor 3

2 Copy each of these diagrams onto squared paper and enlarge it by scale factor 2, using the origin as the centre of enlargement.

a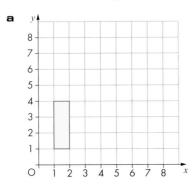

b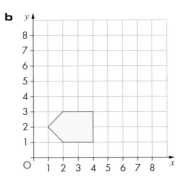

c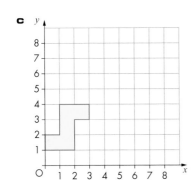

3 Copy each of these diagrams onto squared paper and enlarge it by scale factor 2, using the given centre of enlargement.

a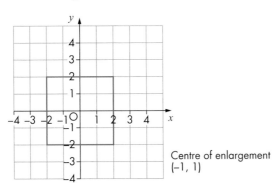

Centre of enlargement
(−1, 1)

b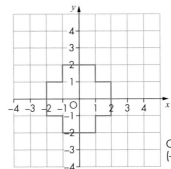

Centre of enlargement
(−2, −3)

4 **a** Draw a triangle ABC on squared paper.

b Mark four different centres of enlargement on your diagram:

one above your triangle
one to the left of your triangle

one below your triangle
one to the right of your triangle

c From each centre of enlargement, draw an enlargement by scale factor 2.

d What do you notice about each enlarged shape?

5 'Strange but True'... you can have an enlargement in mathematics that is actually smaller than the original shape! This happens when you 'enlarge' a shape by a fractional scale factor. For example, triangle ABC on the right has been enlarged by scale factor $\frac{1}{2}$ about the centre of enlargement, O, to give the image triangle A'B'C'.

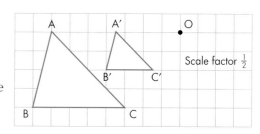

Enlarge the shape below by scale factor $\frac{1}{2}$ about the centre of enlargement, O.

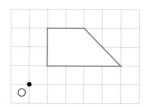

6 Copy this diagram onto squared paper.

a Enlarge the rectangle A by scale factor $\frac{1}{3}$ about the point (–2, 1). Label the image B.

b Write down the ratio of the lengths of the sides of rectangle A to the lengths of the sides of rectangle B.

c Work out the ratio of the perimeter of rectangle A to the perimeter of rectangle B.

d Work out the ratio of the area of rectangle A to the area of rectangle B.

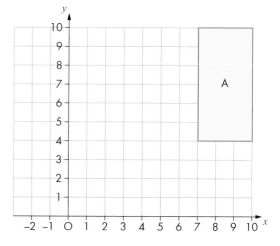

7 a i On squared paper draw a rectangle, label it ABCD

ii Draw enlargements of ABCD

scale factor 2, label $A_2B_2C_2D_2$

scale factor 3, label $A_3B_3C_3D_3$

scale factor 4, label $A_4B_4C_4D_4$

iii Copy and complete the table below, simplify any fractions.

Shape	SF	Perimeter	Ratio of perimeters	Area	Ratio of areas
ABCD	1	?		?	
$A_2B_2C_2D_2$	2	?	$\dfrac{ABCD}{A_2B_2C_2D_2}$ = ?	?	$\dfrac{ABCD}{A_2B_2C_2D_2}$ = ?
$A_3B_3C_3D_3$	3	?	$\dfrac{ABCD}{A_3B_3C_3D_3}$ = ?	?	$\dfrac{ABCD}{A_3B_3C_3D_3}$ = ?
$A_4B_4C_4D_4$	4	?	$\dfrac{ABCD}{A_4B_4C_4D_4}$ = ?	?	$\dfrac{ABCD}{A_4B_4C_4D_4}$ = ?

iv What do you notice about the above ratios?

b Investigate the ratios of perimeter, area and volume when you enlarge any cuboid.

1 The grid shows six shapes A, B, C, D, E and F.

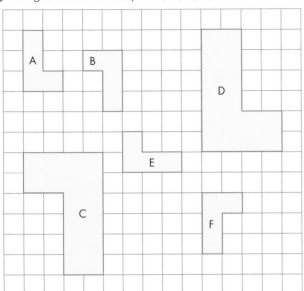

Write down the letters of the shapes that are congruent to shape A.

2

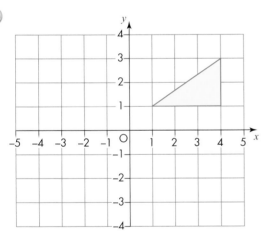

Copy the diagram on to squared paper.

a Draw the reflection of the shaded triangle in the *x*-axis.

b Rotate the shaded triangle 90° anticlockwise about the point O. Label it B.

3 The vertices of triangle T are (1, 1), (1, 2) and (3, 1).

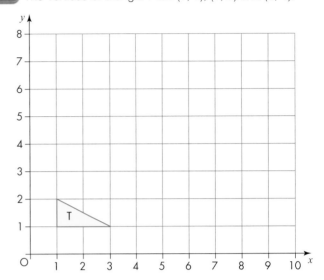

Copy the diagram onto squared paper.

Enlarge triangle T by scale factor 3, with (0, 0) as the centre of enlargement.

4 The diagram shows two identical shapes, A and B.

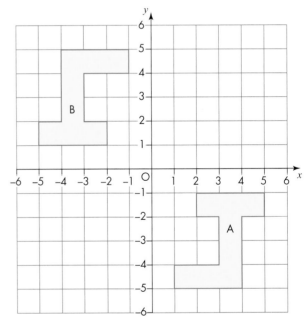

Describe fully the *single* transformation that takes shape A to shape B.

5 Copy this diagram onto squared paper.

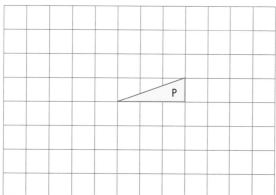

a Translate shape P 3 squares to the left and 2 squares down.

Copy this diagram onto squared paper.

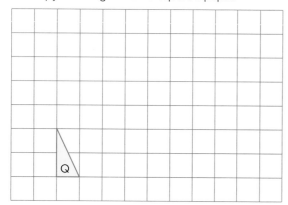

b Enlarge shape Q by a scale factor of 2.

Edexcel, Question 7, Paper 11A Foundation, March 2004

6

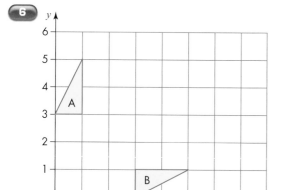

Triangle A and triangle B have been drawn on the grid.

Describe fully the single transformation which will map triangle A onto triangle B.

Edexcel, Question 3, Paper 5 Higher, June 2005

7

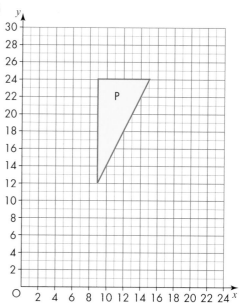

a Copy the grid and translate triangle P by the vector $\begin{pmatrix} 8 \\ -3 \end{pmatrix}$

Label the new triangle Q.

b On your grid enlarge triangle P by a scale factor of $\frac{1}{3}$, centre (0, 0). Label the new triangle R.

Edexcel, Question 2, Paper 10A Higher, March 2005

WORKED EXAM QUESTION

The grid shows several transformations of the shaded triangle.

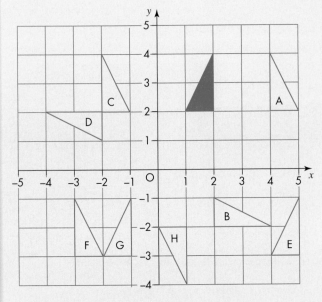

a   Write down the letter of the triangle:

   i   after the shaded triangle is reflected in the line $x = 3$

   ii   after the shaded triangle is translated by the vector $\begin{pmatrix} 3 \\ -5 \end{pmatrix}$

   iii   after the shaded triangle is rotated 90° anticlockwise about O.

b   Describe fully the *single* transformation that takes triangle F onto triangle E.

Solution

a   i   A: $x = 3$ is the vertical line passing through
      $x = 3$ on the x-axis.

   ii   E: move the triangle 3 squares to the right and 5 squares down.

   iii   D: use tracing paper to help when rotating a shape.

b   A reflection in the line $x = 1$, the vertical mirror line passes through $x = 1$ on the x-axis.

451

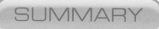
GRADE YOURSELF

G Able to recognise congruent shapes

E Know how to tessellate a 2-D shape

E Able to reflect a 2-D shape in the x-axis or the y-axis

D Able to translate a 2-D shape

D Able to reflect a 2-D shape in a line $x = a$ or $y = b$

D Able to rotate a 2-D shape about the origin

D Able to enlarge a 2-D shape by a whole number scale factor

C Able to translate a 2-D shape by a vector

C Able to reflect a 2-D shape in the line $y = x$ or $y = -x$

C Able to rotate a 2-D shape about any point

C Able to enlarge a 2-D shape by a fractional scale factor

C Able to enlarge a 2-D shape about any point

What you should know now

- How to recognise congruent shapes
- How to tessellate a 2-D shape
- How to translate a 2-D shape
- How to reflect a 2-D shape
- How to rotate a 2-D shape
- How to enlarge a 2-D shape

Constructions

1 Constructing triangles

2 Bisectors

3 Loci

This chapter will show you ...

- how to do accurate constructions
- how to draw the path of a point moving according to a rule

Visual overview

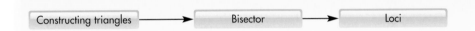

Constructing triangles → Bisector → Loci

What you should already know

- The names of common 3-D shapes
- How to measure lengths of lines
- That a line segment is part of a larger line
- How to measure angles with a protractor

Quick check

1 Measure the following lines.

a _____

b _____

c _____

2 Measure the following angles.

a

b

Constructing triangles

In this section you will learn how to:

- construct triangles using compasses, a protractor and a straight edge

Key words

angle
compasses
construct
side

There are three ways of **constructing** a triangle. Which one you use depends on what information you are given about the triangle.

All three sides known

EXAMPLE 1

Construct a triangle with **sides** that are 5 cm, 4 cm and 6 cm long.

- **Step 1:** Draw the longest side as the base. In this case, the base will be 6 cm, which you draw using a ruler. (The diagrams in this example are drawn at half-size.)

- **Step 2:** Deal with the second longest side, in this case the 5 cm side. Open the **compasses** to a radius of 5 cm (the length of the side), place the point on one end of the 6 cm line and draw a short faint arc, as shown here.

- **Step 3:** Deal with the shortest side, in this case the 4 cm side. Open the compasses to a radius of 4 cm, place the point on the other end of the 6 cm line and draw a second short faint arc to intersect the first arc, as shown here.

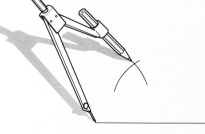

- **Step 4:** Complete the triangle by joining each end of the base line to the point where the two arcs intersect.

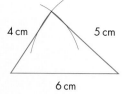

4 cm   5 cm

6 cm

Note: The arcs are construction lines and so are always drawn lightly. They *must* be left in an answer to an examination question to show the examiner how you constructed the triangle.

Two sides and the included angle known

EXAMPLE 2

Draw a triangle ABC, where AB is 6 cm, BC is 5 cm and the included **angle** ABC is 55°. (The diagrams in this example are drawn at half-size.)

- **Step 1:** Draw the longest side, AB, as the base. Label the ends of the base A and B.

  A ———————————— B

- **Step 2:** Place the protractor along AB with its centre on B and make a point on the diagram at the 55° mark.

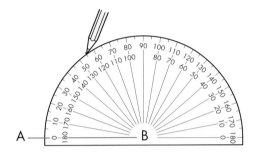

- **Step 3:** Draw a *faint* line from B through the 55° point. From B, using a pair of compasses, measure 5 cm along this line.

- Label the point where the arc cuts the line as C.

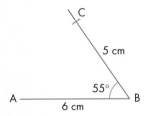

- **Step 4:** Join A and C and make AC and CB into bolder lines.

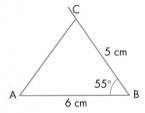

Note: The construction lines are drawn lightly and left in to demonstrate how the triangle has been constructed.

Two angles and a side known

When you know two angles of a triangle, you also know the third.

EXAMPLE 3

Draw a triangle ABC, where AB is 7 cm, angle BAC is 40° and angle ABC is 65°.

- **Step 1:** As before, start by drawing the base, which here has to be 7 cm. Label the ends A and B.

- **Step 2:** Centre the protractor on A and mark the angle of 40°. Draw a faint line from A through this point.

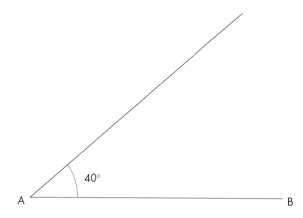

- **Step 3:** Centre the protractor on B and mark the angle of 65°. Draw a faint line from B through this point, to intersect the 40° line drawn from A. Label the point of intersection as C.

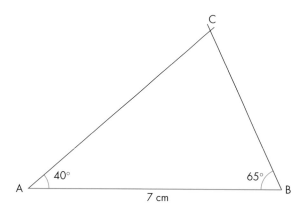

- **Step 4:** Complete the triangle by making AC and BC into bolder lines.

EXERCISE 20A

1 Draw the following triangles accurately and measure the sides and angles not given in the diagram.

> **HINTS AND TIPS**
>
> Always do a sketch if one is not given in the question.

a

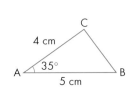

C
4 cm
A 35°
5 cm B

b

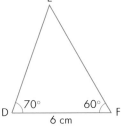

E
D 70° 60° F
6 cm

c

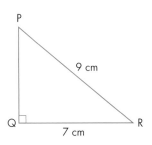

I
8 cm
4 cm
G 6 cm H

d

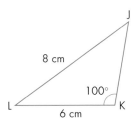

J
8 cm
100°
L 6 cm K

e

O
70°
55°
M 8 cm N

f

P
9 cm
Q 7 cm R

2 a Draw a triangle ABC, where AB = 7 cm, BC = 6 cm and AC = 5 cm.

> **HINTS AND TIPS**
>
> Sketch the triangle first.

b Measure the sizes of ∠ABC, ∠BCA and ∠CAB.

3 Draw an isosceles triangle that has two sides of length 7 cm and the included angle of 50°.

a Measure the length of the base of the triangle.

b What is the area of the triangle?

4 A triangle ABC has ∠ABC = 30°, AB = 6 cm and AC = 4 cm. There are two different triangles that can be drawn from this information.

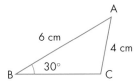

A
6 cm   4 cm
B 30° C

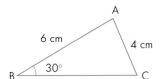

A
6 cm   4 cm
B 30° C

What are the two different lengths that BC can be?

5 Construct an equilateral triangle of side length 5 cm.

a Measure the height of the triangle.

b What is the area of this triangle?

6 Construct a parallelogram with sides of length 5 cm and 8 cm and with an angle of 120° between them.

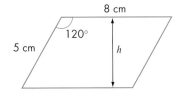

8 cm
120°
5 cm
h

a Measure the height of the parallelogram.

b What is the area of the parallelogram?

Bisectors

In this section you will learn how to:

- construct the bisector of lines and angles

Key words

angle bisector
bisect
line bisector
perpendicular
bisector

To **bisect** means to divide in half. So a bisector divides something into two equal parts.

- A **line bisector** divides a straight line into two equal lengths.

- An **angle bisector** is the straight line that divides an angle into two equal angles.

To construct a line bisector

It is usually more accurate to construct a line bisector than to measure its position (the midpoint of the line).

- **Step 1:** Here is a line to bisect.

- **Step 2:** Open your compasses to a radius of about three-quarters of the length of the line. Using each end of the line as a centre, and without changing the radius of your compasses, draw two intersecting arcs.

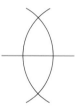

- **Step 3:** Join the two points at which the arcs intersect. This line is the **perpendicular bisector** of the original line.

To construct an angle bisector

It is much more accurate to construct an angle bisector than to measure its position.

- **Step 1:** Here is an angle to bisect.

- **Step 2:** Open your compasses to any reasonable radius that is less than the length of the shorter line. If in doubt, go for about 3 cm. With the vertex of the angle as centre, draw an arc through both lines.

- **Step 3:** With centres at the two points at which this arc intersects the lines, draw two more arcs so that they intersect. (The radius of the compasses may have to be increased to do this.)

- **Step 4:** Join the point at which these two arcs intersect to the vertex of the angle.

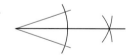

This line is the **angle bisector**.

To construct an angle of 60°

It is more accurate to construct an angle of 60° than to measure and draw it with a protractor.

- **Step 1:** Draw a line and mark a point on it.

- **Step 2:** Open the compasses to a radius of about 4 centimetres.
  Using the point as the centre, draw an arc that crosses the line and extends almost above the point.

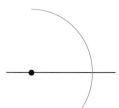

- **Step 3:** Keep the compasses set to the same radius.
  Using the point where the first arc crosses the line as a centre, draw another arc that intersects the first one.

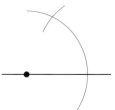

- **Step 4:** Join the original point to the point where the two arcs intersect.

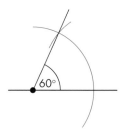

- **Step 5:** Use a protractor to check that the angle is 60°.

To construct a perpendicular from a point on a line

This construction will produce a perpendicular from a point A on a line.

- Open your compasses to about 2 or 3 cm.
  With point A as centre, draw two short arcs to intersect the line at each side of the point.

- Now extend the radius of your compasses to about
  4 cm. With centres at the two points at which the arcs intersect the line, draw two arcs to intersect at X above the line.

- Join AX.

  AX is perpendicular to the line.

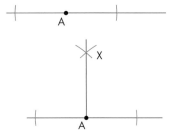

Note: If you needed to construct a 90° angle at the end of a line, you would first have to extend the line.

You could be even more accurate by also drawing two arcs *underneath* the line, which would give three points in line.

To construct a perpendicular from a point to a line

This construction will produce a perpendicular from a point A to a line.

- With point A as centre, draw an arc which intersects the line at two points.

- With centres at these two points of intersection, draw two arcs to intersect each other both above and below the line.

- Join the two points at which the arcs intersect. The resulting line passes through point A and is perpendicular to the line.

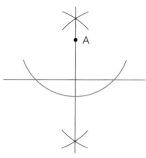

Examination note: When a question says *construct*, you must *only* use compasses – no protractor. When it says *draw*, you may use whatever you can to produce an accurate diagram. But also note, when constructing you may use your protractor to check your accuracy.

EXERCISE 20B

1 Draw a line 7 cm long and bisect it. Check your accuracy by seeing if each half is 3.5 cm.

2 Draw a circle of about 4 cm radius.

Draw a triangle inside the circle so that the corners of the triangle touch the circle.

Bisect each side of the triangle.

The bisectors should all meet at the same point, which should be the centre of the circle.

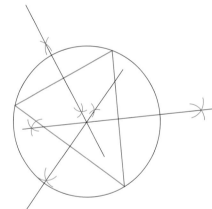

> **HINTS AND TIPS**
>
> Remember that examiners want to see your construction lines.

3 **a** Draw any triangle with sides that are between 5 cm and 10 cm.

b On each side construct the line bisector.

All your line bisectors should intersect at the same point.

c Using this point as the centre, draw a circle that goes through each vertex of the triangle.

4 Repeat question **2** with a different triangle and check that you get a similar result.

5 **a** Draw the following quadrilateral.

b On each side construct the line bisector. They all should intersect at the same point.

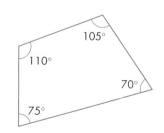

c Use this point as the centre of a circle that goes through the quadrilateral at each vertex. Draw this circle.

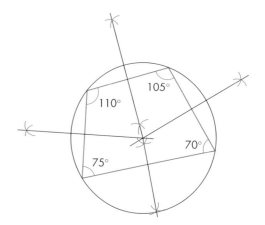

6 a Draw an angle of 50°.

b Construct the angle bisector.

c Check how accurate you have been by measuring each half. Both should be 25°.

7 Draw a circle with a radius of about 3 cm.

Draw a triangle so that the sides of the triangle are tangents to the circle.

Bisect each angle of the triangle.

The bisectors should all meet at the same point, which should be the centre of the circle.

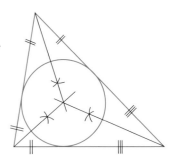

8 a Draw any triangle with sides that are between 5 cm and 10 cm.

b At each angle construct the angle bisector. All three bisectors should intersect at the same point.

c Use this point as the centre of a circle that just touches the sides of the triangle.

9 Repeat question **8** with a different triangle.

20.3 Loci

In this section you will learn how to:	Key words
• draw loci	loci
	locus

What is a locus?

A **locus** (plural **loci**) is the movement of a point according to a rule.

For example, a point that moves so that it is always at a distance of 5 cm from a fixed point, A, will have a locus that is a circle of radius 5 cm.

This is expressed mathematically as:

The locus of the point P is such that AP = 5 cm

Another point moves so that it is always the same distance from two fixed points, A and B.

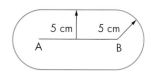

This is expressed mathematically as:

The locus of the point P is such that AP = BP

This is the same as the bisector of the line AB which you have met in Section 20.2.

Another point moves so that it is always 5 cm from a line AB.
The locus of the point P is given as a 'racetrack' shape.
This is difficult to express mathematically.

The three examples of loci just given occur frequently.

Imagine a grassy, flat field in which a horse is tethered to a stake by a rope that is 10 m long. What is the shape of the area that the horse can graze?

In reality, the horse may not be able to reach the full 10 m if the rope is tied round its neck but you can ignore fine details like that. The situation is 'modelled' by saying that the horse can move around in a 10 m circle and graze all the grass within that circle.

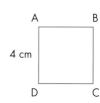

In this example, the locus is the whole of the area inside the circle.

This is expressed mathematically as:

The locus of the point P is such that AP ⩽ 10 m

EXERCISE 20C

1　A is a fixed point. Sketch the locus of the point P for these situations.

　　a　AP = 2 cm

　　b　AP = 4 cm

　　c　AP = 5 cm

> **HINTS AND TIPS**
>
> Sketch the situation before doing an accurate drawing.

2　A and B are two fixed points 5 cm apart. Sketch the locus of the point P for the following situations.

　　a　AP = BP

　　b　AP = 4 cm and BP = 4 cm

　　c　P is always within 2 cm of the line AB.

> **HINTS AND TIPS**
>
> If AP = BP this means the bisector of A and B.

3　**a**　A horse is tethered in a field on a rope 4 m long. Describe or sketch the area that the horse can graze.

　　b　The same horse is still tethered by the same rope but there is now a long, straight fence running 2 m from the stake. Sketch the area that the horse can now graze.

4　ABCD is a square of side 4 cm. In each of the following loci, the point P moves only inside the square. Sketch the locus in each case.

　　a　AP = BP

　　b　AP < BP

　　c　AP = CP

　　d　CP < 4 cm

　　e　CP > 2 cm

　　f　CP > 5 cm

5 One of the following diagrams is the locus of a point on the rim of a bicycle wheel as it moves along a flat road. Which is it?

a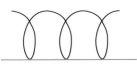

b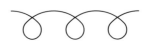

c

d

6 Draw the locus of the centre of the wheel for the bicycle in question **5**.

Practical problems

Most of the loci problems in your GCSE examination will be of a practical nature, as shown in the next three examples.

EXAMPLE 4

Imagine that a radio company wants to find a site for a transmitter. The transmitter must be the same distance from both Doncaster and Leeds, and within 20 miles of Sheffield.

In mathematical terms, this means you are concerned with the perpendicular bisector between Leeds and Doncaster, and the area within a circle of radius 20 miles from Sheffield.

The map, drawn to a scale of 1 cm = 10 miles, illustrates the situation and shows that the transmitter can be built anywhere along the thick green line.

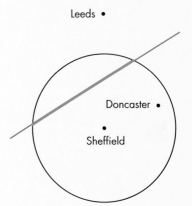

EXAMPLE 5

A radar station in Birmingham has a range of 150 km (that is, it can pick up any aircraft within a radius of 150 km). Another radar station in Norwich has a range of 100 km.

Can an aircraft be picked up by both radar stations at the same time?

The situation is represented by a circle of radius 150 km around Birmingham and another circle of radius 100 km around Norwich. The two circles overlap, so an aircraft could be picked up by both radar stations when it is in the overlap.

EXAMPLE 6

A dog is tethered by a rope, 3 m long, to the corner of a shed, 4 m by 2 m. What is the area that the dog can guard effectively?

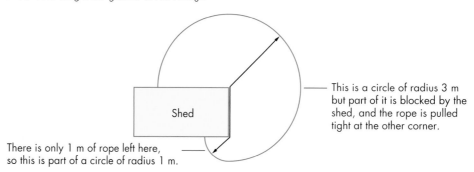

This is a circle of radius 3 m but part of it is blocked by the shed, and the rope is pulled tight at the other corner.

There is only 1 m of rope left here, so this is part of a circle of radius 1 m.

EXERCISE 20D

For questions **1** to **7**, you should start by sketching the picture given in each question on a 6 × 6 grid, each square of which is 2 cm by 2 cm. The scale for each question is given.

1 A goat is tethered by a rope, 7 m long, in a corner of a field with a fence at each side. What is the locus of the area that the goat can graze? Use a scale of 1 cm ≡ 1 m.

2 A horse in a field is tethered to a stake by a rope 6 m long. What is the locus of the area that the horse can graze? Use a scale of 1 cm ≡ 1 m.

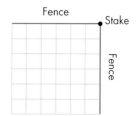

3 A cow is tethered to a rail at the top of a fence 6 m long. The rope is 3 m long. Sketch the area that the cow can graze. Use a scale of 1 cm ≡ 1 m.

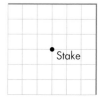

4 A horse is tethered to a stake near a corner of a fenced field, at a point 4 m from each fence. The rope is 6 m long. Sketch the area that the horse can graze. Use a scale of 1 cm ≡ 1 m.

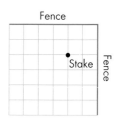

5 A horse is tethered to a corner of a shed, 2 m by 1 m. The rope is 2 m long. Sketch the area that the horse can graze. Use a scale of 2 cm ≡ 1 m.

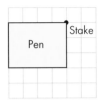

6 A goat is tethered by a 4 m rope to a stake at one corner of a pen, 4 m by 3 m. Sketch the area of the pen on which the goat cannot graze. Use a scale of 2 cm ≡ 1 m.

7 A puppy is tethered to a stake by a rope, 1.5 m long, on a flat lawn on which are two raised brick flower beds. The stake is situated at one corner of a bed, as shown. Sketch the area that the puppy is free to roam in. Use a scale of 1 cm ≡ 1 m.

8 The diagram, which is drawn to scale, A and B, shows two towns, A and B, which are 8 km apart.

A phone company wants to erect a mobile phone mast. It must be within 5 km of town A and within 4 km of town B.

Copy the diagram accurately.

Show the possible places where the mast could be.

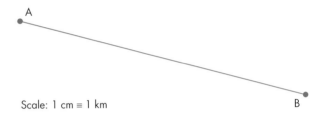

Scale: 1 cm ≡ 1 km

9 The map shows a field that is 100 m by 100 m.

There are two large trees in the field and a power line runs across it.

a Make an accurate scale drawing of the field, using a scale of 1 cm ≡ 10 m.

b Bernice wants to fly a kite.

She cannot fly the kite within 50 m of the power line.

She cannot fly the kite within 30 m of a tree.

Show the area where she can fly the kite.

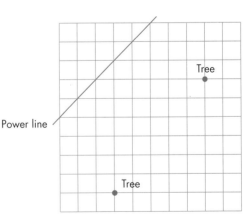

10 A radio station broadcasts from London on a frequency of 1000 kHz with a range of 300 km. Another radio station broadcasts from Glasgow on the same frequency with a range of 200 km.

a Sketch the area to which each station can broadcast.

b Will they interfere with each other?

c If the Glasgow station increases its range to 400 km, will they then interfere with each other?

Use a copy of this map to answer questions **10** to **16**.

For each question, trace the map and mark on those points that are relevant to that question.

11 The radar at Leeds airport has a range of 200 km. The radar at Exeter airport has a range of 200 km.

    a Will a plane flying over Glasgow be detected by the radar at Leeds?

    b Sketch the area where a plane can be picked up by both radars at the same time.

12 A radio transmitter is to be built according to the following rules.

    i It has to be the same distance from York and Birmingham.

    ii It must be within 350 km of Glasgow.

    iii It must be within 250 km of London.

> **HINTS AND TIPS**
>
> The same distance from York and Birmingham means on the bisector of the line joining York and Birmingham.

    a Sketch the line that is the same distance from York and Birmingham.

    b Sketch the area that is within 350 km of Glasgow and 250 km of London.

    c Show clearly the possible places at which the transmitter could be built.

13 A radio transmitter centred at Birmingham is designed to give good reception in an area greater than 150 km and less than 250 km from the transmitter. Sketch the area of good reception.

14 Three radio stations pick up a distress call from a boat in the Irish Sea. The station at Glasgow can tell from the strength of the signal that the boat is within 300 km of the station. The station at York can tell that the boat is between 200 km and 300 km from York. The station at London can tell that it is less than 400 km from London. Sketch the area where the boat could be.

15 One way to construct a regular polygon is inside a circle as illustrated below;

(i)	To construct a regular pentagon inside the circle, centre C	Fig. 1
(ii)	Divide the angle at the centre 360° by the number of sides, 5	360 ÷ 5 = 72
(iii)	Draw one line from centre, C, to the circumference. From there, continue to draw lines at 72° round the circle.	Fig. 2
(iv)	Join up the sides of the polygon from the points on the circumference where the lines have cut through.	Fig. 3

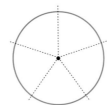

    Fig. 1   Fig. 2   Fig. 3

Use the above process to construct:

    a A regular hexagon in a circle with radius 3 cm.

    b A regular octagon in a circle with radius 3 cm.

    c A regular nonagon (nine sides) in a circle with radius 3.5 cm.

    d A regular decagon (ten sides) in a circle with radius 4 cm.

    e A regular heptagon (seven sides) in a circle with radius 3 cm.

1 The diagram shows a sketch of triangle ABC.

AB = 5.6 cm.

Angle A = 43°.

Angle B = 108°.

Make an accurate drawing
of triangle ABC.

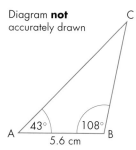

Diagram **not**
accurately drawn

Edexcel, Question 3, Paper 9A Intermediate, March 2005

2 Here is a sketch of a rhombus.

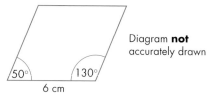

Diagram **not**
accurately drawn

The rhombus has a side of length 6 cm.
One angle of the rhombus is 50°.
Another angle of the rhombus is 130°.

Use a ruler and a protractor to make an accurate
drawing of the rhombus.

Edexcel, Question 8, Paper 8B Foundation, March 2004

3 The diagram below shows a plan of a room.
The dimensions of the room are 10 m and 8 m.

Make an accurate scale drawing of the room, using a
scale of 1 cm representing 1 m.

Two TV sockets are fitted along the walls.
One is at the point marked X. The other is at the point
marked Y.

A third TV socket is to be fitted along a wall.
It must be equidistant from X and Y.

Using ruler and compasses, find the position of the
new socket. Label it Z.

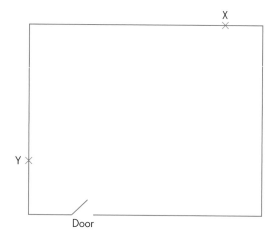

4 a Construct an angle of 60°.

b Copy this diagram and construct the perpendicular
bisector of the line joining the points A and B.

5 The diagram shows a
triangular prism.
The cross-section of
the prism is an
equilateral triangle.

a In the space below,
draw a sketch of a
net for the triangular prism.

b Use ruler and compasses to construct an equilateral
triangle with sides of length 6 centimetres.

You must show all construction lines.

Edexcel, Question 4, Paper 17 Intermediate, June 2005

6 In this question you
should use a ruler and
compasses.

a Copy the diagram and
bisect the angle ABC.

b Construct an angle of 60°.

c Bisect your 60° angle.

7 The diagram, which is drawn to scale, shows a garden
bordered by a house wall.

On the wall there is an electricity outlet (E) and a water
outlet (W).

Frank is installing a pond.

The centre of the pond must be within 4 metres of the
electricity outlet and within 6 metres of the water outlet.

Scale: 1 square ≡ 1 m²

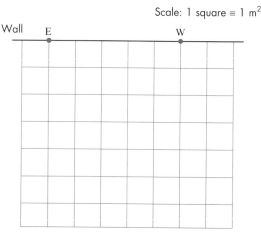

Find the area within which the centre of the pool may
be located.

WORKED EXAM QUESTION

Here is a sketch of a triangle. PR = 6.4 cm, QR = 7.7 cm and angle R = 35°.

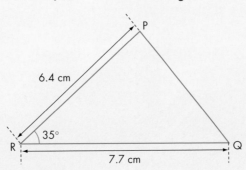

a   Make an accurate drawing of the triangle.

b   Measure the size of angle Q on your drawing.

Solution

a   Make an accurate drawing, using these steps.

Step 2: Measure the angle at R as 35°.
Draw a faint line at this angle

Step 3: Using a pair of compasses, draw an arc 6.4 cm long from R. Where this crosses the line from Step 2, make this P.

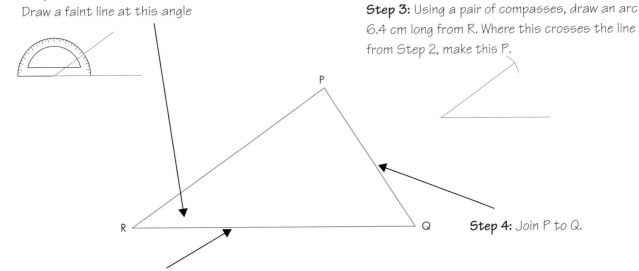

Step 4: Join P to Q.

Step 1: Draw the base as a line 7.7 cm long.
You can draw this and measure it with a ruler,
although a pair of compasses is more accurate.

b   Measure the angle Q. It is 56°.

The street

Bill the builder builds a street of 100 bungalows, with 50 on each side of the street. He builds them in blocks of five.

The bungalows at the ends of the blocks are called end-terraced and the other bungalows are called mid-terraced.

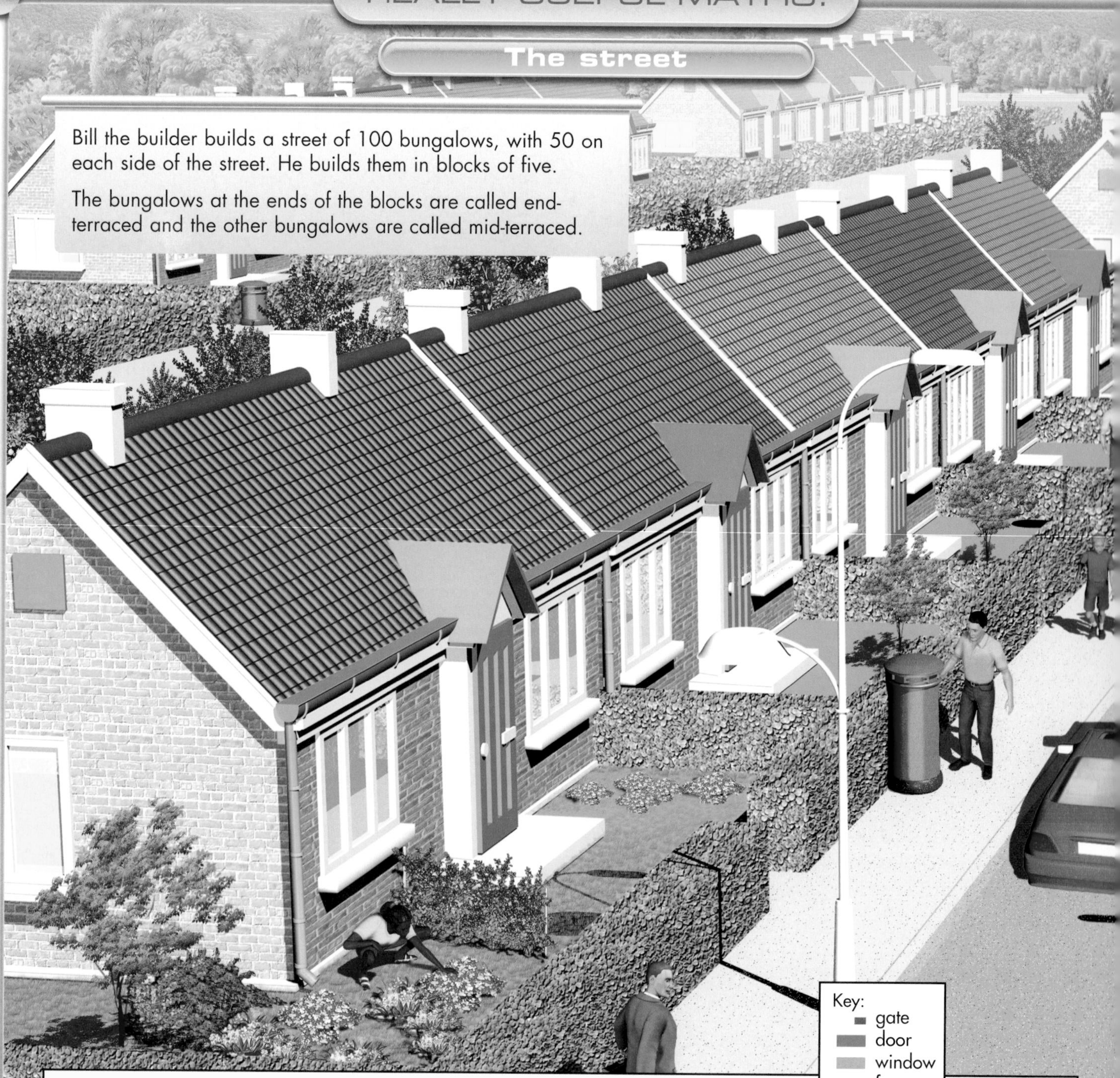

Here is the plan of one block of five.

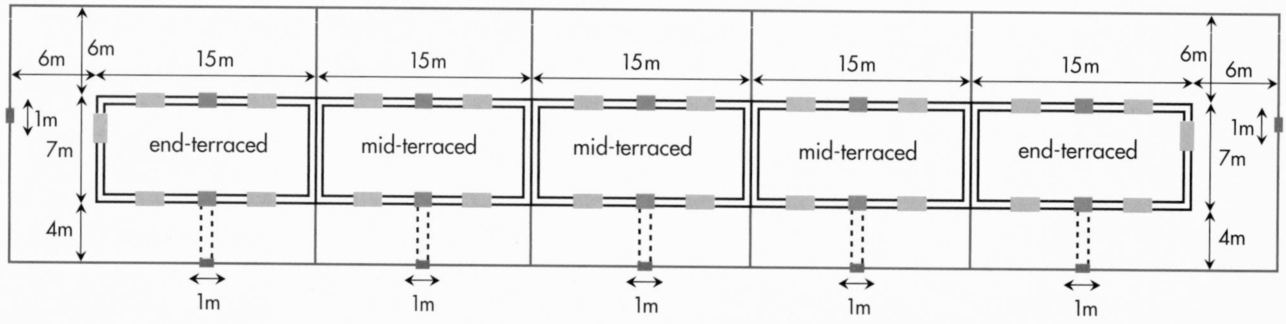
Key:
gate
door
window
fence
6m
6m
15m
15m
15m
15m
15m
6m
6m
1m
7m
4m
1m
7m
4m
end-terraced
mid-terraced
mid-terraced
mid-terraced
end-terraced
1m
1m
1m
1m
1m

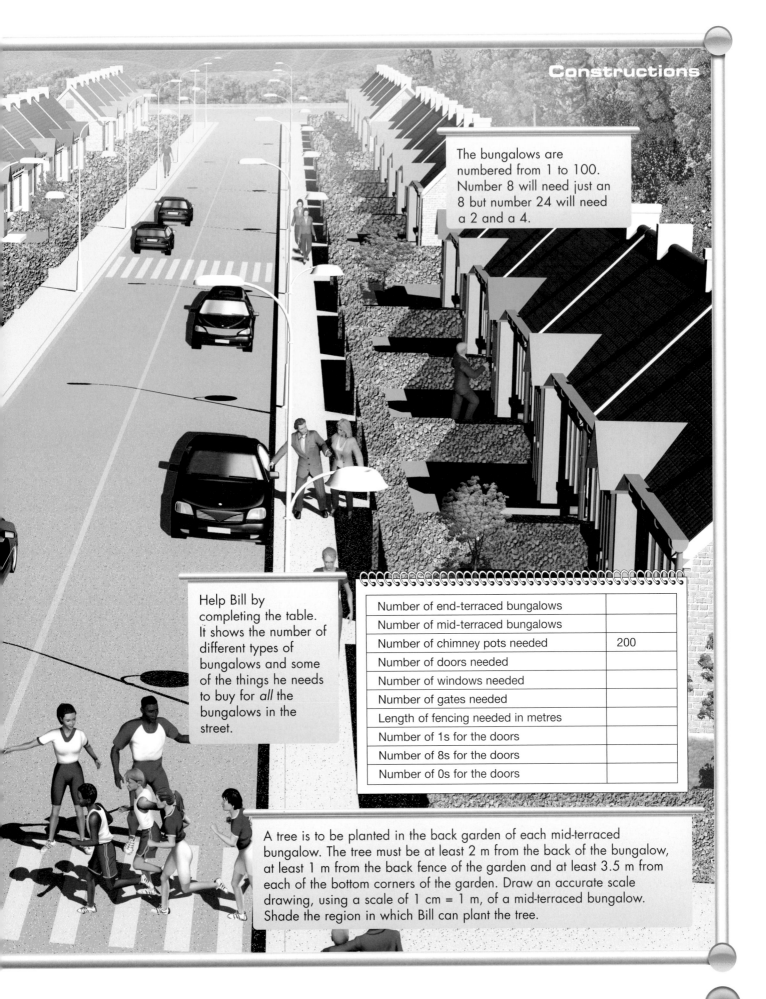

The bungalows are numbered from 1 to 100. Number 8 will need just an 8 but number 24 will need a 2 and a 4.

Help Bill by completing the table. It shows the number of different types of bungalows and some of the things he needs to buy for *all* the bungalows in the street.

Number of end-terraced bungalows	
Number of mid-terraced bungalows	
Number of chimney pots needed	200
Number of doors needed	
Number of windows needed	
Number of gates needed	
Length of fencing needed in metres	
Number of 1s for the doors	
Number of 8s for the doors	
Number of 0s for the doors	

A tree is to be planted in the back garden of each mid-terraced bungalow. The tree must be at least 2 m from the back of the bungalow, at least 1 m from the back fence of the garden and at least 3.5 m from each of the bottom corners of the garden. Draw an accurate scale drawing, using a scale of 1 cm = 1 m, of a mid-terraced bungalow. Shade the region in which Bill can plant the tree.

GRADE YOURSELF

D Able to construct diagrams accurately using compasses, a protractor and a straight edge

C Can construct line and angle bisectors, and draw the loci of points moving according to a rule

What you should know now

- How to draw scale diagrams and construct accurate diagrams, using mathematical instruments
- How to draw loci of sets of points

Units

1 Systems of measurement

2 Metric units

3 Imperial units

4 Conversion factors

This chapter will show you ...

- which units to use when measuring length, weight and capacity
- how to convert from one metric unit to another
- how to convert from one imperial unit to another
- how to convert from imperial units to metric units

Visual overview

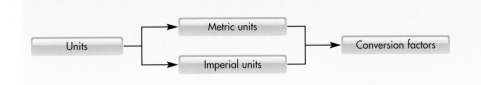

What you should already know

- The basic units used for measuring length, weight and capacity
- The approximate size of these units
- How to multiply or divide numbers by 10, 100 or 1000

Quick check

1 How many centimetres are there in one metre?

2 How many metres are there in one kilometre?

3 How many grams are there in one kilogram?

4 How many kilograms are there in one tonne?

Systems of measurement

In this section you will learn how to:

- decide which units to use when measuring length, weight and capacity

Key words

capacity
imperial
length
metric
volume
weight

There are two systems of measurement currently in use in Britain: the **imperial** system and the **metric** system.

The imperial system is based on traditional units of measurement, many of which were first introduced several hundred years ago. It is gradually being replaced by the metric system, which is used throughout Europe and in many other parts of the world.

The main disadvantage of the imperial system is that it has a lot of awkward conversions, such as 12 inches = 1 foot. The metric system has the advantage that it is based on powers of 10, namely 10, 100, 1000 and so on, so it is much easier to use when you do calculations.

It will be many years before all the units of the imperial system disappear, so you have to know units in both systems.

System	Unit	How to estimate it
	Length	
Metric system	1 metre	A long stride for an average person
	1 kilometre	Two and a half times round a school running track
	1 centimetre	The distance across a fingernail
Imperial system	1 foot	The length of an A4 sheet of paper
	1 yard	From your nose to your fingertips when you stretch out your arm
	1 inch	The length of the top joint of an adult's thumb
	Weight	
Metric system	1 gram	A 1p coin weighs about 4 grams
	1 kilogram	A bag of sugar
	1 tonne	A saloon car
Imperial system	1 pound	A jar full of jam
	1 stone	A bucket three-quarters full of water
	1 ton	A saloon car
	Volume/Capacity	
Metric system	1 litre	A full carton of orange juice
	1 centilitre	A full soup spoon
	1 millilitre	A full teaspoon is about 5 millilitres
Imperial system	1 pint	A full bottle of milk
	1 gallon	A half-full bucket of water

Volume and capacity

The term 'capacity' is normally used to refer to the volume of a liquid or a gas.

For example, when referring to the volume of petrol that a car's fuel tank will hold, people may say its capacity is 60 litres or 13 gallons.

In the metric system, there is an equivalence between the units of capacity and volume, as you can see on page 474.

EXAMPLE 1

Choose an appropriate unit for each of the following.

a your own height	**b** the thickness of this book	**c** the distance from home to school
d your own weight	**e** the weight of a coin	**f** the weight of a bus
g a large bottle of lemonade	**h** a dose of medicine	**i** a bottle of wine

a metres or centimetres	**b** millimetres	**c** kilometres
d kilograms	**e** grams	**f** tonnes
g litres	**h** millilitres	**i** centilitres

EXERCISE 21A

Decide the metric unit you would be most likely to use to measure each of the following.

1 The height of your classroom

2 The distance from London to Barnsley

3 The thickness of your little finger

4 The weight of this book

5 The amount of water in a fish tank

6 The weight of water in a fish tank

7 The weight of an aircraft

8 A spoonful of medicine

9 The amount of wine in a standard bottle

10 The length of a football pitch

11 The weight of your head teacher

12 The amount of water in a bath

13 The weight of a mouse

14 The amount of tea in a teapot

15 The thickness of a piece of wire

Estimate the approximate metric length, weight or capacity of each of the following.

16 This book (both length and weight)

17 The length of your school hall

18 The capacity of a milk bottle

19 A brick (length, width and weight)

20 The diameter of a 10p coin, and its weight

21 The distance from your school to Manchester

22 The weight of a cat

23 The amount of water in one raindrop

24 The dimensions of the room you are in

25 Your own height and weight

21.2 Metric units

In this section you will learn how to:
● convert from one metric unit to another

Key words
millimetre (mm)
centimetre (cm)
metre (m)
kilometre (km)
gram (g)
kilogram (kg)
tonne (t)
millilitre (ml)
centilitre (cl)
litre (l)

You should already know the relationships between these metric units.

Length	10 **millimetres** = 1 **centimetre**	**Weight**	1000 **grams** = 1 **kilogram**
	1000 millimetres = 100 centimetres = 1 **metre**		1000 kilograms = 1 **tonne**
	1000 metres = 1 **kilometre**		
Capacity	10 **millilitres** = 1 **centilitre**	**Volume**	1000 litres = 1 metre^3
	1000 millilitres = 100 centilitres = 1 **litre**		1 millilitre = 1 centimetre^3

Note the equivalence between the units of capacity and volume:

1 litre = 1000 cm^3 which means   1 ml = 1 cm^3

You need to be able to convert from one metric unit to another.

Since the metric system is based on powers of 10, you should be able easily to multiply or divide to change units. Work through the following examples.

EXAMPLE 2

To change *small* units to *larger* units, always *divide*.

Change:

a 732 cm to metres

732 ÷ 100 = 7.32 m

b 410 mm to centimetres

410 ÷ 10 = 41 cm

c 840 mm to metres

840 ÷ 1000 = 0.84 m

d 450 cl to litres

450 ÷ 100 = 4.5 l

EXAMPLE 3

To change *large* units to *smaller* units, always *multiply*.

Change:

a 1.2 m to centimetres

1.2 × 100 = 120 cm

b 0.62 cm to millimetres

0.62 × 10 = 6.2 mm

c 3 m to millimetres

3 × 1000 = 3000 mm

d 75 cl to millilitres

75 × 10 = 750 ml

EXERCISE 21B

Fill in the gaps using the information on page 476.

1 125 cm = … m

2 82 mm = … cm

3 550 mm = … m

4 2100 m = … km

5 208 cm = … m

6 1240 mm = … m

7 4200 g = … kg

8 5750 kg = … t

9 85 ml = … cl

10 2580 ml = … l

11 340 cl = … l

12 600 kg = … t

13 755 g = … kg

14 800 ml = … l

15 200 cl = … l

16 630 ml = … cl

17 8400 l = … m^3

18 35 ml = … cm^3

19 1035 l = … m^3

20 530 l = … m^3

21 34 km = … m

22 3.4 m = … mm

23 13.5 cm = … mm

24 0.67 m = … cm

25 7.03 km = … m

26 0.72 cm = … mm

27 0.25 m = … cm

28 0.64 km = … m

29 2.4 l = … ml

30 5.9 l = … cl

31 8.4 cl = … ml

32 5.2 m^3 = … l

33 0.58 kg = … g

34 3.75 t = … kg

35 0.94 cm^3 = … l

36 21.6 l = … cl

37 15.2 kg = … g

38 14 m^3 = … l

39 0.19 cm^3 = … ml

Imperial units

In this section you will learn how to:

● convert one imperial unit to another

Key words

inch (in)
foot (ft)
yard (yd)
mile (m)
ounce (oz)
pound (lb)
stone (st)
ton (T)
pint (pt)
gallon (gal)

You need to be familiar with imperial units that are still in daily use. The main ones are:

Length	12 **inches**	=	1 **foot**
	3 feet	=	1 **yard**
	1760 yards	=	1 **mile**
Weight	16 **ounces**	=	1 **pound**
	14 pounds	=	1 **stone**
	2240 pounds	=	1 **ton**
Capacity	8 **pints**	=	1 **gallon**

Examples of the everyday use of imperial measures are:

miles for distances by road

gallons for petrol (in conversation)

feet and inches for people's heights

pints for milk

pounds for the weight of babies (in conversation)

ounces for the weight of food ingredients in a food recipe

EXAMPLE 4

● To change *large* units to *smaller* units, always *multiply*.

● To change *small* units to *larger* units, always *divide*.

Change:

a 4 feet to inches

$4 \times 12 = 48$ inches

c 36 feet to yards

$36 \div 3 = 12$ yards

b 5 gallons to pints

$5 \times 8 = 40$ pints

d 48 ounces to pounds

$48 \div 16 = 3$ pounds

EXERCISE 21C

Fill in the gaps, using the information on this page 478.

1 2 feet = … inches   **2** 4 yards = … feet   **3** 2 miles = … yards

4 5 pounds = … ounces   **5** 4 stone = … pounds   **6** 3 tons = … pounds

7 5 gallons = … pints   **8** 4 feet = … inches   **9** 1 yard = … inches

10 10 yards = … feet   **11** 4 pounds = … ounces   **12** 60 inches = … feet

13 5 stone = … pounds   **14** 36 feet = … yards   **15** 1 stone = … ounces

16 8800 yards = … miles   **17** 15 gallons = … pints   **18** 1 mile = … feet

19 96 inches = … feet   **20** 98 pounds = … stones   **21** 56 pints = … gallons

22 32 ounces = … pounds   **23** 15 feet = … yards   **24** 11 200 pounds = … tons

25 1 mile = … inches   **26** 128 ounces = … pounds   **27** 72 pints = … gallons

28 140 pounds = … stones   **29** 15 840 feet = … miles   **30** 1 ton = … ounces

21.4 Conversion factors

In this section you will learn how to:
- use the approximate conversion factors between imperial units and metric units

Key words
conversion factor
imperial
metric

You need to know the approximate conversions between certain **imperial** units and **metric** units.

The **conversion factors** you should be familiar with are given below.

The symbol '≈' means 'is approximately equal to'.

Those you do need to know for your examination are in **bold** type.

Length	**1 inch**	≈ **2.5 centimetres**	**Weight**	1 pound	≈ 450 grams
	1 foot	≈ **30 centimetres**		**2.2 pounds**	≈ **1 kilogram**
	1 mile	≈ 1.6 kilometres			
	5 miles	≈ **8 kilometres**			
Capacity	1 pint	≈ 570 millilitres			
	1 gallon	≈ **4.5 litres**			
	$1\frac{3}{4}$ **pints**	≈ **1 litre**			

EXAMPLE 5

Use the conversion factors above to find the following approximations.

a Change 5 gallons into litres.

$5 \times 4.5 \approx 22.5$ litres

b Change 45 miles into kilometres.

45×1.6 kilometres ≈ 72 kilometres

c Change 5 pounds into kilograms.

$5 \div 2.2 \approx 2.3$ kilograms (rounded to 1 decimal place)

Note: An answer should be rounded when it has several decimal places, since it is only an approximation.

EXERCISE 21D

In questions **1** to **18**, fill in the gaps to find the approximate conversions for the following. Use the conversion factors on page 479

1 8 inches = ... cm

2 6 kg = ... pounds

3 30 miles = ... km

4 15 gallons = ... litres

5 5 pints = ... ml

6 45 litres = ... gallons

7 30 cm = ... inches

8 80 km = ... miles

9 11 pounds = ... kg

10 1710 ml = ... pints

11 100 miles = ... km

12 56 kg = ... pounds

13 40 gallons = ... litres

14 200 pounds = ... kg

15 1 km = ... yards

16 1 foot = ... cm

17 1 stone = ... kg

18 1 yard = ... cm

 19 Which is heavier, a tonne or a ton? Show your working clearly.

20 Which is longer, a metre or a yard? Show your working clearly.

21 The weight of 1 cm^3 of water is about 1 gram.

a What is the weight of 1 litre of water:

i in grams? **ii** in kilograms?

b What is the approximate weight of 1 gallon of water:

i in grams? **ii** in kilograms?

 22 While on holiday in France, I saw a sign that said: 'Paris 216 km'. I was travelling on a road that had a speed limit of 80 km/h.

a Approximately how many miles was I from Paris?

b What was the approximate speed limit in miles per hour?

c If I travelled at the top speed all the way, how long would it take me to get to Paris? Give your answer in hours and minutes.

1 Copy and complete this table. Write a sensible unit for each measurement.

	Metric	Imperial
The length of a football pitch	....	Yards
The weight of a new-born baby	....	Pounds
The length of this book	Centimetres	....

2 a Write down the name of a *metric* unit which is used to measure

  i the distance from London to Brighton

  ii the weight of a bar of soap.

 b i Change 240 millimetres to centimetres.

  ii Change 3.8 litres to millilitres.

  Edexcel, Question 1, Paper 8B Foundation, March 2003

3 a Work out the weight of 12 eggs. Give your answer in kilograms.

 b Work out the total weight of the flour and butter. Give your answer in grams.

  Edexcel, Question 3, Paper 8A Foundation, January 2004

 4 Two villages are 40 km apart.

 a Change 40 km into metres.

 b How many miles are the same as 40 km?

5 A garage has a diagram for converting gallons to litres.

Use the diagram to convert

 a 2 gallons to litres

 b 3.5 gallons to litres.

  Edexcel, Question 4d, Paper 2 Foundation, June 2003

6 A school canteen orders 30 litres of milk, but 30 pints of milk are delivered instead. Does the canteen have enough milk?

7 Brian is driving through Germany. The speed limit on the autobahn is 120 kilometres per hour. Change 120 km/h to miles per hour.

8 The diagram below shows the dimensions of a bookcase. The thickness of all the wood used is 30 mm.

24 cm	90 cm	90 cm	90 cm
28 cm			
36 cm			

 a Calculate the height of the bookcase, giving your answer in metres.

 b Calculate the length of the bookcase, giving your answer in metres

WORKED EXAM QUESTION

Beth weighs 10 stone 5 pounds and her height is 5 feet 4 inches.

a Estimate her weight, to the nearest kilogram.

b Estimate her height, to the nearest centimetre.

Solution

a 1 stone = 14 pounds, so she weighs 145 pounds.

 2.2 pounds ≈ 1 kg

 So, 145 pounds ≈ 145 ÷ 2.2 ≈ 66 kg

b 1 foot = 12 inches, so her height is 64 inches.

 2.5 cm ≈ 1 inch

 So, 64 inches ≈ 64 × 2.5 ≈ 160 cm

GRADE YOURSELF

F Able to convert from one metric unit to another

F Able to convert from one imperial unit to another

E Able to use the approximate conversion factors to change from imperial units to metric units

E Able to solve problems, using conversion factors

What you should know now

- How to convert from one metric unit to another
- How to convert from one imperial unit to another
- How to use conversion factors to change imperial units into metric units
- How to solve problems, using metric units and imperial units

Pie charts, scatter diagrams and surveys

1 Pie charts

2 Scatter diagrams

3 Surveys

4 Social statistics

This chapter will show you ...

- how to draw and interpret pie charts
- how to draw scatter diagrams and lines of best fit
- how to interpret scatter diagrams and the different types of correlation
- how to design a survey sheet and questionnaire
- some of the common features of social statistics

Visual overview

What you should already know

- How to draw and interpret pictograms, bar charts and line graphs
- How to draw and measure angles
- How to plot coordinates

Quick check

1 The bar chart shows how many boys and girls are in five Year 7 forms.

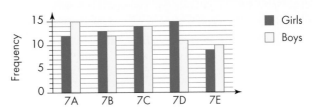

a How many pupils are in 7A?

b How many boys altogether are in the five forms?

2 Draw an angle of 72°.

3 Three points, A, B and C, are shown on the coordinate grid.

What are the coordinates of A, B and C?

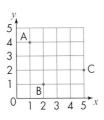

Pie charts

22.1

In this section you will learn how to:

● draw pie charts

Pictograms, bar charts and line graphs (see Chapter 6) are easy to draw but they can be difficult to interpret when there is a big difference between the frequencies or there are only a few categories. In these cases, it is often more convenient to illustrate the data on a **pie chart**.

In a pie chart, the whole of the data is represented by a circle (the 'pie') and each category of it is represented by a **sector** of the circle (a 'slice of the pie'). The **angle** of each sector is proportional to the frequency of the category it represents.

So, a pie chart cannot show individual frequencies, like a bar chart can, for example. It can only show proportions.

Sometimes the pie chart will be marked off in equal sections rather than angles. In these cases, the numbers are always easy to work with.

EXAMPLE 1

Twenty people were surveyed about their preferred drink. Their replies are shown in the table.

Drink	Tea	Coffee	Milk	Pop
Frequency	6	7	4	3

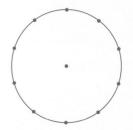

Show the results on the pie chart given.

You can see that the pie chart has ten equally spaced divisions.

As there are 20 people, each division is worth two people. So the sector for tea will have three of these divisions. In the same way, coffee will have $3\frac{1}{2}$ divisions, milk will have two divisions and pop will have $1\frac{1}{2}$ divisions.

The finished pie chart will look like the one in the diagram.

Note:

● You should always label the sectors of the chart (use shading and a separate key if there is not enough space to write on the chart).

● Give your chart a title.

Preferred drinks

EXAMPLE 2

In a survey on holidays, 120 people were asked to state which type of transport they used on their last holiday. This table shows the results of the survey. Draw a pie chart to illustrate the data.

Type of transport	Train	Coach	Car	Ship	Plane
Frequency	24	12	59	11	14

You need to find the angle for the fraction of 360° that represents each type of transport. This is usually done in a table, as shown below.

Type of transport	Frequency	Calculation	Angle
Train	24	$\frac{24}{120} \times 360° = 72°$	72°
Coach	12	$\frac{12}{120} \times 360° = 36°$	36°
Car	59	$\frac{59}{120} \times 360° = 177°$	177°
Ship	11	$\frac{11}{120} \times 360° = 33°$	33°
Plane	14	$\frac{14}{120} \times 360° = 42°$	42°
Totals	120		360°

Draw the pie chart, using the calculated angle for each sector.

Note:

- Use the frequency total (120 in this case) to calculate each fraction.

- Check that the sum of all the angles is 360°.

- Label each sector.

- The angles or frequencies do not have to be shown on the pie chart.

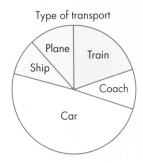

Type of transport

EXERCISE 22A

1 Copy the basic pie chart on the right and draw a pie chart to show each of the following sets of data.

a The favourite pets of 10 children.

Pet	Dog	Cat	Rabbit
Frequency	4	5	1

b The makes of cars of 20 teachers.

Make of car	Ford	Toyota	Vauxhall	Nissan	Peugeot
Frequency	4	5	2	3	6

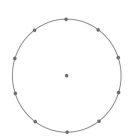

F

c The newspaper read by 40 office workers.

Newspaper	Sun	Mirror	Guardian	Times
Frequency	14	8	6	12

2 Draw a pie chart to represent each of the following sets of data.

a The number of children in 40 families.

No. of children	0	1	2	3	4
Frequency	4	10	14	9	3

HINTS AND TIPS

Remember to do a table as shown in the examples. Check that all angles add up to 360°.

b The favourite soap-opera of 60 students.

Programme	Home and Away	Neighbours	Coronation Street	Eastenders	Emmerdale
Frequency	15	18	10	13	4

c How 90 students get to school.

Journey to school	Walk	Car	Bus	Cycle
Frequency	42	13	25	10

3 Mariam asked 24 of her friends which sport they preferred to play. Her data is shown in this frequency table.

Sport	Rugby	Football	Tennis	Squash	Basketball
Frequency	4	11	3	1	5

Illustrate her data on a pie chart.

4 Andy wrote down the number of lessons he had per week in each subject on his school timetable.

Mathematics 5   English 5   Science 8   Languages 6
Humanities 6   Arts 4   Games 2

a How many lessons did Andy have on his timetable?

b Draw a pie chart to show the data.

c Draw a bar chart to show the data.

d Which diagram better illustrates the data? Give a reason for your answer.

5 In the run up to an election, 720 people were asked in a poll which political party they would vote for. The results are given in the table.

a Draw a pie chart to illustrate the data.

b Why do you think pie charts are used to show this sort of information during elections?

Conservative	248
Labour	264
Liberal-Democrat	152
Green Party	56

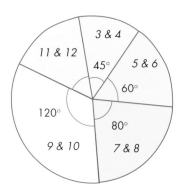

6 This pie chart shows the proportions of the different shoe sizes worn by 144 pupils in Y11 in a London school.

a What is the angle of the sector representing shoe sizes 11 and 12?

b How many pupils had a shoe size of 11 or 12?

c What percentage of pupils wore the modal size?

22.2 Scatter diagrams

In this section you will learn how to:

● draw, interpret and use scatter diagrams

Key words

correlation
line of best fit
negative
    correlation
no correlation
positive
    correlation
scatter
    diagram
variable

A **scatter diagram** (also called a scattergraph or scattergram) is a method of comparing two **variables** by plotting their corresponding values on a graph. These values are usually taken from a table.

In other words, the variables are treated just like a set of (*x*, *y*) coordinates. This is shown in the scatter diagram that follows, in which the marks scored in an English test are plotted against the marks scored in a mathematics test.

This graph shows **positive correlation**. This means that pupils who get high marks in mathematics tests also tend to get high marks in English tests.

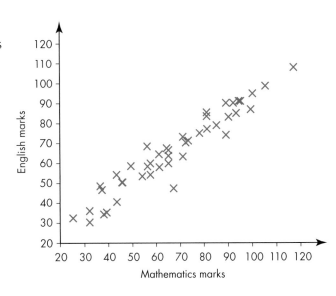

Correlation

There are different types of **correlation**. Here are three statements that may or may not be true.

- The taller people are, the wider their arm span is likely to be.

- The older a car is, the lower its value will be.

- The distance you live from your place of work will affect how much you earn.

These relationships could be tested by collecting data and plotting the data on a scatter diagram. For example, the first statement may give a scatter diagram like the first one below.

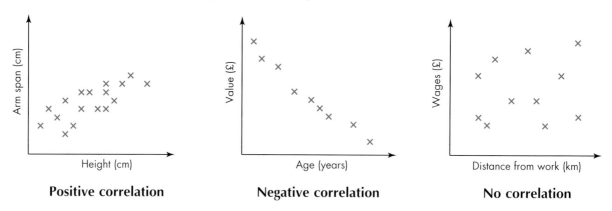

Positive correlation   **Negative correlation**   **No correlation**

This first diagram has **positive correlation** because, as one quantity increases, so does the other. From such a scatter diagram, you could say that the taller someone is, the wider their arm span.

Testing the second statement may give a scatter diagram like the middle one above. This has **negative correlation** because, as one quantity increases, the other quantity decreases. From such a scatter diagram, you could say that, as a car gets older, its value decreases.

Testing the third statement may give a scatter diagram like the one on the right, above. This scatter diagram has **no correlation**. There is no obvious relationship between the distance a person lives from their work and how much they earn.

EXAMPLE 3

The graphs below show the relationship between the temperature and the amount of ice-cream sold, and that between the age of people and the amount of ice-cream they eat.

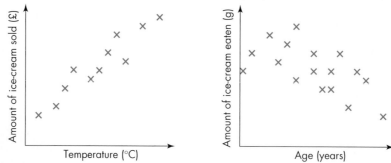

a Comment on the correlation of each graph.

b What does each graph tell you?

The first graph has positive correlation and tells us that, as the temperature increases, the amount of ice-cream sold increases.

The second graph has negative correlation and tells us that, as people get older, they eat less ice-cream.

Line of best fit

A **line of best** fit is a straight line that goes between all the points on a scatter diagram, passing as close as possible to all of them. You should try to have the same number of points on both sides of the line. Because you are drawing this line by eye, examiners make a generous allowance around the correct answer. The line of best fit for the scatter diagram on page 487 is shown below, left.

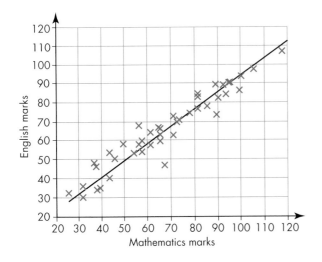
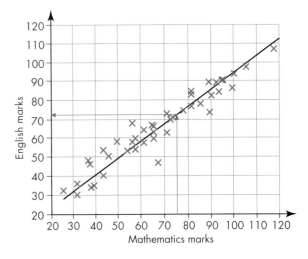

The line of best fit can be used to answer questions such as: "A girl took the mathematics test and scored 75 marks but was ill for the English test. How many marks was she likely to have scored?"

The answer is found by drawing a line up from 75 on the mathematics axis to the line of best fit and then drawing a line across to the English axis as shown in the graph above, right. This gives 73, which is the mark she is likely to have scored in the English test.

EXERCISE 22B

1 Describe the correlation of each of these four graphs.

a

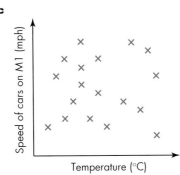

b

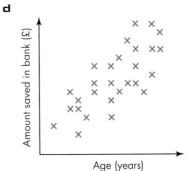

c

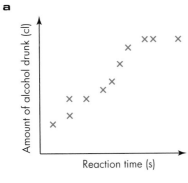

d

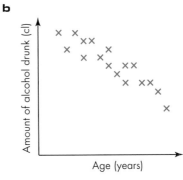

2 Write in words what each graph in question **1** tells you.

3 The table below shows the results of a science experiment in which a ball is rolled along a desk top. The speed of the ball is measured at various points.

Distance from start (cm)	10	20	30	40	50	60	70	80
Speed (cm/s)	18	16	13	10	7	5	3	0

  a Plot the data on a scatter diagram.   **b** Draw the line of best fit.

  c If the ball's speed had been measured at 5 cm from the start, what is it likely to have been?

  d How far from the start was the ball when its speed was 12 cm/s?

> **HINTS AND TIPS**
>
> Usually in exams axes are given and most, if not all, of the points are plotted.

4 The heights, in centimetres, of 20 mothers and their 15-year-old daughters were measured. These are the results.

Mother	153	162	147	183	174	169	152	164	186	178
Daughter	145	155	142	167	167	151	145	152	163	168
Mother	175	173	158	168	181	173	166	162	180	156
Daughter	172	167	160	154	170	164	156	150	160	152

  a Plot these results on a scatter diagram. Take the *x*-axis for the mothers' heights from 140 to 200. Take the *y*-axis for the daughters' heights from 140 to 200.

  b Is it true that the tall mothers have tall daughters?

5 The table below shows the marks for ten pupils in their mathematics and geography examinations.

Pupil	Anna	Beryl	Cath	Dema	Ethel	Fatima	Greta	Hannah	Imogen	Sitara
Maths	57	65	34	87	42	35	59	61	25	35
Geog	45	61	30	78	41	36	35	57	23	34

  a Plot the data on a scatter diagram. Take the *x*-axis for the mathematics scores and mark it from 20 to 100. Take the *y*-axis for the geography scores and mark it from 20 to 100.

  b Draw the line of best fit.

  c One of the pupils was ill when she took the geography examination. Which pupil was it most likely to be?

  d If another pupil, Kate, was absent for the geography examination but scored 75 in mathematics, what mark would you expect her to have got in geography?

  e If another pupil, Lina, was absent for the mathematics examination but scored 65 in geography, what mark would you expect her to have got in mathematics?

A form teacher carried out a survey of twenty pupils from his class and asked them to say how many hours per week they spent playing sport and how many hours per week they spent watching TV. This table shows the results of the survey.

Pupil	1	2	3	4	5	6	7	8	9	10
Hours playing sport	12	3	5	15	11	0	9	7	6	12
Hours watching TV	18	26	24	16	19	27	12	13	17	14

Pupil	11	12	13	14	15	16	17	18	19	20
Hours playing sport	12	10	7	6	7	3	1	2	0	12
Hours watching TV	22	16	18	22	12	28	18	20	25	13

a Plot these results on a scatter diagram. Take the *x*-axis as the number of hours playing sport and mark it from 0 to 20. Take the *y*-axis as the number of hours watching TV and mark it from 0 to 30.

b If you knew that another pupil from the form watched 8 hours of TV a week, would you be able to predict how long they spent playing sport? Explain why.

22.3 Surveys

In this section you will learn how to:

● conduct surveys
● ask good questions in order to collect reliable and valid data

Key words
leading question
primary data
questionnaire
response
secondary data
survey

A **survey** is an organised way of asking a lot of people a few, well-constructed questions, or of making a lot of observations in an experiment, in order to reach a conclusion about something. Surveys are used to test out people's opinions or to test a hypothesis. Data like this, that you have found yourself, is known as **primary data**. Data from other sources, such as libraries, the internet or a census, is known as **secondary data**.

Simple data collection sheet

If you need to collect some data to analyse, you will have to design a simple data collection sheet.

Look at this example: "Where do you want to go for the Y10 trip at the end of term – Blackpool, Alton Towers, The Great Western Show or London?"

You would put this question on the same day to a lot of Y10 students and enter their answers straight onto a data collection sheet, as below.

Place	Tally	Frequency
Blackpool	IIII IIII IIII IIII III	23
Alton Towers	IIII IIII IIII IIII IIII IIII IIII IIII IIII I	46
The Great Western Show	IIII IIII IIII	14
London	IIII IIII IIII IIII II	22

Notice how plenty of space is left for the tally marks and how the tallies are 'gated' in groups of five to make counting easier when the survey is complete.

This is a good, simple data collection sheet because:

● only one question is asked ("Where do you want to go?")

● all the possible venues are listed

● the answer from each interviewee can be easily and quickly tallied, and the next interviewee questioned.

Notice too that, since the question listed specific places, they must all appear on the data collection sheet. You would also lose marks in an examination if you just asked the open question: "Where do you want to go?"

Data sometimes needs to be collected to obtain **responses** for two different categories. The data collection sheet is then in the form of a simple two-way table.

EXAMPLE 4

The head of a school wants to find out how long his students spend doing homework in a week. He carries out a survey on 60 students. The two-way table shows the result.

	0–5 hours	0–10 hours	10–20 hours	More than 20 hours
Year 7				

This is not a good table as the categories overlap. A student who does 10 hours' work a week could tick any of two columns. Response categories should not overlap and there should be only one possible place to put a tick.

A better table would be:

	0 up to 5 hours	More than 5 and up to 10 hours	More than 10 and up to 15 hours	More than 15 hours
Year 7	ЖЖ II	ЖЖ		
Year 8	ЖЖ	ЖЖ II		
Year 9	III	ЖЖ II	II	
Year 10	III	ЖЖ	III	I
Year 11	II	IIII	IIII	II

This gives a more accurate picture of the amount of homework done in each year group.

Using your computer

Once the data has been collected for your survey, it can be put into a computer database. This allows the data to be stored and amended or updated at a later date if necessary.

From the database, suitable statistical diagrams can easily be drawn within the software and averages calculated for you. Your results can then be published in, for example, the school magazine.

EXERCISE 22C

1 "People like the supermarket to open on Sundays."

   a To see whether this statement is true, design a data collection sheet that will allow you to capture data while standing outside a supermarket.

   b Does it matter on which day you collect data outside the supermarket?

2 The school tuck shop wanted to know which types of chocolate it should order to sell – plain, milk, fruit and nut, wholenut or white chocolate.

   a Design a data collection sheet that you could use to ask the pupils in your school which of these chocolate types are their favourite.

HINTS AND TIPS
Include space for tallies.

   b Invent the first 30 entries on the chart.

3 What type of television programme do people in your age group watch the most? Is it crime, romance, comedy, documentary, sport or something else? Design a data collection sheet to be used in a survey of your age group.

4 On what do people of your age tend to spend their money? Is it sport, magazines, clubs, cinema, sweets, clothes or something else? Design a data collection sheet to be used in a survey of your age group.

5 Design two-way tables to show the following. Invent about 40 entries for each one.

HINTS AND TIPS
Make sure all possible responses are covered.

   a How students in different year groups travel to school in the morning.

   b The type of programme that different age groups prefer to watch on TV.

   c The favourite sport of boys and girls.

   d How much time students in different year groups spend on the computer in the evening.

Questionnaires

When you are putting together a **questionnaire**, you must think very carefully about the sorts of question you are going to ask to put together a clear, easy-to-use questionnaire.

Here are five rules that you should *always* follow.

- Never ask a **leading question** designed to get a particular response.

- Never ask a personal, irrelevant question.

- Keep each question as simple as possible.

- Include questions that will get a response from whomever is asked.

- Make sure the categories for the responses do not overlap and keep the number of choices to a reasonable number (six at the most).

The following questions are *badly constructed* and should *never* appear in any questionnaire.

✘ *What is your age?* This is personal. Many people will not want to answer. It is always better to give a range of ages such as:

☐ Under 15   ☐ 16–20   ☐ 21–30   ☐ 31–40   ☐ Over 40

✘ *Slaughtering animals for food is cruel to the poor defenceless animals. Don't you agree?* This is a leading question, designed to get a 'yes'. It is better ask an impersonal question such as:

Are you a vegetarian?   ☐ Yes   ☐ No

✘ *Do you go to discos when abroad?* This can be answered only by those who have been abroad. It is better to ask a starter question, with a follow-up question such as:

Have you been abroad for a holiday?   ☐ Yes   ☐ No

If 'Yes', did you go to a disco whilst you were away?   ☐ Yes   ☐ No

✘ *When you first get up in a morning and decide to have some sort of breakfast that might be made by somebody else, do you feel obliged to eat it all or not?* This question is too complicated. It is better to ask a series of shorter questions such as:

What time do you get up for school?   ☐ Before 7   ☐ Between 7 and 8   ☐ After 8

Do you have breakfast every day?   ☐ Yes   ☐ No

If 'No', on how many schooldays do you have breakfast?   ☐ 0   ☐ 1   ☐ 2   ☐ 3   ☐ 4   ☐ 5

A questionnaire is usually put together to test a hypothesis or a statement. For example: "People buy cheaper milk from the supermarket as they don't mind not getting it on their doorstep. They'd rather go out to buy it."

A questionnaire designed to test whether this statement is true or not should include these questions:

✓ *Do you have milk delivered to your doorstep?*
✓ *Do you buy cheaper milk from the supermarket?*
✓ *Would you buy your milk only from the supermarket?*

Once the data from these questions has been collected, it can be looked at to see whether or not the majority of people hold views that agree with the statement.

EXERCISE 22D

1 These are questions from a questionnaire on healthy eating.

    a *Fast food is bad for you. Don't you agree?*

      ☐ Strongly agree   ☐ Agree   ☐ Don't know

      Give two criticisms of the question.

    b *Do you eat fast food?*   ☐ Yes   ☐ No

      If 'Yes', how many times on average do you eat fast food?

      ☐ Once or less   ☐ 2 or 3 times   ☐ 4 or 5 times   ☐ More than 5 times

      Give two reasons why this is a good question.

2 This is a question from a survey on pocket money:

How much pocket money do you get each week?

☐ £0–£2   ☐ £0–£5   ☐ £5–£10   ☐ £10 or more

a Give a reason why this is not a good question.

b Rewrite the question to make it a good question.

3 Design a questionnaire to test the following statement.

People under sixteen do not know what is meant by all the jargon used in the business news on TV, but the over-twenties do.

4 *The under-twenties feel quite at ease with computers, while the over-forties would rather not bother with them. The twenty-to-forties always try to look good with computers.*

Design a questionnaire to test this statement.

5 Design a questionnaire to test the following hypothesis.

The older you get, the less sleep you need.

> **HINTS AND TIPS**
>
> Keep questions simple with clear response categories and no overlapping.

22.4 Social statistics

In this section you will learn about:
- how statistics are used in everyday life and what information the government needs about the population

Key words
margin of error
national census
polls
retail price index
social statistics
time series

This section will explain about **social statistics** and introduce some of the more common ones in daily use.

In daily life, many situations occur in which statistical techniques are used to produce data. The results of surveys appear in newspapers every day. There are many on-line **polls** and phone-ins that give people the chance to vote, such as in reality TV shows.

Results for these are usually given as a percentage with a **margin of error**, which is a measure of how accurate the information is.

Some common social statistics in daily use are briefly described on the next page.

General index of retail prices

This is also know as the **retail price index** (RPI) and it measures how much the daily cost of living increases (or decreases). One year is chosen as the base year and given an index number, usually 100. The corresponding costs in subsequent years are compared to this and given a number proportional to the base year, such as 103.

Note: The numbers do not represent actual values but just compare current prices to those in the base year.

Time series

Like the RPI, a **time series** measures changes in a quantity over time. Unlike the RPI, though, the actual values of the quantity are used. A time series might track, for example, how the exchange rate between the pound and the dollar changes over time.

National census

A **national census** is a survey of all people and households in a country. Data about categories such as age, gender, religion and employment status is collected to enable governments to plan where to allocate future resources. In Britain a national census is taken every ten years. The most recent census was in 2001.

EXERCISE 22E

 1 In 2000 the cost of a litre of petrol was 78p. Using 2000 as a base year, the price index of petrol for each of the next five years is shown in this table.

Year	2000	2001	2002	2003	2004	2005
Index	100	103	108	109	112	120
Price	78p					

Work out the price of petrol in each subsequent year. Give your answers to 1 decimal place.

2 The following is taken from the UK government statistics website.

In mid-2004 the UK was home to 59.8 million people, of which 50.1 million lived in England. The average age was 38.6 years, an increase on 1971 when it was 34.1 years. In mid-2004 approximately one in five people in the UK were aged under 16 and one in six people were aged 65 or over.

Use this extract to answer the following questions about the UK in 2004.

a How many of the population of the UK *did not* live in England?

b By how much had the average age increased since 1971?

c Approximately how many of the population were aged under 16?

d Approximately how many of the population were aged over 65?

3 The graph shows the exchange rate for the dollar against the pound for each month in 2005.

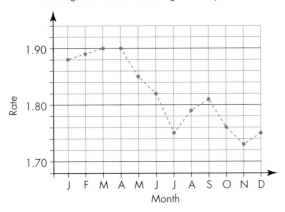

Exchange rate for the dollar against the pound, 2005

a What was the exchange rate in January?

b Between which two consecutive months did the exchange rate fall most?

c Explain why you could not use the graph to predict the exchange rate in January 2006.

4 The general index of retail prices started in January 1987, when it was given a base number of 100. In January 2006 the index number was 194.1.

If the 'standard weekly shopping basket' cost £38.50 in January 1987, how much would it have cost in January 2006?

5 The time series shows car production in Britain from November 2004 to November 2005.

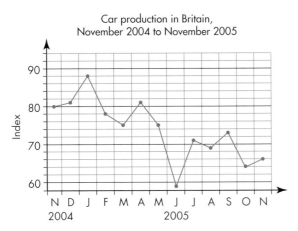

Car production in Britain, November 2004 to November 2005

a Why was there a sharp drop in production in July 2005?

b The average production over the first three months shown was 172 000 cars.

i Work out an approximate value for the average production over the last three months shown.

ii The base month for the index is January 2000 when the index was 100. What was the approximate production in January 2000?

1 A café recorded the different types of drinks sold one Saturday. Here are the results.

Drink	Percentage
Tea	35%
Coffee	22%
Soft drink	33%
Other	10%

a Copy and complete the bar chart to show these results.

b The café sold 300 drinks that day. How many of the drinks were coffee?

c The café did a similar count on another Saturday when they sold 240 drinks. The results are shown on the pie chart.

  i How many coffees did they sell?

  ii What is the probability that a person picked at random from this café had a drink of tea?

Give your answer as a fraction in its simplest form.

2 **a** The nationalities of 45 people on a coach were recorded.

Destination	Number of students
French	9
Spanish	12
Italian	6
Greek	10
American	8

Draw a clearly labelled pie chart to represent this information.

b What percentage of the 45 people were French?

3 Sandra carries out a survey of 90 Year 11 students. She asks them their favourite snack.

She draws this accurate pie chart.

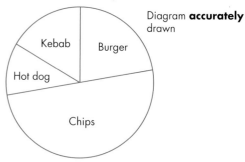

Diagram **accurately** drawn

Copy the table and use the pie chart to complete it.

Favourite snack in Year 11	Frequency	Angle
Burger	20	
Chips	45	180°
Hot dog		
Kebab		
Total	90	

Edexcel, Question 11, Paper 3 Intermediate, November 2004

4 The table gives information about the medals won by Austria in the 2002 Winter Olympic Games.

Medal	Frequency	
Gold	3	
Silver	4	
Bronze	11	

Draw an accurate pie chart to show this information.

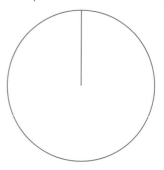

Edexcel, Question 5, Paper 4 Intermediate, June 2005

5 The table below shows how a number of men and women on a cruise ship rated their understanding of the rules of croquet.

	Totally understand	Understand	Understand some	Understand a little	Do not understand at all	Total
Men	160	520	560	320	40	1600
Women	160	240	200	80	40	720

The pie chart for men has been drawn for you.

a Copy and complete the pie chart for women.

b Which group, men or women, do you think had a better overall understanding of the rules of croquet? Give *one* reason to justify your answer.

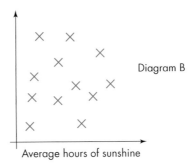

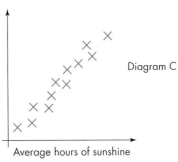

6 The scatter diagrams below show the results of a survey on the average number of hours of sunshine in a week during the summer weeks in Bournemouth.

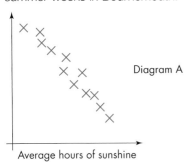

Diagram A

Average hours of sunshine

Diagram B

Average hours of sunshine

Diagram C

Average hours of sunshine

a Which scatter diagram shows the average hours of sunshine plotted against:

i the number of ice creams sold? **ii** the number of umbrellas sold? **iii** the number of births in the town?

b State which one of the diagrams shows a negative correlation.

7 As each customer left a shop the manager gave them a questionnaire containing the following question.

Question: How much did you spend in the shop today?

Response: Less than £10 ☐   Less than £20 ☐
Less than £30 ☐   £30 or more ☐

Write down one reason why the response section of this question is not suitable.

8 Joy wants to find out who eats vegetarian food. She decides to investigate this hypothesis:

Girls are more likely than boys
to eat vegetarian food.

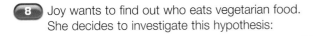

a Design a two-way table that Joy might use to help her do this.

b Joy records information from a sample of 40 boys and 30 girls. She finds that 18 boys and 16 girls eat vegetarian food. Based on this sample, is the hypothesis correct? Explain your answer.

9 Low Storrs School wants to do a survey.

a This is one of the questions.

Do you agree that Low Storrs School has better teachers than Goldale School?

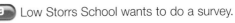

Give one criticism of this question.

b The survey is only carried out on parents of pupils at Low Storrs School. Give a reason why this is *not* suitable.

10 The scatter graph shows some information about six new-born baby apes. For each baby ape, it shows the mother's leg length and the baby ape's birth weight.

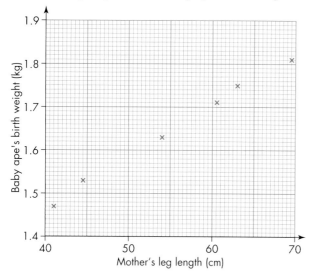

The table shows the mother's leg length and the birth weight of two more baby apes.

Mother's leg length (cm)	50	65
Baby ape's birth weight (kg)	1.6	1.75

a Copy the graph onto graph paper and plot the information from the table.

b Describe the correlation between a mother's leg length and her baby ape's birth weight.

c Draw a line of best fit on your graph.

A mother's leg length is 55 cm.

d Use your line of best fit to estimate the birth weight of her baby ape.

Edexcel, Question 5, Paper 16 Intermediate, June 2005

11 Mr Evans carried out a survey on the weight of his football team. The scatter graph shows the results.

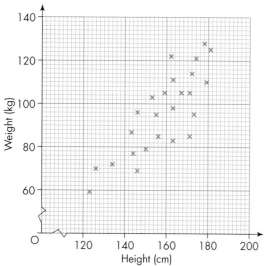

a Write down the highest weight.

b Describe the relationship shown on the scatter graph.

c Copy the scatter graph onto graph paper and draw a line of best fit.

d Leigh was a footballer at a similar club. He was 156 cm tall. Use your line of best fit to estimate Leigh's weight.

12 The table shows the time taken and distance travelled by a taxi driver for 10 journeys one day.

Time (min)	Distance (km)
3	1.7
17	8.3
11	5.1
13	6.7
9	4.7
15	7.3
8	3.8
11	5.7
16	8.7
10	5.3

a Plot on a grid, a scatter diagram with time, on the horizontal axis, from 0 to 20, and distance, on the vertical axis, from 0 to 10.

b Draw a line of best fit on your diagram.

c A taxi journey takes 4 minutes. How many kilometres is the journey?

d A taxi journey is 10 kilometres. How many minutes will it take?

13 Terry and Dora are doing a survey on the types of shows people go to see.

a This is one question from Terry's survey.

> Musicals are just for posh people.
>
> Don't you agree?
>
> Tick (✓) a box.
>
> Strongly agree ☐   Agree ☐   Don't know ☐

Give two criticisms of Terry's question.

b This is a question from Dora's survey.

> Do you go to shows?   ☐ Yes   No ☐
>
> If yes, how many shows do you go to each year?
>   ☐ 2 or less   ☐ 2 or 4   ☐ 5 or 6
>   ☐ More than 6

Give two reasons why this is a good question.

WORKED EXAM QUESTION

The scatter diagram shows the relationship between the age of a laptop and its available free memory.

a Which of the four points, A, B, C or D represents each of the statements below?

Cathy: I have a good laptop. It's quite old but it still has lots of spare memory.

Gary: My laptop is quite new but it doesn't have much spare memory.

Joe: My laptop is old and running out of memory.

b Make up a statement that matches the fourth point.

c What does the graph tell you about the relationship between the age of a laptop and its available free memory?

d Draw scatter diagrams to show the relationship between:

   i   the cost of a laptop and its memory capacity

   ii the age of a laptop and the number of emails received on it per day.

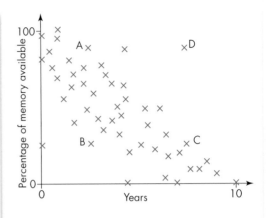

Solution

a Cathy is represented by point D.
  Gary is represented by point B.
  Joe is represented by point C.

> Read both axes. The horizontal axis is the age and the vertical axis is the available memory, so Cathy would be to the right of the horizontal axis and to the top of the vertical axis. Use similar reasoning for the other people.

b 'My laptop is new and has lots of memory'.

> Point A is a fairly new laptop with a lot of memory.
> Any statement that says something like this answer given would get the mark.

c The older a laptop is the less available memory it has.

> The graph basically shows weak negative correlation, so as one variable increases the other decreases.

d i

(scatter diagram: Capacity vs Cost of laptop)

ii

(scatter diagram: Emails per day vs Age of laptop)

> The first diagram shows a positive correlation, as the more a laptop costs, the more memory you would expect it to have.
> The second diagram shows no correlation as there is no relationship.

Mr Owen owns a riding stables. He buys six new horses. He uses the bodyweight calculator to work out the weight, in kilograms, of each horse. He then uses the feed chart to work out how much feed to give each horse.

Help him by completing the table for his new horses.

Summer
Girth: 220 cm
Length: 142 cm
Height: 17 hands 2 inches
Work: medium

Sally
Girth: 190 cm
Length: 95 cm
Height: 14 hands 3 inches
Work: hard

Skip
Girth: 200 cm
Length: 114 cm
Height: 16 hands 0 inches
Work: hard

Simon
Girth: 180 cm
Length: 124 cm
Height: 15 hands 3 inches
Work: medium

Feed chart

Body weight of horse (kg)	Weight of feed (in kg) at different levels of work	
	Medium work	**Hard work**
300	2.4	3.0
350	2.8	3.5
400	3.2	4.0
450	3.6	4.5
500	4.0	5.0
Extra feed per 50 kg	300 g	400 g

Horse	Weight (kg)	Feed (kg)
Summer	850	6.1
Sally		
Skip		
Simon		
Barney		
Teddy		

Instructions

Put a ruler from the girth line to the length line. Where the ruler crosses the weight line is the reading for the approximate weight of the horse.

Give each horse's weight to the nearest 10 kilograms.

Barney
Girth: 160 cm
Length: 110 cm
Height: 15 hands 1 inch
Work: medium

Teddy
Girth: 190 cm
Length: 140 cm
Height: 16 hands 2 inches
Work: hard

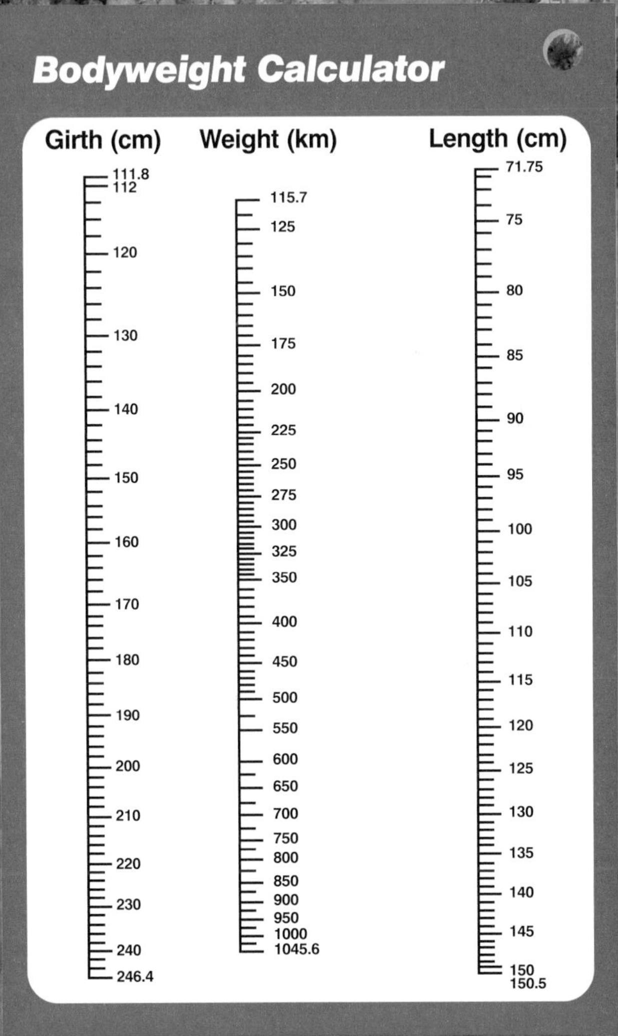

Bodyweight Calculator

Girth (cm)	Weight (km)	Length (cm)
111.8	115.7	71.75
112	125	75
120	150	80
130	175	85
140	200	90
150	225	95
160	250	100
170	275	105
180	300	110
190	325	115
200	350	120
210	400	125
220	450	130
230	500	135
240	550	140
246.4	600	145
	650	150
	700	150.5
	750	
	800	
	850	
	900	
	950	
	1000	
	1045.6	

Mr Owen wants to plan for next year so, during one week in the summer holidays, he keeps a record of the riding abilities of his customers.

Children	45
Female novice	20
Female experienced	61
Male novice	15
Male experienced	39

Draw a pie chart to show the different types of rider that he needs to cater for.

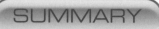

F Able to interpret a simple pie chart

E Able to draw a pie chart

D Able to draw a line of best fit on a scatter diagram

D Able to recognise the different types of correlation

D Able to design a data collection sheet

C Able to interpret a scatter diagram

C Able to use a line of best fit to predict values

C Able to design and criticise questions for questionnaires

What you should know now

- How to read and draw pie charts

- How to plot scatter diagrams, recognise correlation, draw lines of best fit and use them to predict values

- How to design questionnaires and know how to ask suitable questions

Pattern

1 Patterns in number

2 Number sequences

3 The *n*th term of a sequence

4 Special sequences

5 General rules from given patterns

This chapter will show you ...

- some of the common sequences of numbers

- how to recognise rules for sequences

- how to express a rule for a sequence in words and algebraically

Visual overview

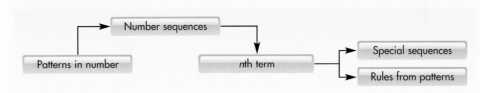

What you should already know

- Basic algebra and how to use letters for numbers

- How to substitute numbers into algebraic expressions

- How to solve simple linear equations

Quick check

1 Angela is x years old. Write down expressions for the ages of the following people, in terms of x.

   a Angela's brother Bill, who is three years older than her.

   b Angela's mother Carol, who is twice as old as Angela.

   c Angela's father Dick, whose age is the sum of Angela's age and Bill's age.

2 Work out the value of the expression $2n + 3$ for:

   a $n = 1$

   b $n = 2$

   c $n = 3$.

In this section you will learn how to:

● recognise patterns in number sequences

Key words

pattern
sequence

Look at these number **patterns**.

$$0 \times 9 + 1 = 1$$
$$1 \times 9 + 2 = 11$$
$$12 \times 9 + 3 = 111$$
$$123 \times 9 + 4 = 1111$$
$$1234 \times 9 + 5 = 11111$$

$$1 \times 8 + 1 = 9$$
$$12 \times 8 + 2 = 98$$
$$123 \times 8 + 3 = 987$$
$$1234 \times 8 + 4 = 9876$$
$$12345 \times 8 + 5 = 98765$$

$$1 \times 3 \times 37 = 111$$
$$2 \times 3 \times 37 = 222$$
$$3 \times 3 \times 37 = 333$$
$$4 \times 3 \times 37 = 444$$

$$7 \times 7 = 49$$
$$67 \times 67 = 4489$$
$$667 \times 667 = 444889$$
$$6667 \times 6667 = 44448889$$

Check that the patterns you see there are correct and then try to continue each pattern without using a calculator. The numbers form a **sequence**. Check them with a calculator afterwards.

Spotting patterns is an important part of mathematics. It helps you to see rules for making calculations.

EXERCISE 23A

In Questions **1** to **10**, look for the pattern and then write the next two lines. Check your answers with a calculator afterwards.

You might find that some of the answers are too big to fit in a calculator display. This is one of the reasons why spotting patterns is important.

1
$$1 \times 1 = 1$$
$$11 \times 11 = 121$$
$$111 \times 111 = 12321$$
$$1111 \times 1111 = 1234321$$

2
$$9 \times 9 = 81$$
$$99 \times 99 = 9801$$
$$999 \times 999 = 998001$$
$$9999 \times 9999 = 99980001$$

> **HINTS AND TIPS**
>
> Look for symmetries in the number patterns.

3 $3 \times 4 = 3^2 + 3$
$4 \times 5 = 4^2 + 4$
$5 \times 6 = 5^2 + 5$
$6 \times 7 = 6^2 + 6$

4 $10 \times 11 = 110$
$20 \times 21 = 420$
$30 \times 31 = 930$
$40 \times 41 = 1640$

HINTS AND TIPS

Think of the numbers as
1 10, 4 20, 9 30, 16 40
...

5
$1 = \ 1 = 1^2$
$1 + 2 + 1 = \ 4 = 2^2$
$1 + 2 + 3 + 2 + 1 = \ 9 = 3^2$
$1 + 2 + 3 + 4 + 3 + 2 + 1 = 16 = 4^2$

6
$1 = \ 1 = 1^3$
$3 + 5 = \ 8 = 2^3$
$7 + 9 + 11 = 27 \ = 3^3$
$13 + 15 + 17 + 19 = 64 \ = 4^3$

7
$1 \qquad\qquad = 1$
$1 + 1 \qquad\quad = 2$
$1 + 2 + 1 \qquad = 4$
$1 + 3 + 3 + 1 \qquad = 8$
$1 + 4 + 6 + 4 + 1 \quad = 16$
$1 + 5 + 10 + 10 + 5 + 1 = 32$

8 $12\ 345\ 679 \times \ 9 = 111\ 111\ 111$
$12\ 345\ 679 \times 18 = 222\ 222\ 222$
$12\ 345\ 679 \times 27 = 333\ 333\ 333$
$12\ 345\ 679 \times 36 = 444\ 444\ 444$

9 $1^3 \qquad\qquad = 1^2 \qquad\quad = 1$
$1^3 + 2^3 \qquad = (1 + 2)^2 \qquad = 9$
$1^3 + 2^3 + 3^3 = (1 + 2 + 3)^2 = 36$

10
$3^2 + 4^2 = 5^2$
$10^2 + 11^2 + 12^2 = 13^2 + 14^2$
$21^2 + 22^2 + 23^2 + 24^2 = 25^2 + 26^2 + 27^2$

HINTS AND TIPS

$4 + 5 = 9 = 3^2$
$12 + 13 = 25 = 5^2$
$24 + 25 = 49 = 7^2$

From your observations on the number patterns in Questions **1** to **10**, answer Questions **11** to **19** without using a calculator.

11 $111\ 111\ 111 \times 111\ 111\ 111 =$

12 $999\ 999\ 999 \times 999\ 999\ 999 =$

13 $12 \times 13 =$

14 $90 \times 91 =$

15 $1 + 2 + 3 + 4 + 5 + 6 + 7 + 8 + 9 + 8 + 7 + 6 + 5 + 4 + 3 + 2 + 1 =$

16 $57 + 59 + 61 + 63 + 65 + 67 + 69 + 71 =$

17 $1 + 9 + 36 + 84 + 126 + 126 + 84 + 36 + 9 + 1 =$

18 $12\ 345\ 679 \times 81 =$

19 $1^3 + 2^3 + 3^3 + 4^3 + 5^3 + 6^3 + 7^3 + 8^3 + 9^3 =$

HINTS AND TIPS

Look for clues in the patterns from questions 1 to 10, for example, $1111 \times 1111 = 1234321$. This is four 1s times four 1s, so what will it be for nine 1s times nine 1s?

Number sequences

In this section you will learn how to:

● recognise how number sequences are building up

Key words

consecutive
difference
sequence
term

A number **sequence** is an ordered set of numbers with a rule for finding every number in the sequence. The rule that takes you from one number to the next could be a simple addition or multiplication, but often it is more tricky than that. So you need to look *very* carefully at the pattern of a sequence.

Each number in a sequence is called a **term** and is in a certain position in the sequence.

Look at these sequences and their rules.

3, 6, 12, 24 … doubling the previous term each time … 48, 96, …

2, 5, 8, 11, … adding 3 to the previous term each time … 14, 17, …

1, 10, 100, 1000, … multiplying the previous term by 10 each time … 10 000, 100 000

1, 8, 15, 22, … adding 7 to the previous term each time … 29, 36, …

These are all quite straightforward once you have looked for the link from one term to the next (**consecutive** terms).

Differences

For some sequences you need to look at the **differences** between consecutive terms to determine the pattern.

EXAMPLE 1

Find the next two terms of the sequence 1, 3, 6, 10, 15, … .

Looking at the differences between consecutive terms:

```
1    3    6    10    15
  ↑    ↑    ↑    ↑
  2    3    4    5
```

So the sequence continues as follows.

```
1    3    6    10    15    21    28
  ↑    ↑    ↑    ↑
  2    3    4    5  └+6┘└+7┘
```

So the next two terms are 21 and 28.

This is a special sequence of numbers. Do you recognise it? You will meet it again, later in the chapter.

The differences usually form a number sequence of their own, so you need to find the *sequence of the differences* before you can expand the original sequence.

EXERCISE 23B

1. Look at the following number sequences. Write down the next three terms in each and explain how each sequence is formed.

   a 1, 3, 5, 7, ...
   b 2, 4, 6, 8, ...

   c 5, 10, 20, 40, ...
   d 1, 3, 9, 27, ...

   e 4, 10, 16, 22, ...
   f 3, 8, 13, 18, ...

   g 2, 20, 200, 2000, ...
   h 7, 10, 13, 16, ...

   i 10, 19, 28, 37, ...
   j 5, 15, 45, 135, ...

   k 2, 6, 10, 14, ...
   l 1, 5, 25, 125, ...

2. By considering the differences in the following sequences, write down the next two terms in each case.

   a 1, 2, 4, 7, 11, ...
   b 1, 2, 5, 10, 17, ...

   c 1, 3, 7, 13, 21, ...
   d 1, 4, 10, 19, 31, ...

   e 1, 9, 25, 49, 81, ...
   f 1, 2, 7, 32, 157, ...

   g 1, 3, 23, 223, 2223, ...
   h 1, 2, 4, 5, 7, 8, 10, ...

   i 2, 3, 5, 9, 17, ...
   j 3, 8, 18, 33, 53, ...

3. Look at the sequences below. Find the rule for each sequence and write down its next three terms.

   a 3, 6, 12, 24, ...
   b 3, 9, 15, 21, 27, ...

   c 128, 64, 32, 16, 8, ...
   d 50, 47, 44, 41, ...

   e 2, 5, 10, 17, 26, ...
   f 5, 6, 8, 11, 15, 20, ...

   g 5, 7, 8, 10, 11, 13, ...
   h 4, 7, 10, 13, 16, ...

   i 1, 3, 6, 10, 15, 21, ...
   j 1, 2, 3, 4, ...

   k 100, 20, 4, 0.8, ...
   l 1, 0.5, 0.25, 0.125, ...

4. Look carefully at each number sequence below. Find the next two numbers in the sequence and try to explain the pattern.

   a 1, 1, 2, 3, 5, 8, 13, ...
   b 1, 4, 9, 16, 25, 36, ...

   c 3, 4, 7, 11, 18, 29, ...
   d 1, 8, 27, 64, 125, ...

> **HINTS AND TIPS**
>
> These patterns do not go up by the same value each time so you will need to find another connection between the terms.

5. Triangular numbers are found as follows.

   1   3   6   10

   Find the next four triangular numbers.

6 Hexagonal numbers are found as follows.

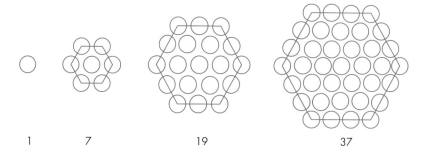

| 1 | 7 | 19 | 37 |

Find the next three hexagonal numbers.

23.3 The *n*th term of a sequence

In this section you will learn how to:

● recognise how number sequences are built up

Key words

coefficient
consecutive
difference
linear
    sequence
*n*th term

Finding the rule

When using a number sequence, you sometimes need to know, say, its 50th term, or even a higher term in the sequence. To do so, you need to find the rule that produces the sequence in its general form.

It may be helpful to look at the problem backwards. That is, take a rule and see how it produces a sequence. The rule is given for the general term, which is called the **nth term**.

EXAMPLE 2

A sequence is formed by the rule $3n + 1$, where $n = 1, 2, 3, 4, 5, 6, \ldots$. Write down the first five terms of the sequence.

Substituting $n = 1, 2, 3, 4, 5$ in turn:

$(3 \times 1 + 1), (3 \times 2 + 1), (3 \times 3 + 1), (3 \times 4 + 1), (3 \times 5 + 1), \ldots$

    4   7   10   13   16

So the sequence is 4, 7, 10, 13, 16, ...

Notice that in Example 2 the **difference** between each term and the next is always 3, which is the **coefficient** of n (the number attached to n). Also, the constant term is the difference between the first term and the coefficient, that is, $4 - 3 = 1$.

EXAMPLE 3

The nth term of a sequence is $4n - 3$. Write down the first five terms of the sequence.

Substituting $n = 1, 2, 3, 4, 5$ in turn:

$$(4 \times 1 - 3), (4 \times 2 - 3), (4 \times 3 - 3), (4 \times 4 - 3), (4 \times 5 - 3)$$

$$1 \qquad\qquad 5 \qquad\qquad 9 \qquad\qquad 13 \qquad\qquad 17$$

So the sequence is 1, 5, 9, 13, 17, … .

Notice that in Example 3 the difference between each term and the next is always 4, which is the coefficient of n.

Also, the constant term is the difference between the first term and the coefficient, that is, $1 - 4 = -3$.

EXERCISE 23C

 1 Use each of the following rules to write down the first five terms of a sequence.

    a $2n + 1$ for $n = 1, 2, 3, 4, 5$ **b** $3n - 2$ for $n = 1, 2, 3, 4, 5$ **c** $5n + 2$ for $n = 1, 2, 3, 4, 5$

    d n^2 for $n = 1, 2, 3, 4, 5$ **e** $n^2 + 3$ for $n = 1, 2, 3, 4, 5$

 2 Write down the first five terms of the sequence which has as its nth term:

    a $n + 3$ **b** $3n - 1$ **c** $5n - 2$

    d $n^2 - 1$ **e** $4n + 5$

>
> **HINTS AND TIPS**
>
> Substitute numbers into the expressions until you can see how the sequence works.

 3 The first two terms of the sequence of fractions $\dfrac{n - 1}{n + 1}$ are:

$$n = 1: \quad \frac{1 - 1}{1 + 1} = \frac{0}{2} = 0 \qquad n = 2: \quad \frac{2 - 1}{2 + 1} = \frac{1}{3}$$

Work out the next five terms of the sequence.

 4 A sequence is formed by the rule $\frac{1}{2} \times n \times (n + 1)$ for $n = 1, 2, 3, 4, …$.

    The first term is given by $n = 1$: $\frac{1}{2} \times 1 \times (1 + 1) = 1$

    The second term is given by $n = 2$: $\frac{1}{2} \times 2 \times (2 + 1) = 3$

    a Work out the next five terms of this sequence.

    b This is a well-known sequence you have met before. What is it?

 5 5! means factorial 5, which is $5 \times 4 \times 3 \times 2 \times 1 = 120$.

    7! means $7 \times 6 \times 5 \times 4 \times 3 \times 2 \times 1 = 5040$.

    a Calculate 2!, 3!, 4! and 6!.

    b If your calculator has a factorial button, check that it gives the same answers as you get for part **a**. What is the largest factorial you can work out with your calculator before you get an error?

Finding the *n*th term of a linear sequence

In a **linear sequence** the *difference* between one term and the next is always the same.

For example:

2, 5, 8, 11, 14, ... difference of 3

The *n*th term of this sequence is given by $3n - 1$.

Here is another linear sequence.

5, 7, 9, 11, 13, ... difference of 2

The *n*th term of this sequence is given by $2n + 3$.

So, you can see that the *n*th term of a linear sequence is *always* of the form $An + b$, where:

- *A*, the coefficient of *n*, is the difference between each term and the next term (**consecutive** terms).

- *b* is the difference between the first term and *A*.

EXAMPLE 4

Find the *n*th term of the sequence 5, 7, 9, 11, 13, ...

The difference between consecutive terms is 2. So the first part of the *n*th term is 2*n*.

Subtract the difference, 2, from the first term, 5, which gives $5 - 2 = 3$.

So the *n*th term is given by $2n + 3$. (You can test it by substituting $n = 1, 2, 3, 4, ...$)

EXAMPLE 5

Find the *n*th term of the sequence 3, 7, 11, 15, 19, ...

The difference between consecutive terms is 4. So the first part of the *n*th term is 4*n*.

Subtract the difference, 4, from the first term, 3, which gives $3 - 4 = -1$.

So the *n*th term is given by $4n - 1$.

EXAMPLE 6

From the sequence 5, 12, 19, 26, 33, ... , find:

    a the *n*th term   **b** the 50th term.

a The difference between consecutive terms is 7. So the first part of the *n*th term is 7*n*.

Subtract the difference, 7, from the first term, 5, which gives $5 - 7 = -2$.

So the *n*th term is given by $7n - 2$.

b The 50th term is found by substituting $n = 50$ into the rule, $7n - 2$.

50th term $= 7 \times 50 - 2 = 350 - 2$
$$= 348$$

6 a Pick any odd number. Pick any other odd number.

Add the two numbers together. Is the answer odd or even?

Copy and complete this table.

+	Odd	Even
Odd	Even	
Even		

b Pick any odd number. Pick any other odd number.

Multiply the two numbers together. Is the answer odd or even?

Copy and complete this table.

×	Odd	Even
Odd	Odd	
Even		

7 The square numbers are 1, 4, 9, 16, 25, … .

a Continue the sequence for another five terms.

b The nth term of this sequence is n^2. Give the nth term of these sequences.

    i 2, 5, 10, 17, 26, …   **ii** 2, 8, 18, 32, 50, …   **iii** 0, 3, 8, 15, 24, …

8 Write down the next two lines of this number pattern.

$$1 = 1 = 1^2$$
$$1 + 3 = 4 = 2^2$$
$$1 + 3 + 5 = 9 = 3^2$$

9 The triangular numbers are 1, 3, 6, 10, 15, 21, … .

a Continue the sequence for another four terms.

b The nth term of this sequence is given by $\frac{1}{2}n(n + 1)$. Use the formula to find:

    i the 20th triangular number   **ii** the 100th triangular number.

c Add consecutive terms of the triangular number sequence.

$$1 + 3 = 4, \; 3 + 6 = 9, \ldots$$

What do you notice?

10 The number p is odd and the number q is even. State if the following are odd or even.

    a $p + 1$ **b** $q + 1$ **c** $p + q$

    d p^2 **e** $qp + 1$ **f** $(p + q)(p - q)$

    g $q^2 + 4$ **h** $p^2 + q^2$ **i** p^3

11 It is known that p is a prime number and q is an even number. State if the following are odd or even, or could be either odd or even.

    a $p + 1$ **b** $p + q$ **c** p^2

    d $qp + 1$ **e** $(p + q)(p - q)$ **f** $2p + 3q$

In this section you will learn how to:

● find the *n*th term from practical problems

Many problem-solving situations that you are likely to meet involve number sequences. So you do need to be able to formulate general rules from given number patterns.

EXAMPLE 7

The diagram shows a pattern of squares building up.

a How many squares will be on the base of the *n*th pattern?

b Which pattern has 99 squares in its base?

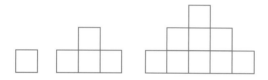

a First, build up the following table for the patterns.

Pattern number	1	2	3	4	5
Number of squares in base	1	3	5	7	9

Looking at the difference between consecutive patterns, you should see it is always 2 squares. So, use 2*n*.

Subtract the difference, 2, from the first number, which gives $1 - 2 = -1$.

So the number of squares in the *n*th pattern is $2n - 1$.

b Now find *n* when $2n - 1 = 99$.

$2n - 1 = 99$

$2n = 99 + 1 = 100$

$n = 100 \div 2 = 50$

The pattern with 99 squares in its base is the 50th.

EXERCISE 23E

1 A pattern of squares is built up from matchsticks as shown.

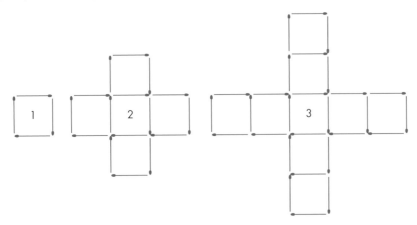

a Draw the fourth diagram.

b How many squares are there in the nth diagram?

c How many squares are there in the 25th diagram?

d With 200 squares, which is the biggest diagram that could be made?

2 A pattern of triangles is built up from matchsticks.

   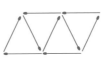

1　　　　2　　　　3　　　　4

a Draw the fifth set of triangles in this pattern.

b How many matchsticks are needed for the nth set of triangles?

c How many matchsticks are needed to make the 60th set of triangles?

d If there are only 100 matchsticks, which is the largest set of triangles that could be made?

3 A conference centre had tables each of which could sit six people. When put together, the tables could seat people as shown.

 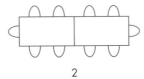 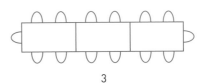

1　　　　　　2　　　　　　　3

a How many people could be seated at four tables?

b How many people could be seated at n tables put together in this way?

c At a conference, 50 people wished to use the tables in this way. How many tables would they need?

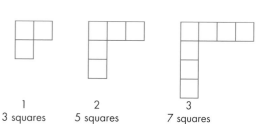

4 A pattern of squares is put together as shown.

a Draw the fourth diagram.

b How many squares are there in the *n*th diagram?

c How many squares are there in the 50th diagram?

d With 300 squares, what is the biggest diagram that could be made?

1
3 squares

2
5 squares

3
7 squares

5 Regular pentagons of side length 1 cm are joined together to make a pattern as shown.

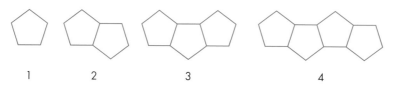

1   2   3   4

Copy this pattern and write down the perimeter of each shape.

a What is the perimeter of patterns like this made from:

i 6 pentagons   **ii** *n* pentagons   **iii** 50 pentagons?

b What is the largest number of pentagons that can be put together like this to have a perimeter less than 1000 cm?

6 Lamp-posts are put at the end of every 100 m stretch of a motorway, as shown.

1   2   3

a How many lamp-posts are needed for:

i 900 m of this motorway   **ii** 8 km of this motorway?

b The contractor building the M99 motorway has ordered 1598 lamp-posts. How long is the M99?

7 **a** The powers of 2 are 2, 4, 8, 16, 32, … .

What is the *n*th term of this sequence?

b A supermarket sells four different-sized bottles of water.

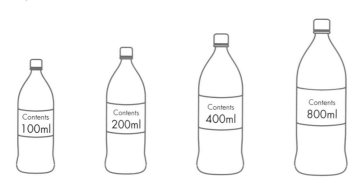

Contents
100ml

Contents
200ml

Contents
400ml

Contents
800ml

Pocket size   Standard size   Family size   Giant size

i Describe the number pattern that the contents follow.

ii The supermarket introduces a super giant size, which is the next sized bottle in the pattern. How much water is there in this bottle?

Dots are used to make a sequence of patterns. The first three patterns are shown.

Pattern 1

Pattern 2

Pattern 3

Pattern 4

a Draw pattern 4.

b Copy and complete the table showing the number of dots in each pattern.

Pattern number	1	2	3	4	5
Number of dots	1	3	6		

c Describe, in words, the rule for continuing the sequence of the number of dots.

 a Here is a sequence of numbers.

    29   25   21   17   13

  i Write down the next two numbers in the sequence.

  ii Write down the rule for continuing the sequence.

b Another sequence of numbers begins:

    2   5   14   41

The rule for continuing this sequence is:

> Multiply by 3 and subtract 1

  i What is the next number in the sequence?

  ii The same rule is used for a sequence that starts with the number 7. What is the second number in this sequence?

  iii The same rule is also used for a sequence that starts with the number −2. What is the second number in this sequence?

 Here are some patterns made from matchsticks:

Pattern number 1   Pattern number 2

Pattern number 3

The graph shows the number of matchsticks m used in pattern number n.

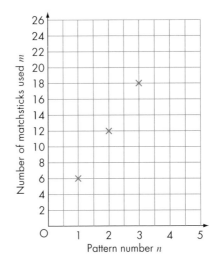

Write down a formula for m in terms of n.

Edexcel, Question 2, Paper 3 Intermediate, June 2003

 The first ten prime numbers are 2, 3, 5, 7, 11, 13, 17, 19, 23, 29.

P is a prime number.
Q is an odd number.
State whether each of the following is always odd, always even or could be either odd or even.

a $P(Q + 1)$

b $Q - P$

 The nth term of a sequence is $4n - 1$.

a Write down the first and second terms of the sequence.

b Which term of the sequence is equal to 19?

c Explain why 78 is not a term in this sequence.

6 a The number E is an even number.
Kira says that $\frac{1}{2}E + 3$ is always even.

Give an example to show that Kira is wrong.

b The letters x and y represent prime numbers.
Is $x + y$ always an even number? Explain your answer.

7 A is an odd number.
B is an even number.

a Explain why $A + B + 1$ is *always* an even number.

b Billy says that $A + B - 1$ *cannot* be a prime number. Explain why Billy is wrong.

Here are the first five terms of an arithmetic sequence.

−1   3   7   11   15

a Find, in terms of n, an expression for the nth term of this sequence.

In another arithmetic sequence the nth term is $8n − 16$

John says that there is a number that is in both sequences.

b Explain why John is wrong.

Edexcel, Question 9, Paper 9B Intermediate, March 2004

 a The nth term of a sequence is $4n − 1$.

    i Write down the first three terms of the sequence.

    ii Is 132 a term in this sequence? Explain your answer.

b Tom builds fencing from pieces of wood as shown below.

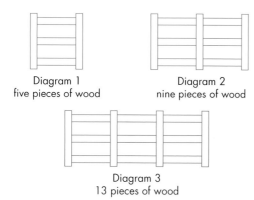

Diagram 1
five pieces of wood

Diagram 2
nine pieces of wood

Diagram 3
13 pieces of wood

How many pieces of wood will be in diagram n?

 The table shows some rows of a number pattern.

Row 1	1		$= \dfrac{1 \times 2}{2}$
Row 2	1 + 2		$= \dfrac{2 \times 3}{2}$
Row 3	1 + 2 + 3		$= \dfrac{3 \times 4}{2}$
Row 4	1 + 2 + 3 + 4		
Row 8			

a Copy the table and complete row 4 of the number pattern.

b In your table, complete row 8 of the number pattern.

Edexcel, Question 7, Paper 4 Intermediate, June 2003

 Look at the patterns made with counters, below.

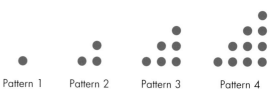

Pattern 1   Pattern 2   Pattern 3   Pattern 4

a Draw pattern 5.

b The numbers of counters used in the patterns are:

1, 3, 6, 10, …

Write down the next two terms in this sequence.

c Consecutive patterns are put together.

Pattern 1 and 2   Pattern 2 and 3   Pattern 3 and 4

    i The numbers of counters in the combined patterns form the sequence:

4, 9, 16, …

How many counters will be in the next combined pattern in the sequence?

    ii What type of numbers are 4, 9, 16, … ?

    iii How many counters will be in the combined pattern formed by patterns 9 and 10?

12 Martin says that the square of any number is always bigger than the number. Give an example to show that Martin is wrong.

13 It is known that n is an integer.

a Explain why $2n + 1$ is always an odd number for all values of n.

b Explain why n^2 could be either odd or even.

WORKED EXAM QUESTION

a   Matches are used to make patterns.

Pattern 1   Pattern 2

Pattern 3   Pattern 4

   i   How many matches would be needed for the 10th pattern?

   ii How many matches would be needed for the *n*th pattern?

b   The patterns are used to make a sequence of shapes.

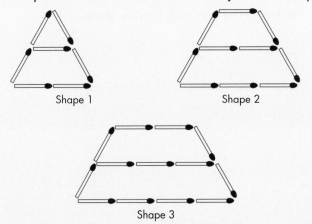

Shape 1   Shape 2

Shape 3

The number of matches needed to make these shapes is
   7, 10, 13, 16, ...

   i   How many matches are needed for the *n*th shape?

   ii What shape number could be made with 64 matches?

Solution

a   i   The number of matches needed is 21.

   ii $2n + 1$

b   i $3n + 4$

   ii 20th shape

The number of matches needed is
3, 5, 7, 9, ... which is going up in 2s.
Continuing the sequence for 10 terms
gives 3, 5, 7, 9, 11, 13, 15, 17, 19, 21.

The sequence goes up in 2s and the
first term is 3, so the *n*th term is $2n + 1$.

The sequence goes up in 3s and the
first term is 7 so the *n*th term is $3n + 4$.

$3n + 4 = 64$, then $3n = 60$, so $n = 20$.

GRADE YOURSELF

F Able to give the next term in a sequence and describe how the pattern is building up

E Able to find any term in a number sequence and recognise patterns in number calculations

D Able to substitute numbers into an nth term rule

D Understand how odd and even numbers interact in addition, subtraction and multiplication problems

C Able to give the nth term of a linear sequence

C Know the nth term of a sequence of powers of 2 or 10

What you should know now

- Be able to recognise a number pattern and explain how the pattern is made
- Be able to recognise a linear sequence and find its nth term
- Be able to recognise a sequence of powers of 2 or 10

This book provides indicators of the equivalent grade level of maths questions throughout. The publishers wish to make clear that these grade indicators have been provided by Collins Education, and are not the responsibility of Edexcel Ltd. Whilst every effort has been made to assure their accuracy, they should be regarded as indicators, and are not binding or definitive.

Surface area and volume of 3-D shapes

1 Units of volume

2 Surface area and volume of a cuboid

3 Density

4 Surface area and volume of a prism

5 Volume of a cylinder

This chapter will show you ...

- the units used when finding the volume of 3-D shapes
- how to calculate the surface area and volume of a cuboid
- how to find density
- how to calculate the surface area and volume of prisms
- how to calculate the volume of a cylinder

Visual overview

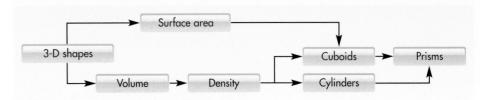

What you should already know

- How to find the area of a rectangle and a triangle (see Chapter 5)
- The units used with area
- The names of basic 3-D shapes
- What is meant by the term 'volume'

Quick check

What are the mathematical names of these 3-D shapes?

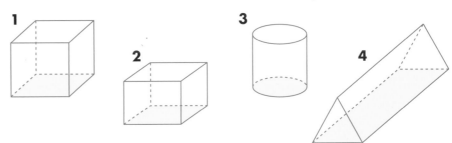

1

2

3

4

Units of volume

In this section you will learn how to:

- use the correct units with volume

Key words
cubic
    centimetre
cubic metre
cubic
    millimetre
edge
face
vertex
volume

Volume is the amount of space taken up inside a 3-D shape.

Volume is measured in **cubic millimetres** (mm^3), **cubic centimetres** (cm^3) or **cubic metres** (m^3).

Length, area and volume

A cube with an edge of 1 cm has a volume of 1 cm^3 and each face has an area of 1 cm^2.

A cube with an edge of 2 cm has a volume of 8 cm^3 and each face has an area of 4 cm^2.

A cube with an edge of 3 cm has a volume of 27 cm^3 and each face has an area of 9 cm^2.

 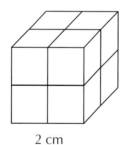 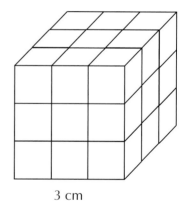

    1 cm   2 cm   3 cm

EXAMPLE 1

How many cubes, each 1 cm by 1 cm by 1 cm, have been used to make these steps? What volume do they occupy?

When you count the cubes, do not forget to include those hidden at the back.

You should count:

    6 + 4 + 2 = 12

The volume of each cube is 1 cm^3.

So, the volume of the steps is:

    12 × 1 = 12 cm^3

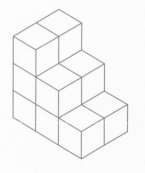

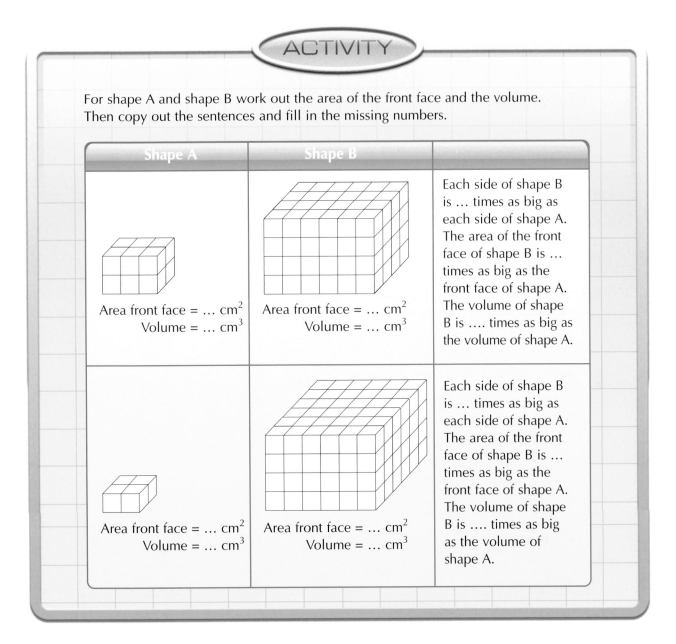

For shape A and shape B work out the area of the front face and the volume.
Then copy out the sentences and fill in the missing numbers.

Shape A	Shape B	
Area front face = … cm^2 Volume = … cm^3	Area front face = … cm^2 Volume = … cm^3	Each side of shape B is … times as big as each side of shape A. The area of the front face of shape B is … times as big as the front face of shape A. The volume of shape B is …. times as big as the volume of shape A.
Area front face = … cm^2 Volume = … cm^3	Area front face = … cm^2 Volume = … cm^3	Each side of shape B is … times as big as each side of shape A. The area of the front face of shape B is … times as big as the front face of shape A. The volume of shape B is …. times as big as the volume of shape A.

EXERCISE 24A

Find the volume of each 3-D shape, if the edge of each cube is 1 cm.

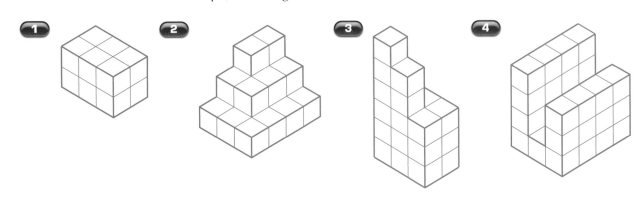

1   **2**   **3**   **4**

G

Many-faced shapes

All 3-D shapes have **faces**, **vertices** and **edges**.
(**Note:** Vertices is the plural of vertex.)

Look at the shapes in the table below and on the
next page. Then copy the table and fill it in.

Remember that there are hidden faces, vertices
and edges. These are shown with dashed lines.

Look at the numbers in the completed table.

- For each shape, can you find the connection
  between the following properties?

  - The number of faces, F

  - The number of vertices, V

  - The number of edges, E

- Find some other solid shapes. Does your connection also hold for those?

Vertex
(a point)

Face
(a surface)

Edge
(a line)

Shape	Name	Number of faces (F)	Number of vertices (V)	Number of edges (E)
	Cuboid			
	Square-based pyramid			
	Triangular-based pyramid (or tetrahedron)			
	Octahedron			

Shape	Name	Number of faces (*F*)	Number of vertices (*V*)	Number of edges (*E*)
	Triangular prism			
	Hexagonal prism			
	Hexagon-based pyramid			

24.2 Surface area and volume of a cuboid

In this section you will learn how to:

- calculate the surface area and volume of a cuboid

Key words
capacity
height
length
litre
surface area
volume
width

A cuboid is a box shape, all six faces of which are rectangles.

Every day you will come across many examples of cuboids, such as breakfast cereal packets, shoe boxes, video cassettes – and even this book.

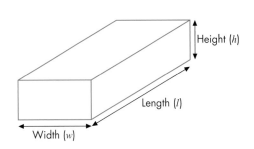

The **volume** of a cuboid is given by the formula:

volume = **length** × **width** × **height**   *or* $V = l \times w \times h$ *or* $V = lwh$

The **surface area** of a cuboid is calculated by finding the total area of the six faces, which are rectangles. Notice that each pair of opposite rectangles have the same area. So, from the diagram at the bottom of the last page:

area of top and bottom rectangles = 2 × length × width = $2lw$

area of front and back rectangles = 2 × height × width = $2hw$

area of two side rectangles = 2 × height × length = $2hl$

Hence, the surface area of a cuboid is given by the formula:

surface area = $A = 2lw + 2hw + 2hl$

EXAMPLE 2

Calculate the volume and surface area of this cuboid.

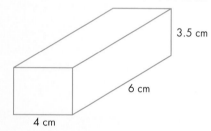

3.5 cm

6 cm

4 cm

Volume = $V = lwh = 6 \times 4 \times 3.5 = 84$ cm^3

Surface area = $A = 2lw + 2hw + 2hl$

$= (2 \times 6 \times 4) + (2 \times 3.5 \times 4) + (2 \times 3.5 \times 6)$

$= 48 + 28 + 42 = 118$ cm^2

Note:

1 cm^3 = 1000 mm^3 and 1 m^3 = 1 000 000 cm^3

The word '**capacity**' is often used for the volumes of liquids or gases.

The unit used for measuring capacity is the **litre**, l, with:

1000 millilitres (ml) = 1 litre

100 centilitres (cl) = 1 litre

1000 cm^3 = 1 litre

1 m^3 = 1000 litres

EXERCISE 24B

1 Find **i** the volume and **ii** the surface area of each of these cuboids.

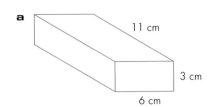

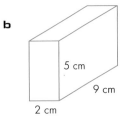

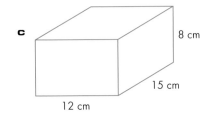

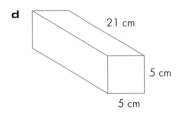

2 Find the capacity of a fish-tank with dimensions: length 40 cm, width 30 cm and height 20 cm. Give your answer in litres.

3 Find the volume of the cuboid in each of the following cases.

   a The area of the base is 40 cm² and the height is 4 cm.

   b The base has one side 10 cm and the other side 2 cm longer, and the height is 4 cm.

   c The area of the top is 25 cm² and the depth is 6 cm.

4 Calculate **i** the volume and **ii** the surface area of each of the cubes with these edge lengths.

   a 4 cm   **b** 7 cm   **c** 10 mm

   d 5 m   **e** 12 m

5 The safety regulations say that in a room where people sleep there should be at least 12 m³ for each person. A dormitory is 20 m long, 13 m wide and 4 m high. What is the greatest number of people who can safely sleep in the dormitory?

6 Complete the table below for cuboids **a** to **e**.

	Length	Width	Height	Volume
a	8 cm	5 cm	4.5 cm	
b	12 cm	8 cm		480 cm³
c	9 cm		5 cm	270 cm³
d		7 cm	3.5 cm	245 cm³
e	7.5 cm	5.4 cm	2 cm	

7 A tank contains 32 000 litres of water. The base of the tank measures 6.5 m by 3.1 m. Find the depth of water in the tank. Give your answer to one decimal place.

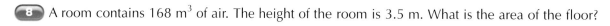

D

8 A room contains 168 m^3 of air. The height of the room is 3.5 m. What is the area of the floor?

9 What are the dimensions of cubes with these volumes?

    a 27 cm^3 **b** 125 m^3 **c** 8 mm^3 **d** 1.728 m^3

10 Calculate the volume of each of these shapes.

a
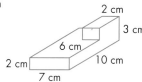

b
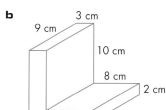

> **HINTS AND TIPS**
>
> Split the solid into two separate cuboids and work out the dimensions of each of them from the information given.

24.3 Density

In this section you will learn how to:
- find the density of a 3-D shape

Key words
density
mass
volume

Density is the **mass** of a substance per unit **volume** and is usually expressed in grams per cubic centimetre (g/cm^3) or kilograms per cubic metre (kg/m^3). The relationship between the three quantities is:

$$\text{density} = \frac{\text{mass}}{\text{volume}}$$

This is often remembered with a triangle similar to that used for distance, speed and time.

Mass = density × volume

Density = mass ÷ volume

Volume = mass ÷ density

Note: Density is defined in terms of mass, which is commonly referred to as 'weight', although, strictly speaking, there is a difference between these terms (you may already have learnt about it in science). In this book, the two terms are assumed to have the same meaning.

EXAMPLE 3

A piece of metal weighing 30 g has a volume of 4 cm^3. What is the density of the metal?

$$\text{Density} = \frac{30}{4} = 7.5 \text{ g/cm}^3$$

EXAMPLE 4

What is the mass of a piece of rock that has a volume of 34 cm^3 and a density of 2.25 g/cm^3?

Mass = 2.25 × 34 = 76.5 g

EXERCISE 24C

1 Find the density of a piece of wood weighing 6 g and having a volume of 8 cm^3.

2 Calculate the volume of a piece of wood that weighs 102 g and has a density of 0.85 g/cm^3.

3 Find the mass of a marble model, 56 cm^3 in volume, if the density of marble is 2.8 g/cm^3.

4 Calculate the volume of a liquid weighing 4 kg and having a density of 1.25 g/cm^3.

5 Find the density of the material of a pebble that weighs 34 g and has a volume of 12.5 cm^3.

6 It is estimated that the statue of Queen Victoria in Endcliffe Park, Sheffield, has a volume of about 4 m^3. The density of the material used to make the statue is 9.2 g/cm^3. What is the estimated mass of the statue?

7 I bought a 50 kg bag of coal and estimated the total volume of coal to be about 28 000 cm^3. What is the density of coal in g/cm^3?

8 A 1 kg bag of sugar has a volume of about 625 cm^3. What is the density of sugar in grams per cubic centimetre?

24.4 Surface area and volume of a prism

In this section you will learn how to:
- calculate the surface area and volume of a prism

Key words
cross-section
prism
surface area
volume

A **prism** is a 3-D shape that has the same **cross-section** running all the way through it, whenever it is cut perpendicular to its length. Here are some examples.

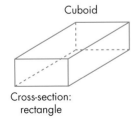

Cuboid

Cross-section:
rectangle

Triangular prism

Cross-section:
isosceles triangle

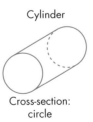

Cylinder

Cross-section:
circle

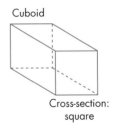

Cuboid

Cross-section:
square

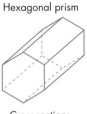

Hexagonal prism

Cross-section:
regular hexagon

The **volume** of a prism is found by multiplying the area of its cross-section by the length of the prism (or height if the prism is stood on end), that is:

volume of prism = area of cross-section × length   *or* $V = Al$

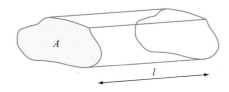

EXAMPLE 5

Calculate the **surface area** and the volume of the triangular prism below.

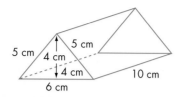

The surface area is made up of three rectangles and two isosceles triangles.

Area of the three rectangles = 10 × 5 + 10 × 5 + 10 × 6 = 50 + 50 + 60 = 160 cm²

Area of one triangle = $\dfrac{6 \times 4}{2}$ = 12, so area of two triangles = 24 cm²

Therefore, the total surface area = 184 cm²

Volume of the prism = Al

Area of the cross-section = area of the triangle = 12 cm²

So, V = 12 × 10 = 120 cm³

EXERCISE 24D

1 For each prism shown:

   i sketch the cross-section

   ii calculate the area of the cross-section

   iii calculate the volume.

> **HINTS AND TIPS**
>
> Look back at page 102 to remind yourself how to calculate the areas of compound shapes

a

b

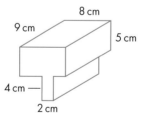

c

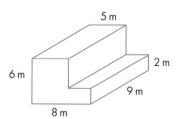

d

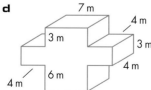

e

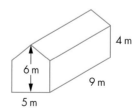

f

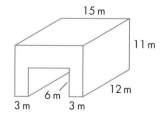

2 Each of these prisms has a regular cross-section in the shape of a right-angled triangle.

   a Find the volume of each prism.   **b** Find the total surface area of each prism.

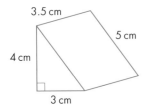
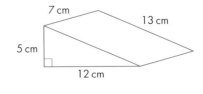

3 The uniform cross-section of a swimming pool is a trapezium with parallel sides of lengths 1 m and 2.5 m, with a perpendicular distance of 30 m between them. The width of the pool is 10 m. How much water is in the pool when it is full? Give your answer in litres.

4 The dimensions of the cross-section of a girder, which is 2 m in length, are shown on the diagram. The girder is made of iron with a density of 7.9 g/cm³. What is the mass of the girder?

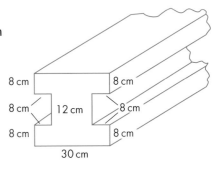

5 Which of these 3-D shapes is the heavier? The density of each shape is given below.

a

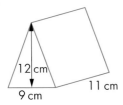

4.8 g/cm³

b

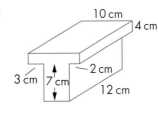

3.2 g/cm³

In this section you will learn how to:

- calculate the volume of a cylinder

Key words

cylinder
height
length
π
radius
volume

The **volume** of a **cylinder** is found by multiplying the area of its circular cross-section by its **height**, that is:

volume = area of circle × height *or* $V = \pi r^2 h$

where r is the **radius** of the cylinder and h is its height or **length**.

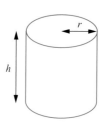

EXAMPLE 6

Calculate the volume of a cylinder with a radius of 5 cm and a height of 12 cm.

Volume = $\pi r^2 h = \pi \times 5^2 \times 12 = 942.5$ cm^3 (to 1 decimal place)

EXERCISE 24E

1 Find the volume of each of these cylinders. Round your answers.

   a base radius 4 cm and height 5 cm

   b base diameter 9 cm and height 7 cm

   c base diameter 13.5 cm and height 15 cm

   d base radius 1.2 m and length 5.5 m

2 Find the volume of each of these cylinders. Round your answers.

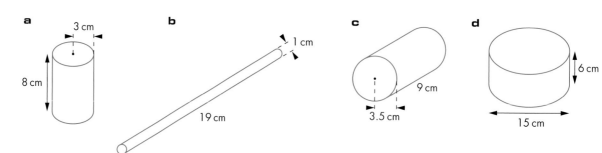

3 The diameter of a cylindrical marble column is 60 cm and its height is 4.2 m. The cost of making this column is quoted as £67.50 per cubic metre. What is the estimated total cost of making the column?

4 Find the mass of a solid iron cylinder 55 cm high with a base diameter of 60 cm. The density of iron is 7.9 g/cm^3.

5 A cylindrical container is 65 cm in diameter. Water is poured into the container until it is 1 metre deep. How much water is in the container? Give your answer to the nearest litre.

6 A cylindrical can of soup has a diameter of 7 cm and a height of 9.5 cm. It is full of soup that weighs 625 g. What is the density of the soup?

7 A metal bar, 1 m long and with a diameter of 6 cm, weighs 22 kg. What is the density of the metal from which the bar is made?

8 What are the volumes of the following cylinders? Give your answers in terms of π.

a with a base radius of 6 cm and a height of 10 cm

b with a base diameter of 10 cm and a height of 12 cm

1 A water tank is a cuboid with length 6 m, width 4 m and height 2 m.

Calculate the volume of the water tank.
Remember to state the units in your answer.

2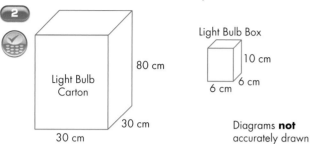

Light Bulb Box

80 cm

Light Bulb Carton

30 cm

30 cm

10 cm

6 cm

6 cm

Diagrams **not** accurately drawn

A light bulb box measures 6 cm by 6 cm by 10 cm.
Light bulb boxes are packed into cartons.
A carton measures 30 cm by 30 cm by 80 cm.

Work out the number of light bulb boxes which can completely fill *one* carton.

Edexcel, Question 3, Paper 12A Intermediate, January 2005

3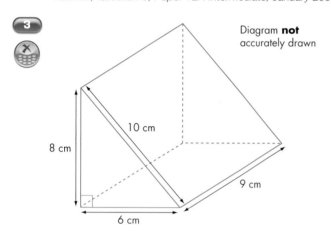

Diagram **not** accurately drawn

10 cm

8 cm

9 cm

6 cm

a Work out the surface area of the triangular prism.
b Work out the volume of the triangular prism.

Edexcel, Question 19, Paper 3 Intermediate, June 2005

4 The diagram shows a cylinder. The diameter of the cylinder is 10 cm. The height of the cylinder is 12 cm.

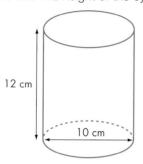

12 cm

10 cm

Work out the volume of the cylinder.
Give your answer in terms of π.

5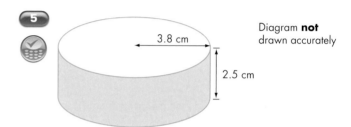

3.8 cm

2.5 cm

Diagram **not** drawn accurately

An ice hockey puck is in the shape of a cylinder with a radius of 3.8 cm, and a thickness of 2.5 cm.

It is made out of rubber with a density of 1.5 grams per cm^3.

Work out the mass of the ice hockey puck. Give your answer correct to 1 decimal place.

Edexcel, Question 19, Paper 4 Intermediate, June 2004

WORKED EXAM QUESTION

The diagrams show two boxes.

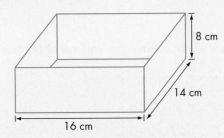
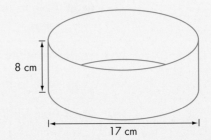

The cuboid box measures 16 cm by 14 cm by 8 cm. The diameter of the circular box is 17 cm. Its height is 8 cm. Which box has the greater volume?

Solution

$V = lbh = 16 \times 14 \times 8 = 1792$ cm^3

$V = \pi r^2 h$

The diameter is 17 cm, so $r = 8.5$ cm.

So, $V = \pi \times 8.5^2 \times 8 = 1816$ cm^3 (to the nearest cm^3)

So, the circular box has the greater volume.

GRADE YOURSELF

G Able to find the volume of a 3-D shape by counting cubes

F Able to find the surface area of 3-D shapes by counting squares on faces

E Know the formula $V = lbh$ to find the volume of a cuboid

E Able to find the surface area of a cuboid

C Able to find the surface area and volume of a prism

C Able to find the volume of a cylinder

C Know how to find the density of a 3-D shape

What you should know now

- The units used when finding volume
- How to find the surface area and volume of a cuboid
- How to find the surface area and volume of a prism
- How to find the volume of a cylinder
- How to find the density of a 3-D shape

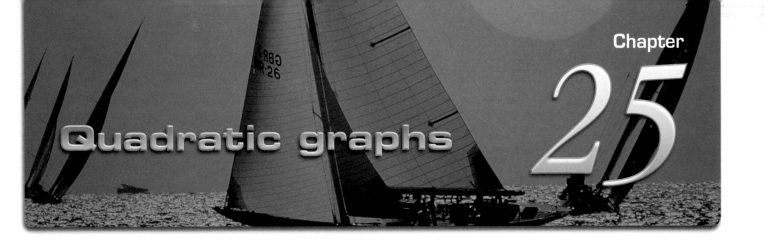

Quadratic graphs

1 Drawing quadratic graphs

2 Solving quadratic equations

This chapter will show you ...

- how to draw a quadratic graph
- how to use a graph to solve a quadratic equation

Visual overview

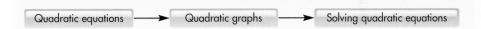

Quadratic equations → Quadratic graphs → Solving quadratic equations

What you should already know

- How to plot coordinate points in all four quadrants (see Chapter 14)
- How to substitute numbers into a formula (see Chapter 7)
- How to draw linear graphs (see Chapter 14)

Quick check

Substitute:

    a $x = 4$

    b $x = -2$ into the following expressions.

1 x^2

2 $x^2 + 4$

3 $x^2 - 2$

4 $x^2 + 2x$

Drawing quadratic graphs

In this section you will learn how to:

● draw a quadratic graph, given its equation

A **quadratic graph** has a term in x^2 in its equation.

All of the following are **quadratic equations** and each would produce a quadratic graph.

$y = x^2$, $y = x^2 + 5$, $y = x^2 - 3x$,

$y = x^2 + 5x + 6$, $y = x^2 + 2x - 5$

EXAMPLE 1

Draw the graph of $y = x^2$ for $-3 \leqslant x \leqslant 3$.

First make a table, as shown below.

x	-3	-2	-1	0	1	2	3
$y = x^2$	9	4	1	0	1	4	9

Now draw axes, with $-3 \leqslant x \leqslant 3$ and $0 \leqslant y \leqslant 9$, plot the points and join them to make a smooth curve.

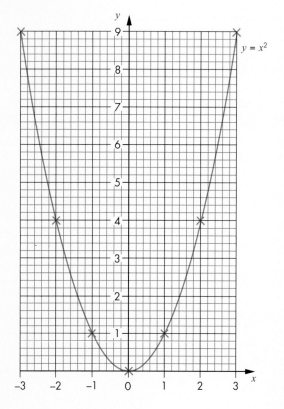

This is the graph of $y = x^2$. This type of graph is often referred to as a 'parabola'.

Note that although it is difficult to draw accurate curves, examiners often work to a tolerance of between 1 and 2 mm.

Here are some of the more common ways in which marks are lost in an examination.

- When the points are too far apart, a curve tends to 'wobble'.

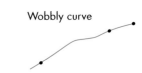
Wobbly curve

- Drawing curves in small sections leads to 'feathering'.

Feathering

- The place where a curve should turn smoothly is drawn 'flat'.

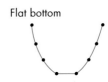
Flat bottom

- A curve is drawn through a point which, clearly, has been incorrectly plotted.

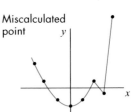
Miscalculated point

A quadratic curve drawn correctly will always be a smooth curve.

Here are some tips that will make it easier for you to draw smooth, curved graphs.

- If you are *right-handed*, turn your piece of paper or your exercise book round so that you draw from left to right. Your hand is steadier this way than trying to draw from right to left or away from your body. If you are *left-handed*, you should find drawing from right to left the more accurate way.

- Move your pencil over the points as a practice run without drawing the curve.

- Do one continuous curve and only stop at a plotted point.

- Use a *sharp* pencil and do not press too heavily, so that you may easily rub out mistakes.

Normally in an examination, grids are provided with the axes clearly marked. Remember that a tolerance of 1 or 2 mm is all that you are allowed. In the following exercises, suitable ranges are suggested for the axes. Usually you will be expected to use 2 mm graph paper to draw the graphs.

EXAMPLE 2

a Draw the graph of $y = x^2 + 2x - 3$ for $-4 \leqslant x \leqslant 2$.

b Use your graph to find the value of y when $x = 1.6$.

c Use your graph to find the values of x that give a y-value of 1.

a Draw a table as follows to help work each step of the calculation.

x	−4	−3	−2	−1	0	1	2
x^2	16	9	4	1	0	1	4
$+2x$	−8	−6	−4	−2	0	2	4
−3	−3	−3	−3	−3	−3	−3	−3
$y = x^2 + 2x - 3$	5	0	−3	−4	−3	0	5

Generally, you do not need to work out all values in a table. If you use a calculator, you need only to work out the y-value. The other rows in the table are just working lines to break down the calculation.

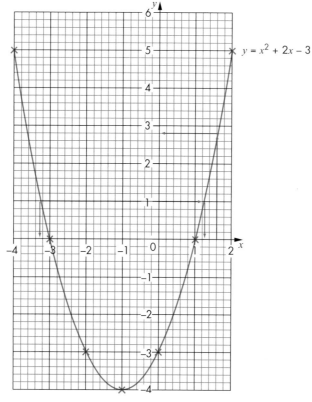

b To find the corresponding y-value for any value of x, you start on the x-axis at that x-value, go up to the curve, across to the y-axis and read off the y-value. This procedure is marked on the graph with arrows.

Always show these arrows because even if you make a mistake and misread the scales, you may still get a mark.

So when $x = 1.6$, $y = 2.8$.

c This time start at 1 on the y-axis and read off the two x-values that correspond to a y-value of 1.

Again, this procedure is marked on the graph with arrows.

So when $y = 1$, $x = -3.2$ or $x = 1.2$.

EXERCISE 25A

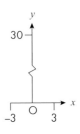

1 Copy and complete the table for the graph of $y = 3x^2$ for $-3 \leqslant x \leqslant 3$.

x	-3	-2	-1	0	1	2	3
$y = 3x^2$	27		3			12	

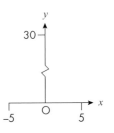

2 Copy and complete the table for the graph of $y = x^2 + 2$ for $-5 \leqslant x \leqslant 5$.

x	-5	-4	-3	-2	-1	0	1	2	3	4	5
$y = x^2 + 2$	27		11					6			

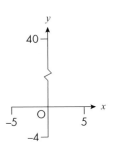

3 a Copy and complete the table for the graph of $y = x^2 - 3x$ for $-5 \leqslant x \leqslant 5$.

x	-5	-4	-3	-2	-1	0	1	2	3	4	5
x^2	25		9					4			
$-3x$	15							-6			
y	40							-2			

b Use your graph to find the value of y when $x = 3.5$.

c Use your graph to find the values of x that give a y-value of 5.

4 a Copy and complete the table for the graph of $y = x^2 - 2x - 8$ for $-5 \leqslant x \leqslant 5$.

x	-5	-4	-3	-2	-1	0	1	2	3	4	5
x^2	25		9					4			
$-2x$	10							-4			
-8	-8							-8			
y	27							-8			

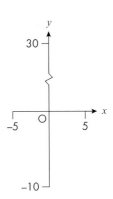

b Use your graph to find the value of y when $x = 0.5$.

c Use your graph to find the values of x that give a y-value of -3.

5 a Copy and complete the table for the graph of $y = x^2 - 5x + 4$ for $-2 \leqslant x \leqslant 5$.

x	-2	-1	0	1	2	3	4	5
y	18		4			-2		

b Use your graph to find the value of y when $x = -0.5$.

c Use your graph to find the values of x that give a y-value of 3.

6 **a** Copy and complete the table for the graph of $y = x^2 + 2x - 1$ for $-3 \leqslant x \leqslant 3$.

x	-3	-2	-1	0	1	2	3
x^2	9				1	4	
$+2x$	-6		-2			4	
-1	-1	-1				-1	
y	2					7	

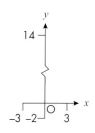

b Use your graph to find the y-value when $x = -2.5$.

c Use your graph to find the values of x that give a y-value of 1.

25.2 Solving quadratic equations

In this section you will learn how to:
- use a graph to solve a quadratic equation

Key word

quadratic
  equation
quadratic
  graph
solution

If you look at the graph of $y = x^2 + 2x - 3$ in Example 2, you will see that the graph crosses the x-axis at $x = -3$ and $x = 1$. Since the x-axis is the line $y = 0$, the y-value at any point on the axis is zero. So, you have found the answers or the **solutions** to the **quadratic equation** $x^2 + 2x - 3 = 0$.

That is, you have found the values of x that make the equation true.

So, in the case of the quadratic equation $x^2 + 2x - 3 = 0$, the solutions are $x = -3$ and $x = 1$.

Checking the two solutions in the equation:

For $x = -3$, $(-3)^2 + 2(-3) - 3 = 9 - 6 - 3 = 0$

For $x = 1$, $(1)^2 + 2(1) - 3 = 1 + 2 - 3 = 0$

So you can find the solutions of a quadratic equation by drawing its **quadratic graph** and finding where the graph crosses the x-axis.

EXAMPLE 3

a Draw the graph of $y = x^2 - 3x - 4$ for $-2 \leqslant x \leqslant 5$.

b Use your graph to find the solutions of the equation $x^2 - 3x - 4 = 0$.

a Set up a table and draw the graph.

x	-2	-1	0	1	2	3	4	5
x^2	4	1	0	1	4	9	16	25
$-3x$	6	3	0	-3	-6	-9	-12	-15
-4	-4	-4	-4	-4	-4	-4	-4	-4
y	6	0	-4	-6	-6	-4	0	6

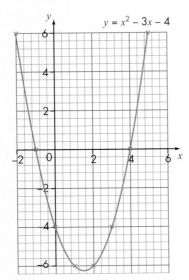

$y = x^2 - 3x - 4$

b The points where the graph crosses the x-axis are at $x = -1$ and $x = 4$.

So, the solution of $x^2 - 3x - 4 = 0$ is $x = -1$ or $x = 4$.

EXERCISE 25B

1 a Copy and complete the table to draw the graph of $y = x^2 - 4$ for $-4 \leqslant x \leqslant 4$.

x	-4	-3	-2	-1	0	1	2	3	4
y	12			-3				5	

b Use your graph to find the solutions of $x^2 - 4 = 0$.

2 a Copy and complete the table to draw the graph of $y = x^2 - 9$ for $-4 \leqslant x \leqslant 4$.

x	-4	-3	-2	-1	0	1	2	3	4
y	7				-9			0	

b Use your graph to find the solutions of $x^2 - 9 = 0$.

C

3 **a** Copy and complete the table to draw the graph of $y = x^2 + 4x$ for $-5 \leqslant x \leqslant 2$.

x	−5	−4	−3	−2	−1	0	1	2
x^2	25			4			1	
$+4x$	−20			−8			4	
y	5			−4			5	

b Use your graph to find the solutions of the equation $x^2 + 4x = 0$.

4 **a** Copy and complete the table to draw the graph of $y = x^2 - 6x$ for $-2 \leqslant x \leqslant 6$.

x	−2	−1	0	1	2	3	4	5	6
x^2	4			1			16		
$-6x$	12			−6			−24		
y	16			−5			−8		

b Use your graph to find the solutions of the equation $x^2 - 6x = 0$.

5 **a** Copy and complete the table to draw the graph of $y = x^2 + 3x$ for $-5 \leqslant x \leqslant 3$.

x	−5	−4	−3	−2	−1	0	1	2	3
y	10			−2				10	

b Use your graph to find the solutions of the equation $x^2 + 3x = 0$.

6 **a** Copy and complete the table to draw the graph of $y = x^2 - 6x + 3$ for $-1 \leqslant x \leqslant 7$.

x	−1	0	1	2	3	4	5	6	7
y	10			−5			−2		

b Use your graph to find the solutions of the equation $x^2 - 6x + 3 = 0$.

1 **a** Complete the table for the graph of $y = x^2 - 5$.

x	-3	-2	-1	0	1	2	3
y	4	-1	-4				4

b Draw the graph on a grid, labelling the x-axis from -3 to +3 and the y-axis from -6 to +6.

2 **a** Complete the table of values for $y = x^2 - 3x - 1$.

x	-2	-1	0	1	2	3	4
y		3	-1	-3			3

b Draw the graph on a grid labelling the x-axis from -2 to 4 and the y-axis from -4 to 10.

c Use your graph to find an estimate for the minimum value of y.

Edexcel, Question 2, Paper 10A Higher, March 2003

3 **a** Complete the table of values for the graph of $y = 4x(11 - 2x)$.

x	0	1	2	3	4	5	6
y	0			60			-24

b On a copy of the grid, draw the graph of $y = 4x(11 - 2x)$

c Use your graph to find the maximum value of y.

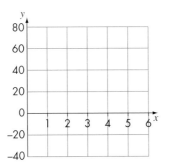

Edexcel, Question 5, Paper 10B Higher, January 2004

4 The graph of $y = x^2 + c$ is shown on the grid below.

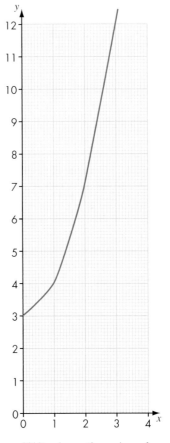

a Write down the value of c.

b Explain what happens to the graph if the value of c decreases by 2.

WORKED EXAM QUESTION

a Complete the table of values for $y = x^2 - 4x + 1$.

x	-1	0	1	2	3	4	5
y	6		-2		-2		6

b Draw the graph of $y = x^2 - 4x + 1$ for $-1 \leqslant x \leqslant 5$.

c Use your graph to solve the equation $x^2 - 4x + 1 = 0$.

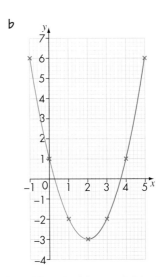

Solution

a When $x = 0$, $y = (0)^2 - 4(0) + 1 = 0 - 0 + 1 = 1$

When $x = 2$, $y = (2)^2 - 4(2) + 1 = 4 - 8 + 1 = -3$

When $x = 4$, $y = (4)^2 - 4(4) + 1 = 16 - 16 + 1 = 1$

c The solution to the equation is where the graph crosses the x-axis. There are two intersections, so the solutions are $x = 0.3$ or $x = 3.7$.

GRADE YOURSELF

D Able to draw a simple quadratic graph

C Able to draw a more complex quadratic graph

C Able to solve a quadratic equation from a graph

What you should know now

● How to draw a quadratic graph

● How to solve a quadratic equation from a graph

This book provides indicators of the equivalent grade level of maths questions throughout. The publishers wish to make clear that these grade indicators have been provided by Collins Education, and are not the responsibility of Edexcel Ltd. Whilst every effort has been made to assure their accuracy, they should be regarded as indicators, and are not binding or definitive.

Pythagoras' theorem

1 Pythagoras' theorem

2 Finding a shorter side

3 Solving problems using Pythagoras' theorem

This chapter will show you ...

- how to use Pythagoras' theorem in right-angled triangles
- how to solve problems using Pythagoras' theorem

Visual overview

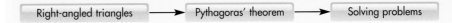

Right-angled triangles → Pythagoras' theorem → Solving problems

What you should already know

- How to find the square and square root of a number
- How to round numbers to a suitable degree of accuracy

Quick check

Use your calculator to evaluate the following, giving your answers to one decimal place.

1 2.3^2

2 15.7^2

3 0.78^2

4 $\sqrt{8}$

5 $\sqrt{260}$

6 $\sqrt{0.5}$

In this section you will learn how to:

- calculate the length of the hypotenuse in a right-angled triangle

Key words

hypotenuse
Pythagoras' theorem

Pythagoras, who was a philosopher as well as a mathematician, was born in 580 BC on the island of Samos in Greece. He later moved to Crotona (Italy), where he established the Pythagorean Brotherhood, which was a secret society devoted to politics, mathematics and astronomy. It is said that when he discovered his famous theorem, he was so full of joy that he showed his gratitude to the gods by sacrificing a hundred oxen.

ACTIVITY

1 Draw a right-angled triangle with sides of 3 cm and 4 cm, as shown.

2 Measure accurately the long side of the triangle (the **hypotenuse**).

3 Draw four more right-angled triangles, choosing your own lengths for the short sides.

4 When you have done this, measure the hypotenuse for each triangle.

5 Copy and complete the table below for your triangles.

Short side	Short side	Hypotenuse			
a	b	c	a^2	b^2	c^2
3	4	5	9	16	25

Is there a pattern in your results? Can you see that a^2, b^2 and c^2 are related in some way?

You should spot that the value of a^2 added to that of b^2 is very close to the value of c^2. (Why don't the values add up exactly?)

You have 'rediscovered' **Pythagoras' theorem**. His theorem can be expressed in several ways, two of which are given on the next page.

Consider squares being drawn on each side of a right-angled triangle, with sides 3 cm, 4 cm and 5 cm.

The longest side is called the **hypotenuse** and is always opposite the right angle.

Pythagoras' theorem can then be stated as follows:

> *For any right-angled triangle, the area of the square drawn on the hypotenuse is equal to the sum of the areas of the squares drawn on the other two sides.*

The form in which most of your parents would have learnt the theorem when they were at school – and which is still in use today – is as follows:

> *In any right-angled triangle, the square of the hypotenuse is equal to the sum of the squares of the other two sides.*

Pythagoras' theorem is more usually written as a formula:

$$c^2 = a^2 + b^2$$

Remember that Pythagoras' theorem can only be used in right-angled triangles.

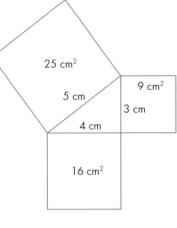

Finding the hypotenuse

EXAMPLE 1

Find the length of the hypotenuse, marked x on the diagram.

Using Pythagoras' theorem gives:

$$x^2 = 8^2 + 5.2^2$$
$$= 64 + 27.04$$
$$= 91.04$$

So, $x = \sqrt{91.04} = 9.5$ cm (1 decimal place)

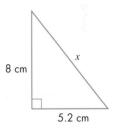

EXERCISE 26A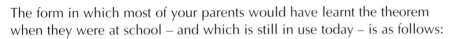

For each of the following triangles, calculate the length of the hypotenuse, x, rounding your answers to 1 decimal place.

1

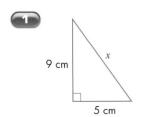

2

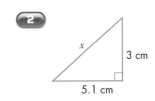

3

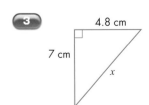

C

C

4

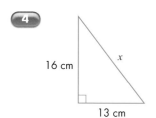

16 cm

x

13 cm

5

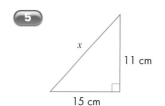

x

11 cm

15 cm

6

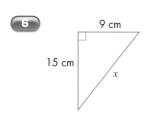

9 cm

15 cm

x

7

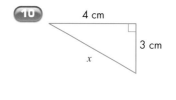

19 cm

x

26 cm

8

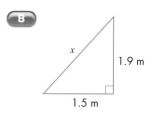

x

1.9 m

1.5 m

9

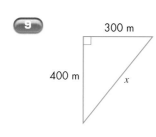

300 m

400 m

x

10

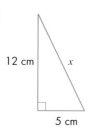

4 cm

3 cm

x

11

12 cm

x

5 cm

12

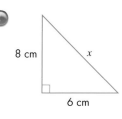

8 cm

x

6 cm

The last three examples give whole-number answers. Sets of whole numbers that obey Pythagoras' theorem are called *Pythagorean triples.* Examples of these are:

3, 4, 5   5, 12, 13   and   6, 8, 10

Note that 6, 8, 10 are respectively multiples of 3, 4, 5.

26.2 # Finding a shorter side

In this section you will learn how to:
- calculate the length of a shorter side in a right-angled triangle

Key word
Pythagoras' theorem

By rearranging the formula for **Pythagoras' theorem**, you can easily calculate the length of one of the shorter sides.

c

a

b

$$c^2 = a^2 + b^2$$

So: $a^2 = c^2 - b^2$ or $b^2 = c^2 - a^2$

EXAMPLE 2

Find the length x.

In the triangle, x is one of the shorter sides.

So, using Pythagoras' theorem gives:

$$x^2 = 15^2 - 11^2$$
$$= 225 - 121$$
$$= 104$$

So: $x = \sqrt{104} = 10.2$ cm (1 decimal place)

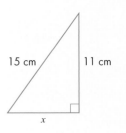

EXERCISE 26B

1 For each of the following triangles, calculate the length x to 1 decimal place.

HINTS AND TIPS

In this question you are finding the length of a shorter side. Subtract the square of the other short side from the square of the hypotenuse in every case.

a

17 cm

x

8 cm

b

24 cm

x

19 cm

c

6.4 cm

x

9 cm

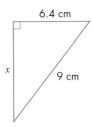

d

31 cm

25 cm

x

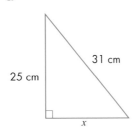

e

x

7.2 cm

9 cm

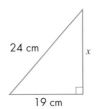

f

500 m

x

450 m

g

x

1 cm

0.9 cm

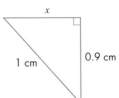

h

17 m

x

15 m

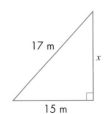

2 For each of the following triangles, calculate the length x to 1 decimal place.

a
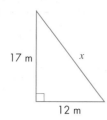
17 m x 12 m

b
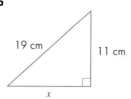
19 cm 11 cm x

c

17 m x 23 m

d
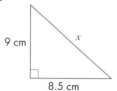
9 cm x 8.5 cm

e

34 m x 41 m

f
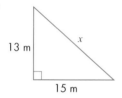
13 m x 15 m

g
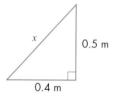
7 m 10 m x

h
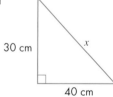
x 0.5 m 0.4 m

3 For each of the following triangles, find the length marked x.

a
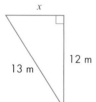
x 12 m 13 m

b
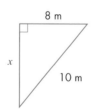
8 m x 10 m

c
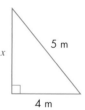
5 m x 4 m

d
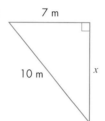
30 cm x 40 cm

26.3 # Solving problems using Pythagoras' theorem

In this section you will learn how to:
• solve problems using Pythagoras' theorem

Key words
Pythagoras' theorem

Pythagoras' theorem can be used to solve certain practical problems. When a problem involves two lengths only, follow these steps.

• Draw a diagram for the problem, making sure that it includes a right-angled triangle.

- Look at the diagram and decide which side has to be found: the hypotenuse or one of the shorter sides. Label the unknown side x.

- If it is the hypotenuse, then square both numbers, add the squares and take the square root of the sum.

- If it is one of the shorter sides, then square both numbers, subtract the smaller square from the larger square and take the square root of the difference.

EXAMPLE 3

A plane leaves Manchester airport and heads due east. It flies 160 km before turning due north. It then flies a further 280 km and lands. What is the distance of the return flight if the plane flies straight back to Manchester airport?

First, sketch the situation.

Using Pythagoras' theorem gives:

$$x^2 = 160^2 + 280^2$$
$$= 25\ 600 + 78\ 400$$
$$= 104\ 000$$

So: $x = \sqrt{104\ 000} = 322$ km (nearest whole number)

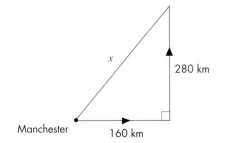

Remember the following tips when solving problems.

- Always sketch the right-angled triangle you need. Sometimes, the triangle is already drawn for you but some problems involve other lines and triangles that may confuse you. So identify which right-angled triangle you need and sketch it separately.

- Label the triangle with necessary information, such as the length of its sides, taken from the question. Label the unknown side x.

- Set out your solution as in the last example. Avoid shortcuts, since they often cause errors. You gain marks in your examination for showing clearly how you are applying Pythagoras' theorem to the problem.

- Round your answer to a suitable degree of accuracy.

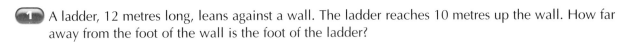

EXERCISE 26C

1 A ladder, 12 metres long, leans against a wall. The ladder reaches 10 metres up the wall. How far away from the foot of the wall is the foot of the ladder?

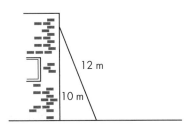

2 A model football pitch is 2 metres long and 0.5 metres wide. How long is the diagonal?

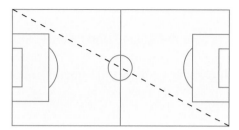

3 How long is the diagonal of a rectangle 6 metres long and 9 metres wide?

4 How long is the diagonal of a square with a side of 8 metres?

5 In a hockey game, after a pass was made, the ball travelled 7 metres up the field and 6 metres across the field. How long was the actual pass?

6 A ship going from a port to a lighthouse steams 15 km east and 12 km north. How far is the lighthouse from the port?

7 A plane flies from London due north for 120 km before turning due west and flying for a further 85 km and landing at a secret location. How far from London is the secret location?

8 Some pedestrians want to get from point X on one road to point Y on another. The two roads meet at right angles.

a If they follow the roads, how far will they walk?

b Instead of walking along the road, they take the shortcut, XY. Find the length of the shortcut.

c How much distance do they save?

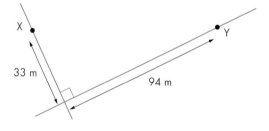

9 At the moment, three towns, A, B and C, are joined by two roads, as in the diagram. The council want to make a road that runs directly from A to C. How much distance will the new road save?

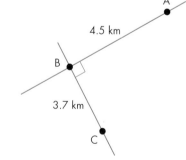

10 A mast on a sailboat is strengthened by a wire (called a stay), as shown on the diagram. The mast is 35 feet tall and the stay is 37 feet long. How far from the base of the mast does the stay reach?

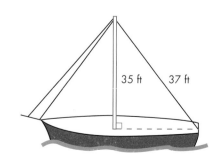

11 A 4-metre ladder is put up against a wall.

    a How far up the wall will it reach when the foot of the ladder is 1 m away from the wall?

    b When it reaches 3.6 m up the wall, how far is the foot of the ladder away from the wall?

12 A pole, 8 m high, is supported by metal wires, each 8.6 m long, attached to the top of the pole. How far from the foot of the pole are the wires fixed to the ground?

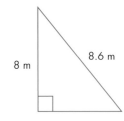

13 A line segment AB is drawn from A(1, 1) to B(13, 6).

    a What are the coordinates of the midpoint of AB?

    b If one grid square is 1 cm^2, what is the length of AB?

14 A line segment PQ is drawn from P(2, 3) to Q(52, 53).

    a What are the coordinates of the midpoint of PQ?

    b If one grid square is 1 cm^2, what is the length of PQ?

15 The regulation for safe use of ladders states that, for a 5 m ladder: *The foot of the ladder must be placed between 1.6 m and 2.1 m from the foot of the wall.*

    a What is the maximum height the ladder can safely reach up the wall?

    b What is the minimum height the ladder can safely reach up the wall?

16 A rectangle is 4.5 cm long. The length of its diagonal is 5.8 cm. What is the area of the rectangle?

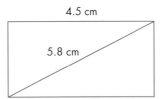

> **HINTS AND TIPS**
>
> First find the width, then the area

17 Two large trees, 5.5 m and 6.8 m tall, stand 12 m apart. A bird flies directly from the top of one tree to the top of the other. How far has the bird flown?

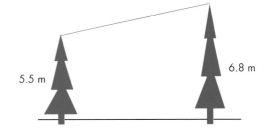

18 Is the triangle with sides 7 cm, 24 cm and 25 cm, a right-angled triangle?

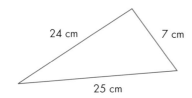

1 A football pitch ABCD is shown. The length of the pitch, AB = 120 m. The width of the pitch, BC = 90 m.

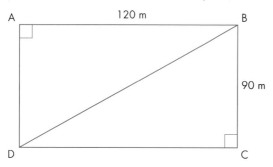

Calculate the length of the diagonal BD.
Give your answer to 1 decimal place.

2 A ladder is leant against a wall. Its foot is 0.8 m from the wall and it reaches to a height of 4 m up the wall.

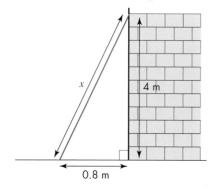

Calculate the length, in metres, of the ladder (marked *x* on the diagram). Give your answer to a suitable degree of accuracy.

3 In the diagram, ABC is a right-angled triangle. AC = 18 cm and AB = 12 cm.

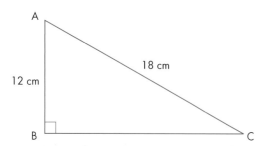

Calculate the length of BC.

4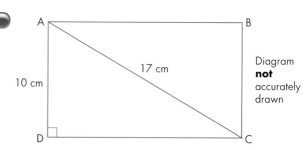

ABCD is a rectangle.
AC = 17 cm.
AD = 10 cm.
Calculate the length of the side CD.
Give your answer correct to 1 decimal place.

Edexcel, Question 20, Paper 4, November 2004

5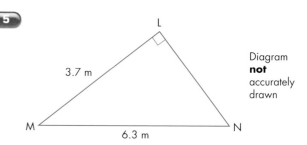

Angle MLN = 90°.
LM = 3.7 m.
MN = 6.3 m.
Work out the length of LN.
Give your answer correct to 1 decimal place.

Edexcel, Question 1, Paper 10B Higher, March 2004

6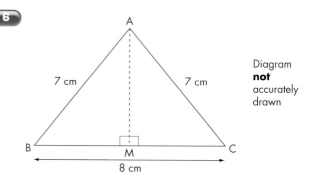

Work out the length, in centimetres, of AM.
Give your answer correct to 2 decimal places.

Edexcel, Question 1, Paper 10B Higher, March 2003

7 The diagram shows a ship, S, out at sea.
It is 30 kilometres East and 25 kilometres North from a
port, P.

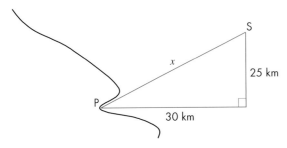

Calculate the direct distance from the port to the ship.
(The distance is marked *x* on the diagram).

Give your answer to 1 decimal place.

8 The diagram shows Penny's house, H, and her school, S.

Penny can get to school by car, by going down the
road to the junction at X and then travelling along the
road XS to school.

She can also walk to school along the footpath HS.

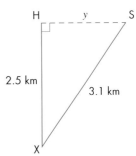

a Calculate the distance along the footpath if she
walks to school. (The distance is marked *y* on the
diagram).

b How much shorter is the journey if she walks to
school?

Give your answers to 1 decimal place.

WORKED EXAM QUESTION

The sketch shows triangle ABC. AB = 60 cm, AC = 61 cm and BC = 11 cm.

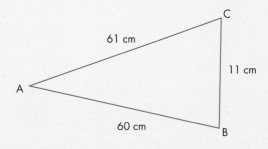

By calculation, show that triangle ABC is a right-angled triangle.

Solution

For triangle ABC to be right-angled, the right angle must be at B and AC must be the hypotenuse.

$60^2 + 11^2 = 3600 + 121 = 3721$ and also $61^2 = 3721$

So $60^2 + 11^2 = 61^2$

Therefore the sides satisfy Pythagoras' theorem and therefore triangle ABC must be right-angled.

GRADE YOURSELF

c Able to use Pythagoras' theorem in right-angled triangles

c Able to solve problems in 2-D using Pythagoras' theorem

What you should know now

- How to use Pythagoras' theorem to find the hypotenuse or one of the shorter sides of a right-angled triangle, given the other two sides
- How to solve problems using Pythagoras' theorem

Coursework guidance

During your GCSE course, you will need to do two coursework tasks. One of the tasks will cover the content from Number and Algebra and/or Shape and Space (Ma1 task), and the other will cover the content from Handling Data (Ma4 task). The tasks will be assessed and marked by your teacher or by the examination board. Each task will carry 10% of the total marks for the examination. Each task has three strands, with a maximum mark of 8 in each strand. The two tables, which follow, will give you some idea of what each strand means and what you need to do in order to obtain a particular mark in each strand.

Ma1 task

- **Strand i**: Decisions. This is about how you decide to solve a particular problem and then how you ask your own questions in order to extend the problem.
- **Strand ii**: Presentation. This is about how you present your work mathematically. It involves making tables of results, drawing graphs, using algebraic notation or using computer software.
- **Strand iii**: Reasons. This is about finding solutions to problems and drawing conclusions. You need to find patterns, rules or formulae and to explain how you obtained them.

Mark	Strand i: Making and monitoring decisions to solve problems	Strand ii: Communicating mathematically	Strand iii: Developing skills of mathematical reasoning
1	You should show that you understand the problem by giving an example.	You should explain how you intend to solve the problem by giving an example or by drawing a diagram.	You should find an easy example that fits the problem.
2	You should plan a suitable method to help solve the problem further by giving at least three examples.	You should write out your results clearly and carefully in a list or show them on diagrams.	You should look for any patterns in your results.
3	You should identify the information needed to solve the problem and check that your results are correct.	You should show your results in a clearly labelled table or by using diagrams and symbols.	You should explain the pattern, or find a rule for your results.
4	You should break down the problem into easier and more manageable stages.	You should link your tables, diagrams or graphs with a clear explanation.	You should test a different example to show that your pattern or rule works and comment on the outcome.
5	You should introduce some questions of your own in order to extend the problem to give a further solution.	You should find an algebraic formula to explain the rule and show by substitution that the formula works.	You should explain why your rule or formula works by using simple algebra, graphs or computer software.
6	You should develop the problem further by using algebra, graphs or trigonometry.	You should introduce more difficult algebra or trigonometry on at least three occasions.	You should comment constructively on your solution to show that you have fully understood the problem.
7	You should analyse a more complex problem by considering approaches which manipulate three variables.	You should show you can present an accurate and convincing mathematical solution or proof.	You should give reasons why you are considering using approaches which use three variables.
8	You should introduce new content or an area of mathematics that is unfamiliar into a more complex problem.	You should use mathematical techniques efficiently to give a complete and concise solution or proof.	You should provide an accurate proof to a more complex problem and explain the conditions under which it remains valid.

Ma4 task

- **Strand i**: Planning. This is about how you decide to design the problem by specifying your aims and hypotheses and planning an overall strategy.
- **Strand ii**: Collection and presentation of data. This is about the methods you use to collect the data for the problem and how you use statistical calculations, diagrams or computer software to illustrate the data.
- **Strand iii**: Interpretation. This is about how you interpret and summarise the results based on your statistical calculations and diagrams. It also involves evaluating your strategy and how you could make improvements.

Mark	Strand i: Specify and plan	Strand ii: Process and represent	Strand iii: Interpret and discuss
1–2	Collect data relevant to the problem. State your overall plan and aims.	Present your results on diagrams such as bar charts or pictograms. Use the mode and range for the data.	Make a comment on the data. Attempt to summarise any results you notice in the data.
3–4	Your plan should include a suitable hypothesis relevant to the problem. Decide how to collect your data and use an appropriate sample size.	Use relevant statistical calculations for the problem, such as mode, median, mean and range. Present your data in a variety of forms, such as stem-and-leaf diagrams, scatter graphs or pie charts, and link them with a relevant explanation.	Interpret any graphs and statistical calculations used and draw sensible conclusions, which relate to your original hypothesis.. Comment on how you could improve your work.
5–6	In a more complex problem, you should develop hypotheses that are linked and where comparisons can be made. Consider how to overcome any practical problems when choosing your sample.	Ensure that your data is relevant, and use more complex statistical calculations, such as the mean for grouped data. Use appropriate diagrams, such as cumulative frequency graphs, box plots or lines of best fit, and give clear reasons for your choice of presentation.	Summarise and correctly interpret your diagrams and statistical calculations. Make relevant comparisons and show that the nature of the sampling method used may have some significance on your results. Evaluate the effectiveness of your strategy.
7–8	In a more demanding problem, you should plan and look for practical problems that you might encounter and consider how to avoid bias, modifying your method of data collection in light of this. Use other suitable data collection techniques and refine these to enhance the problem.	You should ensure that all practical problems are dealt with, and use effectively a wide range of more advanced statistical calculations to present a convincing argument. Use a range of diagrams, such as histograms, to help you to summarise the data and show how the variables are related.	All diagrams and calculations should be correctly interpreted in order to appreciate the significance of the results. You should explain why any possible bias might affect your conclusions, and make suggestions on how you could make an improvement. Comment on any limitations in your work.

For all GCSE mathematics qualifications for first examination in June 2009 with first certification June 2009, coursework does not form part of the assessment. The assessment consists of examination papers only. Therefore these coursework pages are not appropriate for these GCSE mathematics qualifications.

Quick check

1 24   **2** 21   **3** 40   **4** 18   **5** 42

6 27   **7** 30   **8** 6   **9** 12   **10** 5

11 10   **12** 8   **13** 5   **14** 7   **15** 4

16 80   **17** 900   **18** 30   **19** 1400

20 170

Exercise 1A

1 a 45   **b** 43   **c** 40   **d** 45   **e** 45   **f** 36
   g 43   **h** 42   **i** 41

2 a 0, 4, 8   **b** 6, 2, 9   **c** 1, 0, 6   **d** 9, 1, 7, 6
   e 4, 9, 0, 10, 3, 8   **f** 6, 5, 7, 18, 8, 17, 45
   g 8, 6, 12, 1, 7, 22   **h** 1, 8, 0, 13, 5, 19, 43
   i 1, 6, 5, 0, 7, 3, 7, 14, 11 or 1, 6, 5, 7, 14, 3, 0, 7, 11

Exercise 1B

1 a 20   **b** 21   **c** 24   **d** 15   **e** 16   **f** 12
   g 10   **h** 42   **i** 24   **j** 18   **k** 30   **l** 28
   m 18   **n** 56   **o** 25   **p** 45   **q** 27   **r** 30
   s 49   **t** 24   **u** 36   **v** 35   **w** 32   **x** 36
   y 48

2 a 5   **b** 4   **c** 6   **d** 6   **e** 5   **f** 4   **g** 7
   h 6   **i** 2   **j** 3   **k** 7   **l** 8   **m** 9   **n** 5
   o 8   **p** 9   **q** 4   **r** 7   **s** 7   **t** 9   **u** 5
   v 4   **w** 5   **x** 7   **y** 6

3 a 12   **b** 15   **c** 21   **d** 13   **e** 8   **f** 7
   g 14   **h** 3   **i** 30   **j** 6   **k** 35   **l** 5
   m 16   **n** 7   **o** 16   **p** 15   **q** 27   **r** 6
   s 15   **t** 24   **u** 40   **v** 6   **w** 17   **x** 72
   y 46

4 a 30   **b** 50   **c** 80   **d** 100   **e** 120
   f 180   **g** 240   **h** 400   **i** 700   **j** 900
   k 1000   **l** 1400   **m** 2400   **n** 7200
   o 10 000   **p** 2   **q** 7   **r** 9   **s** 17
   t 30   **u** 3   **v** 8   **w** 12   **x** 29
   y 50

Exercise 1C

1 a 11   **b** 6   **c** 10   **d** 12   **e** 11   **f** 13
   g 11   **h** 12   **i** 12   **j** 4   **k** 13   **l** 3

2 a 16   **b** 2   **c** 10   **d** 10   **e** 6   **f** 18
   g 6   **h** 15   **i** 9   **j** 12   **k** 3   **l** 8

3 b 3 + (2 × 4) = 11   **c** (9 ÷ 3) − 2 = 1
   d 9 − (4 ÷ 2) = 7   **e** (5 × 2) + 3 = 13
   f 5 + (2 × 3) = 11   **g** (10 ÷ 5) − 2 = 0
   h 10 − (4 ÷ 2) = 8   **i** (4 × 6) − 7 = 17
   j 7 + (4 × 6) = 31   **k** (6 ÷ 3) + 7 = 9
   l 7 + (6 ÷ 2) = 10

4 a 38   **b** 48   **c** 3   **d** 2   **e** 5   **f** 14
   g 10   **h** 2   **i** 5   **j** 19   **k** 15   **l** 2
   m 20   **n** 19   **o** 54   **p** 7   **q** 2   **r** 7
   s 7   **t** 38   **u** 42   **v** 10   **w** 2   **x** 10
   y 10   **z** 24

5 a (4 + 1)   **b** No brackets needed
   c (2 + 1)   **d** No brackets needed
   e (4 + 4)   **f** (16 − 4)
   g No brackets needed   **h** No brackets needed
   i (20 − 10)   **j** No brackets needed
   k (5 + 5)   **l** (4 + 2)
   m (15 − 5)   **n** (7 − 2)   **o** (3 + 3)
   p No brackets needed   **q** No brackets needed
   r (8 − 2)

6 a 8   **b** 6   **c** 6   **d** 13   **e** 11   **f** 9
   g 12   **h** 8   **i** 15   **j** 16   **k** 1   **l** 7

7 a 2 × 3 + 5   **b** 2 × (3 + 5)   **c** 2 + 3 × 5
   d 5 − (3 − 2) and (5 + 3) ÷ 2   **e** 5 × 3 − 2
   f 5 × 3 × 2

Exercise 1D

1 a 40   **b** 5 units   **c** 100   **d** 90   **e** 80
   f 9 units   **g** 80   **h** 500   **i** 0   **j** 5000
   k 0   **l** 4 units   **m** 300   **n** 90   **o** 80 000

2 a Forty-three, two hundred
   b One hundred and thirty-six; four thousand and ninety-nine
   c Two hundred and seventy-one; ten thousand, seven hundred and forty-four

3 a Five million, six hundred thousand
   b Four million, seventy-five thousand, two hundred
   c Three million, seven thousand, nine hundred and fifty
   d Two million, seven hundred and eighty-two

4 a 8 200 058   **b** 9 406 107   **c** 1 000 502   **d** 2 076 040

5 a 9, 15, 21, 23, 48, 54, 56, 85
   b 25, 62, 86, 151, 219, 310, 400, 501
   c 97, 357, 368, 740, 888, 2053, 4366

6 a 95, 89, 73, 52, 34, 25, 23, 7
   b 700, 401, 174, 117, 80, 65, 18, 2
   c 6227, 3928, 2034, 762, 480, 395, 89, 59

7 a Larger   **b** Larger   **c** Smaller   **d** Larger
   e Larger   **f** Smaller   **g** Larger   **h** Smaller
   i Smaller

8 a 368, 386, 638, 683, 836, 863   **b** 368   **c** 863

9 408, 480, 804, 840

10 33, 35, 38, 53, 55, 58, 83, 85, 88

Exercise 1E

1 a 20   **b** 60   **c** 80   **d** 50   **e** 100
   f 20   **g** 90   **h** 70   **i** 10   **j** 30
   k 30   **l** 50   **m** 80   **n** 50   **o** 90
   p 40   **q** 70   **r** 20   **s** 100   **t** 110

2 a 200   **b** 600   **c** 800   **d** 500   **e** 1000
   f 100   **g** 600   **h** 400   **i** 1000   **j** 1100
   k 300   **l** 500   **m** 800   **n** 500   **o** 900
   p 400   **q** 700   **r** 800   **s** 1000   **t** 1100

3 a 1   **b** 2   **c** 1   **d** 1   **e** 3   **f** 2
   g 3   **h** 2   **i** 1   **j** 1   **k** 3   **l** 2
   m 74   **n** 126   **o** 184

4 a 2000   **b** 6000   **c** 8000   **d** 5000
   e 10 000   **f** 1000   **g** 6000   **h** 3000
   i 9000   **j** 2000   **k** 3000   **l** 5000
   m 8000   **n** 5000   **o** 9000   **p** 4000

q 7000   **r** 8000   **s** 1000   **t** 2000

5 a 230   **b** 570   **c** 720   **d** 520   **e** 910
 f 230   **g** 880   **h** 630   **i** 110   **j** 300
 k 280   **l** 540   **m** 770   **n** 500   **o** 940
 p 380   **q** 630   **r** 350   **s** 1010   **t** 1070

6 a True   **b** False   **c** True
 d True   **e** True   **f** False

7 a Man Utd v West Brom   **b** Blackburn v Fulham
 c 40 000, 19 000, 42 000, 26 000, 40 000, 68 000,
 35 000, 25 000, 20 000
 d 39 600, 19 000, 42 100, 26 100, 40 400, 67 800,
 34 800, 25 500, 20 200

8 a 35 min   **b** 55 min   **c** 15 min   **d** 50 min
 e 10 min   **f** 15 min   **g** 45 min   **h** 35 min
 i 5 min   **j** 0 min

Exercise 1F

1 a 713   **b** 151   **c** 6381   **d** 968   **e** 622
 f 1315   **g** 8260   **h** 818   **i** 451   **j** 852

2 a 646   **b** 826   **c** 3818   **d** 755   **e** 2596
 f 891   **g** 350   **h** 2766   **i** 8858   **j** 841
 k 6831   **l** 7016   **m** 1003   **n** 4450
 o 9944

3 a 450   **b** 563   **c** 482   **d** 414   **e** 285
 f 486   **g** 244   **h** 284   **i** 333   **j** 216
 k 2892   **l** 4417   **m** 3767   **n** 4087
 o 1828

4 a 128   **b** 29   **c** 334   **d** 178   **e** 277
 f 285   **g** 335   **h** 399   **i** 4032   **j** 4765
 k 3795   **l** 5437

5 a 6, 7   **b** 4, 7   **c** 4, 8   **d** 4, 7, 9
 e 6, 7, 9   **f** 2, 7, 6   **g** 6, 6, 2   **h** 4, 5, 9
 i 4, 8, 8   **j** 4, 4, 9, 8

6 a 5, 3   **b** 8, 3   **c** 5, 8   **d** 5, 4, 8
 e 6, 5, 7   **f** 2, 1, 1   **g** 2, 7, 7   **h** 5, 5, 6
 i 8, 8, 3   **j** 1, 8, 8, 9

Exercise 1G

1 a 56   **b** 65   **c** 51   **d** 38   **e** 108
 f 115   **g** 204   **h** 294   **i** 212   **j** 425
 k 150   **l** 800   **m** 960   **n** 1360   **o** 1518

2 a 294   **b** 370   **c** 288   **d** 832   **e** 2163
 f 2520   **g** 1644   **h** 3215   **i** 3000   **j** 2652
 k 3696   **l** 1880   **m** 54 387
 n 21 935   **o** 48 888

3 a 219   **b** 317   **c** 315   **d** 106   **e** 99
 f 121   **g** 252   **h** 141   **i** 144   **j** 86
 k 63   **l** 2909   **m** 416   **n** 251   **o** 1284

4 a 119   **b** 96   **c** 144   **d** 210   **e** 210

5 a 13   **b** 37 weeks   **c** 43 m
 d 36   **e** 45

Really Useful Maths!: Paradise in Pembrokeshire

Totals: £64, £70, £36, £58, £65, £118, £38, £46, £99

Cost of holiday (£): Activities, 594.00; Cottage, 550.00; Petrol, 54.00; Total, 1198

ANSWERS TO CHAPTER 2

Quick check

1 8	**2** 15	**3** 10	**4** 18	**5** 14
6 20	**7** 24	**8** 24	**9** 18	**10** 21
11 5	**12** 6	**13** 8	**14** 4	**15** 10
16 3	**17** 5	**18** 3	**19** 2	**20** 4

Exercise 2A

1 a $\frac{1}{4}$ **b** $\frac{1}{3}$ **c** $\frac{5}{8}$ **d** $\frac{7}{12}$ **e** $\frac{4}{9}$ **f** $\frac{3}{10}$ **g** $\frac{3}{8}$
 h $\frac{15}{16}$ **i** $\frac{5}{12}$ **j** $\frac{7}{18}$ **k** $\frac{4}{8}=\frac{1}{2}$ **l** $\frac{4}{12}=\frac{1}{3}$
 m $\frac{6}{9}=\frac{2}{3}$ **n** $\frac{6}{10}=\frac{3}{5}$ **o** $\frac{4}{8}=\frac{1}{2}$ **p** $\frac{5}{64}$

Exercise 2B

1 a $\frac{3}{4}$ **b** $\frac{4}{8}=\frac{1}{2}$ **c** $\frac{3}{5}$ **d** $\frac{8}{10}=\frac{4}{5}$ **e** $\frac{2}{3}$ **f** $\frac{5}{7}$
 g $\frac{7}{9}$ **h** $\frac{5}{6}$ **i** $\frac{4}{5}$ **j** $\frac{7}{8}$ **k** $\frac{5}{10}=\frac{1}{2}$ **l** $\frac{5}{7}$ **m** $\frac{4}{5}$
 n $\frac{5}{6}$ **o** $\frac{5}{9}$ **p** $\frac{7}{11}$

2 a $\frac{2}{4}=\frac{1}{2}$ **b** $\frac{3}{5}$ **c** $\frac{3}{8}$ **d** $\frac{3}{10}$ **e** $\frac{1}{3}$ **f** $\frac{4}{6}=\frac{2}{3}$

g $\frac{3}{7}$ **h** $\frac{5}{9}$ **i** $\frac{1}{5}$ **j** $\frac{3}{7}$ **k** $\frac{3}{9}=\frac{1}{3}$ **l** $\frac{6}{10}=\frac{3}{5}$
 m $\frac{3}{6}=\frac{1}{2}$ **n** $\frac{2}{8}=\frac{1}{4}$ **o** $\frac{2}{11}$ **p** $\frac{4}{10}=\frac{2}{5}$

3 a (diagram)   **b** (diagram)   **c i** $\frac{3}{4}$ **ii** $\frac{1}{4}$

4 a (diagram)   **b** (diagram)
 c i $\frac{6}{10}=\frac{3}{5}$ **ii** $\frac{8}{10}=\frac{4}{5}$ **iii** $\frac{7}{10}$

Exercise 2C

1 a $\frac{4}{24}$ **b** $\frac{8}{24}$ **c** $\frac{3}{24}$ **d** $\frac{16}{24}$ **e** $\frac{20}{24}$ **f** $\frac{18}{24}$
 g $\frac{9}{24}$ **h** $\frac{15}{24}$ **i** $\frac{21}{24}$ **j** $\frac{12}{24}$

2 a $\frac{11}{24}$ **b** $\frac{9}{24}$ **c** $\frac{7}{24}$ **d** $\frac{19}{24}$ **e** $\frac{23}{24}$ **f** $\frac{23}{24}$
 g $\frac{21}{24}$ **h** $\frac{22}{24}$ **i** $\frac{19}{24}$ **j** $\frac{23}{24}$

3 a $\frac{5}{20}$ **b** $\frac{4}{20}$ **c** $\frac{15}{20}$ **d** $\frac{16}{20}$ **e** $\frac{2}{20}$ **f** $\frac{10}{20}$
 g $\frac{12}{20}$ **h** $\frac{8}{20}$ **i** $\frac{14}{20}$ **j** $\frac{6}{20}$

4 a $\frac{9}{20}$ **b** $\frac{14}{20}$ **c** $\frac{11}{20}$ **d** $\frac{19}{20}$ **e** $\frac{19}{20}$

Exercise 2D

1 a $\frac{8}{20}$ b $\frac{3}{12}$ c $\frac{15}{40}$ d $\frac{12}{15}$ e $\frac{15}{18}$ f $\frac{12}{28}$

  g $\times 2, \frac{6}{20}$ h $\times 3, \frac{3}{9}$ i $\times 4, \frac{12}{20}$ j $\times 6, \frac{12}{18}$

  k $\times 3, \frac{9}{12}$ l $\times 5, \frac{25}{40}$ m $\times 2, \frac{14}{20}$ n $\times 4, \frac{4}{24}$

  o $\times 5, \frac{15}{40}$

2 a $\frac{1}{2} = \frac{2}{4} = \frac{3}{6} = \frac{4}{8} = \frac{5}{10} = \frac{6}{12}$

  b $\frac{1}{3} = \frac{2}{6} = \frac{3}{9} = \frac{4}{12} = \frac{5}{15} = \frac{6}{18}$

  c $\frac{3}{4} = \frac{6}{8} = \frac{9}{12} = \frac{12}{16} = \frac{15}{20} = \frac{18}{24}$

  d $\frac{2}{5} = \frac{4}{10} = \frac{6}{15} = \frac{8}{20} = \frac{10}{25} = \frac{12}{30}$

  e $\frac{3}{7} = \frac{6}{14} = \frac{9}{21} = \frac{12}{28} = \frac{15}{35} = \frac{18}{42}$

3 a $\frac{2}{3}$ b $\frac{4}{5}$ c $\frac{5}{7}$ d $\div 6, \frac{2}{3}$ e $\frac{3}{5}$ f $\div 3, \frac{7}{10}$

4 a $\frac{2}{3}$ b $\frac{1}{3}$ c $\frac{2}{5}$ d $\frac{3}{4}$ e $\frac{1}{3}$ f $\frac{1}{2}$ g $\frac{7}{8}$

  h $\frac{4}{5}$ i $\frac{1}{2}$ j $\frac{1}{4}$ k $\frac{4}{5}$ l $\frac{5}{7}$ m $\frac{5}{7}$ n $\frac{2}{3}$

  o $\frac{2}{5}$ p $\frac{2}{5}$ q $\frac{1}{3}$ r $\frac{7}{10}$ s $\frac{1}{4}$ t $\frac{3}{2} = 1\frac{1}{2}$

  u $\frac{2}{3}$ v $\frac{2}{3}$ w $\frac{3}{4}$ x $\frac{3}{2} = 1\frac{1}{2}$ y $\frac{7}{2} = 3\frac{1}{2}$

5 a $\frac{1}{2}, \frac{2}{3}, \frac{5}{6}$ b $\frac{1}{2}, \frac{5}{8}, \frac{3}{4}$ c $\frac{2}{5}, \frac{1}{2}, \frac{7}{10}$ d $\frac{7}{12}, \frac{2}{3}, \frac{3}{4}$

  e $\frac{1}{6}, \frac{1}{4}, \frac{1}{3}$ f $\frac{3}{4}, \frac{4}{5}, \frac{9}{10}$ g $\frac{7}{10}, \frac{4}{5}, \frac{5}{6}$ h $\frac{3}{10}, \frac{1}{3}, \frac{2}{5}$

Exercise 2E

1 $2\frac{1}{3}$ 2 $2\frac{2}{3}$ 3 $2\frac{1}{4}$ 4 $1\frac{3}{7}$ 5 $2\frac{2}{5}$ 6 $1\frac{2}{5}$

7 $2\frac{2}{5}$ 8 $3\frac{3}{4}$ 9 $3\frac{1}{2}$ 10 $2\frac{1}{7}$ 11 $2\frac{5}{6}$ 12 $3\frac{3}{5}$

13 $4\frac{3}{4}$ 14 $3\frac{1}{7}$ 15 $1\frac{3}{11}$ 16 $1\frac{1}{11}$ 17 $5\frac{3}{5}$ 18 $2\frac{5}{7}$

19 $5\frac{5}{7}$ 20 $8\frac{2}{5}$ 21 $2\frac{1}{10}$ 22 $2\frac{1}{2}$ 23 $1\frac{1}{3}$ 24 $3\frac{1}{8}$

25 $2\frac{3}{10}$ 26 $2\frac{1}{11}$ 27 $7\frac{3}{5}$ 28 $5\frac{3}{7}$ 29 5 30 2

31 $\frac{10}{3}$ 32 $\frac{35}{6}$ 33 $\frac{9}{5}$ 34 $\frac{37}{7}$ 35 $\frac{41}{10}$ 36 $\frac{17}{3}$

37 $\frac{5}{2}$ 38 $\frac{13}{4}$ 39 $\frac{43}{6}$ 40 $\frac{29}{8}$ 41 $\frac{19}{3}$ 42 $\frac{89}{9}$

43 $\frac{59}{5}$ 44 $\frac{16}{5}$ 45 $\frac{35}{8}$ 46 $\frac{28}{9}$ 47 $\frac{26}{5}$ 48 $\frac{11}{4}$

49 $\frac{30}{7}$ 50 $\frac{49}{6}$ 51 $\frac{26}{9}$ 52 $\frac{37}{5}$ 53 $\frac{61}{5}$ 54 $\frac{13}{8}$

55 $\frac{71}{10}$ 56 $\frac{73}{9}$ 57 $\frac{61}{8}$ 58 $\frac{21}{2}$ 59 $\frac{17}{16}$ 60 $\frac{19}{4}$

Exercise 2F

1 a $\frac{6}{8} = \frac{3}{4}$ b $\frac{4}{10} = \frac{2}{5}$ c $\frac{6}{9} = \frac{2}{3}$ d $\frac{3}{4}$ e $\frac{6}{10} = \frac{3}{5}$

  f $\frac{6}{12} = \frac{1}{2}$ g $\frac{8}{16} = \frac{1}{2}$ h $\frac{10}{16} = \frac{5}{8}$

2 a $\frac{12}{10} = \frac{6}{5} = 1\frac{1}{5}$ b $\frac{9}{8} = 1\frac{1}{8}$ c $\frac{9}{8} = 1\frac{1}{8}$ d $\frac{13}{8} = 1\frac{5}{8}$

  e $\frac{11}{8} = 1\frac{3}{8}$ f $\frac{7}{6} = 1\frac{1}{6}$ g $\frac{9}{6} = 1\frac{3}{6} = 1\frac{1}{2}$ h $\frac{5}{4} = 1\frac{1}{4}$

3 a $\frac{10}{8} = \frac{5}{4} = 1\frac{1}{4}$ b $\frac{6}{4} = \frac{3}{2} = 1\frac{1}{2}$ c $\frac{5}{5} = 1$

  d $\frac{16}{10} = \frac{8}{5} = 1\frac{3}{5}$ e $\frac{10}{8} = \frac{5}{4} = 1\frac{1}{4}$ f $\frac{22}{16} = \frac{11}{8} = 1\frac{3}{8}$

  g $\frac{16}{12} = \frac{4}{3} = 1\frac{1}{3}$ h $\frac{18}{16} = \frac{9}{8} = 1\frac{1}{8}$ i $1\frac{3}{4}$ j $3\frac{1}{4}$

  k $6\frac{1}{4}$ l $3\frac{5}{8}$

4 a $\frac{4}{8} = \frac{1}{2}$ b $\frac{6}{10} = \frac{3}{5}$ c $\frac{1}{4}$ d $\frac{3}{8}$ e $\frac{1}{4}$ f $\frac{3}{8}$

  g $\frac{4}{10} = \frac{2}{5}$ h $\frac{5}{16}$ i $\frac{1}{4}$ j $1\frac{2}{3}$ k $2\frac{1}{4}$ l $2\frac{1}{8}$

Exercise 2G

1 $\frac{1}{2}$ 2 a $\frac{1}{4}$ b $\frac{3}{8}$ c Ayesha 3 $\frac{4}{6} = \frac{2}{3}$

4 $\frac{3}{8}$ 5 $\frac{2}{5}$ 6 $\frac{3}{8}$ 7 $\frac{4}{11}$ 8 $\frac{1}{6}$ 9 $\frac{5}{8}$

Exercise 2H

1 a 18 b 10 c 18 d 28 e 15 f 18
  g 48 h 45

2 a £1800 b 128 g c 160 kg d £116
  e 65 litres f 90 min g 292 d h 21 h
  i 18 h j 2370 miles

3 a $\frac{5}{8}$ of 40 = 25 b $\frac{3}{4}$ of 280 = 210

  c $\frac{4}{5}$ of 70 = 56 d $\frac{5}{6}$ of 72 = 60

  e $\frac{3}{5}$ of 95 = 57 f $\frac{3}{4}$ of 340 = 255

4 £6080 5 £31 500 6 23 000 7 52 kg

8 a 856 b 187 675

9 a £50 b £550

10 a 180 g b 900 g

11 a £120 b £240

12 £6400

Exercise 2I

1 $\frac{1}{6}$ 2 $\frac{1}{20}$ 3 $\frac{2}{9}$ 4 $\frac{1}{6}$ 5 $\frac{1}{4}$ 6 $\frac{2}{5}$ 7 $\frac{1}{2}$

8 $\frac{1}{2}$ 9 $\frac{3}{14}$ 10 $\frac{35}{48}$ 11 $\frac{8}{15}$ 12 $\frac{21}{32}$

Exercise 2J

1 a $\frac{1}{3}$ b $\frac{1}{5}$ c $\frac{2}{5}$ d $\frac{5}{24}$ e $\frac{2}{5}$ f $\frac{1}{6}$ g $\frac{2}{7}$

  h $\frac{1}{3}$

2 $\frac{3}{5}$ 3 $\frac{12}{31}$ 4 $\frac{7}{12}$

Exercise 2K

1 a 0.5 b 0.$\dot{3}$ c 0.25 d 0.2 e 0.1$\dot{6}$
  f 0.$\dot{1}$42 85$\dot{7}$ g 0.125 h 0.$\dot{1}$ i 0.1
  j 0.$\dot{0}$76 92$\dot{3}$

2 a i 0.$\dot{5}$71 42$\dot{8}$ ii 0.$\dot{7}$14 28$\dot{5}$ iii 0.$\dot{8}$57 14$\dot{2}$
  b The recurring digits are all in the same sequence but they start in a different place each time.

3 0.$\dot{1}$, 0.$\dot{2}$, 0.$\dot{3}$, 0.$\dot{4}$, 0.$\dot{5}$, 0.$\dot{6}$, 0.$\dot{7}$, 0.$\dot{8}$
  The recurring digit is the numerator of the fraction.

4 0.0$\dot{9}$, 0.1$\dot{8}$, 0.2$\dot{7}$, 0.3$\dot{6}$, 0.4$\dot{5}$, 0.5$\dot{4}$, 0.6$\dot{3}$, 0.7$\dot{2}$, 0.8$\dot{1}$, 0.9$\dot{0}$
  The recurring digits follow the nine times table.

5 $\frac{9}{22} = 0.4\dot{0}\dot{9}$, $\frac{3}{7} = 0.\dot{4}28 57\dot{1}$, $\frac{16}{37} = 0.\dot{4}32$, $\frac{4}{9} = 0.\dot{4}$, $\frac{5}{11} = 0.\dot{4}\dot{5}$, $\frac{6}{13} = 0.\dot{4}61 53\dot{8}$

6 $\frac{7}{24} = \frac{35}{120}$, $\frac{3}{10} = \frac{36}{120}$, $\frac{19}{60} = \frac{38}{120}$, $\frac{2}{5} = \frac{48}{120}$, $\frac{5}{12} = \frac{50}{120}$

7 a $\frac{1}{8}$ b $\frac{17}{50}$ c $\frac{29}{40}$ d $\frac{5}{16}$ e $\frac{89}{100}$ f $\frac{1}{20}$
  g $2\frac{7}{20}$ h $\frac{7}{32}$

8 a 0.08$\dot{3}$ b 0.0625 c 0.05 d 0.04
  e 0.02

9 a $\frac{4}{3} = 1\frac{1}{3}$ b $\frac{6}{5} = 1\frac{1}{5}$ c $\frac{5}{2} = 2\frac{1}{2}$ d $\frac{10}{7} = 1\frac{3}{7}$
  e $\frac{20}{11} = 1\frac{9}{11}$ f $\frac{15}{4} = 3\frac{3}{4}$

10 a 0.75, 1.$\dot{3}$ b 0.8$\dot{3}$, 1.2 c 0.4, 2.5
  d 0.7, 1.$\dot{4}$28 57$\dot{1}$ e 0.55, 1.8$\dot{1}$ f 3.75

11 The answer is always 1.

Quick check

1 0, 1, 2, 4, 5, 8, 9, 17, 19, 51, 92

2 10, 11, 14, 17, 19

3 0, 24, 32, 51, 92

4 12, 56, 87, 136, 288

5 0, $\frac{1}{2}$, 5, 50, 87, 100

Exercise 3A

1 –£5 **2** –£9 **3** Profit **4** –200 m **5** –50 m **6** Above **7** –3 h **8** –5 h **9** After **10** –2 °C **11** –8 °C **12** Above **13** –70 km **14** –200 km **15** North **16** +5 m **17** –5 mph **18** –2

Exercise 3B

1 Many different answers to each part
2 Many different answers to each part
3 a Is smaller than **b** Is bigger than **c** Is smaller than **d** Is smaller than **e** Is bigger than **f** Is smaller than **g** Is smaller than **h** Is bigger than **i** Is bigger than **j** Is smaller than **k** Is smaller than **l** Is bigger than
4 a Is smaller than **b** Is smaller than **c** Is smaller than **d** Is bigger than **e** Is smaller than **f** Is smaller than
5 a < **b** > **c** < **d** < **e** < **f** > **g** < **h** > **i** > **j** > **k** < **l** < **m** > **n** > **o** < **p** >
6 a

b

c

d

e

f

g

h

i

Exercise 3C

1 a –2° **b** –3° **c** –2° **d** –3° **e** –2° **f** –3° **g** 3 **h** 3 **i** –1 **j** –1 **k** 2 **l** –3 **m** –4 **n** –6 **o** –6 **p** –1 **q** –5 **r** –4 **s** 4 **t** –1 **u** –5 **v** –4 **w** –5 **x** –5
2 a –4 **b** –4 **c** –10 **d** 2 **e** 8 **f** –5 **g** 2 **h** 5 **i** –7 **j** –12 **k** 13 **l** 25 **m** –32 **n** –30 **o** –5 **p** –8 **q** –12 **r** 10 **s** –36 **t** –14 **u** 41 **v** 12 **w** –40 **x** –101
3 a 6 **b** –5 **c** 6 **d** –1 **e** –2 **f** –6 **g** –6 **h** –2 **i** 3 **j** 0 **k** –7 **l** –6 **m** 8 **n** 1 **o** –9 **p** –9 **q** –5 **r** –80 **s** –7 **t** –1 **u** –47

Exercise 3D

1 a 6 **b** 7 **c** 8 **d** 6 **e** 8 **f** 10 **g** 2 **h** –3 **i** 1 **j** 2 **k** –1 **l** –7 **m** 2 **n** –3 **o** 1 **p** –5 **q** 3 **r** –4 **s** –3 **t** –8 **u** –10 **v** –9 **w** –4 **x** –9
2 a –8 **b** –10 **c** –11 **d** –3 **e** 2 **f** –5 **g** 1 **h** 4 **i** 7 **j** –8 **k** –5 **l** –11 **m** 11 **n** 6 **o** 8 **p** 8 **q** –2 **r** –1 **s** –9 **t** –5 **u** 5 **v** –9 **w** 8 **x** 0
3 a 3 °C **b** 0 °C **c** –3 °C **d** –5 °C **e** –11 °C
4 a 10 degrees Celsius **b** 7 degrees Celsius **c** 9 degrees Celsius
5 –9, –6, –5, –1, 1, 2, 3, 8
6 a –3 **b** –4 **c** –2 **d** –7 **e** –14 **f** –6 **g** –12 **h** –10 **i** 4 **j** –4 **k** 14 **l** 11 **m** –4 **n** –1 **o** –10 **p** –5 **q** –3 **r** 5 **s** –4 **t** –8
7 a 2 **b** –3 **c** –5 **d** –7 **e** –10 **f** –20
8 a 2 **b** 4 **c** –1 **d** –5 **e** –11 **f** 8
9 a 13 **b** 2 **c** 5 **d** 4 **e** 11 **f** –2
10 a –10 **b** –5 **c** –2 **d** 4 **e** 7 **f** –4
13 a –5 **b** 6 **c** 0 **d** 2 **e** 13 **f** 0 **g** –6 **h** –2 **i** 212 **j** 5 **k** 3 **l** 3 **m** –67 **n** 7 **o** 25
14 a –1, 0, 1, 2, 3 **b** –6, –5, –4, –3, –2 **c** –3, –2, –1, 0, 1 **d** –8, –7, –6, –5, –4 **e** –9, –8, –7, –6, –5 **f** 3, 4, 5, 6, 7 **g** –12, –11, –10, –9. –8 **h** –16, –15, –14, –13, –12 **i** –2, –1, 0, 1, 2, 3; –4, –3, –2, –1, 0, 1 **j** –12, –11, –10, –9, –8, –7; –14, –13, –12, –11, –10, –9 **k** –2, –1, 0, 1, 2, 3; 0, 1, 2, 3, 4, 5 **l** –8, –7, –6, –5, –4, –3, –2; –5, –4, –3, –2, –1, 0, 1 **m** –10, –9, –8, –7, –6, –5, –4; –1, 0, 1, 2, 3, 4, 5 **n** 3, 4, 5, 6, 7, 8, 9; –5, –4, –3, –2, –1, 0, 1
15 a –4 **b** 3 **c** 4 **d** –6 **e** 7 **f** 2 **g** 7 **h** –6 **i** –7 **j** 0 **k** 0 **l** –6 **m** –7 **n** –9 **o** 4 **p** 0 **q** 5 **r** 0 **s** 10 **t** –5 **u** 3 **v** –3 **w** –9 **x** 0 **y** –3 **z** –3

16 a +6 + 5 = 11   **b** +6 + −9 = −3
c +6 − −9 = 15   **d** +6 − 5 = 1
17 a +5 + +7 − −9 = +21   **b** +5 + −9 − +7 = −11
c +7 + −7, +4 + −4

Exercise 3E

1 −12

−1	−9	−2
−5	−4	−3
−6	1	−7

2 0

1	−4	3
2	0	−2
−3	4	−1

3 −15

0	−14	−1
−6	−5	−4
−9	4	−10

4 −9

2	−12	1
−4	−3	−2
−7	6	−8

5 −18

−3	−6	−9
−12	−6	0
−3	−6	−9

6 −21

−2	−18	−1
−6	−7	−8
−13	4	−12

7 −21

−4	−12	−5
−8	−7	−6
−9	−2	−10

8 0

2	1	−3
−5	0	5
3	−1	−2

9 −15

−2	−10	−3
−6	−5	−4
−7	0	−8

10 −26

−8	−1	−3	−14
−8	−9	−7	−2
−11	−6	−4	−5
1	−10	−12	−5

11 −16

−7	5	2	−16
−6	−8	−5	3
−11	−3	0	−2
8	−10	−13	−1

ANSWERS TO CHAPTER 4

Quick check

1 a 6   **b** 12   **c** 15   **d** 18   **e** 21   **f** 24

2 a 8   **b** 16   **c** 20   **d** 24   **e** 28   **f** 32

3 a 10   **b** 45   **c** 25   **d** 30   **e** 35   **f** 40

4 a 12   **b** 54   **c** 64   **d** 36   **e** 63   **f** 48

5 a 14   **b** 63   **c** 72   **d** 42   **e** 49   **f** 56

Exercise 4A

1 a 3, 6, 9, 12, 15   **b** 7, 14, 21, 28, 35
c 9, 18, 27, 36, 45   **d** 11, 22, 33, 44, 55
e 16, 32, 48, 64, 80
2 a 254, 108, 68, 162, 98, 812, 102, 270
b 111, 255, 108, 162, 711, 615, 102, 75, 270
c 255, 615, 75, 270
d 108, 162, 711, 270
3 a 72, 132, 216, 312, 168, 144
b 161, 91, 168, 294
c 72, 102, 132, 78, 216, 312, 168, 144, 294
4 a 98   **b** 99   **c** 96   **d** 95   **e** 98   **f** 96
5 a 1002   **b** 1008   **c** 1008

Exercise 4B

1 a 1, 2, 5, 10   **b** 1, 2, 4, 7, 14, 28
c 1, 2, 3, 6, 9, 18   **d** 1, 17
e 1, 5, 25   **f** 1, 2, 4, 5, 8, 10, 20, 40
g 1, 2, 3, 5, 6, 10, 15, 30   **h** 1, 3, 5, 9, 15, 45
i 1, 2, 3, 4, 6, 8, 12, 24   **j** 1, 2, 4, 8, 16
2 a 1, 2, 3, 4, 5, 6, 8, 10, 12, 15, 20, 24, 30, 40, 60, 120
b 1, 2, 3, 5, 6, 10, 15, 25, 30, 50, 75, 150
c 1, 2, 3, 4, 6, 8, 9, 12, 16, 18, 24, 36, 48, 72, 144
d 1, 2, 3, 4, 5, 6, 9, 10, 12, 15, 18, 20, 30, 36, 45, 60, 90, 180
e 1, 13, 169
f 1, 2, 3, 4, 6, 9, 12, 18, 27, 36, 54, 108
g 1, 2, 4, 7, 14, 28, 49, 98, 196
h 1, 3, 9, 17, 51, 153
i 1, 2, 3, 6, 9, 11, 18, 22, 33, 66, 99, 198   **j** 1, 199
3 a 55   **b** 67   **c** 29   **d** 39   **e** 65   **f** 80
g 80   **h** 70   **i** 81   **j** 50
4 a 2   **b** 2   **c** 3   **d** 5   **e** 3   **f** 3
g 7   **h** 5   **i** 10   **j** 11

Exercise 4C

1 36, 49, 64, 81, 100, 121, 144, 169, 196, 225, 256, 289, 324, 361, 400
2 4, 9, 16, 25, 36, 49
3 a 3   **b** 5   **c** 7   **d** Odd numbers
4 a 50, 65, 82   **b** 98, 128, 162   **c** 51, 66, 83
d 48, 63, 80   **e** 149, 164, 181
5 a 529   **b** 3249   **c** 5929   **d** 15 129
e 23 104   **f** 10.24   **g** 90.25   **h** 566.44
i 16   **j** 144
6 a 25, 169, 625, 1681, 3721
b Answers in each row are the same.

Exercise 4D

1 a 6, 12, 18, 24, 30   **b** 13, 26, 39, 52, 65
c 8, 16, 24, 32, 40   **d** 20, 40, 60, 80, 100
e 18, 36, 54, 72, 90
2 a 12, 24, 36   **b** 20, 40, 60   **c** 15, 30, 45
d 18, 36, 54   **e** 35, 70, 105
3 a 1, 2, 3, 4, 6, 12   **b** 1, 2, 4, 5, 10, 20
c 1, 3, 9   **d** 1, 2, 4, 8, 16, 32
e 1, 2, 3, 4, 6, 8, 12, 24   **f** 1, 2, 19, 38

g 1, 13　　**h** 1, 2, 3, 6, 7, 14, 21, 42
i 1, 3, 5, 9, 15, 45　　**j** 1, 2, 3, 4, 6, 9, 12, 18, 36
4 13 is a prime number.
5 Square numbers
6 2, 3, 5, 7, 11, 13, 17, 19
7 1, 4, 9, 16, 25, 36, 49, 64, 81, 100
8 4 packs of sausages, 5 packs of buns
9 24 seconds
10 30 seconds
11 12 minutes; Debbie: 3 and Fred: 4
12 a 12　　**b** 9　　**c** 6　　**d** 13　　**e** 15　　**f** 14
g 16　　**h** 10　　**i** 18　　**j** 17　　**k** 8　　**l** 21
13 $1 + 3 + 5 + 7 + 9 = 25$
$1 + 3 + 5 + 7 + 9 + 11 = 36$
$1 + 3 + 5 + 7 + 9 + 11 + 13 = 49$
$1 + 3 + 5 + 7 + 9 + 11 + 13 + 15 = 64$
14 b 21, 28, 36, 45, 55

Exercise 4E

1 a 2　　**b** 5　　**c** 7　　**d** 1　　**e** 9　　**f** 10
g 8　　**h** 3　　**i** 6　　**j** 4　　**k** 11　　**l** 12
m 20　　**n** 30　　**o** 13
2 a 5　　**b** 6　　**c** 10　　**d** 7　　**e** 8　　**f** 4
g 3　　**h** 9　　**i** 1　　**j** 12
3 a 81　　**b** 40　　**c** 100　　**d** 14　　**e** 36　　**f** 15
g 49　　**h** 12　　**i** 25　　**j** 21　　**k** 121　　**l** 16
m 64　　**n** 17　　**o** 441
4 a 24　　**b** 31　　**c** 45　　**d** 40　　**e** 67　　**f** 101
g 3.6　　**h** 6.5　　**i** 13.9　　**j** 22.2

Exercise 4F

1 a 27　　**b** 125　　**c** 216　　**d** 1728　　**e** 16
f 256　　**g** 625　　**h** 32　　**i** 2187　　**j** 1024
2 a 100　　**b** 1000　　**c** 10 000　　**d** 100 000
e 1 000 000
f The power is the same as the number of zeros.
g i 100 000 000　　**ii** 10 000 000 000
iii 1 000 000 000 000 000
3 a 2^4　　**b** 3^5　　**c** 7^2　　**d** 5^3　　**e** 10^7　　**f** 6^4
g 4^4　　**h** 1^7　　**i** 0.5^4　　**j** 100^3
4 a $3 \times 3 \times 3 \times 3$　　**b** $9 \times 9 \times 9$　　**c** 6×6
d $10 \times 10 \times 10 \times 10 \times 10$
e $2 \times 2 \times 2 \times 2 \times 2 \times 2 \times 2 \times 2 \times 2 \times 2$
f $8 \times 8 \times 8 \times 8 \times 8 \times 8$　　**g** $0.1 \times 0.1 \times 0.1$
h 2.5×2.5　　**i** $0.7 \times 0.7 \times 0.7$　　**j** 1000×1000
5 a 16　　**b** 243　　**c** 49　　**d** 125
e 10 000 000　　**f** 1296　　**g** 256　　**h** 1
i 0.0625　　**j** 1 000 000
6 a 81　　**b** 729　　**c** 36　　**d** 100 000
e 1024　　**f** 262 144　　**g** 0.001　　**h** 6.25
i 0.343　　**j** 1 000 000
7 10^6
8 10^6
9 4, 8, 16, 32, 64, 128, 256, 512
10 0.001, 0.01, 0.1, 1, 10, 100, 1000, 10 000, 100 000,
1 000 000, 10 000 000, 100 000 000

Exercise 4G

1 a 31　　**b** 310　　**c** 3100　　**d** 31 000

2 a 65　　**b** 650　　**c** 6500　　**d** 65 000
3 Factors of 10 are the same, e.g. $100 = 10^2$
4 a 7.3×10　　**b** 7.3×10^2　　**c** 7.3×10^3　　**d** 7.3×10^5
5 a 0.31　　**b** 0.031　　**c** 0.0031　　**d** 0.000 31
6 a 0.65　　**b** 0.065　　**c** 0.0065　　**d** 0.000 65
7 Factors of 10 are the same, e.g. $1000 = 10^3$
8 a $7.3 \div 10$　　**b** $7.3 \div 10^2$　　**c** $7.3 \div 10^3$
d $7.3 \div 10^5$
9 a 250　　**b** 34.5　　**c** 4670　　**d** 346　　**e** 207.89
f 56 780　　**g** 89 700　　**h** 865　　**i** 10 050
j 999 000　　**k** 23 456　　**l** 98 765.4
10 a 0.025　　**b** 0.345　　**c** 0.004 67　　**d** 3.46
e 0.207 89　　**f** 0.056 78　　**g** 0.0246　　**h** 0.000 865
i 1.005　　**j** 0.000 000 999　　**k** 20.367　　**l** 7.643
11 a 60 000　　**b** 120 000　　**c** 10 000　　**d** 200 000
e 28 000　　**f** 900　　**g** 400　　**h** 8000　　**i** 160 000
12 a 20　　**b** 2　　**c** 1　　**d** 16　　**e** 150　　**f** 12
g 15　　**h** 40　　**i** 5　　**j** 40　　**k** 320
13 i a 2.3×10^7　　**b** 3.4×10^{-2}　　**c** 6.3×10^{10}
d 1.6×10^{-3}　　**e** 5.5×10^{-4}　　**f** 1.2×10^{14}
ii a 23 000 000　　**b** 0.034　　**c** 63 000 000 000
d 0.0016　　**e** 0.00055　　**f** 120 000 000 000 000
14 a 51 000 000 000　　**b** 8160 000 000 000
c 5 3333 3.3333　　**d** 1500 000.000

Exercise 4H

1 a $84 = 2 \times 2 \times 3 \times 7$
b $100 = 2 \times 2 \times 5 \times 5$
c $180 = 2 \times 2 \times 3 \times 3 \times 5$
d $220 = 2 \times 2 \times 5 \times 11$
e $280 = 2 \times 2 \times 2 \times 5 \times 7$
f $128 = 2 \times 2 \times 2 \times 2 \times 2 \times 2 \times 2$
g $50 = 2 \times 5 \times 5$
h $1000 = 2 \times 2 \times 2 \times 5 \times 5 \times 5$
i $576 = 2 \times 2 \times 2 \times 2 \times 2 \times 2 \times 3 \times 3$
j $650 = 2 \times 5 \times 5 \times 13$
2 a $2^2 \times 3 \times 7$　　**b** $2^2 \times 5^2$　　**c** $2^2 \times 3^2 \times 5$
d $2^2 \times 5 \times 11$　　**e** $2^3 \times 5 \times 7$　　**f** 2^7　　**g** 2×5^2
h $2^3 \times 5^3$　　**i** $2^6 \times 3^2$　　**j** $2 \times 5^2 \times 13$
3 1, 2, 3, 2^2, 5, 2×3, 7, 2^3, 3^2, 2×5, 11, $2^2 \times 3$, 13,
2×7, 3×5, 2^4, 17, 2×3^2, 19, $2^2 \times 5$, 3×7, 2×11,
23, $2^3 \times 3$, 5^2, 2×13, 3^3, $2^2 \times 7$, 29, $2 \times 3 \times 5$, 31,
2^5, 3×11, 2×17, 5×7, $2^2 \times 3^2$, 37, 2×19, 3×13, $2^3 \times$
5, 41, $2 \times 3 \times 7$, 43, $2^2 \times 11$, $3^2 \times 5$, 2×23, 47, $2^4 \times 3$,
7^2, 2×5^2
4 a Each is double the previous number.
b 64, 128
c 81, 243
d 256, 1024, 4096
e 3, 3^2, 3^3, 3^4, 3^5, 3^6, …; 4, 4^2, 4^3, 4^4, 4^5, …

Exercise 4I

1 a 20　　**b** 56　　**c** 6　　**d** 28　　**e** 10　　**f** 15
g 24　　**h** 30
2 It is their product.
3 a 8　　**b** 18　　**c** 12　　**d** 30
4 No. Because the numbers in each part have common
factors.

5 a 168 **b** 105 **c** 84 **d** 168 **e** 96
f 54 **g** 75 **h** 144
6 a 8 **b** 7 **c** 4 **d** 14 **e** 4 **f** 9
g 5 **h** 4 **i** 3 **j** 16 **k** 5 **l** 9
7 a i no **ii** yes **iii** yes **iv** no
b i no **ii** no **iii** yes **iv** no

Exercise 4J
1 a 5^4 **b** 5^{10} **c** 5^5 **d** 5^3 **e** 5^{15} **f** 5^9
g 5^6 **h** 5^9 **i** 5^8
2 a 6^3 **b** 6^5 **c** 6^1 **d** 6^0 **e** 6^1 **f** 6^3
g 6^2 **h** 6^1 **i** 6^2
3 a x^8 **b** x^9 **c** x^8 **d** x^5 **e** x^{12} **f** x^{13}
g x^{11} **h** x^{10} **i** x^{16}
4 a x^4 **b** x^5 **c** x^3 **d** x^3 **e** x^6 **f** x^5
g x^2 **h** x^6 **i** x^9

ANSWERS TO CHAPTER 5

Quick check

20 cm, 16 cm^2

Exercise 5A
1 10 cm
2 8 cm
3 14 cm
4 12 cm
5 16 cm
6 6 cm
7 10 cm
8 12 cm
9 12 cm
10 14 cm
11 12 cm
12 12 cm

Exercise 5B
1 a 10 cm^2 **b** 11 cm^2
c 13 cm^2 **d** 12 cm^2 (estimates only)

Exercise 5C
1 35 cm^2, 24 cm
2 33 cm^2, 28 cm
3 45 cm^2, 36 cm
4 70 cm^2, 34 cm
5 56 cm^2, 30 cm
6 10 cm^2, 14 cm
7 53.3 cm^2, 29.4 cm
8 84.96 cm^2, 38 cm
9 a 20 cm, 21 cm^2 **b** 18 cm, 20 cm^2
c 2 cm, 8 cm^2 **d** 3 cm, 15 cm^2
e 3 mm, 18 mm^2 **f** 4 mm, 22 mm^2
g 5 m, 10 m^2 **h** 7 m, 24 m^2
10 a 390 m **b** 6750 m^2
11 a 920 m **b** 1 h 52 min
12 £839.40 **13** 40 cm
14 a 100 mm^2
b i 300 mm^2 **ii** 500 mm^2 **iii** 630 mm^2
15 a 10 000 cm^2
b i 20 000 cm^2 **ii** 40 000 cm^2 **iii** 56 000 cm^2

Exercise 5D
1 30 cm^2 **2** 40 cm^2
3 51 cm^2 **4** 35 cm^2

5 43 cm^2 **6** 51 cm^2
7 48 cm^2 **8** 33 cm^2
9 24 m^2

Exercise 5E
1 a 6 cm^2, 12 cm **b** 120 cm^2, 60 cm
c 30 cm^2, 30 cm
2 40 cm^2
3 84 m^2
4 a 21 cm^2 **b** 55 cm^2 **c** 165 cm^2

Exercise 5F
1 a 21 cm^2 **b** 12 cm^2 **c** 14 cm^2
d 55 cm^2 **e** 90 cm^2 **f** 140 cm^2
2 a 28 cm^2 **b** 8 cm **c** 4 cm
d 3 cm **e** 7 cm **f** 44 cm^2
3 a 40 cm^2 **b** 65 m^2 **c** 80 cm^2
4 a 65 cm^2 **b** 50 m^2
5 For example: height 10 cm, base 10 cm; height 5 cm, base 20 cm; height 25 cm, base 4 cm; height 50 cm, base 2 cm

Exercise 5G
1 96 cm^2
2 70 cm^2
3 20 cm^2
4 125 cm^2
5 10 cm^2
6 112 m^2

Exercise 5H
1 a 30 cm^2 **b** 77 cm^2 **c** 24 cm^2 **d** 42 cm^2
e 40 cm^2 **f** 6 cm **g** 3 cm
2 a 27.5 cm, 36.25 cm^2 **b** 33.4 cm, 61.2 cm^2
c 38.6 m, 88.2 m^2
3 Any pair of lengths that add up to 10 cm
For example: 1 cm, 9 cm; 2 cm, 8 cm; 3 cm, 7 cm; 4 cm, 6 cm; 4.5 cm, 5.5 cm
4 Shape c. Its area is 25.5 cm^2
5 Shape a. Its area is 28 cm^2

Exercise 5I

1 $P = 2a + 2b$
2 $P = a + b + c + d$
3 $P = 4x$
4 $P = p + 2q$
5 $P = 4x + 4y$
6 $P = a + 3b$
7 $P = 5x + 2y + 2z$
8 $P = 2\pi r$
9 $P = 2h + (2 + \pi)r$

Exercise 5J

1 $A = a^2 + ab$
2 $A = \frac{1}{2}bh$
3 $A = bh$
4 $\frac{1}{2}(a + b)h$
5 $A = \pi r^2$
6 $A = 2ad - a^2$
7 $A = \frac{1}{2}bh + \frac{1}{2}bw$
8 $A = 2rh + \pi r^2$
9 $A = \pi d^2 + \frac{1}{2}dh$

Exercise 5K

1 $V = abc$
2 $V = p^3$
3 $V = 6p^3$
4 $V = \pi r^2 h$
5 $V = \frac{1}{2}bhw$
6 $V = \frac{1}{2}bhl$

Exercise 5L

1 **a** A **b** L **c** L **d** A **e** V **f** V **g** V
 h A **i** L **j** V **k** A **l** L **m** V **n** A
 o V **p** A **q** V **r** A **s** A **t** A **u** L
 v A **w** A **x** A **y** V **z** V
2 **a** C **b** I **c** C **d** I **e** C **f** I **g** C
 h I **i** C **j** I **k** C **l** C **m** C **n** C
 o C **p** I

Really Useful Maths!: A new floor

Room	Floor area (m²)	Edging needed (m)
Hall	14	18
Bathroom	9	12
Total	23	30

Room	Floor area (m²)	Edging needed (m)
Lounge	57	32
Sitting room	30	22
Kitchen/diner	50	32
Conservatory	12	14
Total	149	100

	Number of packs	Price per pack	Total cost
Beech flooring	12	£32	£384
Beech edging	3	£18	£54
Oak flooring	75	£38	£2850
Oak edging	9	£22	£198
		Total	£3486

cost after VAT £4096.05

Quick check

a

Size	Tally	Frequency
8	⊞⊞⊞ ⊞⊞⊞ ⊞⊞⊞ I	16
10	⊞⊞⊞ ⊞⊞⊞ II	12
12	⊞⊞⊞ ⊞⊞⊞ II	12
14	⊞⊞⊞ I	6
16	IIII	4

b Size 8

Exercise 6A

1 a

Goals	0	1	2	3
Frequency	6	8	4	2

b 1 goal   **c** 22

2 a

Temperature (°C)	14–16	17–19	20–22	23–25	26–28
Frequency	5	10	8	5	2

b 17–19 °C

  c Getting warmer in the first half and then getting cooler towards the end.

3 a Observation   **b** Sampling   **c** Observation   **d** Sampling   **e** Observation   **f** Experiment

4 a

Score	1	2	3	4	5	6
Frequency	5	6	6	6	3	4

b 30   **c** Yes, frequencies are similar

5 a

Height (cm)	151–155	156–160	161–165	166–170	171–175	176–180	181–185	186–190
Frequency	2	5	5	7	5	4	3	1

b 166 – 170 cm

Exercise 6B

1

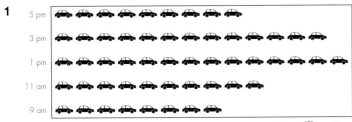

2

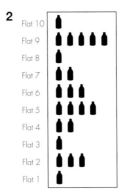

3 a May 9 h, Jun 11 h, Jul 12 h, Aug 11 h, Sep 10 h   **b** July   **c** Visual impact, easy to understand

4 a Simon   **b** £165   **c** Difficult to show fractions of a symbol

Exercise 6C

1 a Swimming   **b** 74   **c** For example: limited facilities   **d** No. It may not include people who are not fit

2 a

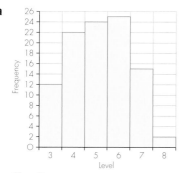

b $\frac{40}{100} = \frac{2}{5}$

c Easier to read the exact frequency

3 a

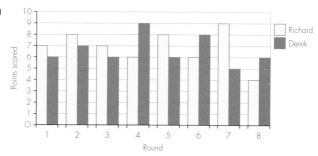

b Richard got more points overall, but Derek was more consistent.

4 a

Time (min)	1–10	11–20	21–30	31–40	41–50	51–60
Frequency	4	7	5	5	7	2

b

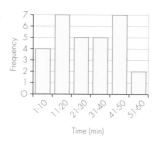

c Some live close to the school. Some live a good distance away and probably travel to school by bus

5 a

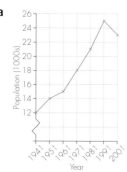

Key = 1 accident

b

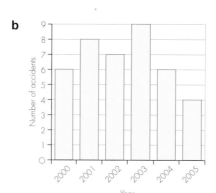

c Use the pictogram because an appropriate symbol makes more impact

Exercise 6D

1 a Tuesday, 52p   **b** 2p   **c** Friday   **d** £90

2 a

b about 16 500
c 1981 and 1991
d No; do not know the reason why the population started to decrease after 1991

3 a

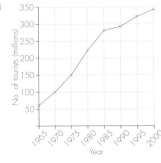

b Between 178 and 180 million

c 1975 and 1980

d Increasing; better communications, cheaper air travel, more advertising, better living standards

4 a

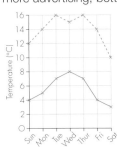

b 7 °C and 10 °C

---- Maximum temperature
— Minimum temperature

Exercise 6E

1 a 17 s **b** 22 s **c** 21 s
2 a 57 **b** 55 **c** 56 **d** 48
  e Boys, because their marks are higher
3 a 2 | 8 9
    3 | 4 5 6 8 8 9
    4 | 1 1 3 3 3 8 8
    Key 4 | 3 represents 43 cm
  b 48 cm **c** 43 cm **d** 20 cm
4 a 0 | 2 8 9 9 9
    1 | 2 3 7 7 8
    2 | 0 1 2 3
    Key 1 | 2 represents 12 messages
  b 23 **c** 9

ANSWERS TO CHAPTER 7

Quick check

1 a 8 **b** 3

2 14

3 a $(2 + 3 + 5) \times 4$ **b** $2 + (3 + 5) \times 4$

Exercise 7A

1 a $2 + x$ **b** $x - 6$ **c** $k + x$ **d** $x - t$
  e $x + 3$ **f** $d + m$ **g** $b - y$ **h** $p + t + w$
  i $8x$ **j** hj **k** $x \div 4$ or $\frac{x}{4}$ **l** $2 \div x$ or $\frac{2}{x}$
  m $y \div t$ or $\frac{y}{t}$ **n** wt **o** a^2 **p** g^2
2 a i $P = 4, A = 1$ **ii** $P = 4x, A = x^2$
    iii $P = 12, A = 9$ **iv** $P = 4t, A = t^2$
  b i $P = 4s$ cm **ii** $A = s^2$ cm^2
3 a $x + 3$ yr **b** $x - 4$ yr
4 $F = 2C + 30$
5 Rule **c**
6 a $C = 100M$ **b** $N = 12F$ **c** $W = 4C$
  d $H = P$
7 a $3n$ **b** $3n + 3$ **c** $n + 1$ **d** $n - 1$
8 Rob: $2n$, Tom: $n + 2$, Vic: $n - 3$, Wes: $2n + 3$
9 a $P = 8n, A = 9n^2$ **b** $P = 24n, A = 36n^2$
10 a £4 **b** £$(10 - x)$ **c** £$(y - x)$ **d** £$2x$
11 a 75p **b** $15x$ p **c** $4A$ p **d** Ay p
12 £$(A - B)$

13 £$A \div 5$ or $\frac{£A}{5}$

14 Dad: $(72 + x)$ yr, me: $(T + x)$ yr

15 a $T \div 2$ or $\frac{T}{2}$ **b** $T \div 2 + 4$ or $\frac{T}{2} + 4$
  c $T - x$
16 a $8x$ **b** $12m$ **c** $18t$
17 Andrea: $3n - 3$, Bert: $3n - 1$, Colin: $3n - 6$ or $3(n - 2)$,
    Davina: 0, Emma: $3n - n = 2n$, Florinda: $3n - 3m$

Exercise 7B

1 $6t$ **2** $12y$ **3** $15y$ **4** $8w$ **5** $3t^2$
6 $5b^2$ **7** $2w^2$ **8** $15y^2$ **9** $8p^2$ **10** $6t^2$
11 $12m^2$ **12** $15t^2$ **13** $2mt$ **14** $3wy$ **15** $5qt$
16 $6mn$ **17** $6qt$ **18** $12fg$ **19** $10hk$ **20** $21pr$
21 y^3 **22** t^3 **23** $3m^3$ **24** $4t^3$ **25** $6n^3$
26 $20r^3$ **27** t^4 **28** h^5 **29** $12n^5$ **30** $10t^7$
31 $6a^7$ **32** $4k^7$ **33** t^3 **34** $6y^2$ **35** $12d^3$
36 $15p^6$ **37** $3mp^2$ **38** $6t^2y$ **39** $6m^2n$ **40** $8m^2p^2$

Exercise 7C

1 a £t **b** £$(4t + 3)$
2 a $10x + 2y$ **b** $7x + y$ **c** $6x + y$
3 a $5a$ **b** $6c$ **c** $9e$ **d** $6f$ **e** $3g$
  f $4i$ **g** $4j$ **h** $3q$ **i** 0 **j** $-w$
  k $6x^2$ **l** $5y^2$ **m** 0
4 a $7x$ **b** $6y$ **c** $3t$ **d** $-3t$ **e** $-5x$
  f $-5k$ **g** $2m^2$ **h** 0 **i** f^2
5 a $7x + 5$ **b** $5x + 6$ **c** $5p$ **d** $5x + 6$
  e $5p + t + 5$ **f** $8w - 5k$ **g** c

h $8k - 6y + 10$

6 a $2c + 3d$ **b** $5d + 2e$ **c** $f + 3g + 4h$
  d $2i + 3k$ **e** $2k + 9p$ **f** $3k + 2m + 5p$
  g $7m - 7n$ **h** $6n - 3p$ **i** $6u - 3v$
  j $2v$ **k** $2w - 3y$ **l** $11x^2 - 5y$
  m $-y^2 - 2z$ **n** $x^2 - z^2$

7 a $8x + 6$ **b** $3x + 16$ **c** $2x + 2y + 8$

Exercise 7D

1 $6 + 2m$ **2** $10 + 5l$ **3** $12 - 3y$
4 $20 + 8k$ **5** $6 - 12f$ **6** $10 - 6w$
7 $3g + 3h$ **8** $10k + 15m$ **9** $12d - 8n$
10 $t^2 + 3t$ **11** $m^2 + 5m$ **12** $k^2 - 3k$
13 $3g^2 + 2g$ **14** $5y^2 - y$ **15** $5p - 3p^2$
16 $3m^2 + 12m$ **17** $4t^2 - 4t$ **18** $8k - 2k^2$
19 $8g^2 + 20g$ **20** $15h^2 - 10h$ **21** $15t - 12t^2$
22 $6d^2 + 12de$ **23** $6y^2 + 8ky$ **24** $15m^2 - 10mp$
25 $y^3 + 5y$ **26** $h^4 + 7h$ **27** $k^3 - 5k$
28 $3t^3 + 12t$ **29** $4h^4 - 4h$ **30** $5g^4 - 10g$
31 $12m^3 + 4m^2$ **32** $10k^4 + 5k^3$ **33** $15d^3 - 3d^4$
34 $6w^3 + 3tw$ **35** $15a^3 - 10ab$ **36** $12p^4 - 15mp$
37 $5m^2 + 4m^3$ **38** $t^4 + 2t^4$ **39** $5g^2t - 4g^4$
40 $15t^3 + 3mt^2$ **41** $12h^3 + 8gh^2$ **42** $8m^3 + 2m^4$

Exercise 7E

1 a $7t$ **b** $9m$ **c** $3y$ **d** $9d$ **e** $3e$ **f** $2g$
  g $3p$ **h** $2t$ **i** $5t^2$ **j** $4y^2$ **k** $5ab$ **l** $3a^2d$
2 a $22 + 5t$ **b** $21 + 19k$ **c** $10 + 16m$
  d $16 + 17y$ **e** $22 + 2f$ **f** $14 + 3g$
  g $10 + 11t$ **h** $22 + 4w$
3 a $2 + 2h$ **b** $9g + 5$ **c** $6y + 11$ **d** $7t - 4$
  e $17k + 16$ **f** $6e + 20$ **g** $7m + 4$ **h** $3t + 10$
4 a $4m + 3p + 2mp$ **b** $3k + 4h + 5hk$
  c $3n + 2t + 7nt$ **d** $3p + 7q + 6pq$
  e $6h + 6j + 13hj$ **f** $6t + 8y + 21ty$
  g $24p + 12r + 13pr$ **h** $20k - 6m + 19km$
5 a $13t + 9t^2$ **b** $5y + 13y^2$ **c** $18w + 5w^2$
  d $14p + 23p^2$ **e** $7m + 4m^2$ **f** $22d - 9d^2$
  g $10e^2 - 6e$ **h** $14k^2 - 3kp$
6 a $17ab + 12ac + 6bc$ **b** $18wy + 6ty - 8tw$
  c $16gh - 2gk - 10hk$ **d** $10ht - 3hp - 12pt$
  e $ab - 2ac + 6bc$ **f** $12pq + 2qw - 10pw$
  g $14mn - 15mp - 6np$ **h** $8r^3 - 6r^2$

Exercise 7F

1 $6(m + 2t)$ **2** $3(3t + p)$ **3** $4(2m + 3k)$

4 $4(r + 2t)$ **5** $m(n + 3)$ **6** $g(5g + 3)$
7 $2(2w - 3t)$ **8** $2(4p - 3k)$ **9** $2(8h - 5k)$
10 $2m(p + k)$ **11** $2b(2c + k)$ **12** $2a(3b + 2c)$
13 $y(3y + 2)$ **14** $t(4t - 3)$ **15** $2d(2d - 1)$
16 $3m(m - p)$ **17** $3p(2p + 3t)$ **18** $2p(4t + 3m)$
19 $4b(2a - c)$ **20** $4a(3a - 2b)$ **21** $3t(3m - 2p)$
22 $4at(4t + 3)$ **23** $5bc(b - 2)$ **24** $2b(4ac + 3ed)$
25 $2(2a^2 + 3a + 4)$ **26** $3b(2a + 3c + d)$
27 $t(5t + 4 + a)$ **28** $3mt(2t - 1 + 3m)$
29 $2ab(4b + 1 - 2a)$ **30** $5pt(2t + 3 + p)$
31 Not possible   **32** $m(5 + 2p)$ **33** $t(t - 7)$
34 Not possible   **35** $2m(2m - 3p)$ **36** Not possible
37 $a(4a - 5b)$ **38** Not possible   **39** $b(5a - 3bc)$

Exercise 7G

1 $x^2 + 5x + 6$ **2** $t^2 + 7t + 12$ **3** $w^2 + 4w + 3$
4 $m^2 + 6m + 5$ **5** $k^2 + 8k + 15$ **6** $a^2 + 5a + 4$
7 $x^2 + 2x - 8$ **8** $t^2 + 2t - 15$ **9** $w^2 + 2w - 3$
10 $f^2 - f - 6$ **11** $g^2 - 3g - 4$ **12** $y^2 + y - 12$
13 $x^2 + x - 12$ **14** $p^2 - p - 2$ **15** $k^2 - 2k - 8$
16 $y^2 + 3y - 10$ **17** $a^2 + 2a - 3$ **18** $t^2 + t - 12$
19 $x^2 - 5x + 4$ **20** $r^2 - 5r + 6$ **21** $m^2 - 4m + 3$
22 $g^2 - 6g + 8$ **23** $h^2 - 8h + 15$ **24** $n^2 - 2n + 1$
25 $x^2 + 10x + 25$ **26** $t^2 + 12t + 36$ **27** $15 - 2b - b^2$
28 $y^2 - 6y + 5$ **29** $p^2 - 8p + 16$ **30** $k^2 - 4k + 4$
31 $x^2 - 9$ **32** $t^2 - 25$ **33** $m^2 - 16$
34 $t^2 - 4$ **35** $y^2 - 64$ **36** $p^2 - 1$
37 $25 - x^2$ **38** $49 - g^2$ **39** $x^2 - 36$

Exercise 7H

1 a 8 **b** 17 **c** 32 **2 a** 3 **b** 11 **c** 43
3 a 9 **b** 15 **c** 29 **4 a** 9 **b** 5 **c** -1
5 a 13 **b** 33 **c** 78 **6 a** 10 **b** 13 **c** 58
7 a 32 **b** 64 **c** 160 **8 a** 6.5 **b** 0.5 **c** -2.5
9 a 2 **b** 8 **c** -10 **10 a** 3 **b** 2.5 **c** -5
11 a 6 **b** 3 **c** 2 **12 a** 12 **b** 8 **c** $1\frac{1}{2}$

Exercise 7I

1 a 11 **b** 17 **c** 13 **2 a** 7 **b** 14 **c** -2
3 a 7 **b** 32 **c** -3 **4 a** 27 **b** 5 **c** 0
5 a 75 **b** 8 **c** -6 **6 a** 900 **b** 180 **c** 0
7 a 5 **b** 8 **c** 1 **8 a** 4.4 **b** 2.6 **c** -1.4

Really Useful Maths!: Walking holiday

Day	Distance (km)	Height climbed (m)	Time (minutes)	Time (hours and minutes)	Start time	Time allowed for breaks	Finish time
1	16	250	265	4 h 25 min	10.00 am	2 hours	4.25 pm
2	18	0	270	4 h 30 min	10.00 am	1 1/2 hours	4.00 pm
3	11	340	199	3 h 19 min	9.30 am	2 1/2 hours	3.19 pm
4	13	100	205	3 h 25 min	10.30 am	2 1/2 hours	4.25 pm
5	14	110	221	3 h 41 min	10.30 am	2 1/2 hours	4.41 pm

Quick check

1 6, 12, 18, 24, 30

2 8, 16, 24, 32, 40

3 15

4 20

5 12

6 a $\frac{4}{5}$ **b** $\frac{1}{4}$ **c** $\frac{1}{4}$ **d** $\frac{8}{25}$ **e** $\frac{9}{25}$ **f** $\frac{2}{3}$ **g** $\frac{8}{25}$

Exercise 8A

1 12 138	**2** 45 612	**3** 29 988	**4** 20 654
5 51 732	**6** 25 012	**7** 19 359	**8** 12 673
9 19 943	**10** 26 235	**11** 31 535	**12** 78 399
13 17 238	**14** 43 740	**15** 66 065	**16** 103 320
17 140 224	**18** 92 851	**19** 520 585	**20** 78 660

EExercise 8B

1 25	**2** 15	**3** 37	**4** 43	**5** 27	**6** 48
7 53	**8** 52	**9** 32	**10** 57	**11** 37 rem 15	
12 25 rem 5		**13** 34 rem 11		**14** 54 rem 9	
15 36 rem 11		**16** 17 rem 4		**17** 23	
18 61 rem 14		**19** 42	**20** 27 rem 2		

Exercise 8C

1 6000	**2** 312	**3** 68	**4** 38
5 57 600 m or 57.6 km	**6** 60 200	**7** 5819 litres	
8 £302.40	**9** 33	**10** 34 h	**11** £1.75
12 £136.80			

Exercise 8D

1 a 4.8 **b** 3.8 **c** 2.2 **d** 8.3 **e** 3.7
   f 46.9 **g** 23.9 **h** 9.5 **i** 11.1 **j** 33.5
   k 7.1 **l** 46.8 **m** 0.1 **n** 0.1 **o** 0.6
   p 65.0 **q** 213.9 **r** 76.1 **s** 455.2 **t** 51.0
2 a 5.78 **b** 2.36 **c** 0.98 **d** 33.09 **e** 6.01
   f 23.57 **g** 91.79 **h** 8.00 **i** 2.31 **j** 23.92
   k 6.00 **l** 1.01 **m** 3.51 **n** 96.51 **o** 0.01
   p 0.07 **q** 7.81 **r** 569.90 **s** 300.00 **t** 0.01
3 a 4.6 **b** 0.08 **c** 45.716 **d** 94.85
   e 602.1 **f** 671.76 **g** 7.1 **h** 6.904
   i 13.78 **j** 0.1 **k** 4.002 **l** 60.0
   m 11.99 **n** 899.996 **o** 0.1 **p** 0.01
   q 6.1 **r** 78.393 **s** 200.00 **t** 5.1
4 a 9 **b** 9 **c** 3 **d** 7 **e** 3
   f 8 **g** 3 **h** 8 **i** 6 **j** 4
   k 7 **l** 2 **m** 47 **n** 23 **o** 96
   p 33 **q** 154 **r** 343 **s** 704 **t** 910

Exercise 8E

1 a 49.8 **b** 21.3 **c** 48.3 **d** 33.3 **e** 5.99
   f 8.08 **g** 90.2 **h** 21.2 **i** 12.15 **j** 13.08
   k 13.26 **l** 24.36

2 a 1.4 **b** 1.8 **c** 4.8 **d** 3.8 **e** 3.75
   f 5.9 **g** 3.7 **h** 3.77 **i** 3.7 **j** 1.4
   k 11.8 **l** 15.3
3 a 30.7 **b** 6.6 **c** 3.8 **d** 16.7 **e** 11.8
   f 30.2 **g** 43.3 **h** 6.73 **i** 37.95 **j** 4.7
   k 3.8 **l** 210.5

Exercise 8F

1 a 7.2 **b** 7.6 **c** 18.8 **d** 37.1 **e** 32.5
   f 28.8 **g** 10.0 **h** 55.2 **i** 61.5 **j** 170.8
   k 81.6 **l** 96.5
2 a 9.36 **b** 10.35 **c** 25.85 **d** 12.78 **e** 1.82
   f 3.28 **g** 2.80 **h** 5.52 **i** 42.21 **j** 56.16
   k 7.65 **l** 48.96
3 a 1.8 **b** 1.4 **c** 1.4 **d** 1.2 **e** 2.13
   f 0.69 **g** 2.79 **h** 1.21 **i** 1.89 **j** 1.81
   k 0.33 **l** 1.9
4 a 1.75 **b** 1.28 **c** 1.85 **d** 3.65 **e** 1.66
   f 1.45 **g** 1.42 **h** 1.15 **i** 3.35 **j** 0.98
   k 2.3 **l** 1.46
5 a 1.89 **b** 1.51 **c** 0.264 **d** 4.265 **e** 1.224
   f 0.182 **g** 0.093 **h** 2.042 **i** 1.908 **j** 2.8
   k 4.25 **l** 18.5
6 Pack of 8 at £0.625 each
7 £49.90
8 Yes. She only needed 8 paving stones.

Exercise 8G

1 a 89.28 **b** 298.39 **c** 66.04 **d** 167.98
   e 2352.0 **f** 322.4 **g** 1117.8 **h** 4471.5
   i 464.94 **j** 25.55 **k** 1047.2 **l** 1890.5
2 a £224.10 **b** £223.75 **c** £29.90
3 £54.20
4 £120.75

Exercise 8H

1 a 0.48 **b** 2.92 **c** 1.12 **d** 0.12
   e 0.028 **f** 0.09 **g** 0.192 **h** 3.0264
   i 7.134 **j** 50.96 **k** 3.0625 **l** 46.512
2 a 35, 35.04, 0.04 **b** 16, 18.24, 2.24
   c 60, 59.67, 0.33 **d** 180, 172.86, 7.14
   e 12, 12.18, 0.18 **f** 24, 26.016, 2.016
   g 40, 40.664, 0.664 **h** 140, 140.58, 0.58

Exercise 8I

1 a $\frac{7}{10}$ **b** $\frac{2}{5}$ **c** $\frac{1}{2}$ **d** $\frac{3}{100}$ **e** $\frac{3}{50}$ **f** $\frac{13}{100}$
   g $\frac{1}{4}$ **h** $\frac{19}{50}$ **i** $\frac{11}{20}$ **j** $\frac{16}{25}$
2 a 0.5 **b** 0.75 **c** 0.6 **d** 0.9
   e 0.333 **f** 0.625 **g** 0.667 **h** 0.35
   i 0.636 **j** 0.444
3 a 0.3, $\frac{1}{2}$, 0.6 **b** 0.3, $\frac{2}{5}$, 0.8 **c** 0.15, $\frac{1}{4}$, 0.35
   d $\frac{7}{10}$, 0.71, 0.72 **e** 0.7, $\frac{3}{4}$, 0.8 **f** $\frac{1}{20}$, 0.08, 0.1
   g 0.4, $\frac{1}{2}$, 0.55 **h** 1.2, 1.23, $1\frac{1}{4}$

Exercise 8J

1 a $\frac{8}{15}$ b $\frac{7}{12}$ c $\frac{3}{10}$ d $\frac{11}{12}$ e $\frac{7}{8}$ f $\frac{1}{2}$
   g $\frac{1}{6}$ h $\frac{1}{20}$ i $\frac{1}{10}$ j $\frac{1}{8}$ k $\frac{1}{12}$ l $1\frac{1}{3}$
   m $\frac{1}{6}$ n $\frac{7}{9}$ o $\frac{5}{8}$ p $\frac{3}{8}$ q $\frac{1}{15}$ r $1\frac{13}{24}$
   s $\frac{59}{80}$ t $\frac{22}{63}$ u $\frac{37}{54}$

2 a $3\frac{5}{14}$ b $10\frac{3}{5}$ c $2\frac{1}{6}$ d $3\frac{31}{45}$ e $4\frac{47}{60}$ f $\frac{41}{72}$
   g $\frac{29}{48}$ h $1\frac{43}{48}$ i $1\frac{109}{120}$ j $1\frac{23}{30}$ k $1\frac{31}{84}$

3 $\frac{1}{20}$ 4 $\frac{1}{6}$ 5 $\frac{13}{15}$ 6 $\frac{1}{3}$ 7 $\frac{3}{8}$

Exercise 8K

1 a $\frac{1}{6}$ b $\frac{1}{10}$ c $\frac{3}{8}$ d $\frac{3}{14}$ e $\frac{8}{15}$ f $\frac{1}{5}$
   g $\frac{2}{7}$ h $\frac{3}{10}$ i $\frac{3}{32}$ j $\frac{1}{2}$ k $\frac{2}{5}$ l $\frac{3}{8}$
   m $\frac{7}{20}$ n $\frac{16}{45}$ o $\frac{3}{5}$ p $\frac{5}{8}$

2 3 km   3 $\frac{1}{12}$
4 $\frac{3}{8}$ 5 21
6 260   7 £51

8 18

9 a $\frac{5}{12}$ b $2\frac{1}{12}$ c $6\frac{1}{4}$ d $2\frac{11}{12}$ e $3\frac{9}{10}$ f $3\frac{1}{3}$
   g $12\frac{1}{2}$ h 30

10 $\frac{2}{5}$ of $6\frac{1}{2} = 2\frac{3}{5}$ 11   £5

12 Three-quarters of 68 = 51

13 7 min   14   £10.40   15   £30

Exercise 8L

1 a $\frac{3}{4}$ b $1\frac{2}{5}$ c $1\frac{1}{15}$ d $1\frac{1}{14}$ e 4   f 4
   g 5   h $1\frac{5}{7}$ i $\frac{4}{9}$ j $1\frac{3}{5}$

2 18   3 40   4   15   5 16

6 a $2\frac{2}{15}$ b 38   c $1\frac{7}{8}$ d $\frac{9}{32}$ e $\frac{1}{16}$ f $\frac{256}{625}$

Exercise 8M

1 a −15   b −14   c −24   d 6   e 14
   f 2   g −2   h −8   i −4   j 3
   k −24   l −10   m −18   n 16   o 36
   p −4   q −12   r −4   s 7   t 25
   u 18   v −8   w −45   x 3   y −40

2 a −9   b 16   c −3   d −32   e 18
   f 18   g 6   h −4   i 20   j 16
   k 8   l −48   m 13   n −13   o −8
   p 0   q 16   r −42   s 6   t 1
   u −14   v 6   w −4   x 7   y 0

3 a −2   b 30   c 15   d −27   e −7
4 a 4   b −9   c −3   d 6   e −4
5 a −9   b 3   c 1
6 a 16   b −2   c −12
7 a 24   b 6   c −4   d −2

8 For example: 1 × (−12), −1 × 12, 2 × (−6), 6 × (−2), 3 × (−4), 4 × (−3)

9 For example: 4 ÷ (−1), 8 ÷ (−2), 12 ÷ (−3), 16 ÷ (−4), 20 ÷ (−5), 24 ÷ (−6)

10 a 21   b −4   c 2   d −16   e 2
    f −5   g −35   h −17   i −12   j 6
    k 45   l −2   m 0   n −1   o −7
    p −36   q 9   r 32   s 0   t −65

Exercise 8N

1 a 50 000   b 60 000   c 30 000   d 90 000
   e 90 000   f 50   g 90   h 30
   i 100   j 200   k 0.5   l 0.3
   m 0.006   n 0.05   o 0.0009   p 10
   q 90   r 90   s 200   t 1000

2 a 65, 74   b 95, 149   c 950, 1499

3 Elsecar 750, 849; Hoyland 950, 1499; Barnsley 150 000, 249 999

4 a 60 000   b 27 000   c 80 000   d 30 000
   e 10 000   f 6000   g 1000   h 800
   i 100   j 600   k 2   l 4
   m 3   n 8   o 40   p 0.8
   q 0.5   r 0.07   s 1   t 0.01

Exercise 8P

1 a 35 000   b 15 000   c 960   d 12 000
   e 1000   f 4000   g 4   h 20
   i 1200

2 a £3000   b £2000   c £1500   d £700

3 a £15 000   b £18 000   c £18 000

4 8

5 £21 000

6 a 14   b 10   c 3 or 4   d $\frac{1}{2}$
   e 6   f 400   g 2   h 20

7 a 40   b 10   c £70

8 1000 or 1200

9 a 28   b 120   c 1440

10 400

11 a 3 kg   b 200

12 a i 850 grams   ii 750 grams
    b i 133   ii 117

Exercise 8Q

1 a 1.7 m   b 6 min   c 240 g
   d 80 °C   e 35 000   f 16 miles
   g 284 519   h 14 m^2

2 82 °F, 5.3 km, 110 min, 43 000 people, 6.2 s, 67th, 1788, 15, 5 s

Really Useful Maths!: The gym

Person	Weight category	Calories in breakfast	Minutes exercising
Dave	Overweight	833	119
Pete	OK	308.6	35
Andy	OK	297	38
Sue	Overweight	685.2	115
Sally	Underweight	440	55
Lynn	OK	607	68

Quick check

1 a $\frac{3}{5}$ **b** $\frac{1}{5}$ **c** $\frac{1}{3}$ **d** $\frac{16}{25}$ **e** $\frac{2}{5}$
f $\frac{3}{4}$ **g** $\frac{1}{3}$

2 a £12 **b** £66 **c** 175 litres **d** 15 kg
e 40 m **f** £35 **g** 135 g **h** 1.05 litres

Exercise 9A

1 a 1 : 3 **b** 3 : 4 **c** 2 : 3 **d** 2 : 3 **e** 2 : 5
f 2 : 5 **g** 5 : 8 **h** 25 : 6 **i** 3 : 2 **j** 8 : 3
k 7 : 3 **l** 5 : 2 **m** 1 : 6 **n** 3 : 8 **o** 5 : 3
p 4 : 5

2 a 1 : 3 **b** 3 : 2 **c** 5 : 12 **d** 8 : 1
e 17 : 15 **f** 25 : 7 **g** 4 : 1 **h** 5 : 6
i 1 : 24 **j** 48 : 1 **k** 5 : 2 **l** 3 : 14
m 2 : 1 **n** 3 : 10 **o** 31 : 200 **p** 5 : 8

3 $\frac{7}{10}$

4 $\frac{10}{25} = \frac{2}{5}$

5 a $\frac{2}{5}$ **b** $\frac{3}{5}$

6 a $\frac{7}{10}$ **b** $\frac{3}{10}$ **7** Amy $\frac{3}{5}$, Katie $\frac{2}{5}$

8 Fruit crush $\frac{5}{32}$, lemonade $\frac{27}{32}$

9 a $\frac{2}{9}$ **b** $\frac{1}{3}$ **c** twice as many

10 a $\frac{1}{2}$ **b** $\frac{7}{20}$ **c** $\frac{3}{20}$

11 James $\frac{1}{2}$ John $\frac{3}{10}$ Joseph $\frac{1}{5}$

12 sugar $\frac{5}{22}$, flour $\frac{3}{11}$, margarine $\frac{2}{11}$, fruit $\frac{7}{22}$

Exercise 9B

1 a 160 g, 240 g **b** 80 kg, 200 kg **c** 150, 350
d 950 m, 50 m **e** 175 min, 125 min
f £20, £30, £50 **g** £36, £60, £144
h 50 g, 250 g, 300 g **i** £1.40, £2, £1.60
j 120 kg, 72 kg, 8 kg
2 a 160 **b** 37.5%
3 a 28.6% **b** 250 kg
4 a 21 **b** 94.1%
5 a Mott: no, Wright: yes, Brennan: no, Smith: no, Kaye: yes
 b For example: *W*26, *H*30; *W*31, *H*38; *W*33, *H*37
6 a 1 : 400 000 **b** 1 : 125 000 **c** 1 : 250 000
d 1 : 25 000 **e** 1 : 20 000 **f** 1 : 40 000
g 1 : 62 500 **h** 1 : 10 000 **i** 1 : 60 000
7 a 1 : 1 000 000 **b** 47 km **c** 8 mm
8 a 1 : 250 000 **b** 2 km **c** 4.8 cm
9 a 1 : 20 000 **b** 0.54 km **c** 40 cm
10 a 1 : 1.6 **b** 1 : 3.25 **c** 1 : 1.125 **d** 1 : 1.44
e 1 : 5.4 **f** 1 : 1.5 **g** 1 : 4.8 **h** 1 : 42
i 1 : 1.25

Exercise 9C

1 a 3 : 2 **b** 32 **c** 80
2 a 100 **b** 160

3 0.4 litres **4** 102 **5** 1000 g **6** 10 125
7 5.5 litres
8 a 14 min **b** 75 min (= $1\frac{1}{4}$ h)
9 11 pages
10 Kevin £2040, John £2720
11 a 160 cans **b** 48 cans
12 lemonade 20 litres, ginger 0.5 litres
13 a $\frac{7}{50}$ **b** 75

Exercise 9D

1 18 mph
2 280 miles
3 52.5 mph
4 11.50 am
5 500 s
6 a 75 mph **b** 6.5 h **c** 175 miles
d 240 km **e** 64 km/h **f** 325 km
g 4.3 h (4 h 18 min)
7 a 120 km **b** 48 km/h
8 a 30 min **b** 6 mph
9 a 7.75 h **b** 52.9 mph
10 a 2.25 h **b** 99 miles
11 a 1.25 h **b** 1 h 15 min
12 a 48 mph **b** 6 h 40 min
13 a 10 m/s **b** 3.3 m/s **c** 16.7 m/s
d 41.7 m/s **e** 20.8 m/s
14 a 90 km/h **b** 43.2 km/h **c** 14.4 km/h
d 108 km/h **e** 1.8 km/h
15 a 64.8 km/h **b** 28 s **c** 8.07
16 a 6.7 m/s **b** 66 km **c** 5 minutes
d 133.3 metres

Exercise 9E

1 60 g **2** £5.22 **3** 45 **4** £6.72
5 a £312.50 **b** 8
6 a 56 litres **b** 350 miles
7 a 300 kg **b** 9 weeks
8 40 s
9 a i 100 g, 200 g, 250 g, 150 g
 ii 150 g, 300 g, 375 g, 225 g
 iii 250 g, 500 g, 625 g, 375 g
 b 24

Exercise 9F

1 a Large jar **b** 600 g tin **c** 5 kg bag
d 75 ml tube **e** Large box **f** Large box
g 400 ml bottle
2 a £5.11 **b** Large tin
3 a 95p **b** Family size
4 Bashir's
5 Mary
6 Kelly

Really Useful Maths!: Party time!

Marinated mushrooms (serves 6)

mushrooms	675 g
wine vinegar	45 ml
olive oil	135 ml

Leek and macaroni bake (serves 6)

macaroni	195 g
butter	75 g
leeks	405 g
flour	45 g
milk	900 ml
cheese	270 g
breadcrumbs	30 g

Crème caramel (serves 6)

sugar	180 g
eggs	6
milk	0.9 litres or 900 ml

There are four possible seating plans:
Bob, Elizabeth, Frank, Alison, Derek, Claire;
Bob, Elizabeth, Derek, Alison, Frank, Claire;
Bob, Claire, Frank, Alison, Derek, Elizabeth;
Bob, Claire, Derek, Alison, Frank, Elizabeth

They will need two bottles of wine.

ANSWERS TO CHAPTER 10

Quick check

a cube **b** cuboid **c** square-based pyramid **d** triangular prism **e** cylinder **f** cone
g sphere

Exercise 10A

1

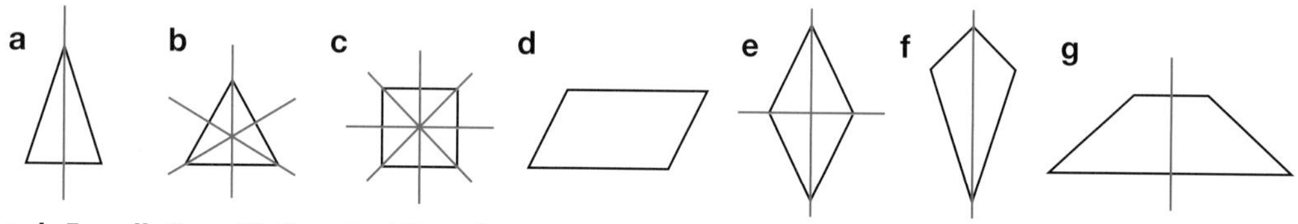

2 **a** **i** 5 **ii** 6 **iii** 8 **b** 10

3 **a**

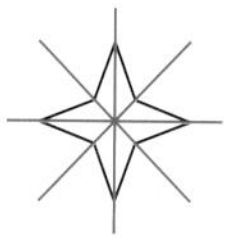

b

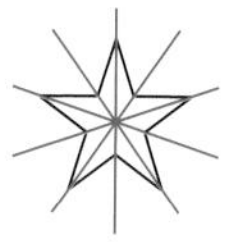

c

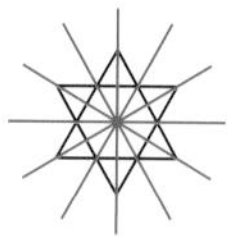

4 **a**

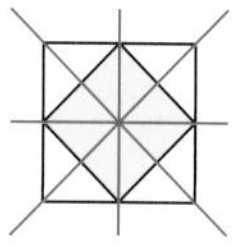

b

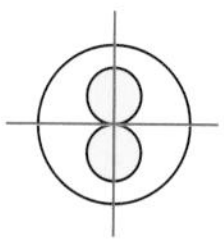

c

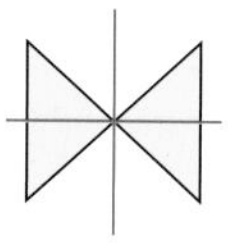

d

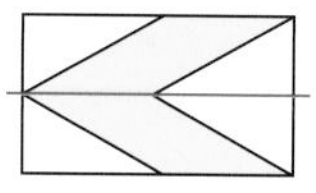

e

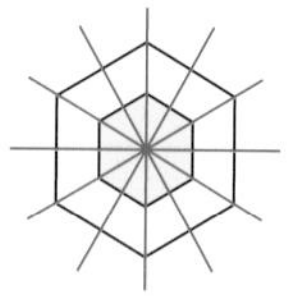

f

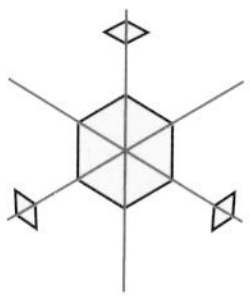

5 2, 1, 1, 2, 0

6 **a**

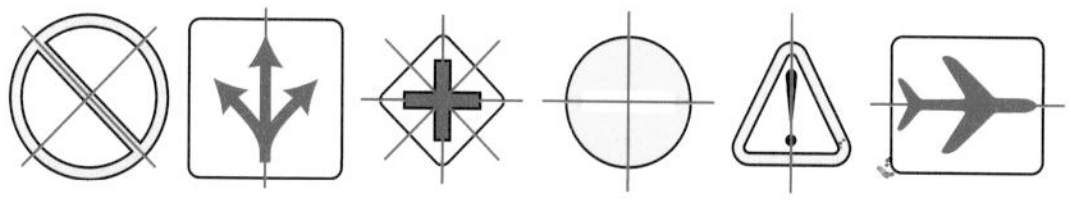

7 **a** 1 **b** 5 **c** 1 **d** 6

8 **c** Infinite number

Exercise 10B

1 **a** 4 **b** 2 **c** 2 **d** 3 **e** 6
2 **a** 4 **b** 5 **c** 6 **d** 4 **e** 6
3 **a** 2 **b** 2 **c** 2 **d** 2 **e** 2
4 **a** 4 **b** 3 **c** 8 **d** 2 **e** 4 **f** 2
5 A, B, C, D, E, F, G, J, K, L, M, P, Q, R, T, U, V, W, Y
6 Infinite number

Exercise 10C

1 a 9 **b** 4 **c** 4

3 a Sphere **b**

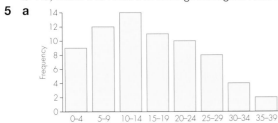

Cylinder   Cone

4 a 3 **b** 1 **c** 1 **d** 1 **e** Infinite **f** 1

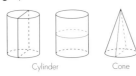
ANSWERS TO CHAPTER 11

Quick check

a 7 **b** 6 **c** 8 **d** 90

Exercise 11A

1 a 4 **b** 48 **c** −1 **d** $\frac{1}{4}$ **e** no mode **f** 3.21

2 a red **b** sun **c** β **d** ★

3 a 32 **b** 6 **c** no

   d no; boys generally take larger shoe sizes

4 a 5

   b no; more than half the form got a higher mark

5 a

(bar chart: Frequency vs intervals 0–4, 5–9, 10–14, 15–19, 20–24, 25–29, 30–34, 35–39 with heights 9, 12, 14, 11, 10, 8, 4, 2)

   b 70 **c** 24

   d cannot tell; know only that 9 households had between 0 and 4 e-mails **e** 10–14

6 The mode will be the most popular item or brand sold in a shop.

7 a 28 **b i** brown **ii** blue **iii** brown

   c Both pupils had blue eyes.

Exercise 11B

1 a 5 **b** 33 **c** $7\frac{1}{2}$ **d** 24 **e** $8\frac{1}{2}$ **f** 0 **g** 5.25

2 a £2.20 **b** £2.25

   c median, because it is the central value

3 a 5 **b i** 15 **ii** 215 **iii** 10 **iv** 10

4 a 13, Ella **b** 162 cm, Pat **c** 40 kg, Elisa

   d Ella, because she is closest to the 3 medians

5 a 12 **b** 13

6 a 21 **b** 16 **d** 15

7 Answers will vary

8 a 22 s **b** 25 s

9 a 56 **b** 48 **c** 49 **d** 45.5

   e Girls have higher average but boys have highest score

10 12, 14, 14, 16, 20, 22, 24

11 53

Exercise 11C

1 a 6 **b** 24 **c** 45 **d** 1.57 **e** 2

2 a 55.1 **b** 324.7 **c** 58.5 **d** 44.9 **e** 2.3

3 a 61 **b** 60 **c** 59 **d** Brian **e** 2

4 42 min

5 a £200 **b** £260 **c** £278

   d median, because the extreme value of £480 is not taken into account

6 a 35 **b** 36

7 a 6

   b 16; all the numbers and the mean are 10 more than those in part **a**

   c i 56 **ii** 106 **iii** 7

8 24

Exercise 11D

1 a 7 **b** 26 **c** 5 **d** 2.4 **e** 7

2 a 5°, 3°, 2°, 7°, 3°

   b variable weather over England

3 a £31, £28, £33 **b** £8, £14, £4

   c not particularly consistent

4 a 82 and 83 **b** 20 and 12

   c Fay, because her scores are more consistent

5 a 5 min and 4 min **b** 9 min and 13 min

   c number 50, because times are more consistent

Exercise 11E

1 a 29 **b** 28 **c** 27.1 **d** 14

2 a i Mode 3, median 4, mean 5 **ii** 6, 7, $7\frac{1}{2}$ **iii** 4, 6, 8

   b i Mean: balanced data

     ii Mode: 6 appears five times

     iii Median: 28 is an extreme value

3 a Mode 73, median 76, mean 80

   b The mean, because it is the highest average

4 a 150 **b** 20

5 a i 6 **ii** 16 **iii** 26 **iv** 56 **v** 96

   b units are the same

   c i 136 **ii** 576 **iii** 435 **iv** 856

   d i 5.6 **ii** 15.6 **iii** 25.6 **iv** 55.6 **v** 95.6

6 a Mean **b** Median **c** Mode **d** Median

   e Mode **f** Mean

7 No. Mode is 31, median is 31, and mean is $31\frac{1}{2}$

8 a i £18 000 **ii** £24 000 **iii** £23 778

   b i The 6% rise, because it gives a greater increase in salary for the higher paid employees

ii 6% increase: £19 080, £25 440, £25 205; +£1500:
£19 500, £25 500, £25 278

9 a Median   **b** Mode   **c** Mean

10 11.6   **11** 42.7

Exercise 11F

1 a i 7   **ii** 6   **iii** 6.4   **b i** 4   **ii** 4   **iii** 3.7
  c i 8   **ii** 8.5   **iii** 8.2   **d i** 0   **ii** 0   **iii** 0.3

2 a 668   **b** 1.9   **c** 0   **d** 328

Exercise 11G

1 a i $30 < x \leq 40$ **ii** 29.5   **b i** $0 < y \leq 100$ **ii** 158.3   **c i** $5 < z \leq 10$ **ii** 9.43   **d i** 7–9   **ii** 8.4

2 a $100 < w \leq 120$ g   **b** 10 860   **c** 108.6 g

3 a 207   **b** 19–22 cm   **c** 20.3 cm

4 a 160   **b** 52.6 min   **c** modal group   **d** 65%

5 a $175 < h \leq 200$ **b** 31%   **c** 193.25   **d** No

6 Average price increases: Soundbuy 17.7p, Springfields 18.7p, Setco 18.2p

7 a Yes average distance is 11.7 miles per day.
  b Because shorter runs will be completed faster, which will affect the average.
  c Yes because the shortest could be 1 mile and the longest 25 miles.

3 a 2.2, 1.7, 1.3   **b** Better dental care

4 a 0   **b** 0.96

5 a 7   **b** 6.5   **c** 6.5

6 a 1   **b** 1   **c** 0.98

7 a Roger 5, Brian 4   **b** Roger 3, Brian 8
  c Roger 5, Brian 4   **d** Roger 5.4, Brian 4.5
  e Roger, because he has the smaller range
  f Brian, because he has the better mean

Exercise 11H

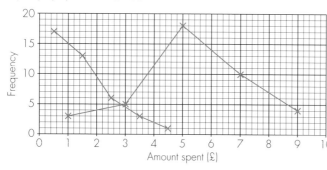

1 a   **b** 1.72   **2 a**   **b** 2.77

3 a
  b boys 12.9, girls 13.1

4 a
  b Mon 28.4, Tue 20.9, Wed 21.3
  c There are more people on a Monday as they became ill over the weekend.

5 a i 17, 13, 6, 3, 1   **ii** £1.45
  b i   **ii** £5.35

  c There is a much higher mean, first group of people just want a paper or a few sweets. Later, people are buying food for the day.

Really Useful Maths!: A pint of milk please

Monthly milk production in thousands of litres		
	2004	2005
mean	62	72
median	63	71
mode	64	62
range	24	24

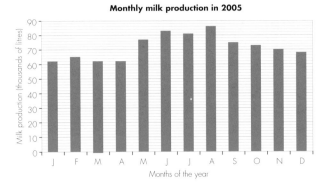

Milk production compared to rainfall: as the rainfall decreases, the milk production increases, and as the rainfall increases the milk production decreases. Milk production compared to sunshine: as the sunshine increases, the milk production increases, and as the sunshine decreases, the milk production decreases.

ANSWERS TO CHAPTER 12

Quick check

1 a $\frac{3}{8}$ **b** $\frac{4}{9}$ **c** $\frac{7}{12}$ **d** $\frac{3}{5}$

2 a 18   **b** 20   **c** 19   **d** 27

3 a 1200   **b** 0.34   **c** 23   **d** 0.047

Exercise 12A

1 a $\frac{2}{25}$ **b** $\frac{1}{2}$ **c** $\frac{1}{4}$ **d** $\frac{7}{20}$ **e** $\frac{9}{10}$ **f** $\frac{3}{4}$
2 a 0.27 **b** 0.85 **c** 0.13 **d** 0.06 **e** 0.8 **f** 0.32
3 a $\frac{3}{25}$ **b** $\frac{2}{5}$ **c** $\frac{9}{20}$ **d** $\frac{17}{25}$ **e** $\frac{1}{4}$ **f** $\frac{5}{8}$
4 a 29% **b** 55% **c** 3% **d** 16% **e** 60% **f** 125%
5 a 28% **b** 30% **c** 95% **d** 34% **e** 27.5% **f** 87.5%
6 a 0.6 **b** 0.075 **c** 0.76 **d** 0.3125 **e** 0.05 **f** 0.125
7 150   **8** none   **9** 20
10 a 77% **b** 39% **c** 63%
11 27%   **12** 61.5%
13 a 50% **b** 20% **c** 80%
14 a 87.5%, 75%, 62.5%, 50%, 25%
   b 12.5%, 12.5%, 12.5%, 12.5%, 25%
15 a 20% **b** 25% **c** 75% **d** 45% **e** 14%
   f 50% **g** 60% **h** 17.5% **i** 55% **j** 130%
16 a 33.3% **b** 16.7% **c** 66.7% **d** 83.3% **e** 28.6%
   f 78.3% **g** 68.9% **h** 88.9% **i** 81.1% **j** 20.9%
17 a 7% **b** 80% **c** 66% **d** 25% **e** 54.5%
   f 82% **g** 30% **h** 89.1% **i** 120% **j** 278%
18 a $\frac{3}{5}$ **b** 0.6 **c** 60%
19 63%, 83%, 39%, 62%, 77%
20 a 80% **b** 20%
21 6.7%
22 25.5%
23 34%, 0.34, $\frac{17}{50}$; 85%, 0.85, $\frac{17}{20}$; 7.5%, 0.075, $\frac{3}{40}$
24 a 0.3, 0.35, 0.75, 0.8   **b** 10%, 0.15, $\frac{1}{5}$, $\frac{1}{2}$
   c $\frac{1}{4}$, 26%, 0.275, 30%   **d** 3%, 0.32, $\frac{3}{8}$, $\frac{3}{4}$
   e 45%, $\frac{1}{2}$, 0.55, 0.6   **f** 9%, $\frac{1}{10}$, 0.111, $\frac{1}{8}$
   g 0.23, $\frac{1}{4}$, 0.275, 28%   **h** 8%, $\frac{1}{8}$, 0.8, 0.88
   i 0.3, 0.325, $\frac{1}{3}$, 35%   **j** $\frac{1}{5}$, 0.35, 50%, $\frac{3}{5}$

Exercise 12B

1 a 0.88 **b** 0.3 **c** 0.25 **d** 0.08 **e** 1.15
2 a 78% **b** 40% **c** 75% **d** 5% **e** 110%
3 a £45 **b** £6.30 **c** 128.8 kg **d** 1.125 kg
   e 1.08 h **f** 37.8 cm **g** £0.12 **h** 2.94 m
   i £7.60 **j** 33.88 min **k** 136 kg **l** £162
4 96   **5** £1205   **6 a** 86% **b** 215
7 8520   **8** 287
9 Each team: 22 500, referees: 750, other teams: 7500, FA: 15 000, celebrities: 6750
10 114
11 Mon: 816, Tue: 833, Wed: 850, Thu: 799, Fri: 748
12 Lead 150 g, tin 87.5 g, bismuth 12.5 g
13 a £3.25 **b** 2.21 kg **c** £562.80 **d** £6.51
   e 42.93 m **f** £24
14 480 cm^3 nitrogen, 120 cm^3 oxygen
15 13   **16** £270

Exercise 12C

1 a 1.1 **b** 1.03 **c** 1.2 **d** 1.07 **e** 1.12
2 a £62.40 **b** 12.96 kg **c** 472.5 g **d** 599.5 m
   e £38.08 **f** £90 **g** 391 kg **h** 824.1 cm
   i 253.5 g **j** £143.50 **k** 736 m **l** £30.24
3 £29 425
4 1 690 200
5 a Bob: £17 325, Anne: £18 165, Jean: £20 475, Brian: £26 565
   b No
6 £411.95   **7** 193 800   **8** 575 g   **9** 918
10 60
11 TV: £287.88, microwave: £84.60, CD: £135.13, stereo: £34.66

Exercise 12D

1 a 0.92 **b** 0.85 **c** 0.75 **d** 0.91 **e** 0.88

2 a £9.40 **b** 23 kg **c** 212.4 g **d** 339.5 m
 e £4.90 **f** 39.6 m **g** 731 m **h** 83.52 g
 i 360 cm **j** 117 min **k** 81.7 kg **l** £37.70
3 £5525
4 a 52.8 kg **b** 66 kg **c** 45.76 kg
5 Mr Speed: £176, Mrs Speed: £297.50,
 James: £341, John: £562.50
6 448
7 705
8 £18 975
9 a 66.5 mph **b** 73.5 mph
10 £16.72, £22.88 **11** 524.8 units
12 TV £222.31, DVD player £169.20

Exercise 12E
1 a 25% **b** 60.6% **c** 46.3% **d** 12.5%

e 41.7% **f** 60% **g** 20.8% **h** 10%
 i 1.9% **j** 8.3% **k** 45.5% **l** 10.5%
2 32% **3** 6.5% **4** 33.7%
5 a 49.2% **b** 64.5% **c** 10.6%
6 17.9% **7** 4.9% **8** 90.5%
9 a Brit Com: 20.9%, USA: 26.5%, France: 10.3%, Other 42.3%
 b total 100%, all imports

Exercise 12F
1 a 0.6, 60% **b** $\frac{7}{10}$, 70% **c** $\frac{11}{20}$, 0.55
2 a £10.20 **b** 48 **c** £1.26
3 a 56% **b** 68% **c** 37.5%
4 a 276 **b** 3204
5 a 20% **b** 30% **c** £13.20
6 a £6400 **b** £5440
7 a 70.4 kg **b** iii

ANSWERS TO CHAPTER 13

Quick check

1 a $6x$ **b** $12x - 4$ **c** $18x + 7$
2 a -4 **b** 2.5

Exercise 13A
1 $x = 4$ **2** $w = 14$ **3** $y = 5$
4 $p = 10$ **5** $x = 5$ **6** $x = 6$
7 $z = 24$ **8** $x = 2.5$ **9** $q = 4$
10 $x = 1$ **11** $r = 28$ **12** $s = 12$

Exercise 13B
1 $\leftarrow \div 3 \leftarrow -5 \leftarrow, x = 2$
2 $\leftarrow \div 3 \leftarrow + 13 \leftarrow, x = 13$
3 $\leftarrow \div 3 \leftarrow + 7 \leftarrow, x = 13$
4 $\leftarrow \div 4 \leftarrow + 19 \leftarrow, y = 6$
5 $\leftarrow \div 3 \leftarrow -8, a = 1$
6 $\leftarrow \div 2 \leftarrow -8 \leftarrow, x = 3$
7 $\leftarrow \div 2 \leftarrow -6 \leftarrow, y = 6$
8 $\leftarrow \div 8 \leftarrow -4 \leftarrow, x = 1$
9 $\leftarrow \div 2 \leftarrow + 10 \leftarrow, x = 9$
10 $\leftarrow \times 5 \leftarrow -2 \leftarrow, x = 5$
11 $\leftarrow \times 3 \leftarrow + 4 \leftarrow, t = 18$
12 $\leftarrow \times 4 \leftarrow -1 \leftarrow, y = 24$
13 $\leftarrow \times 2 \leftarrow + 6 \leftarrow, k = 18$
14 $\leftarrow \times 8 \leftarrow + 4 \leftarrow, h = 40$
15 $\leftarrow \times 6 \leftarrow -1 \leftarrow, w = 18$
16 $\leftarrow \times 4 \leftarrow -5 \leftarrow, x = 8$
17 $\leftarrow \times 2 \leftarrow + 3 \leftarrow, y = 16$
18 $\leftarrow \times 5 \leftarrow -2 \leftarrow, f = 30$

Exercise 13C
1 56 **2** 2 **3** 6 **4** 3 **5** 4 **6** $2\frac{1}{2}$ **7** $3\frac{1}{2}$
8 $2\frac{1}{2}$ **9** 4 **10** 21 **11** 72 **12** 56 **13** 0
14 -7 **15** -18 **16** 36 **17** 36 **18** 60

Exercise 13D
1 1 **2** 3 **3** 2 **4** 2 **5** 9 **6** 5 **7** 6
8 4 **9** 2 **10** -2 **11** 24 **12** 10 **13** 21 **14** 72 **15** 56 **16** 5 **17** 28 **18** 5 **19** 35 **20** 33
21 23

Exercise 13E
1 3 **2** 7 **3** 5 **4** 3 **5** 4 **6** 6 **7** 8
8 1 **9** 1.5 **10** 2.5 **11** 0.5 **12** 1.2
13 -4 **14** -2

Exercise 13F
1 2 **2** 1 **3** 7 **4** 4 **5** 2 **6** -1 **7** -2 **8** 2
9 6 **10** 11 **11** 1 **12** 4 **13** 9 **14** 6

Exercise 13G
1 55p **2** **a** 1.5 **b** 2
3 a 1.5 cm **b** 6.75 cm^2 **4** 17 **5** 3 yr **6** 9 yr
7 3 cm **8** 5 **9** **a** $4x + 40 = 180$ **b** $x = 35°$

Exercise 13H
1 a 4 and 5 **b** 4 and 5 **c** 2 and 3
2 $x = 3.5$
3 $x = 3.7$
4 $x = 2.5$
5 $x = 1.5$
6 a $x = 2.4$ **b** $x = 2.8$ **c** $x = 3.2$
7 $x = 7.8$ cm, 12.8 cm
8 $x = 5.8$

Exercise 13I
1 $k = \dfrac{T}{3}$ **2** $m = P - 7$ **3** $y = X + 1$ **4** $p = 3Q$
5 a $m = p - t$ **b** $t = p - m$
6 $k = \dfrac{t - 7}{2}$
7 $m = gv$ **8** $m = \sqrt{t}$

9 $r = \dfrac{C}{2\pi}$ **10** $b = \dfrac{A}{h}$

11 $l = \dfrac{P - 2w}{2}$ **12** $p = \sqrt{m - 2}$

Exercise 13J

1 **a** $x < 5$ **b** $t > 8$ **c** $p \geqslant 10$ **d** $x < 5$
  e $y \leqslant 3$ **f** $t > 5$ **g** $x < 6$ **h** $y \leqslant 15$
  i $t \geqslant 18$ **j** $x < 7$ **k** $x \leqslant 3$ **l** $t \geqslant 5$
2 **a** 8   **b** 6   **c** 16   **d** 3   **e** 7
3 **a** 11   **b** 16   **c** 16   **d** 3   **e** 7

Exercise 13K

1 **a** $x > 1$ **b** $x \leqslant 3$ **c** $x < 2$ **d** $x \geqslant -1$
  e $x \leqslant -1$ **f** $x < 1$ **g** $x > -1$ **h** $x \geqslant 1$
  i $x \leqslant 2$ **j** $1 < x \leqslant 4$ **k** $-2 < x < 4$
  l $-1 \leqslant x \leqslant 3$

2 **a**  **b**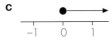

  c  **d**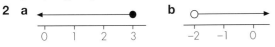

  e 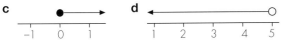 **f**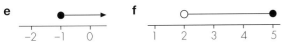

  g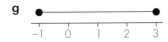

  h 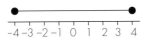 **i**  **j**

3 **a** $x \geqslant 4$  **b** $x < -2$  **c** $x \leqslant 3$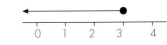

  d $x > 3$  **e** $x > 4$  **f** $x \leqslant 5$

  g $x < 2.5$  **h** $x \geqslant 4.5$ 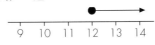 **i** $x \leqslant 10$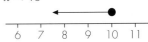

  j $x > 12$  **k** $x \geqslant 12$  **l** $x < 25$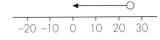

4 **a** $x \leqslant 2$  **b** $x \geqslant 3\frac{1}{2}$  **c** $x > 5$

  d $x < -1$  **e** $x < 4$  **f** $x \geqslant 2$

g $x \geq -1$

h $x \geq 3.5$

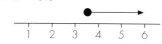

i $x > 15$

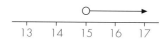

j $x \leq 24$

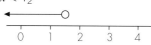

k $x < 12$

l $x \geq 70$

5 a $x < 1\frac{1}{2}$

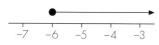

b $x \leq -2$

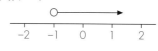

c $x > 50$

d $x \geq -6$

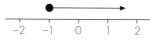

e $x > -1$

f $x \leq 2.5$

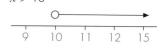

g $x \geq -1$

h $x < 8$

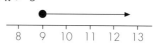

i $x > 10$

j $x \leq 9$

k $x \geq 9$

l $x < 13$

ANSWERS TO CHAPTER 14

Quick check

A(2, 4), B(4, 3), C(0, 2), D(3, 0)

Exercise 14A

1 a i $8\frac{1}{4}$ kg **ii** $2\frac{1}{4}$ kg **iii** 9 lb **iv** 22 lb
b 2.2 lb
2 a i 10 cm **ii** 23 cm **iii** 2 in **iv** $8\frac{3}{4}$ in
b $2\frac{1}{2}$ cm
3 a i \$320 **ii** \$100 **iii** £45 **iv** £78
b \$3.2
4 a i £120 **ii** £82 **b i** 32 **ii** 48
5 a i £100 **ii** £325
b i 500 **ii** 250
6 a i £70 **ii** £29 **b i** £85 **ii** £38
7 a i 40 km **ii** 16 km **iii** 25 miles
iv $9\frac{1}{2}$ miles
b 8 km
8 a i 95 °F **ii** 68 °F **iii** 10 °C **iv** 32 °C
b 32 °F
9 b 2.15 pm
10 b £50

Exercise 14B

1 a i 9 am **ii** 10 am **iii** 12 noon
b i 40 km/h **ii** 120 km/h **iii** 40 km/h
2 a i 125 km **ii** 125 km/h
b i Between 2 and 3 pm **ii** 25 km/h

3 a 30 km **b** 40 km **c** 100 km/h
4 a He fell over or stopped to tie up a shoe lace
b i 333 m/min **ii** 180 s **iii** 5.6 m/s
c i About $8\frac{1}{2}$ min into the race **ii** About 30 s
5 a i Because it stopped several times
ii Ravinder
b Ravinder at 3.57 pm or 3.58 pm, Sue at 4.20 pm,
Michael at 4.35 pm
c i 24 km/h **ii** 20 km/h **iii** 5
6 a Araf ran the race at a constant pace, taking
5 minutes to cover the 1000 metres.
Sean started slowly, covering the first 500 metres in
4 minutes. He then went faster, covering the last
500 metres in $1\frac{1}{2}$ minutes, giving a total time of
$5\frac{1}{2}$ minutes for the race
b i 20 km/h **ii** 12 km/h **iii** 10.9 km/h

Exercise 14C

1 a A(1, 2), B(3, 0), C(0, 1), D(−2, 4), E(−3, 2), F(−2, 0),
G(−4, −1), H(−3, −3), I(1, −3), J(4, −2)
b i (2, 1) **ii** (−1, −3) **iii** (1, 1)
c $x = -3, x = 2, y = 3, y = -4$
d i $x = -\frac{1}{2}$ **ii** $y = -\frac{1}{2}$
2 Values of y: 2, 3, 4, 5, 6
3 Values of y: −2, 0, 2, 4, 6
4 Values of y: 1, 2, 3, 4, 5
5 Values of y: −4, −3, −2, −1, 0
6 a Values of y: −3, −2, −1, 0, 1 and −6, −4, −2, 0, 2
b (3, 0)

7 a Values of y: 0, 4, 8, 12, 16 and 6, 8, 10, 12, 14
  b (6, 12)
8 Points could be (0, −1), (1, 4), (2, 9), (3, 14), (4, 19), (5, 24)
  etc

Exercise 14D
1 Extreme points are (0, 4), (5, 19)
2 Extreme points are (0, −5), (5, 5)
3 Extreme points are (0, −3), (10, 2)
4 Extreme points are (−3, −4), (3, 14)
5 a Extreme points are (0, −2), (5, 13) and (0, 1), (5, 11)
  b (3, 7)
6 a Extreme points are (0, −1), (12, 3) and (0, −2), (12, 4)
  b (6, 1)
7 a Extreme points are (0, 1), (4, 13) and (0, −2), (4, 10)
  b Do not cross because they are parallel
8 a Values of y: 5, 4, 3, 2, 1, 0. Extreme points are
    (0, 5), (5, 0)
  b Extreme points are (0, 7), (7, 0)

Exercise 14E
1 a 2 **b** $\frac{1}{3}$ **c** −3 **d** 1
  e −2 **f** $-\frac{1}{3}$ **g** 5 **h** −5 **i** $\frac{1}{5}$ **j** $\frac{3}{4}$
2 a They are perpendicular and **b** −1
    symmetrical about the axes
3

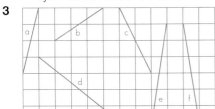

Exercise 14F
1
$y = 2x + 6, y = 3x - 4, y = \frac{1}{2}x + 5, y = x + 7$

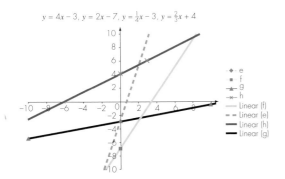

$y = 4x - 3, y = 2x - 7, y = \frac{1}{4}x - 3, y = \frac{2}{3}x + 4$

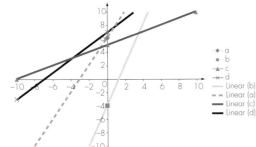

$y = 6x - 5, y = x + 8, y = \frac{4}{5}x - 2, y = 3x - 9$

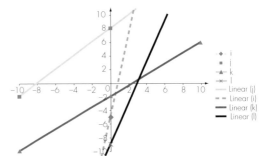

2 a
$y = 3x + 1, y = 2x + 3$

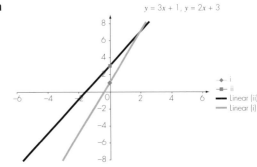

  b (2, 7)
3 a
$y = \frac{x}{3} + 3, y = \frac{x}{4} + 2$

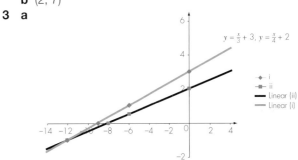

  b (−12, −1)
4 a
$y = x + 3, y = 2x$

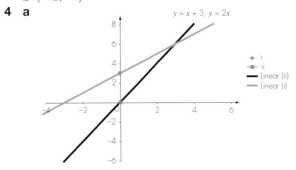

  b (3, 6)

Really Useful Maths!: A trip to France

The quickest and shortest route, avoiding Paris, is Boulogne, Arras, Reims, Dijon, Lyon, Orange, Montpellier, Perpignan, which is 1230 km and takes 11 hours 55 minutes, at an average speed of approximately 103.22 km/h.

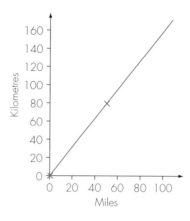

km/h	mph
50	31
80	50
90	56
100	63
110	69
130	81

Tyre pressures: front 2.2 bars, back 2.4 bars

ANSWERS TO CHAPTER 15

Quick check

1 obtuse **2** acute **3** reflex **4** obtuse
5 reflex

Exercise 15A

1 a 40° **b** 30° **c** 35° **d** 43° **e** 100°
f 125° **g** 340° **h** 225°

Exercise 15B

1 48° **2** 307° **3** 108° **4** 52° **5** 59°
6 81° **7** 139° **8** 51° **9** 138° **10** 128°
11 47° **12** 117° **13** 27° **14** 45° **15** 108°
16 69° **17** 135° **18** 58° **19** 74° **20** 23°
21 55° **22** 56°
23 a $x = 100°$ **b** $x = 110°$ **c** $x = 30°$
24 a $x = 55°$ **b** $x = 45°$ **c** $x = 12.5°$
25 a $x = 34°, y = 98°$ **b** $x = 70°, y = 120°$
c $x = 20°, y = 80°$

Exercise 15C

1 a 70° **b** 50° **c** 80° **d** 60° **e** 75°
f 109° **g** 38° **h** 63°
2 a no, total is 190° **b** yes, total is 180°
c no, total is 170° **d** yes, total is 180°
e yes, total is 180° **f** no, total is 170°
3 a 80° **b** 67° **c** 20° **d** 43° **e** 10° **f** 1°
4 a 60° **b** equilateral triangle **c** same length
5 a 70° each **b** isosceles triangle **c** same length
6 $x = 50°, y = 80°$
7 a 109° **b** 130° **c** 135°
8 a missing angle = y, $x + y = 180°$ and
$a + b + y = 180°$ so $x = a + b$

Exercise 15D

1 a 90° **b** 150° **c** 80° **d** 80° **e** 77°
f 131° **g** 92° **h** 131°

2 a no, total is 350° **b** yes, total is 360°
c no, total is 350° **d** no, total is 370°
e yes, total is 360° **f** yes, total is 360°
3 a 100° **b** 67° **c** 120° **d** 40° **e** 40° **f** 1°
4 a 90° **b** rectangle **c** square
5 a 120° **b** 170° **c** 125° **d** 136° **e** 149°
f 126° **g** 212° **h** 114°

Exercise 15E

1 a i 45° **ii** 8 **iii** 1080°
b i 20° **ii** 18 **iii** 2880°
c i 15° **ii** 24 **iii** 3960°
d i 36° **ii** 10 **iii** 1440°
2 a i 172° **ii** 45 **iii** 7740°
b i 174° **ii** 60 **iii** 10 440°
c i 156° **ii** 15 **iii** 2340°
d i 177° **ii** 120 **iii** 21 240°
3 a exterior angle is 7°, which does not divide exactly into 360°
b exterior angle is 19°, which does not divide exactly into 360°
c exterior angle is 11°, which does divide exactly into 360°
d exterior angle is 70°, which does not divide exactly into 360°
4 a 7° does not divide exactly into 360°
b 26° does not divide exactly into 360°
c 44° does not divide exactly into 360°
d 13° does not divide exactly into 360°
5 $x = 45°$, they are the same, true for all regular polygons

Exercise 15F

1 a 40° **b** $b = c = 70°$ **c** $d = 75°, e = f = 105°$
d $g = 50°, h = i = 130°$ **e** $j = k = l = 70°$
f $n = m = 80°$
2 a $a = 50°, b = 130°$ **b** $c = d = 65°, e = f = 115°$
c $g = i = 65°, h = 115°$ **d** $j = k = 72°, l = 108°$

e $m = n = o = p = 105°$ **f** $q = r = s = 125°$

3 b, d, f, h

4 a $a = 95°$ **b** $b = 66°, c = 114°$

5 a $x = 30°, y = 120°$ **b** $x = 25°, y = 105°$
  c $x = 30°, y = 100°$

6 a $x = 50°, y = 110°$ **b** $x = 25°, y = 55°$
  c $x = 20°, y = 140°$

7 Use alternate angles to see b, a and c are all angles on a straight line, and so total 180°

8 a 40°
  b third angle in triangle equals q (alternative angle), angle sum of triangle is 180°.

9 a Angle at CD is 55°, so angles ABC, 85° and 55° add up to 180° (angles on a straight line) and these same angles are the ones in the triangle.
  b In algebraic form, $a + b + c = 180°$

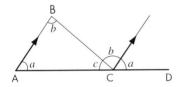

Exercise 15G

1 a $a = 110°, b = 55°$ **b** $c = 75°, d = 115°$
  c $e = 87°, f = 48°$

2 a $a = c = 105°, b = 75°$ **b** $d = f = 70°, e = 110°$
  c $g = i = 63°, h = 117°$

3 a $a = 135°, b = 25°$ **b** $c = d = 145°$
  c $e = f = 94°$

4 a $a = c = 105°, b = 75°$ **b** $d = f = 93°, e = 87°$
  c $g = i = 49°, h = 131°$

5 a $a = 58°, b = 47°$ **b** $c = 141°, d = 37°$
  c $e = g = 65°, f = 115°$

Exercise 15H

2

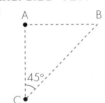

3 a 090°, 180°, 270°   **b** 000°, 270°, 180°

4

Leg	Actual distance	Bearing
1	50 km	060°
2	70 km	350°
3	65 km	260°
4	46 km	196°
5	60 km	130°

ANSWERS TO CHAPTER 16

Quick check

1 27.1   **2** 77.1   **3** 240.3   **4** 3.2
5 8.1   **6** 15.2

Exercise 16A

1 a $1\frac{1}{2}$ cm, 3 cm   **b** 2 cm, 4 cm   **c** 3 cm, 6 cm

5 d regular hexagon

6 d 90°
  f a radius is perpendicular to a tangent at a point

Exercise 16B

1 a 25.1 cm   **b** 15.7 cm   **c** 44.0 cm
  d 22.0 cm   **e** 18.8 cm   **f** 47.1 cm
  g 28.9 cm   **h** 14.8 cm

2 a 6.3 cm   **b** 8.2 cm   **c** 5.3 cm   **d** 7.5 cm

3 a 31.4 cm   **b** 18.8 cm   **c** 9.4 cm
  d 25.1 cm   **e** 5.7 cm   **f** 15.7 cm
  g 81.7 cm   **h** 39.6 cm

4 100.5 cm

5 a A 188.5 m, B 194.8 m, C 201.1 m, D 207.3 m
  b 18.7 or 18.8 m

6 879.6 or 880 cm

7 a 37.7 cm   **b** 3770 cm   **c** 37.7 m
  d 37.7 km

8 100 cm   **9** 24.2 cm   **10** 15.9 cm

11 a 30.8 cm   **b** 17.9 cm

12 a Sue 62.8 cm, Julie 69.1 cm, Dave 75.4 cm, Brian 81.7 cm
  b the difference between the distances round the waists of two people is 2π times the difference between their radii
  c 6.28 m

13 a perimeters of shapes A and B are both 25.1 cm
  b 25.1 cm

Exercise 16C

1 a 78.5 cm²   **b** 28.3 cm²   **c** 7.1 cm²
  d 50.3 cm²   **e** 2.5 cm²   **f** 19.6 cm²
  g 530.9 cm²   **h** 124.7 cm²

2 a 3.1 cm² **b** 5.3 cm² **c** 2.3 cm² **d** 4.5 cm²

3 a 50.3 cm²   **b** 19.6 cm²   **c** 153.9 cm²
  d 38.5 cm²   **e** 28.3 cm²   **f** 176.7 cm²
  g 66.5 cm²   **h** 17.3 cm²

4 a 9.1 cm²   **b** 138   **c** 2000 cm²
  d 1255.8 cm² or 1252.9 cm² using unrounded answer from **a**
  e 744.2 cm² or 747.1 cm², using unrounded answer from **a**

5 3848.5 m²

6 a i 56.5 cm   **ii** 254.5 cm²
  b i 69.1 cm   **ii** 380.1 cm²
  c i 40.8 cm   **ii** 132.7 cm²
  d i 88.0 cm   **ii** 615.8 cm²

7 a 19.1 cm   **b** 9.5 cm
  c 286.5 cm² (or 283.5 cm²)

8 962.9 cm² (or 962.1 cm²)

9 a 56.5 cm²   **b** 19.6 cm²

10 a 50.3 m²   **b** 44.0 cm²   **c** 28.3 cm²

Exercise 16D

1 10π cm

2 **a** 4π cm **b** 20π cm **c** 15π cm **d** 4π cm

3 **a** 16π cm^2 **b** 25π cm^2 **c** 9π cm^2
   d 81π cm^2

4 25 cm **5** 10 cm **6** $\dfrac{200}{\pi}$ cm **7** $\dfrac{5}{\sqrt{\pi}}$ cm

8 **a** 12.5π cm^2 **b** 16π cm^2 **c** $(16\pi + 80)$ cm^2
   b $(50\pi + 100)$ cm^2

9 **a** 32π cm^2 **b** 16π cm^2 **c** 8π cm^2
   d 4π cm^2

ANSWERS TO CHAPTER 17

Quick check

1 cube **2** cylinder **3** triangular prism

Exercise 17A

1 **a** **i** 4 **ii** 16 g **iii** 38 mph **b** **i** 8 kg **ii** 66 mph **iii** 160 g
   c **i** 13 oz **ii** 85 mph **iii** 76 kph **d** **i** 26 **ii** 71.6 **iii** 64

2 **a**  **b**  **c** 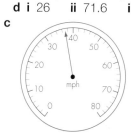 **d**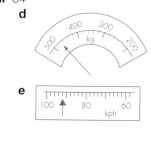
   e 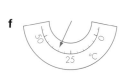 **f**

3 **a** 50 °C **b** 64 °C **c** −10 °C **d** 82 °C **e** −16 °C
4 **a** 8 kg **b** 29 mph **c** 230 g **d** 12.7 kg
5 **a** 1.2 kg **b** 125 g

Exercise 17B

1 **a** bike 2 m, bus 10 m, train 17–18 m
2 height 3.8 m, length 17.5 m
3 250 g
4 **a** 3.8 m **b** 6.5 m **c** 5.5 m
5 9.5 or 10 g

Exercise 17C

1 **c** Onions: 40 m × 10 m, soft fruit: 50 m × 10 m, apple
   trees: 20 m × 20 m, lawn: 30 m × 20 m, potatoes:
   50 m × 20 m

   d Onions: 400 m^2, soft fruit: 500 m^2, apple trees: 400 m^2,
   lawn: 600 m^2, potatoes: 1000 m^2
2 **a** 33 cm **b** 9 cm
3 **a** 8.4 km **b** 4.6 km **c** 6.2 km **d** 6.4 km **e**
   7.6 km **f** 2.4 km
4 **a** **i** 64 km **ii** 208 km **iii** 116 km **iv** 40 km
   b **i** 84 km **ii** 196 km **iii** 152 km **iv** 128 km
5 **a** 50 km **b** 35 km **c** 45 km
6 **a** 30 cm × 30 cm **b** 40 cm × 10 cm **c** 20 cm ×
   15 cm **d** 30 cm × 20 cm **e** 30 cm ×
   20 cm
   f 10 cm × 5 cm

Really Useful Maths!: A place in the sun

Villa	Distance from airport (km)	Distance to coast (km)	Cost per square metre (€/m^2)	Cost (£)	Rental income per year (£)
Rosa	9.5	9.5–10.5	2250	120 000	8750
Cartref	14–15	20	2100	126 000	6000
Blanca	11–12	6.5–7.5	2750	132 000	10 500
Azul	12–13	15–16	2370	158 000	11 700
Amapola	10–11	25–26	2400	168 000	10 000
Hinojos	23.5–24.5	7.5–8.5	2400	176 000	12 000

Quick check

1 a $\frac{3}{4}$ **b** $\frac{1}{6}$ **c** $\frac{1}{4}$ **d** $\frac{4}{5}$ **e** $\frac{2}{3}$ **f** $\frac{1}{4}$

2 a $\frac{1}{2}$ **b** $\frac{2}{3}$ **c** $\frac{2}{9}$ **d** $\frac{7}{18}$ **e** $\frac{3}{4}$

3 GR, GPu, GPi, YR, YPu, YPi

Exercise 18A

1 a unlikely **b** certain **c** likely **d** very unlikely
e impossible **f** very likely **g** evens

2

Exercise 18B

1 a $\frac{1}{6}$ **b** $\frac{1}{6}$ **c** $\frac{1}{2}$ **d** $\frac{1}{13}$ **e** $\frac{1}{4}$ **f** $\frac{1}{2}$ **g** $\frac{1}{3}$
h $\frac{1}{26}$ **i** $\frac{1}{13}$ **j** 0
2 a $\frac{1}{2}$ **b** $\frac{1}{2}$ **c** $\frac{1}{2}$ **d** $\frac{1}{52}$ **e** $\frac{4}{13}$ **f** $\frac{1}{52}$
3 a 0 **b** 1
4 a $\frac{1}{10}$ **b** $\frac{1}{2}$ **c** $\frac{2}{5}$ **d** $\frac{1}{5}$ **e** $\frac{2}{5}$
5 a $\frac{1}{3}$ **b** $\frac{1}{3}$ **c** $\frac{2}{3}$
6 a $\frac{6}{11}$ **b** $\frac{5}{11}$ **c** $\frac{6}{11}$
7 a $\frac{1}{5}$ **b** $\frac{1}{2}$ **c** $\frac{1}{2}$ **d** $\frac{7}{10}$
8 a $\frac{7}{15}$ **b** $\frac{2}{15}$ **c** $\frac{8}{15}$ **d** 0 **e** $\frac{8}{15}$
9 $\frac{1}{50}$
10 a AB, AC, AD, AE, BC, BD, BE, CD, CE, DE
b 1 **c** $\frac{1}{10}$ **d** 6 **e** $\frac{3}{5}$ **f** $\frac{3}{10}$
11 a 2 **b** 7 **c i** $\frac{5}{9}$ **ii** $\frac{4}{9}$
12 a $\frac{1}{13}$ **b** $\frac{1}{13}$ **c** $\frac{1}{2}$ **d** $\frac{2}{13}$ **e** $\frac{7}{13}$ **f** $\frac{1}{26}$
13 a i $\frac{12}{25}$ **ii** $\frac{7}{25}$ **iii** $\frac{6}{25}$
b They add up to 1
c All possible outcomes used
14 35%
15 0.5

Exercise 18C

1 a $\frac{19}{20}$ **b** 55% **c** 0.2
2 a i $\frac{3}{13}$ **ii** $\frac{10}{13}$ **b i** $\frac{1}{4}$ **ii** $\frac{3}{4}$ **c i** $\frac{2}{13}$ **ii** $\frac{11}{13}$
3 a i $\frac{1}{4}$ **ii** $\frac{3}{4}$ **b i** $\frac{3}{11}$ **ii** $\frac{8}{11}$

Exercise 18D

1 a $\frac{1}{6}$ **b** $\frac{1}{6}$ **c** $\frac{1}{3}$
2 a $\frac{1}{4}$ **b** $\frac{1}{4}$ **c** $\frac{1}{2}$
3 a $\frac{2}{11}$ **b** $\frac{4}{11}$ **c** $\frac{6}{11}$
4 a $\frac{1}{3}$ **b** $\frac{2}{5}$ **c** $\frac{11}{15}$ **d** $\frac{11}{15}$ **e** $\frac{1}{3}$
5 a 0.6 **b** 120
6 a 0.8 **b** 0.2
7 a $\frac{17}{20}$ **b** $\frac{2}{5}$ **c** $\frac{3}{4}$
8 Because these are three separate events. Also probability cannot exceed 1.

Exercise 18E

1 a B **b** B **c** C **d** A **e** B **f** A
g B **h** B
2 a 0.2, 0.08, 0.1, 0.105, 0.148, 0.163, 0.1645
b 6 **c** 1 **d** $\frac{1}{6}$ **e** 1000
3 a 0.095, 0.135, 0.16, 0.265, 0.345
b 40 **c** No
4 a 0.2, 0.25, 0.38, 0.42, 0.385, 0.3974 **b** 8
5 a 6
6 a Caryl, threw greatest number of times
b 0.39, 0.31, 0.17, 0.14
c Yes; all answers should be close to 0.25
7 a not likely **b** impossible **c** not likely
d certain **e** impossible **f** 50–50 chance
g 50–50 chance **h** certain **i** quite likely

Exercise 18F

1 a 7 **b** 2 and 12
c $\frac{1}{36}, \frac{1}{18}, \frac{1}{12}, \frac{1}{9}, \frac{5}{36}, \frac{1}{6}, \frac{5}{36}, \frac{1}{9}, \frac{1}{12}, \frac{1}{18}, \frac{1}{36}$
d i $\frac{1}{12}$ **ii** $\frac{1}{3}$ **iii** $\frac{1}{2}$ **iv** $\frac{7}{36}$ **v** $\frac{5}{12}$ **vi** $\frac{5}{18}$
2 a $\frac{1}{12}$ **b** $\frac{11}{36}$ **c** $\frac{1}{6}$ **d** $\frac{5}{9}$
3 a $\frac{1}{36}$ **b** $\frac{11}{36}$ **c** $\frac{5}{18}$
4 a $\frac{5}{18}$ **b** $\frac{1}{6}$ **c** $\frac{1}{9}$ **d** 0 **e** $\frac{1}{2}$
5 a $\frac{1}{4}$ **b** $\frac{1}{2}$ **c** $\frac{3}{4}$ **d** $\frac{1}{4}$
6 a 6 **b i** $\frac{4}{25}$ **ii** $\frac{13}{25}$ **iii** $\frac{1}{5}$ **iv** $\frac{3}{5}$

Exercise 18G

1 a $\frac{1}{6}$ **b** 25
2 a $\frac{1}{2}$ **b** 1000
3 a i $\frac{1}{2}$ **ii** $\frac{1}{13}$ **iii** $\frac{1}{4}$ **iv** $\frac{1}{52}$
b i 260 **ii** 40 **iii** 130 **iv** 10
4 a $\frac{1}{37}$ **b** 5
5 a 150 **b** 100 **c** 250 **d** 0
6 a 167 **b** 833
7 1050
8 a 10, 10, 10, 10, 10, 10 **b** 3,5
c Find the average of the scores ($\frac{21}{6}$)

Exercise 18H

1 a Everton **b** Man Utd, Everton, Liverpool **c** Leeds
2 a

Shape		Shaded	Unshaded
	Circle	3	3
	Triangle	2	2

b $\frac{1}{2}$
3 a 40 **b** 16 **c** 40% **d** 10% **e** 16
4 a

		No. on disc		
		4	5	6
Letter on card	A	3	4	5
	B	4	5	6
	C	5	6	7

b $\frac{4}{9}$ **c** $\frac{1}{3}$

5 a 23   **b** 20%   **c** $\frac{4}{25}$ **d** 480
6 a 10   **b** 7   **c** 14%   **d** 15%
7 a

		Spinner A		
		1	2	3	4
Spinner B	5	6	7	8	9
	6	7	8	9	10
	7	8	9	10	11
	8	9	10	11	12

   b 4   **c i** $\frac{1}{4}$ **ii** $\frac{3}{16}$ **iii** $\frac{1}{4}$
8 a 16   **b** 16   **c** 73   **d** $\frac{51}{73}$

9 a

		Number on dice					
		1	2	3	4	5	6
Coin	H	1	2	3	4	5	6
	T	2	4	6	8	10	12

   b 2 (1 and 4)   **c** $\frac{1}{4}$
10 a larger mean diameter
    b smaller range, so more consistent

ANSWERS TO CHAPTER 19

Quick check

a $x = -2$ **b** $x = 1$ **c** $y = 2$ **d** $y = -1$

e $y = x$ **f** $y = -x$

Exercise 19A

1 a yes   **b** yes   **c** no   **d** yes   **e** no   **f** yes
2 a triangle ii   **b** triangle iii   **c** sector i
3 a 1, 3, 4   **b** 2, 4   **c** 1, 4   **d** 1, 2, 3, 4
4

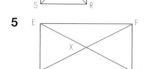

PQR to QRS to RSP to SPQ;
SXP to PXQ to QXR to RXS

5

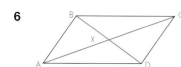

EGF to FHE to GEH to HFG;
EFX to HGX; EXH to FXG

6

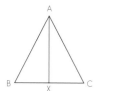

ABC to CDA;
BDC to DBA;
BXA to DXC;
BXC to DXA

7

AXB to AXC

Exercise 19B

3 All quadrilaterals tessellate
4 The interior angle for each shape divides exactly into 360°

Exercise 19C

3 a i $\begin{pmatrix} 1 \\ 3 \end{pmatrix}$ **ii** $\begin{pmatrix} 4 \\ 2 \end{pmatrix}$ **iii** $\begin{pmatrix} 2 \\ -1 \end{pmatrix}$ **iv** $\begin{pmatrix} 5 \\ 1 \end{pmatrix}$ **v** $\begin{pmatrix} -1 \\ 6 \end{pmatrix}$ **vi** $\begin{pmatrix} 4 \\ 6 \end{pmatrix}$

 b i $\begin{pmatrix} -1 \\ -3 \end{pmatrix}$ **ii** $\begin{pmatrix} 3 \\ -1 \end{pmatrix}$ **iii** $\begin{pmatrix} 1 \\ -4 \end{pmatrix}$ **iv** $\begin{pmatrix} 4 \\ -2 \end{pmatrix}$

   v $\begin{pmatrix} -2 \\ 3 \end{pmatrix}$ **vi** $\begin{pmatrix} 3 \\ 3 \end{pmatrix}$

 c i $\begin{pmatrix} -4 \\ -2 \end{pmatrix}$ **ii** $\begin{pmatrix} -3 \\ 1 \end{pmatrix}$ **iii** $\begin{pmatrix} -2 \\ -3 \end{pmatrix}$ **iv** $\begin{pmatrix} 1 \\ -1 \end{pmatrix}$

   v $\begin{pmatrix} -5 \\ 4 \end{pmatrix}$ **vi** $\begin{pmatrix} 0 \\ 4 \end{pmatrix}$

 d i $\begin{pmatrix} 3 \\ 2 \end{pmatrix}$ **ii** $\begin{pmatrix} -4 \\ 2 \end{pmatrix}$ **iii** $\begin{pmatrix} 5 \\ -4 \end{pmatrix}$ **iv** $\begin{pmatrix} -2 \\ -7 \end{pmatrix}$

   v $\begin{pmatrix} 5 \\ 0 \end{pmatrix}$ **vi** $\begin{pmatrix} 1 \\ -5 \end{pmatrix}$

4

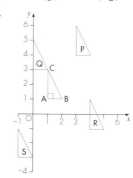

5 a $\begin{pmatrix} -3 \\ -1 \end{pmatrix}$ **b** $\begin{pmatrix} 4 \\ -4 \end{pmatrix}$ **c** $\begin{pmatrix} -5 \\ -2 \end{pmatrix}$ **d** $\begin{pmatrix} 4 \\ 7 \end{pmatrix}$ **e** $\begin{pmatrix} -1 \\ 5 \end{pmatrix}$

  f $\begin{pmatrix} 1 \\ 6 \end{pmatrix}$ **g** $\begin{pmatrix} -4 \\ 4 \end{pmatrix}$ **h** $\begin{pmatrix} -4 \\ -7 \end{pmatrix}$

6 $10 \times 10 = 100$ (including $\begin{pmatrix} 0 \\ 0 \end{pmatrix}$)

Exercise 19D

1 a

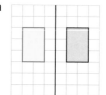

      b

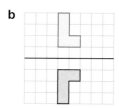

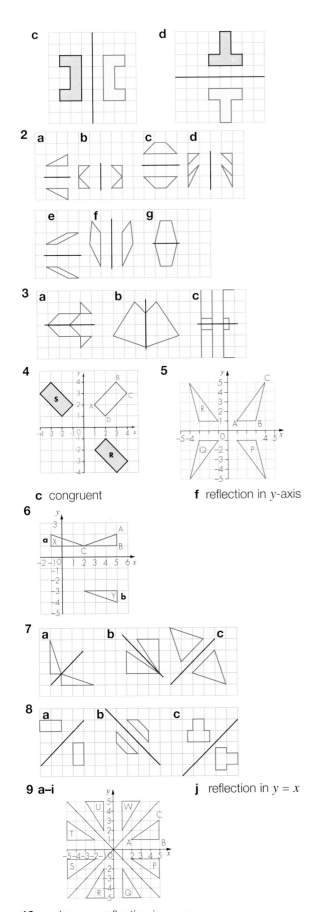

c

d

2 a b c d

e f g

3 a b c

4 **5**

c congruent

f reflection in *y*-axis

6

7 a b c

8 a b c

9 a–i

j reflection in *y* = *x*

10 c always a reflection in *y* = *x*

1 a b c d

2 a b

c d

3

d 90° turn clockwise about O

4 a A(1, 2), B(3, 1), C(4, 3)   b (2, −1), (1, −3), (3, −4)

c (−1, −2), (−3, −1), (−4, −3)   d (−2, 1), (−1, 3), (−3, 4)

e corresponding vertices have same pairs of numbers switching round and changing signs

5 a

b rotation 90° anticlockwise
rotation 270° clockwise

6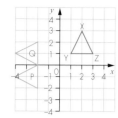

c a rotation of 90° clockwise about the point (0, −1)

7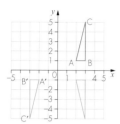

d rotation 180° about O
e yes
f yes

Exercise 19F

1

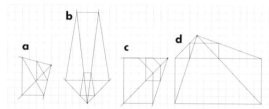

2 a 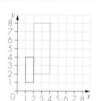   **b**

c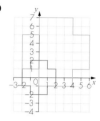

3 a 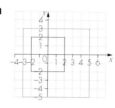   **b**

4 d they are all congruent

5

6 a 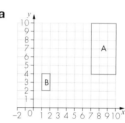   **b** 3:1
c 3:1
d 9:1

7 iii Ratios of perimeters = $\frac{1}{2}, \frac{1}{3}, \frac{1}{4}$
Ratios of areas = $\frac{1}{4}, \frac{1}{9}, \frac{1}{16}$

iv Ratios of perimeter go up according to scale factors, ratios of area go up according to square of scale factors.

ANSWERS TO CHAPTER 20

Quick check

1 a 6 cm   **b** 7.5 cm   **c** 11 cm

2 a 30°   **b** 135°

Exercise 20A

1 a BC = 2.9 cm, ∠B = 53°, ∠C = 92°   **b** EF = 7.4 cm, ED = 6.8 cm   **c** ∠G = 105°, ∠H = 29°, ∠I = 46°
d ∠J = 48°, ∠L = 32°, JK = 4.3 cm   **e** ∠N = 55°, ON = OM = 7 cm   **f** ∠P = 51°, ∠R = 39°, QP = 5.7 cm
2 b ∠ABC = 44°, ∠BCA = 79°, ∠CAB = 57°
3 a 5.9 cm   **b** 18.8 cm²   **4** BC = 2.6 cm, 7.8 cm
5 a 4.5   **b** 11.25 cm²   **6 a** 4.3 cm   **b** 34.5 cm²

Exercise 20B

[No answers needed for this exercise]

Exercise 20C

1 Circle with radius   **a** 2 cm   **b** 4 cm   **c** 5 cm

2 a

b

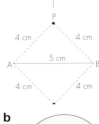

c

3 a Circle with radius 4 m **b**

4 a

b

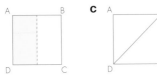

c

d

e

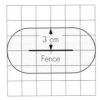

f

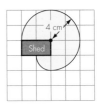

5 Diagram **c**

6 ----------

Exercise 20D

1

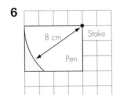

2

3

4

5

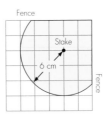

6

7

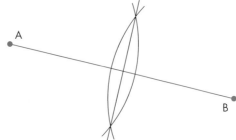

8

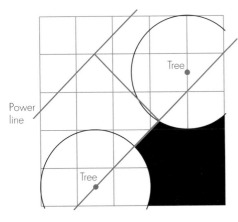

9

10 a

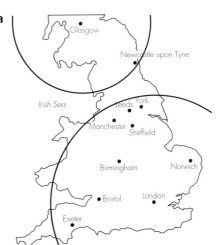

b No   **c** Yes

11 a No

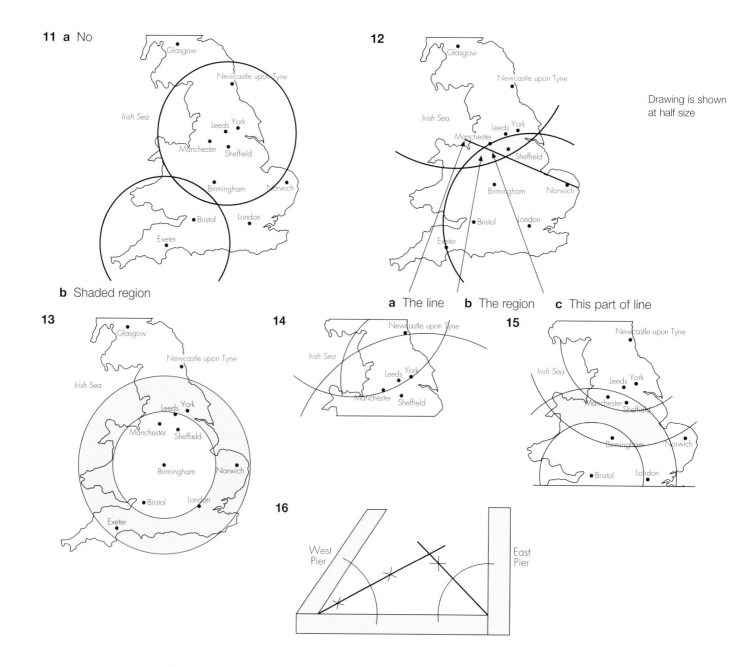

b Shaded region

12

Drawing is shown at half size

a The line   **b** The region   **c** This part of line

13

14

15

16

Really Useful Maths!: The street

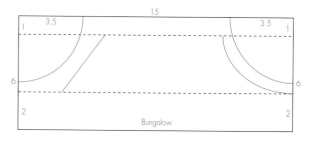

Number of end-terraced bungalows	40
Number of mid-terraced bungalows	60
Number of chimney pots needed	200
Number of doors needed	200
Number of windows needed	440
Number of gates needed	140
Length of fencing needed in metres	4820
Number of 1s for the doors	21
Number of 8s for the doors	20
Number of 0s for the doors	11

Drawing is shown at a reduced size.

Quick check

1 100   **2** 1000   **3** 1000   **4** 1000

Exercise 21A

1 metres   **2** kilometres   **3** millimetres
4 kilograms or grams   **5** litres   **6** kilograms
7 tonnes   **8** millilitres   **9** centilitres   **10** metres
11 kilograms   **12** litres   **13** grams   **14** centilitres
15 millimetres

Exercise 21B

1 1.25 m   **2** 8.2 cm   **3** 0.55 m   **4** 2.1 km
5 2.08 cm   **6** 1.24 m   **7** 4.2 kg   **8** 5.75 t
9 8.5 cl   **10** 2.58 l   **11** 3.4 l   **12** 0.6 t
13 0.755 kg   **14** 0.8 l   **15** 2 l   **16** 63 cl
17 8.4 m^3 **18** 35 cm^3 **19** 1.035 m^3
20 0.53 m^3 **21** 34 000 m   **22** 3400 mm
23 135 mm   **24** 67 cm   **25** 7030 m   **26** 7.2 mm
27 25 cm   **28** 640 m   **29** 2400 ml   **30** 590 cl
31 84 ml   **32** 5200 l   **33** 580 g   **34** 3750 kg
35 0.000 94 l   **36** 2160 cl   **37** 15 200 g
38 14 000 l   **39** 0.19 ml

Exercise 21C

1 24 in   **2** 12 ft   **3** 3520 yd   **4** 80 oz
5 56 lb   **6** 6720 lb   **7** 40 pt   **8** 48 in
9 36 in   **10** 30 ft   **11** 64 oz   **12** 5 ft
13 70 lb   **14** 12 yd   **15** 224 oz   **16** 5 miles
17 120 pt   **18** 5280 ft   **19** 8 ft   **20** 7 st
21 7 gal   **22** 2 lb   **23** 5 yd   **24** 5 tons
25 63 360 in   **26** 8 lb   **27** 9 gal   **28** 10 st
29 3 miles   **30** 35 840 oz

Exercise 21D

1 20 cm   **2** 13.2 lb   **3** 48 km   **4** 67.5 l
5 2850 ml   **6** 10 gal   **7** 12 in   **8** 50 miles
9 5 kg   **10** 3 pints   **11** 160 km   **12** 123.2 lb
13 180 l   **14** 90.9 kg   **15** 1100 yd   **16** 30 cm
17 6.3 kg   **18** 90 cm   **19** ton   **20** metre
21 a i 1000 g   **ii** 1 kg   **b i** 4500 g   **ii** 4.5 kg
22 a 135 miles   **b** 50 mph   **c** 2 h 42 min

Quick check

1 a 27   **b** 62

3 A(1, 4), B(2, 1), C(5, 2)

Exercise 22A

1 a    **b**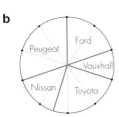

c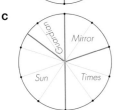

2 a 36°, 90°, 126°, 81°, 27°
b 90°, 108°, 60°, 78°, 24°
c 168°, 52°, 100°, 40°
3 60°, 165°, 45°, 15°, 75°
4 a 36   **b** 50°, 50°, 80°, 60°, 60°, 40°, 20°
d Bar chart, because easier to make comparisons

5 a 124°, 132°, 76°, 28°
b Split of total data seen at a glance
6 a 55°   **b** 22   **c** $33\frac{1}{3}$%

Exercise 22B

1 a positive correlation   **b** negative correlation
c no correlation   **d** positive correlation
2 a a person's reaction time increases as more alcohol is consumed
b as people get older, they consume less alcohol
c no relationship between temperature and speed of cars on M1
d as people get older, they have more money in the bank
3 c about 20 cm/s   **d** about 35 cm
4 b yes, usually (good correlation)
5 c Greta   **d** about 70   **e** about 72
6 b No, becauses there is no correlation

Exercise 22D

1 a leading question, not enough responses
b simple 'yes' and 'no' response, with a follow-up question, responses cover all options and have a reasonable number of choices
2 a overlapping responses
b ☐ £0–£2   ☐ over £2 up to £5
☐ over £5 up to £10   ☐ over £10

Exercise 22E

1 Price: 78p, 80.3p, 84.2p, 85p, 87.4p, 93.6p
2 **a** 9.7 million   **b** 4.5 years   **c** 12 million
   d 10 million
3 **a** £1 = $1.88
   b Greatest drop was from June to July
   c There is no trend in the data so you cannot tell if
       it will go up or down.
4 £74.73
5 **a** holiday month
   b i 138–144 thousand   **ii** 200–210 thousand

Really Useful Maths!: Riding stables

Horse	Weight (kg)	Feed (kg)
Summer	875	6.1
Sally	350	3.5
Skip	550	5.4
Simon	500	4.0
Barney	350	2.8
Teddy	650	6.2

ANSWERS TO CHAPTER 23

Quick check

1 **a** $x + 3$ **b** $2x$ **c** $2x + 3$
2 **a** 5   **b** 7   **c** 9

Exercise 23A

1 $11111 \times 11111 = 123454321$,
   $111111 \times 111111 = 12345654321$
2 $99999 \times 99999 = 9999800001$,
   $999999 \times 999999 = 999998000001$
3 $7 \times 8 = 7^2 + 7$, $8 \times 9 = 8^2 + 8$
4 $50 \times 51 = 2550$, $60 \times 61 = 3660$
5 $1 + 2 + 3 + 4 + 5 + 4 + 3 + 2 + 1 = 25 = 5^2$,
   $1 + 2 + 3 + 4 + 5 + 6 + 5 + 4 + 3 + 2 + 1 = 36 = 6^2$
6 $21 + 23 + 25 + 27 + 29 = 125 = 5^3$,
   $31 + 33 + 35 + 37 + 39 + 41 = 216 = 6^3$
7 $1 + 6 + 15 + 20 + 15 + 6 + 1 = 64$,
   $1 + 7 + 21 + 35 + 35 + 21 + 7 + 1 = 128$
8 $12\,345\,679 \times 45 = 555\,555\,555$,
   $12\,345\,679 \times 54 = 666\,666\,666$
9 $1^3 + 2^3 + 3^3 + 4^3 = (1 + 2 + 3 + 4)^2 = 100$,
   $1^3 + 2^3 + 3^3 + 4^3 + 5^3 = (1 + 2 + 3 + 4 + 5)^2 = 225$
10 $36^2 + 37^2 + 38^2 + 39^2 + 40^2 = 41^2 + 42^2 + 43^2 + 44^2$, 55^2
   $+ 56^2 + 57^2 + 58^2 + 59^2 + 60^2 = 61^2 + 62^2 + 63^2 + 64^2 +$
   65^2
11 12345678987654321   12 999999998000000001
13 $12^2 + 12$ 14 8190   15 $81 = 9^2$
16 $512 = 8^3$ 17 512   18 999 999 999
19 $(1 + 2 + 3 + 4 + 5 + 6 + 7 + 8 + 9)^2 = 2025$

Exercise 23B

1 **a** 9, 11, 13: add 2   **b** 10, 12, 14: add 2
   c 80, 160, 320: double
   d 81, 243, 729: multiply by 3
   e 28, 34, 40: add 6   **f** 23, 28, 33: add 5

g 20 000, 200 000, 2 000 000: multiply by 10
h 19, 22, 25: add 3   **i** 46, 55, 64: add 9
j 405, 1215, 3645: multiply by 3
k 18, 22, 26: add 4
l 625, 3125, 15 625: multiply by 5
2 **a** 16, 22   **b** 26, 37   **c** 31, 43   **d** 46, 64
  e 121, 169   **f** 782, 3907   **g** 22 223, 222 223
  h 11, 13   **i** 33, 65   **j** 78, 108
3 **a** 48, 96, 192   **b** 33, 39, 45   **c** 4, 2, 1
  d 38, 35, 32   **e** 37, 50, 65   **f** 26, 33, 41
  g 14, 16, 17   **h** 19, 22, 25   **i** 28, 36, 45
  j 5, 6, 7   **k** 0.16, 0.032, 0.0064
  l 0.0625, 0.031 25, 0.015 625
4 **a** 21, 34: add previous 2 terms
  b 49, 64: next square number
  c 47, 76: add previous 2 terms
  d 216, 343: cube numbers
5 15, 21, 28, 36   6   61, 91, 127

Exercise 23C

1 **a** 3, 5, 7, 9, 11   **b** 1, 4, 7, 10, 13
  c 7, 12, 17, 22, 27   **d** 1, 4, 9, 16, 25
  e 4, 7, 12, 19, 28
2 **a** 4, 5, 6, 7, 8   **b** 2, 5, 8, 11, 14
  c 3, 8, 13, 18, 23   **d** 0, 3, 8, 15, 24
  e 9, 13, 17, 21, 25
3 $\frac{2}{4}, \frac{3}{5}, \frac{4}{6}, \frac{5}{7}, \frac{6}{8}$
4 **a** 6, 10, 15, 21, 28   **b** Triangular numbers
5 **a** 2, 6, 24, 720   **b** 6

Exercise 23D

1 **a** 13, 15, $2n + 1$ **b** 25, 29, $4n + 1$
  c 33, 38, $5n + 3$ **d** 32, 38, $6n - 4$
  e 20, 23, $3n + 2$ **f** 37, 44, $7n - 5$
  g 21, 25, $4n - 3$ **h** 23, 27, $4n - 1$
  i 17, 20, $3n - 1$ **j** 42, 52, $10n - 8$

k 24, 28, $4n + 4$ **l** 29, 34, $5n - 1$

2 a $3n + 1$, 151   **b** $2n + 5$, 105   **c** $5n - 2$, 248
 d $4n - 3$, 197   **e** $8n - 6$, 394   **f** $n + 4$, 54
 g $5n + 1$, 251   **h** $8n - 5$, 395   **i** $3n - 2$, 148
 j $3n + 18$, 168   **k** $7n + 5$, 355   **l** $8n - 7$, 393

3 a i $4n + 1$ **ii** 401
 b i $2n + 1$ **ii** 201   **c i** $3n + 1$ **ii** 301
 d i $2n + 6$ **ii** 206   **e i** $4n + 5$ **ii** 405
 f i $5n + 1$ **ii** 501   **g i** $3n - 3$ **ii** 297
 h i $6n - 4$ **ii** 596   **i i** $8n - 1$ **ii** 799
 j i $2n + 23$ **ii** 223

4 a 64, 128, 256, 512, 1024
 b i $2^n - 1$ **ii** $2^n + 1$ **iii** $6 \times 2^{n-1}$

5 a They are the same.   **b** 6
 c i $10^n - 1$ **ii** 2×10^n

6 a Odd + even = odd, even + odd = odd,
   even + even = even
 b Odd × even = even, even × odd = even,
   even × even = even

7 a 36, 49, 64, 81, 100
 b i $n^2 + 1$ **ii** $2n^2$ **iii** $n^2 - 1$

8 $1 + 3 + 5 + 7 = 16 = 4^2$, $1 + 3 + 5 + 7 + 9 = 25 = 5^2$

9 a 28, 36, 45, 55, 66   **b i** 210   **ii** 5050
 c They produce square numbers.

10 a even   **b** odd   **c** odd   **d** odd   **e** odd
 f odd   **g** even   **h** odd   **i** odd

11 a either   **b** either   **c** either   **d** odd
 e either   **f** even

Exercise 23E

1 b $4n - 3$ **c** 97   **d** 50th diagram
2 b $2n + 1$ **c** 121   **d** 49th set
3 a 18   **b** $4n + 2$ **c** 12
4 b $2n + 1$ **c** 101   **d** 149th diagram
5 a i 20 cm   **ii** $(3n + 2)$ cm   **iii** 152 cm
 b 332
6 a i 20   **ii** 162   **b** 79.8 km
7 a 2^n
 b i The quantity doubles   **ii** 1600 ml

ANSWERS TO CHAPTER 24

Quick check

1 cube   **2** cuboid   **3** cylinder

4 triangular prism

Exercise 24A

1 12 cm³   **2** 20 cm³
3 23 cm³   **4** 32 cm³

Exercise 24B

1 a i 198 cm³   **ii** 234 cm²
 b i 90 cm³   **ii** 146 cm²
 c i 1440 cm³   **ii** 792 cm²
 d i 525 cm³   **ii** 470 cm²
2 24 litres
3 a 160 cm³   **b** 480 cm³   **c** 150 cm³
4 a i 64 cm³   **ii** 96 cm²
 b i 343 cm³   **ii** 294 cm²
 c i 1000 mm³   **ii** 600 mm²
 d i 125 m³   **ii** 150 m²
 e i 1728 m³   **ii** 864 m²
5 86
6 a 180 cm³   **b** 5 cm   **c** 6 cm   **d** 10 cm
 e 81 cm³
7 1.6 m
8 48 m²
9 a 3 cm   **b** 5 m   **c** 2 mm   **d** 1.2 m
10 a 148 cm³   **b** 468 cm³

Exercise 24C

1 0.75 g/cm³   **2** 120 cm³
3 156.8 g   **4** 3200 cm³
5 2.72 g/cm³   **6** 36 800 kg (36.8 t)
7 1.79 g/cm³   **8** 1.6 g/cm³

Exercise 24D

1 a i

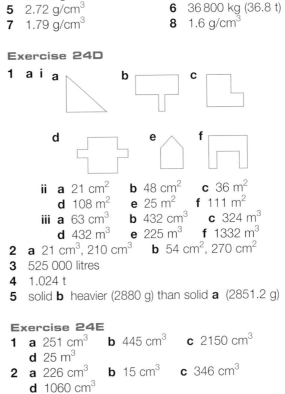

 ii a 21 cm²   **b** 48 cm²   **c** 36 m²
   d 108 m²   **e** 25 m²   **f** 111 m²
 iii a 63 cm³   **b** 432 cm³   **c** 324 m³
   d 432 m³   **e** 225 m³   **f** 1332 m³
2 a 21 cm³, 210 cm³   **b** 54 cm², 270 cm²
3 525 000 litres
4 1.024 t
5 solid **b** heavier (2880 g) than solid **a** (2851.2 g)

Exercise 24E

1 a 251 cm³   **b** 445 cm³   **c** 2150 cm³
 d 25 m³
2 a 226 cm³   **b** 15 cm³   **c** 346 cm³
 d 1060 cm³
3 £80   **4** 1229 kg   **5** 332 l
6 1.71 g/cm³   **7** 7.78 g/cm³
8 a 360π cm³   **b** 300π cm³

Quick check

1 a 16   **b** 4   **2 a** 20   **b** 8

3 a 14   **b** 2   **4 a** 24   **b** 0

Exercise 25A

1

x	−3	−2	−1	0	1	2	3
y	27	12	3	0	3	12	27

2

x	−5	−4	−3	−2	−1	0	1	2	3	4	5
y	27	18	11	6	3	2	3	6	11	18	27

3 a

x	−5	−4	−3	−2	−1	0	1	2	3	4	5
x^2	25	16	9	4	1	0	1	4	9	16	25
$-3x$	15	12	9	6	3	0	−3	−6	−9	−12	−15
y	40	28	18	10	4	0	−2	−2	0	4	10

b 1.8   **c** −1.2, 4.2

4 a

x	−5	−4	−3	−2	−1	0	1	2	3	4	5
x^2	25	16	9	4	1	0	1	4	9	16	25
$-2x$	10	8	6	4	2	0	−2	−4	−6	−8	−10
	−8	−8	−8	−8	−8	−8	−8	−8	−8	−8	−8
y	27	16	7	0	−5	−8	−9	−8	−5	0	7

b −8.8   **c** −1.5, 3.5

5 a

x	−2	−1	0	1	2	3	4	5
y	18	10	4	0	−2	−2	0	4

b 6.8   **c** 0.2, 4.8

6 a

x	−3	−2	−1	0	1	2	3
x^2	9	4	1	0	1	4	9
$+2x$	−6	−4	−2	0	2	4	6
	−1	−1	−1	−1	−1	−1	−1
y	2	−1	−2	−1	2	7	14

b 0.3   **c** −2.7, 0.7

Exercise 25B

1 a 12 5 0 −3 −4 −3 0 5 12
   b $x = \pm 2$

2 a 7 0 −5 −8 −9 −8 −5 0 7
   b $x = \pm 3$

3 a 5 0 −3 −4 −3 0 5 12
   b $x = -4$ or 0

4 a 16 7 0 −5 −8 −9 −8 −5 0
   b $x = 0$ or 6

5 a 10 4 0 −2 −2 0 4 10 18
   b $x = -3$ or 0

6 a 10 3 −2 −5 −6 −5 −2 3 10
   b $x = 0.5$ or 5.5

Quick check

1 5.3   **2** 246.5   **3** 0.6   **4** 2.8

5 16.1   **6** 0.7

Exercise 26A

1 10.3 cm   **2** 5.9 cm   **3** 8.5 cm
4 20.6 cm   **5** 18.6 cm   **6** 17.5 cm
7 32.2 cm   **8** 2.4 m   **9** 500 m
10 5 cm   **11** 13 cm   **12** 10 cm

Exercise 26B

1 a 15 cm   **b** 14.7 cm   **c** 6.3 cm   **d** 18.3 cm
   e 5.4 cm   **f** 218 m   **g** 0.4 cm   **h** 8 m
2 a 20.8 m   **b** 15.5 cm   **c** 15.5 m   **d** 12.4 cm
   e 22.9 m   **f** 19.8 m   **g** 7.1 m   **h** 0.64 m
3 a 5 m   **b** 6 m   **c** 3 m   **d** 50 cm

Exercise 26C

1 6.6 m   **2** 2.1 m   **3** 10.8 m   **4** 11.3 m
5 9.2 m   **6** 19.2 km   **7** 147 km
8 a 127 m   **b** 99.6 m   **c** 27.4 m
9 2.4 km   **10** 12 ft
11 a 3.9 m   **b** 1.7 m   **12** 3.2 m
13 a $(7, 3\frac{1}{2})$
   b 13 cm
14 a (27, 28)
   b 50 cm
15 a 4.7 m   **b** 4.5 m   **16** 16.5 cm^2
17 12.07 m   **18** yes, $25^2 = 24^2 + 7^2$

Index

acute angles 328
addition
  decimals 174
  up to four digit numbers 14–16
  fractions 27–8, 36–7, 181–2
  in grids/columns/rows 2–3
  negative numbers in 56–61
  in order of operations 6
addition rule (probability) 405–7
algebra 143–66, 275–98
  equations *see* equations
  expressions *see* expressions
allied angles 345
alternate angles 345
angles 327–54
  bisectors 458
  measuring and drawing 328–30
  in parallel lines 344–7
  polygons (other than
    triangles/quadrilaterals) 337–44
  quadrilaterals 338, 347–9
  of rotation 440
  of sector in pie chart 484
  60°, construction 459
  triangles 333–7, 455–6
anticlockwise rotation 440
approximation 187–90, 377–9
  calculations 188–90
  see also estimation; rounding
arc 356
  drawn with compasses 459, 460
areas
  circle 363–6, 367
  compound shape 102–3
  dimensions of 111–12
  irregular shape 98–9
  parallelogram 107–8
  quadrilateral 107
  rectangle 100–1
  surface *see* surface area
  trapezium 108–9, 159
  triangles 103–7, 159
average(s) 225–56
  which to use 238–41
  see also mean; median; mode
average speed 202–5, 304
axis (axes)
  bar charts 127
  graphs *see* x-axis; y-axis

balancing ('doing same to both sides of')
    equations 277, 280–2
bar charts 127–30
base in area calculation
  parallelogram 107–8
  triangles 103–5, 159
bearings 349–51
best buy 207–8
best fit, line of 489
bias 413

bisectors, line/angle 458
BODMAS 6–9, 143
box method, long multiplication 168,
    169
brackets, in algebraic expressions 285–6
  expanding *see* expansion
brackets, order of operations with 6–9

C angles 345
calculators
  algebraic equations 160–1
  negative numbers 58
  powers 76, 80, 83
  standard form on 83
  statistical keys 234, 242
cancelling *see* simplifying
capacity *see* volume
carry mark (long multiplication) 169
census, national 496
centilitre 476, 528
centimetres 476, 479
  cubic 524
centre
  of circle 356
  of enlargement 443, 444, 445, 446
  of rotation 439
certainty of outcome 398
chance *see* probability
chord 356
chunking method (repeated subtraction)
    169, 170
circles 355–71
  area 363–6, 367
  circumference *see* circumference
  drawing 356–8
  see also pie charts
circumference 356, 359–63
  calculations 359–63, 367
class intervals (classes) 121, 127
  modal 228
clockwise rotation 440
coefficient of *n* 510, 511
co-interior angles 345
column(s)
  addition in 2–3
  long multiplication 168
column vector 432, 433
comment column with equations 289
common factors
  in algebraic expressions, taking out
    (=factorisation) 155–8
  highest 89
common units 196
compasses
  circle drawing 357
  perpendicular construction 459, 460
  60° angle construction 459
  triangle construction 454, 455, 456
compound shape 97
  area of 102–3

computers, survey data 492
congruent shapes 428–30
consecutive terms 508
  difference between 508, 510, 512
consistency between data sets 236
constructions 453–72
continuous data 248
conversion
  between fractions and decimals 43,
    179–80
  between units 300–3, 479–80
  graphs of 300–3
coordinates 309
  in image enlargement 445–6
correlation, graphs showing 487, 488
corresponding angle 345
cost/price
  per unit weight 207
  retail, index of 496
  unit *see* unit cost
cross-section of prism 531
cube (shape)
  pentomino/hexomino 390
  volume 112
cube (third power) 79
cubic units 524
cuboid 386, 526, 527–30
  volume 112, 527–30
curves, quadratic 539–48
cylinder, volume 112, 534–5

data
  continuous 248
  discrete 134, 248
  experimental 409
  extreme vs representative values
    238
  frequency distribution of *see* frequency
  grouped 121, 245–7
  historical 409
  ordered and unordered 134
  raw 134–6
  spread 236–7
  trends 130–4
data collection sheet 120, 491, 492
decagon 338, 341, 342
decimal numbers (decimals) 172–9
  addition/subtraction 174
  division 175–7
  fractions and, converting between 43,
    179–80
  multiplication 175–9
  percentages expressed as 258–62
  recurring 42, 43
  rounding 173–4, 187, 188, 190
  terminating 42, 43
decimal place 172–4
  in equations 288
decimal point 172
  hidden 174–5

denominators (in fractions) 25, 180
    in addition and subtraction 27
    in cancelling 31
density 530–1
diameter 356, 363, 364
    circumference calculation 359–63
difference between consecutive terms
        508, 510, 512
digits (in number)
    addition/subtraction up to 4 digits
        14–16
    multiplication/division by single-digits
        16–18, 175–7
    place value 9–11
dimensional analysis 110–13
direct proportion 205–6
direction and bearing 349–51
discrete data 134, 248
distance/time/speed relationships 202–5,
        304–8
division (of number/amount)
    decimals 175–7
    fractions 184–5
    long 169–70
    negative numbers 185–6
    in order of operations 6
    powered numbers 81–3
    by ratios of amounts 198–200
    by single-digit numbers 16–18
division(s) (on scale) 374
'doing same to both sides' 277, 280–1
drawing
    angles 328–30
    circles 356–8
    graphs see plotting
    line with gradient 318–20
    pie charts 484–7
    to scale 380–3
    scatter diagrams 487–91
    see also constructions
dual bar chart 128

edges of 3-D shapes 526
elevation (3-D shape) 387
enlargements 443–8
equally likely outcome 400, 409
equations (algebraic) 159–61, 275–98
    quadratic 539–48
    setting up 286–7
equations (of line on graphs) 309
equilateral triangles 335
    isometric grid 386–9
equivalent fractions 28–33
estimation 377–9
    irregularly shaped area 98–9
    of length/weight/volume 474
    see also approximation
even-numbered sequences 513
event 400
    outcomes see outcomes

expansion of brackets (multiplying out)
        152–4
    quadratic expression 156–8
    reversal of process 155–8
expected outcome 416–17
experiment 120
experimental probability 407–13
expressions, algebraic 144, 159, 290
    brackets in see brackets
    quadratic 156–8
    simplifying 148–51, 153–4
    substitution in 159–61
exterior angles of polygons 342
    triangles 337

F angles 345
faces of 3-D shapes 526
    area see surface area
factors 71–2, 76, 77
    common see common factors
    conversion 479–80
    prime 85–90
    scale 380, 443, 444, 445, 446
flow diagrams/graphs 308–14
    inverse 277, 278–80
foot 478, 479
formulae
    algebraic 145, 159, 290–1
    in dimensional analysis 112
fractions 25–48, 179–85
    addition 27–8, 36–7, 181–2
    cancelling 31–3, 182, 258
    decimals and, converting between 43,
        179–80
    division 184–5
    equivalent 28–33
    multiplication 40–1, 182–4
    percentage expressed as 258–62
    probability 400
    proper 33, 36
    of quantity see quantity
    ratios as 196–8
    reciprocals of 43
    of shapes 26
    subtraction 27–8, 37, 181–2
    top-heavy (improper) 33–5, 36
frequency
    averages see average
    diagrams/tables/charts etc. of 120–30,
        241–4, 248–50, 484, 485
    relative 409
function 309

gallon 478, 479
gradient 317–18
    drawing a line with a 318–20
gradient-intercept method 320–1
gram 476, 479
graphs 299–326
    line see line graphs

plotting see plotting
    quadratic 539–48
    see also scatter diagrams
'greater than' (>) sign 291
'greater than or equal to' (≥) sign 291
grids 70
    in addition 2–3
    isometric 386–9
    in long multiplication 170
grouped data 121, 245–7
grouped (grouped frequency) table 121,
        245
guess column with equations 289

height in area calculation
    parallelogram 107
    trapezium 108
    triangles 103–5, 159
height in volume/surface area calculation
    cuboid 527, 528
    cylinder 534
heptagon 338, 341
hexagon 338, 341, 342
hexomino cube 390
highest common factor 89
historical data 409
horizontal axis see x-axis
horizontal lines, equations 309
hypotenuse 550, 551

image (in transformation) 432
    enlarged 443, 444, 445
    reflected see reflections
    rotated 439, 440
imperial system 474, 478–9
    conversion between metric and
        479–80
impossibility of event 398
improper (top-heavy) fractions 33–5, 36
inches 478, 479
indices see powers
inequality
    linear 291–4
    signs for 54
input values 310
integers and linear inequalities 292
interior angles of polygons 338, 341, 342
    triangles 335
inverse flow diagrams 277, 278–80
inverse operations 277–8
isometric grids 386–9
isosceles triangle 335

key
    in pictogram 124
    in stem-and-leaf diagrams 134, 135,
        136
kilogram 476, 479
kilometre 476, 479
kite 348

leading question 493, 494
least common multiple 89
least terms (lowest terms) 31–3, 36
length
    dimensions of 110–11
    imperial units of 474, 478
    metric-imperial conversion 479
    metric units of 474, 476
    rectangle, in area calculation 100–1
    right-angled triangle's sides, finding
        551–4
    in volume calculations 112, 524, 527,
        528, 531, 534
    see also height
'less than' (<) sign 291–4
'less than or equal to' (≤) sign 291
letter in equations see variable
like term in algebraic expressions,
        collecting 149–50
likelihood see probability
likely outcome 398, 399
    equally 400, 409
line
    angles on 330
    of best fit 489
    bisectors 458
    equation of 309
    parallel see parallel lines
    perpendiculars to 459–60
    slope see gradient
    of symmetry (mirror line) 215, 435
line graphs 130–4
    straight (linear graphs) 314–21
linear equations
    graph 309
    simple 276–83
linear graphs 314–21
linear inequalities 291–4
linear sequence, nth term 512
litre 476, 479, 528
locus (loci) 461–7
long division 169–70
long multiplication 168–9
    decimals 177–8
lowest common multiple 89
lowest terms 31–3, 36

magic squares 19
map scales 381
margin of error 495
mass per unit volume 530–1
mean (the average) 226, 233–6, 242
    advantages/disadvantages/use 239
measurement(s) 473–82
    angles 328–30
    on scale drawing 380
    systems of 473–82
median (middle value) 226, 229–33,
        242
    advantages/disadvantages/use 239

metres 476
    cubic 524
metric system 474, 476–7
    conversion between imperial and
        479–80
middle value see median
mile 478, 479
millilitre 476, 528
millimetres 476
    cubic 524
mirror line 215, 435
mirror writing 214
mixed numbers 33–5, 36, 182
modal class 228
modal value/score 226
mode 226, 242
    advantages/disadvantages/use 239
money, value for 207–8
multiples 68–70, 76, 77
    lowest common 89
    recognising 69–70
    see also times tables
multiplication
    with brackets see expansion
    decimals 175–9
    fractions 40–1, 182–4
    long see long multiplication
    negative numbers 185–6
    in order of operations 6
    powered numbers 81–3
    by single-digit numbers 16–18, 175–7
    times tables see multiples; times tables
multiplier, percentage 263, 265, 269
mutually exclusive outcomes 405–7

n see nth term
national census 496
negative coordinates 309
negative correlation 488
negative numbers 49–66
    in equations 281
    multiplying/dividing 185–6
nets of 3-D shapes 384–5
no correlation 488
no possibility (impossibility) of event
        398
nonagon 338, 341, 342
nth term 510–12, 516–18
    of special sequences 513
numbers 1–24, 49–94, 167–94
    basic 1–24
    factors of see factors
    mixed 33–5, 36, 182
    negative see negative numbers
    rational 42–5
    sequences, and their patterns 505–22
    see also decimal numbers; digits
numerators (in fractions) 25, 180
    in addition and subtraction 27
    in cancelling 31

object (in transformation) 432
    reflected 435
    rotated 439, 440
observation 120
obtuse angles 328
octagon 338, 341, 342
odd-numbered sequences 513
operations, order of (BODMAS) 6–9, 143
opposite angles 345
order
    of numbers, place value and 9–11
    of operations (BODMAS) 6–9, 143
    of rotational symmetry 218
ordered data 134
ounce 478
outcomes of event 398, 400, 400
    expected 416–17
    likely see likely outcome
    mutually exclusive 405–7
    probability of see probability
output values 310

parallel lines 344–7
    special quadrilaterals 348
parallelogram 348
    area 107–8
partition method, long multiplication 168
pentagon 338, 341, 342
pentomino cube 390
percentages 257–74
    increasing/decreasing by 265–8
perimeters 96–7, 110
    circle see circumference
perpendicular height of triangles 105
perpendicular line, construction
        459–60
pi (π) 367–8
    area calculations 363–4, 367
    circumference calculations 359–61,
        367
    cylinder volume calculation 534
Pick's theorem 107
pictograms 124–5
pie charts 484–7
pint 478, 479
place value 9–11
plan of 3-D shape 387
planes of symmetry 220–1
plotting graphs 310
    linear graphs 314–21
    quadratic graphs 540–4
points
    angles around 331, 349–51
    bearings and 349–51
    coordinates (on graph) see coordinates
    perpendicular from, on line 459
    perpendicular from, to line 460
    plotted on graph see plotting
    see also centre; locus
polls 495

polygons 248–50, 337–40
  angles 337–44
  frequency 248–50
  regular 341–4
positive correlation 488
pound (weight) 478, 479
powers (indices) 79–81
  multiplying/dividing 81–3, 91
  of ten *see* ten
price *see* cost
prime factor(s) 85–90
prime factor tree 86–8
prime numbers 73, 76, 77, 513
prisms 527, 531–3
probability (chance; likelihood) of
    outcome of event 397–426
  calculating 400–16
  experimental 407–13
  not happening 404–5
  scale of 398–9
  of two/combined events 413–16
probability space diagrams 414
proper fractions 33, 36
proportion, direct 205–6
  see also ratio
protractor
  angle measurement 328
  triangle construction 454, 455, 456
pyramids 526, 527
Pythagoras' theorem 549–60

quadratic equations and graphs 539–48
quadratic expansion and expressions 156–8
quadrilaterals
  angles 338, 347–9
  areas 107
  special 347–9
quantity
  expressed as fraction of another 41–2
  expressed as percentage of another
    268–71
  finding fraction of 38–40
  finding percentage of 263
questions in surveys 491, 493–4

radius 356, 360
  in area calculation 363–7
  in cylinder volume calculation 534
  setting compass to 357
random 400
range 236–7
ratio 196–201
  scales given as 380
  see also proportion
rational numbers 42–5
raw data 134–6
ray method 444–5
rearranging
  equations 277, 283
  formulae 290–1

reciprocals 43
rectangle
  area 100–1
  perimeter 96
recurring decimals 42, 43
reflections 435–9
  mirror line (line of symmetry) 215, 435
reflex angles 328
relative frequency 409
remainder (long division) 170
repeated subtraction (in long division)
    169, 170
responses in surveys 492
retail price index 496
rhombus 348
right-angled triangles 549–60
  area 103–5
  Pythagoras' theorem and 549–60
rotational symmetry 218–20
rotations 439–43
rounding 11–13, 187–8, 190
  decimals 173–4, 187, 188, 190
rows, addition in 2–3

sample collection 120
sample space diagrams 414
scale(s) 374–6
  on axis 311
  drawings made to 380–3
  of probability 398–9
  reading/interpreting 374–6
scale factors 380, 443, 444, 445, 446
scatter diagrams 487–91
sectors 356
  pie charts 484
segment 356
sequence(s)
  of numbers 505–22
  of operations (BODMAS) 6–9, 143
shapes
  angles *see* angles
  areas *see* areas
  compound *see* compound shape
  congruent 428–30
  fractions of 26
  perimeters 96–7, 110
  symmetry 213–24
  tessellations 430–1
  3-D, nets of 384–5
  transformations 432–46
  see also specific shapes
sides of triangle
  in construction 454–6
  of right-angled triangle, finding lengths
    551–4
simplifying
  algebraic expressions 148–51, 153–4
  fractions (=cancelling) 31–3, 182, 258
  ratios (=cancelling) 196
60° angle construction 459

slope *see* gradient
social statistics 495–7
solution to equation 276
  quadratic equation 544–6
speed/time/distance relationships 202–5,
    304–8
spread of data 236–7
square (shape), angles 341, 342
square (square number) 74–7, 79
  in Pythagoras' theorem 550, 551
  sequences 513
square root 78
standard form on calculator 83
statistics 119–42, 225–56, 397–426,
    483–504
  social 495–7
stem-and-leaf diagrams 134–6, 230
stone (weight) 478
straight line
  angles on 330
  graphs of 314–21
subject of formulae 290
substitution, algebra 159–61
subtraction
  decimals 174
  up to four digit numbers 14–16
  fractions 27–8, 37, 181–2
  negative numbers in 56–61
  in order of operations 6
  repeated (in long division) 169, 170
surface area (faces of 3-D shapes)
    524
  cuboid 527–30
  prism 531–3
surveys 491–5
symbols
  algebra 144
  pictograms 124
symmetry 213–24
  line of (mirror line) 215, 435

tally chart (data collection sheet) 120,
    491, 492
tangent 356
ten, powers of 513
  in metric system 474, 477
  multiplying/dividing by 81–3
term(s), in sequence 508
  consecutive *see* consecutive terms
  *n*th *see* *n*th term
terminating decimals 42, 43
tessellations 430–1
three-dimensional (3-D) shapes
  isometric grids of 386–9
  nets of 384–5
  volume 112, 523–38
three-figure bearing 350
time, distance and speed in relation
    202–5, 304–8
time series 496

times tables 4–5, 68
  see also multiples
ton (imperial) 478
tonne (metric) 476
top-heavy fractions 33–5, 36
transformations 432–46
translation 432–6
transposing formulae 290–1
trapezium 348
  areas 108–9, 159
travel graphs 304–8
trends in data 130–4
trial (probability event) 409
trial and improvement method 288–90
triangles 103–7, 333–7
  angles in 333–7, 455–6
  area 103–7, 159
  construction 454–7
  equilateral *see* equilateral triangles
  in polygons 338
  right-angled *see* right-angled triangles
  see also pyramids
triangular numbers 513
two-way tables 418–22

unit(s)
  common 196
  converting between 300–3, 479–80
  imperial system 474, 478–9, 479

metric 474, 476–7, 479
  on scales 374
  of volume *see* volume
unit cost 205, 207
  weight per 207
unit weight, cost per 207
unlikely outcome 398, 399
unordered data 134

variable in equations (=letter)
  on both sides 285–6
  on one side 276–84
variables, two, scatter diagrams 487
vector (for translation) 432, 433
vertical axis *see* y-axis
vertical lines, equations 309
vertically opposite angles 345
vertices
  in Pick's theorem 107
  3-D shapes 526
volume (capacity) 112, 475, 528–38
  dimensions of 112
  imperial units of 474, 478
  metric-imperial conversion 479
  metric units of 474, 476, 524–5
  of 3-D shapes 112, 523–38

weight
  imperial units of 474, 478

metric-imperial conversion 479
metric units of 474, 476
per unit cost 207
unit, cost per 207
width
  cuboid, in area/volume calculation
    527, 528
  rectangle, in area calculation 100–1
word (real-life) problems 37–8, 171–2

X angles 345
x-axis (horizontal axis) 309, 311
  gradients and 317
  in solution to quadratic equations
    544m 544
x-coordinates 309
  gradients and 317
x-values 310, 313
x^y (or y^x key) 76, 80

y-axis (vertical axis) 309, 311
  gradients and 317
y-coordinates 309
  gradients and 317
y-values 310
yard 478
y^x (or x^y key) 76, 80

Z angles 345